SHEFFIELD HALLAM UNIVERSITY
LEARNING & IT SERVICES
ADSETTS CENTRE CITY CAMPUS
SHEFFIELD S1 1WB

RISK

MANAGEMENT

IN BANKING

ONE WEEK LOAN

"Highly recommended to professionals, risk managers and students in risk management who look for a relevant comprehensive view of how risk management expands and evolves towards greater sophistication."
Alain Canac, former Senior Credit Officer at Banque Paribas and IXIS Corporate & Investment Bank

"The recent global financial crisis has highlighted the need for all participants in the banking system to understand and intelligently utilize risk management. Updated and expanded, the new edition of Bessis's Risk Management in Banking *is the best overall guide to the concepts and tools needed to avoid the next banking crisis. Bessis reveals his roots as both academic and practitioner by his combination of intellectual rigor and pragmatic application. Concisely integrating a wide body of work within a comprehensive analytic framework, the careful exposition as well as practical illustrations will be appreciated by students and bankers alike. Highly recommended!"*
Stephen Kealhofer, Co-founder of KMV Corporation

"Risk Management in Banking has been a constant companion in my work. Over my career I have developed three different corporate risk management programs and have found Dr. Bessis's writing to be highly valuable and especially practical. This updated edition expands greatly on previous volumes and benefits from recent international experiences which have greatly challenged some approaches to the understanding of risk. It is essential reading for those managing risks in today's complex banking environment."
David R. Koenig, Chief Executive Officer, The Governance Fund, LLC and Past Chair, Board of Directors, Professional Risk Managers' International Association (PRMIA)

RISK

MANAGEMENT

IN BANKING

THIRD EDITION

Joël Bessis

WILEY

A John Wiley and Sons, Ltd, Publication

This edition first published by John Wiley & Sons Ltd in 2010
Copyright © 2010 John Wiley & Sons Ltd

Registered office
John Wiley & Sons Ltd, The Atrium, Southern Gate, Chichester, West Sussex, PO19 8SQ, United Kingdom

For details of our global editorial offices, for customer services and for information about how to apply for permission to reuse the copyright material in this book please see our website at www.wiley.com

The right of the author to be identified as the author of this work has been asserted in accordance with the Copyright, Designs and Patents Act 1988.

Reprinted June 2010

All rights reserved. No part of this publication may be reproduced, stored in a retrieval system, or transmitted, in any form or by any means, electronic, mechanical, photocopying, recording or otherwise, except as permitted by the UK Copyright, Designs and Patents Act 1988, without the prior permission of the publisher.

Wiley also publishes its books in a variety of electronic formats. Some content that appears in print may not be available in electronic books.

Designations used by companies to distinguish their products are often claimed as trademarks. All brand names and product names used in this book are trade names, service marks, trademarks or registered trademarks of their respective owners. The publisher is not associated with any product or vendor mentioned in this book. This publication is designed to provide accurate and authoritative information in regard to the subject matter covered. It is sold on the understanding that the publisher is not engaged in rendering professional services. If professional advice or other expert assistance is required, the services of a competent professional should be sought.

A catalogue record for this book is available from the British Library.

ISBN 978-0-470-01912-2 (H/B)
ISBN 978-0-470-01913-9 (P/B)

Set in 10/12 pt Times New Roman by Sparks – www.sparkspublishing.com
Printed in Great Britain by CPI Antony Rowe, Chippenham, Wiltshire

SHEFFIELD HALLAM UNIVERSITY
WL
332.1068
BE
ADSETTS LEARNING CENTRE

Contents

About the Author

Joël Bessis is Professor of Finance at HEC, the leading French business school, where he conducts training in risk management throughout Europe, the US and Asia. Over the course of his career Joël has developed a dual expertise – as an academic and as a practitioner, holding permanent consulting assignments in corporations and later, in banks. Joël worked for over fifteen years in risk management departments of financial institutions – as a consultant to the risk departments of several banking institutions in Europe, including the Banque Paribas and the European Bank for Development (EIB). Joël took a leave of absence from HEC Paris between 2000 and 2005 where he held positions as Director of Research at Fitch, and Head of Risk Analytics and Model Validation in the Risk Department of IXIS, a Paris based investment bank. Joël graduated as an Engineer from École Centrale in Paris, before earning a Masters in Business Administration from Columbia University in New York, and a PhD in Finance from the Université Paris-Dauphine. As an academic, Joël has published various papers and books in the fields of corporate finance, industrial economics, and financial markets.

Introduction

Risk management in banks became "the" hot topic after the 2008 financial crisis. The crisis appears as the most important one in the modern period. It is systemic in nature, in that it involves the entire financial system, from capital markets, to banks, funds and insurance companies, and all financial firms. Addressing risk management in this context is challenging given that the magnitude of the crisis suggests that risk management was inefficient, that risk models were inadequate and that regulations failed to meet their goal of avoiding a major crisis. Indeed, it is ironic that the crisis started when the new Basel 2 regulations were enforced in Europe.

Contents

1 BASIC POSTULATES OF THIS TEXT

This book does not address the financial crisis directly, but does not bypass it either. The very first chapter addresses the issue of "what went wrong" in the development of the crisis, starting from the 2007 so-called "sub-prime" crisis and culminating in 2008 into an unprecedented halt of the financial system, a system that was precisely under regulations aiming at avoiding such systemic crisis.

1.1 The Financial Crisis

Some simple facts deserve to be mentioned as a starting point. Criticisms of financial firms, of regulators and regulations, of rating agencies, of governance practices, of short-sighted appetite for profitability, of improper behavior of supervising authorities, of risk models, became commonplace and are seen as major causes of the 2008 crisis. Even financial models, which are supposed to have scientific foundations, are widely blamed today, perhaps because they have been pushed too far, for example by plugging in unreliable data.

In the end, the development of the crisis, as explained in the very first chapter of this text, refers to simple mechanisms that could have been anticipated, some of them being well-known and others resulting from relatively simple adverse effects that were not beyond common sense, but emerged through interactions of new regulations. Presumably critics are right in explaining the crisis by such factors.

This fact supports the positive view that inspires this text. It postulates that there is a major distinction between practices and techniques that are economically sound and the use that financial firms make of these techniques. The financial crisis seems to be an example of what should not be done and strongly reinforces the need for sound practices and sound economics of financial firms, and an enhanced governance of financial firms.

Some implications follow. Risk management is made up from practices and tools, including risk models. Those are extremely different factors. Practices are subject to discretionary judgments and policies, to business development goals, as long as they comply with existing regulations. Technical tools and models are not.

Risk management techniques have made a lot of progress since the best practices were defined by various think-tanks and regulatory bodies. Does the crisis mean that all such progress is useless? Presumably, this is not so. It rather suggests that actual risk practices diverged from best practices, that governance has probably not been up to the standards of sound management policies, and that the growth of the financial sector, with increased risk and appetite for profitability, increased beyond what the financial system can sustain under current rules regulating the industry.

1.2 Scope and Goals of this Text

This introduction reminds one of some basic principles of risk management and explains how this text is positioned within a considerable range of financial literature. Loosely speaking, financial risks designate any uncertainty that might trigger losses.

Risk management designates the entire spectrum of risk management processes and risk models that allow banks to implement risk-based policies and practices. It covers all techniques and management processes required for monitoring and controlling risks, and the required risk models. The spectrum of processes and models extends to all financial risks, the main ones being credit risk, market risk, interest rate risk and liquidity risk. Operational risk, however, is not addressed in this text, essentially because it is a non-financial risk.

The risk prospective differs strongly from the business prospective. Business units focus on development and profit. Risk managers focus on risk control and limits, on potential losses rather than profit. While the former think "profit," the latter think "worst case" situations. The main goal of risk policies and practices is viewed as controlling risk without impairing profitability, or "optimizing" the risk–return trade-off that all financial firms face.

If there were a single key priority to re-emphasize today, it would be risk oversight by bank professionals, supervisors and standards setters. Risk oversight implies awareness of risks embedded in the balance sheets and off the balance sheets of banks. Risk oversight also implies a minimum understanding of risk models and techniques, at least with respect to a sound usage of those, without going as far as turning all professionals into risk modelers.

Buzzwords such as "bank-wide risk management," suggest that risk oversight across giant banks is widely shared and managed consistently across their wide array of business lines. Indeed, models and techniques have been designed for achieving such a goal. But the financial crisis also suggests that risk oversight was not well shared within banks or by other financial firms and regulators. Risk oversight implies knowledge of risks, a forward view on adverse events, plus the capability of enforcing risk controls and limits when risks drift away from guidelines making up banks' policies.

Risk oversight and risk controlling is theoretically and practically feasible today because risk processes, techniques, and models are developed continuously for reaching this goal. Such a postulate is often challenged today in view of the wide underestimation of the magnitude of the crisis.

Last but not least, while risk management techniques have expanded for individual firms, the techniques for early detection of risk at the system-wide level remained nearly nonexistent, with an over-reliance on self-management and self-regulations by firms. It is striking that the target of risk regulations, system-wide risk, is not measured in any way, and that regulations focused on individual specific risk of financial firms. Measuring system-wide risk is a conceptual and practical challenge. Recognition of such a "regulation hole" now finally seems to emerge in current financial reforms.

2 POSITIONING OF THE TEXT

The positioning of this text in the literature should help readers to identify how it complements the multitude of texts and articles that relate to risk and to risk management.

2.1 The "Model Divide"

Current risks are tomorrow's potential losses. Unfortunately, they are not as tangible as revenues and costs, thereby making risk modeling a conceptual and a practical challenge. Risk models and techniques have continuously expanded in recent years, enhancing the ability to monitor and control risk and to develop business activities without a myopic view on profitability. This is the "bright side" of risk models. The "dark side" is that, perhaps, the usage of risk models remained in the hands of a small group of "quants", who used them without caring too much about explaining model risk to non-specialists. This is not a good enough reason to throw everything to the trash can. The modeling effort was productive and a necessary step in the development of better risk practices.

The gap between the technicality of the literature and the capability of risk professionals, who are not model experts, to integrate the complexity of models in their own practices is damaging. Presumably, such a gap exists, and grew through time as the 2008 crisis seems to suggest.

It is noticeable that, instead of a dissemination of model expertise across the entire industry, modeling techniques tended to concentrate in a smaller core of experts. Such a concentration might explain the persisting and growing gaps between "model experts" and practitioners. Experts are "embedded" in banks, but being "embedded" does not imply that expertise is shared.

The book does not take harsh positions against models, even though it is relatively easy to pinpoint some model glitches[1] that were the sources of the financial crisis. Instead, it capitalizes on progress achieved that should allow banks to implement truly efficient risk management. It addresses risk processes and risk models, hoping to narrow the gap between specialists of quantitative finance and risk managers. It builds on a long experience in the risk department of banks and on academic knowledge.

Modelers will find here some reminders on classical finance models, which are pre-requisites to risk models, because there is no need for expanding such finance models beyond the essentials required for understanding risk models. However, risk models are expanded, explaining the rationale of models and illustrating them with examples. The text should help increasing transparency across the technicalities of risk management. It is balanced rather than technical, with a minimal background on risk modeling and an emphasis on how to assemble risk models in a consistent way, and on techniques and processes for making bank-wide risk management achievable.

As a consequence, an important goal of this book, as in previous editions, remains to address the "model divide" between model designers and risk professionals. Experts will find that some of the introductory essentials on modeling are fairly basic in this text. On the other hand, the larger mass of practitioners and students of risk management should find the text helpful because it is largely self-contained and integrated.

2.2 Risk Management versus Risk Instruments

Many risk management texts heavily focus on hedging instruments, mainly derivatives. Jumping to instruments for managing risk without prior knowledge of the source of risks bypasses the risk oversight principle. There is a major distinction between the usage of hedging instruments and the knowledge of what should be hedged in the first place.

Because derivatives are privileged instruments for controlling risks, they are introduced in a dedicated section of this book. But they are not the main focus of this book, because we know, in general, how to hedge a risk exposure once it has been properly identified. Financial institutions develop their business through an ever-changing innovation process of products. Innovation made it feasible to customize products for matching investors' needs. It also allowed both financial and corporate entities to hedge their risks with derivatives. The need for investors to take exposures and, for those holding exposures, to hedge them provided business for both risk takers and risk hedgers.

Did that solve risk management issues in financial institutions? It did not because two basic pre-requisites of a risk management system, risk oversight and tracing risks back to risk drivers, are different issues to understanding how derivatives work. Hence, the gap remains between derivatives that makes risk management feasible and financial firms' risk management focusing on risk oversight, the prerequisite for controlling risks with proper instruments.

---

1 We refer here to unreliable inputs of default correlations in credit portfolio models and, presumably, a lack of stress-testing of valuation models (see the chapters in Section 9 "Dependencies" and Chapter 51 on portfolio modeling).

2.3 Reverting to Better Risk Practices and Lessons of the Crisis

This text proceeds step by step in developing the building blocks of a sound risk management scheme, with the postulate that a sound usage of risk models and techniques is a tangible advance and that the sources of the current issues have to be looked for elsewhere, in the drift of practices and policies away from "best practices," rather than flaws of techniques, even though such flaws are pointed out throughout the text.

Some of the regulatory changes that emerge from the lessons of the crisis are ongoing, and some reforms have already been identified. But it is too early to foresee how regulatory changes will be implemented. A brief overview of future reforms being considered at the time of writing concludes the book. In between, we address risk management from a technical perspective, and maintain that sound risk processes and risk models have to be re-emphasized.

Moreover, the response to the crisis by financial authorities demonstrated that a major crisis implies that gains remain private while losses become publicly shared through massive government injections of cash and capital in ailing giant banks. Such responses, with the unique choices being either the "improvised" dismantling of failing financial firms or facing a financial collapse is unsustainable in the medium and long-term. It reinforces the critical need for sound risk practices and risk models for all financial firms, plus system-wide risk oversight.

3 BOOK STRUCTURE

The structure of the book is in 16 sections, each divided into several chapters. This structure facilitates a clear distinction between related subjects, with each chapter being dedicated to a specific topic. The benefit is that it is possible to move across chapters without necessarily following a sequential process throughout the book. Each chapter, or section introduction, provides a synthesis of the topics that will subsequently be expanded, allowing the reader to get an overview of each one and how it relates to the neighboring context.

The book outline is summarized by the list of sections, each of them divided into a number of different chapters dedicated to the related topics.

1 The Financial Crisis (2007–2008)
2 Business Lines, Risks and Risk Management
3 Financial Products
4 Valuation
5 Risk Modeling
6 Regulations
7 Asset Liability Management (ALM)
8 Fund Transfer Pricing Systems
9 Dependencies and Portfolio Risk
10 Market Risk
11 Credit Risk: Standalone
12 Credit Portfolio Risk
13 Capital Allocation
14 Risk-adjusted Performance
15 Credit Portfolio Management
16 Conclusion

The book addresses risk management in nine core blocks dedicated, respectively, to:

- Bank-wide risk management
- Asset liability management (mismatch risks)
- Risk regulations and accounting standards
- Market risk models
- Credit risk models
- Dependencies modeling
- Credit portfolio models
- Capital allocation
- Risk-adjusted performance
- Credit portfolio management

In between such core blocks are sections of three types. Some are here for providing a minimum background to subsequent issues. Others address parallel issues, many gathered in Sections 1 to 4 on the financial crisis, risk management principles and financial products. Others also provide parallel technical topics with the same purpose. Among other subjects, these sections provide the basics of derivatives, of main distribution functions of random variables, and of valuation. Note that valuation is a topic addressed in a considerable volume of literature whose purpose is to address pricing models, which is not the focus in this book. Rather, what is needed here is a minimum understanding on how to model potential losses and values (Section 4), summarizing some basic principles for valuation of risky assets, and providing minimal links with the pricing literature.

The extensive section on modeling dependencies, which is the foundation of diversification modeling within portfolios, is a transversal building block that applies to all portfolio models. The dependency topic is viewed from several angles, from traditional approaches as correlations and factor models up to the modern copula approach. Dependencies are addressed by keeping the focus on the essentials and on examples throughout a sequence of chapters.

We found that textbooks rarely address risk management in banking and in financial institutions in a comprehensive manner. We have tried to compensate for such gaps, by making a compromise between technicalities and simplicity, without sacrificing scope. Readers will realize that a balanced coverage of major risk models and practices is a goal that has inspired the entire volume.

The text develops many numerical examples, while restricting the analytics to the essentials. Simple examples help in illustrating the essentials better than formal descriptions. Of course, simple examples are no substitutes to full-blown models.

Finally, there is a balance to strike between concepts, analytics and applications. The goal of risk management is to use risk models for instrumental purposes and enriching the risk processes. This principle inspired this text by making it implementation focused. From a risk management prospective, it is important to understand which are the basic data required to model risk, the guidelines for implementing models, what are their outputs and how these should feed risk processes. For example, sample reports useful for management purposes, such as ALM or credit portfolio risk reporting, are included.

4 THE THIRD EDITION

The third edition of this book adds major and voluminous extensions to the previous edition.

The very first chapter deals with the financial crisis, which could not be a better introduction to the challenges of risk management in financial firms. The overview of risk management and risk models has been extended. The financial products section is also a full addition to the previous edition. The valuation section is entirely changed and expanded. The dependency section has been fully expanded to cover all approaches to dependencies, from the traditional techniques and up to the modern, more involved, techniques. The regulations section comprehensively covers the Basel 2 regulations using, as building blocks, the various approaches and sub-approaches. It now includes some essential features of accounting standards. Excerpts of Basel 2 are scattered in different chapters, notably in presenting cash products. Some of the analytics underlying the Basel 2 formulas are expanded in the credit sections.

Note that regulations are not the starting point of this text because these rely on risk management topics and issues. Risk management topics are introduced gradually without distortions between rule-based regulations and risk economics. Regulations are addressed in a dedicated section as they should, as regulatory application of risk models and risk processes.

As it is, the text sticks to the principle that sound models and sound implementation of risk management techniques remain the reference, and that the crisis is a massive evidence of absence of compliance with otherwise sound practices, governance and models. Therefore, the text has no negative view of risk models and practices, which tend to expand today, as expected in times of a major crisis.

SECTION I

The Financial Crisis

I

The 2007–2008 Financial Crisis

The crisis of 2007 and 2008 was a system-wide crisis whose amplitude is unprecedented in modern finance. It is systemic, in that it extends to the entire financial system. The sub-prime crisis should have been contained within the small segment of sub-prime mortgages. Financial risks of regulated firms are subject to strict regulations, whose purpose is precisely to avoid systemic, or "system-wide," crisis. Instead, it extended to the entire financial system and triggered economic contagion. Why did regulations fail? What went wrong?

The crisis expanded through "traditional" contagions, the contaminations of other segments of the system by a local event, and through procyclical effects. Procyclicality refers to the magnification of the amplitude of cycles. Moreover contagion and procyclical effects interacted with each other, revealing unexpected and interconnected effects, as seen in the various papers and official documents[1] used as a starting point for defining reforms of the overall regulation system.

Contagion and procyclicality are joint effects, which make them difficult to segregate. Many contagion effects detailed hereafter contribute to procyclicality and the reverse is also true. In this introductory chapter on the crisis, they are sometimes isolated for convenience.

Accordingly, this chapter starts with a brief overview of the sub-prime market, the classical contagion mechanisms, the financial risks, and the basics of risk regulations and of accounting regulations. The next sections address new contagion effects that emerged from the crisis. Those include adverse effects of accounting standards, the dissemination of risks through securitization, the liquidity crunch and its mechanical contagion effect, the procyclicality resulting from regulations and financial firms' behaviors, the role of lagged rating adjustments, the adverse effects of collateral-based leverage. Although the governance of banks is an issue in this context, we focus on the above effects.

---

1 The Financial Stability Forum [28] focuses on procyclicality, and the White Paper of the White House [79] addresses other aspect of the crisis and proposes reforms. Both are reviewed in the concluding chapter, Chapter 60.

This preliminary chapter also provides an overview of the financial system and regulations, which are subsequently detailed throughout several dedicated chapters on risk, regulations, banks' practices and risk models.

Contents

1.1   THE SUB-PRIME CRISIS

By mid-2007, housing prices in the US began to decline. In previous years, the mortgage industry was flourishing and the sub-prime market developed significantly. Sub-prime loans are simply loans that would not be granted to borrowers under normal standards. They are, as other mortgages, collateralized by real estate property, and rely on the expectation that house prices going up would make the collateral more valuable and transform a sub-prime loan in a prime mortgage. Collateralization is traditionally measured by the "Loan-to-Value" ratio, the ratio of the value of the collateral to the debt contracted, or "LTV." The LTV ratio is below one for mortgages. It was above standards for sub-prime loans.

In earlier years the capital markets performed well and all financial institutions were expanding profitably. Furthermore, the financial system was regulated. The so-called "Basel 2" regulations[2] for banking credit risk were enforced in 2008 in Europe. In the US, banks refrained from full compliance to the new rules, except international banks. But, in both regions, the market risk was under scrutiny by the supervisors.

However, many financial players were considering mid-2007 with some worries because the house market prices stopped inflating and because the interest rates on sub-prime loans, low at inception (teaser rates), were expected to increase after the initial grace period. A crisis in the sub-prime compartment of the market should have had a limited impact. The sub-prime market is a small segment of the huge mortgage US market. Even if some expected some difficulties in this special compartment, nobody expected that it would trigger a system-wide crisis.

In fact, an unprecedented crisis in modern times developed by the end of 2007 and peaked with the failure of Lehman Brothers in the US in September 2008. At that time, it became obvious that the entire financial system was locked into its first systemic crisis of modern times. Bank failures, considered as a "thing of the past," became numerous and spectacular. Northern Rock

---

2   See Chapters 19 and 20 on regulations. Regulations guidelines are defined by the Bank of International Settlements (BIS) in Basel, Switzerland.

went under, an unprecedented event in the booming United Kingdom financial industry within the previous century. Failures extended to all players, funds, and insurance companies.

At first sight, this crisis looks like a puzzle. Indeed, it took some time to get a financial picture of what happened in a narrow time framework, to have a decent perception of the magnitude of expected losses by all financial players, to understand how drastic was the extent of the crisis, to realize that the financial landscape was undergoing a unprecedented shake up in modern times, and that the rules and the perceived "best practices" of governance and risk management proved inefficient.

How come the sub-prime market triggered such a contagion to all financial players and to all financial industries, triggering in turn an economic crisis? Why did regulations fail? How could the "systemic risk," feared by all, actually materialize at a time when regulations – whose purpose is precisely to eliminate it – developed and culminated in the enforcement of the Basel 2 Accord for banks, and with the final stage of the Solvency 2 regulations for the insurance industry?

The sub-prime market size was estimated in 2007 at around $600 billion of the $3 trillion mortgage market. Sub-prime loans are loans which would normally not be granted to borrowers because they have sub-standard credit quality. Sub-prime borrowers originally pay 200–300 basis points (2–3%) above prime mortgage rates ("spread") because they have higher credit risk and because they would not otherwise get a loan. Sub-prime borrowers often pay variable rates, with a grace period (2–3 years) before rates get higher. Such features make loans riskier if borrowers cannot sustain the hike of interest rates and/or if house values move down.

Defaults on loans don't occur in the early stages of a loan, right after inception, nor at a later stage when the loan is almost paid back. Rather, the peak of defaults occurs in between, with historical statistics on non sub-prime loans showing a peak at around 50 to 60 months after origination, and depending on various factors, such as economic conditions prevailing or the nature of interest paid, fixed or adjustable. For lenders, loss in the event of default is mitigated by the real estate property backing the loan.

Default risk, measured by the likelihood of default event and the magnitude of such losses under default, increased progressively. Interest rates started to increase from mid-2004. House prices began to fall from 2005–6 in the US. Both factors reduced the solvency of borrowers and a surge in mortgage defaults showed up in 2007 and accelerated in subsequent months. The potential losses directly related to such defaults, at the date of this writing, remained difficult to evaluate, with estimates ranging initially from $200 million to much bigger figures in 2008.

The specific features of sub-prime loans led to a concentration of reset dates to higher rates after the initial grace period with low rates for sub-prime borrowers. The peak of defaults was expected to occur more or less around the same period, in 2007–2008, given estimates on "normal seasoning," or time profile of mortgage defaults. The home price downturn became visible as early as 2006 and accelerated subsequently. The three factors concurrently increased the default rates in 2007–2008.

Higher defaults in the segment were expected, perhaps not with the magnitude observed, but were also expected to remain within the segment. But they were not. Instead, the segment problems triggered unprecedented numerous "contagions" and adverse effects within the system.

Those adverse effects included a capital market downturn; a liquidity "crunch" or a contraction of liquidity of the funding and the cost of funding for all financial players; a "credit crunch," or a drastic contraction of credit; and, finally, an adverse economic impact with the risk of a strong economic recession.

The summer 2007 crisis turned out to be a major financial crisis in 2008 with a series of bank failures, mergers, losses, and unprecedented intervention of financial authorities "injecting" liquidity in the system and up to nationalization of major institutions. When the crisis peaked, the US authorities set up a major, and unprecedented in modern finance, emergency plan in September 2008, intended to isolate so-called "toxic assets" from the balance sheets of banks and other financial players (insurance), and to avoid a global collapse of the financial system. In other countries, notably the UK, similar plans were implemented. At the same period, US authorities, faced with numerous failures of major institutions, supported some flamboyant Wall Street investment banks but let Lehman Brothers go under. The event seems to have considerably altered the trust in the financial system and brutally accelerated the plunge of the capital markets.

At this stage, it was clear to all that the financial system as a whole was on the verge of collapsing and that the financial landscape had drastically changed within weeks, with investment banks disappearing, trough mergers and failures, inclusive of the biggest ones, and up to the failure the biggest insurance company in the world, AIG.

After-the-fact, casual observation was enough to identify classical "contagion" mechanisms. More puzzling are other contagion mechanisms, which have become the focus of the new wave of regulations taking place today.

1.2 CLASSICAL CONTAGION MECHANISMS

A well-known contagion effect is the "domino effect." The failure of a large financial institution triggers failure in many others who have large exposure, through lending for example, to the ailing institution. The domino effect played a role in the crisis since so many financial organizations failed. It is the foundation of the "too big to fail" principle, which suggests that no large institution can be allowed to fail for fear of contagion to many others. It is noticeable that the principle was not fully implemented when US authorities let Lehman Brothers go under, although they seem to have done whatever they could in other similar cases (Bear Stearns acquired by J.P. Morgan with a Federal Reserve credit line). The domino effect is the effect rather than the cause of the crisis. In this chapter, we try to examine some of the main contagion effects, other than the "domino effect" and some procyclical mechanisms that were seen as the explanation of the amplitude of the crisis.

The capital market downturn was triggered by several well-known factors, which developed with a much larger magnitude than in the recent crises. The usual "flight to quality" is triggered by the fear of investors of further losses from the on-going downturn of markets. Investors sell risky assets and buy Treasury bills and bonds. Such sales further accelerate the capital market downturn.

"Fire sales" of assets were triggered for all funds and leveraged financial firms, by the lower value of their collateralized securities. All leveraged funds, using extensively debt ("leverage") for financing their assets, face a lower ratio of debt to the value of pledged assets. The gap between security values and debt is called the "haircut," and is subject to minimum values below which either debt has to be reduced or additional collateral posted ("margin calls"). In other words, financial debt is over-collateralized, a standard practice for financial players, because the collateral is made of securities of which value varies with market movements. When values of market instruments fall, the ratio falls, triggering a deficiency, making debt unsustainable. In order to comply with lenders' requirements, leveraged institutions have only one way out:

Fire sales of assets for reducing debt and bringing back asset value in line with LTV ratios, thereby adding to the market turmoil.

Banks' equity moved down because of huge markdowns of portfolios, due to the depreciated value of their assets, adding to fear of further losses and inadequate capital of banks. A bank's capital is the foundation of regulations. It is considered as the unique safety cushion capable of absorbing losses. Once capital is deteriorated by losses commensurate with capital size, the bank's solvency and credit standing strongly deteriorates.

All such mechanisms are usually triggered by a downturn of financial conditions. But their effect is usually of limited magnitude and never ended up in systemic risk. Moreover, the recent history of continuous growth of economies fueled by easy financing, have symmetric effects. In the expansive phase, the risk appetite for financially risky assets grows. The value of assets also increases and generates capital gains, rather than capital losses, which allows leveraged institutions to further increase their leverage. Banks' equity is up, fueled by profits. Combining favorable economic conditions with regulations supposed to limit the magnitude of adverse effect tends to make the financial industry more "resilient," as evidence was provided by several crises, which were all feared, such as the downturn in 2002, but ended up with a limited magnitude.

Wealth effects usually follow adverse financial conditions. Faced with reduced wealth, due to the decline of real estate property or of the value of financial assets, spending declines. A financial crisis has always an adverse economical impact, beyond the financial sphere. Consumer spending cannot rely anymore on refinancing mortgages, which is feasible when home values go up making it possible to get another loan extension within acceptable limits for lenders, secured by an increasing home value. Agents, with less wealth, become reluctant to spend. Wealth effect further slows down consumption and, consequently, investment. Consumption and revenue fall; saving rate becomes negative. Doubt on growth becomes stronger and expectations adjust accordingly. Expected recession materializes in lower growth. All economic entities, financial firms and non-financial firms, face lower growth prospects.

1.3 FINANCIAL RISKS

All classical adverse mechanisms are supposed to have limited magnitude because of risk regulations. Risk regulations address the main risks faced by financial players. Risk is defined as a combination of uncertainty and potential losses resulting from adverse scenarios. Major risks are subject to quantification imposed by Basel regulations.

Credit risk is the risk of losses due to borrowers' defaults or deterioration of credit standing. Market risk is the risk of losses due to adverse movements of the value of financial instruments (stocks, bonds, etc.) because of market movements for an horizon that depends on the required time to liquidate them, thereby avoiding further losses. Both risks are regulated in banks. Credit risk is now subject to Basel 2 rules. Market risk has been measured since the 1996–1997 Basel amendments for market risk either by capital charges allocated to each exposure, or the now common "value-at-risk" calculation[3]. Other risks are well defined and supervised, even though they do not require a capital charge.

Interest rate risk is the risk of losses due to adverse movements of interest rates, notably when cost of debt increases. Liquidity risk, or funding risk, refers to the availability of funds when

---

3 See related Chapters 19 and 20 on market risk regulations.

needed. It is the risk of not being able to raise funds at a reasonable cost, and it culminates when a financial entity cannot raise additional funds, with the ultimate stage being bank failure.

Both risks are related to mismatch risk. Mismatch risk results from the maturity of assets being often longer than maturity of financing. Lending or investing long and borrowing short is a common practice because it allows financial institutions to tap the lower rates of the highly liquid short-term market and to benefit from longer rates when lending (when the turn structure of interest rates is upward sloping). Maturity mismatch creates liquidity risk when financial players roll over their short-term debts. It creates as well interest rate risk since the rollover of short-term debts is at prevailing rates, which might increase. Mismatch risk is a common practice even in depository institutions, which benefits from short-term funds and lends for longer maturities. Since mismatch risk was the source of the failure of the saving and loans institutions in the US, when short-term interest rates jumped up when the Chairman of the Federal Reserve in the US, Paul Volcker, decided to increase interest rates to double digit levels for fighting inflation in 1979, it is still surprising that mismatch risk is left to direct control by banks, and entails no capital charge.

Obviously, financial players are aware of such risks and they prepare themselves for market disruptions. A common way of isolating a bank from market disruptions is to hold very liquid assets. Liquid assets are the easiest to sell without risk of significant losses. Short maturity risk-free assets are less exposed to value variations when interest rates increase. High credit quality assets are always in demand at time of uncertainty, when "flights to quality" occur. Assets meeting those two basic requirements are Treasury bills. Holding such assets allows one to rely on sales of such assets to obtain liquidity when market conditions deteriorate. Banks hold a varying fraction of their total assets in highly liquid assets. How much depends on the bank's exposure to such market disruptions and the bank's policies. Regulations do not provide minimum amounts although regulators normally monitor the situations of banks. The drawback for banks is the low return of such liquid assets, which creates a trade-off between the cushion against market disruptions and profitability.

Market liquidity risk is a price risk and refers to the capability of selling traded instruments at a "fair price." Market liquidity is directly related to the volume of trading in capital markets. As long as trading exists with some volume, selling assets without disrupting price remains relatively easy. The recent period demonstrated that market liquidity can dry up just as funding liquidity did.

The absence of stringent regulations on liquidity risk is the "liquidity hole" in regulations, as well as it is in the theory of finance. It proved to be a major weakness that turned a downturn of capital markets into a major liquidity crisis for both the markets and the financial system.

A review of financial reports of banks in various countries, referring to the end of 2006, showed that banks were apparently prepared for such risks. They disclosed the volumes of liquid assets; the mismatch between assets and liability maturities; the measures of regulatory capital; the excess capital buffer over minimum requirement; how they performed their value-at-risk calculations for market risk; and up to the assessment of "economic capital" for credit risk, based on economic assessment rather than regulatory rules. Such disclosures testify of the prevailing confidence in their risk management practices before the crisis.

1.4 REGULATIONS

There are two set of regulations that that apply to financial firms. Risk regulations are designed to prevent failure of individual financial firms by imposing minimum standards to the capital base that are risk driven. Accounting standards affect the value assessment of financial assets and liabilities, and have a direct influence on capital base and the bottom line of the income statement.

1.4.1 Risk Regulations

Financial risks are precisely defined because they are regulated. Regulations impose a quantification of potential losses stemming from risks, and such potential losses are the foundation for determining the capital base of financial institutions. The regulations of the financial system are reviewed in Chapters 19 and 20 of this text. Only the basic principles are summarized here. The core concept of risk regulations is the "capital adequacy" principle, which imposes a capital base commensurate with risks to which each bank is exposed. The principle is sound and makes a lot of sense. Instead of "dos and don'ts"," banks simply need to have enough capital to make their risks sustainable[4].

The rationale of the principle is that lenders can always absorb "statistical losses," such as those that are measurable in retail banking where there are millions of commitments, through adequate provisions. Risk provisioning can go beyond with provisions for general factors, should banks feel that they are exposed to such factors in their portfolios. But what would happen for the first Euro or Dollar of loss beyond the provisions? In the absence of capital, there would be no further buffer for such "average" losses. The rationale of the capital buffer is that banks should have a capital capable of sustaining much higher than average losses. It sounds natural, for ensuring bank solvency, to impose a capital base in line with such unexpected losses. Of course unexpected losses are future and potential losses. They are not supposed to materialize in other than unexpected ways. And they depend on current risks taken by the bank. The challenge of regulators and of banks as well, is in measuring potential losses in line with current risks.

The capital adequacy principle was the starting point of the strong emergence of modern risk management because it requires translating risks, which appear, at first sight, as intangibles, into Euro or Dollar values. Risk quantification and modeling made tremendous advances under the impulse of capital regulations.

Guidelines are defined by a regulators meeting in Basel at the Bank of International Settlement (BIS), hence the name of "Basel" Accords. The sequence of Accords in Basel started 20 years ago with the Accord for credit risk, or Basel 1, which relied on the very simple Cooke ratio. The Cooke ratio stipulated that the capital charge for lending or credit risk in general should be 8% of risk-weighted assets. Risk-weighted assets are the amount at risk, subject to loss, weighted by a coefficient between 0% and 100%. Such values were supposed to match rough proxies of the likelihood of unexpected credit losses, after considering the diversification effect of lending portfolios. Since they were very few weights, the first capital accord was very easy to implement, which was the purpose of its simplicity.

The 1996–1997 amendments targeted market risk, and allowed to use a standard approach using risk weights and, for the first time, the internal model approach, or the value-at-risk model for market risk. The challenge for measuring potential losses is to turn intangible risks into quantified measures in monetary value. The conceptual solution to that challenge is the

---

4 Among others, important documents on risk regulations by the Basel Committee for Banking Supervision (BCBS) are for credit risk in sources [7] and [10] and [8] for market risk, supplemented by publications available on the Bank of International Settlements (BIS) website.

"value-at-risk" concept, which synthesizes risks into a Dollar or Euro value through risk models. Value-at-risk gained popularity because it measures in a single figure the potential losses, a measure imposed by the bank's supervisors. Value-at-risk is the potential loss that is not supposed to be exceeded in more than a very small fraction of all feasible scenarios. It has now a track record of around 10 years and is implemented in most banks as the basis for the calculation of the capital charge against market risk.

In January 2007, the Basel 2 Accord for credit risk was enforced in European counties and for major international banks. The Basel 2 Accord essentially differentiates the capital charge according to the credit risk of the borrowers, using as an intermediate step internal credit ratings assigned by banks to all borrowers (in approaches other than the simpler Standard approach).

Ratings are measures of the "credit standing" as a rank along a scale. For bonds, rating agency scales are widely used. Those are letter grades such as, in the simplified Moody's scale: Aaa, Aa, A, Baa, Ba, B. Detailed scales are also extensively used. Under Basel 2, any borrower from a bank (corporations, banks), should be assigned an internal credit rating, which drives the capital charge. For individuals, in retail banking, the large volume of data allows using statistical measures, or "scores," for measuring credit standing, already used by many banks. Some are nationwide such as the famous FICO (Fair Isaac Corporation) score in the US. Others are proprietary to banks, such as in Europe.

Regulations were stringent, but regulations "holes" remained. Mismatch risk is a case in point, since it is left mainly to the self-discipline of market players, and without any capital charge. In addition, the scope of regulations does not extend to the entire industry. Another case in point is that of hedge funds. Hedge funds use proprietary trading techniques for enhancing their return, providing alternate sources of returns to straight investments in securities. For doing so, they use various techniques, such as betting on convergence of market parameters of different regions, or stock prices, or using event-driven strategies, betting on the outcome of mergers or even elections for example. Creativity has no bounds. Regulations would make proprietary strategies more public than they are, removing the added value of hedge funds policies, as some argue. Head fund management was left to self-discipline as well, contrasting with standard mutual funds subject to stringent restrictions. Moreover, funds can be highly leveraged (using debt financing), posting as collateral the assets held. A well-known effect of debt financing is that, under favorable conditions, it enhances the returns to investors (and to the fund managers as well). This could be fine, except that funds rely a lot on market liquidity and on mismatch risk for enhancing return. As explained subsequently, hedge funds participated to the aggravation of the crisis because of rules applying to collateral-based financing and mismatch risk.

Other entities are supposed to follow a "code of conduct" enforced by the market. The case in point is that of rating agencies. The business model of rating agencies is assigning credit ratings which serve the investors. Since they help issuers of bonds to raise financing, they are paid by issuers. Self-discipline can be powerful enough to impose self-regulation because the reputation of agencies depends on how well they do. At least, this was the prevailing view, since no one regulated rating agencies. Once the role of rating agencies in monitoring risk was heavily criticized, it become a common perception that self-regulation was not enough, and that the "issuer paid" model might raise conflicts of interest for agencies rating issues.

The debate on regulations before the crisis was how to weight self-regulation, or self-discipline, versus rule-based regulations enforced over financial firms. Since the crisis, it became official that regulation could not depend any more on self-discipline or "codes of conduct." Rather, all official documents point to the deficiency of existing regulations, and universally recommend that existing regulations should be more consistent and reinforced[5]. The contrast is striking. Extending the scope of regulation and how stringent regulations should be, have become hot issues.

1.4.2 Accounting Standards

"Fair value accounting," under the new accounting standards, focuses on the price at which an asset can be sold[6]. For market products, stocks, bonds, and derivatives, prices are usually liquidation values unless they are loans and receivables or held until maturity assets. For assets valued at fair values, valuation depends on whether markets are active or not. Active markets are such that the volume of transactions allows defining clear prices. For other instruments, prices can be derived from other traded instruments in active markets. For instruments for which prices cannot be derived from active markets, valuation is model based. The classification in accounting categories is based on management intent.

A main drawback of fair value, as it used to be discussed, was to make the net income more volatile because it was directly related to market movements, thereby blurring the profitability picture. This drawback was addressed by making a distinction between assets held for trading purpose, for which capital gains and losses of traded instruments are transferred to net income, and those for which capital gains and losses are transferred to the capital rather than to the bottom line.

When markets went down, fair value rules triggered markdowns of portfolios, even if there was no intention to sell them, which translated into losses that eroded the capital base of banks.

1.5 CONTAGION THROUGH SECURITIZATIONS

Banks progressively shifted from the "originate and hold" business model to the "originate and distribute" business model. Traditional lending consists of lending and keeping the loans in the "banking portfolio" until maturity. The drawback of such classical practice is that loans withheld in the balance sheet freezes the capital required by regulators, thereby excluding origination of new loans if the bank has capital constraints. The securitizations allowed bank to turnaround the constraint and to keep developing their loan business[7]. The mechanism facilitated the financing of growing economies.

Banks originate new loans but, instead of keeping them in their balance sheets, they sold them into the capital markets, thereby off-loading massive amounts of credit risk in the capital markets. The principle consists of creating a Special Purpose Entity (SPE), a legal entity, alike a fund, which is bankruptcy remote from sponsors (banks or other financial players). The SPE buys the assets and issues "bonds" in the market for financing the acquisition. Loan cash flows serve for compensating investors in such asset-backed securities issued by "SPEs." As a result, banks distributed credit risk to a variety of investors, which was seen as a wider diversification of risks.

---

5   See the concluding chapter, Chapter 61.
6   See Chapter 21 on accounting standards.
7   See Chapter 5 on financial products, for definitions of securitizations, and Chapter 58 detailing the securitization economics.

Banks' original motivation for selling assets, under the "originate and distribute" business models is to free capital, which allows them to expand their lending activities again. Investors look for credit spread of issued bonds (spread of bond yields above risk-free yield) and base their investment decisions on the ratings assigned by rating agencies to such loan-backed bonds. Investors care only about the credit quality of bonds, measured by credit ratings, rather than the composition of the pool of loans, over which they have no direct information, making the role of rating agencies critical in the process. They also had an additional benefit when investing in SPE securities. The credit spreads of notes issued by securitization vehicles have been more attractive than those of comparable corporate bonds with the same rating.

Whatever the risk of the assets securitized, the funding of the SPE can be achieved through the "structuring" of loan-backed bond issues[8]. A series of notes of different seniorities, from AAA to high yield bonds, are issued. Seniority refers to the relative priority of different debt claims on the SPE. The subordinated notes bear the risk of securitized assets, thereby providing insurance against losses for more senior notes. Senior notes can be hit by losses only once the subordinated notes absorbed the first losses. The mechanism allows assigning high ratings to senior notes. It also allows customization of the risks of bonds issued by a single securitization to the differentiated risk appetites of a wide array of investors from conservative pension funds, buying senior bonds, to investors looking for the high spreads of subordinated bonds, at the cost of additional risk.

Securitizations became widely spread. Whatever the risk of the underlying assets, whether they are mortgages or risky loans, they can be securitized. All that securitization arrangers have to do for securitizing riskier assets is to increase the size of subordinated bonds for increasing the safety cushion protecting the senior bonds. With such mechanisms, financing speculative grade debt (high-risk debt) is feasible partially with AAA bonds, the rest of the bonds issued guaranteeing the seniority levels of the high-grade bonds.

The growth of securitization of mortgages has been sustained since the mechanism started to be implemented by banks. For mortgage backed securities, ("MBS"), the early phase was 40 years ago in the US. Securitizations of other assets are more recent, such as consumer loans, or corporate loans. There was an accelerated growth of securitizations of bonds and debts throughout 1996–2002, slowing down in 2002, and breaking down at crisis time.

Securitizations by banks or mortgage institutions are attractive because they save the capital, and because investors benefit from higher spreads for same ratings with loan-backed bonds. As a result of this "win-win" game, both banks and investors gain.

But, as a result of risk distribution through securitizations, no one knows any more who bears the credit risk of the riskier assets, such as sub-prime loans. By disseminating risk across investors, securitizations create a potential for triggering a "contagion" of risks to all investors in those bonds. If securitized pools of assets are perceived as riskier, investors might fear that the risk is much higher than expected. So called "toxic assets," such as sub-prime loans, found their ways into securitized portfolios and became "poison pills" triggering doubt about the securitized portfolios, even though they might represent a small, although unknown, fraction of them.

As a result, securitizations disseminated the risks of toxic assets to the entire industry, and to players who do not know exactly how much risk they were carrying "indirectly." The theory is that credit ratings of rating agencies should provide reliable information about this risk. The practice is that rating agencies might not be well equipped to quantify such risks and that, although they claim to monitor risks when time passes, they might not have the human

---

8 This is the dominant mechanism of securitization. See Chapter 58 for alternate schemes.

resources for doing so. Once it became obvious to all that the risk was higher than expected, it was too late. All that rating agencies could do was accelerating downgrades, for catching up on unexpected risks, which confirmed the fears of investors and created a high risk aversion for the perceived risk of these products.

It is not surprising that all blame securitizations today for having spread credit risk all over the financial system and not providing any way of assessing such risk. Securitizations disseminated risks that should have been contained to some specific segments of the markets. The consequence is that they disappeared when the crisis expanded.

Securitizations were a major source of financing for banks, not only a way of saving capital. Their virtual disappearance dried a major source of funds in the brilliant years of securitizations. It left them with the pressure of capital constraints. This is enough to trigger a credit crunch, no bank being able to extend further credit for lack of financing through securitizations,

Still, the securitization mechanism relies on sound economics. As long as assets provide enough return for compensating investors in line with the risk that they take, SPEs remain sound vehicles. When the asset returns fall below such threshold, when the perceived risk changes drastically, when trust with respect to the assets backing the risk of investors disappears, the mechanism collapses, after having spread distrust everywhere. As a consequence, securitizations virtually stopped since the crisis.

The process was aggravated by the lack of short-term liquidity which also serves in the financing of the pools of assets securitized. In absence of liquidity, some SPEs had to unwind their holding of assets, liquidating them in adverse conditions to pay investors. As an alternate option, banks who originated assets held by the SPEs took them back in their balance sheets to avoid reputation risk, thereby reversing the effect on capital required, which increased again.

1.6 LIQUIDITY CONTAGION

The crisis turned almost instantly into a liquidity crisis. The $1.2 trillion commercial paper market, the most liquid market in the US in 2007, dried up very quickly after the first phases of the crises. Liquidity froze, making funding shrink and turning financing into a major issue for all borrowers.

The first mechanism of this liquidity gridlock appears to be risk aversion of lenders, and this impression was later confirmed when major institutions collapsed. The "who is going to be next to lose" issue made potential lenders reduce their exposures to others, for fear that would suffer of unexpected losses of equally unexpected magnitudes. Mismatch risk, or more simply, relying on short-term funds, exacerbates the effect of a liquidity crunch in the short-term liquidity markets. Banks and other financial firms relying on short-term debt chased liquidity that evaporated suddenly, triggering a liquidity crisis.

In normal periods, the short end of the money market is very liquid. Mismatch risk is of no consequence. But, if rolling over short-term debt becomes difficult because of market disruption, the funding is disrupted. Still, mismatch is common. A bank's so-called "structural position" consists of lending long and borrowing short. Mismatch increases the profitability because the term structure of interest rates, the set of rates applicable to various maturities from the short-term horizon up to the very long-term, is usually upward sloping. This upward sloping curve implies that long-term rates are higher than short-term rates under normal conditions, which indeed prevailed for a long time before the crisis. Mismatches allow capturing the spread between long-term and short-term rates.

Many securitization vehicles rely on "liquidity conduits." Liquidity conduits, attached to SPEs, serve for tapping liquidity in the short end of the market because it is cheaper. The arrangers of such conduits need to make sure that the mismatch risk will not translate into a disruption for the vehicle being financed. The standard manner of doing so is to attach to the conduit "back-up liquidity lines" by so-called "liquidity providers." A liquidity provider, commonly a bank, contracts to provide liquidity up to a maximum amount in the event of market disruption. The contract is subject to various conditions, such as a minimum rating of the portfolio of assets being financed. The length of market disruptions is supposed to be "short," not to last for months.

Once liquidity dried up, all liquidity commitments were triggered. This implies that mismatch risk translated in a lot of "involuntary lending" by banks. Not only did they have to lend to comply with their commitments, but also they faced simultaneously the issue of having insufficient liquidity for themselves. Liquidity did not dry up only because of the "who is next to lose how much" issue. It also dried because of such involuntary lending commitments by lenders. Involuntary lending made liquidity even scarcer.

Liquidity appears to have dried up even after massive injection of liquidity by central banks. Presumably, banks and financial firms were "hoarding liquidity" for fear of a lack of liquidity if they started using it for extending credit. Involuntary lending and liquidity hoarding are effects rather than causes. The cause seems to have been the risk aversion and uncertainty about who was next to lose, an effect to be traced back not only to "toxic assets," which could not explain the magnitude of losses if considered in isolation, but also to fair value accounting standards.

1.7 CONTAGION AND PROCYCLICALITY THROUGH FAIR VALUE RULES

Even though the principle of fair value has a sound basis, it became a contagion factor in exceptionally adverse conditions. The contagion effect results from uncertainty with respect to "who is going to be the next to lose." Most of the losses of financial entities resulted from the markdowns of their portfolios, resulting from the downturn of the market aggravated by extensive fire sales of assets. But losses are also tied to the nature of portfolios held by financial institutions[9].

Many firms held securitizations assets, subject to suspicion because of the house price downturn and because of dissemination of "toxic assets" through securitizations. Finding out which assets are embedded in portfolios, directly or indirectly, and whether they qualify as toxic assets, are no trivial tasks. Bank systems were not designed for the purpose of tracing back underlying assets in securitization notes. Rather they record transactions and valuations, as required for trading and lending.

Many assets, easy to value in active markets, lost perceived value in inactive and illiquid markets. The category of assets subject to model valuation, extended to assets which, otherwise, would have been valued on prices considered as reliable when active markets became inactive. Model prices were themselves subject to a negative perception, since many assets, which were

---

9   The *Financial Times* provided useful articles on the causes of the crisis in the late months of 2008, following the Lehman Brothers collapses in September 2008 and in early 2009. The document of the FSF [28] provides various views on procyclicality.

supposedly properly priced, lost perceived value because confidence in models collapsed in stressed conditions. Fair values failed to provide the actual values of assets, whatever they were. Rather, the perceived values substituted to actual values.

The combined result of dissemination of toxic assets and fair value rules implemented in severe conditions made losses unavoidable. It became impractical to find out what the actual solvency of banks was. Some might see that mechanism as a deterioration of banks' solvency only, which it is. But the substitution of perceived values and credit standing of financial firms to "actual" values and related solvency issues seems to have had a joint effect on liquidity and credit crunches.

Under stressed conditions, solvency and liquidity are intertwined. Solvency uncertainty triggers lack of funding and illiquidity. The reverse is also true. Leveraged firms rely on collateral-based financing, subject to over-collateralization ratios. Should the market move down, whatever the reason, leveraged entities have no other option for complying with the over-collateralization ratio than reducing their debt through "fire sales" of assets under adverse conditions. Fire sales trigger losses that adversely affect solvency. This mechanism was not expected to have so much adverse effect and is further detailed in section 1.9. Whether illiquidity or solvency is the initial cause does not matter. Once the mechanism triggered it operates both ways.

The mechanism makes risk aversion increase. Risk aversion in inter-bank lending and borrowing can be measured by the spread between inter-bank lending and borrowing, which jumped to unprecedented peaks, as high as 10 times the usual spread prevailing in other times.

Without fair value effects in adverse conditions, risk aversion would presumably be lower because the unique issue would have been isolating the toxic assets. Fair values were a contagion factor in that they exposed simultaneously all players to losses that become unpredictable.

Fair value rules are also procyclical. In a downturn of the markets, they trigger markdowns, which trigger losses, which trigger a lower capital base, a lower credit standing and solvency, and a higher cost of financing or a lack of collateral based financing due to lower values of collateral. The mechanisms are reversed in expansion. Fair value triggers markups, gains, a stronger capital base, a higher credit standing and a better solvency, and ends up in easy financing.

The mechanism is procyclical because a first downside move in the market triggers all above effects, resulting in downgrades of credit standing and values, and triggers another downside of markets, which accelerates the initial downside. All effects tend to be cumulative over time. This mechanism is procyclical to the extent that it magnifies the amplitude of movements. Adverse affects, in stressed conditions, magnify the market movements and the industry deterioration. Such effects could be inverted in a favorable environment, and, indeed, they did contribute to the expansion preceding the crisis.

The symmetry can be seen as a good point. After all, when everything goes well, it is normal for the financial system to get stronger and vice versa. The point is valid, but, unfortunately, it cannot be segregated from procyclicality, and procyclicality can end up in major crisis, which is a major drawback. No wonder why fair value rules are under attack today, after having been seen as favorable by many players in the expansion phase.

1.8 CONTAGION THROUGH RATING DOWNGRADES

There were waves of downgrades by rating agencies of banks and other issuers, which accompanied the deterioration of solvency of banks, resulting both from defaults of borrowers and from fair value rules[10]. Credit ratings measure the credit standing and solvency of borrowers. Downgrades correspond to a higher credit risk, commanding a higher cost of funds, and a higher return required by lenders and investors in instruments issued by downgraded entities. Accordingly, downgrades trigger higher cost of funding and lower prices of instruments issued by those who are downgraded, adding to their difficulties. Finally, late or not, downgrades confirm the fears of investors and lenders.

Since the frequency of downgrades increased abruptly, rating agencies seemed not to have anticipated the difficulties and tried to catch up with bad news. Lagged downgrades tend to be concentrated in time, instead of gradually measuring the actual credit standing of issues. Because rating downgrades seemed to have lagged way beyond timely adjustments, such waves of downgrades generated doubts about the value of credit ratings, resulting in lower perceived ratings than gradually adjusted ratings.

Rating downgrades have other indirect effects. Many lenders and investors require a minimum rating for lending and investing. Notably, they trigger additional collateral calls, which requires posting additional collateral. If no additional collateral can be posted, the only open choice is to reduce debt by selling assets under adverse conditions.

Entities hit by rating downgrades were those more exposed to mortgage loan risk. Among those are insurance companies, or monolines, called "credit enhancers." As the name suggests, by providing insurance against loss for certain instruments, they enhance their credit quality. But the "wrapped" instrument quality is as good as the quality of the insurer. Because "monolines" extended so many guarantees to assets, they were highly exposed to the risk which erupted in a short period of time. It was not long before credit enhancers were downgraded.

Downgrades of credit enhancers have a leverage effect: Any instrument "wrapped" in a guarantee by credit enhancers is also downgraded. The scope of downgrades and deterioration of credit quality increased drastically when the value of the guarantee provided by credit enhancers went down.

Procyclicality for credit ratings result from the lag between ratings and actual deteriorations of the credit standing of products and issuers. Credit ratings are well known to be "sticky." Agencies claim that ratings are long-term and that there is no point in adjusting them frequently. Perhaps, but sticky ratings create lags. When some issues are upgraded and other downgraded, the net effect on the system is negligible. When there is a strong cycle, lags amplify the cycle. And monolines downgrades magnified the waves of downgrades by extension to all "wrapped" assets by insurers.

1.9 CONTAGION AND PROCYCLICALITY IN A LEVERAGED INDUSTRY

Most financial firms rely on collateralized debt, subject to an over-collateralization ratio. When the collateral values go down, the only way to comply with the constraint is reducing debt through sales of assets for repaying a fraction of the debt contracted. Fire sales of assets

---

10 The ratings assigned by agencies were relatively stable, and downgrades increased abruptly in the last months of 2007 and throughout the first semester of 2008 when the crisis amplified.

contribute to the contagion to the capital markets. In fact, the de-leveraging process is gradual and continuous when asset values keep declining. To that extent, collateral-based financing has contributed to the downturn of the market, and because it is gradual, it presumably maintained a pressure on the market for several months[11].

The mechanism is strongly procyclical. If asset values move down, sales of assets amplify the downturn. If asset values are up, funds and others can afford to borrow more because the collateral value increases as well. Furthermore, the process is cumulative. A downturn triggers fire sales of assets and fire sales accelerate the downturn, which triggers another round of fire sales and so on. The reverse happens in up-cycles, for the benefit of financial players, but perhaps not for the benefit of the financial system. Asset values go up, allowing additional collateral-based leverage, and additional debt finances and additional assets, which allows more financing and so on. The expansion is easier, but its drawback appears when the cycle reverses, notably when the entire system becomes highly leveraged – as it seems to have been the case.

A leveraged expansion is not necessarily beneficial to the system to the extent that it increases the systemic risk. In an adverse situation, the risks materialize and are cumulative. Although these principles are supposed to be well known, the adverse effect of de-leveraging in stressed conditions has been underestimated, even though it is mechanical.

Procyclicality is exacerbated by investors. Investors are happy when leveraged returns get higher, but when the situation reverses, they contribute to magnify the adverse cycle because of the redemption of shares in funds, which aggravates further the need for liquidity and the necessity of fire sales.

Note that the key point is not leverage. The key point is collateral-based leverage. Debt exists because assets are pledged, otherwise raising debt would not be feasible. In the end, it is the combination of fair value rules, collateral-based leverage, and the associated debt to value ratio that are procyclical.

1.10 SOME IMPLICATIONS

It is still too early to foresee all implications of the crisis. Regulations holes will be filled up with new regulations. Disclosure requirements on banks' portfolios will get more stringent. Fair value rules will be relaxed, at least to a certain extent, trying to strike a balance between faithful image and meaningless values when markets dry up. Liquidity and mismatch risks will be supervised again, as they were at certain periods. Governance and short-term horizon for compensations will evolve.

As the history of regulations shows, there will be a new wave of more comprehensive and stringent regulations, which might be followed by more flexibility. At a time when a drastic crisis requires immediate actions, long-term analysis and views are more necessary than ever. There is a lot of work on financial research, on such hot topics as liquidity and how to define a "better regulation," the regulation that everyone would agree to be required. The reforms are still in the process of being gradually defined. Finance researchers now have a lot of issues

---

11 Although various documents address the procyclicality of accounting standards and of risk regulations, they do not mention the specific mechanism stemming from collateral-based debt, which is the core of this section.

to explore, perhaps not the same areas than before this major crisis. Many mechanisms of the crisis described in this chapter are under scrutiny, at the time of this writing, as the concluding chapter of this text illustrates.

SECTION 2

Business Lines, Risks, and Risk Management

This section covers risk definitions, the risk management process, and the various business lines or "books" of banks.

The purpose of Chapter 2 is to provide an overview of the wide variety of banking business lines, as an introduction to the various risks and the differentiation of risk management processes.

Risks are broadly defined as uncertainties potentially resulting in adverse variations of profitability or in losses. The main financial risks and their definitions are provided in Chapter 3, as inspired by risk regulations. The main financial risks addressed in this text are described in Chapter 3 and include:

- liquidity
- interest rate risk
- market risk for the trading book
- credit risk.

Note that operational risk, mentioned in Chapter 3, is not addressed in this text.

Chapter 4 is dedicated to an overview of risk management practices and organization. The goal of risk management is controlling risks. Classical risk practices consist of setting risk limits to "Amount-at-Risk," or amount subject to losses, and delegations, allowing decentralization of the risk management process. The organization and processes of risk management should be bank-wide, across all business lines, with the risk department providing a central independent oversight of risks with power to oppose decisions proposed by the business lines, the "front-offices," for bringing risk in line with the bank's policy.

2

Banking Business Lines

This chapter describes the main business poles, and, within each pole, the business lines. Regulations make a clear distinction between commercial banking and trading activities, with the common segmentation between "banking book" and "trading book." However, there is a wide spectrum of banking business lines. The main business poles, the investment banking pole and the banking pole, are too global for being representative of the variety of business in banking. For example, lending activities extend from retail banking to specialized finance. Moreover, risk management practices differ significantly across business units. The purpose of this chapter is to provide an overview of business line differentiation, as an introduction to the various risks and risk management processes.

The first section provides a global view of how the main poles sub-divide in different business lines, which address different categories of clients with different products. Because of such differentiation, risk management practices also vary across business lines. The last section provides some details on the accounting practices, for market instruments and lending activities.

Contents

2.1 BUSINESS POLES IN THE BANKING INDUSTRY

The banking industry, and financial firms in general, have a wide array of business lines[1]. The following chart (Figure 2.1) maps these activities, grouping them into three main poles:

---

[1] For a comprehensive review of the financial system in the US, see the textbook of Saunders and Cornett [66].

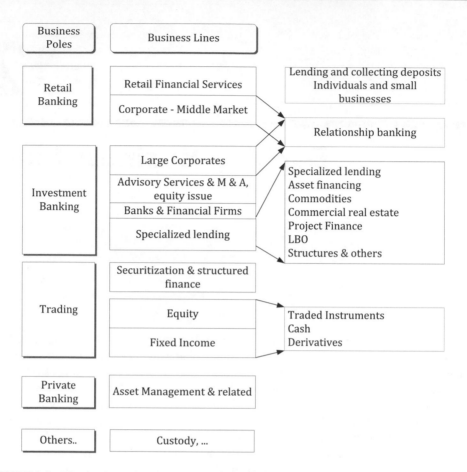

FIGURE 2.1   The variety of business lines in banking

- traditional commercial banking
- investment banking, with specialized transactions
- trading.

The poles subdivide into various business lines (Figure 2.1).

2.2 MANAGEMENT PRACTICES DIFFER ACROSS AND WITHIN BUSINESS LINES

Retail banking tends to be mass oriented and "industrial" because of the large number of transactions. Individual lending decisions rely more on statistical techniques. Management reporting on such large numbers of transactions focuses on large subsets of transactions. Criteria for grouping the transactions include date of origination, type of customers, product family (consumer loans, credit cards, leasing). Banks manage such loans by grouping transactions of similar characteristics into homogenous pools.

For medium and large corporate borrowers, individual decisions require more judgment because mechanical rules are not sufficient to assess the actual credit standing of a corporation. For the large corporate businesses, "relationship banking" prevails. The relation is stable, based on mutual confidence, and generates sales of multiple services to large clients. Risk decisions necessitate individual evaluation of transactions.

Investment banking is the domain of large transactions customized to the needs of big corporates or financial institutions[2]. Large corporations demand a variety of services, some of them being lending facilities and others derivatives for hedging purposes for example. For dealing with such multiple products, banks have account officers who convey the demands from those large clients to trading and lending poles. Investment banking in Europe generally means trading activities and large corporation lending, while the historical tradition in the US separated, originally, lending and trading activities (the former Glass-Steagall Act). In European banks, no such separation existed and large banks group both types and transactions under the generic name of "Corporate and Investment Banking." Still, it remains true that traders and the lending pole are not allowed to share information, for example when confidential inside information on a corporate client would allow investors to trade based on undisclosed information about the corporate policy.

"Specialized finance" extends from specific fields with standard practices, such as export and commodities financing, to "structured financing." They imply specific structuring and customization for making large and risky transactions feasible, such as project finance. "Structuring" designates the assembling of financial products and derivatives, plus contractual clauses for monitoring risk ("covenants"). Without such risk mitigants, transactions would not be feasible.

Trading involves traditional proprietary trading and trading for third parties (sales). In the first case, the bank is trading for itself, taking positions to make gains. Arbitrage means taking advantage of some "disequilibrium" in the markets, for example trading spreads of interest rates that are perceived as disappearing in the near future. Arbitrage, as viewed by practitioners, is not risk free. In the financial theory, arbitrage free prices are equilibrium prices, which are prices that would prevail once risk-free arbitrage trading made them disappear.

Other activities do not generate directly traditional banking risks, such as private banking, or asset management, and advisory services. However, they might generate risks when the financial firm provides a guarantee to a client, a typical example being that of "guaranteed capital funds." They also generate other risks, such as operational risk or legal risk.

Although all main business lines share the common goals of risk-expected return enhancement, practices vary across market segment and business lines. Generally specific, expertise varies across sectors of clients and across products.

Product lines vary within the above broad groups. Retail financial services (RFS) covers all lending activities, from credit card and consumer loans to mortgage loans, to individuals. RFS also extends to very small enterprises, such as those of doctors or home services, for which similar processes are used for decision-making by banks. This is the universe of statistical techniques for assessing credit risk, and lending decisions are based on a combination of automated systems plus management monitoring. When moving to larger size enterprises, each commitment relies on expert and analyst contributions, and analysts tend to specialize according to industry. Individual credit ratings of obligors are used, which include a judgmental component rather than statistical techniques that prevail in retail banking.

---

2 Investment banking refers to the large firms' clients as well as trading, as is the practice in Europe. Its scope is wider than the firms having the "investment bank" status in the US.

Standard corporate lending transactions include overnight loans, short-term loans (less than one year), revolving facilities, term loans, committed lines of credit, or large loans. Such transactions are under the responsibility of credit officers and their reporting lines. Financial institutions, which include banks as well as insurance or brokers, require a different expertise than large corporates. Specialized finance includes project finance, commodities financing, asset financing (from real estate to aircraft), and trade financing, which are dealt with by experts of the industry. Structured finance extends to securitizations, which are different "objects" than corporations and banks. The product assessment, as well the expertise needed, differ radically from standard finance. In general financial engineering prevails for securitizations and trading activities, where transactions are customized to each large client.

In the chapters (5–9) dedicated to banking products, we detail the definitions and the terminology applying to most common products, relying on Basel 2 definitions.

2.3 BANKING REGULATIONS AND ACCOUNTING STANDARDS

The "banking book" refers to commercial banking activities. It includes all lending and borrowing. Customers are mainly non-financial corporations or individuals. Inter-bank transactions occur between financial institutions. The "trading book" groups all trading transactions. Customers include corporations (corporate counterparties) or other financial players belonging to the financial industry (professional counterparties). Many market transactions are over-the-counter instruments, or derivatives such as swaps and options (over-the-counter – OTC – means on a bilateral basis rather than on markets). The rationale for separating these "portfolios" originated from the risk regulations (Chapters 19 and 20).

Trading is either proprietary or client oriented. "Prop" trading designates trades done by the bank for itself. Sales designate trades sold to clients. Accordingly, the following terminology applies: The "sell side" is the bank, because it sells products to end-users. The "buy side" designates the clients, corporations, and asset managers, who buy the products, for example for hedging purposes.

Accounting rules differ with the banking portfolio and the trading portfolio. Accounting rules for lending use accrual accounting of revenues and costs, and relies on book value for assets and liabilities. Trading relies on market values (mark-to-market) of transactions and profit and loss (P&L) measured as variations of the mark-to-market value of transactions between two dates.

The accounting standards further segregates instruments into the basic four classes: Held for trading, available for sale, lending instruments and "held-to-maturity" assets. Valuation rules differ across these categories. Classification of instruments depends on management intentions. Both types of classifications are compared in Chapter 21 on accounting standards.

Capital market products, and mainly derivatives, are detailed in dedicated chapters, where we deal with the engineering of such products and the rationale for using them as end-users (buy-side) or when selling them (sell-side). Note, however, that we do not address the pricing models and valuation issues in this book.

3

Risks and Risk Management

Risks are broadly defined as uncertainties potentially resulting in adverse variations of profitability or in losses. Banking regulations, imposing capital charges against all risks, greatly helped the process of risk modeling because they imposed a quantification of several main risks of the bank. Risk definitions serve as the starting point for both regulatory and economic treatments of risks.

After introducing uncertainty and risks, the basic types of risk are listed before detailing each of them. The risk classification and definitions provided in this chapter are closely inspired by the definitions of risk regulations[1], which aimed at defining risk with enough accuracy for allowing risk quantification and ultimately defining a capital charge to each class of risk.

Contents

---

1 Many definitions are provided in the Basel 2 Accord for explaining the capital treatment of various products [7].

3.1 UNCERTAINTY, RISK, AND EXPOSURE TO RISK

Risk is not identical to uncertainty. Uncertainty refers to the randomness of outcomes. Risk refers to the adverse effect on wealth that such outcomes have. If none, there is uncertainty but not risk. If such adverse effects can materialize, there are both uncertainty and risk. Risk exists only when uncertainty can have a potential adverse effect, which is a possibility of loss.

Similarly, exposure is a loose concept defined as the "amount at risk," or an amount subject to loss of value, or the size of commitments. But exposure is not risk because risk has other components than the size of commitments. In financial terminology, the generic term "exposure" refers to a transaction which generates some risk.

A financial example of the distinction between risk and uncertainty could refer to a situation when there is perfect hedge in place. By definition, hedging means "mitigating chances of financial losses," eventually making them zero whatever happens.

Consider an equity position. A buyer of stock faces losses if the stock price moves down. Holding the stock is a "long" position. Assume now that he or she borrowed the same stock and immediately sold it. This is a "short sale," or the sale of a borrowed stock. At some point, the borrowed stock has to be returned to the lender of the security. If the stock price goes down, the long position on stock generates a loss. Simultaneously, the borrower of stock makes a gain that exactly offsets the loss. In order to return the borrowed stock to the security dealer, one buys back the stock at a lower price than when the borrowed stock was sold, and makes a gain on the borrowed stock. Because the dealer has both a long and a short position in the same stock, gain and loss exactly offset. Since there is no loss, there is no risk. Hence, a perfectly hedged position is subject to uncertainty, but is not exposed to risk because, whatever the market movements, there cannot be any loss.

The above example is case of a zero net exposure, measured by value held or net worth, without risk. The long and short positions on the stock perfectly offset and net worth remains zero whatever happens. Hence, there is no risk for the netted exposure. Another example of zero net exposure associated with risk would simply arise from buying the stock with borrowed fund. Net worth is again zero when the transaction is made. However, there is risk exposure because, should the stock price move down, the stock value would fall below what is needed for repaying the loan.

3.2 TYPES OF RISKS

There are various types of risks, which are differentiated according to the source of losses, market movements or default on payment obligations of borrowers. Each is detailed below. We introduce them in the following order:

- credit risk
- liquidity risk: funding risk
- interest rate risk
- mismatch risk
- market liquidity: market price risk
- market risk
- foreign exchange risk.

Operational risk is not financial to the extent that it arises from internal malfunctions of processes, and is mentioned because it is subject to a capital charge under the risk regulations.

All risks are defined as potential losses and need to be quantified. The assessment of potential losses raises conceptual and technical issues. Most quantification tools are related to the VaR concept[2] and necessitate risk models. Risk measurement and risk models are discussed throughout the book. Here, the focus is on risk definitions only.

Any transaction generally generates risk. When considered in isolation, the risk is qualified as "standalone." When we consider portfolios of transactions, whether market instruments or loans for example, there is always a diversification effect, which diversifies away some of the risk of the individual transactions. All loans will never default simultaneously and it is also unlikely that market movements will generate losses for all instruments making up a trading book.

This is the well-known rule that states that the sum of individual risks is less than the risk of the sum, or, that risks should be sub-additive. Risks do not add up algebraically because of diversification. Diversification effects are intimately related to the concept of dependency, a key concept in risk which raises difficult challenges when trying to move from the intuitive notion to modeling and measuring diversification. Loosely speaking, dependency means that events tend to occur jointly, and independency means that they are unrelated. Diversification effects exist because dependency is never perfect.

For example, defaults on loans depend on some common factors such as economic conditions, which create dependencies between defaults. Assessing risk for portfolios implies some measure of such dependencies. They are often designated as correlation risk, or loss correlations, because correlation is one common measure of how dependent defaults are. In any case, portfolio risk is different from standalone risk and will be considered throughout this book, because all financial players hold portfolios, never a single transaction.

Correlation or dependency risk is one side of the coin for portfolios. Concentration is similar but distinct. A bank can have a large number of small loans, such as in retail banking. Assume that such loans have a high probability of defaulting together. This is not theoretical. The sub-prime loans referred to in the introduction were, from inception, subject to a high dependency on house price and interest rates. If one defaults, the likelihood that others default is high, and this dependency effectively materializes. A large dependency results in large losses.

Large losses can also occur when there are large discrepancies in the size of loans, while losses are not much dependent. The example of large books of small loans is typical of granular portfolios, meaning portfolios where each individual transaction is small compared to the size of the entire portfolio. With portfolios made of large transactions, which is typical in investment banking, a single default can trigger a large loss. This is the case in the investment banking pole because clients are large corporations or large financial institutions. A single loss, whether dependent or not from other losses, can be very large. Concentration risk within portfolio refers to discrepancies of sizes, and the presence of large exposures. Note that the final effect is similar to a high dependency of many small losses resulting in a large loss, but the cause of the large loss is not the same.

In the next sections, we expand the definitions of risks.

---

2 The VaR model is presented first in Chapter 18, before being substantially detailed in the sections on market risk (Section 10) and credit risk (Section 11).

3.3 CREDIT RISK

Credit risk is the most important risk in banking. It is the risk of a counterparty defaulting on payment obligations. Following regulations and the literature on credit risk, credit risk splits up in several "credit risk components":

- default risk
- migration risk
- exposure risk, which designates the uncertainty with respect to the future value of the amount subject to loss at the unknown time of default
- "loss given default" (LGD), or "loss under default," is usually less than the amount due because of recoveries arising from third party guarantees or collateral (assets pledged to the lender)
- counterparty risk is a specific form of credit risk that is encountered with derivative products, which can shift from one counterparty to the other.

Figure 3.1 summarizes the credit risk components. The figure shows "spread risk" in addition to the above. Spread risk designates the changes of spread between the risky return of risky assets and the risk-free rate (of government bonds). As it is explained in the valuation chap-

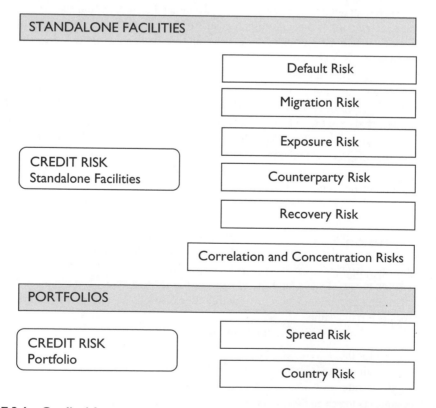

FIGURE 3.1   Credit risk components

ter (Chapter 13), variation of spreads triggers changes of values, positive or negative, hence potential losses.

Next, we expand credit risk components.

3.3.1 Default Risk

Default risk is the risk that borrowers default, meaning that they fail to comply with their obligations to service debt. Default triggers a total or partial loss of any amount lent to the counterparty.

There are various default events such as: delay in payments obligations; restructuring of debt obligations due to a major deterioration of the credit standing of the borrower; bankruptcies. Simple delinquencies, or payment delays, do not turn out as plain defaults, with a durable inability of lenders to face debt obligations. Many are resolved within a short period (say less than 3 months). Restructuring is very close to default when it results from the inability of the borrower to face payment obligations unless its debt structure changes. Plain defaults imply that the non-payment will be permanent. Bankruptcies, liquidation of the firm or acquisition of a distressed firm, are possible outcomes. They trigger significant losses.

Conceptually, defaults are considered as an "absorbing state," that is an event such that the probability of migrating out of the default state is zero. This is not realistic since individuals might default on a consumer loan, for example, but might be able to face their financial obligations at a later date. In the US and other countries, bankruptcy law is designed to maximize the chance of survival of a firm that defaults, and require defining a business plan, possibly with other corporations, that has some chances of success. Therefore the default state might be a transient state.

Default depends on rules and conventions. The prevailing regulatory rule is that non-payment extends over at least 90 days. This is not a universal definition. For example, rating agencies, those organizations that provide rating to investors, consider that default occurs from the very first day of defaulting on the payment obligation of an issue.

"Issuer" risk designates the obligors' credit risk, which is distinct from the risk of a particular issue, among several of the same issuer, depending on the nature of the instrument and its credit mitigants (seniority level and guarantees).

3.3.2 Migration Risk

Credit risk is also the risk of a decline in the credit standing of the issuer of a bond or stock. Such deterioration does not imply default, but it does imply that the probability of default increases. In the market universe, a deterioration of the credit standing of a borrower materializes into a loss because it triggers a value decline. The mechanism is due to the variations of credit spreads, the difference between the risk-free rate and the risky rate of an issue. Credit spreads account for the risk of nonpayment and increase with default risk. Since market values are the present values of promised cash flows discounted at the risky rate, they vary inversely with the discount rate, and hence with spreads. Any migration triggers a value change, and adverse migrations towards a lower (riskier) credit standing trigger losses.

3.3.3 Exposure Risk

Exposure commonly designates the magnitude of the amount subject to risk. For a loan it would be equal to the amount due plus interest accrued.

Exposure risk arises from the fact that future exposures, the size of amount due, are subject to uncertainty. Since only future exposures will trigger losses in the event of default, and since future exposures are uncertain, there is exposure risk. In the terminology of regulations, "Exposure at Default" ("EAD") is the relevant measure of the amount subject to risk.

Exposure uncertainty results from various sources that we address in more detail in the subsequent section on credit risk (Section 11). We consider here only loans. Loans often have contractual repayment schedules, but they are subject to exposure risk since they can be renegotiated by individual borrowers in retail banking. Many other facilities are commitments of the bank to provide funds at the initiative of a borrower, named committed lines of credit. The lender accepts to lend up to a maximum amount over a given period. The drawn amount is cash lent. The undrawn amount is the remaining fraction of the committed line of credit. Both are unknown since draws on the credit line are contingent upon the borrower's willingness to use the credit line.

3.3.4 Counterparty Risk of Derivatives

For over-the-counter instruments, such as derivatives (swaps and options), sale is not readily feasible since, by definition, they are contracted on a bilateral basis rather than on organized exchanges.

The bank faces the risk of losing the positive value of such instruments. Since this value varies constantly with the market parameters, credit risk changes with market movements during the entire residual life of the instrument. This is the well-known case of interaction between credit risk and market risk.

Counterparty risk designates the form of credit risk[3] that is specific to some derivatives. We take the example of an interest rate swap (IRS). This instrument pays a fixed rate and receives a floating rate, such as the Libor (London Inter-bank Offering Rate). By convention, the value of the swap at origination is always zero. After origination, the value of the swap is, intuitively, the present value of remaining cash flows, some fixed and some floating. If the floating rate increases above the fixed rate, the swap has a positive value. The one who receives the floating rate will lose this value if the counterparty defaults. Conversely, if the floating rate declines, the swap might have a negative value. The counterparty who receives the floating rate has no risk. The counterparty that pays the floating rate holds a positive value and will lose in the event of default of the other party. The risk for derivatives is a two-way risk, depending on who owns the positive value. The risk of loss shifts from one counterparty to the other depending on market movements. Moreover, the swap value is uncertain since it fluctuates with the market parameters. Counterparty risk is a two-way risk combined with exposure uncertainty, driven by market movements.

---

3 For example, the BCBS document [9] provides guidelines for addressing this risk after the Group of Thirty made recommendations in 1993.

3.3.5 Recovery Risk

Average recovery rates in percentage of the outstanding debt value (book value or market value if listed in the markets) are positive. Regulators impose using, in the so-called Foundation Approach of Basel 2[4], recovery rates of 25% for subordinated debt and 55% for senior debts. The seniority level of debts sets which debt should be paid first, senior debts being paid back before subordinated debts are. Subordinated debt repayment is subject to prior repayment of other debts. Senior debts have a priority claim.

Economically, the amount of recoveries is not known in advance. It depends on guarantees and economic conditions of borrowers. Recovery risk refers to such uncertainty that arises at the time of default. Here, recovery risk designates the randomness of the proceeds from working out of a borrower's default.

3.3.6 Correlation and Concentration Risks

For portfolio of loans or fixed income instruments, another major driver of credit losses is loss correlation, which designates whether losses tend to occur independently from each other or whether they tend to appear jointly. The higher the loss correlation, the higher is the credit risk.

Loss correlation is similar to concentration risk. Concentration designates the fact that large amounts lent to a small number of borrowers of good credit standing results in very large losses, although with a low probability. A correlation is a different concept, since it applies to all borrowers whatever the size of their debt obligations. But it results in the same effect. If many small borrowers tend to default jointly, this results in a large loss, just as when a very large loan defaults.

3.3.7 Credit Risk in the Trading Portfolio

Capital markets value issuers' or obligors' credit standing according to credit risk. Unlike loans, the credit risk of traded debts is visible through public agencies' ratings, assessing the credit quality of public debt issues, or through changes of the value of their stocks. Credit risk is also explicit in credit spreads, the add-on to the risk-free rate defining the required market yield on credit risky debts.

The capability of trading market assets mitigates the credit risk since there is no need to hold these securities until the deterioration of credit risk materializes into effective default. Traders can liquidate positions as soon as they have bad news on an obligor. If the credit standing of the obligor declines, it is still possible to sell these instruments in the market at a lower value. The faculty of trading the assets limits the loss if sale occurs before default. The loss due to credit risk depends upon the value of these instruments and their liquidity. If the default is totally unexpected, traded instruments decline rapidly. The loss is the difference between the pre- and post-default prices. Unexpected defaults are not the exception, one example being Parmalat, an Italian firm whose default surprised all traders and bankers.

---

4 See Chapter 39 for publicly available data and Chapter 20 on regulations.

3.3.8 Spread Risk

Spread risk is another dimension of credit risk as viewed by the market, and applies to capital market instruments, typically to bonds. Credit spreads designate the spread between the risky yield of a bond and the risk-free rate. Credit spreads might depend on many factors. But they relate also to the uncertainty of contractual payments of debt issues. Credit spreads compensate investors for credit risk. Spreads narrow or widen both due to general economic or industry factors and due to events specific to an issuer. Such risks, general and specific, are sometimes called spread risk, and are evidently important for all books of fixed income instruments (bonds and fixed income derivatives).

3.3.9 Country Risk

Country risk, or sovereign risk, is, loosely speaking, the risk of a "crisis" in a country. Sovereign risk is the risk of default of sovereign issuers, such as central banks or government sponsored banks. Sovereign defaults actually materialize as debt restructuring, with the uncertainty being the duration of frozen debt payments.

In many cases, country risk designates "transfer risk." Transfer risk refers to the impossibility to transfer funds from the country, either because there are legal restrictions imposed locally or because the currency is not convertible any more. A common practice stipulates that country risk is a floor for the risk of a local borrower, or, equivalently, that the country rating caps the ratings of local borrowers. The rationale is that, if transfers become impossible, the risk materializes for all corporations in the country, and the transfer risk applies to the borrower whatever its credit standing.

3.4 LIQUIDITY RISK: FUNDING

Liquidity risk of a firm is the risk that the cost of funding becomes higher, up to the extreme case when raising funds becoming impossible.

Funding risk depends upon how risky the market perceives the issuer and its funding policy. An institution coming to the market with unexpected and frequent needs for funds sends a negative signal, which might restrict the willingness to lend to this institution. The cost of funds also depends on the bank's credit standing. If the perception of the credit standing deteriorates, funding becomes more costly. The credit rating of the firm influences the cost of funds, making it a critical factor for a bank. In addition, it drives the ability to do business with other financial institutions since many investors follow some minimum rating guidelines for investing and lending.

Banks are not supposed to depend on liquidity crunch and should hold assets as an alternate source of funds than the market. In order to fulfill this role, liquid assets should mature in the short-term because market prices of long-term assets are more volatile[5], and more exposed to loss under sale. Banks used to reveal the size of the liquidity asset buffer and how much time

---

5   Long-term interest-bearing assets are more sensitive to interest rate movements. See the duration concept used for capturing the sensitivity of the mark-to-market value of the balance sheet in the related chapter on "Economic Value" of the balance sheet. Duration is introduced in Chapter 15, Sensitivity.

they could sustain market disruption. Actually, the size of liquidity buffers should be related to cash flows and liquidity commitments of banks, including off balance sheet commitments, to make such time estimates meaningful. This is a route that supervisory authorities are considering for monitoring system-wide liquidity[6]. Liquidity risk is also dependent on system-wide market disruptions, as the sub-prime crisis illustrates.

Extreme lack of liquidity results in failure. Extreme conditions are often the outcome of others risks, such as major market or credit losses. Important unexpected losses raise doubts with respect to the solvency of the organization and lenders refrain from further lending to the troubled institution. Massive withdrawals of funds by the public plus the closing of credit lines by others institutions are direct outcomes of such situations.

3.5 INTEREST RATE RISK

The interest rate risk is the risk of declines of net interest income, or interest revenues minus interest cost, due to the movements of interest rates. Most of the loans and receivables of the balance sheet of banks, and term or saving deposits, generate revenues and costs that are driven by interest rates. Since interest rates are unstable, so are earnings.

Anyone who lends or borrows is subject to interest rate risk. This is obvious for borrowers and lenders with a variable rate. But loans and debts that are on fixed rates are also subject to interest rate risk because fixed rate lenders could lend at higher than their fixed rate if rates increase and borrowers could pay a lower interest rate when rates decline. Fixed rate transactions are not exempt of interest rate risk because of the opportunity cost that arises from market movements.

Implicit or explicit options embedded in banking products are another source of interest rate risk. A well-known case is that of the re-negotiation of loan interest rates that carry a fixed rate. The borrower can always repay the loan or borrow at a new rate, a right that he or she will exercise when interest rates decline substantially. Variable rate loans can embed an explicit cap in the interest rates, in which case, the option is explicit. Several loans embed a grace period, such as sub-prime loans beyond which rate hikes occur.

Deposits carry options as well, since deposit holders transfer funds to term deposits earning interest revenues when interest rates increase. Optional risks are "indirect" interest rate risks because they do not depend only from changes of interest rates but also result from the behavior of customers. Notably, prepayment risk depends on geographical mobility or other factors unrelated to interest rates.

3.6 MISMATCH RISK

Mismatch risk designates the gap between maturities and interest rate reset dates of assets and liabilities[7]. The bank's "structural position" illustrates the risk. Banks tend to lend medium or long-term while securing financing in the short end of the market. The rationale is that long-term rates are higher than short-term rates in most usual situations. By taking this posture, banks can capture the positive spread between long-term and short-term rates.

---

6 See Chapter 61.

7 Mismatch risk is addressed by the asset-liability management function in a bank, whose goals and techniques make up the core topics of Section 7.

The mismatch implies both liquidity risk and interest rate risk. Liquidity risk results from the necessity of rolling over short-term debts to maintain a permanent financing in line with the asset maturity time profile. Interest rate risk results from the relative variations of the short-term and long-term interest rates, which make the spread between long-term and short-term rates variable across time, and eventually become negative if there is sudden spike of short-term interest rates relative to long-term rates.

Mismatch risk is not specific to banks. Many financial entities and vehicles, such as securitization vehicles, tap liquidity in the short-term market while asset maturity is much longer. The risk is limited as long as there is no market disruption. In the presence of a severe market disruption, mismatch risk might not be sustainable anymore in a leveraged financial system. The Saving and Loans debacle in the US is an example of adverse effects of mismatch risk, when interest rates suddenly spiked because of anti-inflationary policies by the Federal Reserve in the early 1980s.

3.7 MARKET LIQUIDITY RISK

Market liquidity also designates price risk for those assets for which trading volume is low or does not exist. Market liquidity can be firm-specific but it is more severe when it is system-wide. Some assets are highly liquid, such as Treasury bills or bonds. Other issues suffer from low trading volume and sales might result in significant declines of prices. Market liquidity turns into a price risk for specific issues. Market liquidity is not a source of risk, under normal circumstances, in an "active" market when volume of trading is significant. Market liquidity becomes an issue in "inactive markets," where volume is low, or for certain products, when market prices can drift away from representative prices. Market liquidity and active markets are related notions. Fair value accounting makes a distinction between active and inactive markets for the purpose of determining fair values.

Bank liquidity relies on inter-bank lending and borrowing, which used to be considered as reliable. Market liquidity becomes a system-wide issue when inter-bank lending and borrowing dries up for fear of solvency deterioration by borrowers. The financial crisis demonstrated that highly liquid markets could dry up and require surveillance system-wide.

3.8 MARKET RISK

Market risk is the risk of adverse deviations of the mark-to-market value of the trading portfolio, due to market movements, during the period required to liquidate the transactions[8]. The period of liquidation is critical to assess such adverse deviations. If it gets longer, so do the deviations from the current market value.

Earnings for the market portfolio, the portfolio of assets held for trading, over a period, are the variations of the market value. Any decline in value results in a market loss. The potential worst-case loss is higher when the holding period gets longer because market volatility tends to increase over longer horizons.

However, it is possible to liquidate tradable instruments or to hedge their future changes of value at any time. This is the rationale for limiting market risk to the liquidation period. In

---

8 VaR models have become commonplace for modeling market risk.

general, the liquidation period varies with the type of instruments. It could be short (one day) for foreign exchange, and much longer for "exotic" derivatives. The regulators provide rules to set the liquidation period. They impose a 10-day liquidation period plus a multiple over banks' internal measures of market value potential losses.

Note that liquidation involves asset and market liquidity risks. Price volatility is not the same in high liquidity and poor liquidity situations. When liquidity is high, the adverse deviations of prices are much lower than in poor liquidity environments, within a given horizon. Measures of market risk should include value changes when liquidity dries down, and imposes wider variations of prices under liquidation.

3.9 FOREIGN EXCHANGE RISK

The currency risk is that of incurring losses due to changes in the exchange rates. Variations in earnings results from the indexation of revenues and charges to exchange rates, or of changes of the values of assets and liabilities denominated in foreign currencies. Foreign exchange risk is a classical field of international finance, which relies on traditional techniques. Hedging instruments accommodate both interest rate and exchange rate risk. For market transactions, foreign exchange rates are a subset of market parameters, so that techniques applying to other market parameters apply as well. Translation risk arises from conversion of all foreign currency denominated assets and liabilities of a firm into a base reference currency.

3.10 SOLVENCY RISK

Solvency risk is the risk of being unable to absorb losses, generated by all types of risks, with the available capital. It differs from bankruptcy risk resulting from defaulting on debt obligations, and inability to raise funds for meeting such obligations. Solvency relates to the net worth of a bank and its capital base.

The basic principle of "capital adequacy," promoted by regulators, is to define the minimum capital that allows a bank to sustain the potential losses arising from all risks and complying with an acceptable solvency level. When using economic measures of potential losses, the capital buffer sets the default probability of the bank, or the probability that potential losses exceed the capital base. Solvency risk is impaired by incurred losses and resulted in major capital injections by governments in the financial crisis.

3.11 OPERATIONAL RISK

Operational risks result from malfunctions of the information system, reporting systems, internal risks monitoring rules, and internal procedures designed to take timely corrective actions, or the compliance with the internal risk policy rules. The New Basel Accord of January 2007 defines operational risk as "the risk of direct or indirect loss resulting from inadequate or failed internal processes, people and systems or from external events."

In the absence of an efficient tracking and reporting of risks, some important risks remain ignored, do not trigger any corrective action, and can result in disastrous consequences. In essence, operational risk is an "event risk." There is a wide range of events that potentially trigger losses. The very first step for addressing operational risk is to set up a common classification of events that should serve as a receptacle for data-gathering processes on event frequencies and costs. Such taxonomy is still flexible and industry standards are emerging. What follows is a tentative classification. Operational risks appear at different levels:

- human errors
- processes
- technical
- information technology.

Human errors are understood in a broad sense, which includes lack of expertise and fraud, including lack of compliance with existing procedures and policies. Process risk includes:

- inadequate procedures and controls for reporting, monitoring and decision-making
- inadequate procedures on processing information, such as errors in booking transactions and failure to scrutinize legal documentation
- organizational deficiencies
- risk surveillance and undetected excess limits
- management deficiencies in risk monitoring, such as not providing the right incentives to report risks, or not abiding by the procedures and policies in force
- errors in the recording process of transactions
- technical deficiencies of the information systems or of risk measures.

Technical risks relate to model errors, implementation, and the absence of adequate tools for measuring risks. Technology risk relates to deficiencies of the information systems and system failures.

Operational risk raises data and methodology challenges. Modeling operational risk requires setting up a classification of risk events, plus the assessment of their frequencies and of their monetary impacts. There are sources of historical data on various incidents and their costs, which serve for measuring the number of incidents and the losses attached to such incidents. Beyond external statistics, other sources on operational events are expert judgments, questioning local managers on possible events and what would be their implications, pooling data from similar institutions, and insurance costs that should relate to event frequencies and costs.

The data-gathering phase is the first stage, followed by data analysis and statistical techniques. They help in finding links between various operational risks. For example, business volume might make some events more frequent. The process ends up with some estimate of worst-case losses due to event risks. Under current regulations, operational risk is subject to capital charges, which requires the modeling of loss distributions due to operational risks.

4

Risk Management

The goal of risk management is controlling risks. Control is feasible when quantitative and qualitative assessments of risks exist. Such risk measurements are detailed throughout this book. This chapter is dedicated to a brief overview of bank-wide risk management practices and organization.

Risk oversight is both a major principle of risk management and a challenge for financial firms as well as for regulators. The organization and processes of risk management should be bank-wide, across all business lines. Unfortunately, bank-wide processes face serious challenges, as illustrated by the 2008 financial crisis. On the other hand, most financial firms have adopted standard organizations and processes that should, theoretically, work smoothly. Although the efficiency of risk management organization and processes raises some doubt, the standard organization, properly implemented, serves as a reference. Moreover, there are technical tools that allow moving up and down along the hierarchy and those have added value that is independent of internal discipline.

There are four main sections in this chapter.

- Section 4.1 addresses challenges of bank-wide risk management.
- Section 4.2 introduces the standard risk management organization along the well-known "three lines of defense" concept, and the standard risk processes, which rely on setting up limits and delegations for risk-taking decisions. Limits cap the risk of any single transaction or pools of transactions in retail banking. Delegation allows decentralizing the risk process according to certain rules in order to make the risk decisions smoother and speedier whenever a central assessment of the risk is not necessary. The same basic principles apply to all risks.
- Section 4.3 provides representative criteria for setting limits and enforcing them, for all main financial risks, providing more details on credit limits since other risks rely on similar processes.

- Section 4.4, the final section, discusses the techniques that make bank-wide risk management feasible, allowing moving both top-down and bottom-up along the hierarchy for controlling the risk–return tradeoff that all financial firms face and controls of risks. Two pillars of bank-wide risk management are the fund transfer pricing (FTP) system and the capital allocation system. Together, they allow breaking down global bank earnings and risks into earnings and risk allocations from transactions or pools of transactions in a consistent way. Bank-wide risk management implies the capability of moving bottom-up by aggregation of individual risks and top-down for identifying the sources of aggregated earnings and risks.

Contents

4.1 RISK OVERSIGHT CHALLENGES

Risk oversight is a universal principle that inspires all risk processes and risk management organizations. There are strong incentives motivating risk oversight, not all of them motivated by risk-controlling purposes. Both banks and supervisors share strong motivations for risk oversight. Financial firms want to enhance their risk and return tradeoffs. Regulators want to avoid systemic risk, the risk that the entire system collapses, as it nearly did.

4.1.1 Motivations for Risk Oversight

The classical motivations and incentives for sound risk management practices did not change. These are even reinforced today, once a major crisis revealed that disasters are not far away when bypassing such practices. Banks are "risk machines." They take risks, they transform them, and they embed them in banking products and services.

However, in the financial universe, risk and return are two sides of the same coin. It is always very easy to lend, and to obtain attractive revenues from risky borrowers. The price to pay is a risk higher than the prudent bank's risk. The prudent banks limit risks by restricting business volume and screening out risky borrowers. They save losses but might suffer from lower market shares and lower revenues. However, after a while, less prudent risk takers find out that higher losses materialize, and end up with a lower performance than the prudent lender, and ultimately fail. The financial crisis is a harsh and strong demonstration of adverse effects for careless risk takers and of benefits for more prudent and disciplined financial organizations.

Under a competitive perspective, screening borrowers and differentiating the prices accordingly, given the borrowers' standing and their contributions to the bank's risk–return profile, are key issues. Not doing so results in adverse economics for banks. Banks that do not differentiate risks treat risky and safe borrowers more or less equally, unless their risks are widely different. By over-pricing good risks, they discourage good borrowers. By under-pricing risk to risky customers, they attract them. Discouraging the relatively good clients and attracting the relatively bad ones results in adverse selection.

Those banking institutions that actively manage their risks have a competitive advantage. They take risks more consciously, they anticipate adverse changes, they protect themselves from unexpected events, and they gain the expertise to price risks. They are better prepared for crises than others and are less exposed to failures and takeovers. The competitors who lack such abilities or have less discipline may gain business in the short run and then lose ground with time, when those risks materialize into losses. Again, the crisis reinforces the argument, when considering how various banks expanded and faced the same stressed situation.

This does not mean that pricing the risk is enough if risks are unsustainable. Some financial firms lending aggressively also priced risk aggressively. Aggressive risk-based pricing is no substitute for keeping risk under control, and higher short-term profits are not a "self-contained hedge" against higher future losses.

Without a proper balance between expected return and risks, financial firms adopt, deliberately or not, a "myopic" view of the consequences. Focusing on business development and short-term profitability, while ignoring risks, which is the other side of the coin, is a wide drift away from sound practices. For sub-prime loans, it was simply a double bet: betting that house prices would get higher, or that the "bubble" of house prices would not blow up; and betting that is was feasible to get rid of such loans, through securitizations, early enough to escape the adverse consequences in the "blow up" scenario. This seems to be exactly how some firms behaved in the period preceding the crisis. Originating financial firms simply did not comply with sound practices.

4.1.2 Risk Oversight: Banks' Challenges

There are many pre-requisites for risk oversight, some of them being related to risk data, others to risk models and finally, but not least, to the risk-supervising organization. Risk data is a challenge, notably in credit risk, where data holes with respect to low default portfolios remain. Risk models are equally challenging. Without measures of risks, tracking risks for management purposes would not be feasible. Still, model outputs are no more reliable than the inputs are. Furthermore, transforming model-based measures into instrumental variables for decision makers who perceive models as black boxes, has remained a challenge. Finally, organizational issues refer to the decentralization of the risk management process in large banks.

4.1.2.1 Model Challenges

Tracking risks for management purposes requires models. Even the candid observer would intuitively understand that the only way to quantify risks, which are invisible since they address future random events, is to model them. The same observer would easily understand that many observable risk indicators, such as credit ratings, or economic and industry indexes, are no substitutes for quantified measures, and that they are subject to uncertainty.

Risk models quantify risks in relation with their underlying "risk factors." But risk factors are no substitutes for early warning signals or for risk-controlling tools. Without instrumental tools, risk measures are neither suitable nor sufficient for risk controlling. The value-at-risk is a good example: it provides a measure of risk but is not sufficient to control risks.

Models are often perceived as black boxes by those who do not design them. Models are as good as the data that is being plugged in. Moreover, the "black-box" perception of models does not help. The separation between scientists that design and calibrate models and the immense crowd of end users make the latter feel powerless for lack of instrumental drivers, and lack of transparency and confidence in model valuation. The same remarks apply to portfolio models.

Diversification of portfolios is a natural hedge that has always existed. But modeling diversification of credit risk lagged well behind diversification of market portfolios, even though it has always been the foundation of lending activities. Dependencies are the mirror image of diversification. The less dependent are individual risks, the higher the benefits from diversification are. Dependency measures can vary significantly around their perceived or measured values. As we now know, the diversification effects of portfolios sold by banks and off-loaded onto the financial markets have been strongly underestimated under stress conditions, leaving both banks and rating agencies forced to recognize losses that they did not anticipate.

The separation between model designers and end users mitigates the capability of the bank hierarchy to reveal hidden risks in models due to unreliable data inputs or improper usage of models, leaving the task of assessing model risk, the risk that a model misrepresents reality, in the hands of specialists. This does not mean that models are the culprits of misrepresentation of values. But it does mean that the usage of otherwise sound models can be unreliable.

Understanding of models should be more widespread than it is, and end users would benefit from minimal information about model reliability, or model risk. Whether it is the responsibility of risk modelers or that of end users does not resolve the "black box" effect and results in misperception of how sound models are used. Whoever is in charge, transparency should be enhanced enough so that all parties in risk-taking decisions become better aware of uncertainty built in models. The separation between specialists and end users does not help.

4.1.2.2 Organizational Challenges

The organizational process might not be as bank-wide as it is commonly pretended. Giant banks have to rely on front offices, with their "embedded" risk managers, for controlling risk. Embedded risk managers are close enough to business to understand what is going on. But embedded risk managers might be too close to business to make them a reliable pillar of bank-wide risk management. Distance between the central risk management unit and front offices remained a challenge that embedded risk managers did not resolve.

Putting the pieces together results in a contrasted image. On the one hand, tools and data exist and, on the other hand, one may wonder if bank-wide management is more a concept than a reality. The answer depends on banks and internal transparency, which varies widely with the nature of the bank and its culture. Once implemented in a giant organization, the efficiency of otherwise sound tools could be questioned.

4.1.3 Risk Oversight: Regulators' Challenges

The risk environment drastically changed. Banking failures recessed in most countries since the 1980s and re-emerged abruptly with the financial crisis, shaking up the foundations of the financial system. Banking failures make risks real and convey the impression that the banking industry is always close to disaster. Mutual lending and borrowing, and trading between "highly interconnected[1]" banks, create strong interdependencies between them. An individual failure of a large bank might trigger the "contagion" effect, through which other banks suffer unsustainable losses and eventually fail. This is the foundation of the "too big to fail" principle, which became a rule in the crisis[2], and is a major challenge for the future. From an industry prospective, "systemic risk," the risk of a collapse of the entire industry because of intertwined fates of individual financial firms, is always in the background, and became the foreground in the current context. Regulations focused on systemic risk, but failed to address it efficiently.

The financial crisis changed the financial landscape entirely in a matter of weeks, with major financial firms failing, being bailed out or merging with others. Investments banks disappeared. The financial crisis triggered an economic crisis of which magnitude was compared to the 1929 crisis. Today, corrective financial and economic actions were prompt and massive, raising other issues with respect to the next regulation phase.

Regulators and standard setters face considerable challenges. Not only do they have to correct deficiencies of current regulations, and filling up the holes remaining today, but they also have to address industry-wide risk better instead of focusing only on firm-specific risk. They also need to reinforce market discipline and governance for avoiding maintaining direct support to financial firms that would encourage irresponsible risk behavior, a direct effect of implicit risk insurance by the financial authorities.

4.2 RISK MANAGEMENT PROCESSES

Perhaps a good way to introduce the risk management processes is to rely on representative statements from the annual reports of various banks.

4.2.1 The "Three Lines of Defense" Principle

Control processes use various methods to align risk-taking and risk management throughout the organization. These controls, processes and methods are commonly organized around the so-called "three lines of defense":

- lines of business
- enterprise functions including risk management, compliance, finance, human resources and legal
- corporate audit.

The business lines, or front-office, make up the first line of defense and are responsible for identifying, quantifying, mitigating and managing all risks within their lines of business, while certain enterprise-wide risks are managed centrally.

In large banks, risk managers are embedded within the business lines and report to the central risk department for market risk and credit risk. They might report both to the business lines and to the central risk department. The existence of the risk department would not be enough

---

1 The term is used in the White Paper of the White House (2009) [78].
2 With the notable exception of Lehman Brothers' failure.

to enforce risk practices because it would relieve the business lines from their risk responsibilities. For avoiding such lack of accountability, all risk departments have representatives in the front offices of banks.

The business line management is closer to the changing nature of risks. It is best able to take actions to manage and mitigate those risks. Lines of business prepare periodic self-assessment reports to identify the status of risk issues, including mitigation plans, if appropriate. These reports roll up to executive management and to the risk department, to ensure appropriate risk management and oversight. For large transactions, approval by credit officers and a credit committee is a standard process. Embedded risk managers might be necessary, but they might be too close to business development for ensuring efficient risk control, even if they report to the central risk unit.

Trading-related activities have strong controls at the front office levels because decisions are "real-time." Trading requires daily committees and various levels of control, at the broad level of the trading pole, as well as the levels of "books" of the main broad types of instruments (equity, fixed income or credit), and at the "desk" level where trading is conducted.

Management processes, structures and policies should comply with regulations and provide clear lines for decision-making and accountability. Wherever practical, decision-making authority is often as close to the transactions as possible, while retaining supervisory control functions from both in and outside of the lines of business.

The key elements of the second line of defense are the central units. Risk management is in charge of risk oversight and is accountable for risk-taking guidelines and decisions. Other central functions include compliance, finance, information technology and operations, human resources, and legal functions. These groups are independent of the lines of businesses and are enterprise-wide. For organizational purposes, a senior risk executive might be assigned to each of the lines of business and be responsible for the oversight of all risks associated with that line of business. Enterprise-level risk executives have responsibility to develop and implement policies and practices to assess and manage enterprise-wide credit, market and operational risks.

The finance department is in charge of managing interest rate risk, liquidity risk and mismatch risk. The unit who manages such positions is the asset-liability management (ALM) unit. It has extended responsibilities for ensuring that risks remain within limits bank-wide. ALM is described below and is fully expanded in Section 7 of this text with all required techniques for managing these risks. Because ALM is usually allowed to maintain risk positions open, rather than fully hedge those risks, the risk department extends its oversight to the finance department.

Corporate audit is the third line of defense, and provides an independent assessment of management and internal control systems. Corporate audit activities are designed to provide reasonable assurance that resources are adequately protected; that significant financial, managerial and operating information is materially complete, accurate and reliable; and that employees' actions are in compliance with corporate policies, standards, procedures, and applicable laws and regulations.

Various methods are implemented to manage risks at business level and corporate-wide. Examples of these methods include planning and forecasting, risk committees and forums, limits, models, and hedging strategies, with various roles such as:

- Risk committees are composed of lines of business, risk management, treasury, compliance, legal and finance personnel, among others, who monitor performance, limits, potential issues, and introduction of new products.
- For trading new products, a "product" committee should ensure that the new product is manageable within the risk systems, that risk reporting is feasible and examines accordingly all specifics of the new products, from the pricing tools and up to the pricing risk when model valuation is used.
- Limits, the amount of exposure that may be taken with a product, a client, as well as with a region or industry, seek to align corporate-wide risk goals with those of each line of business and are a key part of the overall risk management process. Limits apply to various risk measures, from market volatility, credit exposure and operational losses.
- Models are used to estimate market value and net interest income sensitivity, and to assess expected and unexpected losses for each product and line of business, where appropriate, down to the level of large transactions. The risk department and the ALM unit are usually in charge of models that aggregate risks bank-wide.
- Planning and forecasting facilitates analysis of actual versus planned results and provides an indication of forecasted risk levels.
- Hedging strategies and enforcements of limits are used to manage the risk of borrower or counterparty risk and to manage market risk in the portfolio. Hedging and limits are both local, at the business level, and global once risks are aggregated and after diversification effects have been assessed.

4.2.2 Risk Management Organization and Central Functions

The emergence of risk models and the enterprise-wide organization of risk management, with the central units such as the risk department and asset-liability management (ALM), allow risk management to extend "bank wide," across all business lines and across different risks. Risk management practices traditionally differ across risks and business lines, so that a bank-wide scope supposes a single unified and consistent framework.

Bank-wide risk management promoted the centralization of risk management and the "clean break" between risk-taking business lines and risk-supervising units. Risk supervision requires independency from business units, since business units face conflicts between expanding business or profitability and risk controlling. A clean break between business lines and a bank-wide supervisory body applies to supervisory processes, such as setting guidelines or resolving conflicts between business units (front offices) and risk controlling. A centralized risk control unit would be over-loaded by the number of risk issues raised by the front offices. Risk managers embedded in business lines within the "first line of defense" should be accountable for risk as well, allowing decentralizing the process.

The risk-supervising unit has full control of risks, possibly at the cost of restricting some of the riskiest business developments. The risk department is under the direct control of the top management. It sets up all guidelines for controlling risk, such as risk limits and reporting, with which all business units should comply. As such, it defines, with the top management, the risk policy and the operational guidelines of the bank.

Two other central units are in charge of risk management, and are subject to the risk department supervision.

- ALM – asset and liability management – is the unit in charge of managing the mismatch risk and the liquidity of the bank. It belongs often to the finance department. Internal funding transfer prices are the responsibility of ALM. They serve for defining the costs of funds used up by all business lines. The fund transfer pricing (FTP) system is bank-wide and plays a key role in that it defines the cost of funding of the business lines.
- Credit portfolio management is a relatively recent function, whose purpose is to reshape the lending portfolio, or a fraction of it, making extensive usage of such techniques as "securitization" and credit derivatives to achieve such rebalancing. Credit portfolio management appears as the most recent evolution of the business model of banks, from the "originate and hold" view to the "originate and distribute" business model. "Distributing risks" means transferring them to other financial players, through securitizations or credit derivatives. Securitizations have been used for decades. Credit portfolio management uses credit derivatives for trading credit risk. When purchasing credit derivatives, it hedges the credit portfolio risk, when there is concentration of credit risk on certain industries or regions for example. When selling such instruments, it takes an exposure on credit risk, for increasing the diversification for example.

Both ALM and credit portfolio management have risk management duties that might generate additional profit for the bank, and can be profit centers. By contrast, the risk department has a supervision role, and might extend its activities to restructuring some transactions jointly with the business lines, for making sure that they comply with risk guidelines. But the risk department cannot be a profit center unlike the other risk management units.

Internal auditors, the "third line of defense," focus on periodical auditing of internal processes, making sure that they comply with internal rules as well as external regulations. Auditors can examine any unit of the bank, from central functions to all business lines. Although introduced here in relation to risk management, auditing has a larger scope of activities since its scope extends to all processes whether or not related to risk management. Auditing has the ability to make recommendations and supervise their execution. Compliance with risk regulations and supervising risk management tools, practices and models, risk data collection and recording in the information system relies on a number of areas of expertise. Internal auditing often relies on validation units for specialized auditing on risk models and information systems.

4.2.3 Limits and Delegations

The process for controlling risks is essentially based on risk limits and delegations. The purpose of limits is to set up an upper bound to the risks of transactions, of books or bank-wide, so that unexpected events cannot impair significantly the credit standing of the bank. Limits serve for capping exposure arising from transactions.

Limits are sometimes called authorizations, while utilizations refer to the extent of exposures within these upper bounds. Utilizations should remain lower than authorizations. The "utilization" of a committed line of credit might be much lower than the authorization, the latter being the limit attached to this product. A positive gap between authorization and utilization allows an increase in utilization by increasing lending and trading volume and/or risk.

For credit risk, limits are used to set upper bounds to credit risk on obligors, or country risk. There are multiple credit risk metrics, the "amount at risk," or exposure, being the simplest, and designating the potential amount that could be lost in the event of a default of the borrower. Other measurements include all components of credit risk: ratings, measuring the credit standing of any borrower, default probability, loss under default, and capital charge, either regulatory or economic. Regulatory capital complies with risk regulations. Economic capital is modeled internally and is not constrained by regulatory rules.

For market risk, limits set upper bounds to market risk sensitivity of market instruments to the various market parameters. In general, limits can apply to any risk measurement. Risk measurements for trading activities include all market risk components, such as sensitivity, volatility, inclusive of market value-at-risk which combines the effect of isolated components.

Risk limits set upper bounds to risks. They also set upper bounds on business volume, except when it is possible to hedge risks and avoid any excess exposure over limits. Hedging makes extensive use of derivative instruments. ALM makes extensive usage of interest rate derivatives, such as swaps, forward contracts and options on interest rates for hedging the interest rate risk arising from the banking portfolio.

For credit risk, there was no hedge until recently. Today, standard insurance contracts, guarantees, credit derivatives, securitizations, discussed later on, offer a wide range of techniques for taking on more risk while still complying with risk limits. Credit default swaps (CDS) are widely traded instruments providing insurance against credit risk losses in exchange for a fixed premium.

All derivatives shape both risk and return since they generate costs and revenues. For instance, a swap receiving the variable rate and paying a fixed rate might reduce the interest exposure, and, simultaneously generate variable rate revenues.

Note that the "originate and distribute" business models allows complying with all limits, including available capital to the extent that it allows off-loading risk from on and off balance sheet. Selling transactions is distinct from selling risks. When hedging, there is a risk transfer to another party, but instruments remain on and off balance sheet. When sales occur and are non-recourse, as is the case for securitizations, the transactions are off-loaded to SPEs financed in the capital markets.

Delegations serve for decentralizing the decision-making process. Delegations, at various levels of the bank, stipulate who has permission to take credit commitments depending on their sizes. Business lines do not need to refer to the central functions to make risk decisions as long as the risk is not too large, which allows delegating risk decisions to business units and risk managers. Delegations follow the same criteria as limits. Typical criteria for delegations are size of commitments or risk classes, defined by credit ratings or credit scores in retail banking. Delegations allow a smooth functioning of risk management but acceptability for risk-taking decisions theoretically remains in the hands of risk or account officers that use such delegations.

4.3 SETTING-UP LIMITS

Credit limits are perhaps the most important to the extent that credit risk is usually considered as the higher source of losses in most banks. As with other activities, they are set up and implemented using criteria and processes that other central units replicate, although with different measures and criteria.

4.3.1 Credit Risk and Lending Activities

Credit limits are defined along various risk metrics. They are set up according to multiple criteria and enforced through credit processes.

4.3.1.1 Credit Limits

Various types of limits are used. Limits can be set for each of the several metrics of risk. The process generates complexities because several limits are implemented simultaneously, one for each measure selected, and because some limits might be hit while others are not. Bank systems address the issue with excess limit reports showing which transaction hits which limit. Any excess limit has to be corrected either by not entering into a new transaction or by hedging (transferring risks).

Often, limits are combined into sub-limits, for example one for each product sold to the same borrower. Each borrower has a global limit and multiple sub-limits. Sub-limits do not need to sum up to the global limit of the counterparty. Only the total utilization of sub-limits should not exceed the global limit of each counterpart. For example, multiple currency facilities are convenient for clients because they allow using financing in several currencies. But the client should not use more than its global limit. Utilizations are bounded by either sub-limits or global limits, whichever is hit first. "Global limit" systems aggregate all risks on any single counterparty, no matter who initiates the risk, through multiple transactions originated by various business lines of the banks, and in different regions.

Bank-wide, global limits have a broader scope – "global limit" systems aggregate all risks on any single counterparty, no matter who initiates the risk, through multiple transactions originated by various business lines of the bank, and in different regions.

4.3.1.2 Defining Credit Limits

Credit limit systems set caps on amounts at risk with any one customer, with a single industry, or with countries, using various risk metrics and based on several criteria. The basic principles are simple and include:

- avoid that any single loss endangers the bank
- diversify the commitments across various dimensions such as customers, industries and regions
- avoid lending to any borrower an amount that would increase its debt beyond its borrowing capacity, the equity of the borrower setting up some reasonable limit to its debt given acceptable levels of debt/equity ratios and repayment ability
- set up some maximum risk level, for example defined by rating, above which lending is prohibited
- risk diversification rules across counterparties are necessary for avoiding "concentrations" of credit risk.

A minimum diversification across rating classes is regarded as necessary, with some floor to the rating of borrowers. For being comprehensive and consistent, the limit system has to be bank-wide. A top-down view of limits would start from the capital of the bank for defining global limits to lending. Regulatory capital is defined for each individual transaction, and total capital sums up the individual capital charges. Available capital can serve for setting a global capital constraint. Within that constraint, the allocation of the bank's commitments across industries, rating classes, types of borrowers, or any other dimension, remains subject to top management guidelines.

"Name lending" applies to big corporations or financial institutions with an excellent credit standing, with few restrictions on volume once the bank has recognized the value of doing business with such well-known big clients.

4.3.1.3 Credit Process

Credit approval processes vary across banks and across transaction types. For large transactions, credit officers and credit committees reach a minimal agreement before authorizing a credit decision by examining in detail significant credit applications. The approval mechanism is either through credit committees or signatures. Credit committees bring together the business line, risk managers and the general management. The front office proposes new transactions, and the committee examines the risk and makes a yes/no decision or might issue recommendations for altering the proposed transaction until it complies with risk standards. This is commonly done by using credit risk mitigants, such as collateral, third party guarantees or contractual clauses that mitigate the risk.

The alternate process is through "signatures" whereby the transaction proposal is circulated and approval requires agreement between all credit officers and front office. Whether signatures or committees are used for approval, risk officers remain accountable for the risk decisions and decisions are recorded, eventually with comments and recommendations of participating executives.

Such processes are applicable for large transaftions. Such time-consuming processes are not applicable for the retail portfolio because of the high number of transactions. Instead credit scoring mechanisms and delegations are used, with committees dealing with guidelines or exceptional decisions.

4.3.2 Market Risk and Trading Activities

The same principles apply to controlling market risk. In these cases, for limiting the potential loss of adverse moves of markets, banks set upper bounds to such parameters as sensitivity of instruments and of portfolios. Limits depend on expectations about market conditions. Market instability might require tighter limits because the chances of large fluctuations are higher. As with credit risk, there are several risk metrics that can serve for defining limits.

Sensitivities are changes of values due to standard shocks on market parameters such as interest rates, foreign exchange rates, or equity indexes. Sensitivities are often measured in monetary values rather than percentages. Because sensitivities drive changes of values, they often serve as a measure of exposure, the size of the transaction value or the notional (face value) being less relevant. Traders prefer to use a broader spectrum of risk measures, which are called "Greeks." Sensitivities are constant with a linear instrument such as a forward contract. The delta of an option measures by how much an option value changes when the underlying asset value changes. Other Greeks are usually defined[3]. For example, convexity is the change of sensitivities due to market movements. Options are non-linear instruments, meaning that their sensitivities to the value of the underlying asset is not constant. The change of the delta is

---

3 Sensitivities are detailed in Chapter 15.

named gamma. In general, the "Greeks" measure how the value of transaction changes when each single parameter that influences the value, or "risk factor," changes. Market value-at-risk combines the effects of the various market risk measurements and serves to define limits for desks, trading books, or at the global level.

Traders comply with such limits by capping trading volume and hedging their risks. Limits are set for the various desks, grouped by books, consistently with aggregate market risk. Excess limits imply hedging, using derivatives or hedging techniques, or limiting trading volume.

Models are essential for defining proper hedges because they provide the Greeks. For example, delta hedging means neutralizing the sensitivity of the hedged instrument with another hedging instrument. Equity options sold can be hedged by holding positions on the underlying stock. How much stock should be bought or sold depends on the delta. Delta hedging does not provide a full hedge against market fluctuations, since options are non-linear, and also depend on other parameters, such as market volatility.

4.3.3 Asset-liability Management (ALM)

Asset-liability management is a central function, usually located within the finance department. Its main goals are to manage liquidity risk, interest rate risk and mismatch risk bank-wide. In terms of interest rate risk, ALM's main target variables are:

- the net interest margin or income (NIM or NII), which is the difference between interest revenues and interest costs
- the economic value of the balance sheet, which is a mark-to-model valuation of assets minus liabilities (mark-to-model is defined in subsequent sections).

For maintaining adequate liquidity and mismatch risk, ALM sets up limits to future funding requirements and manages the debt structure of the banks. For managing the interest rate risk of the target variables, the ALM unit also sets up limits, in conjunction with the risk department, and defines hedging policies. Stress scenarios and contingency planning in both liquidity and interest rate risks are also defined by the ALM unit.

4.4 ENTERPRISE-WIDE RISK MANAGEMENT (ERM)

Bank-wide management implies linking measurements of income and risk at the global bank's level with those used to define income and risk at the business unit, books and transaction levels.

4.4.1 Top-down and Bottom-up Risk Management Processes and Systems

The top-down process starts with global guidelines, with target earnings and risk limits at the bank-wide level. Such guidelines need to be converted into "signals" to business units, such as target revenues, risk limits, and other guidelines with respect to business unit policies. They make it necessary to allocate aggregated income and risks to business units and transactions for linking the global targets with operations.

The monitoring and the reporting of risks is bottom-up oriented, starting with transactions, and ending up with aggregated risks and income. Aggregation is required for supervision purposes and for comparing, at all levels where decision-making occurs, goals with actual realizations.

Navigating top-down or bottom-up from global to transaction level bank-wide requires measurements of risk and profit such that they make aggregated values consistent with the broken-down values of risk and earnings at the various levels for operations, business units, books, or individual transactions (when feasible). Several building blocks need to be assembled for achieving such a goal.

Three of them, expanded in subsequent sections of this book, deserve to be mentioned as necessary for achieving enterprise-wide risk management:

- fund transfer pricing systems
- risk and capital allocation systems
- risk-adjusted performance measures.

Section 8, Chapters 28 and 29, deals with fund transfer pricing; risk allocation of the bank's portfolio risk to subportfolios, business lines or transactions is expanded in Section 13, Chapters 52 to 54; risk-adjusted performance is addressed in Section 14, Chapters 55 and 56. Risk-adjusted performance allows comparing returns across units or transactions of differing risk and making explicit their consistency or discrepancy with the risk guidelines and the target profitability of the bank. Transfer pricing sets up the cost of funding for business lines, and serves to allocate earnings across business lines. Capital allocation designates the allocation of risks across business units. Risk allocation implies modeling because risks do not add up arithmetically due to the diversification effects.

Such building blocks of risk systems allow interactions between risk management and business lines in a consistent bank-wide risk management framework. Without setting them up, there would simply be no way to navigate top-down and bottom-up from business operations to global levels, neither for making decisions nor for monitoring. Without strong economic foundations, they would put the credibility of the risk management at stake and they would create biases between the global goals and business level target variables.

Banks face trade-offs between business volume and risk as well as between business volume and profitability. The target profitability of the bank should be risk-adjusted for providing signals to business units for making business. Risk-adjusted measures of performance require a measurement of risk and are necessary for several purposes such as: comparing performances across business lines; assessing the effect of risk management on performance; achieving a proper balance between risk and profitability in line with risk appetite of the bank and the required profitability.

The allocation of bank's earnings across units is performed with the fund transfer pricing (FTP) system. The risk allocation that serves for risk-adjusted performance measurement is the capital allocation system. Both are expanded in dedicated sections. The sole purpose of mentioning them here is to show how they resolve the technical challenge of enterprise-wide risk management and make it feasible.

4.4.2 Earnings Allocation and Fund Transfer Pricing (FTP) System

For all lending activities, which use up cash, some cost of funds has to be defined. The mechanism relies on internal transfer prices. The purpose of the FTP system is to define income at business unit, book and transaction levels for those transactions using up funds, and to make aggregation of such elementary incomes consistent with the overall bank's income. FTP systems are detailed in Section 8.

With the internal reference prices provided by the FTP system, the income allocation consists in calculating the income as the difference between revenues and internal prices. When aggregating allocated incomes, the internal transfers of funds should net to a zero cost. The mechanisms impose that the cost of funds of business units is identical to the revenue of the FTP unit, the central pool of funds. Target profitability imposes mark-ups over these economic prices.

For trading activities, the earnings are defined by the variations of transaction value over a period, and these add up algebraically to total earnings from trading activities. For some portfolios, the revenue is the spread between the yield of securities held and the cost of funds. Any bias in the cost of funds would result in either a subsidy or a penalty for such portfolios. For the banking portfolio, transfer prices apply to loans and to deposit collection. For the market portfolio, those are all market instruments that are "held to maturity" within the trading portfolio[4]. An example is "spread books" held for capturing the spread between the yield of securities, mainly bonds, and the cost of financing these instruments. For loans, transfer prices allow isolating their net interest income, and for setting a cost for warehousing of loans that pile up in the "ramping period" before they are securitized[5].

There are other difficulties for allocating trading profit to proprietary trading and trading for sales to clients because both activities are managed together within trading portfolios. Such allocations are not dealt with in transfer pricing schemes, but through conventions within the trading unit.

4.4.3 Capital and Risk Allocation System

Risk allocation is less intuitive than income allocation because risks do not add up arithmetically as income does. The risk of the sum (1 + 1) is lower than 2, the sum of risks, due to diversification effects. As a result, both risk aggregation and breaking down global risk into risks allocated to business units, books or transactions, is more complex. The global risk is lower than the arithmetic addition of all elementary risks generated by transactions or by books of transactions because aggregation diversifies away a large fraction of the sum of all standalone transaction risks. Without a proper risk allocation system, there would be a missing link between the risks of transactions and the aggregated enterprise risk that the bank's capital makes sustainable.

At the level of transactions or books, risk is often named "standalone," meaning "as if" the transaction or book were isolated from the rest of the banks' portfolio, that diversifies away a significant fraction of standalone risk. Hence, economically, standalone risks do not sum to total risk.

---

4 See Chapter 21 for the classification of assets within the different categories of portfolios defined according to management intention.
5 See the UBS Shareholder Report [75] which describes in detail how internal cost of funds can affect the policies within the trading book. See also [67].

Note that, for credit risk, the regulatory capital charges are additive since they are calculated for each individual transaction[6]. Total regulatory capital for credit risk is additive and adds up to total regulatory capital for credit risk. Regulatory capital charges applied to single transactions embed a standard diversification effect defined by regulators. The drawback of such simplification is that such standard diversification might differ from the actual diversification effect, which remains specific to each portfolio. On the other hand, regulatory capital for market risk is VaR based, or model-based, and is similar to economic capital.

The purpose of the capital allocation system is to define a risk measurement, serving for allocating the global risk to business units, books and transactions, and to make aggregated risks consistent with the overall bank's risk after diversification effects. Portfolio risk models provide the right technique for calculating economic capital, which is not rule-based, and for capturing risk diversification when moving bottom-up and top-down. Capital allocation is detailed in the dedicated Section 13.

---

6 See Chapters 20 and 21 on risk regulations.

SECTION 3

Financial Products

Risk depends on products and clients. This section has two main purposes:

- providing an overview of financial products
- defining hedging products and explaining how they serve for hedging purposes.

Financial products are traditionally divided into banking portfolio products and capital market instruments. The overview of lending products is largely inspired by the Basel 2 definitions, which are representative of the variety of this class of products.

The purpose of subsequent chapters is entirely different. These chapters provide the basics for understanding derivatives and how they are used for risk management. There are three chapters, respectively dedicated to:

- fixed income derivatives
- foreign exchange derivatives
- credit derivatives.

All three chapters provide a view on the forward contract family of products and of optional products. For forward contracts, they detail how they can be engineered from cash transactions.

Detailed analyses of such products are classical and well developed in many other publications. This text does not address pricing issues. The focus is more on how such products are used for hedging (or speculating) than on simple definitions.

5

Banking and Financial Products

Financial products are traditionally divided into banking portfolio products and capital market instruments. This chapter focuses on traditional lending activities (banking portfolio).

There are several ways of setting up a meaningful classification of lending products relevant from a bank's management and a credit risk perspective. Basel 2 refined the generic classifications for defining which "capital treatment" should be applied. Capital treatment designates the rules used to calculate the regulatory capital charge for credit risk. In most cases, Basel 2 definitions are consistent with a bank's segmentation of products for management purposes.

The first section of this chapter addresses the criteria for differentiating lending products. Although Basel 2 differentiated lending activities with the main goal of defining appropriate capital treatments, the Basel 2 classification[1] is widely used for describing the various types of products because it provides fairly accurate definitions that are generally consistent with bank management. Accordingly, subsequent sections follow the Basel 2 classification. Such presentation allows both describing products and introducing the reader to Basel 2 views of risk. The taxonomy of Basel 2 lending transactions starts from the main asset classes and ends up with some specific cases, such as specialized lending and securitization products.

Contents

---

1   From the final Basel 2 documents from the BIS [7]. Other publications of lending products include Neftci [55].

5.1   CLASSIFICATION OF LENDING PRODUCTS AND BASEL 2 CRITERIA

Basel 2 uses the term "exposure" for designating transactions, or, equivalently, facilities in banking terminology. The term "exposure" refers to the credit risk to which transactions are exposed.

Basel 2 differentiates products based on asset classes, defined by type of counterparty (corporation, sovereign, bank, individual) and in some cases on product characteristics. Basel 2 regulations segregate transactions according to "capital treatment." The asset class is the starting point for implementing capital charge calculations, or "capital treatment." Hence, asset classes are not entirely defined by pure credit risk criteria, but serves for defining "eligibility" to the various capital treatments allowed under Basel 2. In spite of some differences, capital treatment follows generally accepted principles for dealing with credit risk.

If we refer to economic and risk management criteria, the common terminology differs from Basel 2 classification. Lending differs according to whether it is secured or unsecured, whether it is collateral based or not, and whether the risk is more transaction-specific than borrower based. A secured transaction benefits from guarantees, which are named "credit risk mitigants" in Basel 2. All guarantees are generally transaction-specific.

Unsecured lending is therefore primarily credit standing based. Secured lending depends on both borrower's credit standing and transaction-specific guarantees. Many secured transactions have a lower credit risk than the borrower because of the guarantees attached. A transaction can be secured by collateral pledged to the lender or by third party guarantees, or contracts that transfer the credit risk to the guarantor.

Specialized lending is mainly transaction-specific because lending is primarily backed by the transaction collateral and the terms of lending contract, which make up a "term sheet" assembling a variety of contractual clauses that protect the borrowers.

In the definition of lending products, we frequently use the Basel 2 definitions, because they are both comprehensive and specific. The reference document is "International Convergence of Capital Measurement and Capital Standards – A Revised Framework, Comprehensive Version" [7], of which several excerpts are used here. The paragraph references in the text are the references of this document.

Basel 2 uses broad classes of assets with different underlying risk characteristics. Except for the equity asset class, which relates to the nature of the instrument (equity), other asset classes are by type of counterparty. The five main Basel 2 asset classes are:

- corporate
- banks
- sovereign
- retail: individuals and small and medium-sized enterprises (SMEs)
- equity.

Within the corporate asset class, five sub-classes of "specialized lending" are separately identified. Within the retail asset class, three sub-classes are separately identified. The sub-classes are described in subsequent sections.

5.2 SOVEREIGN, BANK, AND EQUITY EXPOSURES

We provide the Basel 2 definitions hereafter, in indented paragraphs. All excerpts are from the comprehensive document issued by the Basel Committee on Banking Supervision, or BCBS (June 2006)[2].

5.2.1 Bank Exposures

This asset class covers exposures to banks and those to securities firms. The definition is self-explanatory. Note that insurance companies are subject to the regulatory treatment of the "corporate" asset class, and there is no "financial institution" category.

5.2.2 Sovereign Exposures

§229. This asset class covers all exposures to counterparties treated as sovereigns under the standardized approach. This includes sovereigns (and their central banks), certain PSEs identified as sovereigns in the standardized approach ("MDB").

Public sector entities (PSEs) are considered "sovereign" if they comply with certain criteria. "MDB" designates Multilateral Development Banks. The "standardized approach" is the simplest of the three Basel 2 approaches[3].

5.2.3 Equity Exposures

The equity asset class refers to equity stakes in other corporations, held by the bank. It does not refer to equity instruments held for trading purposes in the banking portfolio.

§235. In general, equity exposures are defined on the basis of the economic substance of the instrument. They include both direct and indirect ownership interests, whether voting or non-voting, in the assets and income of a commercial enterprise or of a financial institution ….

Note that equity-linked instruments, such as an obligation that can be settled by issuance of issuer's equity shares, are categorized as equity.

---

2 Paragraphs numbering the BCBS document [7] are included for convenience.
3 Basel 2 regulations are detailed in Chapter 20, from Section 6 dedicated to regulations.

5.3 RETAIL PORTFOLIO IN BASEL 2

The retail portfolio is characterized by a large number of small exposures. An exposure is categorized as retail exposure if it meets all the criteria given hereafter, under Basel 2. The retail portfolio is defined according to several criteria, which are mainly product, "granularity" of the retail portfolio, and maximum size of each exposure. The segment includes lending to small corporations, which include individual corporations (such as for physicians or pharmacies). Finally, mortgages are included in the retail portfolio and segregated into sub-classes.

5.3.1 Nature of Borrower or Low Value of Individual Exposures

Exposures are to individuals – such as revolving credits and lines of credit (e.g. credit cards, overdrafts, and retail facilities secured by financial instruments) as well as personal term loans and leases (e.g. instalment loans, auto loans and leases, student and educational loans, personal finance, and other exposures with similar characteristics).

Residential mortgage loans (including first and subsequent lines, term loans and revolving home equity lines of credit) are eligible for retail treatment regardless of exposure size so long as the credit is extended to an individual that is the owner of the property. Loans extended to small businesses and managed as retail exposures are eligible for retail treatment provided the total exposure of the banking group to a small business borrower (on a consolidated basis where applicable) is less than €1 million.

5.3.2 Large Number of Exposures

§232. The exposure must be one of a large pool of exposures, which are managed by the bank on a pooled basis.

The exposure should not exceed 0.2% of the overall regulatory retail portfolio, which imposes a limit to the size of loan. Retail portfolios have to be "granular." Granularity designates the absence of size concentration and wide diversification across a large number of clients. Retail exposures should not exceed €1 million.

SMEs (small and medium-sized enterprises) can be considered as "retail" provided that they are not dealt with on an individual basis when granting credit. When lending is based on a specific credit analysis, the loan falls in the corporate asset class. Accordingly, small business exposures are managed as a part of a pool of exposure for the purpose of risk assessment. For Basel 2 treatment, small business exposures are subject to the €1 million cap.

5.3.3 Retail Portfolio: Further Differentiation for Capital Treatment

§233. Within the retail asset class category, banks are required to identify separately three sub-classes of exposures: (a) exposures secured by residential properties as defined above, (b) qualifying revolving retail exposures..., and (c) all other retail exposures.

Banks divide their retail activities in segments, which are more or less homogeneous, by type of transactions, such as mortgages versus consumer lending, and by type of counterparty, such as SMEs versus individuals. "Qualifying revolving retail exposures" refer to loans which are allowed to fluctuate based on clients' decisions. This includes credit card lending and overdraft of demand deposits.

§234. All of the following criteria must be satisfied for a sub-portfolio to be treated as a qualifying revolving retail exposure (QRRE). These criteria must be applied at a sub-portfolio level consistent with the bank's segmentation of its retail activities generally. Segmentation at the national or country level (or below) should be the general rule.

The exposures are revolving, unsecured, and uncommitted (both contractually and in practice). In this context, revolving exposures are defined as those where customers' outstanding balances are permitted to fluctuate based on their decisions to borrow and repay, up to a limit established by the bank.

The exposures are to individuals.

The maximum exposure to a single individual in the sub-portfolio is €100,000 or less.

5.4 TRANSACTION-SPECIFIC CREDIT RISK

Following common practices, Basel 2 considers two dimensions to credit risk: The borrower's credit standing and the transaction-specific features that "mitigate" borrower's credit risk.

Credit risk in lending activities is primarily driven by the credit standing of the borrower. Credit standing varies across counterparties and is qualified primarily by credit ratings. Under Basel 2, credit ratings are assigned to all borrowers from the bank, corporates, individuals in retail banking, and sovereign. Note that Basel credit ratings are distinct from credit ratings of rating agencies, which are defined for debt issues rather than by borrower (or "issuer").

5.4.1 Credit Risk Mitigants

Most transactions include some specific features which influence their credit risk. Transaction risk is differentiated by techniques that "mitigate" credit risk. There are many common credit risk mitigants, including "debt seniority," collateral pledged to the lender, third-party guarantees, covenants or contractual clauses binding the borrower's obligations.

Seniority is the priority ranking of loans or "claims" of the bank. Senior loans are paid first, while subordinated debt is paid only once senior claims have been repaid in full. Loans can be secured or unsecured. For secured debt, collateral is pledged to the lender. Collateral is used here as a generic term for designating cash, securities, commodities, some other assets (gold...), or physical assets such as residential real estate property. In the event of default, the lender becomes the owner of the collateral, can sell it and use the proceeds as (partial) repayment of its claim on the borrower. Third-party guarantees are provided by "guarantors" who commit to repay debts of borrowers if the latter default.

Covenants are contractual clauses imposed by lenders on various borrowers' debts. They specify lender's obligation with respect to a transaction. Covenants are legal or financial. Legal covenants stipulate the obligations of the borrowers, such as "Do this," "don't do this." Financial covenants are quantitative constraints imposed on borrowers. Some covenants are economic. They impose a minimum diversification of portfolio posted as collateral, or are triggered by credit events such as downgrades. Other financial covenants are the leverage of the borrower, the ratio of debt to equity, or the debt cover ratio (DCR), which is the ratio of cash flows generated by the borrowing entity to the amount due over the same period. DCRs have to be higher than one.

A covenant breach occurs when the borrower does not comply with the constraint. A breach triggers prompt repayment in theory. In practice, a breach provides an opportunity for lenders to restructure the transaction and impose additional restrictions intended to mitigate the risk (more equity from sponsors, etc.). Waivers can be granted by lenders in the event of a breach, allowing the borrower to continue operations.

Collateral-based transactions include all transactions backed by collateralized assets. In the financial system, all players hold a portfolio of securities, which can be eligible for collateral. Such transactions are subject to a minimum ratio of collateral value to the amount of borrowing. The value of collateral is higher than the amount lent. The difference serves as a buffer against the fluctuations of values of securities posted as collateral. The gap between collateral value and loan amount is called the "haircut." It represents the safety cushion required by lenders for lending. Repurchase/reverse repurchases and securities lending/borrowing, or "repo-style transactions," use securities as collateral of the debt and are widely used. Under Basel 2, such transactions are generically designated as securities lending and borrowing, since such securities are exchanged for serving as collateral gain the cash lent or borrowed.

Because such features are transaction-specific, credit risk mitigation is relevant only at the transaction level. Various loans to the same borrowers differ in terms of credit risk because they benefits from different credit mitigants.

5.4.2 Credit Risk Mitigation under Basel 2

Credit risk mitigation in Basel 2 is characterized by loss given default (LGD) equal to amount due, inclusive of interest accrued, minus recoveries from guarantees in the event of default and minus work-out costs. LGD is defined at the transaction level. The LGD is expressed as percentage of the total amount due, principal and interests accrued. The recoveries are 100% minus the LGD in percentage. Loss under default and recoveries cannot be defined at the level of the borrower because various loans have different loss rates. Some debts are more senior than others, some are secured and others are not, etc. The LGD quantifies the transaction-specific risk, the fraction of credit risk that depends on the transaction rather than on the borrower's credit standing.

Agency ratings address investors in debt issues. Accordingly, they are issue-specific, unlike issuers' ratings which characterize the borrowers' credit standings. Note that Basel credit ratings differ from agencies' credit ratings to the extent that they specify the credit standing of the borrower. Issuers' ratings are similar to unsecured debt ratings because such debts are only secured by the credit standing of the borrower. The LGD serves for characterizing the transaction-specific risk.

5.5 SECURITY LENDING AND BORROWING

Security lending and borrowing is a form of collateral-based lending/borrowing that deserves attention because it is a major source of funding for financial institutions and because it further illustrates the mechanisms of collateral-based lending/borrowing.

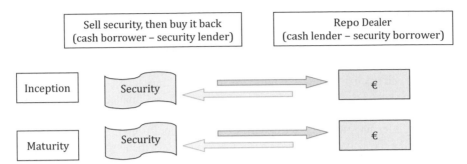

FIGURE 5.1   Repo style transactions

A repurchase or "repo" transaction consists of selling a security and simultaneously committing to repurchase it at the original price at a later date. Repos are used for securing borrowing at a lower cost than straight debt because the transaction is secured by the security. For example, repos are used for financing a "book" of bonds, where the revenues of bonds should exceed the cost of funding, which should be minimized.

The investor buys a security and funds it at lowest cost. Instead of securing the funding before buying the security, the investor follows a reverse sequence, getting the financing based on the acquired security (Figure 5.1). The sequence is: buy the security, repo it out, secure the funds, pay for security. The transaction combines two transactions twice, which occur at inception and at the end. At inception, the investor acquires the security by borrowing cash through repo and commits to return it back to the repo dealer at a predetermined price (same price as at inception) and date. The investor lends the security and borrows cash. The repo dealer lends cash and borrows the security. The repo dealer gets the security and pays cash, and sells it back at the predetermined price (same price as at inception) and date, and receives cash back, plus the interest cost of financing. At maturity, the investor (borrower of cash) receives back the security and pays cash back plus interest. The repo dealer (lender of cash) delivers security and gets back cash plus interest. In such transactions, the lender of cash (the repo dealer) is in fact "borrowing" the security and the borrower of cash is lending the security. Note that such transactions can be subject to haircuts and margin calls because of the fluctuation of the security value. Because they are not exempt of credit risk due to such fluctuations, Basel 2 assigns a capital charge to such transactions. There are variations of repo-style transactions. For example, in security lending/borrowing, the borrower of security lends cash, but does not need the cash and rather wants to earn a return by lending the security.

Because financial organizations often hold large volumes of securities and because of the cost-reducing effect, repo volume is very high. Repo illustrates the "usage" value of a security. The value of a security is its price. The "usage value" relates more to what you can do with the security, in a wider context than the security considered in isolation, in order to create value. When securing financing trough "repo-style" transactions, the cost of funding becomes lower than the cost of financing of the financial entity that holds securities. The process enhances the spread between securities held in the book and the cost of funding. Widening the spread earned from the portfolio creates value. Pledging securities has the same effect. Security lending is also used in "short sales" whereby a trader sells a security that he or she does not own, necessitating borrowing the security.

5.6 SPECIALIZED LENDING

Under Basel 2, the specialized lending activities are differentiated because they have dedicated capital treatment, due to the specific economics of these transactions. Essentially, specialized lending has a credit risk that could be qualified as primarily "transaction-based" and "collateral-based." The five sub-classes of specialized lending are: project finance, object finance, commodities finance, income-producing real estate, and high-volatility commercial real estate.

In specialized lending, the transaction risk is more isolated from the credit standing of the borrower(s) since the actual borrower is a dedicated vehicle which secures the debt with the cash flows generated by its assets. The direct counterparty for lending is a "special purpose entity," or "SPE," which shelters the "object" financed that secures the transaction, and is isolated from the borrower. According to Basel 2, the common features to all specialized lending (SL) transactions are as follows:

§219. The exposure is typically to an entity, often a special purpose entity (SPE) which was created specifically to finance and/or operate physical assets;

The borrowing entity has little or no other material assets or activities, and therefore little or no independent capacity to repay the obligation, apart from the income that it receives from the asset(s) being financed;

The terms of the obligation give the lender a substantial degree of control over the asset(s) and the income that it generates;

As a result of the preceding factors, the primary source of repayment of the obligation is the income generated by the asset(s), rather than the independent capacity of a broader commercial enterprise.

Basel 2 describes the salient features of SPEs as follows:

§552. An SPE is a corporation, trust, or other entity organized for a specific purpose, the activities of which are limited to those appropriate to accomplish the purpose of the SPE, and the structure of which is intended to isolate the SPE from the credit risk of an originator or seller of exposures.

SPEs are commonly used as financing vehicles in which exposures are sold to a trust or similar entity in exchange for cash or other assets funded by debt issued by the trust.

The subsequent descriptions of the five different specialized lending transactions detail the specific features of each sub-class. In many cases, we replicate below the Basel 2 definitions, which are both precise and self-explanatory.

5.6.1 Project Finance

Project finance (PF) (§221) is a method of funding in which the lender looks primarily to the revenues generated by a single project, both as the source of repayment and as security for the exposure. This type of financing is usually for large, complex and expensive installations that might include, for example, power plants, chemical processing plants, mines, transportation infrastructure, environment, and telecommunications infrastructure.

In such transactions (§222), the lender is usually paid solely or almost exclusively out of the money generated by the contracts for the facility's output, such as the electricity sold by a power plant. The borrower is usually an SPE that is not permitted to perform any function other than developing, owning, and operating the installation. The consequence is that repayment depends primarily on the project's cash flow and on the collateral value of the project's assets. In contrast, if repayment of the exposure depends primarily on a well-established, diversified, credit-worthy, contractually obligated end-user for repayment, it is considered a secured exposure to that end-user.

5.6.2 Object Finance

Object finance (OF) (§223) refers to a method of funding the acquisition of physical assets (e.g. ships, aircraft, satellites, railcars, and fleets) where the repayment of the exposure is dependent on the cash flows generated by the specific assets that have been financed and pledged or assigned to the lender. A primary source of these cash flows might be rental or lease contracts with one or several third parties.

In contrast, if the exposure is to a borrower whose financial condition and debt-servicing capacity enables it to repay the debt without undue reliance on the specifically pledged assets, the exposure should be treated as a collateralized corporate exposure.

In object financing, the risk of lending changes over the life of the financing, when both loan principal and price of assets decline. After a while, the LTV gets always lower than 1 even if starting with a LTV above 1, because the loan amortization makes its outstanding balance lower than the asset value at some point in time.

5.6.3 Commodities Finance

Commodities finance (CF) (§224) refers to structured short-term lending to finance reserves, inventories, or receivables of exchange-traded commodities (e.g. crude oil, metals, or crops), where the exposure will be repaid from the proceeds of the sale of the commodity and the borrower has no independent capacity to repay the exposure.

This is the case when the borrower has no other activities and no other material assets on its balance sheet. The structured nature of the financing is designed to compensate for the weak credit quality of the borrower. The exposure's rating reflects its self-liquidating nature and the lender's skill in structuring the transaction rather than the credit quality of the borrower.

§225. The Committee believes that such lending can be distinguished from exposures financing the reserves, inventories, or receivables of other more diversified corporate borrowers. Banks are able to rate the credit quality of the latter type of borrowers based on their broader ongoing operations. In such cases, the value of the commodity serves as risk mitigant rather than as the primary source of repayment.

5.6.4 Income-producing Real Estate

Income-producing real estate (IPRE) (§226) refers to a method of providing funding to real estate (such as, office buildings to let, retail space, multifamily residential buildings, industrial or warehouse space, and hotels) where the prospects for repayment and recovery on the exposure depend primarily on the cash flows generated by the asset. The primary source of these cash flows would generally be lease or rental payments or the sale of the asset.

The borrower may be, but is not required to be, an SPE, an operating company focused on real estate construction or holdings, or an operating company with sources of revenue other than real estate. The distinguishing characteristic of IPRE versus other corporate exposures that are collateralized by real estate is the strong positive correlation between the prospects for repayment of the exposure and the prospects for recovery in the event of default, with both depending primarily on the cash flows generated by a property.

5.6.5 High-volatility Commercial Real Estate

High-volatility commercial real estate (HVCRE) (§227) lending is the financing of commercial real estate that exhibits higher loss rate volatility (i.e. higher asset correlation) compared to other types of SL.

"HVCRE" includes:

- commercial real estate exposures secured by properties of types that are categorized by the national supervisor as sharing higher volatilities in portfolio default rates
- loans financing any of the land acquisition, development and construction (ADC) phases for properties of those types
- loans financing ADC of any other properties where the source of repayment at origination of the exposure is either the future uncertain sale of the property or cash flows whose source of repayment is substantially uncertain (e.g. the property has not yet been leased, occupancy rate is uncertain), unless the borrower has substantial equity at risk.

5.7 SECURITIZATIONS

An entire set of regulatory rules applies to securitizations because neither common criteria applicable to credit risk apply, nor do the regulatory rules for capital treatment.

Securitizations are special transactions whereby assets are sold to investors. In a traditional securitization of loans, for example, a bank sells the loan to an SPE which issues a series of bonds, called "notes," of various seniority levels. Such loan-backed notes are sold to investors, who acquire them based on the rating provided by a rating agency. The financing through a series of notes rather than a single loan-backed note is called the tranching, each note being a "tranche" of total financing provided by investors in the vehicle. Senior notes are paid first, while the subordinated notes are paid last. The most subordinated note is sometimes called the "equity tranche" because it stands to lose all its value since all portfolio losses are routed first to this last tranche. Sometimes, this tranche is called a zero-equity tranche because of the expected loss being 100% of its value.

The economics of securitization are fully expanded in the Chapter 58 of this book. But the basic economics of SPEs are simple. It is possible to securitize an asset or a pool of assets as long as the expected cash flows generated by such assets are sufficient to provide the required compensation to investors for all tranches according to the risk of each tranche. Since cash flows are expected, there is always a risk for investors, which declines when moving up the seniority scale. Both ratings and credit spreads of each class of note depend on its seniority (which one is paid 1st, 2nd and so on), the thickness of the tranche and its ranking in the seniority scale.

According to this principle, any asset can be securitized. The first securitizations were backed by pools of mortgage loans, generally of good quality, and the issued notes were called "mortgage-backed securities." Securitizations expanded considerably and extended to several asset types. Securitized assets include corporate loans, bonds, any type of debt, credit card receivables, leasing receivables, and office building (which generates rents as cash flows). They are designated with abbreviations such as CLO or CDO, meaning, respectively, "collateralized loan obligations" or "collateralized debt obligations." Each type of securitizations has specific features. Credit cards securitizations required to be reloaded periodically (monthly) over 7 years with new credit cards receivables, because consumer lending through cards has an average short maturity, and the cost of setting up the vehicle needs to be amortized over several years.

The expansion of securitizations was a key factor in the shift of the business model of banks from the initial "originate and hold" to the "originate and distribute" business model. The "distribution" term in the new business model refers to the distribution of risk of assets securitized to investors in the notes issued by securitization vehicles. Securitizations came to a halt in the 2007–2008 financial crisis because they were considered as major vector of risk contagion cross the financial system and because some securitizations of the so-called "toxic assets" performed very poorly during the crisis. Their asset-backed bonds were subject to a large number of significant downgrades reflecting their poor quality after the crisis.

In the case of CDOs, securitizations are further differentiated according to the economic rationale for setting up the vehicle. Balance sheet CDOs use balance sheet assets and the rationale for selling those assets is to save the regulatory capital charge, freeing up capital for new business. Balance sheet CDOs aim at capital relief for originating banks. Arbitrage CDOs are used to arbitrage the credit market. In this case, banks sell credit risk to investors at a price higher than "fair" cost of credit risk. The arbitrage is not risk-free and is profitable. The opportunity for such arbitrage exists to the extent that ratings of notes issued do not reflect the exact risk of the tranche. The "exact" risk of the tranche is modeled with credit portfolio models, as explained in the "Credit portfolio model" section of this book (Section 12). It is subject to model risk. But as long as the payments to investors is lower than the expected return matching the rating of each tranche, it is understandable that the vehicle provides an excess return over payments due to investors, which is the proceeds of such arbitrage.

Basel 2 defines precisely traditional securitizations, whereby assets are securitized, and synthetic securitizations which are based on the issuance of credit derivatives, as explained below.

5.7.1 Securitizations: Traditional

§539. A *traditional securitization* is a structure where the cash flow from an underlying pool of exposures is used to service at least two different stratified risk positions or tranches reflecting different degrees of credit risk. Payments to the investors depend upon the performance of the specified underlying exposures, as opposed to being derived from an obligation of the entity originating those exposures.

The stratified/tranched structures that characterize securitizations differ from ordinary senior/subordinated debt instruments in that junior securitization tranches can absorb losses without interrupting contractual payments to more senior tranches, whereas subordination in a senior/subordinated debt structure is a matter of priority of rights to the proceeds of liquidation.

"Tranched structure" refers to the various seniority levels of debts issued, backed by the asset cash flows of the SPE, which are sold to investors providing the funding of the securitization vehicle. The bulk of securitizations are traditional. Synthetic securitizations appeared only when the credit instruments which allow setting up such vehicles emerged.

5.7.2 Securitizations: Synthetic

A synthetic securitization is a portfolio of credit derivatives acquired by the SPE, and sold to buyers looking for credit protection. Credit derivatives are usually credit default swaps (CDS) that provide credit protection to the buyer, a protection, or insurance, sold by the seller of CDS. The credit protection is the payment of losses due to a credit event by the seller to the buyer of the CDS. Credit derivatives are subsequently further detailed in Chapter 9. To understand the basic mechanism of synthetic securitizations, it is sufficient to see them as traded insurance contracts, for which the seller of protection (seller of the credit derivative) receives a securing premium and pays the LGD of the underlying asset, in the event of default of the latter, to the buyer of the CDS. The investors in the SPE bear the credit exposure of sold credit derivatives to buyers of protection. The securitization is synthetic to the extent that it replicates exposure to the credit risk of a portfolio of assets through credit derivatives sold with these underlying assets.

§540. A synthetic securitization is a structure with at least two different stratified risk positions or tranches that reflect different degrees of credit risk where credit risk of an underlying pool of exposures is transferred, in whole or in part, through the use of funded (e.g. credit-linked notes) or unfunded (e.g. credit default swaps) credit derivatives or guarantees that serve to hedge the credit risk of the portfolio. Accordingly, the investors' potential risk is dependent upon the performance of the underlying pool.

When the structure is funded, it means that the investors buy notes paying them the risk-free interest rate plus a spread. The risk-free rate is received by the SPE, and paid to investors, by investing the proceeds of cash received from investors in risk-free assets. The premium from the credit derivatives sold provides the excess revenue over the risk-free rate. Unfunded structures simply pay a premium to investors from the one received by sold credit derivatives.

5.8 OFF-BALANCE SHEET ITEMS

The off-balance sheet elements of banks are commitments of banks that do not imply initial outlays of cash. They include contingencies given and received. Contingencies are third-party guarantees or credit derivatives. Both are triggered by default of direct obligor, resulting in credit exposure to guarantor, whether it is a direct guarantor or whether it is the seller of credit protection through a credit derivative. Because off-balance sheet items have a credit risk, although contingent on some event, they are dealt with under Basel 2, through a dedicated set of regulatory rules. Basel 2 provides definitions of such items, in various paragraphs of the Basel 2 document [7], which include the following:

§25, §26. Direct credit substitutes, e.g. general guarantees of indebtedness (including standby letters of credit serving as financial guarantees for loans and securities) and acceptances (including endorsements with the character of acceptances) lending of banks' securities or the posting of securities as collateral by banks, including instances where these arise out of repo-style transactions (i.e. repurchase/reverse repurchase and securities lending/securities borrowing transactions).

Certain transaction-related contingent items: Standby letters of credit related to particular transactions) …

A guarantee (counter-guarantee) or credit derivative must represent a direct claim on the protection provider and must be explicitly referenced to specific exposures or a pool of exposures. It must be irrevocable and unconditional.

… Short-term self-liquidating trade letters of credit arising from the movement of goods (e.g. documentary credits collateralized by the underlying shipment), …

Derivatives products are detailed in Chapters 6 to 9. A derivative is an asset whose value depends on another asset or a market parameter, called the underlying asset (or the underlying market parameter). They include the above-mentioned credit derivatives, which are the most recent products. Other products, such as forward contracts, swaps, and options, are detailed in dedicated chapters because of their critical importance for risk management purposes.

6

Essentials on Derivative Products

This chapter provides the basics for understanding derivatives and how they are used for risk management. Advanced readers might skip this chapter. Others will find here the basic definitions and terminology[1].

Derivatives are contracts on underlying assets, which are stocks and bonds, or market parameters, such as interest rates and foreign exchange rates. They are two main types of derivatives: forward contracts and options. Forward contracts set today a price for tomorrow for buyers and sellers. Option contracts are rights to buy ("call" option) or to sell ("put" option) the underlying asset at a price set today and up to the maturity of the contract. Derivatives can serve for hedging or for speculating. The seller of an asset at a future date looks for protection against a decline of its value. Both a forward sale and a put option would provide such protection. The same contracts can serve for speculating. A speculator betting that an asset value will be above a certain price can buy forward the asset or buy a call option on the asset. Derivatives are mainly viewed here under a risk management prospective, when derivatives usually serve primarily for hedging purposes. The hedged instruments are the underlying positions, such as stocks in the case of equity contracts.

This review of market products starts from cash positions and moves to basic derivatives. After defining cash and derivative positions, the review of derivatives is organized in two poles: forward contracts and options. All product reviews cover examples, basic properties of the instruments, how such instruments can be used for hedging or for speculative purposes, and pricing principles. Derivative contracts are introduced here with underlying assets being stocks. The next three chapters introduce interest rate, foreign exchange and credit derivatives.

---

1 A useful text for all types of derivatives is Hull [35].

Contents

6.1 ASSETS AND POSITIONS

A position is synonymous to an exposure, which was defined as any transaction that implies a risk of loss. Positions and exposures are "cash" when they imply buying or selling, or lending and borrowing. Holding a cash asset is a "long" position. Being the seller of an asset is a "short" position. For example, a long position in equity means holding a stock. Being short on a bond means that one has sold the bond. The "long/short" terminology applies to any asset. A buyer forward of a call option has a long position in this contract.

Consider equity positions. A long position gains when the stock price goes up. A short position in the stock implies that you need to sell the stock. "Short sales" of equity allow making a gain when the stock price moves down. More specifically, short sales mean borrowing an asset that you do not own, selling it, before buying it back for returning it to lender. An example illustrates how the short seller of equity gains when the equity price declines.

Today, the stock price is 100. The short seller borrows the stock and sells it, with cash proceeds equal to 100. Tomorrow, if stock price is lower, for example 90, the short seller buys back the stock at 90, makes a gain of $100 - 90 = 10$, and returns the asset to the lender of the stock. On the other hand, if the stock price increases, the short seller makes a loss, because he/she buys back the stock at (say) 110, and the loss is $100 - 110 = -10$, for returning the stock to the lender of the security. Losses and gains of the short sale are the reverse than those of a long position. The short sale allows the making of gains in declining markets.

The payoff is the proceeds of the future transaction as a function of the underlying asset on which one has a position. Payoff graphs (e.g. Figure 6.1) show how much you get when the value of a position varies. The x-axis shows the possible values of the asset. The y-axis shows gains or losses when the contract is closed or at maturity.

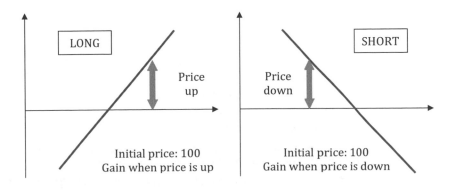

FIGURE 6.1 Long and short positions in stock

Long means buying or holding any asset or contract on an asset. Short means selling or borrowing any asset or contract on an asset. For example, long forward means contracting to buy an asset at a future date and short forward means contracting to deliver (sell) an asset at some future date. The same terminology applies to options. The buyer of the call option on stock has the long option. Conversely, the seller of the call has the short option.

6.2 DERIVATIVES: BASIC DEFINITIONS AND PRINCIPLES

A derivative is an asset whose value depends on another asset or a market parameter, called the underlying asset (or the underlying market parameter). A forward contract on interest rates locks in today a rate applicable tomorrow for a preset period of time. When entering into a forward contract, the buyer or seller has the obligation to comply with the terms of the contract at its maturity. A buyer of a put (call) option on stock has the right to sell (buy) a stock at a preset price until a certain horizon. The seller of an option has an obligation to comply with the contractual rights of the option buyer.

Table 6.1 summarizes the definitions of various common derivatives. Swaps are mentioned, and are defined in the chapter on interest and foreign exchange rates, and belong to the broad family of forward contracts. Derivatives can be written on any underlying:

- stocks
- stock index
- interest rates and foreign exchange rates
- bonds
- options on forward contracts
- commodities
- electricity
- weather
- insurance claims.

Traded instruments are grouped according to the nature of the underlying. The three families are equity, fixed income, which groups all instruments which are interest bearing or depend on foreign exchange, and credit, which is the most recent family of derivatives, of which underlying is the credit risk of an asset. Cross-tabulating the two main families of contracts, forward

TABLE 6.1

Instruments	Definition
Forward contracts	Obligation to buy (sell) and asset at a given price and at a given date, specified at the origin of the contract.
Swaps	The obligation to exchange cash flows at periodical intervals or dates
Options	The right, but not the obligation, of buying (selling) a given asset at a given price over a given period, specified at the origin of the contract.
Futures	Listed forward contracts exchanged on an organized market with standard characteristics.

contracts and options, with the three market segments, covers the spectrum of common instruments. Note that some derivatives are hybrid instruments, with components belonging to two families. For example a quanto instrument eliminates foreign exchange risk: a quanto equity index allows taking a position on a foreign currency equity index, with proceeds in the home currency, without any foreign exchange risk.

The replication principle states that any assets can be replicated by a combination of other financial assets, subject to certain conditions[2]. The replication principle allows one to understand how to engineer, or "construct," products, notably forward contracts and swaps, as illustrated later. The implications are far reaching. A major implication is the "law of one price," which states that the asset price should be the same as that of the replicating portfolio. This is a fundamental law in finance. Another implication is that products can be created synthetically by the replicating portfolio. In these chapters on derivatives, we use the replication principle for showing how simple forward contracts can be constructed as portfolios of other assets.

End users of derivatives are investors and lenders, such as corporations, banks, insurance companies, and funds. Derivatives are used for both hedging and speculation. Typical hedging transactions are those that serve for limiting the uncertainty of certain industrial commercial and industrial transactions, for example by setting a buying price for commodities today for tomorrow. However, the border between speculation and hedging is thin. For example setting today a buying price for tomorrow can also be viewed as a bet that wins when the future price will be lower than the buying price set today for tomorrow. The distinction between hedgers and speculators is that hedgers have an initial position whereas speculators have no initial position.

6.3 FORWARD CONTRACTS

A forward contract is a contract that sets the price of an asset for a future date. Being long the forward contract is a commitment to buy the asset, and being short the forward is a commitment to deliver the asset.

6.3.1 A Simple Example of a Forward Contract

Such contracts are very commonplace, as a non-financial example will illustrate. Assume that you buy a book from a bookshop for delivery in approximately 1 month. You commit to pay the bookshop €10 when the book is delivered. You are buying forward and taking delivery in a month from today. The bookseller is selling you a forward since he promises to deliver in a month at €10. The book is the "deliverable instrument." This forward position entails a risk.

Whichever way the price of the book moves, one party has an interest to default because it suffers a loss. If the price of the book drops to €6, the buyer might prefer to buy at €6, and not at original price of €10 from the bookstore. If the price of the book rises to €15, the bookstore has an incentive not to deliver and so default on its commitment to sell to the buyer at €10. Therefore, an incentive, or obligation, is needed to suppress the temptation not to comply.

Future markets are organized markets of forward contracts. Gains and losses are posted on a margin account. The account is credited and debited for the seller and the buyer as above. The accounts of all traders are centralized in the clearinghouse, which is the unique counterparty

2 See Neftci [55] for a useful source for replication and the "law of one price".

for all buyers and sellers. The gain or loss is settled on a daily basis. The most that the seller can avoid "paying" is the upward movement of price during one day if it fails to post additional cash, should the opportunity cost of trading forward exceed previous day loss. The cash posted out is adjusted incrementally each day. The cumulative gain or loss of each party is the total gain or loss from the forward contract. By posting losses every day for either the seller or the buyer, the incentives for moving away from the contract are reduced to a one day's loss.

Back to the example, where the buyer makes a gain, the gain is the mirror image of the seller's loss. Hence, the cash posted by the seller is credited to the buyer. Should the price decline, such a decline would reduce the seller's loss and eventually turn it into a gain if the price moves below the forward price preset at the time of sale. If the price of the book starts moving up to €11, the buyer makes a gain of €1 and the seller makes a loss of €1. In an organized market, the seller would have to post the loss as €1 in the dedicated margin account. The loss is cashed out and cannot be avoided by the seller.

6.3.2 Spot and Forward Prices

Consider stocks. There are no forward contracts on stocks, although there are on equity indexes. However, it is possible to build a forward price relatively easily. We explain how to construct a forward price for the stock.

Let:

- S_0 be the current price, for example 100
- S_T be the forward price of a stock at time T
- r be the risk-free lending – borrowing rate for 0 to T, for example $r = 10\%$

For constructing a forward price for horizon T, we can enter into the following transactions. Today, we borrow 100 at cost $r = 10\%$ and buy the stock at the current spot price $S_0 = 100$. Tomorrow ($T = 1$), the "fair" forward cost of "carrying" the stock until the date of the forward transaction is the original price paid plus the cost of borrowing. This fair forward price should be: $100 + (10\% \times 100) = 110$. The general formula for such forward price is: $S_0 (1 + r)$.

The unique sustainable, i.e. arbitrage-free, forward price is 110. In order to see why, let the forward price be different from 110. For example, starting with $S_0 = 100$ and forward price $S_T = 115 > 110$, there are risk-free profitable arbitrage opportunities. The seller of stock forward will buy the stock at 100 by borrowing and sell it at 115, making a gain of 5. The sequence of transactions is:

- today: borrow 100 at $r = 10\%$
- buy stock at 100
- tomorrow ($T = 1$): sell at 115 (forward)
- proceeds at $T = 1$: $115 - 110 = +5$

The process will continue and the spot price increases pulled by today's demand for stock, while the supply of stock tomorrow pushes the forward price down. The arbitrage is profitable until the forward price becomes exactly the spot plus interest on borrowing for buying the stock today at spot.

Generalizing, any asset can have a forward price. Such a forward price is determined by the law of supply and demand for this future date. But the forward price remains related to the current (spot) price of the asset and interest rates. The relationship between spot and forward prices results from the possibility of borrowing to acquire the asset and to sell it at a future date inclusive of the cost of the interest. The cost of borrowing until maturity date is the "carrying cost" from now to tomorrow.

6.3.3 Hedging and Speculating with Forward Contracts

The hedging strategy would apply for an owner of the stock. The owner fears a decline of the stock price. He/she can hedge this risk by shorting a forward contract. Doing so implies that he/she has an obligation to deliver the stock at the forward price prevailing for a preset date. As long as the stock price goes below 110, the hedge is winning. Of course, should the price move above the forward price, for example 120, the owner of stock would have to sell at 110 instead of 120, and will lose the 120 – 110, or the positive difference between the future (unknown) spot price and the forward price.

The same forward contract can be used to bet that the future spot price will be above the forward price (will be positive). Consider someone who does not own the stock today. A speculator is willing to bet that the future spot price will be lower than the forward, say 80. The speculator will buy the stock at 80 and sell at 110, making a gain of 30. The forward seller has to deliver the asset tomorrow, whatever its price, since he contracted the obligation to do so. The speculator is exposed to risk, since he/she would lose if the stock price increases above 110, for example 120. Then he/she would buy the stock at 120 and be obligated to sell at 110, making a loss of 110 – 120 = –10. Note that such speculation does not imply any cash outlay when entering into the contract. The difference between the hedger and the speculator is that the former holds the stock while the latter does not.

6.3.4 Payoff of a Forward Contract

The payoff of a forward contract is a horizontal line at maturity, for example 110, when the spot line is the first diagonal and the horizontal axis shows the unknown future spot price. The break-even value making the forward seller win or lose is 110. (See Figure 6.2.) Table 6.2 summarizes the position that a forward buyer or seller would take according to expectations with respect to the future stock price.

6.4 FORWARD CONTRACTS VERSUS OPTIONS

Investors rely on forward prices to lock in a future price today. Forward contracts are obligations: contracting a price today for a future date whatever happens tomorrow might ends up in favorable or unfavorable outcomes for the hedger.

An option is a contract that allows the buyer to buy or sell an asset at a preset price today, up to a certain horizon. The seller is short on the option. Investors use options for investing or for getting protection against a decline of value. Options provide the right, not the obligation, to sell or to buy at a preset price today called the strike price. A call option is the right to buy an asset

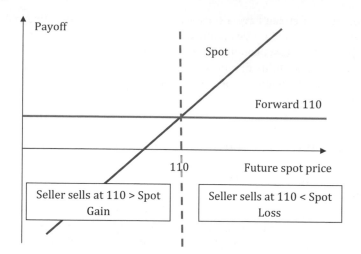

FIGURE 6.2   Payoff of a forward seller

TABLE 6.2

	Buy forward (long contract)	*Sell forward (short contract)*
Hedging	Owe an asset Fear a price increase maturity Lock-in a buying price today	Own an asset Fear a price decline Lock-in a selling price today
Speculating	Bet: future buying price > forward price Buy forward contract	Bet: future selling price < forward price Sell forward contract

at a strike price, allowing investors to gain when the asset price increases, while losing the cost of the call if the stock price remains under the exercise price. A put option is the right to sell an asset at a preset price, protecting investors against price declining below the exercise price.

6.5 OPTIONS

Options are rights, but not obligations (unlike forward contracts), to buy or sell an underlying asset at a pre-determined price. A call option is a right to buy and a put option is the right to sell the underlying asset. The price at which the asset can be acquired or sold is the exercise price. The options have a maturity. Some options can be exercised (the right is used by the holder of the option) only at maturity, and others can be exercised at any time until maturity. There are options on various "underlying" assets or market parameters: stocks, interest rates, foreign exchange rates, etc. The former are called European options and the latter are called American options. The cost of the option is called the "premium" paid by the buyer of the option, usually upfront (at inception).

6.5.1 Options Allow Hedging Risks

Options are often presented as directional instruments, allowing hedging against a trend. For example, an investor in stocks is afraid of the decline of the equity index. The investor buys a put option on stock, from a seller, such as a bank; the investor obtains a protection, or insurance, against a decline in the value of the stock. The buyer of the put has the right to sell the stock at a predetermined price, the exercise price, if the stock value falls down to a lower value than the guaranteed minimum price. If the stock price remains above the minimum guaranteed price, the buyer has paid an insurance of which cost is lost. The seller of the put (a bank) has the obligation to pay the difference between the exercise price and the spot price at maturity if the spot is below the exercise price.

Here is an example of a put option on stock:

- stock X: current value = 100
- strike price of option = 100
- maturity: 1 year
- put premium or price: 5

A put option allows benefiting from the best of both worlds. If the stock price increases, the buyer of the put option benefits from the upside of the stock while remaining protected against the downside.

When the stock price declines, the put option pays off the difference between exercise price and stock price, which becomes positive. The buyer of the put option makes a gain. When the stock price increases, the loss is limited to the premium (in this case 5). For example, if the stock prices declines to 80, the buyer of the put sells at 100, a gain of $100 - 80 = 20$, which offsets the price declines. However, this payoff is the gross proceeds from sale. The net proceeds, ignoring discounting, is netted from the premium paid, 5, and is 15. The put option provides an insurance against the price decline, and costs the premium of such insurance.

The call option has symmetric properties. The buyer buys the right to buy at fixed price equal to strike. If the stock price rises to 120, the gain is $120 - 100 = 20$. The net payoff is $20 - 5 = 15$. If the stock price declines to 105, the option is worthless, because the net proceeds from selling at 105 exactly offsets the premium. If it declines below, the call buyer makes a loss capped to the premium, or 5.

6.5.2 The Payoff of Option Contracts

The payoff graphs of the options show the proceeds, gross and net from the premium paid, from the future buy or sell transactions depending on the value of the underlying stock (Figures 6.3–6.5). The put option is said to be "in-the-money" when it provides a positive gross payoff, or "out-of-the money" if the gross payoff is zero, and "at-the-money" when the strike price is equal to the current stock price.

The call option is said to be "in-the-money" when it provides a positive gross payoff, "out-of-the money" if the gross payoff is zero, and "at-the-money" when the strike price is equal to the current stock price. The net payoff translates downward the gross payoff by the amount of the premium paid.

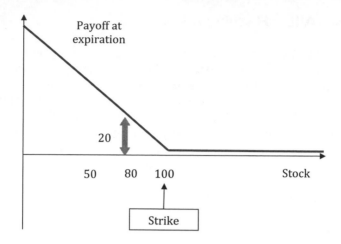

FIGURE 6.3   Payoff of a put option at maturity

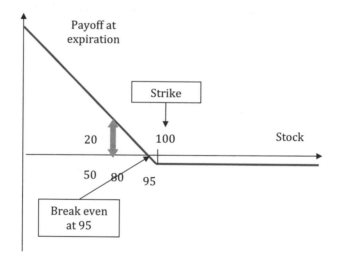

FIGURE 6.4   Net payoff of a put option at maturity

The payoff of the buyer of a put option is:

payoff buyer of put = maximum (strike price – stock price; 0)

The payoff of the buyer of a call option is:

payoff buyer of call = maximum (stock price – strike price; 0)

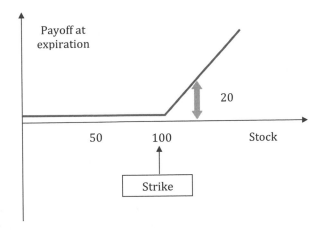

FIGURE 6.5 **Payoff of a call option on stock**

6.5.3 Sellers of Options

Sellers of options, unlike buyers of options, have the obligation to comply with their commitment to the buyer. The seller of a call option on stock will have the obligation to sell the stock to the buyer at the strike price if the buyer exercises. The seller of a put option on stock has the obligation to buy that stock at the strike price if the seller exercises.

The seller, or writer, of the call option has the obligation to pay any positive difference between stock price and strike price when the call option is "in the money," which might be potentially very high. The payoff is the mirror image of the gain of the buyer:

$$\text{payoff seller of call} = -\text{maximum (stock price} - \text{strike price; 0)}$$

The seller, or writer, of the put option has the obligation to pay to the buyer any positive difference between the strike price and the stock price, when the put is "in the money," which might be potentially as high as the strike price. The payoff is the mirror image of the gain of the buyer:

$$\text{payoff seller of put} = -\text{maximum (strike price} - \text{stock price; 0)}$$

Sellers of options are banks. They gain the premium but they have to hedge themselves against the losses that they would incur when the buyer makes a gain. In order to do so, they use a technique called delta-hedging. The delta of an option is the change of value of the option when there is a change in the price of the underlying asset.

$$\text{delta} = \frac{\Delta(\text{option})}{\Delta(\text{stock})}$$

The delta ("δ") changes when the underlying asset price changes. This results from the "kink" observed in the payoff. The value of the option is always above the payoff because, at any point in time before maturity, there is still a chance that the option gets in the money. Accordingly, the price of the option is a curve, such as the one for a call. The difference between the price and the exercise price, which is the payoff from immediate exercise, is called the time value of the option. The delta is the slope of the curve, which is always between 0 (extremely out-of-the-money) and 1 when the call option is well in-the-money. It changes because the curve shows convexity. Because of convexity, options are called non-linear instruments.

The underlying principle for delta-hedging is relatively simple. The seller of a call loses when the option is in the money. If the option has a delta of 0.8, for example, any small variation of the stock price of 1 is matched by a variation of 0.8 of the call option. If the stock price increases further the value of the call also increases, and this makes up an additional loss for the seller of the call. The seller can offset this loss by taking a long position in the stock. Assume that the stock price is $S = 120$, and the strike is 100, the call delta is 0.8, and a call (C) provides the right to buy a single stock. Then being short the call and long by 0.8 the stock, the variation of value of the trader's portfolio is zero. Note that delta-hedging is dynamic, since the delta changes when the underlying changes. This is an application of the replicating principle, whereby the traders replicates a long position in the call by mixing the call with a long position in the stock.

6.5.4 Risk and Return of Option Contracts

We stick to the example of a buyer of a call with the same data as above. The investor invests in the call option. When the call is "out of the money," the payoff is zero. The investor loses entirely the investment, which is the cost of call, 5. When the call is "in the money," the holder of call exercises the option: He/she buys at 100 and sells at 120, with a gross payoff of 20 and a net payoff of 15. The return is 15/5 = 300%.

The loss can be 100% of the invested amount when the option reaches maturity "out-of-the-money." The return is much higher than the stock return. In the example the stock return is 20% and the call return is 300%. This is why options are considered as "leveraged" instruments: They effectively "leverage" the return on the underlying, but the price to pay is a 100% loss risk. Holding the stock would provide a lower return of 20% but the risk of losing entirely the value of the stock is very small.

We summarize the comparison of investing in stock an amount of 100 and investing the same amount in call options on the stock, with the same data of the above example (Table 6.3). Because the cost of the call is 5, the investors would buy 20 calls, each providing the right to buy a single stock at 100, while the same amount allows investing in a single stock.

TABLE 6.3   Leveraged return of options

		Invest in stock	Invest in call
Amount invested		100	100
Stock price 120, call "in-the-money"	Return €	20	15 × 20 = 300
	Return %	20%	300%
Stock price 80, call "out-of-the-money"	Return €	−20	−5 × 20 = −100
	Return %	−20%	−100%

6.5.5 Option Pricing

The value of an option depends on:

- the strike price K
- the spot price of the underlying asset S_0
- the instability of the price of this underlying asset, measured by its volatility σ[3]
- the maturity T
- the risk-free rate r

Valuing an option relies on "pricing models," the well-known model is the "Black–Scholes" model[4], with pricing formulas of a call C and put P being:

$$C = S_0 N(d_1) - K \exp(-rT)N(d_2)$$
$$P = K \exp(-rT)N(-d_2) - S_0 N(-d_1)$$
$$d_1 = [\ln(S_0/K) + (r + \sigma^2/2)T]/\sigma T^{0.5}$$
$$d_2 = [\ln(S_0/K) + (r - \sigma^2/2)T]/\sigma T^{0.5} = d_1 - \sigma T^{0.5}$$

With the pricing formula, we can illustrate how expensive options can be through an example. How can we guarantee that stocks will beat a risk-free investment such as bonds over, say, 10 years? What would be the cost? We use a risk-free rate of 4% and a stock volatility (annualized) of 15%.

The guarantee is equivalent to a put option which allows one to sell the portfolio of stocks, which has a current value of 1000, at a price $= 1000 (1 + 4\%)^{10} = 1480$ after 10 years (strike). This is equivalent to a put option on stock, maturity 10 years, with a strike of 1480. The theoretical value of a put option matching such characteristics is 170, meaning that the guarantee represents about 17% of the total investment value. Note however, that options trade for much less because they have shorter maturities, such as one year or less.

6.5.6 Underlying of Options

There are forward contracts and option contracts for:

- commodities
- interest rate bearing assets such as bonds and bills
- foreign exchange rates.

For options, we have adopted the traditional approach, looking at them as directional instruments, meaning that we bet on a trend. Options are also viewed as volatility instruments because they are implicitly bets on the instability, or volatility, of the underlying asset. As the pricing formulas show, the price of options increases with volatility. Common sense also suggests that the higher the volatility, the higher are the chances than an option gets in the money at some point in time before maturity. Traders view them as volatility instruments. Typical trades are

---

3 The volatility is defined in the chapter on measures of risk.
4 The original article of the Black-Scholes formula is in [13].

betting when the volatility is under-priced or over-priced in traded options. For example, the volatility of markets tends to be lower at end-of-year, with the holiday. In such instances, it can be that options over-price volatility. Then, it makes sense selling options and buying them back when the price declines when volatility declines. Of course, this is a speculative trade.

In the next chapters, we discuss derivatives on interest rate assets and foreign exchange assets.

7

Interest Rate Risk and Interest Rate Derivatives

This chapter summarizes the essentials about interest rate derivatives and how they serve for hedging and speculating. The presentation is limited to simple, or "plain vanilla," generic instruments. The definitions and usages of forward contracts and options on interest rates are discussed with examples illustrating how they can be used by either corporations or banks.

The chapter starts from a definition of interest rate risk for lenders and borrowers, and proceeds, in a second section, with the definitions of interest rates and their term structure. The next section addresses forward contracts and options on interest rates. Forward contracts allow setting today an interest rate for future dates. One can wonder how this is feasible. For addressing the issue, it is explained how such contracts can be engineered from basic cash transactions. The process is called "replication" of a contract by simpler transactions. The valuation follows from the law of one price. Interest rate swaps are within the family of forward contracts. The review of interest rate swaps, in the fourth section, follows the same steps: definition, replication and valuation. The fifth section addresses options and their usages for hedging and speculating, considering also how options can be viewed: as directional instruments allowing "betting" on a trend, or as volatility instruments, since their value depends on how unstable are the underlying interest rates. The sixth section is a generic case study of hedging interest rate risk by a borrower comparing the usage of different instruments. A last section addresses, briefly, the issue of what drives interest rates[1].

---

1 Useful references are Hull [35], Neftci [55], and Das [26].

Contents

7.1 INTEREST RATE RISK FOR BORROWERS AND LENDERS

All lenders and borrowers, whether at fixed or variable rates, are exposed to interest rate risk, as Table 7.1 shows. Lending or borrowing at a fixed rate reduces the uncertainty on interest cost or revenue, but does not eliminate interest rate risk. A lender at a fixed rate faces the risk that rates could go up, in which case the lender has an "opportunity" cost – the cost of not lending at a higher rate. The converse holds for a borrower on a fixed rate: should interest rates decline, the borrower would be better off by borrowing at lower rates. Note that for forecasted future exposures, such as future inflows or outflows, the exposures are identical to floating rate exposures because the future interest rate is uncertain, whether it is fixed or variable.

The only choice is to choose the type of exposure that lenders and borrowers want to have. They can do so and change it according to their perception of interest rates by using fixed income derivatives. The usage of such derivatives is widely spread by corporates as well as financial firms. It is not possible to modify "directly" the variable/fixed interest rate of a loan or a debt. Instead, derivatives are used. They do not modify the original contract (debt or loan), but are new contracts.

TABLE 7.1 Exposure to interest rate risk by lenders and borrowers

Rate	Change of rates	Lender	Borrower
Current exposures			
Floating rate	Rate ↗	+	−
	Rate ↘	−	+
Fixed rate (*)	Rate ↗	−	+
	Rate ↘	+	−
Future exposures			
−	Rate ↗	+	−
−	Rate ↘	−	+

(*) uncertainty with respect to opportunity cost of debt only
+ = gain
− = loss

7.2 INTEREST RATES AND TERM STRUCTURE

The yield curve, or term structure, of interest rates, provides the market rates for all maturities. There are various interest rates, risk-free rates and risky rates for debts issued by non-governmental organizations. Interest rates are also defined in various ways. The yield to maturity provides the return of a bond held until maturity. Zero-coupon rates apply to a unique flow to be received at maturity of a zero bond, without any intermediate cash flows, such as coupons. Such zero-rates are usually derived from the non-zero rates by replication of the zero-coupon bond from other bonds which are liquid. The process is called stripping. The principle consists of calculating the value of the coupon bond minus the present value of coupons, using the rates attached to their dates.

Yield curves exist for risk-free borrower/government and for risky borrowers. The rates paid by a risky borrower include a spread above risk-free rate. The spread accounts, among other factors, for the default risk of the risky debt, and is, accordingly, called a credit spread. It is related to credit rating, among other factors, which measures the credit standing of a particular debt issue. In fact, empirical analysis shows that spreads depend statistically on credit ratings, industry and maturity. The shapes of yield curves are usually upward sloping, downward sloping, with a bump or are simply approximately flat (Figure 7.1).

The graph (Figure 7.2) shows various yield curves and time series across years. The latter illustrate the instability of interest rates, which makes controlling interest rate risk a key issue for corporates for liability management purposes and for banks who are exposed on both sides of the balance sheet. Figure 7.3 shows times series of interest rates in Euros for various maturities. The most stable rates are long-term rates and the most volatile rates are short-term rates. The spreads between the upper and the lower time series shows that yield curves were upward sloping in January to April 2008 and became flat in July 2008.

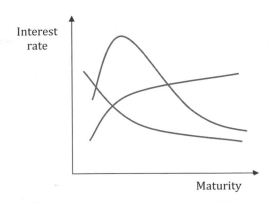

FIGURE 7.1   Typical shapes of term structures of interest rates

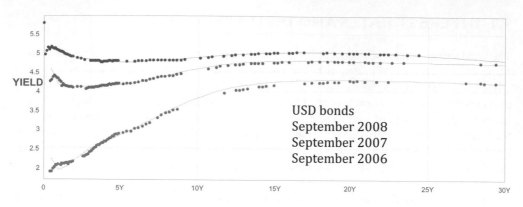

FIGURE 7.2   Bond yields, US, 2006–2008. Source: Lehman Live (Barclays Capital)

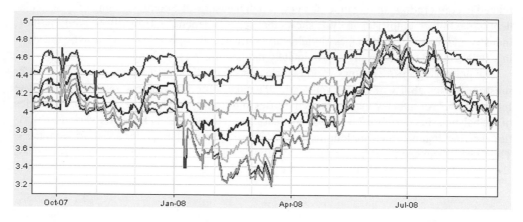

FIGURE 7.3   Time series of interest rates, Euro. Source: Lehman Live (Barclays Capital)

7.2.1 Lending, Borrowing and the Term Structure of Interest Rates

It is easier to introduce interest rate risk to start from the yield curve, which is commonly upward sloping. The basic issues faced by lenders and borrowers who have defined a horizon for borrowing are:

- lenders: lend long or lend short and roll over the loan?
- borrowers: borrow long or borrow short and roll over the debt?

When lenders and borrowers use different maturities than the actual horizon for lending and borrowing, they have a mismatch risk. For example, the two-year lender borrowing for 1 year and rolling over this short-term lending until reaching the two-year horizon is exposed to the risk that interest rates fall in the second one-year period.

For banks which lend and borrow, maintaining a maturity mismatch (borrowing short and lending long) allows capturing the spread between long and short rates. However, such a

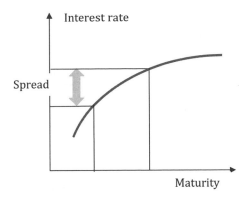

FIGURE 7.4 Mismatch risk and interest rate spread

mismatch implies both interest rate and liquidity risks. This is the typical position of a commercial bank. Short maturities on the liability side come from depositors, which have a short contractual maturity (but a longer effective maturity). It might as well come from short-term financial debt. This is called the "structural position" of commercial banks.

The position economically makes sense as long as the short-term rates are lower than long-term rates. The position is also risky because short-term rates might rise above long-term rates, or rise above historical lending rates of the bank. In both cases, the spread becomes negative. The first case might occur when there is a shift upward of the curve, even though there is still a positive spread between long and short rates. Historical lending rates might become lower than current short-term rates. When the short end of the curve rises above the long end of the curve, the curve becomes inverted. Borrowing short and lending at longer maturities generates a negative spread. Lending short-term and borrowing long-term would generate a positive spread.

Such mechanisms appeared in the debacle of the savings and loans industry in the 1970s, among other factors. The monetary policy became stringent, for fighting double digit inflation. Short-term rates rose above 15% and lending rates remained lower. The inverted curve generated losses which deteriorated the solvency of many savings and loans institutions.

Mismatches between maturities of assets and liabilities imply liquidity risk when liabilities have a shorter maturity than assets. Such liquidity risk materialized with drastic consequences on the financial system in the 2007–2008 crisis, when the short-term liquidity market dried up abruptly. Both short-term financial markets and inter-bank lending/borrowing froze, leaving banks short of liquidity borrowing massively from central banks and fearing to extend credit because of the shortage of liquidity.

7.2.2 Fixed and Variable Rates

Variable rate transactions have a short-term interest rate, since the interest rate is reset periodically. Using short-term debt is similar, because the rate is also reset when debt is rolled-over. However, there is a major difference between a long-term debt that is variable rate and a short-term debt. The latter implies liquidity risk arising from the necessity of raising new debt at maturity.

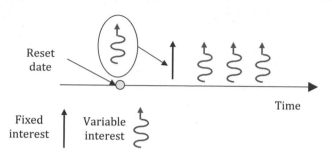

FIGURE 7.5   Fixed and variable interest rates

A variable rate is based upon a market index reset at the beginning of each period for cal-culating accrued and paying interest. Between two sequential reset dates, the variable rate is fixed. Immediately after a reset date, the next interest flow is fixed while subsequent flows remain uncertain. In Figure 7.5 straight lines stand for fixed rates while curved lines represent variables, or unknown, interest rates.

The most typical references for variables rates are Libor rates, or London Inter-Bank Offering Rates. The Libor rates are rates for inter-bank lending and borrowing. They are not risk free, but are rather in line with the average risk of the banks included in the index. There are Libor rates for various maturities up to 1 year: Libor 1-month or the Libor 1-year are reset, respectively, every month or year from initial date. Since market rates are usually defined at the beginning of the period, they are pre-determined at the beginning of the next period.

Sometimes, reference interest rates are more complex to handle than Libor rates because there is no mechanical relationship between these rates and such pre-determined rates as Libor. Some banking reference rates are calculated as an average of historical rates and are therefore known only at the end of the period. Such rates are more complex to handle because they are post-determined. They might be used for indexing the rates paid by individual clients, for example. Some loans to clients refer to the monthly average of daily rates over the last month. Regulated rates are another example of interest rates that are loosely related to market rates. They might be revised, but not at preset dates. Regulated rates on saving deposits might be adjusted at end of month only and vary by steps. The rates depend on a linear combination of benchmarks, such as the short-term interest rate and the inflation rate. The rationale of such rates is to provide some indexation on inflation for savings. Such products are typical in European banks and raise complex issues for hedging them. Note that bank rates charged to clients differ from market rates. Such rates include a spread above the market rates. Notably, in retail banking, short-term rates to clients include a significant margin.

Since all interest rates vary across time and differ across maturities, a common notation for spot (today rates) interest rates are $r(t, T)$, referring both to the date t, today, and the maturity T.

7.3 FORWARD RATES: DEFINITIONS

A forward rate is an interest rate viewed from today (t) applicable between two future dates t_1 and t_2. There are as many forward rates as there are couples of futures dates, for one "today" date. All forward rates can be derived from the current (t) term structure of interest rates.

FIGURE 7.6   Forward rates

Because they can be calculated at date t for two future dates, forward rates are indexed by the 3 dates, as $F(t, t_1, t_2)$. (See Figure 7.6.)

It is useful, for understanding forward rates, to detail how they can be replicated. Assume that a lender expects a future inflow $X = 100$, 1 year from now and that the spot rates for 1 and 2 years are, respectively, 5% and 6%. The lender wants to lock in a rate today for this future loan. A forward contract allows contracting today a rate for tomorrow between 2 future dates 1 and 2. This contract is a forward loan.

7.3.1   Replicating a Forward Loan

The replicating portfolio of a forward loan consists of borrowing today for one year and lending the same amount for two years. One can borrow today at 5% for one year, against the inflow of 100 in one year, an amount of:

$$100/(1 + 5\%) = 95.2381$$

Lending this amount for two years at 6% yields:

$$95.2381 \times (1 + 6\%)^2 = 107.0095$$

Since we get a final value of 107.0095 after lending 100 for 1 year in year 1, the forward rate is 7.0095% for one year and starting at end of year 1. The forward rate is replicated by lending and borrowing the same amount at the current date for two different maturities. (See Figure 7.7.) Note that such replication is static: Once the two borrowing/lending transactions are set up, they do not change. The borrowing today is equal to 95.2381, immediately lent for two years. Figure 7.8 shows the exact calculation of the forward rate. The two subscripts designate the initial and the final dates to which spot interest rates apply. The one-year forward rate applying one year from now is the 12×24 forward, with 12 and 24 designating the number of months for starting and ending dates.

7.3.2   Forward and Spot Rates: No Arbitrage

A forward rate constructed in this way is arbitrage free to the extent that any discrepancy between the prevailing forward at the future date 1 and the above calculated forward would raise risk-free profit opportunities.

For specifying future rates, either prevailing spot rates or forward rates, we need only two subscripts, if we remove the current date. Let us define i_{12} and F_{12} as, respectively, the future

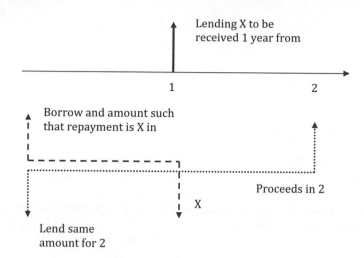

FIGURE 7.7   Replicating a forward loan

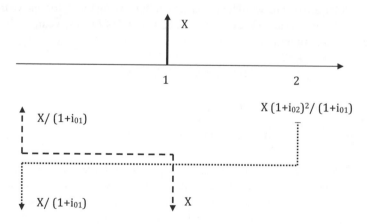

FIGURE 7.8   Calculation of the (12 × 24) forward rate

spot and the forward rates between dates 1 and 2. Date "1" is the starting date, and "2" is the end date. Lending for 2 years is feasible either once or twice for one year. The proceeds, for each one of the two strategies, are:

$$\text{twice, for 1 year: } (1 + 5\%) \times (1 + i_{12}\%)$$

Note that the future 1-year spot rate one year from now, i_{12}, from future date 1 up to future date 2, is unknown as of today. The proceeds of this strategy are uncertain as of today. Lending once for two years, the proceeds are:

$$\text{once, for 2 years: } (1 + 6\%)^2$$

The no arbitrage condition obtains when final proceeds are equal:

$$(1 + 6\%)^2 = (1 + 5\%) \times (1 + F_{12}\%)$$

The value of the forward rate one year from now for one year is $F_{12} = 7.0095\%$. If the expected rate is identical to the forward, the two policies are equivalent. This shows that the forward rate is the break-even rate making the long and short lending policies equivalent.

Consider the case where the forward rate differs from this value. By lending and borrowing at prevailing spot rates, one would replicate a forward transaction. If the proceeds differ from the prevailing forward rate, any discrepancy would lead to riskless arbitrage opportunities. For example, if the forward rate is above the 7.0095%, one can make a forward loan by borrowing and lending today. Such excess supply of forward loan for one year in one year would push the rate down, as well as increase the borrowing spot rate. The implication of the above is that the market perceives as equivalent the future random spot rate and the forward rate.

As a result of the equilibrium equation, forward rates are above spot rates when the yield curve is upward sloping, and forward rates are below spot rates when the yield curve is downward sloping. When the yield curve is flat, the forward rates become identical to the spot rates. Note that there are as many one-year forward rate curves as there are future dates.

Forward rates can be effectively locked in as of today by lenders/borrowers. But lending and borrowing implies transaction costs and cash movements. In fact, one should enter into a "forward rate agreement" contract, or FRA. The FRA will simply exchange the difference between the future spot rate and the forward rate. There are variations with FRA contracts depending upon whether the payment is at 1 or at 2. The usual notations for a FRA are, for example, a FRA (2×3), meaning that the starting date is date 2 and the final date is 3.

It is easy to show that lending fixed is equivalent to lending over sub-periods at the forward rates. In other words, a fixed spot rate is a geometric average of forward rates. The demonstration is based on the equations deriving forward rates from spot rates of various maturities.

Starting with the definition of forward f_{12}, we have: $(1 + s_{01})(1 + f_{12}) = (1 + s_{02})^2$. Next using the definition of the forward f_{23} we have: $(1 + s_{02})^2 (1 + f_{23}) = (1 + s_{03})^3$. Then replacing the expression of the spot 0×2 as a function of forward 1×2 in the definition of forward f_{23}, we obtain: $(1 + s_{02})^2 (1 + f_{23}) = (1 + s_{01}) (1 + f_{12}) (1 + f_{23})$. But f_{01} is identical to s_{01}, and is sometimes called the "trivial forward rate." This shows that compounding 3 forward investments of 1-year, $(1 + s_{01}) (1 + f_{12}) (1 + f_{23})$, is equivalent to investing spot for 3 years: $(1 + s_{03})^3$.

7.3.3 Example of Calculations of the Forward Yield Curves

The spot yield curve provides all yields by maturity. Forward yield curves derive from the set of spot yields for various combinations of dates. The calculations below provide an example of the calculation of several forward yield curves one year from now, as well as two years from now and subsequent maturities. In the first case, we plot the forward rates starting one year from now and for one year (date 2), two years (date 3), three years (date 4), and so on. In the second case, the forward rates are two years from now, for the maturities one year (date 3), two years (date 4), and so on. The general formulas use the term structure relationships. For instance, the forward rates between dates 1 and 3 (one year from now for two years) and between dates 1 and 4 (one year from now for three years) are such that:

TABLE 7.2   The spot and forward yield curves (one year forward rates)

Dates, t	0	I	2	3	4	5
Spot yields	3.50%	4.35%	5.25%	6.15%	6.80%	7.30%
Forward, F_{t1}		5.21%	6.14%	7.05%	7.64%	8.08%
Forward, $F_{t+1,t}$			7.98%	8.28%	8.57%	8.82%

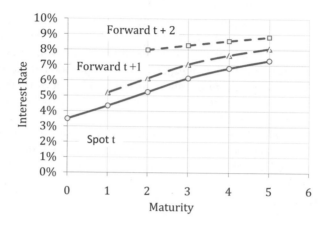

FIGURE 7.9   Spot and forward yield curves

$$(1 + f_{13})^2 = (1 + i_{03})^3/(1 + i_{01})$$

$$(1 + f_{14})^3 = (1 + i_{04})^4/(1 + i_{01})$$

If we deal with yields two years from now, we divide all terms such as $(1 + i_t)$ by $(1 + i_2)^2$ to obtain $1 + f_{2t}$, when $t > 2$.

All forward rates are above the spot rates since the spot yield curve is upward sloping. In addition, the further we look forward; the lower is the slope of the forward curve. Forward yield curves start later than the spot yield curves. Figure 7.9 shows the forward rates embedded in spot rates.

Both Table 7.2 and Figure 7.9 provide the broad picture of investment opportunities, for investors who have recurring positive excess liquidity. When spot yield curves are upward sloping the forward rates are above the spot yield curve. Conversely, with an inverted spot yield curve, the forward rates are below the spot yield curve. When the spot yield curve is flat, both spot and forward yields become identical.

7.3.4 Usages of Forward Rate Contracts

Forward rates are break-even rates for making long/short lending/borrowing decisions. This resolves the issue of choosing between lending once for two years or lending twice for one year. The choice has to do with perceived spot rates at the 1-year horizon. If perceptions are such that the spot rate will be below the forward rate, the choice would be to lend at forward rates. If the spot 1-year rate in one year is believed to be above the forward rate, the correct choice is to lend twice for 1 year.

The forward rates serve a number of purposes:

- they are the break-even rates for comparing expectations with market rates
- it is possible to effectively lock in forward rate for a future period as of today
- they provide lending/borrowing opportunities rather than simply lending/borrowing cash at the current spot rates.

Forward rates offer new lending and borrowing opportunities. Upward sloping curves might offer attractive forward investment opportunities, and downward sloping curves might offer attractive forward borrowing opportunities.

In general, practical decisions have to be made for future funding or investing excess cash. One of the pre-requisites for ALM is to determine what would be such deficits or excesses of funds in the future. It will be explained in the ALM section (Section 7) that raising money too early is not economical. Conversely, investing today excess cash that will exist only in the future is not feasible, because no cash transaction is feasible today. But once such excesses or deficits are projected with a reasonable accuracy, a decision has to be made: Hedging or not? Forward rates are benchmark rates to which one should compare the perception of future spot rates for making a decision.

This rule is general. For making a hedging decision, it is necessary to find the break-even point, here a break-even interest rate prevailing at a future date and unknown as of today, making hedging and no-hedging equivalent in terms of final pay-off. In the case of a forward contract, the break-even rate is equal to the forward rate. The next step is to compare expectations, when there is some consensus, to the break-even rate.

If interest rates for 1-year are expected to be above the 7.0095%, the no-hedge choice (waiting) would be the best. For the previous example, when the choice was to lend once or twice over a shorter period than horizon, it would be better to roll-over the loan twice for 1-year. If there are future excesses of cash to be invested, the decisions would be no hedging, or equivalently, doing nothing. If there is a consensus on a decline of interest rates below the break-even value, the forward hedge is the best solution. In the lend-long versus lend-short decision, hedging would mean lending straight for 2 years. In the case of excess cash forecasted in the future, the hedging decision would be to use a forward contract starting when the excess cash is available and ending at some horizon. There is a last scenario, which is the "myopic" scenario, when there is no consensus on any trend. Then, using forward contracts is a common practice, even though there is a chance that the forward ends up losing because the future spot rates are higher in the end.

Note that this presentation is simplified. It assumes implicitly that the amount of excess cash is constant between the initial and the final dates. This is not the case in practice and several contracts are needed to hedge various amounts matching the time profile of excess cash over different periods. Examples of hedging programs will be provided in the ALM chapter (Chapter 24).

7.3.5 Valuation of a Forward Contract or FRA

A futures contract is similar to a forward contract in that it is an agreement to buy or sell an asset for a specified price on a specified date. But such a contract is traded on an organized exchange and is mark-to-market. A futures contract also differs from a forward contract in that parties to a futures contract must deposit an initial margin at inception of contract, and, subsequently, adjust the cash margin according to the change of the "market value" of the contract. The margin variation is the daily variation of the value of the contract. It is paid to the clearinghouse by the party showing a loss and credited to the party showing a gain. Futures markets are detailed elsewhere and we focus here on the valuation of a forward contract that is over-the-counter (OTC).

The mark-to-market value of an interest rate forward contract (FRA) is derived from the differential between forward and spot rates. At inception, we lend and borrow the same amount. Intuitively, the value should be zero. Formally, the value is zero because the market values equivalently the forward rate and the uncertain spot rate. After inception, when time passes, the contracted flows from lending – borrowing remain constant, but not the interest rates. Since the forward contract is a made of two positions, long 2-year and short 1-year, its value is the net value of these two zero coupon bonds at t, after date of inception 0 and before date 1:

$$\text{FRA value } (t) = \frac{-100}{(1 + i_{t1})^{1-t}} + \frac{100}{(1 + i_{t2})^{2-t}}$$

Note that discounting is from cash flow date 1 until current date t. We assume here that the contract is settled at time 1, when the spot rate at 1 is known. By definition, the portfolio value at inception date is 0. After the initial date, the cash flows remain fixed, but not the interest rates. Therefore, the net value of the two positions fluctuates and might become positive or negative. The one which owns the positive value would lose it if the counterparty defaults. This random exposure to credit risk is discussed in the chapter on counterparty risk (Chapter 44).

7.4 INTEREST RATE SWAPS (IRS)

Lenders/borrowers might wish to exchange their interest rates, swapping from fixed to variable rates and vice versa. When interest rates increase, borrowers would like to pay fixed instead than variable rates and lenders would like to receive floating rather than fixed rates. The converse holds when interest rates decline. Interest rate swaps are contracts exchanging interest rates of different natures.

7.4.1 Definition of Interest Rate Swap

Interest rate swaps exchange a floating rate against a fixed rate, and vice versa, or a specific floating rate (Libor 1-month, for example) against another one (Libor 1 year, for example). A swap always has a "receiving" leg and a "paying" leg. Receiver swaps commonly designate swaps that receive the fixed rate and pay floating. The "notional" of the swap is the reference amount serving for calculating how much one receives and pays. The swap exchanges the cash flows calculated as the product of the notional by the interest rates. (See Figure 7.10.)

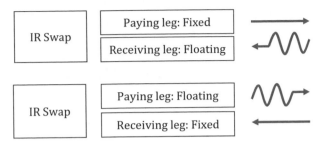

FIGURE 7.10 Interest rate swaps

In general, the swap rates are always set such that the value at inception is always zero. The swap has two legs: the receiving leg and the payer leg. A receiver swap designates a swap that receives the fixed rate. This allows eliminating ambiguity with respect to which interest is received or paid.

Interest rate swaps are useful for all players. Corporations use them for managing the interest rate risk of their debts, which is called liability management for corporations. Banks are exposed to interest rate risk on both sides of the balance sheet. Managing the net exposure is the purpose of asset-liability management for banks and financial institutions.

7.4.2 Replicating an Interest Rate Swap

The basics of interest rate swap engineering are simple. They consist of lending and borrowing the same amount for the same maturity, using a fixed rate in one case and a floating rate in the other case. An interest rate swap can be replicated in two ways. Either we look at streams of interest flows horizontally, or we look at each pair of cash flow vertically.

7.4.2.1 Horizontal View

Let us take the example of a corporation that wants to receive fixed rate and pay a variable rate. The bank could construct the contract by lending fixed and paying variable rate. It would pay the variable rate from the payments of the corporation to the bank. The amounts borrowed and lent are identical. They offset each other when contracting the loan and the debt and, later, when repaying principals of the two transactions at maturity. In reality, lending and borrowing imply transaction costs and bank's lending implies a capital charge for credit risk. It is easier to exchange the interest cash flows. Note that the interest cash flows have to be constructed at the prevailing rates when the swap is contracted. (See Figure 7.11.)

Cash lending and borrowing are non-economical. It is better to exchange only the cash flows. In most cases, a bank has already assets and liabilities that generate fixed rate and floating rate interest flows. The bank manages only the net position in these interest flows, once it has provided the customers with the contracts requested.

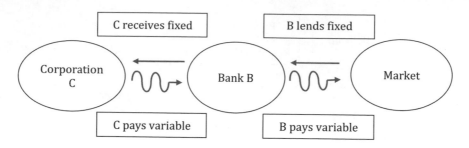

FIGURE 7.11   Engineering an interest rate swap

7.4.2.2 Vertical View

There is an alternate view for understanding how a swap can be engineered (Figure 7.12). Under the "horizontal" view, a swap paying fixed rate and borrowing variable can be viewed as a simultaneous borrowing, say at fixed rate, and lending the same amount floating rate. Under the vertical view, a swap appears as a series of forward rate contracts exchanging floating and fixed rate flows at all dates until maturity. Under the latter view, the series of FRA has a zero value at inception, but not all FRAs have the same signs. Some have a positive value and others have a negative value. In both views, the value at inception is zero and the swap rate is set in such a way, making equivalent the fixed series of interest flows and the floating leg. Up arrows are inflows and down arrows are outflows.

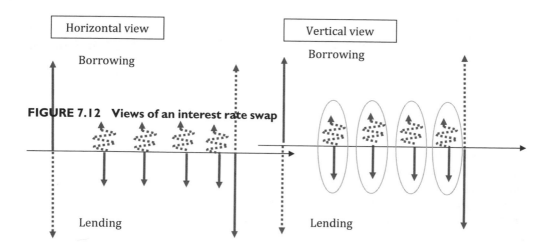

FIGURE 7.12   Views of an interest rate swap

7.4.3 Asset Swaps: Generalization

Swaps can be generalized. An asset swap is an exchange of two series of cash flows. Engineering asset swaps uses a simultaneous sale and purchase of instruments. For example, a client holds a loan and wants to swap Libor against equity index return. The bank could engineer the asset swap by buying the equity index and borrowing floating. The client receives the equity return from the bank and pays to the bank the Libor from its loan.

Fund managers try to track some equity index. One way of doing this is to by buying the underlying portfolio of stocks that replicate the index and constantly adjusting it as the market moves or when new stocks are added or removed from the index, or adjusting is to adjust the fund volume when new funds are received. Using equity swaps is a cost-effective alternative. Under an equity swap, the fund manager receives the equity index return in exchange for a Libor rate over some fixed maturity.

7.4.4 Mark-to-market Value of an IRS

For an IRS receiving fixed rate and paying floating rate, replication can be seen as lending fixed rate and borrowing same amount long fixed rate and short floating rate. This combines a long fixed rate position and a short floating rate position. The mark-to-market value is the net value of a long bond (loan) minus a short floating rate bond (debt).

The value of a floating rate bond is always par. For example, for one year, with rate i, floating, with nominal 1, pays $1 + i$, of which present value is final payment discounted to today, or $(1 + i)/(1 + i) = 1$. The argument is extended to subsequent periods. The value of an IRS is the net value of the two positions. It is zero at inception and becomes positive or negative when fixed is above floating and vice versa. Conceptually, an interest rate swap shows that the market views as equivalent a series of floating rates and a series of fixed swap rate cash flows.

Because a swap can take both positive and negative values when time passes, the one which owns the positive value would lose it if the counterparty defaults. Therefore, it is exposed to credit risk. The modeling of the credit exposure of swaps is discussed in Chapter 44. The situation is similar for a FRA traded OTC.

7.4.5 Derivatives and P & L

Derivatives are always constructed with prevailing market rates. Contracting a swap receiving the fixed rate will imply receiving the current fixed rate for the selected maturity. Contracting a swap receiving the variable rate will imply receiving the current rate for the selected short maturity of the variable rate, 1 month, 3 month, etc.). Therefore, derivatives influence both the nature of interest rates and the level of interest rates paid or received, hence the earnings (P & L) as well. Both impacts have to be assessed carefully before entering into a derivative transaction.

7.5 INTEREST RATE OPTIONS: CAPS AND FLOORS

Interest rates standard options are "caps" and "floors." The "cap" guarantees a maximum rate to the buyer. Borrowers are interested by caps since they set a maximum paid interest cost. A cap is an option: It has value only when the rate is above the guaranteed rate, otherwise, it is worthless. The "floor" guarantees a minimum rate to the buyer. Investors are interested by floors because they are willing to be protected against declining interest revenues. A floor is an option: It has value only when the rate is below the guaranteed rate, otherwise, it is worthless.

7.5.1 Payoff of Interest Rate Options

The mechanism of a cap providing a guaranteed maximum rate is as follows. The borrower has an original variable rate debt, which does not change. Assume that the borrower's debt is indexed to the Libor 3-month. The strike is 8%. If Libor 3-month is 10%, the borrower pays only the strike 8%, and the seller of cap pays the difference: 10% (spot rate) − 8% (strike) = 2%. If Libor 3-month becomes 6%, the borrower pays only 6%.

A floor provides a minimum guaranteed rate. The mechanisms are the same as above. The lender has an original variable rate debt, which does not change. Say the reference rate is Libor 3-month and that the strike is 8%. If Libor 3-month is 10%, the lender receives 10%, and the seller of cap does not pay anything. If Libor 3-month is 6%, the lender receives the strike 8% and the seller of cap pays the difference 8% (guaranteed rate) − 6% (spot rate) = 2%.

7.5.2 Collar

A "collar" combines a cap and a floor. The buyer of a collar buys a cap from the bank and sells a put to the bank. The premium received from the sale of the put reduces the cost of the straight cap. The buyer is typically a borrower floating rate. The borrower is protected against interest rates higher than the cap guaranteed rate, but pays at least the minimum rate guaranteed by the floor to the bank. The borrower pays the prevailing rate within the range of rates of the cap and the floor guaranteed rates, no more than the cap rate, no less that the floor rate. The primary interest of a collar is the lower net premium paid than for a straight cap, since the premium is that of cap minus that of the floor sold to the bank. Such instruments serve for minimizing the cost of the hedge, the drawback being the minimum rate to be paid if rates decline. In Figure 7.13, the holder of the collar does pay less than the floor and does not pay more than the cap.

Another view of the collar would be in payoff terms, as a function of the future spot rates. When the interest rate moves up and hits the strike of the cap, the buyer of the cap pays a fixed rate equal to strike. When the interest rates moves down to the strike of the floor, the buyer of the collar will pay again a fixed, lower rate. In between the rate varies as the market rate. (See Figure 7.14.)

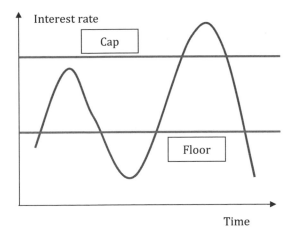

FIGURE 7.13   Collar

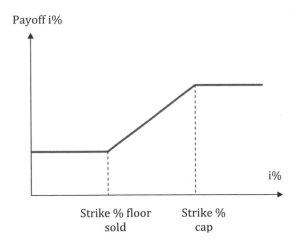

FIGURE 7.14   Payoff of collar

7.5.3 Options as Volatility Instruments

Those are simple examples using simple contracts. They are generic hedges, used with instruments called "plain vanilla," because they have no exotic features embedded in them. There are various ways of combining options on interest rates. Notably, the views of traders will differ from the hedger's view. For example, the trader will see options on interest rates as volatility instruments, and could use options to bet on volatilities. Consider a simple example to illustrate this point. If a trader buys both a cap and a collar, instead of buying one and selling the other one, with the strike price of the cap higher than that of the floor, it has a long position on volatility. The position is long because the trader gains when interest rate volatility increases. The payoff graph would be as shown in Figure 7.15.

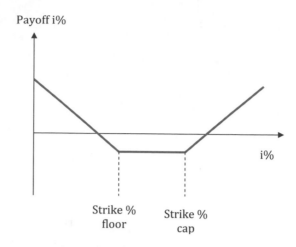

FIGURE 7.15   Payoff of bought cap and floor

As long as the interest rate remains within the strikes, the trader has paid a premium and makes a loss. But if the interest rate moves beyond the strikes, on either side, the trader gains if the gross payoff more than compensates the premium paid (which cumulates the premium of the cap and of the floor). This combination makes up a strangle. The trader is long in the strangle, and wins when the volatility of interest rates is high enough to make either option sufficiently in-the-money. Such combinations apply as well for any underlying, and there are a variety of combinations of options, which allow having payoffs with a variety of shapes.

7.6 HEDGING INTEREST RATE RISK BY CORPORATE BORROWER (CASE STUDY)

Hedging instruments are common hedging products for corporations in their liability management process. A borrower with a variable rate fears an increase of interest rates. In order to hedge its exposure, it is possible to use interest rate swaps, FRAs or options, caps and floors.

Assume, for example, that the borrower's debt is Libor 1-year, currently at 6%, with 3 years residual maturity. The swap fixed rate would be 5% for the remaining maturity. We ignore the fee paid to the bank selling the swap. Assume a forward rate agreement locks in a 6% rate from start date, today, until 3 years. In fact FRAs should start one year from now and last two years, or a 2×3 forward contract. A cap option would guarantee a maximum rate of 7%, but the premium is 1.5%. A collar with a zero net premium would guarantee a maximum rate of 8% and a minimum rate of 5.5%. Such zero-premium collar has not much benefit for the borrower. The bank also proposes a collar with maximum and minimum rates being, respectively, 7% and 5%, the premium being 0.8%. The current base scenario as perceived by the borrower is an increase of Libor.

For the swap to be beneficial, the cost after hedging should be lower than the Libor. The cost of the swap is negligible. In this example, the swap pays a fixed rate equal to 5%. The forward rate agreement becomes profitable if the Libor gets higher than 6%, but should rates declines, it would cost more to the borrower.

The cap option costs 1.5% for a maximum rate of 6.5%. The premium cost has to be included in the all-in cost of the existing debt plus the cap. If the cap lasts two years, the premium averaged over two years would be 0.75%. The maximum all-in cost is when Libor is equal or above the strike 7%. It equals 7% + 0.75% = 7.75%. The break-even value of Libor making the hedge profitable is the premium plus strike rate of the cap, or 7.75%. If Libor is above, the cap is beneficial, since the all-in cost remains at 7.75%, otherwise the all-in cost is above that of debt. It is easy to check that with a Libor equal to 7.25% (6.25% +0.75%), the all-in cost is the same with and without the cap. With the option, the borrower benefits from the downside of Libor, although the all-in cost is always above the cost of original debt.

With the collar, the all-in cost of debt plus collar depends upon whether the Libor moves up or down. If the Libor moves up, the all-in cost equals the cost of existing debt plus annualized premium (0.4%) when Libor remains below 7% and the maximum cost is equal to the strike plus annualized premium, or 7.4%. The break-even value of Libor making the all-in cost equal to the Libor occurs when Libor equals the strike plus the premium, or 7.4%. When the Libor moves down, the all-in cost is Libor + 0.4%, except that the minimum value is equal to the strike of the floor plus premium , or 5% + 0.4% =5.4%. For an intermediate value between the two strikes, the debt with collar costs the Libor plus annualized premium, or Libor + 0.4%, always above Libor by the amount of the premium. When the Libor becomes 4%, the cost of debt with collar remains at 5.4%, and is always above the cost of the original debt. Therefore, the collar has a break-even value of 7.4%. If Libor is above, the borrower makes a gain. If Libor is below, the borrower is better off without the collar, since the all-in cost with collar is the minimum of Libor + 0.4% or 5.4% (Libor equals the strike of the floor, 5%).

The various break-even points of Libor can be shown with payoff graph for all three hedges. Figure 7.16 shows the prevailing Libor rate on the x-axis and the actual cost when entering into a hedge, or no hedge. If no hedge is set, the payoff is simply the cost of debt, or Libor. The highest break-even value is that of the cap, and the lowest is for FRA or the swap, at 6%. Under

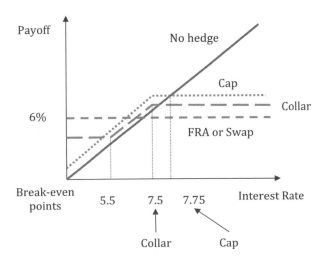

FIGURE 7.16 Comparing interest rate hedges

a scenario of increasing rate, the lowest break-even value is the best, because it is the lowest possible rate paid by the borrower. This makes the FRA or the swap the best hedges.

7.7 WHERE DO INTEREST RATES COME FROM?

Monetary policy is the major driver of interest rates, since the prevailing view is that high interest rates are the best way to fight inflation. Monetary policy has a direct effect on the short end of the curve because central banks tend to act upon those rates. They do so by setting their own discount rate and by lending or borrowing on such maturities. Public deficits are normally financed by debt. Government debt tends to be spread over all maturities, and higher deficits tend to raise the term structure of rates. For managing foreign exchanges, the differentials between interest rates across countries make investing in interest rate instruments relatively more or less attractive. For reducing the pressure on depreciation of the home currency, the central bank might increase interest rates, making lending in the home currency more attractive than in foreign currencies. This scheme was consistently used when the system imposed that European currency exchange rates fluctuate within preset bounds. The fundamentals of the economy also play a role. The better they are, the lower will the interest rates be. Expectations are a major driving factor. If most think that interest rates will increase, they will because all players will be willing to borrow before they do. This is the self-fulfilling prophecy that applies in all markets. For the mechanism to take place, it is necessary, however, that there is a consensus on the market. (See Figure 7.17.)

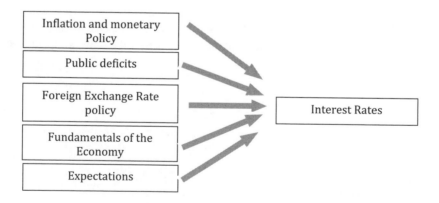

FIGURE 7.17   Drivers of interest rates

8

Foreign Exchange Risk and Foreign Exchange Derivatives

This chapter discusses foreign exchange rates and related derivatives, which are forward exchange rates and options to buy or sell a currency[1]. The most common instruments for controlling foreign exchange risks are forward contracts, foreign exchange swaps and currency options. Forward contracts set up, as of today, future foreign exchange rates. Swaps exchange one currency into another at a rate set today. Currency swaps exchange all the debt flows, interest and principal in one currency into their values in another currency at preset exchange rates. Currency options are options to buy or sell a foreign currency against home currency at a preset strike rate.

The chapter discusses first foreign exchange contracts, which allow setting up today a foreign exchange rate for a future date. A forward exchange contract is used subsequently to illustrate the principles of the derivation of market VaR for contracts that depend non-linearly on several risk factors. Foreign exchange options, or rights to buy or sell a foreign currency at an exercise price, are detailed next. The third section is a case study of hedging foreign exchange exposures using the various instruments. The last short section lists the main drivers of foreign exchange rates.

Contents

---

1 The same sources as in the previous chapter are suitable: Hull [35], Neftci [54].

8.1 FOREIGN EXCHANGE RATES AND FORWARD CONTRACTS

Foreign exchange rates are prices of one currency (foreign currency) in terms of another (home currency). Selling a foreign currency (e.g. USD) to get the home currency (e.g. EUR) is identical to buying the home currency (e.g. EUR) with the foreign currency (e.g. USD). For example, an exchange rate of 0.8 EUR/USD is equivalent to 1.25 USD/EUR. Foreign exchange risk arises because of fluctuations of foreign exchange rates. For example, an exporter receives an inflow of 1 million USD (foreign currency) to be converted into EUR (home currency). The exporter will sell 1 million USD at 0.8 EUR for each USD or, equivalently, buy 800,000 EUR with 1 million USD.

A forward exchange rate is a rate set today for a future date. The benefits are immediate for hedgers. Forward rates lock in the future exchange rate as of today, but they imply an obligation to sell or buy the currency at this exchange rate at the expiration of the contract. They are used when expecting a future inflow in foreign currency ("long" position) or when expecting a future outflow in foreign currency ("short" position).

Currency swaps exchange two debts, principal and interests, in two currencies at a given rate as of today. They serve for changing the currency of a debt issue: borrow in one currency and convert it into another. Foreign exchange swaps exchange currencies at a given horizon at a given rate as of today. Foreign exchange swaps can be viewed as a series of forward contracts for each cash flow to be exchanged in the future.

The usage for hedging purposes is easy to understand. Typical hedging strategies rely on forward prices. We use the example of corporation exporting and receiving foreign currency. The exporter is "long" in the foreign currency and exposed to the risk of a decline of the value of the foreign currency in term of the home currency.

The exporter expects a future inflow in USD in 6 months. Its home currency is the EUR. He is afraid of a decline of the spot exchange rate in EUR/1 USD. The exporter is selling USD and buying EUR forward. He buys a forward contract on foreign exchange, agreeing to exchange, say, USD 1 into EUR 0.80 from a seller of forwards, a bank, in 6 months. The exporter is now hedged against a decrease of the spot exchange rate of USD into EUR below the contracted forward exchange rate. The drawback of the forward hedge is that, if the future spot exchange rate is above the forward rate, the exporter has the obligation to convert USD at the pre-determined forward rate and loses the positive difference between the spot rate and the forward rate. This type of hedge is very common.

8.1.1 Replicating a Forward Exchange Rate

We can find out how a forward contract is constructed and valued using again the static replication principle. A forward contract is equivalent to borrowing and lending the same amount in two different currencies and converting the proceeds in the home currency. Since one borrows and lends the same amount, the initial value has to be zero, as is usual for a forward contract when the forward price is equal to the forward exchange rate under no arbitrage.

The forward exchange rate contract implies three transactions and combines two positions, for which all terms are known and set today (Figure 8.1).

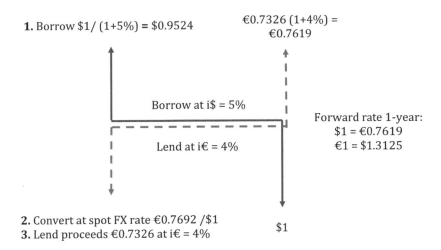

FIGURE 8.1 Forward foreign (FX) rate

- Borrowing in $ at $i\$\%$ (5%) for 1 year such that, in 1 year, we get exactly 1$ to pay, paid by the expected inflow of $1: $1/(1 + 5\%) = \$0.9524$.
- Converting the proceeds of borrowing in $ into € at the spot prevailing exchange rate S €/$: $S = 0.7692$ €/$ or exactly $1/1.3$ $/€: Proceeds in € are € 0.7326.
- Lending the proceeds in € at $i€\%$ (4%) for 1 year, which results in 0.7692 € $\times (1 + 4\%) = 0.7619$ € in 1 year.

The implied forward exchange rate is such that $1 = 0.76190$ € or €1 = \$1.31250. The forward rate F_1 €/$ is above the spot (1.3) because the "carrying cost" is the difference between interest rates in $ and €, here positive.

According to the law of one price, this exchange rate is the only one sustainable. Assume that the forward rate differs from the calculated value and is, for example, 0.79 €/$ instead of 0.76190€/$. A trader could earn money without risk. To do so, one would borrow $1, sell spot, and invest the proceeds in Euros. The gain would be 0.79€/$ – 0.76190€/$. By borrowing more and selling forward more USD will push the forward $/€ rate down, push the interest rate in USD (i_s) up, and push the EUR interest rate (i_e) down, until equilibrium. The fair exchange rate is such that the discrepancy between the forward rate and the one replicated by those transactions disappears.

8.1.2 Mark-to-market Valuation of Forward Contracts

We detail here the valuation of the forward contract after inception. The example will be used subsequently for illustrating the calculation of market VaR.

A forward foreign exchange (FX) contract for $10,000,000, with the forward rate 0.7619048 €/1$, would result in proceeds in € in 1 year of €7,619,048. The forward combines a long (lending) position at € rate with a short position (borrowing) at $ rate. The mark-to-market value is the present value of the two transactions over the life of the transaction. The flows are fixed at inception. After inception, the market parameters i_s, i_e, spot €/$ change and the present value fluctuates.

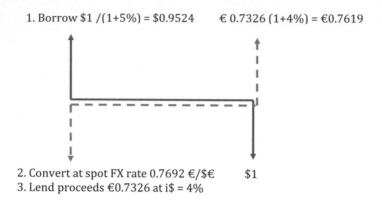

1. Borrow $1 /(1+5%) = $0.9524   € 0.7326 (1+4%) = €0.7619

2. Convert at spot FX rate 0.7692 €/$€ $1
3. Lend proceeds €0.7326 at i$ = 4%

FIGURE 8.2   Forward exchange rate

We value such forward contract in Euros since we convert the borrowing in $ into € at the known spot rate. The mark-to-market (MTM) forward value is that of the portfolio of replicating transactions. Let t be current time and T be the maturity. The forward value in € is:

$$F_t(€) = -S_t(€/\$) \frac{10,000,000\ (\$)}{(1 + i_\$)^{T-t}} + \frac{7,619,048\ (€)}{(1 + i_€)^{T-t}}$$

Note that the value of the forward at inception is simply zero since it combines two identical amounts lent and borrowed with exactly the same values in Euros by definition. The value after inception changes randomly, and becomes positive or negative, because the market parameters change randomly until maturity. We represent these transactions with arrows, with the usual conventions (Figure 8.2): arrows pointing up are inflows and arrows pointing down are outflows.

The proceeds in one year should be equivalent, meaning that $1 is equivalent to €0.7619, which provides the forward exchange rate. Any discrepancy would result in riskless arbitrage.

8.2 FOREIGN EXCHANGE OPTIONS

Options are simple instruments for hedging. An option to sell the foreign currency and buy home currency at a preset exchange rate 0.82 €/$, cost has a premium 0.02 €/$ and maturity set at inception. If the foreign currency appreciates, the option is out-of-the-money and is worthless, but we get the upside of foreign currency above 0.82 €/$. If the foreign currency depreciates, the option is in-the-money, and we get the preset exchange rate 0.82 €/$. The premium, 0.02 €/$ should be deducted from such gross payoffs.

A foreign exchange "collar" would serve as lower premium optional hedge. A collar consists of buying a put and selling a call at different strikes. Consider the seller of USD (foreign currency) against EUR (home currency). The seller would like to buy a put, or right to sell the USD at a preset price. The put strike is 0.82 EUR/USD. In order to reduce the cost of the put (right to sell the foreign currency), he/she sells a call to the bank (an option to buy a foreign currency at a preset exchange rate set to 0.90 EUR/USD). The sale generates revenue reducing his/her cost.

Below 0.82, the protection of the put applies. However, above 0.90, the buyer of the call buys the dollars at 0.90€/$ even though they are worth more. The seller of the call cannot sell USD at more than 0.90 EUR/USD since he has contracted to sell at this exchange rate with the buyer of the call. The combined two options make up a collar providing a downside protection and a limited upside gain.

8.3 HEDGING A CORPORATE LONG EXPOSURE IN FOREIGN CURRENCY (CASE STUDY)

The usage of hedging instruments for corporations is straightforward. An exporter expects a cash inflow of 1 million USD in six months. The exporter has a long position in the USD. The exporter fears a decline of the USD versus the Euro. The current spot exchange rate is 0.80 EUR/USD. Various choices are open for hedging this long exposure against a depreciation of the USD in terms of Euro.

- Doing nothing.
- Selling forward USD at the current forward rate, assumed to be 0.81 EUR/USD.
- Buying a put option: The option provides the right to sell USD against Euros, with a premium of 0.02 EUR/USD, with strike 0.82 EUR/USD.

The put option allows taking advantage of the upside of the USD whereas the forward contract is an obligation to sell forthcoming USD at the forward exchange rate. Payoff graphs are very convenient for comparing the three solutions. The spot (unknown exchange rate) at the time of the USD inflow is along the x-axis. The payoff is in EUR/USD on the vertical axis. (See Figure 8.3.)

Doing nothing means that the exporter will use the prevailing exchange rate, whatever it is. The payoff is the first diagonal, where the future exchange rate is equal to the prevailing spot rate at the future date. The forward contract payoff is a horizontal line with a constant payoff

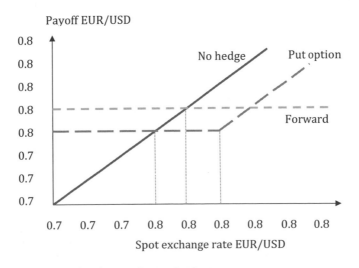

FIGURE 8.3   Comparing foreign exchange hedges

of 0.81. The put option payoff is a kinked line. When the USD hits the strike 0.82, the payoff is the strike minus the premium paid, or $0.82 - 0.02 = 0.80$ EUR/USD. When the exchange rate becomes higher than the strike, the option is out-of-the-money and the exchange rate is the spot exchange rate minus the premium paid upfront 0.02. The payoff is shown as a straight line parallel to the first diagonal but lower by 0.02.

As usual, one can consider both break-even values, such that no hedging is equivalent to hedging, and compare those with expectations. If expectations are such that a decline of the value of USD is likely, the best hedge is the one with the higher break-even point, which is the forward contract. No hedge at all is best when expectations are that the USD appreciates. Under a myopic view of the market, with no consensus at all on the direction, most corporations would opt for the forward because they know, at least, how to set up their budgets.

8.4 THE FOREIGN EXCHANGE MARKET AND RATES

Foreign exchange rates fluctuate according to some macroeconomic drivers and expectations. The excess/deficit of the exports/imports of one country influence foreign exchange rates because trade unbalances generate symmetric unbalances between purchases and sales of the currency. Interest rate differentials between countries also influence foreign exchange because they make investing in one country relatively more or less attractive. Expectations about prospective exchange rates also drive the rates. An expected depreciation of a currency is an incentive to sell it before it depreciates, and, conversely, an expected appreciation is an incentive to purchase the currency at a cheaper rate today. In both cases, expectations tend to be confirmed by the actions they trigger (self-fulfilling prophecy).

9

Credit Derivatives

This chapter is a broad overview of credit derivatives. Credit derivatives are products which serve for trading the credit risk of cash assets independently of the asset themselves[1]. As other derivatives, they serve for hedging purposes and for trading purposes. Such products provide protection against default of a credit risky bond or a portfolio of bonds. The seller of the derivatives is the seller of protection and the buyer of credit risk. The buyer of the derivative is the buyer of protection and the seller of credit risk. Hedgers are protection seekers, investors and traders are sellers of credit derivatives and take exposure to credit risk for various purposes.

There are three basic types of credit derivatives. Credit default swaps, or CDS, provide a specified payment under default events, and are by far the most commonly used products. Total return swaps exchange the revenues and capital gains/losses of the underlying assets between two parties. Credit spread products allow taking positions on future spreads. Other products provide further flexibility, the main ones being "basket swaps."

The chapter starts with an overview of credit derivatives, with the main distinctive feature being that they allow trading the credit risk of cash instruments by isolating the credit risk component from the underlying cash instrument. The next five sections describe five types of credit derivatives. The most commonly used credit derivatives, credit default swaps (CDS), come first in the list. For standardizing such contracts and making them tradable, several issues, with respect to payment under default of the underlying assets, events triggering the derivatives, among others, had to be resolved. The last section addresses issues raised by the pricing of such derivatives.

The main applications of credit derivatives, other than providing insurance against default or allowing gaining exposure through credit derivatives rather than cash exposures, are expanded in Section 15 of this text on credit portfolio management.

---

1 Useful references include Duffie and Singleton [28], Das [25] plus, for pricing, Schönbucher [67].

Contents

9.1 DEFINITIONS OF CREDIT DERIVATIVES

This section provides a broad overview of what credit derivatives are, what functions they fulfill, who has interest in them and why.

Credit derivatives are instruments serving to trade credit risk by isolating the credit risk from the underlying transactions. Credit derivatives allow separating the trading of the credit risk of assets from trading the asset itself since it is possible to trade them without trading the reference assets. Other features of credit derivatives are: they are off-balance sheet; they do not necessitate entering directly into loan arrangements or purchases of bonds; nor do they necessitate prior agreement of the issuer of the reference asset.

For defining the protection, a reference asset, typically a traded bond, serves as underlying asset. When a default event occurs for the underlying asset, buying a credit derivative is like insurance. The seller of the derivative provides a payment to the party suffering the loss. Credit derivatives are similar to insurance on credit risk only, except that they are traded over-the-counter.

Simple cash transactions cannot disentangle the various risk components embedded in them. We can try to hedge the credit risk of a bond by selling short another similar bond. However, this transaction does not eliminate the interest rate risk component. Note that a standard put does not perform the same function since the strike is the price, without disentangling the effect of credit deterioration and a change of market rates.

A credit derivative provides protection against credit events, such as default event. Credit derivatives also provide protection against a rating downgrade, thereby guaranteeing that the minimum target rating holds through the horizon of the reference asset, whether held in the portfolio or not. These options on spread work like covenants triggering default if the credit standing deteriorates beyond some threshold. However, covenants necessitate interactions with the lender with smaller chances of success if the lender cannot do much. Then the loan will simply accelerate (be repaid) and the loss materializes. On the other hand, a spread option will work.

The terminology deserves some attention. Credit derivatives involve a protection seller, a protection buyer and the underlying risk. The seller of a credit derivative is the seller of protection, or insurance, and the buyer of credit risk. The buyer of a credit derivative is the buyer of protection, or insurance, and the seller of credit risk. In other words, the buyer of the instrument is the seller of credit risk and vice versa.

The intermediate player making the market is the protection seller. The underlying asset of which default triggers payment is the underlying asset, typically a bond. The buyer of protection does not need to have the asset in their portfolio. He/she buys protection on the default of the bond, of which credit risk might be correlated to credit exposures to which the buyer is exposed.

The products are generally classified into three broad categories: credit default swaps; total return swaps; credit spread products. Credit default swaps are described below.

In a total return swap, the protection seeker exchanges the "total return" of an asset, which combines both current revenues and capital gains or loss, with a fee paid to the protection seller. It provides a protection against a downside move of the value of the reference asset. The investor looks for an enhanced return.

Credit spread derivatives exchange a risky spread against the risk-free rate, or a risky spread against another one. The protection provider, or investor, looks for enhanced revenue, while the buyer seeks protection against a loss of asset value due to a widening of credit spreads or a downgrade.

Basket derivatives provide protection against the defaults within a basket, or portfolio. The seller of the derivatives pays upon the "N-to-default" asset. For example, a "first to default" derivatives provides payment if a single asset within the basket is the first to default.

9.2 CREDIT DEFAULT SWAPS (CDS)

The majority of credit derivatives are credit default swaps, or CDSs. The buyer of a credit derivative pays a recurring premium and receives payment equal to loss under default if the underlying asset defaults, or is subject to a credit event that qualifies for triggering the CDS. The derivative has a paying leg and a receiving leg, like a swap. For the buyer of a CDS, the paying leg is the premium and the receiving leg is the payment contingent upon default of the underlying asset. (See Figure 9.1.)

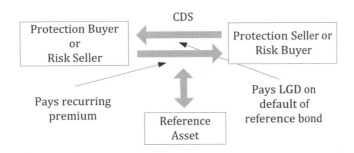

FIGURE 9.1   Credit default swap (CDS), protection seller and buyer, and reference asset

9.3 TOTAL RETURN SWAPS

A total return swap (TRS) exchanges the total return, current yield plus any change in value, whether positive or negative, between two assets. The exchange of cash flows occurs whether or not there is a default event. The swap exchanges flows and changes in asset value periodically or at some fixed dates.

The buyer of the TRS receives an "algebraic" total return, interest plus capital gain or loss of some specified underlying asset (a bond). When the credit standing of the bond deterio-

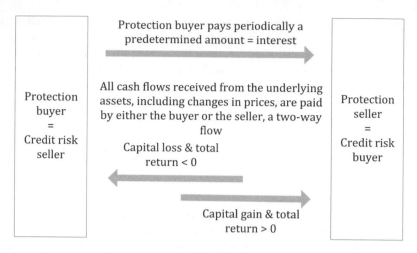

FIGURE 9.2 Two-way flows with a total return swap

rates, there is a capital loss for the bond and the TRS seller pays the loss to the buyer, who is protected against such loss. When the credit standing of the bond improves, the buyer pays to the seller the capital gain. This is a "two-way" flow. The buyer of the TRS pays to the seller a fixed premium for the insurance.

The seller of the total return swap is also as the seller of the protection of the buyer of risk. The same terminology as for CDS applies for the buyer of the swap, who is also a protection buyer and a seller of risk. The credit risk buyer gains full exposure to the underlying asset. The risk materializes through a depreciation of value or a default. The buyer of the protection receives the interest while the seller suffers a loss. (See Figure 9.2.)

9.4 CREDIT SPREAD PRODUCTS

Credit spread derivatives refer to the credit spread relative to the risk-free benchmark or to the differential of credit spreads of two risky assets. Credit spread derivatives isolate the effect of spreads as opposed to contracts on prices subject to the entire change yield, combining both interest rate variations and spread variations. Credit spread options provide the right to buy a future credit spread, as do other forward and option contracts.

The seller of a credit spread swap pays to the buyer a predetermined fixed spread while the buyer pays to the seller the spread of a risky asset over the risk-free rate or another security. The buyer is insensitive to spread variations. The seller gains if the spread widens and suffers a loss if the risky spread narrows.

Credit spread options are options whose payoff depends on the spread between a risky bond and a risk-free bond. Cash transactions do not disentangle the price variations due to interest rate variations from spread variations. A put on the risky debt does not work because of the effect of interest rate risk in addition to that of the spread risk. This is a protection against a fall in the price of the asset if the yield, inclusive of credit spread, moves in the opposite direction.

Only credit spread options strip the risk and isolate spread risk. Credit spread options have the usual value drivers: notional, maturity, underlying, strike spread, and premium. In addition, duration is important because it measures the sensitivity to a credit spread change.

9.5 BASKET SWAPS, FIRST-TO-DEFAULT, N-TO-DEFAULT

Basket swaps refer to credit events of assets within a portfolio (basket) rather than single asset credit events. A "first to default" derivative is triggered by the first default event of any asset in the basket.

First-to-default products are correlation products. Diversification reduces the risk of the basket but it does not reduce the risk of first-to-default derivative. In fact, it is the reverse. The probability of triggering a basket derivative is higher than for a single asset. Consider a basket of two assets only. The rationale is based on joint survival probability[2]. The probability of zero default within the basket is the joint probability that all survive. The joint survival probability is higher when correlation is positive. The complement to one of the joint survival probability is the probability that any one of the assets defaults. Equivalently it is the probability that asset one, or asset two, or that the two assets default. If correlation increases, the joint survival probability increases, and the basket risk decreases. The probability that at least one asset defaults, triggering the derivative, also decreases. The credit risk of the basket varies inversely with correlation.

If we have two independent assets of default probabilities, 1% and 2%, the joint default probability is the product of the two default probabilities. The survival probability of both is the joint survival probability, or 99% × 98% = 97.02%. The probability that either one of the two assets defaults is simply 1– 97.02% = 2.98% if the events are independent. This is higher than any one of the two single default probabilities, which shows that the risk of first-to-default baskets is greater than for single assets. If the credit correlation is positive the joint survival probability increases above 97.02% and the probability that any one defaults is lower than 2.98%. The probability of triggering a first-to-default product is inversely related to correlation. Sometimes, the seller of such products is considered as selling default correlation, and is "short" correlation. Conversely, the buyer is "long" correlation.

This analysis explains the rationale for such derivatives. From the protection buyer standpoint, there might be very large exposures of high-grade obligors to hedge. Putting them together makes sense. From the protection seller standpoint, there is some comfort in finding high-grade exposures in the basket. In fact, the portfolio of high-grade exposures has a lower credit quality in terms of first-to-default events. Nevertheless, it remains an eligible investment in low-risk assets with an enhanced return compared to that of individual high-grade assets.

Other N-to-default products provide payments when at least N assets default. There are triggered when several assets default, such as 2, 3 or more assets of a portfolio. When N defaults are reached, the seller pays the loss to the buyer.

---

2 The discussion of joint probabilities and conditional probabilities is detailed in Chapter 31.

9.6 SOVEREIGN RISK CREDIT DERIVATIVES

Sovereign risk has grown with exposures to emerging markets. Country risk is somehow hybrid in nature. It can be an economic crisis, a currency crisis, a political crisis. A well-defined aspect of country risk is inconvertibility risk, or transfer risk. Because of the various aspects of country risk, it is important to define exactly which is the risk purchased or sold. Convertibility products address the ability of payments in another country. Such events appear as political events, but their consequences are equivalent to a credit event. A well-identified element is the non-transferability of funds outside the country, should some country event occur.

Credit derivatives hedge currency inconvertibility. The agreement provides protection for a determined period. The protection buyer pays a premium. If there is no currency inconvertibility during the agreed period, the contract terminates without benefit for the protection buyer. If there is a currency inconvertibility event, the protection buyer gets the face value of the funds in "hard" ("strong") currency. In return, the protection seller gets property of the face value in the "soft" ("weak") currency. Receiving the hard currency effectively protects the owner of the weak currency from not being able to get the money back. The protection seller should have some local usage of the inconvertible currency to make a deal. Investors in the country might have such a position.

9.7 MAIN SPECIFICS AND KEY TERMS

The main specifics of credit derivatives are, besides the nature of the contract:

- the underlying asset
- the payment terms
- the value of payment under a credit event
- the conditions defining a credit event
- the risk materialization
- legal issues with respect to risk transfers.

9.7.1 The Underlying Assets

Credit derivative contracts exchange payments triggered by a credit event or an underlying asset or a basket of assets. The credit event always entails a loss of value, a downgrade or a default. The underlying asset can be a bond, a loan, or any credit asset, including baskets of assets. As with other derivatives, there is a notional amount. The notional amount might be identical to the principal of a loan or it can differ from the value of the underlying asset. This allows leveraging transactions. For instance, it is possible to insure the spread of a bond for an amount that is a multiple of the face value of the underlying bond. This allows speculation and return (or loss) enhancement because the ratio notional/face value of the underlying asset is higher than 1.

9.7.2 Payment Terms

The investor, or, equivalently, the risk buyer or the protection seller, receives fees from the buyer of protection plus the interest payments of the underlying assets. The buyer of protection, or the risk seller, receives from the investor the recurring premium. Termination payments are settlement payments if the credit risk of the underlying actually materialized. They require the definition of the post-default value. When assets are tradable with a reasonable liquidity, prices are a sound basis for calculating the payment. This leads to choosing underlying assets complying with such conditions, or to agreeing in advance to a payout payment (such as fixed amount). In addition, the determination of the price based on securities needs to be transparent, necessitating some polling of dealer prices to have an objective reference.

9.7.3 Legal Issues

The legal separation of the derivatives from the underlying loan of bond, allows transferring the risks without prior consent of the borrower. This transfer extends to economic rights related to the borrower obligation. This extension raises legal issues since the holder of the total return swap might exercise rights that could affect the profile of the obligation (in case of distress restructuring or any dispute). Because of this issue, the investor in the issue might not have directly such information and any right of representation.

Credit derivatives allow transferring risk without transferring the cash assets. This offers potential whenever it is more difficult to transfer assets than credit risk through derivatives. The development of synthetic structures in Europe for off-loading credit risk, by selling credit derivatives, without sales of assets illustrates the benefit of this differential legal treatment.

9.7.4 Payments under a Credit Event

There is some initial reference price, either a nominal value for a loan, or a bond price reflecting the current credit standing of the issuer as well as the contractual payments of this asset. Since listed assets do not have a single price, several dealers' quotes serve for determining a price. Payments relate to the current value of the asset.

For traded assets, the post-default price defines the loss under default, a standard practice of rating agencies for publishing LGD. With total return swaps, payments cumulate the capital appreciation or depreciation with the normal asset return. For credit-spread derivatives, the payments are a function of the difference between initial and final credit spreads needs conversion into a value. The value is the difference in spreads times a multiple for converting this change into a price change. The multiplier is the duration since it measures the price sensitivity of a bond to a unit change in discount rate.

The relationship to the asset does not imply matching the asset price with the derivative notional. Users can leverage the actual exposure of the underlying by using a notional different from the actual asset value. This allows customizing the exposure. Lenders can reduce their excess exposure. Investors in credit derivatives can leverage their investments and customize their expected return. Delivery is in cash, or with securities considered as acceptable substitutes of the defaulted asset.

9.7.5 Credit Events

For trading such instruments, credit events triggering a credit derivative and payments once triggered have to be defined in a standard way.

Credit events triggering a credit derivative are not identical to those related to the underlying asset. In general, credit events have a wider scope than default events. For the reference asset, credit events include: payment obligation default, bankruptcy or insolvency event, restructuring or equivalent, rating downgrades beyond a specified threshold, and change of credit spread exceeding a specified level. Failure to pay is a default event. Not all such events are necessary for triggering a credit derivative payment. A subset of those events might be enough for triggering a credit derivative.

Events that trigger exercise of the derivative obligations overlap with the credit events of the reference asset, but might differ in practice. For example, any deterioration of the credit standing of the underlying asset might serve for triggering the derivative obligations. Mergers or split-offs might weaken the credit standing of firms and might be looked at as a potential relevant event for a credit derivative. Basel 2 specified the conditions for credit derivatives to be recognized as valid credit risk protection allowing relief of capital charges[3].

§191. In order for a credit derivative contract to be recognized, the following conditions must be satisfied:

(a) The credit events specified by the contracting parties must at a minimum cover:

Failure to pay the amounts due under terms of the underlying obligation that are in effect at the time of such failure (with a grace period that is closely in line with the grace period in the underlying obligation);

Bankruptcy, insolvency or inability of the obligor to pay its debts, or its failure or admission in writing of its inability generally to pay its debts as they become due, and analogous events; and

Restructuring of the underlying obligation involving forgiveness or postponement of principal, interest or fees that result in a credit loss event (i.e. charge-off, specific provision or other similar debit to the profit and loss account).

§193. Only credit default swaps and total return swaps that provide credit protection equivalent to guarantees will be eligible for recognition.

The main credit events triggering payment are default, restructuring of debt or bankruptcy. The payment under default is the loss given default of the underlying asset.

9.7.6 Materialization

Such events might be uneasy to define precisely, because of potential disputes. Materiality clauses help to avoid triggering a "false" credit event by specifying the observable consequences of a credit event. Common facts are minimum variations of prices or changes in spreads, legal notices, and publicly available information. Price materiality refers to a minimum difference between the initial price of the reference asset and the current price. Spread materiality refers to a minimum difference between the spread at inception and the final spread.

---

3 Paragraph references are those of the main Accord document [7].

9.8 PRICING CREDIT DERIVATIVES

A credit derivative, such as the common CDS, is similar to an option because it has a contingent leg, which is the payment contingent on default of the reference asset. The pricing mechanism is based on modeling the time to default of the derivative using time intensity models. The recurring premium should be equal to the expected value of the contingent leg. Time-to-default models[4] allow modeling directly the expected value of the random leg. Through such a pricing mechanism, it can be shown that the recurring premium should be theoretically identical to the credit spread of the underlying asset.

Some pricing issues remain difficult to address. Any correlation between the credit risk of the seller of protection and the issuer of the reference assets weakens the value of the protection because the likelihood of joint default is higher. The issue is identical with any insurer of credit risk. In other words, entering into a CDS does not fully eliminate the credit risk. There can be a joint adverse credit event (downgrade or default) of the underlying asset and of the seller of protection. The joint risk depends on correlation of credit events of obligor and seller of protection and is low as long as credit events do not correlate positively and significantly.

---

4 Time-to-default models are explained in Chapters 10, 12 and 43.

3.4 PRICING CREDIT DERIVATIVES

SECTION 4

Valuation

Valuation plays a central role in risk management because it drives gains and losses for both the banking and the trading portfolios. Most risk models aim at modeling potential losses deriving from current risk. Accordingly, the valuation block is central in such models.

When looking forward, asset values and market parameters are random and follow probability distributions. Rather than introducing such distributions in steps, when progressing through risk models, the most common distributions are reviewed in the first chapter of this section.

The basic valuation mechanism of certain future payoffs of an asset relies on discounting. Discounting is the mirror image of capitalization, whereby we invest an amount and expect a return. Valuation under certainty relies on the simple discounted cash flow (DCF) model, which discounts to present future cash flows.

Because we deal with risky assets in this text, valuation under uncertainty is even more important. Valuation raises issues because both the payoffs and the risk premium embedded in risky returns are generally unknown. Valuation under uncertainty is addressed last, with sample applications that will be used later on in this text.

The five chapters of this section address those topics in sequence.

- The overview of the main distributions used in this text (Chapter 10).
- Basic discussion on returns, discrete and continuous, plus the discounted cash flow model (Chapter 11).
- Common stochastic processes which model the variations over time of random returns on assets or of market parameters are reviewed next (Chapter 12).
- The basic techniques for valuation under uncertainty rely on forming risk-free portfolio or on risk-neutral valuation, which consists as behaving as if investors were indifferent to risk (Chapter 13).
- Sample applications that are used in this text follow in Chapter 14, illustrating basic valuation techniques for credit risky debt, simple options, and modeling of interest rates.

Advanced readers might skip those chapters, since there is a considerable amount of literature dealing with these topics in a much more detailed and advanced way. The sole purpose of this section is to provide some basic background for relating risk management topics to the rest of the literature, at the sacrifice of accuracy.

Other readers might skip, in a first stage, some technical development of financial theories to progress faster towards risk models, which follow in the next section. The review of probability distributions (Chapter 10) can be used as a reference chapter when needed while progressing through the text. The understanding of returns and simple stochastic processes is recommended in the first stage reading (Chapters 11 and 12) – valuation under uncertainty leads to well-known conceptual results, such as risk-neutral valuation, forming risk-free portfolios, and so-called "lattice trees" for describing uncertain future payoffs. Readers can proceed and check that they understand these end results and methodologies when applied later in the text.

10

Distribution Functions

This chapter covers the main definitions and properties of probability distributions that are relevant for risk management techniques. Examples of risk applications are also introduced when possible. The first section provides generic definitions and terminology, plus conventions used in the text for representing random variables. The inverse functions, presented in Section 10.2 serve repeatedly in this text for simulation purposes. The section also relates to uniform distributions from Section 10.4. Each section is dedicated to distributions that are of interest in risk management. There are numerous publications on statistical distributions, statistical sampling and properties of well-known distributions[1].

Putting together the distributions simplifies subsequent developments. Readers can refer to this chapter when needed, as long as they have in mind the basic definitions of random variables, of distribution functions, and of moments.

Contents

---

1 Basic properties are shown in reference 78 (for example), which includes sampling errors distributions. Very detailed presentations of all univariate continuous distributions are in references 41 and 42, which can serve as reference for most distributions and the related methodologies to deal with most statistical issues.

10.1 RANDOM VARIABLES AND PROBABILITY DISTRIBUTION FUNCTIONS

Deterministic variables take a value fully determined by the existing information. Random variables, also called stochastic variables, can take various values associated with probabilities. Probabilities characterize the chance that a random variable falls within a preset range of values.

Random variables are conditional on an information set that evolves with time. For example, the stock price as of date t is conditioned by the set of information available as of t. When t increases, the information set increases and the stock price adjusts accordingly to good and bad news. Random variables are designated by capital letters and their particular values are designated by small letters. Hence X is a random variable which can take a value x.

A random variable takes values associated with a probability. The probability measures the "chances" of a random variable taking any particular value or falling within a range of values. The probability that a random variable falls within the allowed range of possible values is always 1. The range of permissible values is the "support" of the distribution. Hence all probabilities assigned to all permissible values sum up to 1.

10.1.1 Discrete Variables

Some random variables are discrete, meaning that they take discrete values such as 0 or 1 for example. A probability distribution is discrete if it can take only specific values, commonly integer values for example. In the case of discrete functions, possible values of the random variables X are, for example, integers. One could define a default event as a random variable taking value 1 if there is a default and 0 under survival. Or, extending the idea to a portfolio of loans, the number of defaults within a portfolio over a certain horizon, the total number of defaults within a time range can only take integer values. There is a probability $P(x)$ assigned to each value x: $P(X = n)$ is the probability attached to n, a particular discrete value.

The probability assigned to a value is the probability density function (PDF), usually designated by $f(x)$. For discrete variables: $P(X = n) = f(n)$. A cumulative distribution function (CDF) is the probability that the variable be inferior or equal to an upper bound and is usually designated by $F(n)$. The definition of such cumulative probability is: $F(x) = P(X \leq x)$. For defining CDF, the values of the random variable are ranked from lowest to highest. The CDF is monotonously increasing when starting from the lowest bound. The value of cumulative distribution function is monotonously increasing from 0 to 1 when we reach the highest possible value. In the case of discrete variables, the CDF only increases in jumps.

10.1.2 Continuous Variables

In the case of continuous functions, possible values of the random variable X are real numbers, within a certain range. For example, a normal variable can take any real value between minus infinity and plus infinity. The normal distribution is very commonly used in many instances. Another example is that of the lognormal distribution, which characterizes stock prices, of which value is always positive and is defined over the range of positive real values from zero to infinity.

For continuous distributions, the probability that the random variable X falls within a range is derived from the cumulative distribution and is characterized by a probability density function, or PDF. Usual generic notations use $F(X)$ for the CDF and $f(x)$ as the density function, x being a real number. By definition, the probability $P(X \le x)$ is the cumulative distribution function $F(x)$. For continuous variables, the CDF is defined as an integral. An integral can be loosely defined as summation over very small intervals tending towards zero. When starting from the lower bound, which can be minus infinity or the lowest possible value, the CDF is:

$$\text{CDF}(x) = P(X \le x) = F(x) = \int_{-\infty}^{x} f(x)\,dx$$

The probability that x falls between two values is derived from the CDF.

$$P(x_1 < X \le x_2) = F(x_2) - F(x_1)$$

The probability density function, $f(x)$, or PDF, is the limit of $F(x, x + dx)$ when dx tends towards zero. It is the probability that x falls within a very small interval of which size tends towards zero at value x. In the continuous variable case, $P(X \le x) = \text{CDF}(x)$. The PDF derives from the CDF by taking the first derivative:

$$P(X \le x) = F(x) \text{ implies that } P(X = x) = f(x) = F'(x) = dF/dx$$

F' stands for the first derivative dF/dx of the CDF, $F(x)$.

The reciprocal is that the CDF $F(X)$ is obtained by integrating the PDF $f(x)$ from the lower bound of X to its upper bound. The CDF is monotonously increasing with the value x of the random variable X:

$$F(x) = \int_{\text{lower bound}}^{x} f(u)\,du$$

In this equation, u is the variable used for integration, while x is the upper bound and the CDF is the probability that $X \le x$. For example, the CDF of a standard normal variable, with notations F for CDF and f for PDF, and an upper bound x_1 is defined as:

$$F(x_1) = \int_{-\infty}^{x_1} f(u)\,du$$

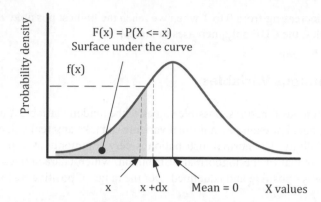

FIGURE 10.1   Distribution function and percentiles

When the upper bound is $x_1 = \infty$, F is the CDF for the range covering all possible real values of X equals 1. Those notions are easily illustrated for the well-known bell-shaped normal distribution (Figure 10.1).

10.2 INVERSE FUNCTIONS

Taking the example of a standard normal distribution, the CDF is S-shaped when the value of the random normal variable increases from minus infinity to plus infinity (Figure 10.2). A CDF always tends towards 1 when we move from the lower bound of the random variable up to the upper bound. Note the notation $x = F^{-1}(u)$ in the graph of the CDF of the normal standard definition: u is a number between 0 and 1 since those are respectively the lower and upper bounds of any CDF.

Assume that, instead of starting from x, we start from a value u of $F(x)$ which is between 0 and 1. Then $x = F^{-1}(u)$ provides the value of x such that the cumulative probability that $X \le x$ is equal to u. $F(x)$ monotonously increases with u. Therefore, there is unique relation between u and x. The value x represents a particular value of the random variable X and u represents the cumulative probability $P(X \le x) = u$. The relationship between a value of u between 0 and 1 and x is the inverse cumulative function. Such properties apply to all distributions.

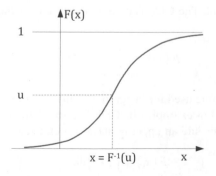

FIGURE 10.2   Inverse function

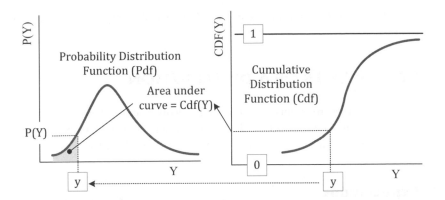

FIGURE 10.3 Converting a modeled variable into a (0, 1) number with a Cdf

A uniform function is a distribution function that can take any value between a lower bound "a" and an upper bound "b" with the same constant probability (Figure 10.3). It is a continuous function. Such random number follows a uniform distribution, which is called "standard" if we pick up numbers within the interval [0, 1].

The properties of inverse functions are used for simulating random variables following any distribution function. The process consists of generating uniform random numbers between 0 and 1, all intermediate values having an equal probability. The value of any cumulative distribution function $F(X)$ can be considered as the value u of a uniform standard distribution $U(0, 1)$. This means that any value u of U matches a value x of X such that:

$$u = F(x)$$

The reciprocal is also true. Each value of a random variable x can be written as the inverse of the cumulative uniform distribution applied to a uniform standard distribution value u:

$$x = F^{-1}(u)$$

One should keep in mind that u represents a cumulative probability and that x represents that value of the variable such that this cumulative probability is equal to u. Therefore, the argument of F is always a value of the variable, while the argument of F^{-1} is always a probability.

The random variable $F^{-1}(U)$ has the same distribution function as X. The reciprocal is that $F^{-1}(X)$ is a uniform standard variable[2] $U(0, 1)$. The relationships between X and U can also be written in various forms. First, we always have $x = F^{-1}(u)$. Second, the cumulative distribution functions of U and X are such that: $P[U \leq F(x)] = P(X \leq x)$, because $P(X \leq x) = P (U \leq = u)$. We use these general properties in subsequent sections.

For some specific distributions, alternate notations might be used. The standard cumulative normal distribution is $\Phi(0, 1)$ where the mean of the random variable X is 0 and the standard

---

2 For showing that, we need to have: $P(X \leq x) = P[F^{-1}(U) \leq x]$. Since $x = F^{-1}(u)$, we write: $P(X \leq x) = P[F^{-1}(U) \leq F^{-1}(u)] = P(U \leq u)$. Since the probabilities that $X \leq x$ and $U \leq u$ are identical, $F^{-1}(U)$ has the same distribution function as X.

deviation is 1. The corresponding notations are: $\Phi(x) = P(X \le x)$ and $\varphi(x)$ is the Gaussian density function.

10.3 THE MOMENTS OF A DISTRIBUTION

Any distribution has several moments. The moments of a distribution characterize its shape. The moments are the weighted averages of the deviations from the mean, elevated at power 2, 3, 4, etc., using the discrete probabilities of discrete values or the probability density as weights.

10.3.1 Expectations

The first moment is the expectation, or mean, of the function. The second moment is the variance. It characterizes dispersion around the mean. The square root of the variance is the standard deviation. It is identical to the "volatility." The third moment is skewness, which characterizes departure from symmetry. The fourth moment is kurtosis, which characterizes the flatness of distribution.

The expectation of a random variable X is $E(X)$, where E represents the expectation operator. The expectation is the weighted average of all values using probabilities as weights. For discrete distributions, the probability assigned to a value x_i of random variable X is $P_i(X = x_i)$, or p_i.

$$E(X) = \sum_{1}^{n} p_i x_i$$

For continuous distributions with density $f(x)$, the expectation is:

$$E(X) = \int_{-\infty}^{+\infty} x f(x) \, dx$$

When using time series, it is common to assign to each observation an identical probability, specifically $p = 1/n$ when there are n observations:

$$E(X) = \frac{1}{n} \sum_{1}^{n} x_i$$

The mean is a probability weighted average of all possible values.

10.3.2 Variance and Volatility

The variance σ^2, where σ is the volatility, is the sum of the probability weighted squared deviations to the mean. The volatility σ is the square root of the variance. The probability of occurrence of x_i of random variable X is $P(X = x_i)$, or p_i.

The volatility characterizes the dispersion around the mean, named $E(X) = \mu$. It is a convenient measure of risk because it measures the magnitude of possible fluctuations around the mean. With discrete distributions:

$$\sigma^2(X) = \sum_i p_i \left[x_i - E(X) \right]^2$$

For continuous distributions with density $f(x)$, the variance is:

$$V(X) = \int_{-\infty}^{+\infty} (x - \mu)^2 f(x) dx$$

The standard deviation σ is the square root of variance:

$$\sigma = \sqrt{V(X)}$$

When using time series, it is common to assign to each observation an identical probability $p = 1/n$ when there are n observations. In general: $\sigma^2(X) = \Sigma_i p [x_i - E(X)]^2$. A useful property facilitating the calculation of the variance is that:

$$\sigma^2(X) = E(X^2) - [E(X)]^2$$

Another property of variance is that it is scaled by a constant, using the square of the constant α^2:

$$\sigma^2(\alpha X) = \alpha^2 \sigma^2(X)$$

This implies that the volatility is also multiplied by the constant α: $\sigma(\alpha X) = \alpha\sigma(X)$.

10.3.3 Skewness and Kurtosis

In general the k central moment of a distribution is the expectation of the deviation from the mean, with power k:

$$\mu_k = E[(X - \mu)^k]$$

The expectation is the first moment and measures the central tendency. The variance is the second moment and measures the dispersion around the expectation. The third and fourth moments are central moments divided respectively by moment is σ^3 and σ^4. The skewness is:

$$\tau = \frac{E\left[(X - \mu)^3\right]}{\sigma^3} = \frac{\mu_3}{\sigma^3}$$

The kurtosis is:

$$\kappa = \frac{E\left[(X - \mu)^4\right]}{\sigma^4}$$

The skewness is 0 and the kurtosis is 3 for the standard normal distribution. The skewness measures the symmetry of the distribution. The kurtosis measures how thick are the tails of the distribution and how narrow is the central section of the distribution. Excess kurtosis is the kurtosis minus 3, and serves for comparing the shape of a distribution to the normal curve. Figure 10.4 illustrates the effect of skewness and excess kurtosis compared to a normal distribution.

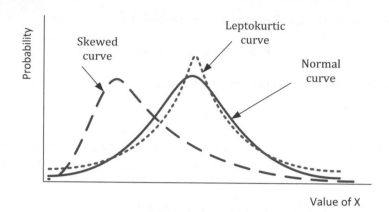

FIGURE 10.4   Effect of skewness and excess kurtosis compared to a normal distribution

In finance, kurtosis of periodical returns on a stock, for instance, measured by the relative change of value over a small interval of time t and $t + \Delta t$, or $(V_{t+\Delta t} - V_t)/V_t$, can arise from "jumps" in the stock prices, or from serial dependence of consecutive returns. Many jumps make extreme values more frequent. Serial dependence means that high returns tend to be followed by large higher returns (in absolute value, either positive or negative), creating higher frequencies of large returns than if returns were independent.

10.4 UNIFORM DISTRIBUTION

A uniform function is a distribution function that can take any value between a lower bound "a" and an upper bound "b" with the same constant probability. It is a continuous function. The expectation of a standard uniform distribution between values a and b is $(b - a)/2$ and its variance is $(b - a)^2/12$, and its standard deviation is $(b - a)/\sqrt{12}$.

Let $u(x)$ be the uniform probability density function and $U(X)$ the cumulative distribution function. The standard uniform distribution is $U(0, 1)$ and is a distribution of a random variable talking values between 0 and 1 with equal probability. The expectation of the standard uniform function is ½ and the standard deviation is $1/\sqrt{12}$. The standard uniform distribution is $U(0, 1)$ is of special interest when simulating random variables with various distribution functions because each random value between 0 and 1 can be seen as the value of cumulative distribution function CDF of another variable, or a probability. Starting from any random uniform standard number, we can derive the value x of the other variable using $x = F^{-1}(u)$.

10.5 APPLICATION TO LOSS DISTRIBUTIONS AND LOSS PERCENTILES

If we assign a value to $F(x)$, such as $F(x) = u$, a percentage value representing the probability that X is lower or equal to x, the percentage is usually called a quantile or percentile. It is always between 0 and 1. Given the above equations, the value of x that matches a given percentile is the inverse function of that percentile, or $x = F^{-1}(u)$.

In finance, percentiles are used for VaR-based measures of risk. A percentile is often called a confidence level α. A loss percentile is an upper bound $L(\alpha)$ of the random loss L which is not exceeded with probability α, hence such that $P(L \leq L(\alpha)] = \alpha$. $L(\alpha)$ designates the threshold which is not exceeded with probability $1 - \alpha$, and, equivalently, which is exceeded with the low probability α. Cumulative distribution functions provide the probability that the random variable does not exceed the upper bound, and refer to $1 - \alpha$.

A common practice in risk management for designating loss percentiles is to refer to the "low" probability of exceeding an upper bound, or 1%, while cumulative distribution functions provide the probability of being lower or equal than this upper bound. If the confidence level is $\alpha = 1\%$, then $1 - \alpha = 99\%$ and the corresponding probability of not exceeding the threshold value is $F(99\%)$. Hence, if we use α as a confidence level equal to the "low" probability of exceeding an upper bound, we should use $1 - \alpha$ as argument of the CDF of the random loss L, or $F(1 - \alpha)$. For avoiding any confusion, it is easier to refer to probabilities directly:

$$L(\alpha) \text{ is such that: } P[L \leq L(\alpha)] = \alpha \text{ and that } P[L > L(\alpha)] = 1 - \alpha.$$

The threshold loss $L(\alpha)$ is such that: $F[L(\alpha)] = 1 - \alpha$. When using 1% as the "low" probability $1 - \alpha$ that the loss exceeds the threshold $L(1\%)$, the probability that L be lower or equal to $L(1\%)$ is $F(99\%)$. Therefore, $L(1\%) = F^{-1}(99\%)$. For illustrating, we refer to the simple example of a random loss following a normal standard distribution and we use "low" probabilities of exceeding the threshold value. The standard normal variables thresholds matching various confidence levels are embedded in the normal distribution as multiples of its standard deviation σ:

$$P[L \leq L(1\%)] = 1\% \text{ and } L(1\%) = -2.33\sigma$$

$$P[L \leq L(2.5\%)] = 2.5\% \text{ and } L(2.5\%) = -1.96\sigma$$

This is equivalent, using the normal distribution for F, to writing that:

$$F(-2.33\sigma) = 1\% \text{ and } F(-1.96\sigma) = 2.5\%$$

10.6 BERNOULLI VARIABLE

A Bernoulli variable is a variable that can take only two values, such as 0 and 1 with probabilities $(1 - d)$ and d. Bernoulli variables serve notably for characterizing any discrete couples of "true" and "false" states. A Bernoulli variable represents for example a default event and could take value 1 if a default occurs and 0 if no default occurs. When considering a portfolio of loans, the number of defaults would be the number of default events, each one characterized by a Bernoulli (default, no default) variable.

Let us calculate the expectation and variance, when d is the probability that the Bernoulli variable takes value 1 (default) and $(1 - d)$ is the probability that the variable takes the value 0 (no default).

$$E(X) = 1 \, d + 0 \, (1 - d) = d$$

Using

$$\sigma^2(X) = E(X^2) - [E(X)]^2$$

we find:

$$V(X) = d - d^2 = d(1 - d) \text{ and } \sigma(X) = \sqrt{d(1-d)}$$

These are, respectively, the expected loss and the loss volatility of a facility which has loss under default equal to 1. If the loss under default is LGD, simply, multiply expectation and volatility by LGD and obtain:

$$E(X) = \text{LGD } d \text{ and } \sigma(X) = \text{LGD} \sqrt{d(1-d)}$$

10.7 INDICATOR FUNCTION

The indicator function is not a random variable, nor a distribution but a mathematical function. A more general way of writing such a discrete variable with two possible values is as an indicator function which takes a value 1 if a certain event occurs and 0 otherwise. The indicator function is usually defined for a set of values of continuous or discrete variable. For example, the event "x belongs to a certain range of values" and the alternate event "x does belong to this set of values" can be the arguments of the function. In abbreviated notations we would write $x \in A$ and $x \notin A$, where A is a specified set of values. The indicator function is:

$$\mathbf{1}_A = 1 \text{ if } x \in A$$

$$\mathbf{1}_A = 0 \text{ if } x \notin A$$

The indicator function can be seen as a Bernoulli variable if we assign probabilities to each of these two events that sum up to 1.

10.8 BERNOULLI DISTRIBUTION

The Bernoulli distribution is a discrete probability distribution, which can be seen as a sum of k Bernoulli variables. Considering again a portfolio, suppose that the default events are independent. We can make various trials, or economic scenarios, and see how many defaults would occur. The sum of defaults would be distributed as a Bernoulli distribution.

The common way of introducing this distribution is to say that we make a series of trials, each trial meaning taking a ball from a set of such balls, some being white and other black. A success is getting a white ball and a failure a black one. Obviously the chances of getting a white ball depend on the fraction p of white balls and the fraction $1 - p$ of black balls. The probability of success (white ball) is p and the probability of failure (black ball) is $q = 1 - p$. A single trial is a Bernoulli variable with probabilities p and $q = 1 - p$. If we make k trials, the probability of k successes is $f(k, p) = p^k(1 - p)^{1-k}$. The expected value of a Bernoulli random variable X is $E(X) = p$ and its variance is $V(X) = p(1 - p)$.

10.9 BINOMIAL DISTRIBUTION OF SUM OF BERNOULLI VARIABLES

The binomial distribution is the probability of the sum Y of n Bernoulli variables X_i that are independent. Let n be number of binomial trials, p the probability of success. The first two moments of the binomial distribution are:

$$E(X) = np$$

$$V(X) = np(1 - p)$$

If $X_1, X_2, X_3, \ldots$ are independent, identically distributed (i.i.d.) random variables, all Bernoulli distributed with "true" probability p, then:

$$Y = \sum_{i=1}^{i=n} X_i$$

The binomial distribution is characterized by the number n of Bernoulli variables and the probability p of a "true" value. Hence Y is binomial (n, p).

Using again default events as an example, each one is a Bernoulli variable. When default events are independent, and have the same probability, the distribution of the random number of defaults in a portfolio of loans is the binomial distribution. The binomial distribution applies to a sum of random independent losses of equal size since it is the distribution of a count of defaults.

Using a simple default probability of 1%, and 100 obligors, Figure 10.5 shows the distribution of the number of defaults. Although the distribution has the fat tail characterizing credit risk loss distributions, this distribution falls short from realistic correlated losses distribution. Nevertheless, the binomial distribution provides a good introduction to credit risk loss distributions.

Binomial distributions are distributions of the number of defaults within a portfolio when all defaults are independent. Using the uniform default probability $d = 1\%$, uniform across the portfolio, and n by the number of firms, say 100, we find that the expected number of defaults

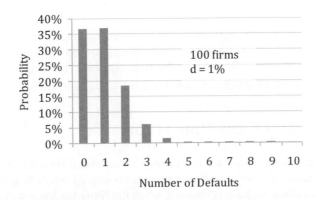

FIGURE 10.5 **Binomial distribution of the number of independent defaults**

is $100 \times 1\% = 1$ and the variance of the number of defaults is $100 \times 1\% \times 99\% = 0.99$. The number of defaults is the sum of n variables taking values 1 for default and 0 under no default for the n obligors of the portfolio.

10.10 NORMAL DISTRIBUTION

The normal distribution has generally the form $N(\mu, \sigma)$, where μ is the mean and σ is the standard deviation. The standard normal distribution has mean 0 and standard deviation 1. For transforming a normal distribution, with random variable Y, into a standard normal distribution, we simply write that $Y = \sigma X + \mu$. Then $X = (Y - \mu)/\sigma$ has mean zero and standard deviation 1, noted $\Phi(0, 1)$.

The cumulative probability density of a distribution is $N(\mu, \sigma) = P(X \leq x)$:

$$N(x) = \int_{-\infty}^{x} \frac{1}{\sigma\sqrt{2\pi}} \exp\left[\frac{(u - \mu)^2}{2\sigma^2} \right] du$$

It collapses to the simpler form in the case of a normal standard distribution:

$$\Phi(x) = \int_{-\infty}^{x} \frac{1}{\sigma\sqrt{2\pi}} \exp\left(\frac{u^2}{2} \right) du$$

The normal distribution is the most well-known distribution. It serves for modeling a large number of financial uncertainties. In general, the distribution of a sum of a large number of random variables is an approximately normal distribution. Many loss percentiles for defining VaR use the loss percentiles of the normal distribution as a first approximation, at least for market risk.

The distribution of asset returns, defined as the percentage difference between two prices in percentage of the beginning price. Let V represent an asset value, such as a stock price, and the subscript designates time point. Using time points 0 and 1, the percentage asset return $(V_1 - V_0)/V_0$, (equity or asset values). For stock prices, percentage returns are supposed normal in general and serially independent (each value is independent of the preceding one). As a result, the value at some horizon follows a lognormal distribution, discussed later on.

Drawbacks of the normal distribution in risk applications include:

- symmetry, which does not fit highly skewed distributions of credit risk losses;
- tails for large deviations from the mean are too thin and are not representative of the fat tails (or higher probabilities than normal probabilities assigned to extreme deviations) of actual distributions of market or credit risk losses.

10.11 LOGNORMAL DISTRIBUTION

The lognormal distribution usage is very common for market values because it results from the assumptions of independent periodical returns following a normal distribution over small intervals. A lognormal distribution is obtained when the Neperian logarithm (ln) of a random variable follows a normal distribution.

Hence, X at some horizon H is lognormal. This implies that $\ln(X) \sim N(\mu, \sigma)$ where ln is the Neperian logarithm and $N(\mu, \sigma)$ the PDF of the normal distribution. It can be shown that the expectation and variance of a lognormal variable are:

$$E(X) = \exp\left(\mu + \frac{\sigma^2}{2}\right)$$

$$V(X) = \exp(\sigma^2 - 1)\exp(2\mu + \sigma^2)$$

10.12 THE POISSON DISTRIBUTION

The Poisson distribution is a discrete probability distribution that expresses the probability of a number of events occurring in a fixed period of time if these events occur with a known average rate and are independent of each other.

10.12.1 Definition

The Poisson distribution serves for modeling the distribution of events having a preset time intensity. The random variable X is the count of a number of discrete occurrences (sometimes called "arrivals") that take place during a time-interval of given length. If the expected number of occurrences in this interval is λ, then the probability of exactly $X = k$ occurrences (k being a non-negative integer, $k = 1, 2 \ldots$) is equal to:

$$f(k,\lambda) = \frac{\lambda^k e^{-\lambda}}{k!}$$

The parameter λ is a positive real number, equal to the expected number of occurrences that occur during a given interval. It is also called an intensity or hazard rate. The time intensity is the number of events occurring per unit of time. The Poisson distribution serves, for instance, for assigning a probability to the number of typos when the rate of typos per unit of time is given.

10.12.2 Financial Applications

The Poisson distribution is the law of rare events when used in finance. It serves for modeling the behavior of prices, for assigning a probability to "jumps," or large price deviations, during a given time interval. The Poisson distribution also serves for modeling the number of claims in insurance.

For defaults, the intensity is analogous to a default probability. For example, if we say that the annual default probability is 1% for a portfolio of 1000 borrowers, the default intensity for one year is $1\% \times 1000 = 10$. The default intensity is the number of defaults per unit of time, of the portfolio. It is equivalent to a default probability measured over a time interval such as 1 year. However, the Poisson distribution requires defaults to be independent, as for the binomial distribution, when using the same default intensity for a portfolio of borrowers.

The Poisson distribution can be derived as a limiting case of the binomial distribution as the number of trials goes to infinity and the expected fraction of successes remains fixed. Therefore it can be used as an approximation of the binomial distribution if n is sufficiently large and p is sufficiently small. The Poisson distribution is a good approximation of the binomial distribution if n is at least 20 and p is smaller than or equal to 0.05. For sufficiently large values of n (say $n > 1000$), the normal distribution is an approximation to the Poisson distribution. The hazard rate is $\lambda = n \times p$ and is a constant. For example, $\lambda = 1$ for $n = 100$ and $p = 1\%$, or $n = 1000$ and $p = 0.1\%$.

The mean of a Poisson distribution is identical to its variance, and to the square of its standard deviation.

$$E(\text{Poisson}) = V(\text{Poisson}) = \lambda$$

The sum of Poisson variables is also a Poisson variable of which Poisson parameter is the summation of all Poisson parameters. This property is used in portfolio models of credit risk.

10.12.3 Number of Default Events over a Given Horizon

The Poisson distribution is notably used in the modeling of time to defaults and in the modeling the number of defaults over a given horizon.

If the number of yearly defaults is 3 out of 100 exposures, this corresponds to a yearly default intensity of 3% and a Poisson parameter equal to 3 per year. The probability of observing 8 defaults is:

$$P(K = 8) = e^{-3}3^8/8! = 0.8\%$$

The mean of a Poisson distribution is the Poisson parameter, 3 in this case, and its volatility is its square root or $\sqrt{3} = 1.732$. Table 10.1 shows the probabilities of the numbers of defaults

TABLE 10.1   The Poisson probability function, Poisson parameter = 3

Number of defaults, k	PDF	CDF
0	4.979%	4.979%
1	14.936%	19.915%
2	22.404%	42.319%
3	22.404%	64.723%
4	16.803%	81.526%
5	10.082%	91.608%
6	5.041%	96.649%
7	2.160%	98.810%
8	0.810%	99.620%
9	0.270%	99.890%
10	0.081%	99.971%
11	0.022%	99.993%
12	0.006%	99.998%
13	0.001%	100.000%

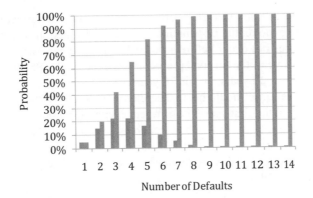

FIGURE 10.6 Poisson distribution (hazard rate: 3 per year)

k with a mean of 3 defaults per year, and Figure 10.6 charts the probability density and the cumulative density functions.

10.13 THE EXPONENTIAL DISTRIBUTION AND TIME TO DEFAULT

The exponential distribution is a continuous probability distribution. It describes the waiting time between events in a Poisson process, i.e. a process in which events occur continuously and independently at a constant average rate, the intensity or hazard rate, λ. The probability density function (PDF) of an exponential distribution has the form, for $x \geq 0$:

$$f(x, \lambda) = \lambda e^{-\lambda x} \text{ if } x \geq 0 \text{ and } 0 \text{ if } x < 0$$

The distribution is supported on the interval $[0, \infty)$. The probability of no event over a time interval Δt is the exponential function. Hence the probability of no event up to t is the summation, or, at the limit, the integral of $\lambda \exp(-\lambda t)$ between 0 and t:

$$\int_0^t e^{-\lambda u} du$$

This cumulative distribution function (CDF) is the probability of no event until t. It is given by the integral of this exponential density function and is equal to:

$$F(t, \lambda) = e^{-\lambda t} \text{ if } t \geq 0 \text{ and } 0 \text{ if } t < 0$$

This formula results from the using the Poisson probability of observing k events and setting $k = 0$. The probability of a single occurrence[3] is the complement to 1: $1 - \lambda \exp(-\lambda t)$.

The standard deviation of the exponential distribution is $1/\lambda$, equal to the mean. Consider as rare event a default with intensity λ. For example, for 1 year, the intensity is the default probability 1% for one year. Let t be the time to default t. The CDF of the exponential function

---

3 Alternatively, the direct calculation is: $\int_0^t e^{-\lambda u} du = \left| -\frac{1}{\lambda} e^{-\lambda u} \right|_0^t = e^0 - e^{-\lambda t} = 1 - e^{-\lambda t}$.

is the probability of default not occurring between dates 0 and t, or survival probability from 0 to t. The CDF of an exponential distribution is a survival function. It represents the probability that a default does not occur before horizon 1 year, here $\exp(-\lambda t)$. For example, if $\lambda = 5\%$ and the horizon is 1 year, the survival probability is $\exp(-5\%) = 95.123\%$. The average of the default time is $1/5\% = 20$ years, or 1 in 20 years.

Note that the survival time should be, in discrete time, exactly 95% and the discrete probability of default is 5% in the first year. The difference with the values comes from continuous intensity to default. The intensity to default matching exactly the 5% discrete default probability is such that $\exp(-\lambda t) = 95\%$, with $t = 1$ year, or $\lambda = -\ln(95\%) = +\ln(5\%) = 5.129\%$. In other words, the discrete probability of default in 1 year of 5% is equivalent to a continuous intensity of default of 5.129%.

10.14 THE BETA DISTRIBUTION

The beta distribution depends upon two parameters, n and r. The formula of the beta density is:

$$F(X) = [(n-1)!/(r-1)! \ (n-r-1)!]X^{r-1}(1-X)^{n-r-1}$$

X is the random variable, with values between 0 and 1. The expectation and the variance of the beta distribution are:

$$E(X) = r/n$$

$$V(X) = \frac{r(n-r)}{n^2(n+1)}$$

The beta distribution models continuous variables between 0 and 1. It notably applies to random recovery rates. It can be bell-shaped, U-shaped, skewed, or even flat between 0 and 1. These are attractive properties for recoveries of which distributions can have all these shapes. If recovery data is available, it is possible to attempt fitting a beta distribution on the data. In addition, modeling recovery uncertainty serves for enhancing the modeling of the loss under default, which depends on exposures, default event and recoveries. Uncertain recoveries increase the volatility of such losses.

10.15 THE STUDENT DISTRIBUTION

The Student distribution is, as the normal distribution, characterized by σ and μ, plus ν, the degree of freedom. It is a symmetric curve that becomes identical to the normal curve when the degrees of freedom increase. The degree of freedom controls fat tails, or the degree of leptokurtosis. The smaller is ν, the fatter is the tail. When the degree of freedom ν gets larger, the Student distribution converges towards the normal distribution. Student distributions are usually considered as a better fit of actual distributions of stock returns. They are designated as t_ν where ν is the degree of freedom.

10.16 A SUMMARY

TABLE 10.2

Distribution	Parameters	PDF	Mean	Variance (σ^2)
Bernoulli	$K = 0, 1$	p if $k = 1$ $q = 1 - p$ if $k = 0$	p	$p(1-p)$
Binomial	$K = 0, 1, 2, \ldots$ $0 \le p \le 1$	$\dfrac{n!}{k!(n-k)!} \, x \, p^k n - p^{n-k}$	np	$np(1-p)$
Poisson	$K = 0, 1, 2, \ldots$	$\dfrac{\left[\exp(-\lambda)\lambda^k\right]}{k!}$	λ	λ
Uniform	$a, b \, (-\infty, +\infty)$	$\dfrac{1}{(b-a)}$	$\dfrac{a+b}{2}$	$\dfrac{(b-a)^2}{12}$
Normal	$\sigma > 0 \, (-\infty, +\infty)$	$\dfrac{1}{\sqrt{2\pi}} \exp\left[\dfrac{-(x-\mu)^2}{2\sigma^2}\right]$	μ	σ^2
Lognormal	$(0, +\infty)$	$\dfrac{1}{x\sigma\sqrt{2\pi}} \exp\left[-\dfrac{\left(\ln(x)-\mu\right)^2}{2\sigma^2}\right]$	$\exp\left(\mu + \sigma^2/2\right)$	$\left[\exp\left(\sigma^2-1\right)\right]\exp\left(2\mu+\sigma^2\right)$
Exponential	$\lambda > 0$	$\lambda e^{-\lambda x}, x > 0$ $0, x < 0$	$\dfrac{1}{\lambda}$	$\dfrac{1}{\lambda^2}$

10.17 APPENDIX: CALCULATION OF STANDARD DEVIATION FROM TIME SERIES

The formulas for calculating the mean and the standard deviations when using observed values of a random variable, the usual case when using times series of observations, are shown below. The random variable is X, the mean is $E(X)$. Say it represents monthly earnings and we are interested in the volatility of these earnings. It is calculated as the arithmetic average of a time series of observations when all are considered of equal probability. For n observations:

$$E(X) = (\textstyle\sum_i x_i)/n$$

The volatility, or standard deviation, is:

$$\sigma = (1/n) \sum_i [x_i - E(X)]^2$$

With time series, the probabilities are estimated by the frequencies of observing any given value. The probability of a single observed value is therefore $1/n$. In other cases, probabilities have to be assigned to values, for instance by assuming that the distribution curve is given. The variance $V(X)$ is identical to σ^2.

The example in Table 10.3 shows how to calculate a yearly volatility of earnings over a 12-month time series of earnings observations. The expectation is the mean of all observed values. The variance is the sum of squared deviations from the mean, and the standard deviation is the square root. The following is a sample of calculations using those definitions. Monthly observations of earnings are available for one year, or 12 observed values. Volatilities are in the same unit as the random variable. If, for instance, the earnings are in Euros, the standard deviation is also expressed in Euros, here €7.71.

TABLE 10.3 Example of a calculation of mean and volatility with a time series of observed data

Dates	Earnings (dollars)	Deviations from mean	Squared deviations
1	15.00	12.08	146.01
2	12.00	9.08	82.51
3	8.00	5.08	25.84
4	7.00	4.08	16.67
5	2.00	−0.92	0.84
6	−3.00	−5.92	35.01
7	−7.00	−9.92	98.34
8	−10.00	−12.92	166.84
9	−5.00	−7.92	62.67
10	0.00	−2.92	8.51
11	5.00	2.08	4.34
12	11.00	8.08	65.34
Sum	35.00	Sum	712.92
Statistics*			
Mean	2.92	Variance	59.41
		Volatility	7.71

*The mean is the sum of observed values divided by the number of observations (12). The variance is the sum of squared deviations divided by 12. The volatility is the square root of variance.

11

Discrete and Continuous Returns

The basic valuation mechanism of future payoffs of an asset relies on discounting. Discounting is the mirror image of capitalization, whereby we invest an amount and expect a return. Valuation under certainty relies on the discounted cash flow (DCF) model, whereby we discount to present future cash flows. In finance, the discount rates are the returns. Under certainty, the returns are risk free, equal to the interest rates of risk-free assets such as Treasury bills and government bonds. The understanding of returns and discounting are pre-requisites for valuation under uncertainty, which we address in the next chapters.

This chapter has two main purposes.

- Discussing returns, and compounding returns, both under a discrete time framework and in a continuous time framework which is extensively used in finance.
- Introducing the DCF model, both in discrete time and in continuous time, under certainty. When introducing the DCF model, we discuss the so-called zero-coupon rates that apply to single future flows and the yield-to-maturity, which is the return applicable to a series of cash flows.

The chapter discusses first discrete and continuous returns. The second main part is the discounted cash flow model, implemented here under certainty, under discrete time or continuous time. The related concepts of yield-to-maturity and zero-coupon rates are introduced here. These basic mechanisms are implemented next for valuation under uncertainty. When using risky returns, the same basic formulas apply, except that we have to deal first with the risk premium embedded in risky returns.

Contents

11.1 DISCRETE AND CONTINUOUS RETURNS

A discrete process applies over a sequence of time points, commonly 1, 2, 3, etc. In what follows R is a discrete return and r is a continuous return. Between two sequential time points, a discrete return R_i is the relative variation $R_i = (V_{i+1} - V_i)/V_i$. Next, consider a time interval between two successive time points getting smaller and tending towards zero. The time points are designated $t + \Delta t$ and t, with the time interval Δt tending towards zero. The relative variation becomes a continuous return $r_t = (V_{t+\Delta t} - V_t)/V_t$ when Δt tends towards zero.

11.1.1 Single Period Discrete Return

We take the example of a stock return. The return over a discrete period is the relative variation of value between two dates, 0 and 1, or a percentage. The single period return depends on the random final value. The original date is 0, and, at that date, we know the original value of the stock, V_0. Both final value and relative returns are random at date 1. The discrete return is $R(0, 1)$ and the random value at horizon is V_1. The return $R(0, 1)$, between the two dates, and the value at horizon, are related:

$$R(0, 1) = (V_1 - V_0)/V_0$$

Dropping the indices of R: $V_1 = V_0(1 + R)$. With a single period return, the value distribution at 1 derives from that of the return because $V_1 = V_0(1 + R)$.

11.1.2 Compounding Discrete Returns over Multiple Periods

Consider a discrete period and using a normal distribution for the return. The obvious limitation of this technique for modeling returns and final values is that a normal distribution allows the random return to hit values lower than -100%, resulting in non-acceptable negative values of the asset.

Compounding discrete returns over a sequence of time intervals, between 0 and t, the return $R(0, t)$ from 0 to t becomes:

$$[1 + R(0, t)] = [1 + R(0, 1)][1 + R(1, 2)] \ldots [1 + R(1, t)]$$

Compounding a constant discrete return R over t periods would result into a final amount of $(1 + R)^t$.

11.1.3 From Discrete to Continuous Returns

Any time interval can be divided into m equal shorter sub-periods. For the horizon h divided in m equal sub-periods, each one having an equal length $\Delta t = h/m$, the final value at h compounds the constant return m times:

$$V_h = V_0(1 + R/m)^m$$

In this formula, R/m is the proportional discrete return matching the constant period $\Delta t = h/m$. The final value is obtained by compounding m times the discrete return R. The proceeds from compounding m times the return over each of the m sub-periods become: $[(1 + R/m)]^m$.

When compounding once for 1 year with $R = 10\%$ per year, the terminal value of 1 invested originally is: $1(1 + 10\%) = 1.10$. Next, compound twice the original amount within a year in two equal periods of 6 months. The proportional return becomes $R/2 = 5\%$ and the terminal value of 1 becomes: $1(1 + 5\%)(1 + 5\%) = 1.1025$. Compounding four times a year at a rate $R/4 = 2.5\%$ results in a terminal value: $1(1 + 2.5\%)^4 = 1.1038$.

When the frequency tends towards infinity, compounding becomes continuous, and over an infinite number of infinitely small sub-periods. The exact formal relation between discrete returns and continuous returns is obtained by taking the limit of compounding m times the proportional discrete return over an increasing number m of sub-periods of duration h/m, using the proportional discrete return R/m. Compounding m times results in $(1 + R/m)^m$. When m gets large, the time interval $\Delta t = h/m$ becomes infinitesimally small. In the formula, the proportional discrete returns tends towards zero but is compounded a number of times that grows to infinity.

The mathematical limit of the expression $(1 + R/m)^m$, when m increases to infinity, is $\exp(r)$. When m increases to infinity, the limit of the expression within brackets tends towards some limit, according to the mathematical formula[1]: $\mathrm{Lim}(1 + x/m)^m \to \exp(x)$. Replacing x by R:

$$\mathrm{Lim}[(1 + R/m)]^m \to \exp(R/m) \to \exp(r) \text{ when } m \to \text{infinity.}$$

$$(1 + R/m)^m = \exp(r)$$

The continuous compounding formula uses the continuous rate r, when the number of sub-periods m tends towards infinity, which is defined from the limit of the left-hand side in the above equation.

The continuous rate r such that $\exp(r) = \mathrm{Lim}[(1 + R/m)]^m$ when $m \to$ infinity is easily calculated when considering a single year. Starting from the discrete annual rate $R = 10\%$, the value of r such that terminal values are identical is such that:

$$\exp(r) = (1 + R) = 1 + 10\%$$

---

1 A mathematical limit $f(x)$ of an expression $f(x, n)$ exists when we can prove that and when we can define a value of n big enough so that $\mid f(x, n) - f(x) \mid < \varepsilon$ no matter how close to zero ε is. The mathematical notation is limit $[f(x, n)]n \to \infty = f(x)$. Mathematically, $\exp[\ln(a)] = \ln[\exp(a)] = a$. Use $a = (1 + x/m)$, then $a^m = \exp[m \ln(a)]$. Replace a by its value $(1 + x/m)$ and obtain: $(1 + x/m)^m = \exp[m \ln(1 + x/m)]$. Then using limit $[\ln(1 + u)] u \to 0 = u$, $\ln(1 + x/m)$ $m \to \infty = x/m$. Finally: $(1 + x/m)^m = \exp\{m \ln[1 + (x/m)]\} = \exp[m(x/m)] = \exp(x)$.

The equivalent continuous rate r, to the discrete one-year rate R, is 9.531% because exp(9.531%) = 1.1. This value can be derived from the mathematical rule that states that, if $y = \ln(x)$, then $x = \exp(y)$. Taking the Neperian logarithm of above equation shows that:

$$r = \ln(1 + R) = \ln(1 + 10\%) = 9.531\%$$

The general formula would use any date t. Assuming constant returns, the future value of 1 at date t is $(1 + R)^t$ with discrete returns, where R matches the time unit, and $\exp(rt)$ when using the continuous return. The present values of 1, as of date 0, are, respectively, $(1 + R)^{-t}$ and $\exp(-rt)$.

The formula can be extended to returns varying over time. Consider all intermediate dates, u, between 0 and t. The continuous equivalent of the future value of one unit is:

$$\exp\left(\int_0^t r(u)\,du\right)$$

Continuous returns formulas are generally used in finance because of their convenient properties.

11.1.4 Logarithmic Returns

Continuous returns are identical to logarithmic returns. The logarithmic return is defined as the Neperian logarithm of the ratio of two values distant in time by a very small interval:

$$r_t = \ln\left(\frac{V_{t+\Delta t}}{V_t}\right)$$

The instantaneous return at time t becomes $r_t = dV_t/V_t$, where dV_t is the small change of value, $dV_t = V_{t+\Delta t} - V_t$, between time points t and $t + \Delta t$. The continuous compounding equation applied to a small time interval is: $V_{t+\Delta t} = V_t \exp(r_t \Delta t)$. It implies that $\exp(r_t \Delta t) = V_{t+\Delta t}/V_t$. Taking the Neperian logarithm, we find that the continuous return is the logarithm of the ratio of final value to initial value:

$$r_t = \ln\left(\frac{V_{t+\Delta t}}{V_t}\right)$$

The logarithm of the ratio is the logarithmic return. It is identical to the continuous return.

With small time intervals, the logarithmic return is approximately equal to the discrete return over the same interval. The ratio $V_{t+\Delta t}/V_t$ is a function of the discrete return $R(t, t + \Delta t)$ over the small period Δt:

$$\frac{V_{t+\Delta t}}{V_t} = 1 + \frac{V_{t+\Delta t} - V_t}{V_t} = 1 + R(t, t + \Delta t)$$

For example, taking $\Delta t = 1$, $V_1 = V_0(1 + R)$, $\ln(V_1/V_0) = \ln(1 + R)$. The logarithm of $1 + R$ is approximately equal to R, using the proxy relation $\ln(1 + R) \cong R$ when R is small. The logarithmic return is approximately equal to the discrete return, and it becomes identical when the time interval gets infinitely small. The approximation follows the Taylor expansion formula, which is in the appendix.

11.1.5 Compounding Continuous Returns

Compounding logarithmic returns over small intervals characterized by time points 1, 2, 3 and up to t, each equal interval being Δt, results in the compounded return from 0 to t. The compounded continuous return collapses into a simple formula:

$$r(0, t) = \ln(V_t/V_0) = \ln[(V_1/V_0)(V_2/V_1)(V_3/V_2) \dots (V_t/V_{t-1})]$$

The logarithmic return over several sub-periods is the sum of intermediate logarithmic returns because the logarithm of a product is the sum of logarithms:

$$\ln(V_t/V_0) = \ln(V_1/V_0) + \ln(V_1/V_0) + \ln(V_2/V_1) + \ln(V_3/V_2) + \dots + \ln(V_t/V_{t-1})$$

$$r(0,t) = \ln\left(\frac{V_t}{V_0}\right) = \sum_{i=0}^{t-1} \ln\left(\frac{V_{i+1}}{V_i}\right)$$

Simplifying notations, the compounded logarithmic return is simply the sum of intermediate logarithmic returns:

$$r(0, t) = r(0, 1) + r(1, 2) + r(2, 3) + \dots + r(t - 1, t)$$

Finally, note that $r(0, t) = \ln(V_t/V_0)$ implies that:

$$V_t = V_0 \exp(rt) \text{ and } V_0 = V_t \exp(-rt)$$

Those are the equivalent expressions of the compounding and discounting formulas with discrete returns:

$$V_t = V_0(1 + R)^t \text{ and } V_0 = V_t/(1 + R)^t$$

Note that compounding discrete returns k times would result in a product:

$$\frac{V_t}{V_0} = \left(1 + \frac{R}{k}\right)^{kt} = \prod_{i=1}^{k} \left(1 + \frac{R}{k}\right)^i$$

11.1.6 Comparing Continuous and Discrete Returns

We use an example of only two periods and compare discrete returns and logarithmic returns. The continuous cumulative return is:

$$r(0, 2) = \ln(V_2/V_1) + \ln(V_1/V_0) = r(0, 1) + r(1,2)$$

The cumulative discrete return is:

$$[(V_2 - V_1)/V_1]((V_1 - V_0)/V_0] = V_0(1 + R_{01})(1 + R_{12})$$

Table 11.1 Cumulating arithmetic and logarithm returns

	V_t	V_t/V_{t-1} $= 1 + R$	$\ln(V_t/V_{t-1})$ $= r$
V_0	1.00		
V_1	1.20	20.00%	18.232%
V_2	1.08	−10.00%	−10.536%
		$(V_2/V_0) - 1$	$\ln(V_2/V_0)$
Cumulative return		8.00%	7.696%

If, for instance, $V_1/V_0 = 120\%$ and $V_2/V_1 = 90\%$, with $V_0 = 1$, then $V_1 = 1.2$ and $V_2 = 90\% \times 1.2$ $= 1.08$. The overall compounded discrete return is 8%. This is very close to the logarithm cumulative return $\ln(V_2/V_0) = 7.696\%$, which is the exact summation of single period logarithmic returns (Table 11.1).

11.2 THE DISCOUNTED CASH FLOW MODEL

The basic technique of valuation under certainty is the so-called discounted cash flow models. The model simply expresses the value of a riskless asset as the present value of all its contractual and future flows calculated at the riskless rates. The process uses the set of discount rates that are applicable for each date of the future cash flows. The set of risk-free rates by maturity forms the term structure of risk-free rates. In practices such risk-free rates are derived from the prices of such risk-free assets such as Treasury bills and Government bonds. This section is a remainder of the valuation of future risk-free payoffs.

In a first stage, we use the zero coupon rates that apply to single cash flows. Then, we extend the discounting formulas to the yield-to-maturity (Ytm), and we extend the same conclusions to a multiple period framework with simple examples. The familiar discounted cash flow (DCF) model is first introduced used in a discrete time framework. The extension to continuous time is straightforward and reminded below.

11.2.1 Valuation in Discrete Time and the Rationale of Discounting

The value of an asset is the discounted value of the stream of future flows that it generates. The discount rates are market risk-free rates corresponding to the dates of the cash flows. The array of risk-free discount rates over all maturities forms the term structure of interest rates. Since they apply to single cash flows, they are also called zero-coupon rates because such zero-bonds have only one cash flow at maturity, all other intermediate payments, such as coupons for coupon bonds, being zero. Using the term structure of risk-free zero rates, the present value $B(t, T)$, as of t, of a stream of future flows F_k where k varies from t to the maturity T of the asset:

$$B(t,T) = \sum_{k=1}^{T} \frac{F_k}{[1+r(t)]^k}$$

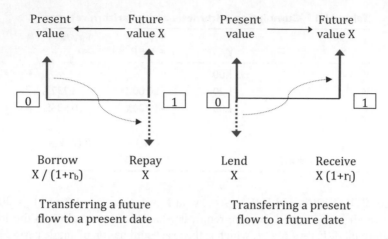

FIGURE 11.1 Discounting and borrowing or lending at market rates

The DCF rationale is directly related to financial transactions that would allow converting future cash flows into present cash flows and vice versa. The relevant discount rates are those that allow transferring flows across time through borrowing and lending. This is why market rates are relevant. For instance, consider a single flow at date 1. We can transfer it to today by borrowing against this flow, or borrowing an amount such that repayment exactly equals the future flow X. In the graph (Figure 11.1), up arrows are inflows and down arrows are outflows. The present value of X is obtained by borrowing today and repaying exactly X tomorrow. Capitalization transforms a present flow into a future flow. By lending today the present flow, the net flow today becomes zero and we get a future inflow at the future date equal to the proceeds of lending. The present value of 1000 at date 1 is $1000/(1 + y_b)$, where y_b is the borrowing rate. When lending, we use the lending rate. Hence, market rates are relevant for the DCF model.

11.2.2 The Case of Floaters

The value of a floater providing interest revenues calculated at a rate equal to the discounting rate does not depend on prevailing rates. This is obvious in the case of a single period, since the asset provides $1 + r$ at the end of the period and this flows discounted at r has a present value of $(1 + r)/(1 + r) = 1$. The property extends to any multi-period floater, since such a bond can be replicated by a series of one-period bonds. At each date, a one-period bond is repaid and the proceeds reinvested in another one.[2] The payoff of a multiple period floating rate note can be replicated by entering into a series of one period floating rate notes. At the end of each period, we borrow again for another period with the proceeds of the preceding period floating rate note. Since, at the beginning of each period, the value of the floating rate debt is par, all single period notes have values equal to par value. Moving recursively back in time from one period to the previous one, the value of the floating rate note today is also par value.

---

2 This is an application of the replication principle, which allows replicating assets by simpler ones, as illustrated in the chapters on derivatives.

11.2.3 Continuous Time

When using continuous compounding instead of discrete compounding, the basic formulas for future and present values are very simple, with a continuous discount rate r_c and a horizon T:

$$B(t, T) = \exp[-r(T - T)]$$

The future value of a today flow is obtained as the exponential of $r(T - t)$, or $\exp[r(T - t)]$. Using discounted cash flow formulas for valuing the present value of a stream of cash flows simply substitute $\exp(-rt)$ to the discount factor $1/(1 + R)^t$. The formulas in continuous time for several cash flows occurring at date k, k being between t and T are:

$$B(t,T) = \sum_{k=t}^{T} F_k \exp\left[-r(k)k\right]$$

Note that the rate r is allowed to vary across dates.

11.2.4 Asset Value and Market Required Return

Since the asset value is the discounted value of all future cash flows at market rates, there is an inverse relationship between a fixed rate bond value and interest rates. By shifting all rates by the same amount, one can see that the discount factors $1/(1 + r + \Delta r)^t$ decrease, making the value lower (Figure 11.2). The only exception is that of a bond of which rate is variable, since it has constant value.

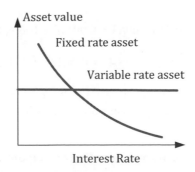

FIGURE 11.2   Fixed rate asset value and interest rate

11.2.5 Yield-to-Maturity and Zero-coupon Rates

A risk-free bond can be valued by discounting each of its cash flows at a discount rate specific to each cash flow date. The zero-coupon rates apply to each individual future flow. An alternate valuation technique consists of using the same rate for all cash flows. This common unique rate is the "yield-to-maturity" $y(t, T)$, which depends on the current date t and the maturity date T. The yield-to-maturity is a proxy of the actuarial return for an investor buying today the bond and holding it until maturity. The yield-to-maturity is only a proxy because it ignores the fact that intermediate cash flows will be reinvested at rates differing from the yield-to-maturity[3]. It is the unique discount rate making the present value of all future flows identical to the observed price.

The following uses as example a bullet bond generating coupons equal to 6% of face value, with a face value equal to 1000, and maturing in 3 years. The bond coupon rate is 6%. The stream of cash flows is 60, 60 and 1060, the last one including the principal repayment. In this example, we assume that cash flows are certain (risk free) and we use either market yield to maturities applicable to the 3-year maturity or zero-coupon interest rates.

First note that discounting all flows at 6% provides exactly 1000, implying that the yield-to-maturity of the bond valued at 1000 is 6%. It is equal to its coupon rate 6%. This is a general property. When discounting at a rate equal to the asset contractual return $r = 6\%$, we always find the face value 1000 as long as the bond repays without any premium or discount the principal borrowed.

If the market yield-to-maturity for 3 years asset rises up to 7%, the value of the asset cash flows declines to 973.77. If the required yield is above the book return of 6%, the value falls below par. The interpretation is that the market value providing the required yield-to-maturity to investors has to be 973.77. An investor paying this value would have the 7% yield-to-maturity in line with the market required yield. If the value were higher, investors would get a return lower than market rate, and vice versa. The reverse would happen with a lower than 6% yield-to-maturity. The value would be above the book value 1000.

Yield-to-maturity and zero rates have to be consistent. Discounting each cash flow with the zero interest rate matching its date and discounting all cash flows at a unique rate, differing from zero rates, provides the same value (Table 11.2).

Using the market zero-coupon interest rates of the table we find that the discounted value of the bond flows is:

$$V = 60/(1 + 5.00\%) + 60/(1 + 6.00\%)^2 + 1060/(1 + 7.00\%)^3$$

$$V = 57.14 + 53.40 + 865.28 = 975.82$$

The value has no reason to be identical to 1000. It represents a mark-to-market valuation of a contractual and certain stream of cash flows. There is a yield-to-maturity making the

TABLE 11.2   Term structure of "zero-coupon" market rates

End of period	1	2	3
Market rate, date t	5.00%	6.00%	7.00%

---

3 Any discounting formula assumes implicitly that intermediate cash flows are reinvested until maturity and discounted back to present at the same discount rate. This is a mathematical property of a discounting formula since we can always write the same formula in two alternate ways:

$$V = \sum_{t=1}^{T} \frac{F_t}{(1+y)^t} = \sum_{t=1}^{T} F_t \frac{(1+y)^{T-t}}{(1+y)^T}$$

value identical to the discounted value of cash flows, using it as unique discount rate across all periods. It is such that:

$$975.82 = 60/(1 + y) + 60/(1 + y)^2 + 1060/(1 + y)^3$$

The value is $y = 6.920\%$[4]. It is higher than the 6% on the face value, because we acquire this asset at a value below par (975.82). The 6.920% yield is the "averaged" return of an investor buying this asset at its market price, with these cash flows, and holding it to maturity.

11.3 VALUATION UNDER UNCERTAINTY

In general, assets are risky and cannot be valued using contractual future payoffs as if they were certain because they are contingent. Stock payoffs are capital gains and dividends which are not contractual. Credit risky bonds pay the contractual promised payment only if they do not default; otherwise the investors get the recovery value of the bond. Option payoffs are contingent upon the underlying asset price. An option on a stock pays off something if the stock price is above the strike price before or at maturity; otherwise, the option does not pay anything. For addressing risky payoffs, whatever the source of risk, which is market risk for stocks and credit risk for risky debts, other valuation principles apply. Discounting future payoffs transform them into their economic value as of today.

If investors were indifferent to risk, they would not make any difference between risky payoffs and risk-free payoffs. The standard example illustrating risk aversion is that of a single uncertain payoff, one period ahead, of which values can be 50 or 150 with equal probabilities. The expected payoff is 100. Under risk neutrality, investors would be indifferent between a certain payoff of 100 and the expected random payoff of 100 (the average of the two possible payoffs). In practice, investors dislike risk and would always prefer the certain payoff of 100. They value the expected payoff at a lower value than the certain payoff of 100. The difference of value between the expected payoff under real world probabilities and the certain payoff of 100 is due to risk aversion, and it measures risk aversion. Assume that the so-called "certainty-equivalent" of the random payoff is 90. The certainty equivalent is the value of the random outcome for investors. The value of risk aversion is the difference between 100 and 90 or 10.

The next chapter reminds the principles for valuation of risky payoffs, given that the risk aversion and the risk premium that it commands over risk-free rate are generally unknown.

11.4 APPENDIX: THE TAYLOR EXPANSION FORMULA

Any function value $f(x)$ has a value $f(a)$ that can be approximated by a Taylor expansion, provided that it is infinitely differentiable in the neighborhood of a, a real number:

$$f(x) = f(a) + \frac{1}{1!}\frac{df}{dx}(x-a)^1 + \frac{1}{2!}\frac{d^2f}{dx^2}(x-a)^2 + \frac{1}{3!}\frac{d^3f}{dx^3}(x-a)^3 + \ldots$$

---

4 It is easy to check that, discounting all contractual flows at this rate, we actually find the 975.82 value. The rate y is the internal rate of return of the stream of flows when using 975.82 as initial value.

$$f(x) = \sum_{n=0}^{\infty} \frac{1}{n!} \frac{d^n f}{dx^n} (x-a)^n$$

If we take $a = 1$:

$$f(x) = f(1) + \frac{1}{1!} \frac{df}{dx} (x-1)^1 + \ldots$$

If $f(x) = \ln(x)$, and $a = 1$, then $\ln(1) = 0$ and $d\ln(x)/dx = 1/a = 1$, so that: $\ln(x) = (x-1)$. Replacing $x = 1 + u$, $\ln(1 + u) \sim u$ when u is small. Similarly, is can be shown that $\exp(u) \sim 1 - u$ when u is small.

12

Stochastic Processes

Risk often refers to the distribution of random asset values at some future horizon. In many instances, risk models are based on simulations of asset values or of risk factors over time. The dynamics of returns and of asset prices are used in this text with the main purpose of assessing such distributions.

Specific applications to risk models include the distribution of asset values when asset returns follow a normal distribution, the simulation of defaults when defaults follow a "rare event" process, or the simulation of interest rates. There is a considerable amount of publications on asset pricing and stochastic processes[1]. This chapter is no substitute to such texts. Rather it covers the minimum pre-requisites of common stochastic processes that serve for risk modeling and simulations, and relate risk modeling to the rest of the literature.

The starting point is a review of the common properties of the time process followed by random variables. The next step is to explain the Ito process that applies to all variables having normal instantaneous returns, such as stock prices, the mean-reverting processes that apply to variables that tend towards long-term value, such as interest rates, and the "rare event process" because it relates directly to default models. Simpler processes are described before because they help understanding these main processes. Two sections provide typical examples of applications, for stock prices and interest rates. The last section briefly introduces the Ito lemma widely used in the literature, because it allows deriving the process of any function of any underlying process. It serves, notably, for deriving the process followed by a derivative from the process of the underlying asset.

---

1 See Hull [36] for an overview of common stochastic processes. Neftci [55] provides more details on the underlying concepts and properties. The book from Grimmett G. R, Stirzaker, D. R. [35] is also a useful introduction.

Contents

12.1 STOCHASTIC PROCESSES

Any variable whose value changes in a random way while time passes follows a stochastic process. When changes can occur at any time, we have a continuous process. When the changes can occur only at certain times, we have a discrete stochastic process. The variables can be stock prices or interest rates, or default events which are Bernoulli variables taking values 0 or 1. The random variable can have continuous values which are real numbers or only discrete values. The range of discrete values can be bounded or unbounded. An example of the last case is the stock price, which cannot have negative real values but can theoretically grow without any upper bound.

Stochastic processes have been introduced to model the randomness of market variables. These serve as the foundations of pricing models as well as for simulating the time path of a random variable. Because they model time paths of values, they serve determining the distribution of the final values of random variable at a future time horizon.

In risk management, we are often interested in the distributions of a random value of a portfolio of market instruments at various time points in the future. For ALM, we are interested in the simulation of interest rates which drive the net interest income of the bank. In general, any risk model based on the VaR methodology relies on modeling a distribution at a given horizon of random values of instruments.

A stochastic process is defined by the equation making the random variation in a small interval a function of the time interval and of a random term. The discrete form of a stochastic process uses small discrete intervals of time. We divide the horizon T into n equal intervals $\Delta t = T/n$ of time. As of time t, we know the value of all variables and the value of the coefficients of the linear equation that are dated as of t. Because all is known as of t, the process is said to be I_t-adapted. But at $t + \Delta t$, the variable $S_{t+\Delta t}$ is unknown. Considering the above process S_t, we have: $\Delta S_t = S_{t+\Delta t} - S_t$ and $\Delta z_t = z_{t+\Delta t} - z_t$. According to the form of a stochastic process, the variation of the process S_t is:

$$S_{t+\Delta t} - S_t = a(t)\Delta t + b(t)(z_{t+\Delta t} - z_t)$$

When the time interval tends towards zero, the the equation has the continuous form:

$$dS_t = a(t)dt + b(t)dz_t$$

The coefficient of time, with general form $a(t)$, is the drift. The drift measures the deterministic change of the process that is due to time. In the above formula, the random process increases by $a(t)$ per unit of time. The drift coefficient can be constant, which would imply a constant increment per unit of time, but it is in general a function of time and of the random variable itself.

The unpredictable component, dz_t multiplied by $b(t)$, is called the innovation or the diffusion term. "Unpredictable" means that, as of time t, the diffusion term cannot be inferred from past information. For defining the process, a distribution has to be defined for this random term. The variations of z, Δz, have the form:

$$\Delta z_t = \varepsilon \sigma(t)\sqrt{\Delta t}$$

The variable ε is standard normal, or $\Phi(0, 1)$. It is the random term embedded in z. But the random term z does not have unit variance. When implementing such process, the variance has the form $\sigma^2(t)\Delta t$ and its standard deviation is $\sigma(t)\sqrt{\Delta t}$. Such a specification allows the variance to be time dependent and proportional to the time interval.

The random term Δz_t has some special properties. $E[\Delta z_t]^2$ is its variance since the mean of Δz_t is zero. Variance is the "size" of a typical Δz_t^2. Assuming that this square difference is negligible would be equivalent to assuming that its variance will be zero. The process would become deterministic. Using above specifications, Δz_t has variance proportional to Δt.

For moving from date 0 and horizon T, we cumulate changes across discrete intervals between 0 and T. The final values cumulate random changes. In between current and future dates, the process follows a time path joining all time points. The example of the time path followed by stock prices is illustrated after the review of the main processes.

Depending on the random variable, a stock price, the asset value of a firm or an interest rate, the coefficient $a(t)$ and $b(t)$ take various forms. Typical stochastic processes are now detailed.

12.2 COMMON STOCHASTIC PROCESSES

The most basic process is the Wiener process. Other processes of interest include the generalized Wiener process and the Ito process. The stock price process is a special case of the Ito process. Other processes, such as interest rate processes and jump processes are relatively straightforward extensions. In what follows, the process is called S_t and the innovation term is $\Delta z_t = \varepsilon \sigma(t)\sqrt{\Delta t}$. The differences between processes result from the definitions of the coefficients, a and b, applied, respectively, to the drift and the diffusion terms. Some basic processes are described to illustrate simple cases. But the most common processes include the Ito process which applies to asset returns, the mean-reverting process which applies to interest rates, and the jump process because it applies to rare events.

12.2.1 The Wiener Process

The Wiener process, also called Brownian motion, is the random process followed by a variable $z(t)$, such that the random change is $\Delta z(t) = z(t + \Delta t) - z(t) = \varepsilon$, where ε follows a normal distribution $\Phi(0, 1)$ or $\Phi(0, \sigma)$. Its drift is zero. Its variance is constant per unit of time. Because all successive random changes are independent and follow the same distribution, the process is said to be "identically independently distributed, or "i.i.d." The distribution is stationary when time passes, meaning that it is identical when starting from any time point.

Dividing the horizon t into n equal sub-periods $\Delta t = T/n$, and considering as time interval $[0, t]$, we observe that cumulating the $\Delta z(t)$ from 0 to T, we have a summation of n random normal variables, starting from some value $z(0)$ known as of time point 0.

The expectation of each increment of z is 0. The expectation of the cumulated increments is the summation of the expectations of each change between 0 and T, each of them being 0, and is equal to zero: $E[z(t)] = 0$. The Brownian motion follows an erratic path around the initial value.

At each time point, we move from the current value to the next "abruptly," always starting from the previous point. The path is continuous but not smooth. It can be obtained by generating independent standard normal variables. Cumulating the random standard normal changes over some period generates the time path of the process. Because the process has no drift term, the time path varies randomly around 0. Other processes combine a drift plus a function of the basic Wiener process.

12.2.2 Application: The Square Root of Time Rule for the Simple Wiener Process

The Wiener process follows $\Phi(0, 1)$. When the coefficient $\sigma_t = \sigma$ is constant, the variable is again stationary. Consider any variable that has a constant variance per unit of time, with independent random increments at each time point. This could be the case for a stock return, notably. Under such a process, the uncertainty measured by the standard deviations increases as the square root of time.

Let S_t represent an asset return with zero drift. The market efficiency hypothesis postulates that all prices reflect all information available at the initial date. Consider two consecutive time intervals of duration 1 (unit of time). Two consecutive random changes between two consecutive time points are independent. Assume that the volatility does not depend on time. The random term over two time intervals has mean zero since it sums up two random variations at each interval with zero mean. The variance over two time intervals is the sum of the variances, or $2\sigma^2$, since variances of independent variables are additive. Hence the standard deviation over the two time intervals is $\sigma\sqrt{2}$. This is the rationale for so-called "square root of time rule for uncertainty," which says, loosely speaking, that the uncertainty measured by the standard deviation of returns increases like the square root of time. Generalizing to several time points, up to T, the variance of the summation of the diffusion terms is the summation of the variances of each change.

$$V[z(t)] = N\sigma^2 = \sigma^2 T$$

$$\sigma[z(t)] = \sigma\sqrt{T}$$

The standard deviation unit has to be consistent with the time unit. If $t = 1$ year, then σ is the annual standard deviation, and so on. Under these assumptions, the process is "stationary," meaning that it remains the same though time.

12.2.3 The Generalized Wiener Process

The generalized Wiener process includes a drift and a constant standard deviation per unit of time. This simple process considers that the drift, a, and the coefficient of the innovation term, b, are constant. The process has now the form:

$$dS = a\ dt + b\ dz$$

Taking the expectation, $E[dx] = a\ dt$, is the constant drift. The incremental change of value is constant per unit of time. The constant drift represents a trend. The standard deviation is $b\sigma\sqrt{t}$. The time path is a steady trend with random variations at each time point around this trend.

The discrete equivalent of this equation serves for simulating the time path of the process. The horizon T is divided into n small intervals of same length $\Delta t = T/n$. The continuous equation takes a discretized form such that all small variations are related by the same relation:

$$\Delta S = a\ \Delta t + b\ \Delta z$$

The random innovation term is $\sigma\varepsilon\sqrt{\Delta t}$. A time path for S can be simulated by incrementing the variable by a Δt at each step and adding a random number, normally distributed with mean zero and standard deviation $\sigma\sqrt{\Delta t}$.

12.2.4 The Ito Process

The Ito process is a generalized Wiener process where the coefficients, a and b, are function of the underlying variable S and of the time t:

$$\Delta S = a(S_t, t)\Delta t + b(S_t, t)\Delta z$$

Drift and variance are, respectively $a(S_t, t)\Delta t$ and $b(S_t, t)\Delta z$, with variance being $b^2(S_t, t)\Delta t$. The drift and the variance rate are now dependent on S_t and time. The stock price process is a special case of an Ito process.

12.2.5 The Stock Price Process

For stock prices, the return is randomly distributed normally and i.i.d. because stock price returns are supposed to have a positive trend plus random deviations independent from past deviations, in line with the efficiency hypothesis of stock markets. Under the efficiency hypothesis, the return reacts to innovations, not to past information, which is embedded in the stock price.

The instantaneous return is dS/S_t, where S_t represents a stock price. The return has a drift μ and a constant variance σ. Hence, the drift and the diffusion coefficients are $a(S_t, t) = \mu S_t$ and $b(S_t, t) = \sigma S_t$. The process for the stock return is:

$$dS_t/S_t = \mu\ dt + \sigma\ dz$$

In the equation of the stochastic process of the stock price, the drift, $a(S_t, t)$, and the diffusion coefficient, $b(S_t, t)$, are now proportional to the stock price:

$$dS_t = \mu S_t \, dt + \sigma S_t \, dz$$

The coefficients μ and σ are constant, but the drift and the diffusion terms depend on S_t. The return follows a generalized Wiener process, with constants $a = \mu$ and $b = \sigma\sqrt{\Delta t}$. The trend is exponential because it is such that $dS/S = \mu^2$. But the stock price follows an Ito process. The variance of S_t increases as the square of S_t.

12.2.6 The Mean Reverting Process

A mean reverting process intends to model processes that cannot drift away of some long-term value by a large magnitude for long periods:

$$dS_t = \lambda(\mu - S_t)dt + \sigma S_t \, dz$$

S_t designates here a process followed by a market parameter, typically an interest rate, not a stock price. Such a model is inconsistent with the market efficiency which implies that stock returns are independent from past returns.

When S_t is above the constant μ, the drift term is negative, making negative variations of S_t more likely. The random variable might decline and revert to μ. If S_t is below μ, the drift term is positive and the random variable might increase and revert to μ. The parameter μ represents a long-term trend. When moving away from this long-term trend the asset price tends to revert to it.

The deviations from the trend last for a period that depends on the value of λ. The higher is λ, the stronger is the force making the process reverts to the long-term parameter. Hence deviations last longer when λ is low and are shorter when λ is high. This process applies to interest rates of which deviations cannot be extremely high as they can be for stock prices.

12.2.7 The "Rare Event" Process

The "jump process" is used to model rare events. Rare events are abnormal jumps of stock prices. In this text, rare events also include defaults which follow a jump process. Rare events occur unexpectedly and their probability of occurrence increases with the time interval elapsed. The size of the event is not small, as it is with the usual normal distribution, even when the time interval is very small, but its probability becomes zero when the time interval gets near to zero.

Assume that the rare event is a default. For stock prices, the random change was noted $z_{t+\Delta t}$ or $\Delta z_t = z_{t+\Delta t} - z_t$. For a process counting rare events, we use n_t instead of z_t because n_t takes only discrete values. The variation between n_t and $n_{t+\Delta t}$ is either 1 or 0. The probability that the rare event occurs, with size 1, is $\lambda \Delta t$. In other words:

$$P(n_{t+\Delta t} - n_t = 1) = \lambda \Delta t$$

---

2 If $S = S_0 \exp(\mu t)$, $\ln(S) - \ln(S_0) = \mu t$ and the derivative of $\ln(S)$ is $dS/S = \mu$.

$$P(n_{t+\Delta t} - n_t = 0) = 1 - \lambda \Delta t$$

The counting variable n_t depends on the intensity λ. The intensity and the event do not depend on past information. Such a process serves for modeling in continuous time the value of a contract that depends on default events.

As a reminder, over a time horizon, the random variable takes integer values k which represents the count of rare events. The probability of observing k rare events is the Poisson distribution: $f(k, \lambda) = \lambda^k e^{-\lambda}/k!$. The parameter λ is a positive real number, equal to the expected number of occurrences that occur during a given interval, called intensity or hazard rate. The time intensity is the number of events occurring within a unit of time. The exponential distribution describes the times between events following a Poisson process with constant rate λ. The probability that a rare event occurs from now and up to date t is $\exp(-\lambda t)$.

12.3 APPLICATION: STOCK VALUE DISTRIBUTION

Under the efficient market hypothesis, all stock values reflect all past information available. Consequently, returns of successive periods are independent from one period to the other because the flow of new information, or "innovations," is random. In addition, small period returns follow approximately normal distributions with a positive mean. The mean is the expected return. Over very small intervals, returns follow a generalized Wiener process, with constants $a = \mu$ and $b = \sigma\sqrt{\Delta t}$. This particular process is:

$$dS_t/S_t = \mu \, dt + \sigma \, dz$$

This equation shows that the return follows a normal distribution around the time drift defined by the expected return $\mu \, dt$.

The formula makes it easy to generate time paths of the S_t by generating normal standardized dz and cumulating them until date t, with preset values of the instantaneous expected return μ and its volatility σ. This simple process applies to asset prices and market parameters of which variance increases over time.

The simulation of time paths of value drivers allows modeling the future values of any asset following the same process. We illustrate here the mechanism with the simple Wiener process, which results into a lognormal distribution. First, the horizon is divided into small intervals. Then, for each time interval, the drift is cumulated with a random term. Finally, all small increments are added up until horizon. The final asset value distribution at horizon results from cumulative returns along each time path.

For generating a discrete path, we use a unit value for $\Delta t = t - (t - 1)$ and the standard $\Phi(0, 1)$ normal variable for the innovations Δz. With several time intervals, we obtain the intermediate values of the price. The process uses the following inputs:

- initial price: $S_0 = 100$
- time interval: $\Delta t = 1$ day
- expected return: 10% annualized, or 10%/250 per day = 0.04%
- volatility of the random component: 30% annualized, or 30%/$\sqrt{250}$ = 1.90% daily.

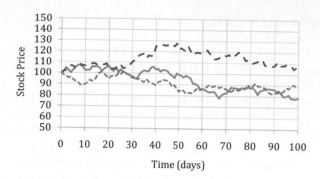

FIGURE 12.1   Time paths of value

The innovation at each time interval Δz is a standardized normal distribution with volatility $30\%\sqrt{250}$. The price variation in each step is the drift 0.04% per day plus the random noise Δz equal to a normal standard distribution (ε) times the daily volatility:

$$S_t - S_{t-1} = S_{t-1}(\mu\Delta t + \sigma\Delta z) = V_{t-1}(0.04\% \times 1 + \varepsilon\, 30\% \sqrt{250})$$

Simulating a time path over one year requires generating a time series of random draws of innovation values. For simulating several time paths, the process is repeated as many times as necessary. This allows calculating any final value that depends on past values, such as the value of a look back option on the stock. Figure 12.1 shows various time paths and the final price at horizon 100 days. If we generate enough time paths, we observe the distribution of the final values at horizon, which is lognormal.

12.4   INTEREST RATE PROCESSES

Interest rate processes are more complex than the basic stock price processes for two reasons.

- There are several interest rates, so that we need to model the behavior of several parameters rather than only one.
- Interest rates tend to reverse to some long-term average over long periods.

For capturing the behavior of interest rates, we need to model the entire time structure of rates, with models using "mean-reverting" stochastic processes.

Several stochastic processes apply to interest rates. Mean reversion implies that rates revert to some long-term average and avoid wide drifts away of the long-term value of the interest rate for mimicking the actual behavior of rates. This contrasts with stock prices, which can drift away from initial value without bounds. A "term structure model" describes the evolution of the yield curve through time. Models generate the entire yield curve using one or two factors.

One-factor models involve only one source of uncertainty, usually the short-term rate. The following equation represents a one-factor model of short term rates r_t. Using such a model implies that all rates correlate with this short-term rate. The random dz_t term follows a standard-ized normal distribution and makes the rate changes stochastic:

$$dr_t = \lambda\left(\mu - r_t\right)dt + \sigma r_t^k dz_t$$

The parameter $\lambda < 1$ determines the speed of mean reversion to a long-term mean μ. When the parameter k is 0, the change of rate is normally distributed as the random term. When $k = 0.5$, the variance of the rate is proportional to its level, implying that low rates are less volatile than high interest rates.

The Vasicek's model is the first model of the term structure (1977):

$$dr = \lambda(\mu - r)dt + \sigma\, dz$$

Vasicek's model is an equilibrium model in that it eliminates any inconsistency between rates of different maturities. The rates might differ from actual rates.

The other family of no-arbitrage models fit the current term structure of rates, which pro-vides the benefit of starting from actual rates that can serve for pricing purpose. This constraint implies that the current shape of the yield curve drives to a certain extent the future short rates. Two-factor models assume two sources of uncertainties[3]. The current practice uses the Libor market model.

For VaR or asset-liability management purposes, it is not practical to use elaborated interest rate models. Simpler techniques are necessary. Principal component analysis use historical data on market parameters to define components that explain the movements. It is particularly suit-able when we deal with highly correlated data, such as interest rates. A full example is given subsequently in Chapter 37 when dealing with simulations of interest rates.

12.5 SPECIFICS OF STOCHASTIC PROCESSES AND ITO LEMMA

The main stochastic processes have been explained. The valuation and modeling of returns relies also on stochastic differentiation, notably on Ito lemma, which derives the process of a derivative from the process of another underlying asset. The purpose of this section is to high-light the differences between standard calculus and stochastic calculus. This is a brief summary of a topic which is expanded in many other publications.

12.5.1 Deterministic Calculus

In deterministic calculus, the small variation of any function $f(x + \Delta x) - f(x)$ can be approxi-mated by a Taylor function around the value x of the variable x, as long as we can calculate the derivatives, which are the response of the function to a small change of the variable. The

---

3 Among useful coverage of various models are [61] from Risk Publications. The current practice is based on the Libor market model, with the formal presentation in [15]. For modeling purposes, in this text, we use Vacisek [75] and Frye Principal Component Analysis of term structure [30] for simulations. The Black, Derman and Toy model [12] is not used in this text, but it is traditionally mentioned because of its conceptual simplicity and for illustrating calibration.

small variation of a function depending on time t and a deterministic variable z could also be approximated by taking the derivative with respect to t and z of the function. When these variables deviate by small amounts Δt and Δz, the variation of the function can be approximated by a linear function of these deviations. The equation becomes exact at the limit when the small variations of the two variables tend towards zero.

The Taylor expansion formula provides an approximation of the variation $f(x + \Delta x, y + \Delta y) - f(x,y)$ around the values x and y, using only the first- and second-order expansion around x and y, assuming that the function can be differentiated twice:

$$f\left(x+\Delta x, y+\Delta y\right)-f\left(x, y\right)=\frac{\partial f}{\partial x}\Delta x+\frac{\partial f}{\partial y}\Delta y+\frac{1}{2}\left[\frac{\partial^2 f}{\partial x^2}\left(\Delta x\right)^2+\frac{\partial^2 f}{\partial y^2}\left(\Delta y\right)^2+2\frac{\partial^2 f}{\partial x\partial y}\Delta x\Delta y\right]$$

In ordinary calculus, squared terms are much smaller than first-order terms and are ignored and it is acceptable to keep only the two first-order terms.

$$f\left(x+\Delta x, y+\Delta y\right)-f\left(x, y\right)=\frac{\partial f}{\partial x}\Delta x+\frac{\partial f}{\partial y}\Delta y$$

This is not so in stochastic calculus because the square of the random innovation term has the dimension of a variance and cannot be ignored.

12.5.2 Stochastic Calculus

Standard notations use S_t for the random price of an asset that depends on time and $F(S_t, t)$ for another asset with underlying S_t. When time passes, both asset and derivative prices fluctuate randomly, and have also drift components that depend on time. The derivative is a function of two variables, one of them being random.

The major difference between standard calculus and stochastic calculus is that the variable S_t is now random and has non-zero variance. The second-order expansion becomes useful to understand what happens. Starting from the standard Taylor expansion, some second-order derivatives are not ignored. In the general equation of the Taylor expansion, x now becomes S_t and y becomes t.

$$F\left(S+\Delta S, t+\Delta t\right)-F\left(S, t\right)=\frac{\partial F}{\partial S}\Delta S+\frac{\partial F}{\partial t}\Delta t+\frac{1}{2}\left[\frac{\partial^2 F}{\partial S^2}\left(\Delta S\right)^2+\frac{\partial^2 F}{\partial t^2}\left(\Delta t\right)^2+2\frac{\partial^2 F}{\partial S\partial t}\Delta S\Delta t\right]$$

The two first terms are the standard first-order approximations. The variable t is not random and its square can be ignored. The issue is mainly with $(\Delta S)^2$. This term has a positive variance. Assuming that it is negligible would be equivalent to considering it as not random. The randomness results from Δz. Stochastic calculus considers this term as non-negligible as it would be in standard calculus.

12.5.3 Ito Lemma

The Ito lemma, which serves mainly for considering the stochastic processes of a function $F(S_t, t)$ of a stochastic variable, following one of the standard stochastic processes, resolves the difficulty. The stock price follows an Ito process, with drift and diffusion terms dependent on the stock price and on time, which we summarize in a single subscript "t":

$$dS_t = a_t\, dt + \sigma_t\, dz_t$$

For moving from the simple Taylor expansion, second-order terms have to be considered, using the expression of ΔS. Summarizing, without expanding, some intermediate steps, we can provide some intuition of how the Ito lemma deals with the differentiation. The first-order terms remain, as in ordinary calculus. Second, the term $(\Delta z)^2$ is its variance and cannot be neglected any more, as reminded above. Third, it can be shown that it has an expectation proportional to the time interval, or: $E[(\Delta z)^2] = \sigma^2 \Delta t$. The term σ^2 is the variance of the asset return, which can depend on time. This is why the second derivative with respect to S remains, times $\sigma^2 \Delta t$. Finally, we make all discrete intervals tend towards zero and replace discrete variations by their limits.

The final result is the Ito formula, which provides the process followed by a function $F(S_t, t)$, when the underlying variable, a stock price for example, follows an Ito process. Starting from:

$$dS_t = a_t\, dt + \sigma_t\, dz_t$$

$$dF_t = \frac{\partial F}{\partial S_t}\, dS_t + \frac{\partial F}{\partial t}\, dt + \frac{1}{2}\frac{\partial^2 F}{\partial S_t^2}\sigma_t^2\, dt$$

We can replace dS_t by its expression, and we have:

$$dF_t = \left[\frac{\partial F}{\partial S_t} S a_t + \frac{\partial F}{\partial t} + \frac{1}{2}\frac{\partial^2 F}{\partial S_t^2}\sigma_t^2\right] dt + \frac{\partial F}{\partial S_t}\sigma_t dz$$

This looks like a complex expression. It is easier to handle using a compact form, by changing the notations as follows:

$$F_s = \frac{\partial F}{\partial S_t},\, F_t = \frac{\partial F}{\partial t},\, F_{ss} = \frac{\partial^2 1}{\partial S_t}$$

And the formula for Ito lemma becomes:

$$dF_t = F_s dS_t + F_t dt + \frac{1}{2}F_{ss}\sigma_t^2 dt$$

$$F_t = \left(F_s dS_t + F_t dt + \frac{1}{2}F_{ss}\sigma_t^2\right) dt + F_s \sigma_t dz$$

An important remark stems from this formula, which we use repeatedly subsequently. The underlying asset depends on a random term dz. The Ito lemma shows that the derivative depends on the same random term. This property will, notably, be used for forming risk-free portfolios by combining the underlying asset and the derivative with weights such that the random terms cancel out. Such portfolios become risk-free and earn the risk-free rate. This property is the foundation of pricing techniques.

12.5.4 Example: Stock Price Distribution

A standard application is to use the Ito formula to derive the stock price distribution from the process of $F = \ln(S)$:

$$\frac{\partial F}{\partial S} = \frac{1}{S}, \frac{\partial^2 F}{\partial S^2} = -\frac{1}{S^2}, \frac{\partial F}{\partial t} = 0$$

$$dF = \left(\mu - \frac{1}{2}\sigma^2\right)dt + \sigma dz$$

Since μ and σ are constant, F follows a generalized Wiener process with a constant drift $a = \mu - \frac{1}{2}\sigma^2$ and diffusion with standard deviation $\sigma\sqrt{t}$. For such process, with a and b constant, we know that the distribution at t is a normal distribution. Hence $\ln(S)$ follows a normal distribution. By definition, S follows then a lognormal distribution. The change of $\ln(S)$ between 0 and T is normally distributed with mean $(\mu - \sigma^2/2)T$ and standard deviation $\sigma\sqrt{T}$, or $\ln(S/S_0)$ follows $N[(\mu - \sigma^2/2)T, \sigma\sqrt{T}]$, N being the normal distribution.

13

Valuation and Pricing Risk

The chapter on returns introduced the discounted cash flow model as a valuation tool under certainty. In presence of uncertainty, valuation is an issue because future payoffs as well the appropriate discount rate are unknown. The discount rate should be the return of risky assets, which is often unknown because it includes a risk premium. Because we do not know, in general, the risk premium, we cannot apply the discounted cash flow model without a proper discount rate. Because we constantly deal with risky assets in this text, the main lines implemented for valuation have to be repeated. Because valuation is not the main purpose of this text, we provide a minimum background without relying on formal demonstrations that can be found elsewhere.

Note that this technical chapter can be skipped in a first stage. For facilitating progress through the text, application of the conceptual background has been isolated from the theory (in Chapter 14 and in other subsequent chapters). The end results of the financial theory, which are routinely applied, are summarized here (section 13.3).

Valuation of risky assets relies on two general methodologies. This chapter provides a minimum background to be used when the risk premium is unknown.

The first methodology consists of combining assets into a portfolio that are risk-free because they depend on the same random term. The methodology relies on Ito lemma because we need to relate the first process to the second one. When writing that such portfolios are risk-free, we obtain an equation of which the unknown is the value of an asset as a function of time and the risk-free rate. Solving that equation resolves the issue. Note that forming such a portfolio combines a hedging instrument with another hedged instrument, a property that serves for risk management.

The second methodology relies on risk-neutral valuation. Under this alternate methodology, the valuation proceeds as if all assets earned the risk-free rate. Future payoffs are derived using this rule, and they are discounted back to present at the risk-free rate. The value is the expectation of such discounted payoffs.

Representative applications follow in the next chapter.

Contents

13.1 CONSTRUCTING A RISK-FREE PORTFOLIO

The first valuation methodology constructs risk-free portfolios by combining assets that follow processes depending on the same random term. The idea is that both a derivative and the underlying asset depend on the same random diffusion term, since Ito lemma shows that both asset processes share the same random term. By adjusting the weights assigned to the derivative and the underlying asset, one can form a portfolio which is instantaneously risk-free. Such portfolio earns the risk-free rate. The starting point is the process of the underlying asset and the process of the derivative is obtained from Ito lemma.

Writing that such a portfolio earns the risk-free rate translates into an equation involving partial derivatives, called a partial differential equation (PDE). The equation has no random term because it was eliminated when forming the portfolio. The unknown of such equations is a function which relates the price of the derivative, the price of the underlying asset, and time, plus all coefficients involved in Ito lemma. Resolving partial differential equations is sometimes feasible analytically, sometimes not. When there is no simple formula for the unknown function, numerical procedures are used. The main point of this section is the derivation of the PDE[1]. Numerical procedures are illustrated for options in the next chapter.

13.1.1 How to Form Risk-free Portfolios

This section explains how to form a risk-free portfolio with a put option. The technique is widely used in practice for hedging the risk of the seller of the put option. It is known under "delta-hedging"[2] because it relies on the "delta" (δ) of the put, which is the ratio of the variation of the put value to the value of the underlying stock. But it serves as well for pricing the option.

In the case of a put option on stock, constructing the risk-free portfolio implies combining the put option on stock with a short position on the stock. We know the "delta" from the pricing formula of an option, but it can also be derived from the conceptual framework expanded hereafter for forming risk-free portfolios. Assume for example that the delta is −0.5. The delta is negative for a put option because the value of the put increases when the stock price declines. A portfolio formed by a short position of 0.5 stocks and short in one put would be risk-free.

The seller's position is short one put. Assume the stock price is 10 and the put price is 1. The seller of the put fears that the stock declines below the strike price, because he or she would pay to the buyer the positive gap between the exercise price and the stock price. The seller wants to preserve its wealth and avoid any loss. The solution is to take an offsetting position.

---

1 The most common example is the Black-Scholes formulas as developed originally [13]. Since then, numerous publications built on the techniques, as mentioned in all pricing textbooks, such as Hull [36].
2 Delta hedging is a common technique addressed in various publications. Hull [36] and Taleb [72] are good introductions.

Because the delta is negative, this implies selling short delta units of stock, which generates cash that is lent risk-free. The delta-neutral portfolio P is:

$$- 1 \text{ put} - 0.5 \text{ stock} + \text{loan (value of } 0.5 \text{ stocks)}$$

The invested amount is 5, since the seller of the put sold short 0.5 stocks. The portfolio value is originally: $-1 + 0.5 \times 10 - 5 = -1$. When the stock price decreases by 1, $\Delta S = -1$ and the variation of values of the call and the stock position exactly offset:

$$\Delta(-1 \text{ put}) = -0.5 \times 1 = -0.5$$

$$\Delta(-0.5 \text{ stock}) = -0.5 \times (-1) = +0.5$$

The variation of value of the portfolio is:

$$\Delta(P) = -0.5 + 0.5 + (\text{interest revenue of lending } 5) = \text{risk-free rate on } 5$$

Because the seller needs to short the stock proportionally to δ, the position needs to be adjusted dynamically when the stock price changes. In general, if F is the put and S is the stock, the portfolio P would be:

$$P = -F + \frac{\partial F}{\partial S} S$$

In this equation the coefficient of S is the delta, or the first derivative of the put value with respect to the stock price. Remember that in the case of a put, the ratio is negative because the put gains value when stock price declines. Hence the position on the stock is negative, or a short position.

Note that, by constructing the portfolio, the option seller has replicated the option sold since it is being hedged. Referring to the replication principle, unlike static replications that apply to forward contacts, the present replication is dynamic. It has to be adjusted continuously when the delta of the option changes. It is not surprising that it is easy to construct a risk-free portfolio. The Ito lemma shows that both the underlying and the derivative F depend on the same diffusion term. All that we need to do is combining the asset and the derivative in such a way that the coefficients of the random term cancel out. With one put, it is necessary to sell short $\partial F/\partial S$ units of stocks, and $\partial F/\partial S$ is the delta.

13.1.2 How to Derive the Pricing PDE

The pricing PDE is derived by writing that the portfolio P earns the risk-free rate. Although, we do not address analytical solution in this text, it is useful to show how the equation is derived. The equation results from a straight application of Ito lemma, because all that we need to do is deriving the process for the derivative and combining it with the one of the underlying stock. The stock price process is:

$$dS_t = a(S_t, t)dt + \sigma(S_t, t)dz$$

The Ito lemma provides dF_t:

$$dF_t = (F_t + \tfrac{1}{2}F_{ss}\sigma^2)dt + F_s dS_t$$

Substituting for dS_t, and isolating the drift term from the random term, we obtain the stochastic process for the derivative:

$$dF_t = (F_t + \tfrac{1}{2}F_{ss}\sigma^2)dt + F_s[a(S_t, t)dt + \sigma(S_t, t)dz]$$

We group terms for isolating the drift and the diffusion terms:

$$dF_t = [F_t + F_s a(S_t, t) + \tfrac{1}{2}F_{ss}\sigma^2]dt + F_s\sigma(S_t, t)dz$$

The diffusion term appears in both processes, with coefficient $\sigma(S_t, t)$ in the stock process and with coefficient $F_s\sigma(S_t, t)$ in the derivative process. For eliminating the unpredictable element, we use these coefficients in forming a portfolio P_t combining one unit of the stock and $-F_s$ of the derivative: $P_t = F - F_s S_t$. The coefficient of the random term cancels out and we are left with the deterministic drift term:

$$dP_t = [F_t + \tfrac{1}{2}F_{ss}\sigma^2]dt$$

For a stock providing only capital gain and no dividend, the expected capital gain of this portfolio is $rP_t\,dt$. Writing that the portfolio earns the risk-free rate provides the PDE, after removing the drift dt which is common to all terms:

$$rP_t = F_t + \tfrac{1}{2}F_{ss}\sigma^2$$

Since $P_t = F - F_s S_t$, we obtain the final form of the partial differential equation:

$$-rF_t + rF_s S_t + F_t + \tfrac{1}{2}F_{ss}\sigma^2 = 0$$

This equation is a partial differential equation. It is completed with additional conditions, since we know that, at expiration T, the expiration price of a call is the positive gap between the final stock price and the exercise price K, or $\max(S_T - K, 0)$. The unknown function is F. The equation can be solved in various ways, from analytical solutions to numerical procedures. The original Black–Scholes methodology for pricing an option was derived by an analytical method. It is often more intuitive to solve such PDE with numerical procedures.

13.1.3 How to Solve Numerically a PDE

Numerical solutions are easier to implement. They rely on lattice trees or on finite difference methods. We provide an example using lattice trees for valuing an option in the next chapter[3].

---

3 Cox and Rubinstein use this approach for their presentation of simple valuation techniques of options [21]. Finite difference methods are presented in accessible ways in Hull [36] and Neftci [55].

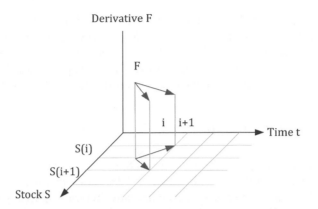

FIGURE 13.1   How the derivative value changes when stock and time vary by small increments

Lattice trees are simpler ways of using the finite difference method. Here, we simply explain the principle.

Any differential equation can be discretized, replacing the infinitesimally small variations by small discrete variations. The principle of difference equations consists of calculating small variations of the underlying asset, the stock, and the derivative, and writing that they comply with the discretized PDE. The first step is to define a range of feasible values for each variable, S_t and t, by selecting some maximum and minimum values. There are two axes, for S_t and t respectively, plus the vertical axis measuring $F(S_t, t)$ (Figure 13.1). When the variables change, the derivative value moves along a surface, of which coordinates are the stock price and time for the horizontal plane and the derivative value on the vertical axis.

The time axis extends to the maturity of the option. The stock value axis extends between bounds that will not be exceeded. Each range of values is divided in small increments, transforming the partial differential equation into a difference equation. For example, the first derivative of F with respect to S_t is the ratio of the change of F to a small variation of S_t, or $\Delta F / \Delta S_t$ between any consecutive pair of points along the surface. Such ratios can be calculated numerically along the grid. The second derivative is the derivative of the first derivative. It is also a ratio of the variation of $\Delta F / \Delta S_t$ to ΔS_t between any consecutive pair of points along the surface.

The basic idea is to calculate numerically a number of points along this surface, starting from points for which we know the value. We know the values at the frontiers of the surface. Those are called "boundary values." For example, for an option, we start at maturity and derive the final payoffs that depend on the stock price and the exercise price when we select the grid points matching the maturity. Starting from there, we calculate all other points moving step by step backward along the grid and starting from the known values. The technique is analogous to the lattice method, which is simpler, as illustrated in the next application chapter.

13.2 RISK-NEUTRAL VALUATION: THE CASE OF A STOCK PRICE

Stocks are expected to provide a higher return than the risk-free rate, the risk premium being equal to the β of the stock times the differential between the equity index return and the risk free return. In this case, the CAPM (capital asset pricing model) provides the risk premium. But we use this example for illustrating the methodology relying on risk-neutral probabilities even though such methodology is usually used for other assets and derivatives. The case of the stock price is the simplest one and suffices for illustrating the principles. The presentation explains how the stochastic equation and the risk-neutral valuation are equivalent[4].

13.2.1 Risk-neutral Probability

Consider a stock with instantaneous return μ and volatility σ and initial value S_0. The random return of a stock is normally distributed, with mean μ and diffusion term σdz. The return between the initial date 0 and the final date t is Y_t. This cumulative return is normally distributed, as instantaneous returns are. The drift and the variance are proportional to the time t. Hence Y_t follows the normal distribution $N(\mu t, \sigma^2 t)$. The return is equal to the logarithm of the ratio of final to initial price S_t/S_0. Therefore S_t can be expressed as $S_t = S_0 \exp(Y_t)$. The stock value follows a lognormal distribution, with a random return Y_t.

Using standard statistical results for lognormal distributions, the expectation of this function can be calculated as:

$$E\left[\exp(Y_t)\right] = \exp\left(\mu t + \frac{1}{2}\sigma^2 t\right)$$

The stock expected value as of date t is:

$$E\left(S_t\right) = S_0 \exp\left[\mu t + \frac{1}{2}\sigma^2 t\right]$$

This expectation is conditional on the known value of the stock at date 0 and is calculated with real-world probabilities. The formula does not help valuing the stock because the return μ contains a risk premium, which we assume unknown.

Since we need the stock value today, we can discount both terms at the risk-free rate by multiplying by $\exp(-r)$, which is known and can be entered as a constant under the expectation sign.

$$E\left[S_t \exp(-rt)\right] = S_0 \exp\left[\left(\mu - r + \frac{1}{2}\sigma^2\right)t\right]$$

Note that discounting makes the risk premium embedded in the risky required return of the stock explicit. It is the excess of the risky return above the risk-free rate r.

The original probability distribution of Y_t is normal with mean μt and variance $\sigma^2 t$, or $N(\mu t, \sigma^2 t)$. We can define a new probability distribution, normal with mean ρt and same variance $\sigma^2 t$, or $N(\rho t, \sigma^2 t)$. Because doing so shifts the mean return, the real world probabilities do not apply any more. In fact, it is possible to use the same probability distribution, but shifting only the mean of the distribution. The expectation is now E^*, the "*" referring to the new probability distribution. The same equation becomes with the new drift:

$$E^*\left[S_t \exp(-rt)\right] = S_0 \exp\left[\left(\rho - r + \frac{1}{2}\sigma^2\right)t\right]$$

---

4 This presentation is inspired by the treatment provided by Neftci in [55].

If we pick a value of $\rho = r - \sigma^2/2$, the term within brackets cancels out:

$$(r - \sigma^2/2) - r + \sigma^2/2 = 0$$

The expectation E^* of the future stock prices discounted at the risk-free rate becomes:

$$E^*\left[S_t \exp(-rt)\right] = S_0$$

This sounds trivial. Why should we calculate the theoretical value of a stock at a date when it can be observed? In fact, such transformation applies to any assets with random payoffs and makes it general. The point is that the current stock price results from all future stock values at horizon by assuming that the growth rate of the stock is the risk-free rate. Such values form a distribution obtained, for example, by simulating the time paths of the stock price. Once this is done, the current stock price is the expectation of all these values discounted at the risk-free rate.

The growth rate of the stock has shifted down compared to what it is under real-world probabilities. The distribution of S_t is lognormal with a new mean $(r - \sigma^2/2)t$ and same volatility $\sigma^2 t$. By changing the mean of the probability distribution, it becomes possible to calculate the expectation of the value of the stock, and by-passing the fact that the risk premium was unknown.

This result can be generalized. By changing the growth rate of the stock, we are able to calculate its value as the expectation of all future values discounted at the risk-free rate. The result applies to other assets. By changing the drift parameter to the risk-free rate, the value of an asset is the expected value of all its payoffs, calculated as if the return was the risk-free rate, and discounted at the risk-free rate. Therefore, valuing an option can be done by shifting the drift to the risk-free rate and calculating the payoffs at maturity, then discounting them back to present at the risk-free rate. The procedure applies to Monte Carlo simulations, when simulating all possible scenarios, deriving the payoffs for each of them, and discounting at the risk-free rate.

Under modern finance terminology, the stock price behaves as a martingale under the new probabilities. Martingales are random variables with only unpredictable component and no drift. Hence, the best forecast of the future value is the current value. Formally, it means that the expected value at date t of the future payoffs is equal to the current value, which can be written as:

$$E_t^*\left[S(t)\right] = S(0)$$

The star "*" with the expectation operator makes explicit that we changed the probability distribution. The above technique of valuation consists of transforming the stock process into a martingale. The process of a martingale is I_t-adapted, meaning that all information until t is embedded in the expectation as seen from t. In the case of the stock price above, S_t is not a martingale because it has a drift term. Even $S_t \exp(-rt)$ is not a martingale because the stock provides an excess return over the risk-free rate. The martingale was obtained by using new probabilities such that the stock value is exactly the expected value of its payoffs at the risk-free rate, and discounted at the same risk-free rate, or:

$$E_t^*\left[S(t)\right] = S(0)$$

Martingales are commonly used, by switching probabilities, because the value becomes the expected value of future payoffs discounted at the risk-free rate. Another view of the risk-neutral probabilities is that they measure the price of risk. They are such that the drift rate declines from the actual risky return to the risk-free return. The difference is the risk premium.

13.2.2 Stock Price Dynamics under Risk-neutral Probabilities

The process of the stock can be derived from the stochastic process of the return. The cumulative return Y_t from 0 to t is normally distributed, and follows the normal distribution $N(\mu t, \sigma^2 t)$. The stock price S_t is a function of the return: $S_t = S_0 \exp(Y_t)$. The stochastic process for the return is:

$$dY_t = \mu dt + \sigma dz$$

Since the stock price is a function of the random Y_t and since we know the process for Y_t, Ito lemma can be used for deriving the process of $S_t = S_0 \exp(Y_t)$. The Ito lemma states that when $F = S_t$ is a function of another process Y_t, the process of S_t is:

$$dS(Y_t, t) = \frac{\partial S}{\partial y} dY_t + \frac{\partial S}{\partial t} dt + \frac{1}{2} \frac{\partial^2 S}{\partial Y^2} \sigma_t^2 dt$$

The term dY_t is the above process. The partial derivatives are:

$$\partial S / \partial t = 0$$

$$\partial^2 S / \partial Y^2 = S_0 \exp(Y_t)$$

$$dS_t = S_0 \exp(Y_t)(\mu dt + \sigma dz) + \tfrac{1}{2} S_0 \exp(Y_t)\sigma^2 dt$$

After substitution:

$$dS_t = \left(\mu + \frac{1}{2}\sigma^2\right) S_t dt + \sigma S_t dz$$

At this point, it is possible to shift the mean from μ to another value ρ provided that the diffusion term dz is replaced by a new diffusion term, dz^*, because the probabilities change. The new equation is:

$$dS_t = \left(\rho + \frac{1}{2}\sigma^2\right) S_t dt + \sigma S_t dz^*$$

Using a value of $\rho = r - \sigma^2/2$, the drift rate collapses to the risk-free rate, and the stock process becomes:

$$dS_t = rS_t dt + \sigma S_t dz^*$$

The same shift of drift that allowed valuing the stock as the expectation of all its future values, using a growth term equal to the risk-free rate and discounting at the risk-free rate, transforms the drift of the stock price process into the risk-free rate.

The risk premium is eliminated and the random drift parameter is the risk-free plus the volatility term, both being known. The transformation of real-world probabilities into risk-neutral probabilities allows eliminating the unknown risk premium. Moreover, we know how to determine such probabilities. We have simply switched the mean to the lower value equal to the risk-free rate. Under risk-neutral probabilities the dynamics of the stock price have a drift equal to the risk-free rate.

The transformation can be performed for all assets, changing their return to the risk-free rate to model the asset process under risk-neutral probabilities. Note the analogy with the technique of forming risk-free portfolio with derivatives for valuing them. The resulting PDE does not depend on risky return, only on the risk-free rate. In fact, this is equivalent to assuming that the stock price grows at the risk-free rate.

13.3 VALUATION: END RESULTS

Real-world probabilities are the actual or natural probabilities. Risk-neutral probabilities are used for valuation purpose under risk aversion and are implied in the value of assets. Real world default probabilities, or natural default probabilities, are those observed in the real world, and do not serve for valuation.

The shift of probabilities provides a general method for valuing risky payoffs. The mechanism proceeds as if the expected return is the risk-free rate. Payoffs are determined using this rule under various scenarios. The current value is the expectation of those discounted payoffs at the risk-free rate. What happens when moving back to the real-world probabilities is that the asset returns gets higher but that the discount rate becomes a risky rate embedding a risk premium and the two changes offset.

The issue becomes how to simulate all possible payoffs under risk neutrality. Various methodologies are implemented. We illustrate some implementations in the next chapter.

A well-known application is the Black-Scholes equation. Instead of constructing a risk-free portfolio of which return is the risk-free rate, it is possible to derive the same formula by calculating the expectation of the payoffs of a call option on stock under risk-neutral probabilities. The payoffs are the positive differences between the stock price and the strike price and zero. The stock price is assumed to grow at the risk-free rate. The equation simply discounts the payoffs at maturity at the risk-free rate. This is exactly what is done in the next chapter for valuing a call option on stock, using the lattice tree methodology.

Risk-neutral valuation applies to any asset, by simulating payoffs and discounting them back to present at the risk-free rate. The Monte Carlo methodology for deriving payoffs is analogous to calculating payoffs using lattice trees or finite differences.

The generalization has conceptual foundations, based on the Girsanov theorem[5]. The theorem states that we can always deduct a drift from any asset and operate under a framework where the drift equals the risk-free rate.

---

5 The Girsanov theorem is explained in an accessible way in Neftci [55]. The same text treats all basics for valuation of risky assets using the risk-free portfolio, the risk-neutral valuation and the stochastic processes.

14

Some Applications of Valuation Techniques

This chapter illustrates some examples of valuation techniques which complement the valuation framework. All examples relate to subsequent applications in this text. The first example deals with the case when we know the price of risk from observation of market prices. Notably, we know the yield of credit risky debt. The first section summarizes the principle of valuation of credit risky debt from credit spreads or under risk-neutral valuation. The second example relies on the risk-neutral valuation methodology for valuing a stock option. Instead of using closed-form formulas, we use the classical binomial trees technique for simulating the random option payoffs and calculating the expectation of the discounted payoffs in a risk-neutral world. The model is used, later on, for valuing the interest rate options embedded in banking mortgages. Finally, the third example deals with interest rates. The Vasicek model of interest rates provides a simple example of closed-form solution to stochastic differential equations obtained by forming risk-free portfolios of bonds. The model can be used for simulating interest rates, although alternate methodologies are used subsequently for the same purpose[1]. The first section summarizes the principles and the next sections deal with these three cases.

Contents

---

[1] Chapter 37 deals with interest rate simulations for market VaR and for ALM. The methodology used is the principal comment analysis, which explains the variations of a target variable with independent factors. Factor models are discussed in Chapter 32.

14.1 VALUATION OF RISKY DEBT FROM CREDIT SPREADS AND RISK-NEUTRAL PROBABILITIES

The value of a credit risky debt is always lower than the value of risk-free debt with same payoffs. The difference is materialized by a higher discount rate of contractual payoffs than the risk-free rate, the difference being the "credit spread" equal to the excess of the risky rate over the risk-free rate. It equivalently appears in implied probabilities in values that make the payoffs of the risky debt depend on default and, eventually, lower than the actual contractual payoffs under the real-world probabilities.

There are two ways to value risky debt. Either we discount the expected future flows subject to default risk at the risk-free rate, or we discount the contractual flow at the risky market rate. These two values should be identical. This imposes a condition on the probabilities used to value the expected flows. The equivalence allows deriving "implied" risk-neutral probabilities in credit risky debt prices.

We illustrate the mechanism of valuation using the example of a credit risky debt for a single period under discrete time. A credit risky debt has current value 100, an annual 8% risky coupon and is a zero coupon bond with 1-year maturity. The risk-free rate is 6%. Recovery under default is 30% of the contractual flow due under default (a percentage value). Assume that the risky yield of this debt is 8%, same as coupon. There are only two credit states at horizon: survival or default. The real world, or "natural," survival and default probabilities, are, respectively $1 - d = 98.5\%$ and $d = 1.5\%$ (Table 14.1).

TABLE 14.1

Credit state	Payoff	Natural probability
Survival	108	$1 - d = 98.5\%$
Default	$30\% \times 108$	$d = 1.5\%$

By definition of risky yield, the value of the credit risky debt is the present value at the risky yield of the contractual payoff:

$$\text{value of risky debt} = 108/(1 + 8\%) = 100$$

Instead of including the risk in the discount rate, we can introduce the risk in the uncertain future payoffs. If we use the real-world probabilities, the expected payoff in one year is $E(F_1)$, where F_1 is the contractual payoff 108 as of horizon. The two possible payoffs at horizon are:

under default: $100 (1 + 8\%) \times 30\% = 32.4$

under survival: $100 (1 + 8\%) = 108$

Weighting each payoff by its probability, we get:

$$E(F_1) = 100 [1.5\% \times 32.4 + 98.5\% \times 1.08] = 106.87$$

If we discount the expected payoff at the risk-free rate 6%, we will find a value above 100, the actual value of the bond. There exists a set of risk-neutral probabilities such that the expected payoff, weighted by such probabilities, and discounted at the risk-free rate, is exactly the value of the debt, or 100. The star ("*") stands for "risk-neutral." $E*$ is the expectation under risk-neutral probabilities (default or survival). The risk-neutral probabilities of default and survival are $d*$ and $1 - d*$.

The risk-neutral default probability $d*$ is such the expected payoff at horizon discounted at the risk-free rate is equal to the value of the risk-free debt:

$$d*(1 + 8\%) \times 30\% \times 100 + (1 - d*) \times (1 + 8\%) \times 100 = 106.0$$

Extracting the risk-neutral default probability from the above equation results in:

$$d* = 2.65\% \text{ and } 1 - d* = 97.35\%$$

The risk-neutral default probability is higher than the natural default probability 1.5%. The difference between 2.65% and 1.5%, or 1.15%, is a measure of risk aversion.

It is obvious from this example that the credit spread applying for defining the risky rate is related to risk-neutral probabilities and to recoveries under default. The theoretical relationship is explained in Chapter 43 dealing with the modeling of default using the "rare event" process, called in this case the intensity model of defaults.

14.2 VALUATION OF AN OPTION UNDER RISK-NEUTRAL PROBABILITIES

When the risk premium is unknown, either we use the risk-neutral methodology for valuing expected payoffs in a risk-neutral world or we rely on stochastic differential equations. The martingale approach uses a simple setup.

- Consider that an asset has a return equal to the risk-free rate, and replace the risky return by the risk-free rate.
- Simulate all future payoffs under this assumption.
- Discount them at the risk-free rate.
- Calculate the expectation of these discounted payoffs.

For valuing a derivative, we assume that the return equals the risk-free return and that its value is the present value of the expected payoffs at the risk-free rate. For generating payoffs, simulations of simpler lattice trees are used. Note that closed form formulas exist for standard options. Instead of using the formula, we replicate here the standard simplest procedure using lattice trees.

A "tree"[2] represents the behavior of the stock price in a risk-neutral world. For the tree to be meaningful, it needs to be calibrated for complying with real-world data. The procedure shifts the mean drift and maintains the volatility. The construction of binomial trees is based on the assumption that the stock price either moves up or down over consecutive periods of time, while its return is the risk-free rate r. The probabilities of ups and down moves are

---

2 See, among many publications designed to "optimize" calibration of various trees, Cox and Rubinstein [22] and Hull [36] for lattice trees.

derived from calibration of the volatility. Standard notations for the stock price are S_u for the upward move and S_d for the downside move. S_u and S_d are derived from the current value by using coefficients u and d such that $S_u = uS_0$ and $S_d = dS_0$, where 0 is the current date. Dividing the horizon from 0 to the maturity of the derivative into small steps, up and down moves are allowed at each step. It is simpler to use $u = 1/d$, so that the tree is recombining. In other words, an up move followed by a down move results in the same original value than before the two consecutive movements.

The payoff of the stock capitalizes the starting value S_0 at the risk-free rate so that the expected payoff after one step equals $\exp(r\Delta t)$. Since we have only two payoffs, the up movement with risk-neutral probability p^* and the down with probability $1 - p^*$, the basic equation between payoffs and original value is:

$$S_0 \exp(r\Delta t) = p^* S_u + (1 - p^*)S_d$$

The stochastic process requires that the volatility over a small time interval Δt is $\sigma\sqrt{\Delta t}$, the same as in the real world. The variance of the return of the stock is calculated as $E(S^2) - [E(S)]^2$ and should be equal to $\sigma^2 \Delta t$:

$$p^* u^2 + (1 - p^*)d^2 - [p^* u + (1 - p^*)d]^2 = \sigma^2 \Delta t$$

We now have two conditions on p^*, u and d, plus $u = 1/d$. The three conditions imply that:

$$p^* = \exp[(r\Delta t) - d]/(u - d)$$

$$u = \exp(\sigma\sqrt{t})$$

$$d = \exp(-\sigma\sqrt{t})$$

This allows constructing the binomial tree of the stock price (Figure 14.1).

The example uses an initial stock price of €100 over only three periods, a monthly interval (0.0833 year), an annual volatility of 30%, and an annual risk-free rate of 5% (Table 14.2). The first step calculates all necessary parameters.

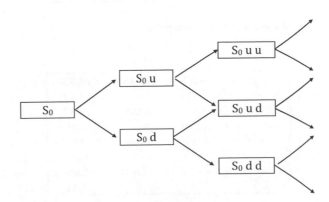

FIGURE 14.1   The binomial tree for the stock price

TABLE 14.2 Parameters
defining the binomial tree

exp($r\Delta t$)	1.0084
exp($-rDt$)	0.9917
u	1.0905
d	0.9170
p^*	0.5266
$1 - p^*$	0.4734

The binomial tree of the stock price is constructed from these parameters (Figure 14.2). For example, the up move, starting from 50 results in a stock price of: $50 \times 1.0905 = 54.52$. The down move results in a stock price of: $50 \times 0.9170 = 45.85$. The same u and d are applied at each step. Two sequential up and down moves result in the same price as the starting price which precedes two up and down moves. From the stock prices, we derive the payoff of the call option as the positive value of stock price minus exercise price, or $S - K = S - 40$ (Figure 14.3).

The valuation process starts from final values which are known at maturity of the option, and moves backward until we reach the current value. When moving back one step, the option value is the expected value of the next step payoffs discounted at the risk-free rate over the time interval. The discount factor is constant for all steps and equal to exp($-r\Delta t$) = 0.9917. For example, starting from the top right-hand corner of the table, we have two payoffs of 24.83 and 14.52. The value of the option is the discounted expected value of these payoffs:

$$(0.5266 \times 24.83 + 0.4734 \times 14.52) \times 0.9917 = 19.79$$

50	54.52	59.46	64.83
			54.52
		50.00	54.52
			45.85
	45.85	50.00	54.52
			45.85
		42.05	45.85
			38.56

FIGURE 14.2   Binomial values of the stock price

10	14.52	19.46	24.83
			14.52
		10.00	14.52
			5.85
	5.85	10.00	14.52
			5.85
		2.05	5.85
			0.00

FIGURE 14.3   Binomial values of the payoff of a call option on stock

11.14	15.18	19.79	24.83
			14.52
		10.33	14.52
			5.85
	6.83	10.33	14.52
			5.85
		3.06	5.85
			0.00

FIGURE 14.4   Binomial tree of the call option value

We proceed in the same way for all cells moving backward, always using the same probabilities, applied to the two next payoffs (Figure 14.4).

When we reach the initial date 0, we find the discounted expected value of all payoffs, which is the value of the option, or 11.14. This is slightly above the payoff at date 0, which is $S - K = 50 - 40 = 10$. The difference is the time value of money. In proceeding backward, we assumed that exercise was feasible only at maturity. We relax this assumption in the example of renegotiations of fixed loan rate by the customers of a bank in Chapter 24.

14.3 THE VASICEK MODEL

The Vasicek one-factor model[3] uses the short-term rate as single factor for modeling bond prices and simulating interest rates. It poses that the rate for maturity T is the continuously compounded instantaneous short-term rates. The Vasicek model is the first model on term structure of rates. The major benefit of the model is that it provides bond prices and rates as closed-form formulas.

The model is an "equilibrium" model that relies on a process for the short rate $r(t)$ in a risk-neutral world, where investors earn $r(t)$, over the small period $(t, t + dt)$. It differs from other models that use a different form for the process driving interest rates, as illustrated by the sample of models mentioned above. It also differs from other types of models, or "arbitrage" models, which aim at modeling the prices of fixed income assets or derivatives.

The basic idea of the model is to form a risk-free portfolio based on two rates of different maturities. Since the rates are correlated, it is easy to derive such a portfolio. The process for $r(t)$ relies on a single source of uncertainty dz. The drift of the process is dependent on $r(t)$, but not on time. The random term is proportional to $\sigma\Delta t$, the volatility of the short-term rate. The model is mean-reverting through a drift factor $\lambda(\mu - r)$, where μ is the long-term value for the short-term rate, supposed given, and λ is the mean-reversion parameter. The process for the short-term interest rate is described by the diffusion equation:

$$dr = \lambda(\mu - r)dt + \sigma dz$$

---

3 See Vasicek [75].

The parameter, λ, is the positive mean reversion term which ensures that the rate $r(t)$ tends to reverse to the mean whenever it is above or below the long-term value μ. The partial differential equation results from the construction of a risk-free portfolio. The equation has a closed-form solution. The value as of t of a zero bond with principal 1 and maturity T is:

$$B(t, T) = E^*[\exp r(T - t)]$$

The "*" denotes the expectation in a risk-neutral world. The continuously compounded interest rate $R(t, T)$ over the maturity $T - t$ is such that the bond value is:

$$B(t, T) = \exp[-R(t, T)(T - t)]$$

By varying T, we generate the entire time structure of rates at t. The value of $R(t, T)$ is:

$$R(t,T) = \frac{1}{T-t} \ln B(t,T)$$

We can illustrate the process of the short-term rate $r(t)$ by plugging in the required inputs: $\lambda = 0.03$, $\mu = 5\%$, $\sigma = 0.05\%$. Simulating the drift of the short-term rate is straightforward. The innovation term is normally distributed, and can be simulated from a random uniform standard number, times the volatility. Then, we cumulate variations across small time steps. For example, starting at $r(t) = 10\%$, we simulate a normal standard innovation dz, -0.7227, from the standard normal inverse function $\Phi^{-1}(U)$, and the innovation term by multiplying by the input $\sigma = 0$. 5%. We obtain a new value for the short-term rate, or 4.639%. Starting from this new value, we run another simulation and so on. The trajectory of the short-term rate is random, as illustrated with 50 time steps. It is shown in Figure 14.5.

The Vasicek closed-form equations provide both the bond price $B(t, T)$ and the interest rate $R(t, T)$ as seen from date t. The zero-coupon bond prices allow calibrating the model with a series of prices of various maturities. The calibration process requires finding the mean-reversion parameter from the bond prices, inputting the long-term rate and the volatility of the short-

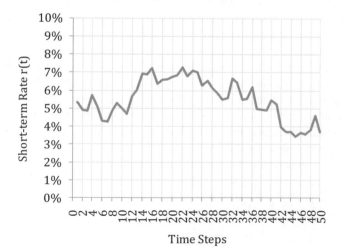

FIGURE 14.5   Short-term rate with 50 time steps

term rate. Once the mean reversion λ is obtained, we derive both $B(t, T)$ and $R(t, T)$ from the formulas. By varying $R(0, T)$, we derive the entire term structure of zero-coupon rates.

The inputs are $\lambda = 0.3$, $\mu = 0.1$, $r(0) = 10\%$ to 1%, by steps of 1%. The mean reversion rate was calibrated in this example from the Euro zero-coupon rates, using the maximum likelihood function[4]. The equations for the bond prices and the interest rate are as follows:

$$P(t,T) = A(t,T)\exp\left[-B(t,T)r(t)\right]$$

$$R(t,T) = \frac{1}{T-t}\ln\left[A(t,T)\right] + \frac{B(t,T)r(t)}{T-t}$$

The bond prices and the interest rates depend on the functions:

$$B(t,T) = \frac{1}{\lambda}\left\{\exp\left[-B(t,T)r(t)\right]\right\}$$

$$A(t,T) = \exp\left\{\left[\frac{1}{\lambda^2}\right]\left[B(t,T)-T+t\right]\left[\lambda^2\mu-\left(\frac{\sigma^2}{2}\right)\right] - \frac{\sigma^2\left[B(t,T)\right]^2}{4\lambda}\right\}$$

In the application, we set t at 0, the current date.

The term structure of the interest rate is generated once we have the simulation process calibrated. They can be upward or downward sloping and show a bump, depending on the inputs and the calibration. With the above values, we show various curves that depend on the initial value of $r(0)$, which can be generated randomly, as illustrated above. The values used for generating these curves are shown in Table 14.3.

For obtaining each curve, we start from a random value of $r(0)$ and we calculate $R(0, T)$ using the model formulas (Figure 14.6).

The model allows simulating the term structure of interest rates. It depends on only one factor, which is restrictive.

For simulations of interest rates, for ALM and VaR application, a common practice is to use the principal component analysis method, which is described in Chapter 32 on factor models, and implemented later on the chapter on interest rate simulations (Chapter 37).

TABLE 14.3

λ	0.300
μ	0.050
σ	0.020
$r(0)$	0.100
t	0.000

---

4 The principle of the maximum likelihood function is explained in the Chapter 16 on modeling volatilities.

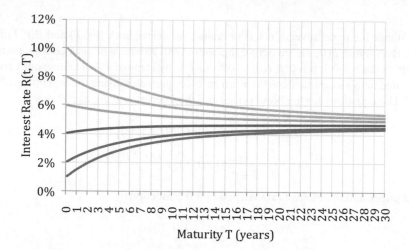

FIGURE 14.6 Simulation of term structure of interest rates (Vasicek's model)

SECTION 5

Risk Modeling

Risk models use different metrics. All are widely used. They include:

- sensitivity: a measure of the response of an asset value to a shock on the underlying market parameters, commonly called "risk factors"
- volatility: a measure of the magnitude of variations of an asset value or of its risk factors – volatility is the second moment of probability distribution, or standard deviations
- downside risk or, more commonly, "value-at-risk," or "VaR": value-at-risk is the modeled value of potential losses in monetary value which synthesizes all risk metrics in a single potential loss figure.

VaR became a building block of risk models. Pre-requisites for modeling VaR are sensitivities and volatilities. The principle for determining VaR is to find a value of potential losses that will not be exceeded on more than a very small fraction of all possible scenarios. When relying on value, or loss, distributions, the VaR is always based on a value, or loss, percentile. A percentile of a distribution is a value defined by the probability that the random values are lower or equal to that value.

The sequence used to model VaR is as follows (Figure S5.1). The same sequence is used in the chapters of this section.

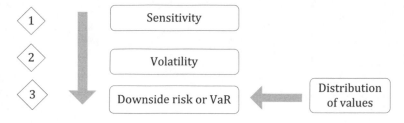

FIGURE S5.1

This section comprises four chapters addressing:

- sensitivity measures (Chapter 15)
- volatilities measures and models (Chapter 16)
- VaR calculations, combining these measures, for market risk VaR and a simple application to credit risk, rely on much simplified examples, representative of more elaborated VaR models as expanded in the market risk and the credit risk sections (Chapter 17)
- VaR and risk-based capital for market risk and credit risk, using the standard terminology for characterizing loss distributions as implemented in risk management practices as well as in regulations (Chapter 18).

15

Sensitivity

Risk management relies on quantitative measures of risks. There are various risk metrics. Sensitivities measure the response of a target variable to a unit movement of a single market parameter, for instance, an interest rate shift of 1%. They are the inputs of the market VaR calculations for linear instruments. In general, asset values depend on several market parameters or on underlying asset values. Those are called "risk factors."

In some cases, sensitivities can be calculated from closed-form formulas providing the price of an asset, such as the Black-Scholes formula for options. In other cases, sensitivities can be approximated from the Taylor expansion formula, which makes variations of value a function of the changes of its arguments multiplied by the first-order partial derivatives with respect to each risk factor. Sensitivities can also be calculated numerically by applying a change of one risk factor and calculating the numerical variation of value of the target asset.

This chapter provides examples of well-known sensitivities for stocks, bonds and mark-to-market values of loans, and options. Sensitivities for some instruments such as forward contracts can be derived from the replicating portfolio. The general Taylor expansion formula can show how asset values vary due to changes in risk factors, considering both first-order terms, which are the sensitivities, and second-order terms. Linear instruments are those which depend linearly on changes of risk factors. The last section explains briefly the applications of sensitivities for hedging, which implies matching the sensitivities of the hedged instrument with those of the hedging instruments.

Contents

15.1 SENSITIVITY DEFINITIONS

Sensitivities are responses of a target variable to changes of risk factors. Variations of values can be expressed in monetary units or in % of initial value. Percentage sensitivities are ratios of the relative variation of value to a shock on the underlying parameter. For instance, the sensitivity of a bond price with respect to a unit interest rate variation of 1% is equal to 5. This sensitivity means that a 1% interest rate variation generates a relative price variation of the bond of $5 \times 1\% = 5\%$. The sensitivity can be measured in monetary units as the change of the value of an instrument for a given change in the underlying parameter. If the bond price is €1000, its variation is $5\% \times 1000 = €50$.

Let V be the market value of an instrument. This value depends upon one or several market parameters, m, that can be prices (such as indexes) or percentages (such as interest rates). By definition:

$$S(\text{value}) = \Delta V / \Delta m$$

$$s(\% \text{ change of value}) = [\Delta V / V] / \Delta m$$

From the above formulas, there is a simple relationship between percentage sensitivities and value sensitivities since:

$$s(\% \text{ change of value}) \times V = \Delta V / \Delta m = S(\text{value})$$

The sensitivity is only an approximation because it provides the change in value for a small variation of the underlying parameter. It is a "local" measure because it depends on current values of both the asset and the market parameter. If they change, both S and s do.

Most assets depend on several risk factors, and their variation of value is a function of several market parameters m_k:

$$\Delta V = \sum_{1 \text{ to } K} S_{ik} \Delta m_k$$

The index k refers to the market parameters, with k varying from 1 to K.

15.2 COMMON SENSITIVITIES

Sensitivities, generically named "deltas," are well known. Some common sensitivities for plain vanilla instruments are reviewed in this section.

15.2.1 Stocks

The sensitivities for stocks relate percentage variations of values, or returns, to percentage variations of a stock index, or stock index returns. They are statistical measures. The "beta" (β) relates the change in stock price to the change of the market index for the same period. It is the sensitivity of the equity return (a percentage change) to the index return (a percentage change). The capital asset pricing model (CAPM)[1] provides the theoretical required return by the market as a function of risk measured by β. The required return on stock, r_i, is equal to the risk-free rate plus a risk premium equal to β times the excess index return r_m over the risk-free rate r_f:

$$r_i = r_f + \beta(r_m - r_f)$$

The β is the coefficient of the regression of historical equity returns against the historical index returns measured over the same time intervals. Both returns are measured as percentage variations or logarithmic returns.

$$r_i = \beta_i r_m + \alpha + \varepsilon_i$$

The β equals 1 by definition for the equity index. The general risk of stock returns results from the general market index changes. The error term is the specific risk, or the fraction of the risk independent of the index. The variance of stock return sums up the variance due to general risk and the variance due to the error term, or specific risk, because they are independent. It is:

$$\sigma^2(r_i) = \beta_i \sigma^2(r_m) + \sigma^2(\varepsilon_i).$$

The betas of stock returns are mostly important for stock portfolio management. If a stock has a beta of 1.2, a change of the index return Δr_m of 1% results, in the average, into a 1.2% increase of the price return r_i. High beta stocks should be selected by portfolio managers in bullish (up) markets and low beta stocks in bear (down) markets.

15.2.2 Bonds and Loans

The sensitivity of bond prices to interest rate shocks is the "duration." If the duration of a bond is 5, it means the bond value will changes by 5% when all rates deviates by 1%. A common measure of sensitivity for bond is the basis point "DV01" measure of bond sensitivity. A basis point ("bp") is 1% of 1%, or 0.0001. In the previous example, the basis point change of the bond value is 5 bp for 1 bp change of all interest rates.

Since bonds depend on interest rates of various maturities, it is convenient to assume a parallel shift of all rates. The sensitivity of a bond to a parallel shift of all rates is the duration. The duration formula relates the change of the bond value to the shock on interest rates[2]:

$$\Delta B = -D\,B\,\Delta i$$

In this formula, B is the bond value, D is the duration and Δi is the common shock to all rates. The cash flows are F_t for the different dates t, and r_t are the market rates. The asset value V is:

$$V = \sum_{t=1,N} \frac{F_t}{(1+y_t)^t}$$

---

1 The original presentation is in Sharpe (1964).
2 The book of Bierwag is entirely dedicated to duration [11].

Consider that a common shock Δy applies to all rates y_t, which become $y_t + \Delta y$, and we take the derivative with respect to Δy rather than with respect to each rate y_t. This derivative is the duration:

$$Duration = \frac{\sum_{t=1,N} t\, F_t / (1 + y_t)^t}{\sum_{t=1,N} F_t / (1 + y_t)^t}$$

The duration is the weighted average of the present values of cash flows, weights being the dates of the cash flows, divided by the bond value. The duration formula seems complex. It represents the weighted average maturity of future flows, using the ratio of the present value of each flow to the present value of all flows as weights for the different dates[3]. The duration of a zero-coupon bond is equal to maturity T, which results from the above theoretical formula when using a single cash flow.

It is easy to derive the variation of value when a single interest rate changes. We simply derive one of the above terms summing up to the value, with respect to this particular rate. This is the rule followed by such measures as "DV01," which measure the change of value for an interest rate change of 1 basis point. But it is convenient to have changes of value when the entire curve shifts.

Since a bond discounts cash flows, each one with the interest rate matching the maturity of the cash flow, the sensitivity due to a shock in any particular interest rate is the variation of value of this discounted cash flow. The bond value sums up all discounted cash flows, the term for the cash flow at date t, F_t, being $F_t / (1 + i_t)^t$. Using the proxy formula $1/(1 + r) \sim 1 - r$, the variation of value of the bond to a change of i_t is approximately $F_t (1 - t\Delta i_t)$. The exact formula is the derivative of this single discounted cash flow with respect to i_t.

Since bond values are sensitive to credit spread, any widening of spreads reduces the value. The sensitivity of bonds with respect to credit spreads is also the duration.

For non-tradable assets, such as banking loans, sensitivities to interest rates also apply to their mark-to-market, or mark-to-model[4], values and are durations. A case in point is the economic value of the banking portfolio balance sheet. The economic value (EV) of the balance sheet is the net mark-to-model value of assets minus liabilities, using as discount rate the risk-free rate. Both assets and liabilities have durations, and the sensitivity of EV to interest rate change depends on their relative durations.

Note that the duration is not constant when interest rates change. The duration is a local measure. The change of the sensitivity of a bond or a loan when interest rates change is the second derivative of the value with respect to a common shift of all interest rates. Finally, the duration of a variable rate bond is zero because such bond values remain constant when interest rates change[5].

---

3   This is different from the simple time-weighted average of flows because of discounting.
4   Marking to market uses all market parameters for valuation, while mark-to-model uses only a subset and cannot produce market prices. For examples, loans can be market-to-model but not fully mark-to-market because there are no trading prices for loans.
5   This is demonstrated in Chapter 7 on interest rates and interest rate derivatives.

15.2.3 Options

The value of options depends upon a number of parameters, as shown originally in the Black–Scholes model: the value of the underlying, the horizon to maturity, the volatility of the underlying, the risk-free interest rate. The model is in line with intuition. The option value increases with the underlying asset value, with its volatility, with the maturity, and decreases with the interest rate. Options sensitivities are known as the "Greek letters."

The sensitivity with respect to the underlying asset is the "delta" (δ). The formula for the delta of stock options is simply Δ call (put) = $\delta\Delta S$. The delta is low if the option is "out-of-the-money" (asset price below strike) because we do not get any money by exercising unless the asset value changes significantly. However, when exercise provides a positive payoff, δ gets closer to 1 because the payoff of the option increases by the same amount as the underlying asset.

The sensitivity can be anywhere in the entire range between 0 and 1, and the highest change of the sensitivity occurs when underlying value is close to the strike price. The variation of δ is the "convexity" of the option. Gamma (γ) is the change of the delta when the underlying changes. It is the change of the slope of the curve representing the option value as a function of the underlying. The option is sensitive to the time-to-maturity because a longer horizon increases the chances that the stock moves above the strike price. The sensitivity with respect to residual maturity is theta (θ). The Greek letter θ measures the "time decay" of the option value. The higher the volatility of the underlying asset, the higher is the chance that the value moves above the strike during a given period. Hence, the option has also a positive sensitivity to the underlying asset volatility, which is the "Vega" (ν). Since any payoff appears only in the future, today's value requires discounting, which implies a negative sensitivity to the level of the risk-free interest rate. "Rho" (ρ) is the change due to a variation of the risk-free rate.

Other options on interest rates or exchange rates follow similar principles. There are closed-form formulas for plain vanilla options. Accordingly, there are sensitivities similar to the delta of stock options and others.

15.2.4 Forward Contracts and Interest Rate Swaps

For all instruments that can be replicated by a portfolio of other instruments, the sensitivities are derived from those of the components of the replicating portfolio. For the forward family of contracts, the replicating portfolio is static. This makes it easy to derive the sensitivities of these instruments.

All forward contracts can be replicated with static portfolios. Hence, they have a closed-form valuation formula. The sensitivities are derived either analytically or numerically using such formulae. For example, a forward exchange contract depends on three risk factors, the spot rate and the two interest rates in the two currencies. Similarly a forward interest rate contract is replicated from lending and borrowing the same amount in the same currency for differing maturities. It has a long and a short leg, each with a single final cash flow. The sensitivities of each leg are the durations of those cash flows with the appropriate signs.

Interest rate swaps (IRSs) can be seen as borrowing and lending the same amount in a single currency for the same maturity, with different interest rates. Under the "horizontal" view, the sensitivity with respect the fixed rate is that of the fixed rate leg. Note that the sensitivity of an IRS is entirely due to the fixed leg since the variable rate leg has zero duration.

15.3 SENSITIVITY AND RISK FACTORS

Sensitivities are ratios of the variation of a target variable, such as interest margin or change of the mark-to-market values of instruments, to a shock of the underlying random parameter driving this change. This property makes them very convenient for measuring risks, because they link any target variable of interest to the underlying sources of uncertainty that influence these variables. Those sources of uncertainty are underlying assets for derivatives or market parameters. They are called "risk factors."

The basic formula for understanding sensitivities and their limitations is the Taylor expansion formula. The formula expresses the value of any function $f(x)$ as equal to its value when the argument has value x_0 plus various terms that depend on the difference between x and x_0. The formula is primarily used for small variations around x_0, otherwise it becomes a proxy. The function is commonly the value of an asset, such as an option.

The Taylor expansion formula was introduced in Chapter 12, when introducing Ito lemma for a function of two variables. With a single variable, it simplifies into:

$$f(x) - f(x_0) = \frac{1}{1!} \frac{\partial f(x_0)}{\partial x}(x - x_0) + \frac{1}{2!} \frac{\partial^2 f(x_0)}{\partial x}(x - x_0)^2 + \ldots + \frac{1}{n!} \frac{\partial^n f(x_0)}{\partial x}(x - x_0)^n$$

Notations are abbreviated by writing the small variation of x as:

$$f(x + \Delta x) - f(x) = \frac{1}{1!} \frac{\partial f(\Delta x)}{\partial x} \Delta x + \frac{1}{2!} \frac{\partial^2 f(\Delta x)}{\partial x} \Delta x^2 + \ldots + \frac{1}{n!} \frac{\partial^n f(\Delta x)}{\partial x} \Delta x^n$$

The formula says that, with deterministic variables, a small change of the variable results in a change than can be approximated by the first term which is a function of Δx. A better approximation is obtained by using the second-order term.

The first derivative applied to Δx is the sensitivity, or the first-order term. The second-order term is the change of the sensitivity when Δx is not negligible. The second-order derivative is the first derivative of the sensitivity. The Taylor series makes explicit the change of value of instruments as a function of the first-, second-, third-order derivatives and so on. For large changes, it is preferable to consider additional terms, beyond first-order terms, of Taylor expansion of the equation relating the value to these parameters. In all cases, using terms beyond the first derivative provides better proxies of any non-linear relation between value and risk factors.

When the second-order terms can be neglected, the instrument is called "linear" because its variation of value relates linearly to the risk factors. Options are non-linear instruments because of the "kink" of the payoff when the underlying asset has a value equal to the strike price. The option value shows smoother variations than payoff because of the time value of options, but the delta changes significantly with the underlying value.

The above formula can be extended to any number of variables. For example, if we have two variables, the formula extends and seems more complex, but first-order changes are always the first derivatives. The generic formula with two variables is well known because it serves as a starting point for the Ito lemma. In the two-variable case, the function is $f(x, y)$, and when moving x and y slightly away from the initial point (x_0, y_0), the variation of the function is approximated by the Taylor expansion. Derivatives are now partial derivatives with respect to either one of the variables, and so on, as follows. The function and partial derivatives are calculated at the starting point (x_0, y_0) and $\Delta x = x - x_0$ and $\Delta y = y - y_0$:

$$f(x, y) = f(x_0, y_0) + \frac{\partial f}{\partial x} \Delta x + \frac{\partial f}{\partial y} \Delta y + \frac{1}{2!} \left[\frac{\partial^2 y}{\partial x^2} \Delta x^2 + \frac{\partial^2 y}{\partial y x^2} \Delta y^2 + \frac{\partial^2 y}{\partial x \partial y} \Delta x \Delta y + \ldots + \ldots \right]$$

Typical Greek letters are notably used for options, but extend to other assets as well. In general, value depends on several factors, for which first-order and second-order derivatives are calculated with respect to each of the risk factors. Considering the example of an equity option:

- delta or δ is the first-order change
- gamma, or γ, is the second-order derivative: it measures by how much the sensitivity changes when the variations of Δx are not small enough to ignore the second order
- vega, ν, is the variation of value of an option due to a change of volatility: volatility is a measure of the instability of a risk factor, which is detailed in the next chapter.

Market risk models widely use sensitivities, these "Greek letters," relating market instrument values to the underlying risk factors that influence them. Delta-VaR for market risk and linear instruments relies on sensitivities or first-order proxies of change of the value of positions exposed to market risk.

Sensitivities apply as well to non-market instruments. For example, the variable rate gap model is the sensitivity of the net interest income, NII, to a shock of an interest rate in the banking portfolio[6]. The gamma also exists for NII because there are options embedded in banking products.

First-order sensitivities have two major drawbacks:

- They always refer to a given change of risk factors (such as a 1% shift of interest rates), without considering that some parameters are quite unstable (or "volatile") while others are not.
- They depend on the prevailing conditions, and are "local" measures. If the market conditions change or if time drifts, the sensitivities are not constant. This is notably true for options where a small change of the underlying asset, such as a stock, might result in significant changes of sensitivities.

The chapter on market VaR (Chapter 35, Delta-normal VaR) uses the sensitivities of a forward foreign exchange contract for calculating VaR, and starts with the decomposition into "elementary" positions depending on each one of the risk factors, the spot exchange rate and the two interest rates of each currency, using sensitivities with respect to these risk factors.

15.4 SENSITIVITIES AND RISK CONTROLLING

Risk controlling implies controlling sensitivities to risk by taking offsetting positions to the same risk factors. The size of the hedging position depends on the relative sensitivities of the hedged instruments and the hedging instruments, as it was the case for hedging a short position on an option, for example. Delta hedging refers to offsetting the option value by a position on the underlying instrument, as a direct implication of forming risk-free portfolios for option valuation purpose. Since an option has several sensitivities, other sensitivities than delta remain

---

6 The gap model is presented in Chapter 23.

un-hedged, such as the vega. Hedging positions should consider all sensitivities, notably delta, gamma and vega for options.

When the hedging instruments do not depend exactly on the same factors as the hedged position, there is basis risk, implying that the two positions do not offset exactly (for example when using traded futures on assets different than those being hedged but which are correlated). In hedge accounting, a hedge is recognized based on its effectiveness. Effectiveness is measured by the adequacy of the hedging instruments in offsetting variations of value of the hedged instrument, which depends on how much is offset, for how long and on the correlation between the risk factors of the two instruments.

Portfolios of instruments are sensitive to potentially hundreds of risk factors. All interest rates, exchanges rates, stocks, etc. Risk management implies considering sensitivities to all factors, while individual instruments are sensitive only to a fraction of all risk factors.

16

Volatility

Volatility is a critical variable in risk because it measures the magnitude of deviations from the mean of a market variable. Sensitivities only measure the response of a market variable to a given shift of risk factors, but they ignore the volatility of risk factors. Combining sensitivity with volatility provides a more comprehensive view of how unstable a market variable is depending on risk factors. Hence both sensitivities and volatility are required to measure the instability of a market variable depending on risk factors.

The first section covers the definition of volatility. The simplest definition of the volatility of random variables is the standard deviation. Volatilities are generally calculated for returns, which can be measured by discrete returns or logarithmic returns. Such volatilities are equally weighted sample historical volatilities. When the distribution of returns is stationary, the historical volatility measure is subject to the sampling error. Implicit volatilities are embedded in the price of options.

Unfortunately, volatilities, whatever the measure, are unstable[1]. In a second step, we focus on time-varying volatilities. The second section introduces the simplest method for addressing time variations, the exponentially weighted moving average (EWMA). The technique assigns higher weights to the most recent observations. The second methodology is based on GARCH models, which do not rely on stationary distributions. It is presented in the third section. The estimates of both EWMA and GARCH volatilities rely on the maximum likelihood estimation, which is introduced in the fourth section. The last section provides an estimate of EWMA, viewed as a specific case of the GARCH volatility, using actual data on equity indices.

---

1 There are a number of publications on modeling volatilities. The Risk publication on "Volatility" addresses all modeling issues [39]. The RiskMetrics document [38] provides a number of insights for modeling volatilities. The text of Brooks (2008) covers all financial series econometrics [13].

Contents

16.1 VOLATILITY

The variance is the second moment of a distribution of a random variable. The standard deviation is the square root of the variance. Both measure the dispersion of random variables around the mean. The volatility is the standard deviation of a market variable.

Measuring volatility raises several issues. First volatility is unobservable. Considering a market variable, the direct measure of standard deviation would proceed from historical time series of observations. The time series is defined by the frequency of observations and the time window over which observations are collected. The simplest scheme for calculating historical volatility is to use equal weights to all observations, the common weight being the inverse of the number of observations k, or $1/k$.

Because time series are samples of all observations, the "true" value of volatility is not observable. The sampling error decreases with the number of observations. Standard sampling theory provides the confidence interval for the range of values within which the estimate of volatility should range within some confidence interval. The best estimate over a sample is obtained by dividing the sum of squared deviations by $k-1$ instead of k, as the theory of sampling implies. This estimate of variance, or volatility, is an equally weighted sample variance or an equally weighted sample historical volatility.

Historical volatilities assume the random variable follows a stochastic process through time that this is identically independently distributed, or "i.i.d.," with, notably, constant variance. When a distribution does not change over time, it is "stationary." Practitioners know that distributions are not stationary and use various techniques for capturing volatility that is most relevant in current conditions. The most obvious and simple technique is to use a window of observations that shifts when times passes, for example using only the most recent daily observations over a year. This is the familiar moving average technique, assigning equal weights to all observations within the time window.

There are other volatilities than historical volatilities. The implied volatility is the volatility embedded in the value of options. It is obtained by inverting the Black-Scholes formula, looking for which value of volatility matches observed prices. Implied volatilities in option prices vary depending on strike and maturity ("the volatility surface") at any given date. Series of implied volatility are calculated with at-the-money options. Implicit volatilities look forward by definition, as market prices do, but they might be very unstable.

We need to expand the "i.i.d." assumptions and make explicit its implications. Next, we address the issue of the constant volatility assumptions. Casual calculation observations of historical volatilities show that sample measures are volatile through time and that such variations exceed the sampling errors. Time-varying volatilities are of major importance. When looking at market behavior, it is easy to see that market variables are relatively stable over some periods and become much higher in crisis times. There are spikes in volatilities. When volatility cannot be considered constant, we need to factor in the stochastic behavior of volatility and give up on the constant variance and the stationary assumptions. The most common techniques for addressing this issue consist of changing the weighting scheme, giving up the equal weight rule for calculating volatility, and the GARCH family of models, the most common being the so called GARCH (1, 1) model.

16.2 EQUALLY WEIGHTED HISTORICAL VOLATILITY

Measuring historical volatility over long periods would provide the long-term estimate of volatility, or "unconditional" volatility. Unfortunately, volatilities are time varying and such long-term volatility is not representative of current conditions. Calculating volatilities over the short-term is the simplest way of capturing volatility conditional on current conditions. The number of observations cannot be too small otherwise the sampling error would be too large. A common practice is to use daily observations over a year, or 250 working days.

If we use daily, weekly or annual observations, we find daily, weekly and annual volatilities, respectively. When time passes, the instability of a random variable should increase when the horizon gets longer. The longer the time band, the higher the chance of observing large deviations. Because weekly observations over a year are much less numerous than daily observations, the sampling error would be larger. The practical rule of using daily observations over a year, or approximately 250 daily observations, is a good compromise.

Volatilities over different periods than a day are required. For example, regulations require comparing volatilities over 60 days and over 250 days and using 10-day volatilities. We need a rule for moving from daily volatilities to volatilities over t days. The "i.i.d." assumption resolves the issue, based on theoretical foundations for returns, discussed as an intermediate step. Volatility applies to any random variable, but is often applied to random returns.

16.2.1 Continuous Returns and Variance

When returns are "i.i.d.," the successive returns are independent, which fits the foundations of efficient markets. Consider the variance of the logarithmic return $\ln(V_h/V_0)$. The variance is the sum of the variances of intermediate logarithmic returns $\ln(V_{i+1}/V_i)$, since these returns are independent. Using $r(i) = \ln(V_{i+1}/V_i)$, we assume that the continuous expected return is constant r and has constant variance σ^2. Assume that we have n sub-periods. The compounded logarithmic return has a variance equal to n times the variance of the instantaneous return, or $n\sigma^2$. Accordingly, the uncertainty measured by the standard deviation of continuous return rises as the square root of time, following the simplified formula:

$$\sigma(n) = \sigma(1)\sqrt{n}$$

In this formula, the variance, or the volatility, is that of the logarithmic return.[2]

---

2 The formula is identical to the formula in Chapter 12, where it was derived as a simple application of a Wiener process, without drift.

The standard framework considers that returns are identically independent distributed (or i.i.d.). Successive logarithmic returns are independent with same variance if the distribution is stationary. The variance grows proportionally to time and the volatility grows proportionally to the square root of time. This is summarized by the statement: "uncertainty grows as the square root of time," where uncertainty is measured by standard deviation or return volatility.

The practical application is to scale up daily volatility over any time horizon, as long as the i.i.d. assumption holds. The typical rule is to use daily observations over a year for determining the equally weighted daily historical volatility. Daily volatilities can be scaled over various horizons t using the square root of time rule $\sigma(t) = \sigma(1)\sqrt{t}$.

For example, the 10-day volatility, the horizon used for regulations for market risk, would be obtained by scaling by $\sqrt{10} = 3.162$, the daily volatility. The annualized historical volatility, starting from daily volatilities, is $\sigma(250) = \sigma(1)\sqrt{250} = 15.8114\sigma(1)$, where the argument within brackets is the time period in days. This annualized volatility is commonly used for characterizing volatilities. Assume that the daily volatility or daily standard deviation of stock index return for the last 250 working days is 2%. The 10-day volatility is $\sigma_{10} = \sigma_1\sqrt{10} = 2\% \times 3.16 = 6.32\%$, using as subscript the number of days. The annualized volatility is $\sigma_{250} = \sigma_1\sqrt{250} = 2\% \times 15.81 = 31.62\%$. The time coefficients applying to volatility are the square roots of time, time being measured with same unit as volatility (in days for daily volatilities and so on).

16.2.2 Historical Volatility with Equally Weighted Observations

The historical volatility, under i.i.d. assumptions, can be calculated using moving windows of time periods. The standard method uses moving windows of observations. For example, we use 250 daily observations, and the window moves when time passes. Assume that there is a spike at some past date. As long as the spike is within the observation window, it will affect the historical volatility estimate. As soon as the spike moves out from the windows, the volatility estimate decreases.

There are other pitfalls with the historical volatility. Successive returns are assumed to be independent, but they might actually be serially correlated. Serial correlation means that high returns tend to be followed by high or low returns. For the long-term horizon, the volatility derived from the square root of time rule would become infinite, which is unacceptable. Many phenomena are "mean-reverting," such as interest rates. Mean-reversion means that when deviation from a long-term value grows larger, a term adds up to the random variation that tends to offset partially such deviations and makes them more likely to revert to zero.

In addition, real phenomena are not "stationary," implying that volatilities are not stable over time, and the assumption does not hold. More elaborated approaches try to capture the instability of volatility over time. They use a moving average with or without assigning higher weights to the most recent observations, or GARCH models of the time behavior of observed volatilities.

16.3 EXPONENTIALLY WEIGHTED MOVING AVERAGE (EWMA) MODEL

Volatilities are unstable. Depending upon the period, they can be high or very low. There are a number of techniques for dealing with this issue. Some are very simple, such as taking the highest between a short-term volatility (3 months) and a long-term volatility (say 2 years). If volatility increases, the most recent one serves as reference. If there are past periods of high volatility, the longer period volatility serves as a reference. The exponentially weighted moving average model (EWMA) use weights decreasing exponentially when moving back in time. RiskMetrics use a variation of these "averaging" techniques[3].

Let us define σ_t as the volatility of a market variable on day t as estimated from day $t - 1$. The square is the variance σ_t^2. Let r_i be the continuous return between day $i - 1$ and day i. $r_i = \ln(S_i/S_{i-1})$. Use a sequence of information:

$$\sigma_t^2 = \frac{1}{k-1} \sum_{i=1,k} \left[r_{t-i} - E(r) \right]^2$$

Setting $E(r) = 0$, since the expectation of the return is smaller than r over short time intervals, the equally weighted estimate of volatility is:

$$\sigma_t^2 = \frac{1}{k-1} \sum_{i=1,k} r_{t-i}^2$$

It is acceptable to consider that $E(r) = 0$ when the standard deviation of returns is smaller than a daily return. The square of the return becomes the last estimate of the variance under this. The denominator $k - 1$ can be changed to k if we use the maximum likelihood estimate, as shown below, since $k - 1$ is appropriate for statistical sample estimators.

The EWMA assigns higher weights to most recent observations: most recent observations weigh more, old observations weigh less. Old spikes in volatility have a lower influence on volatility with equally weighted averages since they have a lower weight. The EWMA methodology was introduced with RiskMetrics from JP Morgan in 1996.

The formula relies on a parameter, λ, between 0 and 1. The formula for estimating variance over the horizon t and moving back from t to date 0 is:

$$\sigma_t^2 = (1 \times r_{t-1}^2 + \lambda \times r_{t-2}^2 + \lambda^2 \times r_{t-3}^2 + \ldots + \lambda^{t-1} \times r_0^2)/(1 + \lambda + \lambda^2 + \ldots + \lambda^{t-2})$$

In the formula, there are t terms, since the estimates of t depend on all previous squared returns from $t - 1$ to 0. Since $\lambda < 1$, the coefficient applied to past observations is lower than for recent observations and the weights decline when moving backward. When extending the horizon to infinity, the formula simplifies because the sum of a geometric progression with λ equal to $1/(1 - \lambda)$:

$$(1 + \lambda + \lambda^2 + \ldots + \lambda^{t-2} + \lambda^{t-1} + \lambda^t + \ldots) = 1/(1 - \lambda)$$

The expressions of σ_t^2 and σ_{t-1}^2 sum up terms from $t - 1$ to 0 and from $t - 2$ until 0 respectively:

$$\sigma_t^2 = (1 \times r_{t-1}^2 + \lambda \times r_{t-2}^2 + \lambda^2 \times r_{t-3}^2 + \ldots + \lambda^{t-2} \times r_1^2 + \lambda^{t-1} \times r_0^2)(1 - \lambda)$$

$$\sigma_{t-1}^2 = (1 \times r_{t-2}^2 + \lambda \times r_{t-3}^2 + \ldots + \lambda^{t-3} \times r_1^2 + \lambda^{t-2} \times r_0^2)(1 - \lambda)$$

3 JP Morgan, RiskMetrics Technical Document, 1995 [64].

Taking the difference $\sigma^2_t - \lambda\sigma^2_{t-1}$, intermediate terms, except the first term of σ^2_t, or r^2_{t-1}, cancel out: $\sigma^2_t - \lambda\sigma^2_{t-1} = (1 - \lambda)r^2_{t-1}$. The formula of the estimate of the variance of returns as of t becomes:

$$\sigma^2_t = \lambda\sigma^2_{t-1} + (1 - \lambda)r^2_{t-1}$$

According to this formula, updating the variance estimate requires only the previous estimate of variance plus one additional observation.

This leads to a simple interpretation of λ. When λ is high, the estimate reacts less to the last recent observation of return r^2_{t-1}, while the previous estimate of variance σ^2_{t-1} counts more. Conversely, a low λ puts more weight on the most recent observations of return and less weight in last estimate of variance. Since the weight of variance is lower than 1, high variances are followed by decreasing variances until a next spike occurs, a scheme that is commonly observed on variance behavior. Finally, the weighting scheme does not allow any more a one shot drop in volatility due to an old spike of volatility when time passes, as is the case when we use moving time windows to estimate equally weighted historical variances.

EWMA does not change the assumption of constant variance. At the limit, $\lambda = 1$ would make the EWMA exactly equal to the equally weighted estimate. Another intuition for showing that EWMA does not change the i.i.d. assumption would be to consider that EWMA is similar to an equally weighted average when the decay parameter is lower than 1. Distant lagging terms will quickly fall down to zero making the calculation closer to a historical volatility estimate over a time window, which moves forward when time passes. But the decay parameter smoothes out abrupt variations, making the estimate move smoothly. The RiskMetrics document suggest some relatively high values of λ, of 0.94 and 0.97. Such values are sufficient to provide estimates significantly different from the equally weighted 250 days daily data.

16.4 GARCH MODELS

The GARCH family of models[4] aims at modeling the time behavior of volatility. Volatilities seem to follow a mean-reverting process, so that high values tend to smooth out after a while. The models attempt to capture these patterns assuming that the variance calculated over a given period as of at t depends on the variance as of $t - 1$, over the same horizon, plus the latest available observations.

The GARCH model differs from EWMA in that it combines a long-term variance rate with the last estimate of the variance and the last return. GARCH (1, 1) indicates that σ^2_t is based on the most recent observation of the squared return and the most recent estimate of the variance rate, without adding more lagged terms. The (1, 1) model refers to the same lag of one period for squared return and for variance estimate. It can be generalized by using more lagged observations of both variables, but GARCH (1, 1) is the most common. The formula for the GARCH model is:

$$\sigma_t^2 = \gamma\sigma_L^2 + \beta\sigma^2_{t-1} + \alpha r^2_{t-1}$$

---

4   A review of GARCH models can be found in [16]. The current Chapter deals with the simplest form.

The distribution of the return is not identically distributed anymore since its variance now depends on the date t. The variance σ_t^2 is a "conditional variance," dependent upon past observations. The long-term variance is unconditional.

Since the variance changes, we cannot any more use a sampling, weighted or not, for estimating the variance. The appropriate methodology for estimating the variance is the maximum likelihood function expanded in the next section.

Comparing the EWMA model with the GARCH model, we see that, for EWMA, $\gamma = 0$, $\beta = \lambda$ and $\alpha = 1 - \lambda$. We have a single parameter, λ, to estimate. The same process should be used to estimate this single EWMA parameter than for the GARCH (1, 1) model, but it is much simpler to execute. The process for estimating both models is detailed below, after explaining the basics of maximum likelihood estimation.

Before moving to the estimation of variance, note that the model is subject to a number of constraints. In the special case where σ is constant and equal to the long run variance $\sigma_L^2 = \sigma$, we can substitute all terms by this long-term variance. Such variance is also unconditional to the extent that it does not depend on any factor that conditions the variance at date t. Writing that the variance is identical in all terms of the above equation, we find a first constraint:

$$\sigma_L^2 = \gamma \sigma_L^2 + \beta \sigma_L^2 + \alpha \sigma_L^2$$

Therefore, $\gamma + \beta + \alpha = 1$, and $\gamma = 1 - (\alpha + \beta)$. The constraint $(\alpha + \beta) \leq 1$ is required for the weight of the long term variance to be positive. It has to be factored in when estimating the coefficients.

The formula can be used iteratively to show that the GARCH model is consistent with declining weights for lagged terms as we move backward in time. For example, if we substitute the lag 1 estimate of the variance as a function of lagged estimate of variance and squared return as of $t - 2$, we find:

$$\sigma_t^2 = \gamma \sigma_L^2 + \alpha r_{t-1}^2 + \beta \sigma_{t-1}^2 = \gamma \sigma_L^2 + \alpha r_{t-1}^2 + \beta (\gamma \sigma_L^2 + \alpha r_{t-2}^2 + \beta \sigma_{t-2}^2)$$

The coefficient of the r_{t-2}^2 is $\beta \alpha$ and that of lagged σ_{t-2}^2 is β^2. The weights applied to the lag 2 squared returns and variance decline exponentially. A recursive operation shows that the current σ_t^2 becomes a function of lagged r_{t-i}^2 and of lagged σ_{t-i}^2.

16.5 MAXIMUM LIKELIHOOD METHODOLOGY

Because we cannot rely anymore on sampling for GARCH models, we need to use an alternate fitting method than usual statistical method for calibrating the GARCH family of models. Since EWMA is a special case of GARCH (1, 1), the methodology might be used for both, but is simpler when having to estimate only the single decay parameter, λ. We expand here the maximum likelihood methodology and we show an example of data series next.

The maximum likelihood methodology involves choosing parameters that maximize the chances of the observing the data. Assume that we can assign probabilities to each observation and derive the probability of observing the entire set of data. For example, when observations are independent, the probability of observing k values is the product of the probabilities of observing each one. The maximum likelihood methodology finds the parameters of the probability distribution that best match the data set. The methodology can be illustrated for finding the maximum likelihood estimate of a constant variance, as an intermediary step. This would apply to EWMA.

Assume that the returns r_t have a constant variance σ. For assigning a probability, it is assumed that returns follow a normal distribution with mean zero and variance σ. The density of the distribution is:

$$-\frac{1}{\sigma\sqrt{2\pi}}\exp\left(\frac{-r_t^2}{\sigma^2}\right)$$

The probability of observing the k observations of returns is the product of the probabilities of observing each one, since all r_i are independent:

$$\prod_{t=1,k}\frac{1}{\sigma\sqrt{2\pi}}\exp\left(\frac{-r_t^2}{\sigma^2}\right)$$

We need to estimate the variance $V = \sigma^2$. The best estimate of σ^2 is the value that maximizes this expression. Maximizing the product is equivalent to maximizing the logarithm of the product:

$$\ln\left[\prod_{t=1,k}\frac{1}{\sigma\sqrt{2\pi}}\exp\left(\frac{-r_t^2}{\sigma^2}\right)\right]$$

The logarithm is a simple summation, and, leaving aside the constant $1/\sqrt{2\pi}$:

$$\sum_{t=1,k}\ln\left(\frac{1}{\sigma^2}\right)-\sum_{t=1,k}\ln\left(\frac{r_t^2}{\sigma^2}\right)=-k\ln(\sigma^2)-\sum_{t=1,k}\ln\left(\frac{r_t^2}{\sigma^2}\right)$$

The maximum likelihood problem is:

$$\max\left(-k\ln(\sigma^2)-\sum_{t=1,k}\frac{r_t^2}{\sigma^2}\right)$$

For maximizing, we derive with respect to $V = \sigma^2$ and obtain the equation:

$$-k/\sigma^2=-\sum_{t=1,k}(r_t^2/\sigma^4)$$

Or:

$$\sigma^2=\frac{\displaystyle\sum_{t=1,k}r_t^2}{k}$$

The maximum likelihood estimate is the average of squared returns, which matches the statistical calculation of variance over the entire set of return data. Note that the best statistical estimate would impose to divide by $k-1$ instead of k.

16.6 ESTIMATING EWMA VOLATILITY

We now move to non-stationary variance, and the maximum likelihood methodology. The equations are the same as above with similar assumptions, except the constant variance.

Under the GARCH model, the return at date t is normally distributed and the variance σ_t^2 is conditional on time. Since returns are normally distributed and independent, the same equation as above applies, except that the conditional variance changes with time. Observations are indexed with subscript t. The probability of observing k data is:

$$\prod_{t=1,k} \frac{1}{\sqrt{2\pi\sigma_t^2}} \exp\left(\frac{-r_t^2}{\sigma_t^2}\right)$$

For estimating the conditional variance, we maximize the likelihood as above.

$$\max \sum_{t=1,k} 1/\sqrt{2\pi\sigma_t^2} \exp\left(\frac{-r_t^2}{\sigma_t^2}\right)$$

The process requires calculating the time series of returns, deriving the squared returns, then the variance estimate. The graph below fits the EWMA model to the entire time series of stock index return data, using the maximum likelihood estimate, following the steps detailed below. The fit of the EWMA model over the index CAC 40 provides the EWMA variance for the CAC 40 from March 1, 1990 and up to February 25, 2009. Spikes are observed, and the spike for the recent period is much higher. Squared returns are not the variance, but they measure the updating term in the GARCH equation. Figure 16.1 shows the typical time pattern of variance, with variance declining slowly after each spike. The biggest spike is in the recent crisis period, as expected.

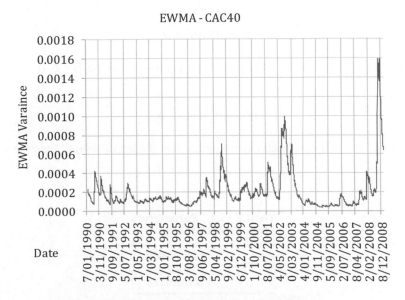

FIGURE 16.1 EWMA estimates of the equity index (CAC 40)

Estimating the GARCH model for the recent period might not be very meaningful because the turmoil of the market created very large deviations. The EWMA smoothly fits time-varying volatilities because the simple weighting scheme depends on a single parameter.

The process for estimating the GARCH $(1, 1)$ model is identical to the process for estimating EWMA. The difference is in the parameters estimated. The parameters to be estimated in the GARCH $(1, 1)$ model are the weighted long term variance $\omega = \gamma \sigma_L^2$ and α and β. The constraints are: $\alpha > 0$, $\beta > 0$ and $(\alpha + \beta) \leq 1$. The parameters for the EWMA model are $\gamma = 0$, $\beta = \lambda$ and $\alpha = 1 - \lambda$. The steps are similar with EWMA and GARCH, except for the coefficients. The calculations are conducted with the EWMA model because there was an exceptional instability of markets in the recent data.

Once we have the time series, we calculate the argument under the maximum operator by summing up across time the terms within brackets. Next we calculate numerically the parameters of the model, factoring in the constraints with which they have to comply. The daily returns are calculated as logarithmic returns $\ln(I_t/I_{t-1})$, where t the time and I the equity index value at date t, or as discrete returns $(I_t - I_{t-1})/I_t$, since both are very close for small variations. The table looks like Table 16.1, with a much longer time series of observations. We show only the first lines, where all calculations start. Dates are moving forward, starting from the oldest date, March 1, 1990. The final date is February 25, 2009. From the two first observations, I_1 and I_2, we derive the first return, as of second date, $r_2 = (I_2 - I_1)/I_1$. The first logarithmic return is calculated in the second line (column "r_t") as $r_2 = \ln(1860/1832) = 0.015168$. The first estimate of variance is the square r_2^2 of the second date return. It is the first value in the σ_t^2 column, or 0.002301.

The next lines of this same third column use the formulas of EWMA model. The process requires plugging in values of the coefficients so that we can determine the maximum likelihood function. By maximizing the likelihood function, we find the right values of the parameters. The calculations shown in Table 16.1 use the best estimate of λ. Starting at the third observation, we calculate the new estimate of the instantaneous variance σ_3^2. Under GARCH, the formula would be:

$$\sigma_3^2 = \omega + \beta \sigma_2^2 + \alpha r_2^2$$

Under EWMA estimates, the GARCH parameters collapse to: $\omega = 0$, $\beta = \lambda$, $\alpha = 1 - \lambda$ and the formula is:

$$\sigma_3^2 = \lambda \sigma_2^2 + (1 - \lambda) r_2^2$$

In this example, α and β have been determined so that the log likelihood function was maximized.

TABLE 16.1   Parameters of the EWMA model

ω	0.00000000
α	0.02918817
β	0.97081183

Using such values, we obtain the second value of the lagging estimate of instantaneous variance, 0.0002250. For all subsequent dates, the same formula is used step by step until we reach the end of the series of observations. The log likelihood function sums k times,

$$\sigma_t^2 - \sum_{t=1,k} (u_t^2 / \sigma_t^2),$$

where k is the total number of observations of the instantaneous variance:

$$-k \ln(\sigma_t^2) - \sum_{t=1,k} (u_t^2 / \sigma_t^2)$$

If we have a total of $t + 2$ observations of returns, the sum adds up t times this log likelihood function. The value of log likelihood function, maximized by choosing λ, appears on top of the last column, as 13138.6. The corresponding value of the parameter is $\lambda = 0.9708$, which is in line with usual estimates (Table 16.1).

Since the function may have several local maxima, the issue is to find the maximum of these maxima. Some algorithms perform better than others. In the example, the solver function of Excel™ was used, which does not guarantee finding the single maximum.

The same procedure serves for estimating the GARCH (1, 1) model, by imposing the above constraints on the maximum algorithm. The GARCH (1, 1) constraints on the coefficients were mentioned above. Summing up, the constraints for the maximization algorithm are:

$$\alpha \geq 0; \; \beta \geq 0; \; \alpha + \beta \geq 0; \; \omega \geq 0$$

The long-term variance should be positive or zero. For estimating the GARCH model, we would proceed with these constraints and maximize the log-likelihood function. Note that it would be possible to reduce the number of parameters to be estimated by setting a value for the long-term variance σ_L^2, which sets $\gamma \sigma_L^2 = \omega$ and $\gamma = 1 - (\beta + \alpha)$. Using $\sigma_L^2 = \omega/\gamma$, the same two parameters remain, with $(\beta + \alpha) < 1$ since $(\beta + \alpha) = 1 - \gamma$.

TABLE 16.2 Calculation of log likelihood function of the EWMA or GARCH models

Date	CAC 40	r_t	σ_t^2	$-\ln(\sigma_t^2) - r_t^2/\sigma_t^2$
		0.000591	0.0001255	13138.6
01/03/1990	1832	$\ln(r_t/r_{t-1})$	$\sigma^2 = r_1^2$	
02/03/1990	1860	0.015168	$\omega + \alpha r_{t-1}^2 + \beta \sigma_{t-1}^2$	
05/03/1990	1874	0.007499	0.0002301	8.133
06/03/1990	1872	−0.001068	0.0002250	8.394
07/03/1990	1880	0.004264	0.0002185	8.346
08/03/1990	1917	0.019490	0.0002126	6.669
09/03/1990	1921	0.002084	0.0002175	8.413
12/03/1990	1912	−0.004696	0.0002113	8.358

17

The Value-at-Risk Measure

This chapter completes the preceding chapters with the calculation of VaR in very simple cases. The purpose is to provide a preliminary view of the VaR modeling framework, without getting into the technicalities of actual VaR models, and to show that the VaR concept applies to different risks. A first simplification is that we only consider the standalone risk of a transaction or a firm, without considering portfolio effects. Another simplification is that we assume that VaR is driven by a single factor, while the actual VaR model depends on a large number of factors. VaR models are expanded on in Section 10 for market risk and in Section 12 for credit portfolios.

Any VaR modeling starts from percentiles of the distribution of the target value. Accordingly, we detail the percentile measure in the first section of this chapter. For market risk, the relevant distribution is that of normally distributed returns of linear instruments. The second section details the process for determining the VaR of a standalone "elementary position" that depends on a single risk factor. This section shows the sequence of steps leading to VaR by combining the previous risk measures, sensitivity and volatility. Value percentiles can also apply to the firm value. Any adverse variation of the firm value can be seen as impairing its solvency and credit standing. The final section shows how VaR for credit risk can be developed for a standalone firm. The methodology is a much simplified view of credit risk VaR in that we do not expand either the details of the Merton model (see Chapter 46) that inspires this example, or portfolio effects.

Contents

17.1 MODELING POTENTIAL VARIATIONS AND PERCENTILES

Because risks are always potential adverse deviations of earnings or of losses, defining "potential" variations is a common module of most risk models. Notably, VaR is the upper bound potential loss not exceeded with some predetermined low probability, called a confidence level.

17.1.1 Modeling Potential Variations of Value

Embedded in VaR models is the rationale of modeling deviations of any parameter at a given confidence level. In the case of VaR, the target variable is the P & L for market risk or credit losses for credit risk. But the same methodology can apply to any other random factor that is of interest. The rationale of measuring adverse deviations has a much wider set of applications than VaR. For example, we might be interested in adverse deviations of value of collateral in collateral-based lending, for assessing the likelihood of collateral deficiency and limiting the probability of such deficiency to a low level. We might be interested in earnings-at-risk, or adverse losses than are not exceeded in more than a fraction of all possible cases. We might want to define the minimum capital required for ensuring a portfolio of credit assets. We might have to stress risk factors to extreme levels with values not exceeded except in a very small fraction of all possible cases. For market-driven exposures, such as those of OTC derivatives (swaps), we might need to define some upper bound of these exposures not likely to be exceeded in more than a small fraction of scenarios.

All such risk issues rely on the same methodology: defining percentiles of the random target variable, which has become a common tool in risk methodology, independently of VaR itself. A percentile of a target random variable is a threshold value of this variable that, depending on the issue, is an upper bound not exceeded with a predetermined probability, or, alternatively, is a lower bound such that the probability of the target variable being higher is predefined.

Because percentiles of a target variable are so commonly used and are important for risk models, including VaR, we redefine them more precisely, as a pre-requisite for illustrating applications in VaR models.

17.1.2 Value Percentile

The methodology used to define potential deviations relies on defining upper or lower bounds to the variable of interest.

The terminology is confusing because risk addresses losses or negative earnings: we look for upper bounds of losses or for lower bounds of earnings. Second, upper or lower bounds are modeled with probabilities of not exceeding upper bounds, or of being lower than lower bounds. This requires defining a couple of associated values: the particular value of the target variable serving as upper or lower bound, and the probability of the variable exceeding the upper bound, or being lower than lower bound.

The standard modeling of potential variations of a target variable is through percentiles, which are probabilities. The target random variable is X. The pre-requisite for defining percentiles is

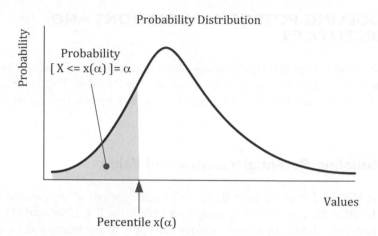

FIGURE 17.1   Probability distribution and percentile

the definition of a distribution. A percentile is always defined as the probability (α) of a variable being lower or equal to an upper bound that we name $x(\alpha)$. By definition of α and $x(\alpha)$.

$$P[X \leq x(\alpha)] = \alpha$$

With these notations, $x(\alpha)$ is the upper bound of x not exceeded with probability α. As a consequence:

$$P[X > x(\alpha)] = 1 - \alpha$$

Therefore, $x(\alpha)$ is also the lower bound exceeded with probability $1 - \alpha$. The cutoff point of X, $x(\alpha)$, paired with probability α, is the α percentile of X. In this expression, α is always a probability of being lower than $x(\alpha)$ and $x(\alpha)$ is the cutoff point of the random variable X of interest.

Figure 17.1 shows the α percentile of X, $x(\alpha)$. The probability that X is lower than this upper bound is the area under the curve, or the cumulative probability density of X at $x(\alpha)$. The probability that X exceeds $x(\alpha)$, considered as a lower bound, is $1 - \alpha$, and is the remaining area on the right-hand side of $x(\alpha)$. Finally, note that percentiles are often called "confidence levels".

17.2 THE VAR METHODOLOGY: MARKET RISK

In this section, we show how to combine the various measures of risk for defining market risk VaR in the case of a very simple position as a percentile of the P & L of the position.

Consider an asset that depends on a single risk factor. There are not many such assets. An example would be a zero-coupon bond whose value depends on the single interest rate applicable at maturity of the bond. For assets which depend on several risk factors and portfolios, we need to fully expand the VaR model, as in the market risk section 10. The single risk factor position is "elementary" because there is no need to go through all technicalities of VaR calculations and we can focus on the three major steps required for deriving market risk VaR.

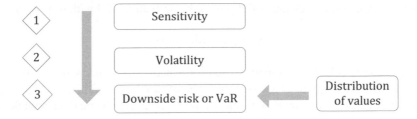

FIGURE 17.2

The three steps combine the previous measures of risk, sensitivity and volatility, for deriving the "value-at-risk," VaR, a measure of potential loss, or "downside risk" (Figure 17.2). VaR or downside risk is the most "comprehensive" measure of risk. It integrates sensitivity and volatility with the adverse effect of uncertainty, but it also relies on assumptions with respect to the distribution of values. The three main steps for an "elementary" position are:

1 measure the sensitivity of the position with respect to the risk factor
2 measure the volatility of the risk factor, and combine the sensitivity of the position and the volatility of the risk factor for deriving the volatility of the position
3 determine a loss percentile at confidence level α, based on an assumption with respect to the distribution of value.

The loss percentile at α is the VaR at the confidence level selected.

This presentation is a prerequisite, starting with an elementary position and using basic assumptions. It is extended to multiple factors positions or portfolios of position in the chapter on delta-normal VaR (Chapter 35).

17.2.1 Sensitivity

Sensitivities measure the response to a given shock of the underlying random parameter, or risk factor referring to a given change of risk factors (such as a 1% shift of interest rates).

Sensitivities are not constant and vary when market conditions change. They are "local" measures and considering them as constant is only a proxy. The zero-coupon bond depends on a single risk factor, the 2-year interest rate applicable as of current date t, or $i(t, T)$, where t is the current date and T the maturity date equal to 2 years. The interest rate is, for example, a risk-free rate: $i(t, 2) = 5\%$. The value of the risk-free zero-coupon bond with maturity $T = 2$ years is the discounted value of the final cash flow $F(T)$:

$$B(t, T) = F(T)/[1 + i (t, T)]$$

Dropping subscripts, t being current date and T being equal to 2 years, and using a final cash flow of 100, the risk-free zero-coupon bond value is:

$$B(0, 2) = 100/(1 + i)^2 = 90.703$$

The response of value B to a change of i by Δi is the derivative of B with respect to i.

$$\Delta B(0, 2) = (\partial B/\partial i)\Delta i$$

The derivative can be calculated from the closed-form theoretical formula. In the case of a bond, it is the duration. The duration of a zero-coupon bond equals its maturity $T = 2$. The random value variations of the zero-coupon bond are a linear function of the random deviations of the interest rate. Using D as duration, with $D = 2$:

$$\Delta B = -D \, B \, \Delta i$$

With $B = 90.703$, and $\Delta i = 1\%$, the monetary value of the bond sensitivity for a 100 basis points change of i is €1.81 or 1.81% of current value.

17.2.2 From Sensitivity to Volatility

The volatility of a position depends on both its sensitivity and the volatility of the underlying risk factors. When there is a single risk factor, the relation is quite simple. When there are several risk factors, all sensitivities to all factors and their dependencies have to be considered. Dependencies are dealt with a separate set of chapters (see Section 9).

The volatility measures the magnitude of the variations of a random variable, such as returns or market parameters. Measuring volatility is discussed in the previous chapter (Chapter 16). In this example, we rely on the common simple measure of historical volatility. The historical volatility is the standard deviation of a time series of observations. The daily historical volatility of interest rate i, $\sigma_1(i)$, is calculated as the standard deviation of the interest rate observed over 250 working days in a year.

There is a linear relation between random value variations and random interest rate variations: $\Delta B = -D \, B \, \Delta i$, considering the initial value of the bond as known as well as its duration, and assuming that the duration is approximately constant. Both ΔB and Δi are random variables. From the relationship, the magnitude of the changes of the bond value depends on both its sensitivity and the magnitude of the variations of interest rates. The standard deviation of a random variable multiplied by a constant is the product of the constant and the volatility of the variable. From above relation, we find the relationship between the volatilities of the two random variables is straightforward.

$$\sigma_1(\Delta B) = +D \, B \, \sigma_1(\Delta i)$$

For proceeding, the daily volatility of i is required. It can be measured in percentage terms or in absolute terms. Let us use 0.1% as the daily volatility of the 2-year rate. The volatility is in monetary units, like the value of the bond. The monetary value of the sensitivity of the zero-coupon is:

$$\sigma_1(\Delta B) = + 2 \times 90.703 \times 0.1\% = €0.1814$$

17.2.3 From Daily Volatility of the Position to Daily VaR

The VaR at confidence level α is the cutoff point of negative P & L variations such that the probability of the P & L being lower than this cutoff point is equal to α. It is the α percentile of the P & L. Let us call X the random P & L. The VaR is the cutoff point of X, $x(\alpha)$, such that $P[X \leq x(\alpha)] = \alpha$.

Back to the example, the determination of VaR at α requires defining a distribution of value for (ΔB). The normal distribution is convenient because it is defined by only two parameters, its mean and its standard deviation or volatility. The one-tailed confidence level α, or α percentile, is embedded in the normal distribution. For each value of α, there is unique deviation from mean equal to a multiple of the standard deviation. The process requires defining the distribution of the P & L. The normal distribution is an acceptable distribution for the short-term horizon and for a zero-coupon bond whose sensitivity is approximately constant when interest rate variations are not too big.

An attractive property of the normal distribution is that the α percentiles are easily defined as multiples of the volatility of the distribution, as described in Figure 17.3. Under this framework, defining the VaR is straightforward. Looking for a VaR at 1% one-tailed confidence level, for a daily horizon, all we need to do is to use the 2.33 multiple matching the 1% percentile for the normal distribution.

$$\text{VaR (1\%, daily)} = 2.33 \times €0.1814 = €0.4227$$

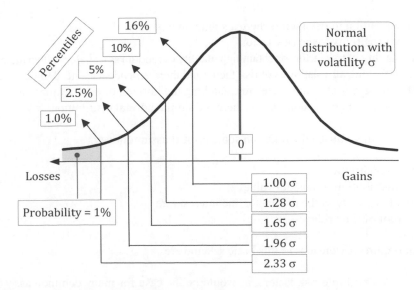

FIGURE 17.3   Normal distribution and one-tailed confidence levels

17.2.4 VaR at Different Horizons

The daily VaR results from the daily volatility. Under some simple assumptions, the volatility was shown to increase as the square root of time. Following this formula, where H is the VaR horizon:

$$\sigma_H = + \sigma_1 \sqrt{H}$$

Taking $H = 10$ days, the horizon selected for the Basel Accord on Market Risk, the 10-day volatility, follows using the "square root of time rule:"

$$\sigma_{10} = \sigma_1 \sqrt{10} = 3.162 \times \sigma_1 = €1.337$$

The 10-day VaR is the multiple of the normal distribution matching the confidence level, or 2.33 for 1%.

$$\text{VaR } (1\%, 10 \text{ days}) = 2.33 \times €1.337 = €3.115$$

Note that using the square root of time rule applies only when sensitivities are approximately constant. With options, it cannot be used. Details are in the market risk chapters (Chapter 35 and 36).

17.2.5 Summary and Extensions

The derivation of VaR shows the basic steps used to derive the VaR.

- Map the position to risk factors, here a single interest rate.
- Measure sensitivity to the risk factor.
- Input volatility of risk factor for obtaining volatility of random asset value. When there are multiple risk factors, all volatilities of risk factor and their dependencies need to be included.
- Use the "square root of time rule" for matching the horizon of the VaR measure.
- Use a distribution of random values, here the simple normal distribution.

As calculated, this VaR model relies on some critical assumptions:

- constant sensitivities
- normal distribution of random values
- historical volatility of the risk factor, the interest rate
- square root of time rule.

The main required extensions of this basic scheme are:

- dealing with multiple risk factors, as would be the case for many common assets and for portfolios of assets
- dealing with non-linear positions, whereby sensitivities cannot be used anymore as a proxy of the change of values
- dealing with dependencies across risk factors and individual positions, which drive the diversification effect of individual risks.

The section dedicated to dependencies (Section 9, Chapters 30 to 34) addresses the issue of portfolio and multiple risk factors that are dependent. The chapters on market risk, notably the delta-normal VaR chapter (Chapter 35), use the same method with several factors and portfolios. This requires modeling dependencies between risk factors and the portfolio variance as a pre-requisite (Section 9). Alternate VaR modeling methodologies, such as non-linearity and other techniques not based on the normal distribution are addressed in Chapter 36.

17.3 CREDIT RISK VAR

The same global methodology can serve for modeling the standalone credit risk of a single firm. Consider a firm whose global value is the present value of its free cash flow at its cost of capital under the framework of valuation defined by Modigliani and Miller [53]. There is no need here to adopt a more general framework, because the actual credit risk models will be expanded in detail in the sections dedicated to standalone credit risk and to credit risk for portfolios (Sections 11 and 12).

17.3.1 The Firm Value

The value of the firm is random because its future cash flows are random. In their simplest setup, Modigliani and Miller assume a static no-growth and no-decay world without tax. Relaxing such assumptions has been done and is found in textbooks of corporate finance. The free cash flow of the firm is the cash flow available to shareholders after other claims from debt holders have been taken care of. Under this simple world, the free cash flow is constant. The firm is all equity funded or has a fraction of debt. This is not important at this stage, because it is shown that the weighted cost of capital (Wacc or w) of the firm depends only on operating risk and is constant whatever the leverage of the firm. If there is no debt, the firm cannot default and the cost of capital is the required return on equity, which depends only on the business risk of the firm. If there is debt, the firm defaults if the asset value falls below the contractual debt payment due at some horizon, which we assume is a given. The value of the firm is the present value of the constant cash flow F at the cost of capital, which collapses to F/w when the cash flow is constant and perpetual.

The firm's solvency is measured by its equity value. Suppose the random cash flow is driven by a single factor, which is the state of the economy. The firm asset value loss is the adverse deviation from its expected value. The firm has an expected cash flow such that its expected return on investment is $E(r)$.

The cumulative yield on investment, from initial date 0 and final date 1, is random and has mean $E(r)$ and standard deviation $\sigma(r)$. The yield is defined as the discount rate that makes the present value of the free cash flows equal to the initial investment, which is the book value of assets A_0. The cash flow is $F = rA_0$, with mean $E(r)A_0$ and standard deviation $\sigma(r)A_0$. As long as the yield of the investment is above the cost of capital, the firm creates value. The value is derived from the random value of the cash flow, and it is random. The loss point is when the firm destroys value. As long as $F > wA_0$, the firm creates value. When the yield on investment becomes equal to the cost of capital, the firm's creation of value is zero because the net present value[1] of the investment is zero. If the yield on investment is lower than the cost of capital, the firm destroys value.

The yield on investment r is random. The firm's value at date 1 is $A_1 = F/w = rA_0/w$. It has mean $E(r)A_0/w$ and standard deviation $\sigma(r)A_0/w$. The loss point for r is w. As long as $F > wA_0$, the firm creates value, otherwise it destroys value. The value of the firm is random. The distribution of value is that of the cash flow, which is driven by r. The firm's solvency is impaired when it destroys value, which occurs when the final value moves below the initial investment. The lower the firm's value below that point, the more is the firm's value impaired, as well its equity value.

17.3.2 The Distribution of Firm Value

The final value is random. Its VaR is adverse deviation of its value matching a percentile derived from the distribution of the firm's final value. Any adverse deviation of the final value can be seen as impairing its credit risk since a lower value implies a lower credit standing. If the firm has debt, the firm's value is still the present value of its free cash flow. If the final value gets below the debt payment obligation due at the horizon, the firm fails because it has not enough value to repay debt. Note that we consider here the face value of debt repayment, not the debt value, which would fall as well when the firm destroys value.

For determining the VaR of the firm's value, we need to plug in a distribution of the firm's value. Since the firm's value is driven by r, the cumulative return from the original date to the final date, the distribution is that of r. The yield of the firm's assets can be considered, like any other continuous return, as following a stochastic process, with a drift and a standard deviation. The ratio of final to initial value is A_1/A_0. From $A_1/A_0 = \exp(rT)$, we find $\ln(A_1/A_0) = rT$. The mean of the logarithm of the ratio is $E(r)T$ and its variance is $\sigma(r)T$. We take $T = 1$, for example one year.

Once we know the mean and the standard deviation of $\ln(x)$, we can derive its distribution, which is log normal (Figure 17.4). The log normal distribution is the normal standard distribution of $[\ln(x) - m]/s$, where m is the mean of $\ln(x)$ and s is its standard deviation[2]. For example, we can set $E(r) = 12\%$ and $\sigma(r) = 30\%$. Such values are those of the mean and standard deviation of the ratio A_1/A_0. Since we know the log normal distribution of the ratio, which is entirely determined by the mean and standard deviation of $\ln(A_1/A_0)$, it is easy to derive the percentiles of the ratio, which should be lower than 1 for the firm losing value.

Table 17.1 shows the percentiles of the ratio: when $\alpha = 90\%$ the final to initial value is 120%. The percentage 90% is the probability that the ratio has a value lower or equal to 120%. When the percentile is 1%, the ratio has a value of 41%: the probability that the ratio is lower or equal to 41% is equal to 1% since $P(A_1/A_0 \leq 41\%) = 1\%$. When the ratio is 41%, the downside variation of value, or loss, is the complement to 1, or $1 - 41\% = 59\%$. The VaR at the 1% confidence level is this loss of value, or 59% of initial asset value. In the case of the log normal

---

1   The net present value of the investment is the present value of future cash flows at the cost of capital w minus the initial investment. It is here equal to $F/w - A_0$. The internal rate of return, or yield of the investment, is such that the present value of cash flows at r equals the initial investment, or $F/r = A_0$. If $r = w$, $F/w = F/r = A_0$. If r is lower than w, $F/w = rA_0/w < A_0$ and the firm's value becomes lower than the investment and the firm destroys value.
2   The general derivation of lognormal percentile is also detailed, with an equivalent methodology, in Chapters 47 and 51, when default risk is modelled through the structural model (chapter 47).

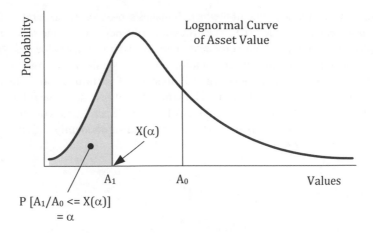

FIGURE 17.4   Distribution of the ratio of initial to final asset value

distribution, the percentiles do not match multiples of volatility since they depend on several parameters: the expected asset value or return, the volatility σ and the horizon.

Now assume that there is a payment obligation due in one year of 60. The firm can face this obligation only if the asset value is higher than the contractual debt payment due. The probability that asset value falls below 60 is around 20%. This is the default probability of the firm.

When considering a threshold of the ratio of final asset value to initial asset value, we see it in different ways. The value percentile is the probability that the value will be lower than this

TABLE 17.1   Percentiles of the ratio of final asset value to initial asset value (expected return 10%, volatility 30%, horizon 1 year)

α	A_i/A_0
99.0%	165%
95.0%	134%
90.0%	120%
80.0%	105%
70.0%	96%
60.0%	88%
50.0%	82%
40.0%	76%
30.0%	70%
20.0%	64%
10.0%	56%
1.0%	41%

threshold. This is a VaR for the value of the firm. It makes sense to view such ratios lower than 1 as a measure of solvency and credit risk. They measure solvency because the ratio represents the decline of equity value. They measure credit risk because, when equity value falls significantly, solvency is so much impaired that credit standing has to be significantly impaired.

This is even more obvious when looking at a threshold of the ratio equal to the ratio of debt contractual repayment to initial asset value. The same percentile making the ratio hit the debt to asset value ratio is simply the default probability of the firm. Such framework for assessing the risk of firms was originally developed by Merton [51] and subsequently called the "structural model of default" (Chapter 47).

18

VaR and Capital

The VaR methodology serves for defining risk-based capital, or economic capital. Economic capital is the capital required to absorb potential unexpected losses at a preset confidence level. The confidence level reflects the risk appetite of the bank. By definition, it is also the probability that the loss exceeds the capital, triggering the bank's insolvency. Hence, the confidence level is equivalent to the default probability of the bank.

In this chapter we lay down the basic definition underlying measures of future losses. Section 18.1 details the merits and drawbacks of the VaR measures. Section 18.2 contrasts the general shapes of the distribution of losses for market risk and credit risk. Section 18.3 defines the standard generic risk measures, expected loss and unexpected loss, derived from such distributions that are implemented throughout this text. The next section explains the direct relationship between VaR and risk-based capital. The last section mentions the "Earnings-at-Risk" measure, which is similar to VaR, as an example of a methodology that can be easily implemented, but which not as comprehensive as VaR.

Contents

18.1 THE CONTRIBUTIONS OF VAR-BASED MEASURES

The VaR concept shines for three major reasons:

- it provides a complete view of portfolio risk
- it measures economic capital
- it assigns fungible values to risks.

Because VaR captures the downside risk, it is the basis for measuring economic capital, the ultimate safety cushion for absorbing losses.

"Earnings-at-Risk," or "EaR," was a much simpler version of VaR. EaR measures provide the potential adverse deviations of earnings and are relatively easy to measure[1]. There is a major distinction between EaR and VaR. EaR does not relate the adverse deviations of earnings to the underlying risk factors, because EaR variations result from all risk factors. By contrast, VaR requires linking losses to risk factors. Although the VaR is an aggregated measure, it can be broken down according to the sources of risk, and, indeed it should be for controlling risks.

VaR has many benefits when compared to traditional measures of risk. It assigns a monetary value to risk, it is synthetic, and it is fungible. Instead of capturing risks through multiple quantitative and qualitative indicators (sensitivities, ratings, watch lists, excess limits, etc.), VaR is a monetary value, making all risk measures fungible, even when the sources of uncertainty differ. Figure 18.1 lists some of the various indicators of risk serving various purposes for measuring or monitoring risks. Traditional measures of market risk for a transaction are the sensitivity of its

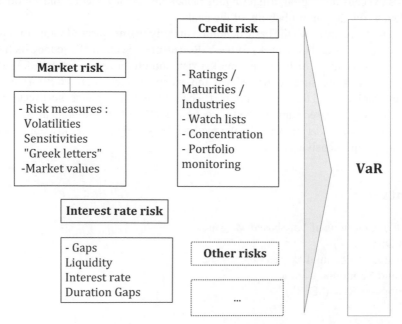

FIGURE 18.1   From traditional measures of risks to VAR

---

1   See for example Matten, 2000, in [50].

value to the variations of market parameters, called risk factors, the volatility, which measures the magnitude of the variations of values or of risk factors (the so-called Greek letters). For credit risk, credit ratings assign a rank to the credit standing of a borrower, and risk management uses watch lists of borrowers which seem to become riskier than predicted, concentration of the credit portfolio in certain industries or regions, etc. Such indicators or quantified measures are not fungible, and it is not possible to convert them into potential losses. By contrast, VaR synthesizes all of them and represents a monetary value.

Because VaR is synthetic it is not a replacement for such specific measures, but it summarizes them and provides a global view.

There are several types of potential losses:

- expected loss "EL"
- unexpected loss "UL"
- exceptional losses.

All three measures require referring to loss distributions. VaR is defined as unexpected loss. For illustrating how the concept is implemented, after this generic presentation we use the well-known normal distribution.

VaR drawbacks are the mirror image of its benefits. Without providing an insight on the sources of risk, it does tell which factors a portfolio is mostly sensitive to. Because it synthesizes risk, it is not adequate for risk management, except for setting up limits on aggregated VaR. But since VaR models do not guarantee backward traceability to sources of risks, it is not suited for other than global limit risk management.

18.2 LOSS DISTRIBUTIONS

Here we consider loss distributions and how they are used for VaR types of measures. Loss distributions differ for market risk and credit risk.

For market risk, losses are adverse price deviations of instruments and portfolios of instruments. There are approximately as many chances that values increase or decrease, and deviations tend to be bell-shaped, with some central tendency. The loss distribution is the truncated distribution of P & L, limited to adverse deviations only. When addressing the measurement of potential losses, the normal distribution is a convenient proxy for actual profit and loss distributions. As is seen later, it forms the basis of the so-called delta-normal VaR, which is acceptable under restricted conditions.

For credit risk, loss distributions result primarily from defaults. Small losses are frequent while large losses are much less likely. This is obvious when considering a single loan. A loan has a loss distribution characterized by a zero loss with probability of, say, 98% and a 100% loss with a 2% probability, this is the default probability of the borrower. When aggregating loans, losses have an asymmetrical distribution whose shape would look like that Figure 18.2. There is a peak close to zero, at 98% along the x-axis which measure losses, and the full loss has only a 2% probability on the far right of the loss x-axis.

Loss distributions can be observed historically for market risk and for credit losses in retail financial activities. The historical observations allow one to find out whether the modeled loss distributions are in line with actual loss realizations. For low-default portfolios, such as those

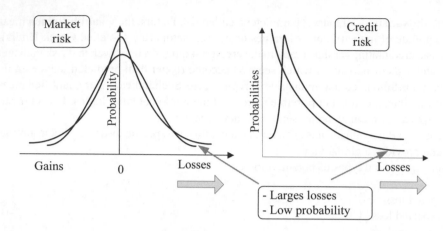

FIGURE 18.2   Loss distributions, fat tails and extreme losses

resulting from lending activities to large corporates, defaults are rare events. Historical defaults are not numerous enough to have a significant number of historical observations, except in retail financial services. Low default portfolios always require models to find out what the loss distribution could be.

18.3 MEASURES OF POTENTIAL LOSSES

There are various measures of potential losses: Expected loss (EL), loss percentiles, unexpected loss (UL) and exceptional losses. Some other measures can also be defined, one of them being the "expected shortfall," or the expected loss beyond a loss percentile. All such measures are defined formally later on, and we provide here broad definitions.

18.3.1 Expected Loss

Expected loss is the probability weighted average of all possible losses. It is widely used for credit losses, notably when there is a large portfolio of loans. In retail financial services, the portfolio is "granular," meaning that all exposures are small compared to the portfolio size and that none has a "large" value.

Expected loss is the mean of the loss distribution. Expected loss provides the foundation for economic provisioning. The expected loss measure used in Basel 2 as a benchmark for provisioning, applies to credit losses. For market risk, the horizon is shorter than with credit risk and expected P & L from the trading portfolio is usually not considered.

Credit losses will never equal such expectation. Sometimes they will be higher and sometimes lower. For a single exposure, the real loss is never equal to the average, since it would be either zero or the loss under default. On the other hand, for a portfolio, the expected loss is the mean of the distribution of losses. It makes sense to charge this average to each transaction, because each one should contribute to the overall loss.

18.3.2 Loss Percentiles

A potential loss is a loss percentile defined with the preset confidence level. The loss threshold is $L(\alpha)$, where α is the one-tailed[2] probability of exceeding $L(\alpha)$, or percentile. For example, if $L(1\%)$ equals 100, it means that the loss will not exceed the value of 100 in more than 1%, or 1 out of 100 possible scenarios. Determining potential losses at various confidence levels requires the loss distribution of the portfolio. The loss distribution provides the frequency of the various possible values of losses. It is highly sensitive to dependencies between positions. This is the major technical challenge raised by measuring loss percentiles in credit portfolio models, and addressed in Section 9 (dependencies) and Section 12 (credit portfolio models).

18.3.3 Unexpected Loss and VaR

Unexpected losses are loss percentiles in excess of the expected loss. The expected loss is an average used for provisioning. The unexpected loss is the additional loss beyond the expected loss and up to the loss percentile used for defining VaR.

$$\text{VaR}(\alpha) = L(\alpha) - \text{EL}$$

VaR applies both to market and credit risk. For market risk, for example, where the 1% confidence level is used, 1% of all 250 trading days would designate a loss not exceeded in more than 2 to 3 days within a year. The expected tail loss or expected shortfall is the expectation of the losses beyond the VaR. All these measures are discussed in the chapters dedicated to market risk and credit risk (Sections 10 and 11).

18.3.4 Exceptional Losses

Unexpected loss does not include exceptional losses beyond the loss percentile defined by a confidence level. Exceptional losses are in excess of the sum of expected loss plus the unexpected loss, which is equal to the loss percentile $L(\alpha)$. Only stress scenarios, whereby we need to consider all effects of extreme situations, help finding out the order of magnitude of such losses.

18.3.5 Loss Distributions, Potential Losses and VaR

If we assemble those definitions in a single graph, the three measures would appear as in Figure 18.3. The distribution is asymmetric, with a fat tail extending to the right, and matches the general shape of portfolio losses for credit risk. For market risk, the loss distribution would be an earnings distribution truncated towards losses only.

Losses appear on the right-hand side of the zero level along the x-axis. The VaR at a given confidence level is a loss percentile in excess of expected loss. The area under the curve between

---

2 Only adverse deviations count as losses. Opposite deviations are gains and do not value risk.

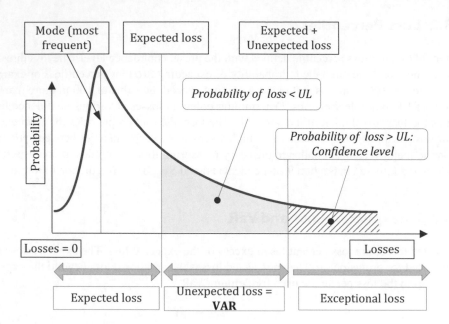

FIGURE 18.3   Unexpected loss and VAR

EL and VaR value on the *x*-axis represents this probability. The maximum total loss at the same confidence level is the sum of the expected loss plus the unexpected loss (or loss percentile).

18.4 VAR AND ECONOMIC CAPITAL

The VaR represents the capital in excess of expected loss necessary for absorbing unexpected deviations from average losses with a given one-tail confidence level. Economic capital is the capital required to absorb losses in excess of expected loss due to current risks and is defined by the VaR at a given confidence level, or UL. Economic capital differs from regulatory capital which is rule based.

The rationale is that the first loss above the average would trigger default. Unexpected loss is a measure of potential losses beyond the expectation. For preserving solvency of financial institutions in adverse conditions, capital should be capable of absorbing such excess losses. If capital is VaR-based, the confidence level is simply the default probability of the bank, since losses will exceed the VaR-based capital in a fraction of all scenarios equal to this confidence level. Using 1% for VaR would imply that capital is not high enough to absorb losses two or three times a year, since there are 250 business days in a year.

For market risk, regulators allow the use of internal VaR models using the 1% confidence level. But they impose a capital higher than VaR by a multiple. The multiple for market risk is currently between 3 and 4. The usage of a multiple is not model based. When the confidence level becomes very small, the value of VaR depends on the shape of the fat tail of the loss distribution and becomes unreliable for extreme and unlikely losses. The rule for a conservative multiple follows. "Back tests" serve for comparing after-the-fact when was the VaR exceeded, and "stress-tests" are intended to see what happens under some extreme conditions. The multiple of the 1% VaR is intended to be conservative enough so that it becomes very unlikely that losses actually exceed the VaR times the multiple.

From a solvency prospective, the confidence level is identical to default probability of the financial firm. Default probabilities, for the best credit standing, are very low. For example, an order of magnitude for a "Aa" credit rating would be a chance of default around 0.03%, which implies measuring a loss percentile at this very low confidence level. The VaR-based economic capital matching a target credit standing should use a confidence level equal to the associated low default probability. Economic capital measures need to measure extreme loss along the tail of the loss distribution in line with such very low confidence level.

18.5 EARNINGS-AT-RISK ("EAR")

An attractive methodology for measuring loss percentiles is Earnings-at-Risk, or "EaR." It is based on historical distributions of earnings. The wider is the dispersion of time series of earnings, the higher is the risk. Earnings at risk have benefits and drawbacks.

Several measures of earnings can be used: accounting earnings, interest margins, commercial margins, cash flows, and market values, notably for the trading portfolio. Of course, the larger the data set, the more relevant the measure will be. The concept applies to any sub-portfolio as well as for the entire bank portfolio. Once earnings distributions are obtained, it is easy to derive loss percentiles by looking for some aggregated level of losses that is not likely to be exceeded in more than a given fraction of all outcomes.

The major benefits of EaR are that they are relatively easy to measure because they are obtained from accounting data. There are some technical difficulties. For example, the volatility calculation raises technical issues, for instance when trends make times series, unadjusted for trends, look highly volatile. In fact, the volatility comes from the trend rather than instability. Hence, relative or percentage variations of earnings are a better measure of their volatility around the trend. The technique requires assumptions, but it remains tractable and easy.

EaR provides a number of outputs. The earnings volatility shows the magnitude of variations. The reduction of earnings volatility, when the perimeter of aggregation increases, measures the diversification effect. The capital is a loss percentile, or the amount not exceeded by adverse deviations of earnings in more than a fraction equal to confidence level. It is difficult to conceive a simpler method of producing a number of outputs without too much effort.

However, the major drawback of EaR relates to risk management. It is not possible to define the sources of the risk making the earnings volatile. Various types of risks materialize simultaneously and create adverse deviations of earnings. The contributions of these risks to the final earning distribution remain unknown. Unlike VaR models, EaR captures risk as an overall outcome of all risks. Without connection to the sources of risk, market, credit or interest rates, EaR does not allow tracing risks back to where they come from. EaR is an additional tool for risk management, but not a substitute.

SECTION 6

Regulations

This section covers both risk regulations and new accounting standards, or IFRS (International Financial Reporting Standards). The first two chapters in this section address regulations for credit risk and market risk. A pre-requisite is to detail the challenges faced by the regulators and how they addressed them over various periods, for providing some prospective on current regulations and how they could evolve in the future.

Risk regulations address several challenges:

- improving the safety of the banking industry, by imposing capital requirements in line with banks risks
- leveling the competitive playing field of banks through setting common benchmarks for all players
- promoting sound business and supervisory practices.

Risk regulations had a decisive impact on risk management. The regulatory framework sets up the constraints and the guidelines that inspire risk management practices, and stimulates the development and the enhancement of the internal risk models and processes of banks. Regulations promoted better definitions of risks, created incentives for developing better methodologies for measuring risks. They imposed the core concept of the capital adequacy principle and of "risk-based capital," stating that banks capital should be in line with risks.

Accounting standards have been developed nearly as if independent of risk regulations. But accounting standards aiming at fair value are critical for valuation purposes and cannot be ignored. They concentrate attention, following the 2008 financial crisis and are presented in this section, close to the risk regulations as they interact with them so much.

Starting from crude estimates of capital charges, with the initial so-called "Cooke ratio," the regulators evolved towards increasingly "risk-sensitive" capital requirements. The section addresses the topic with three chapters.

- The challenges of regulators and how they responded with the first "accord" on credit risk dates from 1988 [10], named Basel 1 and with the Accord Amendment for market risk enforced in 1996 and 1997. It is convenient and relevant to address separately the Basel 1 Accord (Chapter 19) because it laid the foundations for the more sophisticated Basel 2 Accord.
- The Basel 2 Accord (Chapter 20) builds on the Basel 1 chapter giving the basic principles and product definitions for Basel 2 as discussed in the financial product section (Section 3). The Basel 2 Accord is fully detailed in an official document published in 2006 [7], which serves as the basis for detailing the accord. Replicating the details of the document would be useless and Chapter 20 adopts rather a building block structure based on the various approaches and sub-approaches of the accord.
- The main lines of IFRS accounting standards, summarizing the key points required to understand the implications, are detailed in Chapter 21.

19

Banking Regulations: Basel 1 and Market Risk

This chapter describes the main features of the Basel 1 Accord and of the accord on Market Risk. Because of the importance of Basel 2, the "New Accord" is discussed in the next chapter.

At the time of a major crisis that demonstrates how regulators failed to achieve their goal of avoiding systemic risk, it is worth reiterating some of the basic challenges facing the regulators, which were supposed to be properly addressed by the capital-based regulations. In this chapter, section 19.1 offers a brief reminder of the difficult issues faced by regulators, whilst 19.2 describes how regulators addressed their challenges at several periods before the Basel I Accord was implemented.

The capital adequacy principle is the foundation of the recent regulations. Because it is a pre-emptive regulation aiming at avoiding failures rather than managing them when they occur, it was perceived as resolving most of the issues that former regulations could not resolve. Moreover, ensuring a proper level of capital fostered the emergence of sound risk management practices and imposed risk models, or models that quantify risk, rather than relying on judgmental assessments of risks, and it had a series of implications that seemed to be in line with the goal of regulators. The third section expands these ideas.

The final two sections address the former Basel 1 Accord for credit risk (19.4) and its 1996–97 amendment for addressing market risk (19.5), which allowed banks to rely on their own models for defining capital for market risk[1]. Chapter 20 addresses the New Accord for credit risk, or Basel 2, enforced at the end of 2007 in Europe and for major international banks.

---

1 The sources are mainly the documents [7] and [8]. Other related publications are accessible on the website of Bank of International Settlements (BIS).

Contents

19.1 REGULATORY ISSUES

The primary purpose of risk regulations is to prevent "systemic risk," or the risk of collapse of the entire system due to interconnections between financial firms. However, controlling systemic risk raises difficult challenges and dilemmas[2].

Regulations and competition might be conflicting, since many regulations restrict the operations of banks. On the other hand, new rules may create unpredictable behaviors to bypass the constraints. Providing more freedom to financial firms has been a long-standing argument for avoiding too many regulations. But relying on "codes of conduct," rather than rules, implies relying on self-discipline, or "self-regulation," which are not likely to inspire trust in the system.

Deposit insurance by regulation is effective for depositors but not for banks. The protection of bank depositors is a "free" insurance that generates "moral hazard:" because of the insurance, there is no penalty for taking risks. The insurance mechanism can be seen as an incentive for risk taking because the depositors cannot impose a real discipline on banks.

Any significant increase of risk can potentially lead to maximizing risks. When risks are already high, shareholders have not much to lose and they might prefer making riskier bets that increases the chances of not failing. When banks face serious difficulties, the barriers that limit risks disappear. Simultaneously, losses of shareholders and managers do not increase because of limited liability. In the absence of risk regulations, beyond deposit insurance, there would be nothing preventing banks from taking too much risk and subsequently failing, triggering a contagion to other financial players.

Finally, whatever the regulations, the "too big to fail" issue remains a weakness of regulations. The principle refers to the "domino effect" of the failure of large institutions. The failure of large institutions is likely to trigger larger losses and failures to all financial payers that have exposures on the failing bank. Because of fear of such a "domino effect", the regulators might not allow large institutions to fail, thereby generating moral hazard for the major financial firms.

For resolving such issues, the regulators who designed the Basel 1 and the Basel 2 Accord innovated by implementing the new principle of "preemptive" rules for avoiding failure. The principle appeared convincing for a long time, at the time of the continuous and speedy development of the financial system, until the collapse of 2008. The foundations of the new rules became the "capital adequacy" principle, which made it a rule that the capital of banks should be at least in line with the current risk exposures of the bank. The rationale is simple. Capital is the last "line of defense" for avoiding failure in stressed conditions. If it can absorb unexpected losses, the solvency of banks is guaranteed and large losses do not trigger failure.

---

2 The textbook of Saunders and Cornett provides a comprehensive review of regulations issues [65].

Instead of addressing failures "after the fact," the capital adequacy principle imposes "before the fact" protection against failure.

Such regulations worked until the 2008 crisis, which made it obvious that regulations failed to achieve their main goals. Many deficiencies of the new regulations were immediately pointed out. Most of them are addressed in the introduction of this text (Section 1). At this stage, it is helpful to describes how the regulators addressed their challenges at different periods, before the Basel 1 and the Basel 2 accords were enforced.

19.2 THE DILEMMAS OF THE REGULATOR

A number of factors helped stabilize the banking environment in the 1970s. Strong and constraining regulations weighed heavily on banks. Commercial banking was separated from investment banking in the US. Commercial banks collected resources and lent. The commercial banking industry was fragmented, being allowed to operate state wide but not across states. Limited competition facilitated a fair and stable profitability. The rules limited the scope of the operations of the various credit institutions and limited their risks as well. In Europe, no such rules were enforced, and large banks operating nationwide in capital markets and acting as commercial banks were far more common.

The waves of deregulation and re-regulation were more drastic in the US than in Europe. Continental Europe kept relatively conservative rules enforced while the US favored deregulation to resolve specific issues raised by rules that segmented the market. Increased deregulation allowed entry of new players unprepared by their past experiences, resulting in increasing risks for the system. Re-regulation in the 1980s aimed at setting up a regulatory framework reconciling risk control and fair competition.

19.2.1 Regulation and Competition

Too many regulations refrain competition. Those who are constrained by regulations are at a disadvantage compared to other players. Regulations limited the scope of operations of commercial banks, interfering directly with free competition. Examples of inconsistencies between competition and regulations were numerous. A well-known example was the unfair competition between commercial banks, subject to the old regulation Q in the US imposing a ceiling to the interest paid on deposits, and investment bankers offering money market funds earning market interest rates, creating a shift of depositors from bank deposits to money market funds. The motivation of regulation Q was to cap the cost of funds for banks. But it could not prevent other players than commercial banks from offering products more attractive to depositors.

The unfair competition resulting from non-economic rules combined with competition among players motivated the deregulation and the barriers to competition were progressively lifted. The 1970s and the 1980s were the periods of the first drastic waves of changes in the industry. The disappearance of old rules created a vacancy.

Deregulation drastically widened the range of products and services offered by banks. In the US, the Glass-Steagall Act enforced a separation between commercial banking and the capital markets. Similar segmentation existed in Japan. Such cleavages were progressively lifted. For those countries where "universal banking" existed, the transition was less drastic, but segmentation was a heritage of the past rather than being imposed by rules, and was also progressively dismantled.

Most credit institutions diversified their operations out of their original businesses. The pace of creation of new products remained constantly high, especially for those acting in the financial markets, such as derivatives. The research for new market opportunities and products stimulated the growth of other fields than intermediation by banks. The banks entered new business fields and faced new risks. The market share of classical bank lending decreased with the development of capital markets. The competition for market share rose abruptly.

Risks increased because of new competition, of product innovations, of shift from financial intermediation by banks to capital markets, and because of the disappearances of old barriers. New competition generates new risks during the transition period. The deregulation of the 1980s allowed players to freely enter in new markets, including those players that were less ready to do so.

A well-known episode of deregulation, combined with high interest rates, was the failure of the former Savings and Loans institutions which lasted for a decade. Originally, the trigger of these failures was mismatch risk between fixed rate loans and short-term funding at prevailing rates, which materialized when the US monetary policy raised interest rates to unprecedented levels for fighting inflation. Authorities allowed more freedom to surviving institutions, allowed banks to take over some of them while authorizing local banks to extend their activities in other states, for example when taking over ailing institutions.

19.2.2 Preemptive Risk Control versus Risk Insurance

Risk control should be preemptive, while insurance is passive, or "after the fact." Deposit insurance mechanisms exist in most countries, for ensuring the safety of depositors. But risk insurance generates moral hazard and creates a bias towards risk-taking behavior. Theoretically, if depositors had their money at risk with the banks, they would closely monitor the bank behavior, just as any lender does. In practice, if depositors' money is perceived at risk, any sign of increased risks triggers withdrawals of funds that maximize the difficulties, leading to failures. And such old-time "bank runs" were again observed in 2008. This adverse effect is a good reason to insure depositors against bank failure, but it is not sufficient.

Insurance complements the preemptive policies that create disincentives for taking too much risk and avoid failure. For the regulator, the goal became to minimize the risk of failures instead of managing them once they occurred.

The theoretical solution is that financial firms impose enough incentives to control their risks within acceptable bounds. The regulators started redefining new rules along those lines. The BIS (Bank of International Settlements), in Basel, designed new regulations and national regulators relayed them for implementation within the national environments.

19.3 CAPITAL ADEQUACY

A number of rules aiming at limiting risks in a simple manner have been in force for a long time. For instance, several ratios were subject to minimum values. The liquidity ratio imposed that short-term assets be greater than short-term liabilities and that the ratio of long-term lending to long-term debt had a minimum value in Europe. Such ratios limited mismatch risk. They progressively disappeared at times of easy financing, before being again perceived as a necessity in 2008[3].

The main "pillar" of new regulations is "capital adequacy." By enforcing a capital level in line with risks, regulators focused on limiting the risk of failure. The rationale is simple. Capital serves for protecting banks against unexpected losses, or losses beyond the statistically expected losses. Loan loss provisions, in line with statistical losses, provide a first level of protection against credit risk. But any Euro of loss in excess of expected loss will make the bank fail in the absence of capital. The logical consequence is that capital should be sufficient to absorb unexpected losses, beyond expected losses.

Guidelines are defined by a group of regulators meeting in Basel at the Bank of International Settlement (BIS), hence the name of "Basel" Accord. The first accord to be implemented focused on credit risk, with the famous "Cooke ratio." The "Cooke ratio" set up the minimum required capital as a fixed percentage of assets weighted according to their nature in 1988. The scope of regulations extended progressively later. The extension to market risk was a major step for market risk in 1996–97 because it allowed banks to use value-at-risk models for assessing capital charge for market risk. The Basel 2 Accord of January 2007 considerably enhanced the credit risk regulations. The schedule of successive accords is as follows:

- 1988: current accord published
- 1996: Market Risk Amendment allowing usage of internal models
- 1999: First Consultative Package on the New Accord
- 2007: Implementation of the "Basel 2" Capital Accord.

The next sections refer to the 1988 "Current" accord plus the market risk capital regulations. The next chapter expands the "New Accord," which refines capital requirements for credit risk.

19.3.1 Risk-based Capital Regulations

The capital base is not limited to equity plus retained earnings. It includes any debt subordinated to other commitments by the bank. Equity represents at least 50% of the total capital base for credit risk. Equity is also the "tier 1" of capital or the "core capital."

The Cooke ratio stipulates that the capital base should be at least 8% of weighted assets. The weights depend upon the credit quality of the borrowers and the transaction, as described below. For market risk, the rules are more complex because the regulations aim at capturing the economics of market risk, taking advantage of the widely available information on market parameters and prices. The basic idea was the same, defining the minimum amount of the capital charge, as a function of risks assessed either through rules defining capital charge by transaction or VaR-based risk models for market risk. After bank VaR-based models were authorized in 1996–97, they became widespread in the banking industry from the late 1990s.

---

3 See the conclusion, Chapter 60.

19.3.2 Capital Requirements

Traditionally, capital represents a very small fraction of total assets of banks, especially when comparing the minimum requirements to similar ratios of non-financial institutions. A capital percentage of 8% of assets, the now famous "Cooke" ratio of capital to risk-weighted assets, is equivalent to a leverage ratio (debt/equity ratio) of $92/8 = 11.5$. The high leverage of banking institutions results from a number of factors. Smooth operations of banks require easy and immediate access to financial markets, as long as the perceived risk by potential lenders remains acceptable.

The 8% ratio of capital to weighted assets seems too high if compared to average observed default rates in good conditions, and perhaps too low with portfolios of high-risk borrowers under stressed conditions. But the 8% ratio makes sense when considering diversification effects. Regulators' 8% ratio shows that they estimated that a bank could not lose more than 8% of their total risk-weighted portfolio of loans for credit risk, given diversification.

19.3.3 Risk-based Capital and Growth

There is a trade-off between risk taking and risk control. Available capital puts a limit to risk taking, which, in turn, limits the ability to develop business. The available capital might not suffice to sustain new business developments. This rationale was applicable under the "originate and hold" business model of banks.

The capital constraint might require raising new equity, or liquidation of assets, or risk-reduction actions. Raising additional capital implies that profitability of shareholders be in line with their expectations. Moreover, when funding capital growth through retained earnings only, the profitability should be high enough for the capital base to grow in line with the regulatory requirements. Those two constraints are distinct.

A common proxy for the minimum required return of shareholders is the accounting return on equity (ROE), with the 15% after tax, or approximately 25% before tax, benchmark. Profitability limits the sustainable growth if outside sources of capital are not used. The ROE is equal to the growth rate of capital if no dividends are paid[4]. Therefore, any growth above ROE is not sustainable when funding through retained earnings only, under constant average risk. Hence, the first implication of capital requirements is that the ROE caps the growth of banks when they rely on retained earnings only. The second implication is that capital should provide the required market return to stockholders given the risk of the bank's stock. Sometimes, the bank growth is too high to be sustainable given capital requirements. Sometimes, the required compensation to shareholders is the "effective" constraint, while funding capital growth internally is not[5].

---

4 If the leverage is constant, capital being a fixed fraction of total liabilities, the growth rate of accounting capital is also the growth rate of the total liabilities. Leverage is the debt/equity ratio, or $L = D/E$ where D is debt, E is equity plus retained earnings, and L is leverage. The ROE is the ratio of net income (NI) to equity and retained earnings (E), or $ROE = NI/E$. ROE is identical to the sustainable growth rate of capital since it is the ratio of potential additional capital (net income) to existing capital. Since L is constant, total liabilities are always equal to $(1 + L)E$. Hence, they grow at the same rate as E, which is identical to ROE under assumptions of no dividends and no outside capital.
5   In fact, the both constraints are equivalent when the growth rate is exactly 15%, if this figure is representative of both accounting return on equity and the required market return to shareholders.

The only options available to escape the capital constraints are to liquidate assets, or to reduce risks. Direct sales of assets or securitizations serve this purpose, among others. With the expansion of securitizations and the emergence of the "originate and distribute" business model of banks, banks were able to turn around such mechanical constraints, freeing up capital by selling their loans or other assets onto the capital markets, and expanding business while complying with the capital rules.

19.4 THE "BASEL I ACCORD" FOR CREDIT RISK

The Basel 1 Accord remained in force until the end 2007 in Europe, until the "New Accord," or "Basel 2 Accord," was enforced. But Basel 2 was essentially enforced in Europe, and only for major international banks in the US. The Basel 1 regulation remained in force until Basel 2 was enforced, and still is used in regions less prepared to follow Basel 2 guidelines and rules. A quick summary of the Basel 1 Accord plus the description of the amendment to market risk are an adequate introduction to the details of the Basel 2 Accord.

19.4.1 The Cooke Ratio and Credit Risk

The 1988 accord requires internationally active banks in the G10 countries to hold capital for credit equal to, at least, 8% of weighted assets. This is the Cooke ratio for credit risk. Weighted assets are the product of risk weights (RW) by the value of the facility. A risk weight of 100% corresponds to a ratio of capital to asset value of 8%. Hence:

$$\text{capital} = \text{risk weight} \times \text{value}$$

For example, a loan of value 1000 with a risk weight equal to 100% has a capital charge of 80.

The weight scale starts from zero, for commitments with sovereign counterparties within OECD, at the time when Basel 1 was implemented, up to 100% for private businesses. Other weights are 20% for banks and municipalities within OECD countries, and 50% for residential mortgage-backed loans. Off-balance sheet outstanding balances are weighted 50%. There is also a grid of capital charges for off-balance sheet exposures through guarantees, commitments, forward claims, etc.

The 1988 accord requires a two-step approach whereby banks convert their off-balance sheet positions into credit equivalent amounts through a scale of conversion factors, which are then weighted according to the counterparty's risk weighting. The factor is 100% for direct credit substitutes such as guarantees and decreases for less stringent commitments.

The bank has to hold at least half of its measured capital in Tier 1 form. Tier 1 capital is subject to a minimum constraint of 3% of total assets. The calculation of the ratio uses asset weights for differentiating the capital load according to their quality in terms of credit standing.

The capital calculation under Basel 1 Accord is simple. Consider a loan to a corporation of 1000, risk weighted 100%. The capital charge for credit risk is:

$$100\% \times 8\% \times 1000 = 80$$

For a mortgage, backed by property, the same loan would have a capital charge of:

$$50\% \times 8\% \times 1000 = 40$$

19.4.2 Derivatives and Credit Risk

Many derivatives are over-the-counter instruments (interest rate swaps, currency swaps, and options), not as liquid as market instruments. Theoretically, banks hold these assets until maturity, and bear credit risk since they exchange flows of funds with counterparties subject to default risk. For derivatives, credit risk interacts with market risk in that the mark-to-market (or liquidation) value depends on market movements.

The regulators consider those as "hold-to-maturity" positions. The principle is to define the exposure to credit risk as the potential positive value that the derivative can reach during its life. If a derivative has a positive value, the counterparty stands to lose this value if the other counterparty defaults. But values vary randomly with markets, and there is a need to define a methodology for finding out potential positive values.

The G30 group, in 1993, defined the framework for monitoring OTC derivative credit risk. The G30 report recommended techniques for better assessing uncertain exposures, and proposed a framework for modeling the potential deviations of portfolios of derivatives over long periods. The principle is to determine the time profile of upper bounds that future values will not exceed in more than is a preset probability, or confidence level [6]. The final result of this approach is a time profile of potential positive values of the OTC derivatives, updated continuously. Such time-varying exposures are treated as "credit equivalents," that is as if they were loans. The current credit risk exposure is the current liquidation value. There is an additional risk due to the potential upward deviations of liquidation value from the current value.

Regulators defined standard "add-ons," or percentages of notional depending on the underlying parameter and the maturity buckets. Underlying risk factors are interest rate, foreign exchange, equity and commodities. The maturity buckets are up to 1 year, between 1 and 5 years and beyond 5 years. The capital charge is based on current credit exposure plus the add-on for the potential upward drift of the exposure of the derivative. Such add-ons are proxies. In addition, they are added arithmetically, which does not allow capturing dependencies across credit exposures, thereby providing a strong incentive for full-blown modeling of derivative exposures.

Current best-practices rely on such full-blown models of potential credit exposures of derivatives, and those are accepted as exposure inputs under the Basel 2 Accord.

19.4.3 Basel 1 Drawbacks

The major strength of the Cooke ratio is simplicity. There are several major drawbacks, however, which the new Basel Accord addressed. There is no differentiation between the risks of private corporations of different risks. An 8% ratio applying both for a large Aa corporation and for a small business does not make much sense economically. In other words, the accord is not risk-sensitive enough. In addition, short facilities have zero weights, while long facili-

---

6 See Chapter 44 on derivative exposures.

ties have a full capital load. This unequal treatment leads to artificial arbitrage by banks, such as renewing short loans rather than lending long. There is limited allowance for recoveries if a default occurs, even in a case where recoveries are likely, such as for securities collateral. Diversification effects are embedded in the 8% ratio, but the same ratio applies to all credit risk portfolios, whatever their degree of diversification. The regulatory body recognized these facts and reviewed these issues, leading to the New Basel Accord – detailed in the next chapter.

19.5 THE ACCORD FOR MARKET RISK

A significant amendment was enacted in 1995–6, when the Committee introduced a measure whereby trading positions in bonds, equities, foreign exchange and commodities became subject to capital charges for market risk related to the bank's open positions in each instrument [7]. The amendment made explicit the notions of banking book and trading book, defined capital charges for market risk, and allowed banks to use a tier 3 capital in addition to the previous two tiers, 1 and 2.

The 1995 proposal introduced capital charges to be applied to the current market value of open positions (including derivative positions) in interest rate related instruments and equities in banks' trading books, and to banks' total currency and commodities positions. The extension to market risk provides two alternate options for assessing capital charges. The "Standardized Approach" allows measuring the four risks, interest rate, equity, foreign exchange and commodity risk, using sets of standard capital charges. The alternate method allows banks to use risk measures derived from their own internal risk models, or VaR models, subject to a number of conditions, related to qualitative standards of models and processes.

19.5.1 The Standardized Approach

The standardized approach relies exclusively on sets of standard percentages of value for assessing potential losses as percentage of current exposures. Those are summarized in grids for capturing the differences in sensitivities of various market instruments, and on offsetting rules allowing netting the risks within a portfolio whenever there is no residual "basis" risk[7]. For example, for stocks, capital charge is 8% of the net balances, after allowed offsetting long and short comparable exposures. For bonds, the 8% is used with various weights depending upon maturity buckets, because sensitivity differs across maturities.

Within a given class of instruments, such as bonds, equity, and foreign exchange, regulators allow offsetting risks to a certain extent. For instance, being long and short on the same stock results is zero risk, because the gain on the long leg offsets the loss in the short leg when the stocks goes up, and vice versa. Offsetting is limited to exact matches of instrument characteristics. The regulators rely on the "specific" versus "general" risk distinction, following the principle of adding up specific risk while allowing the offsetting of effects for general risk. The rationale is that the general risk represents co-movements of prices driven by the equity index, while specific risk is unrelated to underlying market parameters.

---

7 Basis risk refers to the mismatch between the risk factors of two offsetting positions, for example when one position depends on Libor 3-month and another on Libor 6-month.

The capital charges calculated under the standardized approach remain conservative because they do not allow capturing the full extent of diversification effects. This is the main incentive for moving on to VaR models.

The standardized approach uses a complex grid of weights for interest rate instruments, equity, derivatives, foreign exchange and commodities. The 8% ratio remains the reference when there are no offsetting positions. For interest rate instruments, the grid of coefficients depends on the duration of the bonds, unless they are credit risk-free. Offsetting is permitted within bands of durations and partially across bands. For derivatives which can be replaced by a static portfolio (swaps for example), the capital charge applies to each component of such portfolio (each leg of an IRS for example). Dealing with options implies using scenarios for defining worst-case loss. For equity, the capital charge is 8% for specific risk unless there is a wide diversification, allowing using a 4% capital charge. The general risk capital charge is also 8% but offsets across positions are allowed. Foreign exchange positions in the same currency are offset and the 8% weight applies to the net exposure. Commodity risk is more complex than market instrument risks because it combines a pure commodity price risk with other risks, such as basis risk (mismatch of prices of similar commodities), interest rate risk (for carrying cost of exposures), forward price risk, plus directional risk in commodities price (trends). The capital charges are defined by breaking down the portfolio according to maturities and offset is allowed if there is no basis risk (no mismatch).

19.5.2 Proprietary Models of Market Risk VaR

The economics of market risk are easy to grasp. Tradable assets have random variations of which distributions result from observable sensitivities of instruments and volatilities of market parameters. The standalone market risk of an instrument is a VaR capturing its P & L distribution derived from the underlying market parameter variations. Things get more involved for portfolios because risks offset to some extent due to portfolio diversification, making portfolio risk lower than the sum of all individual standalone risks.

When considering by how much the value of a portfolio of instruments can change, we have to consider all three ingredients: co-movements of market parameters (called risk factors), sensitivities to those of each instruments, and the volatilities of the risk factors. The distinction between "general" versus "specific" risk follows. "General" risk is the risk dependent on risk factors driving all prices. This dependency generates price co-movements since all prices depend, to some extent, on a common set of market parameters. The price volatility unrelated to market parameters is the specific risk, or price variations unrelated to market movements. Factor models allow modeling statistically variations of values due to risk factors, or general risk. The remaining fraction of the price volatility is the specific risk. Market risk VaR models address these issues.

The principles of the extension to proprietary market risk models are as follows.

- Market risk is the risk of loss during the minimum period required to liquidate transactions in the market. The regulatory period is 10 days.
- The loss is the 99% loss percentile (one tailed) for market risk models. The 99% refers to the probability that losses are lower than VaR or, equivalently, that the probability that the market loss exceeds the VaR is 1%.

Models should incorporate historical observations over at least one year. In the event of spikes in volatility, the more recent period should be used. A multiplication factor, between 3 and 4, applies to this modeled VaR. It accounts for potential weaknesses in the modeling process or exceptional circumstances. Reliable models get a "premium" in capital with a lower multiplier of VaR. In addition, the regulators emphasize:

- stress-testing, for assessing the effect of stressed conditions
- back-testing, or checking that the VaR is in line with the historical deviations of values, looking backward. The 1% percentile implies that losses should not exceed the VaR more than 2 to 3 times over one year (1% of 250 days).

20

Banking Regulations: The Basel 2 Accord

The New Basel Accord, or Basel 2, enforced in 2007, focuses on capital requirement definitions (Pillar 1), with major enhancements to credit risk measures, a first coverage of operational risk, disclosure, supervisory review process (Pillar 2), and market discipline (Pillar 3). Simultaneously, it enhances some features of the 1988 "Accord."

This chapter does not follow the complex set of intertwined rules as expanded in the final version of the Accord [7]. Rather, it focuses on the main building blocks of Basel 2 for providing an overview of the principles implemented in the accord. Basel 2 offers several approaches and sub-approaches that banks may select. The entry point is the asset class for describing approaches (available on the BIS site). This chapter is based on the document: Basel Committee on Banking Supervision, (June 2006), "International Convergence of Capital Measurement and Capital Standards – A Revised Framework, Comprehensive Version," Bank for International Settlements, Basel, Switzerland.

For having a comprehensive overview of regulatory issues, the reader should also refer to the introduction and conclusion of this text, which summarizes some main features of current proposals at the time of writing.

Contents

20.1 THE NEW BASEL ACCORD

The New Basel Accord sets new rules for making credit risk capital charges more risk sensitive, recognizing various form of credit risk mitigation, providing various enhancements to the former Basel 1 Accord credit risk measures, adding capital requirements to operational risk, and detailing the "supervision" and the "market discipline" "pillars." The new accord is not simple, with several approaches and sub-approaches differentiated across several asset classes, and adding up as well sub-approaches for credit risk mitigation and dedicated approaches to specialized finance and securitizations.

The new accord defines capital charges for credit risk and operational risk. It treats interest rate risk of the banking book under Pillar 2 (supervisory review process), rather than imposing capital requirements.

The new accord provides a more "risk-sensitive" framework that should considerably reduce distortions between the standard capital charges of Basel 1 and the actual credit risk of counterparties and facilities. It differentiates the risk according to the credit standing of borrower and the transaction-specific guarantees.

The new accord comprises three pillars:

- Pillar 1: minimum capital requirements
- Pillar 2: supervisory review process
- Pillar 3: market discipline.

The accord provides three main approaches for Pillar 1: the "Standardized" approach and the "Foundation" and "Advanced" approaches, which are internal ratings-based (IRB) approaches. A distinctive feature of Basel 2 is to rely on credit ratings for making capital more risk-sensitive. Only the foundation and the advanced approaches use internal credit ratings assigned by the bank to all counterparties, while the standardized approach relies on external ratings when available.

The standardized approach is used only for banks that have no eligible credit rating system, and capital charges are driven by supervisory rules in this case. Basel 2 allows a broader recognition of guarantees for reducing the capital charge. This is the credit risk mitigation (CRM) building block of Basel 2.

Pillar 1 is dedicated to capital treatment. For capital treatment, asset classes are the entry point. Each portfolio of facilities of a bank is assigned an asset class. Capital charge for credit risk proceeds from there and depends, among other factors, on credit ratings of borrowers and on CRM, by asset class. Specialized lending and securitization exposures have a special capital treatment.

The calculation of capital is based, as in Basel 1, on risk weights (RW). A risk weight of 100% corresponds to a ratio of capital to asset value of 8%. The capital charge is calculated as:

$$capital = RW \times exposure \times 8\%$$

The risk weights, under the IRB approaches, depend on "credit risk components," except for specialized lending and securitizations, the main ones being the size of exposure, the default probability, and the loss under default after recoveries. The Basel 2 Accord requires an extensive usage of credit risk data, and imposed a significant enhancement of existing data. It extends the scope of required data as well as their quality. For operational risk, the risk data had to be collected according to a new taxonomy of such risks for quantification purposes.

This chapter presents the major Basel 2 building blocks. The purpose is to introduce the main features of the accord, without blurring the description with the overwhelming amount of rules and conditions imposed in the detailed accord. In some instances, excerpts of the Basel 2 Accord are used, which are self-explaining.

20.2 ASSET CLASSES

The calculation of capital is covered in Pillar 1 of Basel 2. The entry point for capital treatment is the asset class or sub-class. The asset classes have been defined in the chapter on lending activities. The five main Basel 2 asset classes are:

- corporate
- banks
- sovereign
- retail: individuals & small and medium-sized enterprises (SMEs)
- equity.

Within the corporate asset class, five sub-classes of "specialized lending" are defined. Within the retail asset class, three sub-classes are defined. In addition, specialized lending and securitizations have a specific treatment under Basel 2 and are dealt with separately. A pre-requisite for proceeding to the capital charge calculation for credit risk is that each portfolio, or "book," of the bank be assigned to one of these asset classes and sub-classes for capital treatment.

Credit risk mitigation is recognized for capital relief purposes, through two main approaches, called simple and comprehensive. Capital charges are calculated using "risk-weight" functions. There are several risk-weight functions differentiated by asset class or sub-class, plus specific treatments for specialized lending and securitizations.

20.3 CREDIT RISK COMPONENTS

Basel 2 defined four main risk components:

- probability of default (DP)
- exposure at default (EAD)
- loss given default (LGD)
- credit conversion factor (CCF).

Credit risk components are used under the IRB approaches as inputs to the "risk-weight functions" which define the applicable risk weights based on these main inputs and some other parameters. Note that credit risk components of historical public data is provided in Chapter 44. The economic views of credit risk components are detailed in various chapters of Section 11 dealing with standalone credit risk (the credit risk of individual exposure).

In the standardized approach, risk weights are regulatory defined according to external ratings when they exist, and the grid of risk weights is provided by the accord.

20.3.1 Probability of Default (DP) and Default Event

A probability of default quantifies the chances of a borrower's default. Various definitions of default events could be used. They include a default of payment at due date, bankruptcy, or debt restructuring driven by a borrower's difficulties to face debt obligations. Basel 2 defines a default event as non-payment of debt obligations for 90 days.

A default probability refers to a period. The longer is the horizon, the higher are the chances of defaulting. Basel 2 imposes the usage of annualized default probability. Default probabilities depend on prevailing conditions, either general economic conditions or the firm's conditions. Under adverse economic conditions, chances of defaulting grow higher, and conversely. Basel 2 requires using "through-the-cycle" default probabilities, or probabilities that represent some average through the various phases of the economic cycle. Through-the-cycle probabilities of default can be higher or lower than "point-in-time" probabilities of default.

Basel 2 adopts a long-term prospective for defining chances of defaulting over a 1-year period, presumably for reducing pro-cyclicality of capital charge, which would otherwise be lower in expansion and higher in recession. Such sensitivity to economic conditions would require raising more capital in adverse conditions and reducing capital in favorable conditions, which is economically inefficient. Note that, in spite of such rules, many consider that Basel 2 capital remained pro-cyclical and one goal of the ongoing reforms of regulations is further smoothing capital requirements.

Normally, default probabilities should be related to credit ratings, but credit ratings are letter-grades ranking the credit risk, or ordinal measures. A default probability quantifies the risk (a cardinal measure). In retail activities, scoring techniques rely on numerous statistics which serve for quantifying default probabilities, based on historical data. For large corporations or banks, default statistics are not large enough to define default probabilities.

There is a variety of methodologies and data sources that banks may use to associate an estimate of DP to each of its internal grades. The three broad approaches are (i) use of data based on a bank's own default experience; (ii) mapping to external data; and (iii) use of statistical default models. Hence, a bank can use the foundation approaches as long as it maps, in a sound manner, its own assessment of ratings with default probabilities. A common practice, for "low-default-portfolios," relies on "mapping" of internal credit ratings to default frequencies based on historical data, mainly those of rating agencies. The approach has obvious drawbacks, one being that few corporations are rated and another that the bank's portfolio might not have the same composition as the portfolio of rated companies. The methodologies used for mapping credit scores and credit ratings to default probabilities are further discussed in Chapters 45 and 46. For corporate and bank exposures, the DP is the one-year DP associated with the internal borrower grade with a floor of 0.03%. For sovereign exposures, the DP is also associated with the sovereign risk grade, but the floor is zero.

20.3.2 Exposure at Default (EAD)

The exposure at default measures the maximum amount that can be lost under default. Such an amount is generally unknown as of current date. It is measured using rules and models. Sources of uncertainty with respect EAD are numerous. For example, for lending products, the fraction drawn on a committed line of credit depends on the borrower's willingness to use the line. For derivatives traded over-the-counter, the amount subject to default risk is market driven, and can be determined either using simplifying rules or using models.

20.3.3 Loss Given Default (LGD)

Transaction-specific risk is captured by LGD in Basel 2. The LGD is the fraction of the amount at risk that is effectively lost under default, after work-out efforts and recoveries from guarantees. The recovery rate is 1– LGD in percentage of exposure. LGD depend on the type of guarantees attached to a transaction, and is subject to uncertainty. LGD models are mainly based on empirical data, and the financial industry is building up data to make LGD estimates more reliable.

Because of uncertainty attached to LGD, Basel 2 offers several ways for calculating LGD. Under the foundation approach, senior claims on corporates, sovereigns and banks not secured by recognized collateral are assigned a 45% LGD and all subordinated claims on corporates, sovereigns and banks are assigned a 75% LGD. Own estimates of LGD by banks are allowed only in the advanced approach. Otherwise, supervisory rules have to be applied.

LGD reduces directly the capital charges based either on eligible collateral or eligible third party guarantors. For third party guarantees, the credit protection is recognized for sovereign entities, PSEs, banks with a lower risk weight than the counterparty and for other entities rated A– or better. For collateral-based transactions, it is possible to offset a fraction of the exposure by a risk-adjusted value assigned by the collateral[1]. Conservative rules are used to consider drifts of value due to market movements. Supervisory methods are dealt with in the credit mitigation building block of this chapter.

20.3.4 Credit Conversion Factors (CCFs)

Credit conversion factors serve, as in Basel 1, for addressing exposures that are commitments rather than cash exposures, or contingencies and off-balance sheet commitments. Contingencies include guarantees given and received by a lender or any counterparty, whereby a guarantor commits to substitute to the borrower should the latter default on debt obligations. Other off-balance sheet items include derivatives and options.

---

1 See the subsequent section on credit-risk mitigation.

20.3.5 Credit Components and Risk Weights

Capital charge is calculated as 8% times the risk weight of a transaction. In the standardized approach, the risk weights are defined by the regulators. In the IRB approaches, the regulator provides risk-weight functions, differentiated according to asset classes and sub-classes. For specialized lending and securitization exposures, risk weights are defined by specific rules.

20.4 THE STANDARDIZED APPROACH

In the standardized approach to credit risk, exposures to various types of counterparties – sovereigns, banks and corporates – have risk weights based on external credit assessments, or credit ratings, by external credit assessment institutions (ECAIs), or rating agencies, or export credit agencies (ECAs).

20.4.1 Regulatory Risk Weights for Corporates, Sovereigns and Banks

In the standardized approach risk weights are supervisory defined by asset class. The standardized approach is more risk sensitive than the Basel 1 Accord, through the inclusion of an additional risk bucket (50%) for corporate exposures, plus a 150% risk weight for low rating exposures. Un-rated exposures have a 100% weight, lower than the 150% weight. The higher risk bucket (150%) also serves for certain categories of assets. The standardized approach does not allow weights to vary with maturity, except in the case of short-term facilities with banking counterparties in the mid-range of ratings, where weights decrease from 50% to 20% and 100% to 50%, depending on the rating[2].

A majority of corporates have no external rating. The rationale for unrated borrowers is that the absence of external rating simply means that the borrower does not issue listed debt and does not imply a lower credit standing. A 100% risk weight is proposed for unrated counterparties. Because the capital charge is lower for those counterparties than for low-rated entities, the discrepancy could be seen as inconsistent. The accord stipulates that national supervisors have some flexibility in adjusting this weight.

TABLE 20.1 Risk weights of sovereigns

	AAA to AA–	A+ to A–	BBB+ to BBB–	BB+ to B–	Below B–	Unrated
Risk weights	0%	20%	50%	100%	150%	100%

TABLE 20.2 Risk weights of corporates

	AAA to AA–	A+ to A–	BBB+ to BB–	Below BB–	Unrated
Risk weights	20%	50%	100%	150%	100%

---

2 By contrast, the Advanced Internal Ratings Based approach makes risk weights sensitive to maturity and ratings through the default probabilities.

For banks, there are two options. Under the first option, all banks incorporated in a given country are assigned a risk weight one category less favorable than that assigned to claims on the sovereign of that country. However, for banks in countries with sovereigns rated BB+ to B– or unrated, the risk weight is capped at 100%. The second option bases the risk weighting on the external credit assessment of the bank itself, with unrated banks being risk weighted at 50%. Securities firms are treated as banks and insurance companies are treated as corporations.

For an external rating to be used, it has to be equivalent to an issuer's rating. An issuer rating is considered equivalent to that of senior unsecured debt. When there are several external ratings, the selected rating should be most conservative.

20.4.2 The Retail Portfolio

Retail exposures are eligible for the so-called top-down approach, which allows treating them as a pool rather than individually as for corporate exposures. If the regulatory retail portfolio is sufficiently diversified, risk weights is 75%. Lending fully secured by mortgages on residential property is risk weighted at 35%. Mortgages on commercial real estate are assigned a 100% weight.

The unsecured portion of any loan (other than a qualifying residential mortgage loan) that is past due for more than 90 days, net of specific provisions, has a 150% or a 100% risk weight depending on the level of provisions.

20.4.3 Effective Maturity (M)

Effective maturity is relevant only in the foundation or advanced approaches. In general, effective maturity is 2.5 years except for certain short-term transactions. For example, for repo-style transactions, the effective maturity will be 6 months. Otherwise, M is defined as the greater of one year and the remaining effective maturity in years, defined below, subject to a 5-year cap. For an instrument subject to a determined cash flow schedule, effective maturity M is defined as the weighted average of payments dates, with weights equal to cash flows:

$$M = \frac{\sum_t t\, CF_t}{\sum_t CF_t}$$

When such calculation cannot be performed, a longer maturity is used such as the maximum remaining maturity (in years).

20.4.4 Off Balance Sheet Items

Under the standardized approach, credit exposure on OTC derivatives is converted into credit equivalents through the use of "credit conversion factors" (CCF). The CCFs are 20% and 50%, respectively, for commitments with an original maturity up to one year and commitments with an original maturity over one year. Any commitments that are cancellable at any time receive a 0% CCF.

Direct credit substitutes and general guarantees, including standby letters of credit and acceptances, receive a CCF of 100%. Sale and repurchase agreements, where the credit risk remains with the bank, receive a CCF of 100%. Repo-style transactions (i.e. repurchase/reverse repurchase and securities lending/securities borrowing) have a special treatment detailed in the CRM subsequent section. Short-term self-liquidating trade letters of credit arising from the movement of goods (e.g. documentary credits collateralized by the underlying shipment), have a 20% CCF.

20.5 INTERNAL RATINGS BASED FRAMEWORK

The IRB approaches rely on internal ratings assigned by banks to all counterparties. The capital charge is derived from the risk-weight functions applying to each supervisory portfolio, or asset class. Provisions for expected loss are allowed and capital charge is in excess of expected loss. Eligibility to IRB approach is subject to supervisory approval.

For each of the asset classes covered under the IRB framework, there are three key elements.

- Risk components: estimates of risk parameters provided by banks, some of which are supervisory estimates. Risk components include DP, EAD, LGD, effective maturity (M), plus other parameters embedded in the risk-weight functions.
- Risk-weight functions: the means by which risk components are transformed into risk-weighted assets and therefore capital requirements. There are several risk-weight functions depending on the asset class.
- Minimum requirements: the minimum standards that must be met in order for a bank to use the IRB approach for a given asset class.

For the retail portfolio, there is no foundation approach. The treatment is either standard or advanced. In the latter, for retail exposures, banks must provide their own estimates of DP, LGD and EAD. There is no distinction between a foundation and an advanced approach for this asset class.

For other than retail portfolios, under the foundation approach, banks provide their own estimates of DP and rely on supervisory estimates for other risk components. Under the advanced approach, banks provide their own estimates of DP, LGD and EAD, and of M, subject to meeting minimum standards. For both the foundation and advanced approaches, banks must always use the risk-weight functions for the purpose of deriving capital requirements.

As a result, the advanced approach relies on simpler rules than the foundation approach because own-estimates are allowed, while a combination of rules applies under the foundation approach. Under the foundation approach, banks must provide their own estimates of DP associated with each of their borrower grades, but the other risk components are LGD, EAD and M are regulatory defined.

The Basel 2 Accord lists some "benchmark risk weights," or BRWs. The function depends on the probability of default (DP). The benchmark example refers to the specific case of a 3-year asset, with various default probabilities and an LGD of 50% (Table 20.3). Three representative points shows the sensitivity of risk weights to the annualized default probability. For DP = 0.7%, the BRW is 100%, and the maximum risk weight, for DP = 20%, reaches 625%. This value is a cap for all maturities and all default probabilities. The weight profile with varying

TABLE 20.3 Sensitivity of risk weights with maturity: benchmark case (3 years asset, 50% LGD)

DP (%)	0.03%	0.7%	20%
BRW (%)	14%	100%	625%

DP is more sensitive than the standardized approach weights, which vary in the range 20% to 150% for all maturities over one year.

20.6 CREDIT RISK MITIGATION

The credit risk mitigation rules are common to all approaches, and include several options. It is easier to separate this treatment from the broad approaches of Basel 2. Credit risk mitigants are called CRM in Basel 2 terminology. Credit risk mitigation designates transaction-specific features that mitigate, or reduce, the credit risk of the transaction. Eligible guarantees include:

- eligible collateral on trading – cash, securities
- third party guarantees
- credit derivatives

Approaches vary:

- standard: risk weights are standard
- foundation: standard recovery rates are 55% for senior debt and 25% for subordinated debts
- advanced: recovery rates are defined by banks.

Regulations impose minimum operational standards because a poor management of operational risks – including legal risks – would raise doubts with respect to the actual value of such mitigants. For credit risk mitigation to be recognized, eligibility criteria have to be met: transactions must be fully documented and guarantees or credit derivatives must be binding and legally enforceable. Further, banks are required to hold capital against residual risks resulting from any mismatch between credit risk hedges and the corresponding exposure. Mismatches refer to differences in amounts, maturities, or currencies between the exposure and the hedge.

20.6.1 Credit Risk Mitigation: Guarantees and Credit Derivatives

For a bank to obtain any capital relief from the receipt of credit derivatives or guarantees, the credit protection must be direct, explicit, irrevocable and unconditional.

The "substitution approach" provided in the 1988 Accord applies for guarantees and credit derivatives, but the capital floor, w, applies. The substitution approach simply substitutes the risk of the guarantor to that of the borrower subject to full recognition of the enforceability of the guarantee.

The new accord recognizes that banks only suffer losses in guaranteed transactions when both the obligor and the guarantor default. The "double default" approach reduces the credit risk if there is a low correlation between the default probabilities of the obligor and the guarantor[3].

20.6.2 Credit Risk Mitigation: Collateral Treatment

The CRM rules for collateral are more complex than for third party guarantees to the extent that an exposure is divided into a collaterized fraction and the remaining fraction. Furthermore, the breakdown into those two fractions depends on "haircuts," for measuring the amount of over-collateralization. Haircuts calculations are subject to various rules. Finally, the risk weight and the LGD vary for the collateralized portion of an exposure and the unsecured portion.

20.6.2.1 General Rules for Collateral CRM

The Committee has adopted for the standardized approach a definition of eligible collateral that is broader than that in the 1988 Accord. In general, banks can recognize the following as collaterals:

- cash
- a restricted range of debt securities issued by sovereigns, public sector entities, banks, securities firms and corporates
- certain equity securities traded on recognized exchanges
- certain mutual funds holdings
- gold.

There is a capital floor, denoted "w," because a collateralized transaction can never be totally without risk (except for cash). A normal w value is 0.15.

Basel 2 recognizes collateral only if its value is not dependent on the credit standing of the counterparty. The credit quality of the counterparty and the value of the collateral cannot have a material positive correlation. For example, securities issued by the counterparty would provide little protection and would be ineligible.

In securities lending and borrowing, the lender of cash holds securities as collateral, of which value might fall below amount lent even when the transaction is originally over-collaterized.

Supervisory rules allow offsetting exposure with collateral values, subject to "haircuts." Haircuts are percentage of value that account for time changes of exposure and collateral and for mismatches of maturities and of currencies between the exposure and the collateral. They are two sets of haircuts: standard supervisory haircuts; and banks' "own estimates" of collateral volatility[4].

---

3 Chapter 50 on recoveries provides details on the technique for assessing the default probability reduction resulting from "double" or "joint" default of the primary borrower and the guarantor.
4 See Chapter 50 on the modeling of collateral risk-mitigating effect.

As a general rule, the portions of claims collateralized by the haircut-adjusted value of collateral receive the risk weight applicable to the collateral instrument. This risk weight on the collateralized portion is subject to a floor of 20%, except in certain cases, for example when the collateral is cash or when it is made of a sovereign or PSE (public sector entity) securities, which are eligible for a 0% risk weight. The remainder of the claim is unsecured and is assigned the risk weight of the counterparty. In presence of multiple collaterals, the exposure should be divided into fractions, each one being assigned only one CRM type.

Credit risk mitigation is subject to two approaches: the "simple approach" and the "comprehensive approach." Under the simple approach, banks substitute the risk weight of the collateral for the risk weight of the counterparty for the collateralized portion of the exposure (subject to the 20% floor), which is similar to the 1988 Accord.

The comprehensive approach allows a fuller offset of collateral against exposures. Banks may effectively reduce the exposure amount by the value assigned to the collateral. Banks can use either one of these approaches in the banking book, but only the comprehensive approach in the trading book. Partial collateralization is recognized. Mismatches in the maturity of the underlying exposure and the collateral are allowed only under the "comprehensive approach."

For being conservative, the regulatory rules maximize the gap between exposure value and collateral value in order to take into consideration adverse market movements, using a combination of haircuts that account for possible variations of values.

The rationale of haircuts and volatility is expanded in the credit risk chapters[5]. The value of a security depends on the market volatility, on the sensitivity of the value to market movements, and on the length of the period before the collateral can be adjusted. Basel 2 requires that values be volatility-adjusted through haircuts.

Using haircuts, banks are required to adjust both the amount of the exposure to the counterparty and the value of any collateral received to take account of possible future fluctuations in the value of either. Except for cash, the volatility-adjusted amount for the exposure will be higher than the exposure and, for the collateral, it will be lower. Additional haircuts are required for residual risk resulting from currency and maturity mismatches between collateral and exposure. The positive difference between exposure and volatility-adjusted value of collateral is assigned the risk weight of the counterparty.

The general formula for calculating netted exposure to which the risk weight of the counterparty is applied is as follows:

$$E^* = \max\left\{0, \left[E\left(1 + H_e\right) - C\left(1 - H_c - H_{fx}\right)\right]\right\}$$

Where:

- E^*: the exposure value after risk mitigation
- E: current value of the exposure
- H_e: haircut appropriate to the exposure

---

5   See Chapter 50.

- C: the current value of the collateral received
- H_c: haircut appropriate to the collateral
- H_{fx}: haircut appropriate for currency mismatch between the collateral and exposure.

The same formula can be written:

$$E^* = \max\left\{0,\left[\left(E-C\right)+\left(E\,H_e\right)+\left(C\,H_c\right)+\left(C\,H_{fx}\right)\right]\right\}$$

The formula shows that the exposure subject to capital charge is the difference between exposure value and collateral value to which an add-on is applied. The add-on sums up the various haircuts. It assumes that the exposure value can grow by the amount of the haircut and that the collateral value can decrease by the amount of the haircuts. The combined effect is to maximize the gap between exposure and collateral values.

Banks must continue to calculate EAD without taking into account the presence of any collateral, unless otherwise specified. Hence, exposure is always fully recorded in the bank's system, and it is not allowed to record only exposures netted from collateral.

20.6.3 Collateral: Haircut Calculations

Posted collateral is subject to margin calls, or the obligation to post additional collateral when it becomes lower than required. The magnitude of variations of collateral value depends on how long the collateral is allowed to deviate before a margin call is triggered. Accordingly, Basel 2 stipulates additional rules for defining haircuts.

20.6.3.1 Standard Supervisory Haircuts

Basel 2 makes the haircuts dependent on the frequency of "re-margining" or the frequency of the margin call since market deviations depend on the period elapsed between two margin calls. As seen in Chapter 16, under common assumptions, the volatility increases with time as the square root of time. Supervisory standard haircuts build on these rules.

The size of the individual haircuts depends on the type of instrument, the type of transaction and the frequency of mark-to-market and re-margining. For example, repo-style transactions subject to daily mark-to-market and to daily re-margining will receive a haircut based on a 5-business day holding period and secured lending transactions with daily mark-to-market and no re-margining clauses will receive a haircut based on a 20-business day holding period. These haircut numbers are scaled using the square root of time formula depending on the frequency of re-margining or marking-to-market.

Most haircuts are in the range of 0.5% to 15% and are provided in a grid. They depend on the rating of securities, on the type of counterparty, and on the nature of mismatches between exposure and collateral.

20.6.3.2 Own Estimates for Haircuts

Supervisors permit banks to calculate haircuts using their own internal estimates of market price volatility and foreign exchange volatility.

The haircut is the difference between current value of exposure and a lower bound for collateral. The lower bound is defined by a confidence level of 99%. In other words, there is no more than 1% chance that, over the calculation period, the collateral value falls below this lower bound[6]. Referring to the definition of VaR, under simple assumptions, the deviation from current value down to the lower bound is a multiple of the risk factor volatility. Volatilities are higher over longer periods. If the daily volatility is σ_1, the volatility for t days would be simply be $\sigma_1\sqrt{t}$. If haircuts are multiples of volatilities, they are also scaled according to the same square root of time rule.

20.6.4 Effective LGD for Collateral-based Transactions

For any collateral-based exposure, a portion is exposed to the collateral and the remaining portion of exposure is exposed to the counterparty. Hence, both risk weights and LGD differ for these two portions.

The general rule for assigning risk weights to the collateralized and the remaining fraction of exposures is mentioned above: The first fraction receives the risk weight of the collateral and the remaining fraction receives that of the borrower.

The same idea applies for determining LGD. The LGD of a collateralized transaction depends on that of the borrower for the unsecured portion of exposure and on the size of the collateral for the other portion – the "effective LGD" combines both. In all cases, the portion of the exposure regarded as unsecured receives the LGD of the borrower.

20.7 COUNTERPARTY CREDIT RISK

For counterparty credit risk, applying to OTC derivatives, the exposure should consider both the current exposure, which is the current value of the derivative, plus an add-on as in Basel 1. This method is similar to the Basel 1 method, since standard add-ons are defined according to the nature of the underlying asset and the maturity of the derivative. The volatility-adjusted eligible collateral, if any, might offset the resulting "potential exposure." This is called the current exposure method.

The alternate method recognizes the modeling of potential future exposures of derivatives, as explained in the exposure chapter on credit risk[7].

20.8 CAPITAL CALCULATION

Capital calculation starts from the asset class and differs according to the broad approaches. In the standardized approach, risk weights are supervisory, depending on external ratings when

---

6   An economic calculation of haircuts is detailed in Chapter 50.
7   See Chapter 49 on Potential Future Exposure of OTC Derivatives.

applicable. In the IRB approach, risk-weight functions depend on all credit risk components and differ by asset class. In the advanced approach, banks have the flexibility of using their own estimates, both for the inputs of the risk-weight functions and for credit risk mitigation, which make the rules much simpler. We provide below risk-weight functions and inputs in some main cases.

20.8.1 Risk-Weighted Assets for Corporate, Sovereign, and Bank Exposures

The formula is detailed in steps in the Accord, using the Excel™ format. The detailed calculations of risk weights are as follows for corporate exposures.

The general formulas for IRB risk weights (RW), for corporate entities, without complexities such as CRM, are as follows. The core part of the risk-weight function is:

$$RW = LGD\left\{N\left[\frac{N^{-1}(PD)}{\sqrt{1-R}} + \sqrt{\frac{R}{1-R}}N^{-1}(0.999)\right] - (PD\,LGD)\right\}$$

This core part of the full formula is multiplied by a factor with a maturity adjustment:

$$\frac{1+(M-2.5)b}{1-1.5b}$$

$$b(DP) = [0.1582 - 0.0578\ln(DP)]^2$$

The correlation R is a function of DP and size of obligor:

$$\text{Correlation}(R) = 0.15 + \left[0.12\frac{1-e^{-50PD}}{1-e^{-50}} + 0.24\left(1-\frac{1-e^{-50PD}}{1-e^{-50}}\right) - 0.04\left(1-\frac{S-5}{45}\right)\right]$$

In these formulas:

- DP and LGD are measured as decimals, and EAD is measured as currency (e.g. Euros), except where explicitly noted otherwise.
- the firm-size adjustment is:

$$0.04\left(1-\frac{(S-5)}{45}\right)$$

It applies to the corporate risk-weight formula for exposures to SME borrowers. S is expressed as total annual sales in millions of Euros with values of S falling in the range of equal to or less than €50 million or greater than or equal to €5 million.
- $N(x)$ denotes the cumulative distribution function for a standard normal random variable. $G(z)$ denotes the inverse cumulative distribution function for a standard normal random variable, $N^{-1}(x)$, or the value of x such that $N(x) = z$.

Note that this risk-weight function is the one applying to corporate exposures. There are other risk-weight functions. For retail portfolios, there are three risk-weight functions: for residential mortgage exposures, for qualifying revolving retail exposures, and for other retail exposures.

20.8.2 Interpretation of Basel 2 Formulas for Risk Weights

It is feasible to simulate what happens when those parameters change. We focus here on the essentials, since the next paragraph provides a broader picture of Basel 2 risk weights.

20.8.2.1 Capital Charge Depends on Stressed Default Probabilities

The core portion of the formula in the calculation of capital charge is written in the text in Excel™ formula language:

$$N[(1 - R)^\wedge{-}0.5 \times G(DP) + (R/(1 - R))^\wedge 0.5 \times G(0.999)]$$

With standard mathematical notations, using Φ and Φ^{-1} for the standard normal cumulative distribution and factoring out the term $1/\sqrt{(1 - R)}$:

$$\frac{\Phi\left[\Phi(PD) + \sqrt{R}\,\Phi^{-1}(0.999)\right]}{\sqrt{1 - R}}$$

We show in the Chapter 54 (on loss distributions) that the core formula for risk weight uses a stressed default probability that would apply to granular portfolios with uniform correlation. When multiplying this core formula by LGD and deducting the expected loss $EL = 1 - DP \times LGD$, we find the risk-weight formula.

20.8.2.2 Specific Risk Increases for Low Credit Standing Obligors

Basel 2 correlation is a function of DP. The formula, leaving aside the size adjustment, is again built around a core part, which is written:

$$0.24\left[1 - \frac{1 - e^{-50PD}}{1 - e^{50}}\right]$$

When DP increases, the correlation decreases. The formula implies a higher effect of specific risk for low credit grades obligors. Correlation is between 12% and 24%. The size adjustment allows for smoothing out the effect of small sizes.

20.8.2.3 Maturity Adjustment and Migration Risk

The maturity adjustment is a factor applied to the capital charge net of expected loss, and is written:

$$\frac{1-b(M-2.5)}{1-1.5b}$$

Note that b is a function of DP. But when a loan has an effective maturity M of 1 year the factor collapses to 1. Longer maturities translate into higher capital charges and conversely. The maturity is bounded 5 years, except for short-term transactions. The additional charge for long maturity addresses migration risk, which becomes more significant when the horizon becomes longer.

20.8.3 Retail Portfolio

The retail portfolio is subject to the top-down approach, starting from homogeneous segments defined by the nature of the transaction and of the borrower. This implies that the assessment of risk components is done at the segment level rather than at the individual exposure level, as for corporate exposures.

For retail exposures, the Accord also proposes, as an alternate assessment of risk, to evaluate directly "expected loss." Expected loss is normally the product of DP and LGD. This approach bypasses the separate assessment for each segment of the DP and LGD. The maturity (M) of the exposure is not a risk input for retail banking capital.

20.8.4 Equity Exposures

Equity exposures in the trading book are subject to the market risk capital rules. For equity exposures not held in the trading book, there are several approaches.

Equity exposures can be weighted using supervisory standard weights. A 300% risk weight is to be applied to equity holdings that are publicly traded and a 400% risk weight is to be applied to all other equity holdings.

Alternatively, there are two model-based approaches to calculate risk weights for equity: the market-based approach and the DP/LGD approach. In IRB approaches, banks may use internal risk measurement models (VaR-based models) to calculate the risk-based capital requirement. The capital charge equals the potential loss on the institution's equity holdings subject to the 99th percentile, one-tailed confidence interval of the difference between quarterly returns and an appropriate risk-free rate computed over a long-term sample period. Under the DP/LGD approach, banks estimate the DP of the corporate entity, and use a 90% LGD for deriving risk weight. If the bank does not hold debt of the entity, the risk weight is scaled by a factor of 1.5. The minimum risk weights are 100%, 200% for publicly traded equity and 300% for all other equity holdings. When the risk weight is zero, equity exposure can be excluded from the equity approach, or if equity exposures are not material. Materiality refers to the size of equity exposures relative to bank's capital. The materiality threshold is 10% or 5% of aggregated tier 1 plus tier 2.

The measure of an equity exposure on which capital requirements is based on the value presented in the financial statements, which, depending on national accounting and regulatory practices, may include unrealized revaluation gains.

20.9 SAMPLE COMPARISON BETWEEN BASEL I AND BASEL 2 CAPITAL FOR CORPORATE ASSET CLASS CREDIT RISK

For calculating capital, we need a set of default probabilities per rating class. The comparison is meaningful under the same framework. Capital charge is calculated with a risk weight of 100% for Basel 1 and without any credit risk mitigation effect.

Figure 20.1 provides the comparison. The bars are the capital charges. The *x*-axis shows the corresponding ratings. The default probabilities are implicit in the graph, since they map to ratings for the calculation to be feasible. We used a sample mapping of default probabilities to the detailed rating scale. The sample mapping of default probabilities to external ratings is provided in Table 20.4. The methodology for obtaining such mapping is expanded in Chapters 40 and 41.

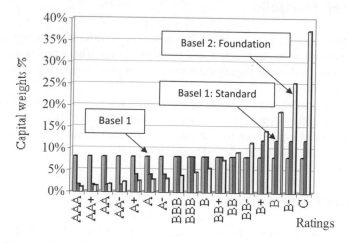

FIGURE 20.1 Comparison of capital charges per rating class: Basel I, Basel 2 standard, Basel 2 advanced approach

20.10 SPECIALIZED LENDING

For SL categories (PF, OF, CF, IPRE, and HVCRE) banks may estimate the DP under the corporate foundation approach, or they use the "supervisory slotting criteria approach." In the second method, they map their internal risk grades to five supervisory categories. Each supervisory category is associated with a specific risk weight. A sample of supervisory risk weights is shown in Table 20.5.

20.11 SECURITIZATIONS

Securitization exposures are treated separately with a hierarchy of three approaches.

• The rating-based approach (RBA) must be applied to securitization exposures that are rated, or where a rating can be inferred.

TABLE 20.4   Sample mapping of default probabilities to ratings

Rank	S & P	Moody's	First-year DP
1	AAA	Aaa	0.020%
2	AA+	Aa1	0.031%
3	AA	Aa2	0.047%
4	AA–	Aa3	0.073%
5	A+	A1	0.077%
6	A	A2	0.081%
7	A–	A3	0.085%
8	BBB+	Baa1	0.101%
9	BBB	Baa2	0.120%
10	BBB–	Baa3	0.142%
11	BB+	Ba1	0.362%
12	BB	Ba2	0.919%
13	BB–	Ba3	2.335%
14	B+	B1	4.040%
15	B	B2	6.989%
16	B–	B3	12.090%
17	C	Caa1	14.629%
18	D	Caa2	17.702%

TABLE 20.5   Supervisory categories and risk weights for SL exposures

Strong	Good	Satisfactory	Weak	Default
70%	90%	115%	250%	0%

- Where an external or an inferred rating is not available, either the supervisory formula (SF) or the internal assessment approach (IAA) must be applied.

Securitization exposures to which none of these approaches can be applied must be deducted from capital.

The accord imposes the "clean break" principle through which the non-recourse sale of assets should be unambiguous, limiting the temptation of banks to support sponsored structures for reputation motives (reputation risk[8]).

The accord assigns risk weights in line with the seniority of structured notes issued by such structures. The credit enhancement note concentrates a large fraction of the risk of the pool of securitized assets. Other issues with securitizations relate to operational risk. Revolving securitizations, with early amortization features, or liquidity lines provided to structures (commitments to provide liquidity for funding the structure under certain conditions), generate some residual risks. There is a standard capital loading for such residual risk.

---

8 Reputation risk is the risk of adverse perception of the sponsoring bank if a structure explicitly related to the bank suffers from credit risk deterioration or from a default event.

20.11.1 Standardized Approach

In the standardized approach, the risk weights are defined by the regulator according to external ratings. The risk weights range from 20% for AAA– to AA-rated notes up to 350% for BB+ to BB= notes, and full deduction of capital for those notes that are rated below BB–. For unrated exposures, there are various provisions extending from full deduction from capital to the "look-through" treatment for senior exposures. The look-through approach consists of determining the risk weight for senior unrated exposures as the average risk weights of underlying exposure of the pool of asset backing the securitization is known.

20.11.2 IRB Approaches

The rating-based approach (RBA) relies on supervisory risk weights. The supervisory risk weights depend on external ratings, the granularity of the underlying pool of assets, and the seniority in the position held by the bank. The risk weights to be used under RBA range from 7% and up to 100% for BBB– and below exposures. When the underlying assets form a non-granular portfolio, the minimum risk weight is 20%.

The internal assessment approach (IAA) relies on inputs provided by banks. The capital charge is given by the supervisory formula (SF). The supervisory formula relies on key elements that determine the credit risk according to the seniority level of notes. There are five bank-supplied inputs:

- the IRB capital charge had the underlying exposures not been securitized (named K_{IRB})
- the tranche's credit enhancement level (L) and thickness (T)
- the pool's effective number of exposures (N)
- the pool's exposure weighted average loss-given-default (LGD).

The inputs K_{IRB}, L, T and N are defined below.

- K_{IRB} is the ratio of the IRB capital requirement including the EL portion for the underlying exposures in the pool to the exposure amount of the pool.
- The credit enhancement level (L) is measured (in decimal form) as the ratio of the amount of all securitization exposures subordinate to the tranche of interest to the amount of exposures in the pool. It refers to the protection provided to the tranche considered, since all subordinated tranches have a lower priority claim and are hit by portfolio losses first.
- Thickness of exposure (T) is measured as the ratio of the nominal size of the tranche of interest to the notional amount of exposures in the pool. The thickness is the difference between two consecutive credit enhancement levels. The higher the thickness, the riskier the tranche.
- The effective number (N) of exposures in the pool is the ratio of the sum of squared exposures to the sum of exposures[9] or:

$$N = \frac{\left(\sum_i EAD_i \right)^2}{\sum_i EAD_i}$$

9 This is a diversity score measure, interpreted as the number of equal exposures equivalent to actual exposures given size discrepancies. The rationale of diversity score is further detailed in Chapter 63 on portfolio analysis.

As a substitute, banks may use the instead the inverse of the largest exposure.
- The exposure weighted average LGD is the average of LGD of each individual underlying exposure with weight equal to the ratio of its exposure to total exposure of the pool.

The capital charge is calculated as $S(L + T) - S(L)$, where S is the function of the supervisory formula.

The supervisory formula is equal to L, the credit enhancement, when $L \leq K_{IRB}$ or becomes a function of all inputs when $K_{IRB} \leq L$. The capital charge is the increment between the capital charge if the bank were exposed to all exposures below $L + T$ minus the capital charge assigned to the subordinated notes (L), which is consistent with seniority rules across tranches.

When the credit enhancement is lower that the capital charge of the underlying pool under IRB approaches, the capital charge is $S(L + T) - S(L)$, but $S(X)$ becomes a function of all inputs. When the capital charge of the underlying pool under IRB approaches is lower than the credit enhancement, regulators make an adjustment for the fact that the IRB treatment of the underlying pool would result in a capital lower than credit enhancement.

20.12 INTEREST RATE RISK

The accord considers it more appropriate to treat interest rate risk in the banking book under Pillar 2, rather than defining capital requirements. This implies no capital load, but an enhanced supervisory process. The guidance on interest rate risk considers banks' internal systems as the main tool for the measurement of interest rate risk in the banking book and the supervisory response. To facilitate supervisors' monitoring of interest rate risk across institutions, banks should provide the results of their internal measurement systems using standardized interest rate shocks. If supervisors determine that a bank is not holding capital commensurate with the level of interest rate risk, they can require that the bank reduces its risk, or holds an additional amount of capital, or combine the two.

20.13 OPERATIONAL RISK

The Committee adopted a standard industry definition of operational risk: "The risk of direct or indirect loss resulting from inadequate or failed internal processes, people and systems or from external events."

As a first approximation in developing minimum capital charges, the Committee estimates operational risk at 20% of minimum regulatory capital as measured under the 1988 Accord. The Committee proposes a range of three approaches to capital requirements for operational risk of increasing sophistication:

- basic indicator
- standardized
- internal measurement.

The "basic indicator approach" links the capital charge for operational risk to a single indicator that serves as a proxy for the bank's overall risk exposure. For example, if gross income is the indicator, each bank should hold capital for operational risk equal to a fixed percentage ("alpha factor") of its gross income.

The "standardized approach" builds on the basic indicator approach by dividing a bank's activities into a number of standardized business lines (e.g. corporate finance and retail banking). Within each business line, the capital charge is a selected indicator of operational risk times a fixed percentage ("beta factor"). Both the indicator and the beta factor may differ across business lines.

The "internal measurement approach" allows individual banks to rely on internal data for regulatory capital purposes. The technique necessitates three inputs for a specified set of business lines and risk types:

- an operational risk exposure indicator
- the probability that a loss event occurs
- the losses given such events.

Together, these components make up a loss distribution for operational risks. Nevertheless, the loss distribution might differ from the industry-wide loss distribution, thereby necessitating an adjustment.

20.14 PILLAR 2: SUPERVISORY REVIEW PROCESS

The second pillar of the new framework aims at ensuring that each bank has sound internal processes to assess the adequacy of its capital based on a thorough evaluation of its risks. Supervisors are responsible for evaluating how well banks are assessing their capital needs relative to their risks. The Basel Committee regards the market discipline through enhanced disclosure as a fundamental part of the new accord. It considers that disclosure requirements and recommendations will allow market participants to assess key pieces of information for the application of the accord.

The risk-sensitive approaches developed by the new accord rely extensively on banks' internal methodologies giving banks more discretion in calculating their capital requirements. Hence, separate disclosure requirements become prerequisites for supervisory recognition of internal methodologies for credit risk, credit risk mitigation techniques and others areas of implementation. Disclosure prerequisites will also apply to the advanced approach of operational risk. In the view of the Committee, effective disclosure is essential to ensure that market participants can better understand banks' risk profiles and the adequacy of their capital positions.

The Committee formulated four basic principles that should inspire supervisors' policies.

- Banks should have a process for assessing their overall capital in relation to their risk profile and a strategy for maintaining their capital levels.
- Supervisors should review and evaluate banks' internal capital adequacy assessments and strategies, as well as their ability to monitor and ensure their compliance with regulatory capital ratios. Supervisors should take appropriate supervisory actions if they are not satisfied with the results of this process.
- Supervisors should expect banks to operate above the minimum regulatory capital ratios and should have the ability to require banks to hold capital in excess of this minimum.
- Supervisors should intervene at an early stage to prevent capital from falling below the minimum levels required to support the risk of a particular bank and should require corrective actions if capital is not maintained or restored.

20.15 PILLAR 3: MARKET DISCIPLINE

The third major element of the Committee's approach to capital adequacy is market discipline. The accord emphasizes the potential for market discipline to reinforce capital regulations and other supervisory efforts in promoting safety and soundness in banks and financial systems.

Given the influence of internal methodologies on the capital requirements established, it considers that comprehensive disclosure is important for market participants to understand the relationship between the risk profile and capital of an institution. Accordingly, the usage of internal approaches is contingent upon a number of criteria, including appropriate disclosure.

For these reasons, the accord is setting out a number of disclosure proposals as requirements, some of them being prerequisites to supervisory approval. Core disclosures convey vital information for all institutions and are important for market discipline. Disclosures are subject to "materiality." Information is "material" if its omission or misstatement could change or influence the assessment or decision of any user relying on that information. Supplementary disclosures may convey information of significance for market discipline actions with respect to a particular institution.

20.16 ADDITIONAL PROPOSALS

In the June 2008 "Principles for Sound Liquidity Risk Management and Supervision" (Draft version), the Basel Committee emphasized the critical role of liquidity, which does not imply yet any capital charge. The paper refers to liquidity funding risk and mismatch risk and explicitly mentions that "banks failed to take account of a number of principles of liquidity management when liquidity was plentiful" (§3). The document mentions 17 principles. Amongst the main ideas, the report emphasizes:

- the requirement of a high liquid assets capable of withstanding a range of stress events
- the definition of a liquidity risk tolerance by the banks
- the incorporation of liquidity costs, benefits and risk in product pricing, performance approval and new product approval
- a sound process for projecting cash flows (which refers to asset and liability management practices)
- diversification of sources of funding
- settlement risk
- the design of a formal contingency plan
- disclosure of liquidity positions.

This is no more than a restatement of otherwise sound principles that were in force when banks were less aggressive in terms of mismatch risk.

Special mentions refer to off balance sheet commitments, which include:

- liquidity lines to SPE and liquidity lines to such vehicles, which are liquidity commitments
- asset "wrapped" by monolines of which liquidity depends on the credit standing of the monolines
- drawdown on letters of credit.

However, there is no capital charge on liquidity funding risk and measures are not well defined, presumably relying on usual bank "sound" practices for measuring liquidity risk as developed in the ALM section of this book.

A number of proposals are being defined to address the sources of the financial crisis. Some blame the procyclicality of current regulations, as in [34], and the Financial Stability Forum report [29] starts from a conceptual framework that emphasizes procyclicality. Procyclicality relates as well to fair value accounting standards addressed in the next chapter. A summary of the proposals is provided at the end of this book (Chapter 60).

21

Accounting Standards

The banks' financial statements "follow" the same basic principles as those of corporations, but there are major differences. Both assets and liabilities of banks are financial contracts; banks' capital is much smaller in relation to the size of the balance sheet than for non-financial firms, and off-balance sheet commitments of banks have a size of comparable magnitude as their balance sheets. We review quickly the structure of the balance sheet and the income statements in the first section.

This chapter expands the new accounting standards, or International Financial Reporting Standards (IFRS). They are of major importance for financial institutions because, due to strong focus on "fair value" accounting, they drive the markups or markdowns of banks' portfolios that alter significantly either the capital base or the bottom line of the P&L statement. Such valuation rules have a direct impact on banks' solvency.

The review of IFRS is based on banks' annual reports and on consultants' reviews of basic principles [57] and [58]. This overview of new accounting standards includes four sections: Initial recognition of financial assets and liabilities; valuation rules; impairment rules for assets; and hedge accounting. The last section provides comparisons of classifications for risk regulations and for accounting treatment.

Contents

21.1 BANKS' FINANCIAL STATEMENTS

The financial statements of banks differ widely from those of a corporation. The principles are the same. The differences relate to the nature of assets and liabilities, and some other features. The capital of banks is quite small compared to that of corporations, since banks should be able to raise funds for their current operations without going through the lengthy processes that non-financial entities face. On-balance sheet transactions include all transactions that generate an outflow of cash for assets and an inflow of cash for liabilities.

The balance sheet provides a snapshot view of all assets and liabilities at a given date. The income statement summarizes all revenues and costs for determining the income of a period. In a simplified view, the balance sheet includes four basic levels, in addition to off-balance sheet, which divide the balance sheet horizontally (Table 21.1):

- treasury and banking transactions
- intermediation (lending and collecting deposits)
- financial assets (trading portfolio)
- long-term assets and liabilities – fixed assets, investments in subsidiaries, and equity plus long-term debt.

The relative weights of the major compartments vary from one institution to the other, depending upon their core businesses. Equity is typically low in all banks' balance sheets. Lending and deposits are traditionally large in retail and commercial banking. Investment banking, including both specialized finance and trading, typically fund operations in the market. In European banks, "universal banking" allows banking institutions to operate over the entire spectrum of business lines, contrasting with the separation between investment banking and commercial banking in the United States.

For banks, off-balance sheet refers to a large number of other transactions, generically named contingencies. They are off-balance sheet to the extent that they did not trigger any cash inflow of outflow, except for costs and revenues related to such transactions, which are recorded in the income statement. For banking transactions, contingencies include guarantees given to customers or to third parties, committed credit lines not yet drawn by customers, or backup lines of credit. Those are contractual commitments, which customers use at their initiative. Contingencies also include guarantees. A guarantee is the commitment to fulfill the obligations of an obligor, contingent on failure to face payment. Guarantees are given or received by a bank.

TABLE 21.1 Simplified balance sheet

Assets	Equity and Liabilities
Cash	Short-term debt
Lending	Deposits
Financial assets	Financial assets
Fixed assets	Long-term debt
	Equity
Off-balance sheet (contingencies received)	Off-balance sheet (contingencies given)

TABLE 21.2 Income statement and earnings

Interest margin plus fees
capital gains and losses
– operating costs
= operating income[a]
– depreciation
– provisions
– tax
= net income

[a]Earnings before tax and depreciation

"Given contingencies" generate revenues. Those are either upfront and/or periodic fees, or interest revenues or costs calculated as percentages of outstanding balances. The outflows occur conditionally on what happens to the counterparty. For example, if a borrower draws on a credit line, the drawn fraction moves up on the balance sheet and an additional interest income adds to revenues from lending.

Derivatives are "off-balance sheet" market transactions. They include swaps, futures contracts, foreign exchange contracts and options. As other contingencies, they are obligations to make contractual payments, which, for options, are contingent upon occurrence of a specified event.

For the banking portfolio, the traditional accounting measures of earnings are contribution margins calculated at various levels of the income statement. They move from the "net interest income" of the bank, or NII, which is the difference between all interest revenues and all interest costs, down to net income. The total revenue cumulates the net interest income with all fees of the period. The interest margin of commercial banking commonly serves as the main target for management policies of interest rate risk because it is entirely interest driven. Banks tend to increase the fraction of revenues as fees for making the net income less interest rate sensitive. Table 21.2 summarizes the main revenues and costs of the income statement.

Provisions for loan losses should ideally be an indicator of the current credit risk of banking loans. However, provisions have to comply with accounting and fiscal rules and differ from economic provisions. Impairment rules under the new accounting standards are based on the "incurred loss" model, once losses become likely.

21.2 INITIAL RECOGNITION OF FINANCIAL ASSETS AND LIABILITIES

Under financial accounting rules, a financial asset is any contract with right to receive cash or another financial asset, a right to exchange a financial instrument into another or an equity instrument of another entity. An instrument is a liability when the issuer is or can be required to deliver either cash or another financial asset to the holder. This is the critical feature that distinguishes a liability from equity. An instrument is classified as equity when it represents a residual interest in the net assets of the issuer, with no maturity.

TABLE 21.3   Categories of financial assets

Fair value through profit and loss
Loans and receivables
Available for sale
Held to maturity investments

Financial assets are initially measured at fair value, as discussed below. There are four categories of financial assets that are defined according to the management intention of the bank (Table 21.3).

Moreover valuation rules and changes of values are subject to different treatments. Value changes are either directed to the P & L item of the income statement or to the equity of the bank. All assets are also subject to "impairment rules," which also change their values. The treatments of valuation, of value changes and impairment are detailed hereafter.

Financial liabilities are either at fair value, or other financial liabilities. Financial liabilities held for trading include derivatives liabilities that are not used for hedging purposes, obligations to deliver securities or other assets borrowed by a third party, financial liabilities with the intention to repurchase them in the short-term, or financial liabilities that are part of a portfolio for which there is an intention of short-term profit making. Note that liabilities, except those held for trading, are recognized at "amortized cost," as explained below, and fair value changes are not recorded, except impairment. Accordingly, the debt funding of the bank is not part of such financial liabilities.

The original classification is generally irrevocable. The reclassification of assets across categories is accepted only in exceptional circumstances. In other words, initial recognition is permanent and applies to all balance sheet dates. There are forced reclassifications when there are doubts with respect to management intention for a portfolio, in which case the portfolio is said to be "tainted."

Special treatments apply to hybrid securities, such as convertible debt. In such cases, there is a derivative embedded in the instrument, or "host contract." Standalone derivatives that are not used for hedging are always categorized as held for trading. Embedded derivatives follow the classification of the host contract, unless it is not "closely related" to the host contract.

21.2.1 Financial Assets and Liabilities at Fair Value through Profit or Loss

A financial asset is held for trading if acquired or originated principally for the purpose of generating a profit from short-term fluctuations in price or if it is part of a portfolio of identified instruments that are managed together and for which there is intention of short-term profit-taking. Derivatives are always categorized as held for trading unless they are accounted for as hedges. This designation is irrevocable. The asset cannot be moved to another category during its life.

Securities in this category are measured at fair value at the balance sheet date. Changes in fair value (excluding accrued interest on fixed income securities) are presented in the profit and loss account under "Net gain/loss on financial instruments at fair value through profit or loss," along with dividends from variable-income securities and realized gains and losses on disposal. This implies that value changes affect directly the profit and loss of the bank.

21.2.2 Loans and Receivables

Loans and receivables are non-derivative financial assets with fixed or determined payments that are not quoted in listed markets. Loans and receivables include loan assets, trade receivables and other debt investments. They typically arise when an entity provides money directly to an obligor with no intention of trading the receivable. Income earned on fixed-income securities classified in this category is shown under "Interest income" in the profit and loss account.

21.2.3 Held-to-maturity Financial Assets

Held-to-maturity investments are financial assets with fixed or determined payments and fixed maturity (for example, debt securities and redeemable preference shares) that an entity has the positive intent and ability to hold to maturity. This category excludes loans and receivables. Equity securities cannot be classified as held-to-maturity because they do not have a fixed maturity date. The intent and ability is assessed not only when the assets are initially acquired but also at each subsequent balance sheet date. A positive intent to hold assets to maturity is a much stronger constraint than simply having no present intention to sell.

The assets held under this category are subject to severe restrictions. Rules impose that any sale of such asset might lead to reclassification of the entire portfolio into available-for-sale assets. If an entity sells more than an insignificant amount of held-to-maturity securities, other than in exceptional circumstances, this casts doubt on its intent or ability to hold investments to maturity. All held-to-maturity investments are reclassified as available for sale and measured at fair value. There is a possibility to revert again to this classification only after a period (originally, two years).

21.2.4 Available-for-sale Financial Assets

All financial assets that are not classified in another category are classified as available for sale. The available-for-sale category includes all equity securities other than those classified as at fair value through profit or loss. An entity also has the right to designate any asset, other than a trading one, to this category at inception.

Available-for-sale financial assets are fixed-income and equity securities other than those classified as "fair value through profit or loss" or "held-to-maturity." Assets included in the available-for-sale category are initially recorded at fair value plus transaction costs. At the balance sheet date, they are re-valued to fair value, with changes in fair value (excluding accrued interest) shown on a separate line in shareholders' equity, "Unrealized or deferred gains or losses." In other words, the gains or losses of those assets appear explicitly in the capital, but do not appear in the bottom line of profit and loss statement because they are unrealized. On

disposal, or on recognition of an impairment loss, these unrealized gains and losses are transferred from shareholders' equity to the profit and loss account, where they are shown on the
line "Net gain/loss on available-for-sale financial assets."

Income recognized using the effective interest method1[1] derived from fixed-income available-
for-sale securities is recorded in "Interest income" in the profit and loss account. Dividend
income from variable-income securities is recognized in "Net gain/loss on available-for-sale
financial assets" when the group's right to receive payment is established.

21.3 VALUATION RULES

The subsequent valuation rules of financial assets and liabilities depend on the classification. Trading assets and liabilities and available-for-sale assets are measured at "fair value."
Loans and receivables, and held-to-maturity investments are carried at "amortized cost." The
easiest method for fair value assessment is the existence of listed prices in active markets.
Whenever market prices are not available other valuation techniques using market data are
implemented.

The alternate valuation method is called "amortized cost." The amortized cost is essentially
derived from the amount to be repaid at maturity. In addition, values are subject to impairment
losses when there is objective evidence of losses due to past events. The correspondences
between classification and valuation and impairment rules are summarized in Table 21.4.
Impairment is irrelevant for a traded asset because it is embedded in the fair value. Fair value
changes, other than impairment, are directed either to capital or to the bottom line according
to rules detailed above.

21.3.1 Amortized Cost

For assets valued at amortized cost, the amortized cost is the amount to be repaid at maturity,
usually the principal of face value, plus or minus any unamortized premium or discount and
net of transaction cost, less principal repayments and any impairment.

The amortization schedule uses the effective interest rate method. The effective interest rate
is the yield-to-maturity, or the value of the discount rate making the value of the instrument

TABLE 21.4 Classification and valuation rules

Financial assets	Measurement	Changes in carrying amount	Impairment (if objective evidence)
Financial assets at fair value	Fair value	Income statement	No
Loans and receivables	Amortized cost	Income statement	Yes
Held-to-maturity investments	Amortized cost	Income statement	Yes
Available-for-sale financial assets	Fair value	Equity	Yes

---

1 See section "Amortized Cost".

exactly equal to all future expected payments, including discounts and premium. This rate is applied to the carried amount at each reporting date for determining the interest income (for assets) or cost (for liabilities), for the elapsed period. The yield-to-maturity, and the cash flows, do not include any potential loss for the instrument. It is a contractual yield. Transaction costs include fees, commissions and taxes paid to other parties.

21.3.2 Method of Determining Fair Value

Financial assets and liabilities classified as fair value through profit or loss, and financial assets classified as available-for-sale, are measured and accounted for at fair value, defined as the amount for which an asset could be exchanged between knowledgeable, willing parties in an arm's length transaction. On initial recognition, the value of a financial instrument is generally the transaction price.

Fair value is determined:

- on the basis of quoted prices in an active market
- or using valuation techniques involving mathematical calculation methods based on accepted financial theories, parameters derived in some cases from the prices of instruments traded in active markets, and from statistical estimates or other quantitative methods.

The distinction between the two valuation methods is made according to whether or not the instrument is traded in an active market. A market for an instrument is regarded as active, and hence liquid, if there is regular trading in that market, bids and offers are matched, or instruments are traded that are very similar to the instrument being valued. There is a hierarchy of fair valuation techniques, in three main categories:

- category 1: observed prices in active markets
- category 2: observed prices in active markets of instruments that can replicate the instruments of which value is to be assessed
- category 3: when there are no observable prices, model valuation is implemented, using generally accepted models.

The existence of public price quotations is considered as the best evidence of fair value. Active markets are such that listed prices are readily and regularly available from an exchange, dealers or brokers. Those prices should represent actual transactions at "arm's length." In the event of multiple trading places, the most favorable price can be used. The IASB (International Accounting Standards Board) redefined fair value as the price that would be received to sell an asset in orderly transactions between market participants.

Inactive markets are those that do not satisfy those conditions, or in plain words, illiquid markets with no reliable prices. Inactive markets exist notably for complex instruments and when liquidity dries down.

21.3.3 Instruments Traded in Active Markets

If quoted prices in an active market are available, they serve for determining fair value. This method is used for quoted securities and for derivatives traded on organized markets such as futures and options. Derivatives, swaps, forward rate agreements, caps, floors and standard options are traded in active markets.

Valuations are determined using generally accepted models (discounted cash flows, Black-Scholes model, interpolation techniques) based on quoted market prices for similar instruments or underlying instruments. The valuation derived from these models is adjusted for liquidity and credit risk. Starting from valuations derived from median market prices, price adjustments are used to value the net position in each financial instrument at bid price in the case of short positions, or at asking price in the case of long positions. Bid price is the price at which the counterparty would buy the instrument, and asking price is the price at which a seller would sell the same instrument. A counterparty risk adjustment is applied to the valuation derived from the model in order to reflect the credit quality of the derivative instrument.

21.3.4 Instruments Traded in Inactive Markets

Two cases are considered when there is no active market. If an instrument can be replicated by other simple instruments traded in active markets, the price is derived from those of these instruments (category 2). If an instrument is not traded in active markets and cannot be valued indirectly by replicating transactions, valuation becomes model-based (category 3).

Products traded in inactive markets are valued using internal valuation models based on parameters that are not observable or only partially observable. A non-observable parameter is defined as a parameter whose value results from assumptions or correlations, which are not based on observable current market transactions or on observable market data at that date.

Some complex financial instruments, which are usually tailored, illiquid or have long maturities, are valued using internally developed techniques or techniques relying on data partially observable on active markets. In the absence of observable data, these instruments are measured on initial recognition in a way that reflects the transaction price, regarded as the best indication of fair value. Valuations derived from these models are adjusted for liquidity risk and credit risk.

The so-called "day-one" gain or loss is defined as the difference between the transaction price and the fair value. It should be recognized at the time of the transaction in active markets.

The margin generated when these complex financial instruments are traded (day one profit) is deferred and taken to the profit and loss account over the period during which the valuation parameters are expected to remain non-observable. When parameters that were originally non-observable become observable, or when the valuation can be substantiated by comparison with recent similar transactions in an active market, the unrecognized portion of the day-one profit is released to the profit and loss account.

21.4 IMPAIRMENT OF FINANCIAL ASSETS

An impairment loss is recognized against loans and held-to-maturity financial assets when there is objective evidence of a measurable decrease in value as a result of an event occurring after inception. Expected losses are not considered as impairment. Objective evidence for impairment includes financial difficulties of the issuer, higher probability of default, and breach of a contract.

If there is objective evidence that impairment has been incurred and the carrying amount of a financial asset carried at amortized cost exceeds its estimated recoverable amount, the asset is impaired. At an individual level, the amount of the impairment is the difference between the carrying amount before impairment and the present value, discounted at the original effective interest rate of the asset, of those components (principal, interest, collateral, etc.) regarded as recoverable. The carrying amount is reduced to its recoverable amount either directly or through the use of an allowance account. The amount of the loss is included in net profit or loss for the period. Impairment appears in financial statements either as "impairments," or "loan losses provisions," or "cost of risk."

Impairment of available-for-sale financial assets (which mainly comprise securities) is recognized on an individual basis if there is objective evidence of impairment as a result of one or more events occurring since acquisition. If there is objective evidence of impairment of available-for-sale financial assets carried at fair value, the cumulative net loss that has previously been recognized in equity is transferred to the bottom line, even though the asset has not been sold. Impairment losses are recognized as a component of net income on the line "Net gain/loss on available-for-sale financial assets."

In the case of variable-income securities quoted in an active market, a prolonged or significant decline in the quoted price below acquisition cost is regarded as objective evidence of impairment. Any subsequent decline in fair value constitutes an additional impairment loss, recognized in the profit and loss account.

Loans are assessed for evidence of impairment initially on an individual basis and on a portfolio basis. Individual impairments apply when the asset subject to impairment is identifiable. Collective impairment of a pool of assets is applicable to assets that have similar credit risk characteristics. Counterparties that are not individually impaired are risk assessed on the basis of portfolios of loans with similar characteristics. The entity identifies groups of counterparties which, as a result of events occurring since inception of the loans, have collectively acquired a probability of default at maturity that provides objective evidence of impairment of the entire portfolio, but without it being possible at that stage to allocate the impairment to individual counterparties[2].

Changes in the amount of impairment losses are taken to the profit and loss account under "impairment." Any subsequent decrease in an impairment loss that can be related objectively to an event occurring after the impairment loss was recognized is directed to the profit and loss.

---

2 Note that the impairment assessment might result from the internal rating system based on historical data, adjusted as necessary to reflect circumstances prevailing at the balance sheet date.

21.5 HEDGE ACCOUNTING

Hedge accounting defines the usual basis for recognizing gains and losses (or revenues and expenses) associated with a hedged instrument and a hedging instrument. It enables the off-setting of gains and losses of the two instruments, the hedging instrument and the hedged instrument. In order to apply hedge accounting, strict criteria, including the existence of formal documentation and the achievement of "effectiveness tests," must be met. Effectiveness tests are intended to provide evidence of a strong enough relationship between the hedged instrument and the hedging instrument.

21.5.1 Types of Hedges

There are three types of hedges that can be recognized:

- fair value hedges
- cash flow hedges
- hedges of a net investment in a foreign operation.

Fair value hedges apply to changes in fair value. Gains and losses of the hedged instruments and of the hedging instrument are recognized immediately and offset, provided that the hedge is effective. Under fair value hedges, the gains and losses or the revenues and expenses of both instruments are recognized over the same accounting period. In a fair value hedging relationship, the derivative instrument is revalued at fair value in the balance sheet, with changes in fair value taken to profit or loss in "Net gain/loss on financial instruments at fair value through profit or loss," symmetrically with the revaluation of the hedged item. A micro-hedge applies to individual instruments. Under special circumstances, macro-hedges, or hedges that apply to a portfolio, can be recognized.

Cash flow hedges are used for reducing the exposure to cash flow variability, and in particular to hedge interest rate risk on floating-rate assets and liabilities, including rollovers, and foreign exchange risk on highly probable forecast foreign currency revenues. Cash flow hedges imply deferring recognized gains and losses of the hedging instrument until the hedged items affect earnings. In a cash flow hedging relationship, the derivative is stated at fair value in the balance sheet, with changes in fair value taken to shareholders' equity on a separate line, "Unrealised or deferred gains or losses." The amounts taken to shareholders' equity over the life of the hedge are transferred to the profit and loss account under "Net interest income" when the cash flows from the hedged item impact profit or loss.

Hedges of net foreign currency investments in subsidiaries and branches are accounted for in the same way as cash flow hedges.

At the inception of the hedge, the group prepares formal documentation of the hedging relationship, identifying:

- the instrument (or portion of the instrument or portion of risk) that is being hedged
- the hedging strategy and the type of risk covered

- the hedging instrument and
- the methods used to assess the "effectiveness" of the hedging relationship.

Whatever the hedging strategy used, any ineffective portion of the hedge is recognized in the profit and loss account under "Net gain/loss on financial instruments at fair value through profit or loss."

21.5.2 "Effectiveness" of Hedge

"Effectiveness" of hedge has to be documented to allow recognition of hedge. On inception and at least quarterly, the group assesses, consistently with the original documentation, the actual (retrospective) and expected (prospective) effectiveness of the hedging relationship. Retrospective effectiveness tests are designed to assess whether actual changes in the fair value or cash flows of the hedging instrument and the hedged item are within a range of 80% to 125%. Prospective effectiveness tests are designed to ensure that expected changes in the fair value or cash flows of the derivative over the residual life of the hedge adequately offset those of the hedged item. For highly probable forecast transactions, effectiveness is assessed largely on the basis of historical data for similar transactions.

21.6 COMPARISONS OF CLASSIFICATIONS: RISK REGULATIONS AND IFRS

It is useful to contrast the regulatory treatment before and after IFRS, as well as the classifications used by IFRS and the classification under risk regulations. Both are summarized in Tables 21.5 and 21.6.

The current debate, arising from the financial crisis, with fair value accounting cannot be dismissed easily. This effect is well defined in an article from *The Economist*, dated September 18th, 2008:

TABLE 21.5 Comparison of accounting treatment and regulatory treatment by asset category: before and after IFRS

Before IFRS		After IFRS	
Accounting treatment	Risk regulatory treatment	Accounting treatment	Risk regulatory treatment
Market value	Trading portfolio, market risk amendment	Fair value through P&L	Trading portfolio, market risk amendment
Amortized cost	Banking portfolio Credit capital charge	Fair value through equity	Banking portfolio Credit capital charge
		Amortized cost	Banking portfolio Credit capital charge

TABLE 21.6 Comparison of accounting treatment and regulatory treatment by asset category

IAS 39	Accounting treatment	Risk regulatory treatment
Fair value or trading portfolio	Fair value through P & L	Trading portfolio
Available for sale	Fair value through equity	Market risk amendment
Loans and receivables	Amortized cost	Banking portfolio
Held-to-maturity	Amortized cost	Credit capital charge

"Bankers say that in a downturn fair value accounting forces them to recognize losses at the same time, impairing their capital and triggering fire sales of assets, which in turn drive prices and valuations down even more. Under traditional accounting, losses hit the books far more slowly."

All's Fair – The crisis and fair value accounting

The IASB and the FASB also committed themselves, in October 2008, to a joint approach to dealing with reporting issues arising from the global financial crisis. They set up the Financial Crisis Advisory Group (FCAG) in December 2008, to advise the two boards about standard-setting implications of the global financial crisis and potential changes to the global regulatory environment. Topics being discussed include fair value accounting, loan provisioning, structured entities and other off-balance sheet vehicles.

SECTION 7

Asset Liability Management (ALM)

Much before VaR appeared as a central concept, asset liability management (ALM) developed and provided tools for capturing liquidity and interest rate risk at the global balance sheet level. It extends to the definition of economic transfer prices, serving as benchmarks for pricing and for allocating revenues. Note that there is no capital charge for mismatch risk that ALM addresses.

ALM is neither a subset of market risk, as sometimes suggested, nor a trivial technique that can be bypassed by addressing the more sophisticated techniques of market risk and credit risk modeling. There are not so many extensive publications on ALM[1]. The financial crisis will presumably enhance and reinforce the role of ALM as a critical function because of its major role of mismatch risk. ALM addresses mismatch risk in its two dimensions, liquidity risk and interest rate risk. ALM provides the very first picture of the liquidity position of a bank, through the time profiles of excesses of deficits of funds in all currencies. ALM also tracks interest income fluctuations by relating them to interest rates. It applies to retail banking, commercial banking, and merchant banking.

The ALM Committee, or "ALCO," decides all related policies with respect to balance sheet structure, funding, regulatory constraints, and relate those with interest income.

Contents

ALM GOALS

The goal of ALM is to provide measures of the exposure to mismatch risk, and to maintain it within bounds, while optimizing the risk–return profile of the balance sheet, both through on-balance sheet actions (business policy) and off-balance sheet instruments (derivatives).

The target variables of mismatch risk include the liquidity position plus target variables subject to interest rate risk (IRR).

1 Net interest income (NII): NII = interest revenues – interest costs.
2 Economic value (EV) of balance sheet: net value of the mark-to-model (MTM) values of assets and liabilities.

ALM risks, liquidity and interest rate, are not subject to capital charges under Basel 2. Basel 2 considers supervision of ALM risks only under pillar 2 ("market discipline"):

§762 The Committee remains convinced that interest rate risk in the banking book is a potentially significant risk which merits support from capital …

---

1 The *Handbook of Asset and Liability Management*, by Alexandre Adam in 2007, John Wiley & Sons, is an example of extensive coverage of the topics.

§763 The revised guidance on interest rate risk recognizes banks' internal systems as the principal tool for the measurement of interest rate risk in the banking book and the supervisory response. To facilitate supervisors' monitoring of interest rate risk exposures across institutions, banks would have to provide the results of their internal measurement systems, expressed in terms of economic value relative to capital, using standardized interest rate shocks.

Basel 2 did not allocate any risk-based capital to ALM risks which played a major role in the 2008 financial crisis. Today, regulations rightly consider minimum simple measures for addressing both financial firm and financial system risks (macro-prudential monitoring), which compensates the relative lack of attention on ALM risks.

FTP systems link global risk management to business units and transactions. As such, they are an important block of bank-wide risk management systems and are generally within the broad scope of ALM.

ALM SCOPE AND STRUCTURE OF THE SECTION

ALM covers a wide scope from the management of liquidity risk to that of the economic value of the balance sheet and up to internal transfer pricing. The overall scope of ALM is subdivided according to ALM roles. This ALM section breaks down the scope of ALM into distinct blocks, which address its different roles, into chapters dedicated to each mission of ALM.

There are six chapters in this section.

- Traditional gap management or liquidity mismatches (Chapter 22).
- Interest rate gap management or interest rate mismatches, with its simple relation to the first target variable of ALM, NII (Chapter 23).
- Hedging interest rate risk based on simple gap analysis (Chapter 24).
- Embedded options in banking products, and, beyond, the so-called "convexity risk," which is unfortunately always adverse to the bank, requiring to move beyond simple gaps, to duration and convexity gaps (Chapter 25).
- Economic value of the balance sheet, a second target variable of ALM that relates to the time profile of net interest incomes across periods (Chapter 26).
- Hedging of economic value convexity risk, through convexity or optional gaps (Chapter 27).

The funds transfer pricing (FTP) scheme, which makes up a separate building block, is addressed in a separated next section.

THE ALM FUNCTION

ALM is usually located in the finance department. The latter deals with all financial issues: interest rate risk, funding risk, internal transfers of funds, allocation of risks across business units, management control and reporting. The finance department might also extend its activities to securitizations and capital management, together with the risk department. ALM might opt for open positions with respect to mismatch risk. Such open exposures should comply with limits set in conjunction by ALM and the risk department. The ALM unit can also be a profit center and independent to the extent that it enhances the risk–return profile of the bank, subject to above limits.

Its organization is summarized in figure 7.1. The ALM committee (ALCO) is in charge of implementing ALM decisions, while a technical unit prepares all analyses necessary for taking decisions and runs the ALM models. The ALCO agenda includes "global balance sheet management," and the guidelines to business lines for making their business policy consistent with the global bank's policy.

The ALCO is the implementation arm of ALM. It groups heads or business lines together with the top management and sets up the guidelines and policies with respect to interest rate risk, liquidity risk for the banking portfolio, and extends its scope to business policies (on-balance sheet). Execution is delegated to a central treasury department.

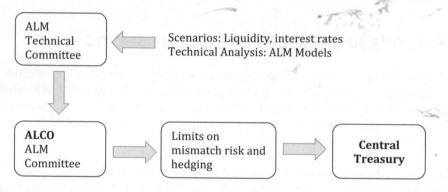

FIGURE S7.1

22

Liquidity Management and Liquidity Gaps

Liquidity risk results from size and maturity mismatches of assets and liabilities. Section 22.1 defines liquidity and liquidity risks. Section 22.2 introduces liquidity gap analysis, which relies on the projected time profiles of excess or deficits of liquidity of the existing assets and liabilities. Such gaps provide the very first image of a liquidity posture of a bank.

There are three basic situations that characterize a bank's liquidity posture and its mismatch risk: either the bank generates future deficits of funds, or it generates excesses of funds, or the amortization of existing assets and liabilities approximately match so that the passage of time does not generate any deficits or excesses of funds. Open projected liquidity gaps imply interest rate exposure because future deficits or excesses of funds will be financed or invested at interest rates unknown today. Cash matching implies zero mismatch risk and is the reference situation. In general, the "structural position" of banks results from the maturity mismatch of assets and liabilities.

The next section (Section 22.3) details liquidity gap calculations and provides sample liquidity gap reports. Section 22.4 addresses liquidity gap management. It shows how liquidity gaps can be closed or maintained with limits by structuring adequately the maturity structure of financial debts or investments. In some cases, projected cash deficits cannot be entirely closed by cash transactions. The bank might still hedge its interest rate risk arising from projected open gaps by entering into forward contracts. Section 22.5 addresses the issue of interest rate risk arising from structural positions characterized by recurring excesses of liquidity. Such excesses necessitate "optimum" rules for investing excesses that pile up with time, which, typically, aim at smoothing out interest rate fluctuations. Section 22.6 addresses the limitations and drawbacks of the liquidity gap models that depend on conventions. The last section (Section 22.7) addresses contingency plans for liquidity.

Contents

22.1 LIQUIDITY DEFINITIONS

Liquidity is the ability to raise cash sufficient to finance lending opportunities and face deposit withdrawals at a reasonable cost in a reasonable time frame. Banks face liquidity needs by collecting deposits or raising financial debt. Liquidity risk is the risk of not being able to raise liquidity or of raising liquidity at a high cost.

For isolating themselves from market disruptions, banks also rely on liquid assets. Liquid assets are assets that can be sold easily without loss of value. Typical liquid assets include Treasury bills, which are riskless and short-term, of which value is less sensitive to interest rate variations. Holding liquid assets has a drawback, in that the return on such assets is the short-term risk-free rate.

Because short-term financial markets were highly liquid, including in the inter-bank market, liquidity risk might have been under-estimated by banks in recent years. The cost of inter-bank liquidity and a measure of risk aversion in inter-bank lending and borrowing is the TED spread, or Treasury bill versus Euro/Dollar spread. The spread is typically at 50 basis points but jumped to values as high as 10 times as much during the financial crisis, which turned out to be a liquidity crunch, triggering such measures as government guarantees for inter-bank lending and borrowing.

Under normal conditions, liquidity management relies on liquidity gaps, which should be completed by "stress tests" on liquidity, for assessing what could happen under an extreme crisis shortage. Contingent liquidity crisis plans have to be set up, and are briefly discussed in the final section.

22.2 LIQUIDITY GAP TIME PROFILES

The liquidity gaps are the differences, at all future dates, between the balances of assets and liabilities of the banking portfolio. When referring only to existing assets and liabilities, they amortize over time, and their time profiles are declining lines. Such gaps are called "static" because new loans and deposits or debts at future dates are ignored. The difference between projected assets and liabilities can have three basic shapes.

22.2.1 Three Basic Liquidity Positions

The very first view of the liquidity position of a bank is the static liquidity gap time profile. There are three basic situations: cash matching, underfunding and overfunding. Figure 22.1 summarizes these typical situations. Any excess funds, or any deficit of funds, at the starting date, are supposed fully funded or invested, making the current gap zero, and non-zero gaps appear only at future dates. The liability time profile hits the level of capital once all debts amortize completely. The diagrams ignore the gap between fixed assets and equity.

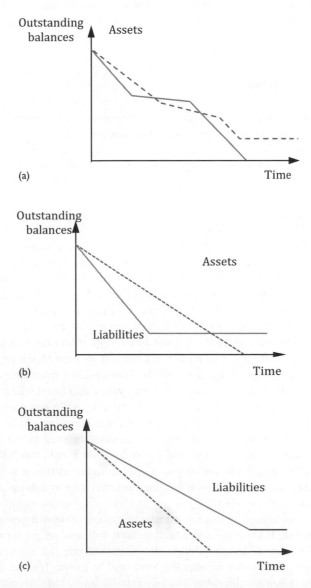

FIGURE 22.1   Three basic situations (a) near zero liquidity gaps, cash matching (b) deficits (c) excess funds. The typical "structural position" of banks is the case when asset average maturity is longer than liability average maturity – this case is shown in (b)

The liquidity gaps are algebraic differences between the projected outstanding balances of existing assets and liabilities. Note that we do not consider here the interest rate flows generated by existing assets and liabilities. Therefore, a positive gap between assets and liabilities is equivalent to a deficit, and vice versa. There are as many gaps as there are time points in the future, and for each date:

$$\text{liquidity gap}(t) = \text{assets}(t) - \text{liabilities}(t)$$

It is implicitly assumed here that the future balances of assets and liabilities are known at future dates. This is an unrealistic assumption, which requires some conventions or modeling in certain cases.

22.2.2 Mismatch Risk

Cash matching implies that the time profiles of amortization of assets and liabilities are (approximately) identical. In such a case there is no maturity mismatch. All liquidity gaps are equal to zero. When the balance sheet amortizes over time, it does not generate any deficit or excess of funds and the repayment schedule of debt replicates the repayment schedule of assets. Equivalently, the static balance sheet melts down over time, remaining balanced without generating any need or investment of funds.

The so-called "structural position" of banks consists of lending for longer maturities than those of liabilities. This is the natural position of commercial banks because of the zero (legal) maturity of demand deposits and because banks often try to take advantage of upward sloping yield curves, and capturing the spread between long-term and short-term rates.

Mismatch generates both liquidity risk and interest rate risk. Consider the case of a single loan, rather than for the entire bank. Assume that the bank grants a bullet loan to a client. If the debt replicates the time profile of the loan, it will have exactly the same amount and maturity. When time passes, there is no liquidity gap due to the loan plus the replicating debt. Assume that both loan and debt are fixed rate. The loan rate will usually be higher than the debt rate, the difference being the net interest income (NII), or interest revenue minus interest cost, of the portfolio made of the loan plus the mirroring debt. The NII of the loan is locked for the life of the loan since the cost is also fixed when the loan is originated. The loan can also be variable rate. It would be indexed to some market rate such as Libor 3-month. Over a year, there will be four reset dates inclusive of the date at which the loan is granted. At each reset date, the loan rate remains indexed to the prevailing Libor. If the debt has the same reference rate, the Libor 3-month index, the NII is again locked from origination. Matching both liquidity and interest rates results in a NII locked in and no liquidity risk. This is why cash matching and interest rate matching are considered as the benchmark case.

Alternatively, any mismatch between maturities and interest rate will generate both liquidity risk and interest rate risk. If loans are under-funded, there will positive gaps, or deficits, at future dates. Those deficits generate both liquidity risk and interest rate risk since there is no way to know at which rate the funds that balance the loans will be raised. If there is excess funding, there is no liquidity risk, since liquidity was raised in advance, but there is interest rate risk, since we do not know at which rate those excess funds will be lent at future dates.

The target funding profile depends upon whether the ALM wishes to close all liquidity gaps, or maintain a mismatch. Any mismatch should be consistent with expectations on interest rates. For instance, in a fixed rate universe, keeping a balance sheet under-funded makes sense only because short-term rates are lower than long-term rates, or when betting on declining interest rates so that deferring funding is consistent with interest cost savings. Conversely, keeping the balance sheet over-funded implies either an inverted yield curve or expectations of raising interest rates, because the investment of excess funds will occur in the future. Sometimes, the balance sheet remains over-funded for long periods because there is an excess of deposits over loans. In such a case, the excess funds will be invested in the market, and the investment policy should follow guidelines with respect to target interest revenue and interest rate risk on future investments.

22.3 LIQUIDITY GAP CALCULATIONS

There are liquidity gaps and marginal gaps, static and dynamic gaps, and other details that need to be considered for projecting liquidity gaps. The most common liquidity gap profiles are static gaps calculated by projecting the balances of existing assets and liabilities. Dynamic gaps include in the projection the new loans or debts as projected from today.

22.3.1 Static Liquidity Gaps

Static liquidity gaps are differences of projected future balances of existing assets and liabilities. Incremental, or marginal gaps, are differences in variations between two adjacent time points. Both simple and marginal gaps are calculated. The cumulated value over time of the marginal gaps is equal to the gap between the current outstanding balances of assets and liabilities. Table 22.1 is an example of a gap time profile.

TABLE 22.1 Time profiles of outstanding assets and liabilities and of liquidity gaps

Dates	1	2	3	4	5	6
Assets	1000	900	700	650	500	300
Liabilities	1000	800	500	400	350	100
Gap[a]	0	100	200	250	150	200
Assets amortization		−100	−200	−50	−150	−200
Liabilities amortization		−200	−300	−100	−50	−250
Marginal gap[b]		100	100	50	−100	50
Cumulative marginal gap[c]		100	200	250	150	200

[a]Calculated as the difference between assets and liabilities. A positive gap is a deficit that requires funding. A negative gap is an excess of resources to be invested.
[b]Calculated as the algebraic variation of assets minus the algebraic variation of liabilities between t and $t - 1$. With this convention, a positive gap is an outflow, and a negative gap is an inflow.
[c]The cumulative marginal gaps are identical to the gaps calculated with the outstanding balances of assets and liabilities.

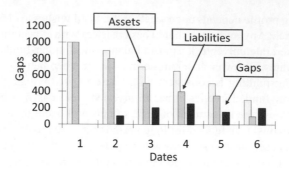

FIGURE 22.2   Time profile of liquidity gaps

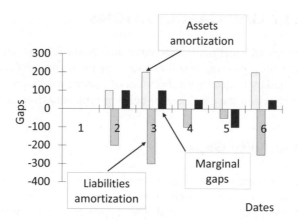

FIGURE 22.3   Time profile of marginal liquidity gaps

In Table 22.1, assets amortize slower than liabilities. Therefore, the inflows from repayments of assets are less than the outflows used to repay the debts, calculated with the outstanding balances of asset and liabilities. A deficit cumulates from one period to the other, except in period 5. Figures 22.2 and 22.3 show cumulative and marginal gap time profiles.

Marginal, or incremental, gaps are the differences between the variations of assets and liabilities during a given period (Figure 22.2). A positive marginal gap means that the algebraic variation of assets exceeds the algebraic variation of liabilities: It is an inflow. A negative marginal gap means that assets amortize at a slower pace than liabilities at that period: It is an outflow[1].

The marginal gaps represent the new funds required, or the new excess funds of the period available for investing. The implicit assumption is that all previous gaps have been financed or invested up to some management horizon. Then, a new marginal gap represents the new financing required or the new investment of lending required for closing the liquidity gaps assuming previous lending/borrowing contracted in previous time points stay in place. The new

---

1   For instance, if the amortization of assets is 3, and that of liabilities is 5, the algebraic marginal gap, as defined above, is $-3 - (-5) = +2$, and it is an outflow. Sometimes the gaps are calculated as the opposite difference. It is important to keep a clear convention, so that the figures can be easily interpreted.

funding, say between the dates 2 and 3, is not the cumulated deficit between dates 1 and 3, or 200, because the debt contracted at date 2, for example 100, does not necessarily amortize at date 3. If the debt is still outstanding at 3, the deficit at date 3 is only 100. This is the rationale for using marginal gaps. They represent the amounts to raise or invest over a given horizon, and for which new decisions are necessary.

The cumulated gaps are easier to interpret, however. Such cumulative gaps represent only the cumulated needs for funds required at all dates, not the new financing or investment at each date (Figure 22.3). This would be the case only when debts or investment of previous periods would amortize at the next time point.

Table 22.2 shows a sample liquidity gap profile from annual report of KBC, 2006. The time buckets are quite large in this sample table. Most tools provide gaps over more frequent time points, at least monthly for up to 1 to 3 years. The next diagram (Figure 22.4) shows the output of a standard ALM software. The top part shows how asset and liabilities amortize through time by monthly steps. The assets are shown on the up section (dark grey area) of the y-axis and time is along the x-axis. Liabilities appear in the down section as a shaded area. The lines show the average interest rates of assets and of liabilities respectively. The liquidity gap time profile is the difference between assets and liabilities. Figure 22.5 shows the time profile of

TABLE 22.2 Sample liquidity gap time profile

Net liquidity gap, KBC group banks								
In millions of EUR	≤1 month	1–3 months	3–12 months	1–5 years	5–10 years	>10 years	Not defined	Total
31-12-2005								
Assets*	90,044	25,163	32,168	53,836	29,167	29,938	36,271	304,587
Liabilities*	133,253	40,492	37,355	39,252	11,487	8,736	34,012	304,587
Net liquidity gap*	−35,209	−15,329	−5,188	14,583	17,680	21,203	2,260	0
31-12-2006								
Assets*	95,950	24,797	31,279	65,215	34,428	26,006	40,622	318,298
Liabilities*	137,731	30,682	37,884	47,961	15,924	9,828	38,289	318,298
Net liquidity gap*	−41,781	−5,884	−6,605	17,254	18,504	16,178	2,333	0

*Excluding derivatives
Source: KBC Annual Report, 2006

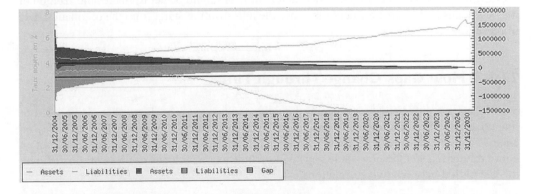

FIGURE 22.4 Time profiles of assets and liabilities

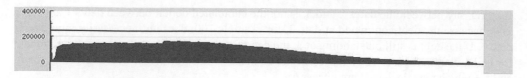

FIGURE 22.5   Time profile of liquidity gap and limits

the liquidity gap, magnified from Figure 22.4. Liquidity gaps are subject to limits. The gap limit is the horizontal line.

Note that software providers embed a number of useful functionalities in their products. For example, it is possible to drill down in any one gap for any date for finding out which transactions contribute to the gap. Any spike in the gap profile can be allocated to the corresponding transactions, which make such tools essential for balance sheet management.

22.3.2 Dynamic Liquidity Gaps

Static liquidity gaps results from existing assets and liabilities only. Dynamic liquidity gaps add the projected new credits and new deposits to the amortization profiles of existing assets.

New assets and liabilities generated at future dates are added to existing assets and liabilities and change the liquidity gaps. Total assets and liabilities, existing plus new ones, tend to increase in general, rather than amortize. This new gap time profile is the "dynamic gap." Gaps for both existing and new assets and liabilities are required to project the total excesses or deficits of funds. In general balance sheet projections are used for budgeting purposes rather than liquidity risk management.

For liquidity management purposes, it is a common practice to focus first on the existing assets and liabilities to calculate the gap time profile because there is no need to obtain funds in advance for new transactions, or to invest resources that are not yet collected. Funding the deficits or investing excesses from new business occurs when they appear in the balance sheet. Since the liquidity gap time profile is continuously updated, any new loan or debt will appear anyway in the updated static liquidity gap profile.

Figure 22.6 shows the new transactions plus the existing assets and liabilities. When projecting new business, volumes of new assets and liabilities should be net from the amortization of the new loans and of the new deposits, since the amortization starts from the origination date of these transactions.

22.3.3 How Gaps Change Through Time

Static gaps are sufficient for managing liquidity for two reasons. First, there is no need to pile up excess funds for financing new loans in advance and it is not possible to act today on excess funds which are not yet here. Second, the static gaps are updated frequently, at least on a monthly basis, and the new static gaps will include any new loans or debts originated over the last period between two calculations.

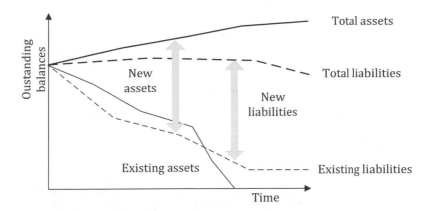

FIGURE 22.6   Gap profile with existing and new business

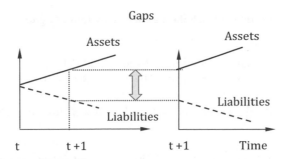

FIGURE 22.7   Gap profile changes

When time passes, the gap profile changes: existing assets and liabilities amortize, and new business comes in. The gap, which starts from 0 at t, might widen up to some positive value at $t+1$. The positive gap at $t+1$ is a pre-funding gap, or "*ex ante.*" In reality, the funding closes the gap at the same time that new business and amortization open it.

In Figure 22.7, the gap at date t is funded, as of current date, and assets and liabilities are equal. At date $t+1$, a new deficit appears which requires new funding. Such a gap will be closed before it actually appears, and at the new date, both asset and liability lines start again from the same point.

22.3.4 Fixed Assets and Equity

Fixed assets and equity are not interest-bearing assets and liabilities. But they contribute to the liquidity gap. In Figure 22.8 they generate a point in time gap of $15 - 30 = -15$. The overall gap includes the 15 excess funds.

The liquidity gap is the difference between total assets and liabilities:

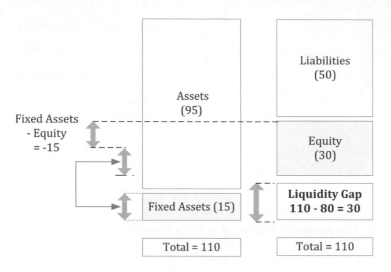

FIGURE 22.8   The structure of the balance sheet and liquidity gap

$$\text{liquidity gap} = \text{total assets} - \text{total liabilities}$$
$$= 95 + 15 - (50 + 30) = 110 - 80 = +30$$

The liquidity gap is also the gap between assets and liabilities plus the gap between fixed assets and equity:

$$\text{liquidity gap} = (\text{assets} - \text{liabilities}) + (\text{fixed assets} - \text{equity})$$
$$= (95 - 50) + (15 - 30) = +30$$

In what follows, we ignore the bottom section of the balance sheet and other items which are not interest bearing.

22.4 LIQUIDITY MANAGEMENT

Liquidity risk exists when there are deficits of funds. Controlling liquidity risk implies spreading over time the required amounts of funding, and avoiding unexpected important needs for raising additional funds. Usually, limits are set for liquidity gaps for making sure that raising funds will remain within acceptable boundaries. Liquidity management aims at a target time profile of gaps after raising new resources, which complies with liquidity gap limits. Such limits depend on the amount that can be raised periodically without raising funding issues.

The minimum liquidity to be raised is the amount that bridges the gap at $t + 1$ and all future dates up to the management horizon. Active management by the Treasury department is usually from now up to 1 or 2 years. Beyond that horizon, the bank should monitor gaps for making sure that no one gap of various subsequent periods peaks to high levels beyond limits. We concentrate here on the short term. Any cash raised today for bridging current gaps can be raised in various ways, depending on the structuring by maturity of the corresponding debt across maturities. The funding decision reshapes the entire amortization profile of liabilities.

The example below shows two examples of profiles of existing assets and liabilities with initial deficits. In both cases, the resources amortize quicker than assets and the deficits are maintained up to the short-term horizon.

We assume that ALM wishes to raise the resources profile up to that of assets because expectations with respect to interest rates have changed or for minimizing liquidity requirements in the future. The issue is to define the structuring of the new debts consistent with the new goal. The target resources profile should become the same as that of assets. The process starts from the horizon and requires moving backward for finding out which debts are required. The treasurer then piles up "layers" of debts starting from the horizon in order to raise the liabilities time profile until it reach the one of assets.

22.4.1 Structuring Debt Maturities

Figure 22.9 illustrates two different cases. In the left-hand side, the gap continuously decreases until the horizon. Then, layers of debts, raised today, pile up, moving backward from the horizon, so that the resources amortization profile replicates the asset profile. Small steps remain, so that this hedge is not perfect. In the second case, it is not feasible to hit the target asset profile with debt contracted as of today (spot debt). This is because the gap increases with time, peaks, and then narrows down when getting closer to the management horizon. We can raise enough debt to match the level of existing assets today. Any additional debt contracted today would result in excess funds over assets, which would be inconsistent with cash matching. On the other hand, limiting funds to what is necessary today does not fill the gap in intermediate periods between now and the horizon.

In a fixed-rate universe, this intermediate mismatch generates interest rate risk. Suppose that it is decided to lock in the NII over all intermediate periods. This is feasible with forward hedges[2]. A forward contract could lock in the rates for each of the intermediate periods. Such hedge should start at future dates and correspond to the amounts of debts represented in gray, those amounts of debts which, raised when needed, would fill in the remaining gaps not yet closed today.

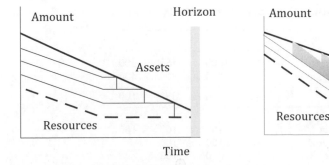

FIGURE 22.9 Closing liquidity gaps (deficit)

---

2 See Chapter 7 on interest rate derivatives and hedging.

22.4.2 Numerical Example

Table 22.3 shows a numerical example of the first case above with three periods. The existing gap is 200, and the cash-matching funding necessitates debts of various maturities. The "layer 1" is a bullet debt extending from now to the end of period 3. Its amount is equal to the gap at period 3 or 50. A second bullet debt from now to period 2, of amount 50, bridges the gap at period 2. Once those debts are in place, there is still a 100 gap left for period 1. In the end, the treasurer contracted three bullet debts: 50 for 3 periods, 50 for 2 periods, and 100 for 1. Once this is done, the time profile of resources becomes identical to that of assets over the total horizon.

In the second case above, the same process does not apply because the gap increases and, after a while, decreases until the horizon (Table 22.4). It is not possible to reach cash matching with resources raised today. One bullet debt, of 100, partially bridges the gaps from now up to the final horizon. A second 100 bullet debt starts today until the end of period 2. Then, the treasurer needs a third forward starting debt of 150. In a fixed-rate universe, a forward contract should lock in its rate as of today if the Treasury wants to eliminate interest rate risk. However, liquidity will be raised only at the beginning of period date 2 up to the end of period 2.

TABLE 22.3 Bridging the liquidity gaps

Periods	1	2	3
Assets	1000	750	500
Resources	800	650	450
Gap	200	100	50
New funding			
Debt 1	50	50	50
Debt 2	50	50	
Debt 3	100		
Total funding	200	100	50
Gap after funding	0	0	0

TABLE 22.4 Bridging the liquidity gap

Periods	1	2	3
Assets	1000	750	500
Resources	800	400	400
Gap	200	350	100
New funding			
Debt 1	100	100	100
Debt 2	100	100	
Debt 3	0	150	
Total funding	200	350	100
Gap after funding	0	0	0

22.5 STRUCTURAL EXCESSES OF LIQUIDITY

Similar problems arise with excesses of funds when there are more resources than uses of funds. ALM should structure the timing of investments and their maturities according to some guidelines.

The expectations about interest rates are important since the interest rates vary across maturities. It is possible to invest all excess funds for a given maturity. However, this would generate an interest income dependent on current rates for the horizon of investment. Such policy makes sense if interest rates are expected not to rise further or to decline because it would crystallize current rates in the NII. However, this is a bet on the future. An alternative policy consists of minimizing the risk while trying to invest for long-term in order to benefit from higher rates, when the term structure of rates is upward sloping.

A common practice is to spread investments over successive periods. For example, an investment policy for core deposits that enhances the return and smoothes out the variations of interest rates consists of lending several fractions of the deposits over several maturities and rolling over the investment of each fraction with the same maturity when it matures. A fraction of the available funds is invested up to 1 year, another fraction for 2 years, and so on up to long maturities for which rates are usually higher. At the first date when such investments are made, the current term structure of interest rate in the portfolio is crystallized in the investment portfolio. But after 1 year, the funds invested for 1 year will be invested again, at new 1-year rates. After 2 years, the amount invested is also rolled over again for another 2 years, and so on up to 10-year or more maturities. When rolling over all investments at the time when they mature, the investment policy captures the new rates of each maturity. This is the "ladder" policy. It avoids crystallizing the current yield curve in large blocks of investments, such as investing the whole block of core deposits up to a 10-year maturity, because the layers are being rolled over at new interest rates when each one of them reaches maturities. Applying this policy over time consistently captures both high and low rates. The rates of investments become averages of the rates of all maturities. This policy captures the variations of interest rates across time and has a smoothing effect on the volatility of rates embedded in the assets.

22.6 ISSUES FOR DETERMINING THE LIQUIDITY GAP TIME PROFILE

There are many technicalities with liquidity gaps. Some are easy to deal with while the main issue is that of lines without maturities.

22.6.1 Lines without Maturity

The outstanding balances of all existing assets and liabilities and their maturity schedules are the basic inputs to build the gap profile. Existing balances are known, but not their maturities. Many assets have contractual repayments schedules, but many others have no explicit maturity. Such assets without maturity are overdrafts, credit card consumer loans, renewed lines of credit, and committed lines of credit. The usage of such lines depends upon customer initiative, subject to limits set by the lender.

Even for amortizing loans, mortgages for example, the effective maturity is not contractual because such loans can always be renegotiated at the client's initiative. In the end, most lending lines are subject to uncertainty. Relying on contractual maturities, when they exist, results in incorrect gaps. Statistical models are required for determining the effective maturity schedule of such loans.

For liabilities, except for financial debts contracted in the market, other resources from commercial activity have no defined maturities. Demand deposits are liabilities with a legal zero maturity and are, in fact, stable resources. Demand deposits have no contractual maturity, and they can be instantly withdrawn from the bank. They can also increase immediately. However, a large fraction of current deposits are stable over time, and represents the "core deposit base." Without proper projections, demand deposits can potentially alter the liquidity gaps up to the point where they become useless because of the embedded uncertainty. We detail below some of the above issues.

22.6.2 Demand Deposits

There are several solutions to deal with deposits without maturity. The simplest solution is to make conventions with respect to their amortization, for example with a yearly amortization rate of 5%, or 10%. This convention generates an additional gap equal to this amortization every year, which, in general, is not in line with reality. This is a common practice because it is conservative.

Note that such a convention has a strong implication in terms of the so-called "economic value" (EV) of the balance sheet. The EV is the discounted value of all cash flows generated by assets and liabilities, as explained in Chapter 26. It depends on the dates of the cash flows. When amortizing deposits over time, we create cash flows which are conventions. By changing the maturity over which we amortize such deposits, we change the EV.

Another approach is to divide deposits into stable and unstable balances. The core deposits represent the stable balance that remains as a permanent resource. The volatile fraction is treated as short-term debt. Separating core deposits from others is closer to reality than the above assumptions, even though the rule for splitting deposits into the core deposits and the remaining balance might be crude. Core deposits can be amortized as above for being conservative and the short fraction of deposits can be amortized over a short period, for example a month.

In large universal banks, pooling all deposits from all branches will reduce the instability of the aggregated balance. Deposits of some branches might increase and deposits of others decline. Such moves offset partially. Of course, this implies setting rules for transferring funds from one unit to the other and making sure that the process does not leave branches with deficits and others with excesses of funds. Offset excesses and deficits of funds across branches is the purpose of fund transfer pricing schemes, expanded later (see Chapter 28).

The last approach is to make projections of the balance sheet. Some observable variables correlated with the outstanding balances of deposits would help. Such variables include the trend of economic conditions and some proxy for the short-term variations in interest rate conditions. Such analyses use multiple regression techniques, or time series analyses. Note that time series analysis does not require external explaining variables. Time series models help in removing seasonal effects, which are important because the level of demand deposits tend to peak at some months and decline at others. The trend of the overall balance of deficits is also relatively easy to model as well as month to month seasonal effects. Models also provide the uncertainty for such projections. A convenient variable to model is the periodical relative variation of demand deposits because it eliminates the trend. Models using a constant relative variation do not work well. This allows defining some confidence intervals[3] to various levels of projected deposits.

There are some limitations to this approach. All parameters that have an impact on the market share deposits are not explicitly considered. Changes in economic conditions, or new fiscal regulations on specific tax-free interest earnings of deposits, alter the allocation of customers' resources between types of deposits. But, overall, this approach is closer to reality than any other.

22.6.3 Contingencies Given (Off-balance Sheet)

Contingencies generate outflows of funds that are uncertain by definition, since they are contingent upon some event, such as the willingness of the borrower to use committed lines of credit. There are many such lines of credit, including rollover short-term debts, or any undrawn fraction of a committed credit line. Only the authorization and its expiring date are fixed. Statistics, experience, knowledge of the account of customers (individuals or corporate borrowers) and of its needs help to make projections on the usage of such lines. The same rules apply for determining the Basel 2 EAD. Otherwise, assumptions are required. However, these are variable rate, so that funding uncertain volumes of loans at variable rates eliminates the interest rate risk.

22.6.4 Amortizing Loans

There are bullet loans and others that amortize progressively. Prepayment risk results in an effective maturity very different from contractual maturity at origination. The effective maturity schedule is more realistic. Historical data help to define such effective maturities. Prepayment models also help. Some are simple, such as the usage of a constant prepayment ratio applicable to the overall outstanding balances. Others are more sophisticated because they make prepayments dependent upon several variables, such as the interest rate differential between the loan and the market, or the time elapsed since origination, and so on. The interest margin of the bank is at risk whenever a fixed rate loan is re-negotiated at a lower rate than the original fixed rate. The chapter of the book dealing with the interest rate risk generated by options embedded in banking products discusses the pricing of this risk (Chapter 25).

22.6.5 Multiple Scenarios

Whenever the future outstanding balances are uncertain, it is tempting to use conventions and make assumptions. The problem with such conventions and assumptions is that they hide the risks. Making those risks explicit with several scenarios is a better solution. For instance if the

---

3 Confidence intervals are upper and lower bounds around the projected values within which projected values fall should be with a probability derived from the model.

deposits' balances are quite uncertain, the uncertainty can be captured by a set of scenarios, such as a base case plus other cases where the deposits' balances are higher or lower. If prepayments are uncertain, multiple scenarios could cover high, average, and low prepayment rate assumptions.

The use of multiple scenarios makes more explicit the risk with respect to the future volumes of assets and liabilities. The price to pay is an additional complexity. The scenarios might become judgmental, notably for the long term. The choices should combine multiple sources of uncertainty, such as volume uncertainty, prepayment uncertainty, plus the uncertainty of all commercial projections for new business. In addition, it is not easy to deal with interest rate uncertainty with more than one scenario. There are relatively simple techniques for dealing with multiple scenarios, embedded in ALM models detailed in the Chapter 24 on ALM simulations.

22.7 LIQUIDITY SCENARIOS

Liquidity management has to be considered under a broader view than simple liquidity gaps, which are necessary but not sufficient. The framework for addressing liquidity management, notably under stressed conditions, is now expanding. Several publications address the issue. They include the FSA report of 2009 [31], the draft document of BCBS in 2008 [6]. The publication in 2003 on "liquidity black holes" [62] addressed the difficulty earlier.

22.7.1 Liquid Assets

Banks publish the level of liquid assets serving as a cushion against market disruption. In order to be meaningful, the amount of liquid assets should be related to the periodical funding over the next period, allowing one to find out for how long the bank can sustain a market disruption. A review of annual reports for 2006 showed that banks published periods of one month up to one year. The financial crisis showed that most banks could not sustain such periods of liquidity crunch. This period relies on many assumptions with respect to projected net outflows. It should be calculated based on stressed assumptions, for example in inter-bank lending and borrowing, to be meaningful.

Borrowing long to hold short-term assets is uneconomical. A more appropriate source of financing liquid assets consists of using repos, which allow the bank to isolate the cost of funding liquid assets from the cost of funding of the bank. The repo cost is cheaper than the bank's funding cost. Furthermore, the repo cost matches the reset dates of the interest rate of liquid assets. The technique is used for financing hold-to-maturity securities.

22.7.2 Liquidity Crises and Stress Test Scenarios

An unexpected release of information might cause normal funding sources to cut down their credit lines. A block in the national or global financial markets could result in a system-wide "run on deposits"; a liquidity crunch caused by some failures; fear of contagion effect to other financial institutions causing an increase of risk aversion and reluctance to lend.

There are several examples of such crises:

- the Russian debt crisis
- the "Y2K" fear of information systems failure
- the 9/11 crisis, and, of course
- the sub-prime crisis of August 2007, which showed that a freeze of the most liquid markets could effectively happen.

For addressing such liquidity crises, stress testing is the appropriate methodology. Stress testing consist of simulating what could happen in a worst case event. The possible origins of a crisis and the historical events provide some examples of such factors. In the event of a system-wide crisis, the unique safety cushion against market disruptions is liquid assets because they always provide a source of funding. Liquid assets are also the source of repo transactions, widely used in the financial system, though which securities are used for collateral-based financing.

Note that liquidity crises might be triggered for a single bank, and not necessarily be system-wide. Examples of such events include unexpected and sudden losses for a single bank that threatens its solvency, disrupting the willingness to lend by other financial players. A downgrade of the bank's rating can also have major effects on both the asset and the liability sides. The cost of funding will increase and the bank might become not eligible for further lending by other institutions which follow lending rules based on a minimum ratings. The same cause can trigger margin calls, through which the bank is supposed to post more collateral in its debt or, alternatively reduce its debt. On the asset side, the bank might become ineligible for some deals when a minimum rating is required, such as providing guarantees. This illustrates the complexity of liquidity stress testing. Credit risk, solvency and liquidity issues are intertwined. A comprehensive stress test would include all such effects on liquidity, combining various scenarios and cumulating their effects on liquidity.

The Royal Bank of Scotland Statement on stress testing (Annual Report, 2006) is an illustration of how banks can define stress testing for liquidity.

> The maintenance of high-quality credit ratings is recognized as an important component in the management of the Group's liquidity risk. Credit ratings affect the Group's ability to raise, and the cost of raising, funds from the wholesale market and the need to provide collateral in respect, for example, of changes in the mark-to-market value of derivative transactions.
>
> Given its strong credit ratings, the impact of a single notch downgrade would, if it occurred, be expected to have a relatively small impact on the Group's economic access to liquidity. More severe downgrades could have a progressively greater impact but have an increasingly lower probability of occurrence.
>
> As part of stress testing of its access to sufficient liquidity, the Group regularly evaluates the potential impact of a range of levels of downgrades in its credit ratings and carries out stress tests of other relevant scenarios and sensitivity analyses.
>
> Royal Bank of Scotland

Such conservative rules did not prevent the RBS from being short of liquidity and from failure triggering government actions.

Contingent plans serve for assessing the ability to generate cash flows to meet loan commitments and deposit withdrawals, or margin calls on collaterals, under extreme circumstances. In order to provide some practical inputs to such plans, banks have to consider the size of their liquid asset portfolio, balance sheet and funding limits, maximum repos that can be contracted, the diversification of sources of funding and the levels of unsecured funding. Once these are identified, a bank can further diversify sources of funding, increase the base for repo financing, etc. The recent reports on sound liquidity management practices and the FSA document provide a number of criteria for addressing such contingency plans.

23

Interest Rate Gaps

This chapter introduces the interest rate gap model, which is the simplest measure of the interest rate risk of the net interest income, which is one main target variable of ALM. Interest rate gaps are defined in Section 23.1 as projected time profiles of the difference between assets and liabilities sharing a common reference interest rate. Section 23.3 introduces the "gap model," which relates interest income to the variations of interest rates. The gap model is extremely simple and provides simple rules for managing the interest rate exposure of the balance sheet. Since open projected liquidity gaps are also open positions on interest rates, they should be included with interest rate gaps for the gap model to be consistent with variations of the net interest income, as explained in the third section. Sample interest rate gap reports are included in this third section. The next section provides, using a simple example, the direct calculation of the net interest income and checks that its variations with interest rates are consistent with the gap model. Section 23.6 lists the drawbacks and the limitations of interest rate gaps, which, notably, implies using various scenarios for the balance sheet for examining the outcomes of various conventions embedded in interest gap calculations. Such conventions lead to simulations (last section) and are developed in Chapter 24.

Contents

23.1 DEFINITION OF INTEREST RATE GAPS

The interest rate gap is a standard measure of the exposure to interest rate risk. There are two types of gaps.

- The fixed interest rate gap, for a given period, is the difference between fixed rate assets and fixed rate liabilities.
- The variable interest rate gap, for a given period, is the difference between interest sensitive assets and interest sensitive liabilities.

As with liquidity gaps, static interest rate gaps are derived from projections of existing assets and liabilities, while dynamic gaps include new transactions. Both are time profiles at various future dates resulting from the projected balance sheets at these dates. The time profile of assets and liabilities is declining with static gaps due to amortization, but the projected gaps can have any time profile. The focus is on static gaps because there is usually no need to hedge today future transactions. Moreover, static gaps are updated frequently and include any new business within consecutive dates.

Variable interest rate gaps are be defined according to the variable rate references (1-month Libor, 1-year Libor, etc.). They are calculated over the management horizon, but projections should also extend beyond for making sure that projected assets and liabilities do not generate unsustainable positions (or very large gaps). Time bands should not be long because the gap calculation over a time band does not show at which exact date, within each time band, a variable rate is reset. A typical choice is one month over management horizons extending to 1 to 3 years. The Treasury department works with shorter time horizons since it manages the day-to-day cash flows and eventually uses short-period hedges.

Let us define a future period by its beginning and end dates (t and $t + 1$). The interest rate gaps are calculated from the beginning of the period. The convention in this book is to calculate interest rate gaps as a difference between assets and liabilities, either with known fixed rates as of today or using those which are interest rate sensitive (IRS).

$$\text{fixed interest rate gap}(t, t + 1) = \text{fixed rate assets}(t) - \text{fixed rate liabilities}(t)$$

$$\text{variable interest rate gap}(t, t + 1) = \text{interest rate sensitive assets}(t) - \text{interest rate sensitive liabilities}(t)$$

23.2 CALCULATIONS OF INTEREST RATE GAPS

The calculation is straightforward once proper interest rate references have been defined. Fixed rates gaps are easier to calculate because there is no need to define interest rate references over horizons such that interest rates attached to assets and liabilities remain fixed. Note that non-interest bearing assets and liabilities should not be included in interest rate gaps. Figure 23.1 shows a point in time balance sheet, as of t, a future date. All rates which are known as of this date are "fixed." Note that balances of assets and liabilities might be at a point in time or be averages over the time band for which the gap applies.

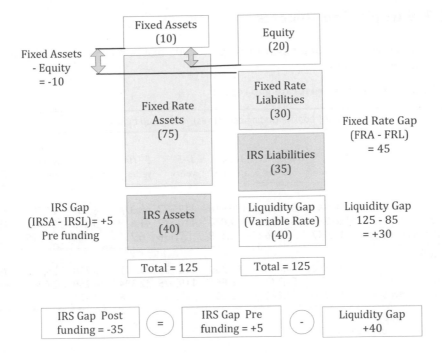

FIGURE 23.1   Interest rate gap

23.2.1 Interest Rate Gap and Liquidity Gaps

If there is no liquidity gap, the fixed rate gap and the variable rate gap are identical in absolute values. Any liquidity gap generates an interest rate gap. Excess funds will be invested, or deficits will be funded, at a future date, at an unknown rate. A projected deficit of funds is equivalent to an interest sensitive liability. An excess of funds is equivalent to an interest sensitive asset.

In the example, the variable rate gaps differ, before and after the deficit, by the liquidity gap, equivalent here to a variable rate liability:

$$\text{variable rate gap before liquidity gap} = 40 - 35 = +5$$

$$\text{variable rate gap after liquidity gap} = +5 - 40 = -35$$

In general, the variable rate gap post funding is the variable rate gap before liquidity gap minus the liquidity gap:

$$\text{variable rate gap post funding} = \text{variable rate gap before funding} - \text{liquidity gap}$$
$$= -35 = +5 - 40$$

23.2.2 Sample Gap Reports

Table 23.1 shows a simplified report of KBC in 2006 that is representative of what banks disclose in their annual reports.

TABLE 23.1 Sample interest rate gap report

Interest sensitivity gap of the ALM book (including derivatives), KBC group banks

In millions of EUR	≤1 month	1–3 months	3–12 months	1–5 years	5–10 years	>10 years	Non-interest-bearing	Total
31-12-2005								
Assets*	110,942	55,572	120,418	117,677	48,374	16,969	26,557	496,509
Liabilities*	120,989	63,858	117,070	110,542	41,619	13,495	28,936	496,509
Interest sensitivity gap	−10,047	−8,286	3,348	7,136	6,755	3,474	−2,379	0
31-12-2006								
Assets*	94,252	56,648	82,360	116,136	49,972	20,730	25,976	446,075
Liabilities*	110,271	51,372	78,861	119,475	42,394	16,259	27,443	446,075
Interest sensitivity gap	−16,020	5,276	3,500	−3,339	7,578	4,471	−1,467	0

*Including derivatives
Source: KBC Annual Report, 2006

Internal models provide far more details as illustrated by Figure 23.2. Figure 23.2 uses average balances of assets and liabilities over each time band. The x-axis shows dates, the calculation being done on a monthly or narrower period basis. The assets and liabilities shown here are fixed rate, as seen from today. Similar to liquidity gaps, static interest rate gaps show only existing assets and liabilities. The top section shows assets and the bottom section shows the liabilities, the difference making up the fixed interest rate gap. Figure 23.2 also shows the projected average rates of fixed rate assets and liabilities. The graphs are data intensive, but the basic calculations remain very simple.

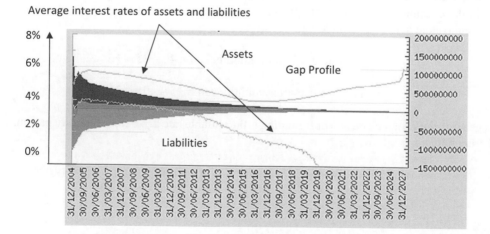

FIGURE 23.2   Interest rate risk and dates of flows

As usual, internal models provide capabilities for drilling down into the gaps and finding out which subsets of transactions contribute the gaps. Subset of transactions can be defined by product type, such as consumer loans, mortgage loans or any other type.

23.3 THE GAP MODEL

Interest rate gaps are very popular because they measure the sensitivity of the net interest income (NII) to a shift of rates. At this stage it is convenient to assume that all rates unknown as of today move by the same amount (parallel shift).

When the variable rate gap (interest rate sensitive assets minus interest rate sensitive liabilities) is positive, the volume of assets that is interest rate sensitive is larger than the volume of liabilities that are rate sensitive. If the index is common to both assets and liabilities, the NII increases with interest rates, and conversely when the variable rate gap is negative. When the variable rate gap is zero, the NII is insensitive to changes in interest rates. It is said to be "immune" to variations of rates. The variable rate gap is the sensitivity of NII to a shift of interest rates. The notations are:

- NII = net interest income
- IRSA and IRSL are interest rate sensitive assets and liabilities
- i = interest rate.

The change of net interest income (NII) due to the change in interest rate Δi is:

$$\Delta NII = (IRSA - IRSL)\Delta i$$

Assume that the variable rate gap is +200. The variation of the NII in the above example is 2 when the rate changes by 1% or $100 \times 1\%$. The basic formula relating the variable rate gap to net interest income is:

$$\Delta NII = (IRSA - IRSL)\Delta i = (\text{interest rate gap})\Delta i$$

The above formula is only an approximation. Several adjustments are required for improving the accuracy of the gap model.

Using a global gap assumes that there is a single reference, and, notably, a parallel shift of all rates. Regulations impose testing the effect of parallel shifts on NII, using shifts of 1% or 2%. However, since there are several interest rate references, there are as many variable rate gaps as there are references. Breaking down the variable rate gap into gaps by interest rate reference provides the sensitivities of NII to these references, for example rates applying to different maturities.

A gap is calculated over time bands, for example a month. The change of interest accrued modeled with the gap assumes that the reset date occurs at the beginning of the time band. If the reset date is close to end of month, the change of interest revenue or cost would be overestimated. The correct change of NII depends on any concentration of reset dates other than beginning of month. The appendix shows the exact calculation of the NII when the interest rate gap is zero but reset dates differ: the NII remains sensitive to a change of interest rates in spite of the zero gap.

The gap nets values of assets and liabilities. Over a month, these amounts change. A gap derived from values as of the beginning of the month would assume that such changes do not occur. A common practice is to use values of assets and liabilities that are averages of daily values over the month for smoothing out within-period variations.

The gap model is very popular because it is very simple and because it measures the sensitivity of the NII to the interest rate movements. Hedging the interest rate risk of the NII becomes very simple since it implies changing the gap, which can be achieved with hedging instruments such as interest rate swaps or forward contracts.

23.4 NET INTEREST INCOME AND INTEREST RATE GAPS

The example below calculates directly the NII with two interest rate scenarios and checks the consistency with the gap model. For making calculations simple, we use assumptions that are not restrictive: Constant commercial spreads and a shift of a flat term structure of rates. The assumptions are not restrictive since we could use gaps for each interest rate reference and differentiate spreads.

Table 23.2 provides a sample set of data for a simplified balance sheet, projected at date 1, one year from now. There is no need to use the balance sheet at date zero for gap calculations. All subsequent interest revenues and costs calculations use the end of year balance sheet. We assume that there is no hedge contracted for the forthcoming year. Note that the projected balance sheet is such that both interest rate gaps and liquidity gaps are open. Both should be considered for interest rates gap calculations since open liquidity gaps generate an interest rate position.

23.4.1 Projected Gaps

The gaps result from the one-year balance sheet projections (Table 23.3). All gaps are algebraic differences between assets and liabilities. The liquidity gap shows a deficit of 12. The variable rate gap before funding is +8, but the deficit of 12 counts as a variable rate liability as long as its rate is not locked in advance, so that the post-funding variable interest rate gap is −4.

TABLE 23.2 Balance sheet projections for the banking portfolio

Dates	I
Interest rate insensitive assets (a)	19
Interest rate sensitive assets (b)	17
Total assets ($c = a + b$)	36
Interest rate insensitive resources (d)	15
Interest rate sensitive resources (e)	9
Total liabilities ($f = d + e$)	24

TABLE 23.3 Gap calculations

Dates	I
Banking portfolio	
Fixed rate assets (a)	19
Interest sensitive assets (b)	17
Total assets(c = a + b)	36
Fixed rate resources (d)	15
Interest sensitive resources (e)	9
Total liabilities (f = d + e)	24
Liquidity gap (c − f)[a]	+12
Variable interest rate gap (b − e)	+8
Variable interest rate gap after funding (b − e) − (c − f)[c]	−4
Liquidity gap[b]	+12
Interest rate gap[c]	−4

[a]Liquidity gaps are as algebraic differences between assets and liabilities.
[b]Interest rate gaps are interest sensitive assets minus interest sensitive liabilities, or "variable rate" interest rate gaps.
[c]Funding is assumed to be variable rate before any hedging decision is made.

23.4.2 Projected Net Interest Income

The net interest income depends on commercial margins, which are spreads between the reference rates used internally and the clients' rates. Hence variations of NII depend on both variations of these interest rates and of the spreads over such reference rates. Usually, such spreads are fixed at inception and do not change over the life of assets and liabilities. Note that reference rates might not be identical to market rates. In the fund transfer pricing chapter (Chapter 28), it is shown that correct internal reference rates are distinct from market rates but should remain related to those. We assume here that they vary as market rates.

In Table 23.4 we stick to the easy solution of only two flat yield curve scenarios. The example uses a flat yield curve at possible levels 8% and 11%. With real yield curves, we would differentiate rates according to maturities and multiplying the number of scenarios would result in similar calculations. But the mechanics would be the same.

TABLE 23.4 Interest rate scenarios

Scenarios	Rate (%)
I (stability)	8
2 (increase)	11

Note: Flat term structure of interest rates

23.4.3 Commercial Spreads

Commercial spreads are the differences between the customer rates and the market rates. They are expressed in percentages of volumes of assets and liabilities. Positive commercial margins for lending mean that the banks lend at higher than market rates. Negative commercial margins for liabilities mean that the rates paid to customers are below market rates.

In this example, we use round figures. Commercial spreads are 3% for assets and –3% for liabilities. This means that the average customer rate for assets is 3% above the market rate, and that the customer rate for demand and term deposits is, on average, 3% less that the market rate. When the market rate is 8%, those rates are 11% and 5%[1]. In practice, percentage margins differ according to the type of asset or liability, but the calculations will be identical across products with varying spreads. The commercial margin, before closing the liquidity gap, results from the customer rates and the outstanding balances of assets and liabilities of the banking portfolio. It is:

$$36 \times 11\% - 24 \times 5\% = 3.96 - 1.20 = 2.76$$

The bank's NII differs from commercial margins because it is after the cost of funding. The cost of funding is the market rate[2]. Since the yield curve is flat, the cost of funds does not depend on maturity in this example. The NII after financing the liquidity gap is the commercial NII minus the cost of funding a deficit of 12. This cost is $8\% \times 12 = 0.96$. The bank's NII is therefore $2.76 - 0.96 = 1.80$.

23.4.4 The Sensitivity of NII and Interest Rate Gap

The percentage commercial spreads remain constant when the interest rate changes because they are fixed at the inception of transactions. Note that if we use the balance sheet model for budgeting purposes, we would need to set them as inputs and make them a function of the bank's business policy.

For all interest insensitive items, the customers' rates remain unchanged when market rates move. For interest sensitive items, the customers' rate variation is identical to the market rate variation because of constant commercial spreads. The value of the NII after the change of interest rate from 8% to 11% results from the new customers' rates once market rate rose. It should be consistent with the interest rate gap calculated previously. The calculations are shown in Table 23.5.

The values of the commercial margins, before and after the interest rate rise, are 2.76 and 3.00. This variation is consistent with the gap model. The change in commercial margin is 0.24 for a rate increase of 3%. According to the gap model, the change is also equal to the interest rate gap multiplied by the change in interest rate. The interest rate gap of the commercial portfolio is +8 and the variation of the margin is $8 \times 3\% = 0.24$, in line with the direct calculation.

The NII, after funding cost, decreases by $1.80 - 1.68 = -0.12$. This is because the funding cost of the liquidity gap is indexed to the market rate and increases by $12 \times 3\% = 0.36$. The

---

1 These figures are used to simplify the example. The actual margins obviously differ for various items of assets and liabilities.
2 Plus any credit spread that applies to the bank, assumed to be included in the rates scenarios.

TABLE 23.5   NII and interest rates

	Volume	Initial rate	Revenues/costs	Final rate	Revenues/costs
Fixed rate assets	19	11%	2.09	11%	2.09
Interest sensitive assets	17	11%	1.87	14%	2.38
Revenues			3.96		4.47
Fixed rate resources	15	5%	0.75	5%	0.75
Interest sensitive resources	9	5%	0.45	8%	0.72
Costs			1.20		1.47
Commercial NII			2.76		3.00
Liquidity gap	12	8%	0.96	11%	1.32
Net interest income			1.80		1.68

commercial margin increase of 0.24, minus the financing cost increase, results in the –0.12 change. Alternatively, the interest gap after funding is that of the commercial portfolio alone minus the amount of funding, or +8 – 12 = –4. This gap, multiplied by 3%, also results in a –0.12 change in margin.

Static gaps are relevant for hedging purposes since they influence the sensitivity of NII to reference market rates. When new transactions pile up with existing assets and liabilities the static gaps are updated, and the hedges can be adjusted. Hedging consists of using derivatives for controlling the magnitude and the sign of the interest rate gaps.

Assume that we have a positive variable interest rate gap in excess of a limit. This implies an excess of variable rate assets over variable rate liabilities. We might prefer to offset such excess with a contract generating fixed rate revenues rather than variable rate revenues. The appropriate instrument is a swap. The swap would receive the fixed rate and pay the variable rate. The notional should be such that any excess gap over the limit is offset by the swap. Simple examples of setting up limits and hedging excess gaps are provided in the next chapter (Chapter 24).

23.5 STATIC VERSUS DYNAMIC GAPS

A dynamic gap will factor in the projections of new business and model the behavior of the balance sheet according to commercial projections. Obviously, the magnitude and signs of interest rate gap would change. Such projections remain useful for hedging, since we can set up hedges according to projected dynamic gaps rather than static gaps. Note, however, that future transactions have an unknown rate as of today, whether they are fixed or variable rates. Future fixed rate loans will earn an interest that depends on future market rates, and they should be considered as variable rate assets as of today. New liabilities would also carry an unknown rate as of today. Therefore, new transactions affect the magnitude of the variable rate gap, not that of the fixed rate gap.

Such projections requires many inputs and introduce business risk, which is the risk attached to new business. Simulations or business scenarios become more appropriate to consider both interest rate risk and business risk, as explained in the simulation chapter (Chapter 24). Often, balance sheet projections are used for budgeting purposes primarily because the budget depends on the new business that accrues over the next years. For this reason, we concentrate in what follows on static gaps and we deal with business risk and scenarios in Chapter 26.

23.6 LIMITATIONS OF INTEREST RATE GAPS

There are several limitations to interest rate gaps. However, gap reports remain common and regulations make it mandatory to monitor gaps and to specify all assumptions underlying the calculations.

23.6.1 Embedded Options in Banking Products

A severe limitation of interest rate gaps is due to options embedded in banking products. Such options embedded in banking products include floating rate loans that have a cap on the interest paid by the client. This is an explicit option. Others are implicit options, notably the ability of a client to renegotiate the fixed rate of their loans when interest rates decline. In such a case, the bank can charge a penalty. In competitive environments, banks tend to comply with the clients' requests because they are reluctant to give up the revenues from other products sold to the clients.

Embedded options, whether explicit or implicit, change the nature of interest rates. For example, if a rate hits a cap, the rate, which was previously variable, becomes fixed. When renegotiating the rate of a fixed rate loan, the rate was initially fixed and becomes variable. Since interest rate gaps are based on the nature of rates, they do not account for changes of variable to fixed rates and vice versa. Optional risk is discussed in Chapters 25 and 27.

23.6.2 Lines without Maturity

As with liquidity gaps, interest rate gaps require maturities. With all lines without maturity, the best proxy that we can have is using effective maturity when it differs from a contractual maturity or when there is no maturity at all. Conventions might help, such as for demand deposits, but do not resolve the issue. Multiple business scenarios are required and they require simulations rather than gap models.

23.6.3 Mapping Interest Rates to Selected Risk Factors

It is difficult to deal with all interest rates serving as references for assets and liabilities. Banks select specific vertices along the yield curve, or risk factors. All rates that do not match those selected reference rates are correlated with them, but not perfectly. The usage of a small number of selected interest rates requires mapping all balance sheet items to those. The process creates basis risk, or the residual risk due to differences between selected and actual rates. One solution is to relate actual rates, by product segment, to the selected reference rates and to use sensitivities for calculating "standardized gaps."

Statistical techniques provide the sensitivities. The average rate of return of a sub-portfolio, for a product family for instance, is the ratio of interest revenues (or costs) to the total outstanding balance. It is feasible to construct times series of such average rates over as many periods as necessary. A statistical fit to observed data provides the relationship between the average rate of the portfolio and the selected rates. A linear relation is such as:

$$rate = \beta_0 + \beta_1\, index_1 + \varepsilon$$

The coefficient β_1 is the sensitivity of the loan portfolio rate with respect to the $index_1$. The residual ε is the random deviation between actual data and the fitted model. A variation of the market index of 1% generates a variation of the rate of the loan portfolio of $\beta_1 \times 1\%$. It captures the basis risk, except for the residual error.

A standardized gap weights the assets and liabilities by their sensitivities to the selected reference rates. For example, if the return of a segment of loans has a sensitivity of 0.8 with respect to the short-term market rate, it will be weighted with 0.8 in the gap calculation.

The alternate solution is to use directly the reference rates of contracts at the level of individual transactions. Vendors' software dedicated to asset liability management provides the capability of calculating exact reset dates with multiple reference rates, as long as banks have the information.

23.6.4 Regulated Rates

The same methodology applies to rates which are not market rates. An example is the rate of regulated saving deposits in European countries. This rate is a linear function of the inflation rate and the short-term 3-month rate. Such liabilities are broken down into two fractions, one indexed to the Libor and the other to the inflation rate. Note that such regulations create exposure to inflation rate. Inflation-indexed hedges (such as inflation swaps) might be used, which are usually derived from government bonds of which rate is indexed to inflation. Such techniques do not fully resolve the issue, because regulated saving rates move by steps, for example, they change only when the composite index moves by at least 0.5%. Stepwise functions are not consistent with the gap model.

23.6.5 Mark-ups and Mark-downs over Reference Rates

Simple interest rate gaps assume that variable rate assets and liabilities carry rates following selected indexes for modeling changes of NII with gaps. Percentage mark-ups over market rates changes as well as rates, for new transactions. When ALM is used for budgeting purposes, projections of new transactions are required for projecting the balance sheet and the NII. Gaps and NII projections use commercial margins as inputs.

23.6.6 Intermediate Flows and NII Calculations

Periodical gaps generate inaccuracies for calculating the NII. The gap model does not accurately date the flows within a period. It does not capture the effect of the reinvestment or the funding of flows across periods. In some cases, both approximations can have a significant impact

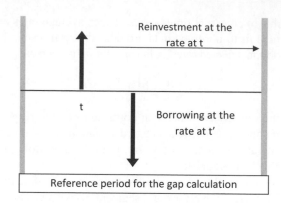

FIGURE 23.3   Interest rate risk and dates of flows

over NII. This section shows that time bands used by interest rate gap models generate errors because actual reset dates do not match the time points defining a period.

Gaps group flows within time bands as if they were simultaneous. In reality, there are different reset dates for liquidity flows and interest rates. They generate interest revenues or costs, which are not properly valued in the gap–NII relationship. Figure 23.3 shows that revenues and costs assigned to intermediate reinvestments or borrowings depend upon the length of the period elapsed between the date of a flow and the final horizon.

A reset date at the end of the period has a negligible influence on the current period margin. Conversely, when the reset occurs at the beginning of the period, it has a significant impact on the margin. For instance, assume that a flow of 1000 occurs at the beginning of the period, and another flow of 1000, with an opposite sign, occurs at the end of the period. These flows are indexed to current rates and are variable rate. The periodical variable rate gap of the entire period will be zero. Nevertheless, the NII of the period will be interest sensitive, since the first flow generates interest revenue over the whole period that does not match the smaller interest cost of the second flow (Figure 23.4).

Figure 23.5 illustrate the error when the goal is to immunize the interest margin. In the preceding example, the gap is zero, but the NII is interest sensitive. In the next example, we have an opposite situation. The gap differs from zero, but the interest margin is immune to interest rate changes. The gap is negative, which suggests that the NII should increase when the interest rate decreases, for example from 10% to 8%. However, this ignores the reinvestment of the positive intermediate flow of date 90 at a lower rate for 270 days. On the other hand, the negative flow generates a debt that costs less over the remaining 180 days. The NII is interest rate sensitive if we calculate interest revenues and costs using the accurate dates of flows.

The interest revenues and costs are:

$$\text{inflow at day 90: } 1000 \times (1.10^{270/360} - 1.08^{270/360}) = -14.70$$

$$\text{outflow at day 180: } -1536 \times (1.10^{180/360} - 1.08^{180/360}) = +14.70$$

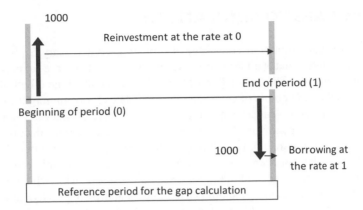

FIGURE 23.4   Zero gap and interest sensitive margin

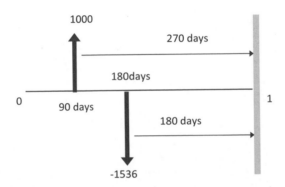

FIGURE 23.5   Negative gap and fixed NII

They match exactly because interest revenues and costs are proportional to the size of flows and to the residual period of reinvestment or funding. The first flow is smaller than the second flow but generates interest revenues over a longer period. The values are such that the residual maturity differential compensates exactly the size differential.

The example shows that gaps lead to errors. In the first example, the NII is interest sensitive, which is inconsistent with a zero gap. In the second example, the gap model suggests plugging another flow of 536 to hedge the NII. Actually, doing so would put the margin at risk. The exact condition under which the margin is insensitive to interest rates is relatively easy to derive for any set of flows. It differs from the zero gap rule. The condition uses the duration concept, discussed in Chapter 27 on the risk management of the economic value of the balance sheet.

23.7 FROM GAPS TO SIMULATIONS

Because gaps have many limitations, the usage of simulations is necessary. Simulations project the balance sheet at future dates under various scenarios. They also serve for plugging in various interest rate scenarios. The calculation of the NII should embed the effect of options and time lags between the time points of gaps and the actual dates for beginning the calculation of interest costs and interest revenues. Simulations cannot resolve all issues. The balance sheet changes according to the behavior of clients. For example, unless rates decline significantly below the fixed rate of a loan, clients will not initiate a renegotiation of rates. This opens the door to behavioral models for clients' decisions. Moreover, uncertainty with respect to outstanding balances of projected assets and liabilities create a "business risk," which combines with interest rate risk. Some methodology should be defined for addressing such double uncertainty. The simulation methodology is addressed in Chapter 24.

24

ALM and Hedging Policies

This chapter illustrates hedging policies and interest rate gap management. Since banks keep interest rate gaps open, they need to define limits to such gaps. Limits are derived from setting a cap to downside risk, with risk being measured as the adverse deviation of the NII, used as target variable. Limit setting is discussed in Section 24.1.

Hedging programs use derivatives to make gap comply with limits across periods. Section 24.2 provides two examples of hedging solutions, one over a single period, and another when the horizon extends over multiple periods.

When considering hedging, entire changes of the term structure of interest rates have to be considered, notably given that bank's structural position is borrowing on the short end and lending on the long end. The gap model can accommodate changes of the steepness of the term structure as well as other transformations, as long as interest rate references used for gap models are spread along the curve. Section 24.3 provides a case study for illustrating hedging opportunities when the entire curve and its steepness changes through time. This section does not deal yet with simulations of the term structure, which are deferred to Chapter 37.

Finally, it is possible to account for uncertainty with respect to the future volume of assets and liabilities, or address business risk, jointly with interest rate risk, by using multiple scenarios and finding an optimum hedge. Section 24.4 provides a methodology for addressing the two risks jointly by cross-tabulating discrete numbers of business scenarios with interest rate scenarios, and finding the best hedges, defined as those which maximize expected NII at a given risk level.

Contents

24.1 MANAGING GAPS: SETTING UP LIMITS

Banks often keep interest rate gaps open, notably when they have mismatch risk for capturing the positive spread between long-term interest rates and short-term interest rates (the "structural position"). In such a case, the variable rate gap would be negative on short-term rates and positive for long-term interest rates (those which are considered fixed over a long period). Open positions implies the usage of limits for capping the risk borne by the bank.

Gap limits have the effect of capping the variations of the net interest income. Limits are set by the ALCO. Either they follow some basic rules or they use some earning-at-risk modeling of the NII for setting limits. In both cases, the management would set up a limit, whose purpose is to set a maximum downside move of the NII.

24.1.1 The Basic Mechanism of Limits

Assume the management does not want the variation of the net interest income to vary adversely by more than 25% of NII current value, for a given shift of interest rates: $\Delta\text{NII} \leq 25\% \times$ current NII. The linear relation holds:

$$\text{NII} = \text{variable rate gap} \times \Delta(\text{interest rate})$$

The current variable rate gap is 3000 and the current NII is 20. For proceeding with such rules, we need to input some benchmark variations of interest rates. Assuming that we use as a relevant scenario a parallel shift of the term structure of $\Delta i = 100$ basis points. The limit imposes: $\Delta\text{NII} \leq 25\% \times 20 = 5$. With the 1% shift of interest rates, $\Delta\text{NII} = \text{gap} \times \Delta i = 1500 \times 1\% = 15 > 5$. The variation exceeds the maximum variation of NII because the gap is too high. If the gap becomes 500, $\Delta\text{NII} = \text{gap} \times \Delta i = 500 \times 1\% = 5$. The bank should close the gap to 500 by hedging the excess gap $1500 - 500 = 1000$ in order to comply with the limit. Hedging uses interest rate derivatives.

24.1.2 Limits and "NII at Risk"

The above calculation requires as input some benchmark variations of interest rates. But standard shifts do not capture the volatility of interest rates, which sometimes might be stable, sometimes highly unstable. Using the earning at risk concept and a measure of the downside movement of NII dependent on interest rate volatility, plus a confidence level is more appropriate. Setting limits involves capping the maximum downward variation of the NII at the preset confidence level.

Let us assume that the gap with respect to a single certain reference market rate is set. The sensitivity of NII with respect to this interest rate i is:

$$\Delta\text{NII} = \text{gap} \times \Delta i$$

Once the gap is set, the probability distribution of the NII results from the distribution of the interest rate. The expectation of the NII depends on the expected variation of interest rate and the volatility of the NII is a function of the gap and the volatility of interest rates:

$$E(\Delta NII) = gap \times E(\Delta i)$$

$$\sigma(\Delta NII) = |gap| \times \sigma(\Delta i)$$

The vertical bars stand for absolute value. The maximum deviation of the margin at a preset confidence level results directly from the maximum deviation of the interest rate at the same confidence level.

The usual VaR, or EaR, framework applies to NII. The NII volatility results from that of interest rates. Let us assume that the annualized interest rate volatility is 2%. Using a normal distribution as a proxy for the distribution of interest rate, confidence levels for the interest rate are multiples of the interest rate volatility. The interest rate will be in the range defined by ± 2.33 times volatility from the mean in 1% of all cases. With a gap equal to 1500, the NII volatility is: $\sigma(NII) = 1500 \times 2\% = 30$. The upper bound, at the 1% confidence level, of the one-sided deviation is 2.33 times this amount, or $2.33 \times 30 = 70$ (rounded). The NII at risk is the unexpected loss in excess of expected NII. Starting from an expected NII at 20 for example, the unexpected loss declines to $20 - 70 = -50$. For setting up limits to gaps for the current year, the management could consider the NII at risk and a confidence level rather than an arbitrary shift of interest rate for setting the gap limit.

Note that the management will consider not only the NII but the earnings, which are calculated after operating costs. Assuming operating costs independent of interest rates, the percentage variation of pre-tax and post-operating costs income is higher than the percentage change of the interest margin at the top of the income statement. For instance, starting with a NII of 20, a maximum downside of 10 represents a 50% decrease. If operating costs are 8, the original pretax income is $20 - 8 = 12$. If the NII declines to 10, the remaining pretax income becomes $10 - 8 = 2$. The percentage variation of pretax income is $-(12 - 2)/12 = -83\%$, while that of interest margin is only -50%.

Instead of using such mechanical calculations, and considering only parallel shift of the interest rates, the ALCO might prefer relying on worst case discrete scenarios of interest rates. The basic calculations would remain similar. The simulation of interest rates is also necessary to investigate the effects of worst case scenarios. Section 24.4 of this chapter can accommodate any number discrete scenarios of interest rates. Full simulations of interest rates would proceed along the lines of Chapter 37.

24.2 HEDGING: CLOSING INTEREST RATE GAPS

Hedging aims at reducing the net interest income volatility by setting limits on gaps. We address the issue in two steps: the first step considers a single period starting at a future date, and, in the second step, we consider several periods ahead. In general, ALM policies tend to reduce the risk for the immediate horizon, while keeping open gaps of increasing value when the horizon extends, for taking advantage of beneficial variations of interest rates.

24.2.1 Single Period

The example of a single period allows differentiating the steps for constructing hedging programs. It would apply, notably, for the short-term horizon, say the current year. For illustrating gap management, we use the simple example of the previous chapter on interest rate gaps (Table 24.1). The liquidity gap shows a deficit of 12. The variable rate gap before funding is +8, but the deficit of 12 counts as a variable rate liability as long as its rate is not locked in advance, so that the post-funding variable interest rate gap is –4 (Table 24.2).

TABLE 24.1   Balance sheet projections for the banking portfolio

Dates	1
Banking portfolio Fixed rate assets (a) Interest rate sensitive assets (b)	19 17
Total assets ($c = a + b$)	36
Fixed rate resources (d) Interest rate sensitive resources (e)	15 9
Total liabilities ($f = d + e$)	24

TABLE 24.2   Liquidity and interest rate gaps

Dates	1
Banking portfolio Fixed rate assets (a) Interest sensitive assets (b)	19 17
Total assets($c = a + b$)	36
Fixed rate resources (d) Interest sensitive resources (e)	15 9
Total liabilities ($f = d + e$)	24
Liquidity gap ($c - f$)[a] Variable interest rate gap ($b - e$)	+12 +8
Total balance sheet	
Variable interest rate gap after funding ($b - e$) – ($c - f$)[c]	–4
Gaps	
Liquidity gap[b] Interest rate gap[c]	+12 –4

[a]Liquidity gaps are algebraic differences between assets and liabilities.
[b]Interest rate gaps are interest-sensitive assets minus interest-sensitive liabilities, or "variable rate" interest rate gaps.
[c]Funding is assumed to be variable rate before any hedging decision is made.

TABLE 24.3   Hedging the liquidity and the interest rate gaps

Liquidity gap	+12
Interest rate gap of the banking portfolio	+8
Fixed rate debt	4
Floating rate debt	8
Total funding	12
Liquidity gap after funding	0
Interest rate gap after funding and hedging	0

The liquidity gap is –12. The variable rate gap is +4 before funding and –4 post-funding, considering that the interest rate of funds to be raised at a future date is unknown. Let us assume that we wish to close both liquidity and interest rate gaps simultaneously. We assume that the above gaps calculated at a point in time are valid for some period after the date of the above projection (for example 1 year).

In order to close the liquidity gap, we need to raise funds for an amount of 12 at the starting date of above gaps. The positive variable rate gap of existing assets and liabilities means that the NII of existing assets and liabilities increases when interest rates shift upward. In reality, this is not so because 12 have to be raised, at a rate unknown today. Post-financing, the variable rate gap becomes –4, which shows that a rise of interest rates would actually make the NII decline.

In order to obtain immunization, the post-funding gap should be zero. In other words, the funding and hedging policies should generate a gap offsetting the commercial portfolio positive gap. The incremental variable rate gap due to funding is equal to the fraction of debt remaining variable rate after hedging, with a minus sign. Since the gap is +8 before funding, the variable rate debt should be set at 8 to offset this gap. This implies that the remaining fraction of debt, 12 – 8 = 4 should have an interest rate fixed as of today. An equivalent approach is to start directly from the post-funding gap. This gap is +8 – 12 = –4. Setting this gap to zero requires reducing the amount of variable rate debt from 12 to 8. We find again that we need to fix the rate today for the same fraction of debt raised, or 4, leaving the remaining fraction of debt, 8, with a floating rate. The solution "variable rate for 8 and locked rate for 4" neutralizes both the liquidity gap and the interest rate gap (Table 24.3).

In order to lock in the rate for an amount of debt of 4, various hedges apply. In this case, we have too much variable rate liabilities, or not enough variable rate assets. A forward swap converting 4 of the floating rate debt into a fixed rate debt is a solution. The swap would pay the fixed rate and receive the floating rate. Alternatively, we could increase the variable rate fraction of assets by 4. A swap paying the fixed rate and receiving the variable rate would "transform" 4 of fixed rate assets into 4 of variable rate assets. This is the same swap.

24.2.2 Hedging Over Multiple Periods

A hedging program should hedge the gaps over several periods so that they comply with limits. Hedges can be forward starting for future periods. Since the interest rate gap can change from one time band to the next, the hedges should also change. As for closing liquidity gaps, we need to start from a final horizon and move backwards.

In Table 24.4, we provide data for calculating the variable rate gap for 8 periods. Any liquidity gap is included in Figure 24.1 as a variable rate asset or liability and variable rate gaps are

TABLE 24.4   Time profile of variable rate gaps

Period	1	2	3	4	5	6	7	8
IRS assets	5000	4800	4800	3800	2400	2300	2300	2300
IRS liabilities	3500	3450	3100	3100	3100	3000	1200	1000
IRS gap	1500	1250	1700	700	−700	−300	1100	1300
Limit	1000	1000	1000	1000	1000	1000	1000	1000
Excess gap	500	250	700	−300	−1700	−1300	100	300

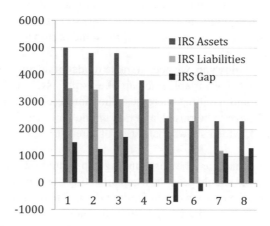

FIGURE 24.1   Time profile of variable rate gaps

after funding or investing any deficit or excess. The table shows the variable rate assets, the variable rate liabilities and the resulting variable rate gaps. The upper part shows the same time series. The lower part shows the limit and the variable rate gap. Any variable rate gap above the upper limit is an excess gap. We do not consider a lower negative limit since all negative variable rate gaps are lower, in absolute value, than 1000.

Excess gaps are shown in Figure 24.1. The limit is materialized by the set of bars with same size 1000. Excess positive gaps are hedged by using forward starting swaps that receive the fixed rate and pay floating. The hedges offset all excess gaps over the horizon, setting the gap after hedging at the limit.

Looking at the three first excess gaps, 500, 250 and 700, we need three swaps for making all three first gaps equal to the limit. The first swap hedges the excess gap of 250, common to all three first periods and extends from period 1 to 3. The second swap offsets the remaining excess gap of 250 (or 500 − 250) for the first period only. The third one offsets the gap of period 3 in excess of 250, the notional of the first swap, or 700 − 250 = 450. All three swaps start at 1. The periods of each of these three swaps are materialized by the horizontal lines above Figure 24.2 showing the gaps. Other swaps are required for hedging the excess gaps of periods 7 and 8. All five swaps make up the hedging program. The five swaps are represented on top of the graph with starting and ending dates only.

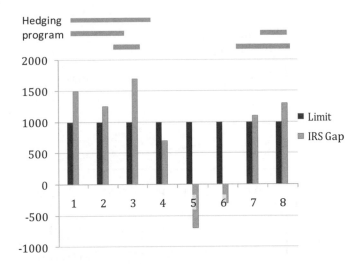

FIGURE 24.2 Setting a hedging program complying with limits

In practice, the limit might be higher for longer horizons than for shorter horizons, as mentioned before. The excess gaps will change accordingly and similar hedging programs will be used, although the hedges would decline in volume with the horizon.

24.3 HEDGING THE VARIATIONS OF THE TERM STRUCTURE OF INTEREST RATES (CASE STUDY)

Forward rates are of interest to banks that collect excess deposits over lending. Such banks have recurring net cash inflows which are positive. They know that new deposits will be collected in a recurring manner at future dates. Should they want to invest excess cash, they have a choice of waiting until the excess cash comes in or lending it forward. The second option is beneficial if they perceive that future spot rates will remain below forward rates, used as break-even rates for hedging decisions.

A case in point is that of the European term structures of interest rates in the years preceding the Euro event. The national yield curves were upward sloping a few years before the Euro. The slope of the spot yield curve was steep, and declined when approaching the Euro, and moving down until it became almost flat when reaching the date of the creation of the Euro. Such movement was interpreted as a convergence of rates of various European countries towards the lowest rates prevailing, which were the German rates.

When the slope was very steep, there was an opportunity to shift from lending to investing forward at high rates. With upward sloping curves, the forward rates were above the spot rates. As long as spot rates do not rise above forward rates, lending forward future excess cash is beneficial. Since rates were declining, chances of reversal of the trend seemed remote. The situation is summarized in Figure 24.3 (which show only trends, not actual figures). After the Euro event, possible scenarios were that rates would remain low or increase again. But the point of the example is determining the best hedging policy in the period of declining interest rates.

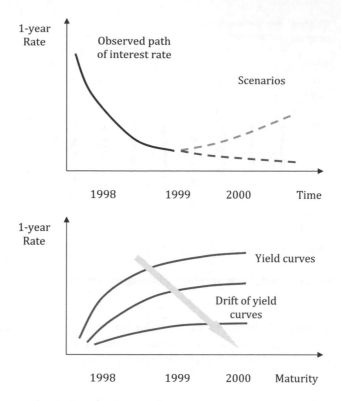

FIGURE 24.3   Matrix of scenarios: cross-tabulating business scenarios and interest rate scenarios

Many banks had recurring excess deposits. They could either wait or lock in forward rates in advance for such recurring excess deposits. Some banks preferred to wait until excess cash from new deposits came in before investing. The rationale was that rates were close to low historical rates and that they should start rising again. Another option was to hedge gradually, progressively entering into swaps receiving the fixed rate, as the decline of interest rates continued. Early swaps would have captured the higher rates of the beginning of the period. Later swaps would still have captured higher rates than at end of the period, but lower than at an earlier stage. Another choice was to enter into out-of-the-money floors.

Note that at a late stage, none of these policies would have helped. Floors become much more expensive if the strike rate becomes too close to spot rates. Furthermore, low rates at the end of the period might not be high enough to absorb operating costs of banks. Late swaps would end up with prevailing fixed rates, which were too low. When hedges receive fixed rates which barely absorb operating costs, some banks might decide not to hedge anymore and bet that rates will finally rise again after hitting a bottom. In general, late hedges are useless and the value of waiting for hedging is negative.

Gradually hedging with swaps was used but was not optimal. Some banks invested at forward rates at an early stage, thereby capturing the spread between forward rates and the declining spot rates. Such a policy was the best one. It allowed investing excesses of funds at high forward rates. Forward rates were much higher than spot rates when the yield curve slope was very steep. These rates also remained much higher than the spot rates prevailing later at subsequent dates because the yield curves kept shifting downward. The policy seemed relatively safe once the downward trend proved to extend over several years.

Of course, when interest rates reached the bottom line in late 1999 and early 2000, the yield curve became lower and flatter. The spread between forward and spot rates narrowed down. The "window of opportunity" for investing in forward rates much higher than subsequent spot rates closed. This case illustrates the cost of waiting and contrasts the gradual policy of using swaps versus the best policy of using forwards. Taking such "directional" positions was possible because the trend of interest rates persisted for several years in a row.

This case is an extreme example because there was an exceptional event ahead. Whenever a trend is identified and when the risk of drifting away from the trend is low, directional bets remain the best policy. When there is no trend or too much uncertainty, simulations or scenarios of the term structure or scenarios should be used. Typical scenarios assume a parallel shift plus a change in the slope of the yield curve because of mismatch risk. The basic gap model applies using gaps for all interest references that are relevant.

The simulation of interest rates might use any number of discrete scenarios, and use full-blown simulations of the entire yield curves. The matrix methodology expanded next can accommodate any number of interest rate scenarios. Full-blown simulations could use the principal components analysis developed in Chapter 37.

24.4 HEDGING BUSINESS RISK AND INTEREST RATE RISK

Business scenarios are required whenever there is too much uncertainty with respect to the behavior of clients, resulting in static gaps that are varying significantly across scenarios, as well as when dealing with projections of new business, for which several scenarios need to be considered. Using multiple scenarios for business volume allows dealing with business risk. This section presents the "matrix" methodology for cross-tabulating business scenarios and interest rate scenarios, and identifying the best hedging solutions. The methodology relies on discrete scenarios, but can accommodate any number of such scenarios.

It is illustrated with a simple example combining two simple interest rate scenarios with two business scenarios only, for illustrating the principle, but the methodology is easily extended to higher numbers, except that the volume of calculations increases.

The process involves the calculation of interest income, and of its summary statistics, expectation and volatility, across the matrix cross-tabulating interest rate scenarios with business scenarios. The next step simulates the effect of hedging solutions for optimizing the hedging policy. Again, the example is limited to the comparisons of two hedging solutions, which is enough to understand how to extend the same process to a larger number of hedging scenarios. The last paragraph summarizes the process and shows how the concept of "efficient frontier" can be used for optimization purposes.

24.4.1 Multiple Business and Interest Rate Scenarios

The gap methodology assumes that the gap value is known for a given time point. This implies that we consider a unique business scenario as if it were certain, since the unique value of the gap results directly from asset and liability volumes. Ignoring business risk is not realistic, and results in hiding risks rather than revealing them.

Gap volume depends on clients' behavior for static gaps and on business projections for dynamic gaps. The ALCO deals with business issues and cannot ignore business uncertainty. Multiple business scenarios address the issue and are materialized by several projections of the balance sheet, at various dates, plus liquidity and interest rate gaps profiles.

Risk management becomes more complex, with interest income volatility resulting from both interest rate risk and business risk. Still, it is possible to characterize the risk–return trade-off, where return refers here to the NII of the banking portfolio. Hedging policies now depend on how both interest rate and business risks influence the interest income. It is interesting to note that financial instruments can help hedging some of the business risk as it will be explained.

The starting point of the method is made up of several interest rate scenarios and business scenarios. The principle of this methodology consists in simulating all values of the target variable, the interest income, across all combinations of interest rate and business scenarios. Because we cross-tabulate interest rate scenarios and business scenarios, the methodology is called the "matrix" methodology.

The values of NII in each cell of the matrix depend on any existing hedge that generates its own interest costs and revenues. When hedging solutions change, the entire set of value changes. Hedging adds a third dimension. If we have two business scenarios and two interest rate scenarios, we need to consider four combinations and calculate the NII for each one of them. If we consider two hedging solutions, we need to consider two sets of four values of NII, or eight cases.

The first step sets up the matrix cross-tabulating interest rate and business scenarios. For each pair of such scenarios, the value of the target variable is determined. For turning around the complexity generated by considering a large number of combinations, the basic idea is to summarize the entire set of values of the target variable within the matrix, whatever their numbers, by a couple of values. One is the expected value of the target variable and the second is its volatility across the entire matrix. For each hedging solution, the values within the matrix changes, and there is a new pair of expected NII and volatility of NII across the matrix. The third step consists of changing hedging solutions and recalculating accordingly the values of expected NII and the volatility across each matrix matching a hedging program.

When hedging changes, the pair of values changes and moves in the "risk–return" space. The last step consists of selecting the hedging solutions that best suit the goals of the ALCO, such as minimizing the volatility, or targeting a higher expected profitability by increasing the exposure to interest rate risk. Those solutions that maximize expected profitability at constant risk or minimize risk at constant expected profitability make up a set of hedging solutions called the "efficient frontier." All other hedging solutions are discarded. It is up to the management to decide which level of risk is acceptable.

The technique allows investigating the impact on the risk–return profile of the balance sheet under a variety of assumptions. For example:

- what is the impact on the risk–return profile of assumptions on volumes of demand deposits, of loans with prepayment risk, or of committed lines of which usage depends upon customers' initiatives?
- which funding and hedging solutions minimize the risk when only interest rate risk exists, when there is business risk only, and when both interact?
- how can the hedging solutions help to optimize the risk–return combination?

The ALM simulations also capture optional risks to the extent that we embed in balance sheet scenarios the effect of options transforming fixed rates into variables rates and vice versa. The gaps will change accordingly. However, this makes the calculation overly complex and other techniques such as valuing the embedded options of optional gaps might be preferable (see Chapter 27).

24.4.2 Matrix Methodology and The Risk–Return Profile of the Balance Sheet

For the first step, we consider that there are no new hedges other than the existing ones. Once we have defined the relevant scenarios, we proceed to the cross-tabulation and summarize the matrix by NII expectation and NII volatility, as illustrated in Table 24.5. However, since the interest income depends upon the funding, investing and hedging solutions, there are as many matrixes as there are hedging solutions as illustrated in Figure 24.4. We proceed with a simple example for illustrating the methodology.

TABLE 24.5 Matrix of scenarios: cross tabulating business scenarios and interest rate scenarios

Interest rate scenarios	Business scenarios			
	A	B	C	NII average and volatility
1	NII	NII	NII	
2	NII	NII	NII	
3	NII	NII	NII	

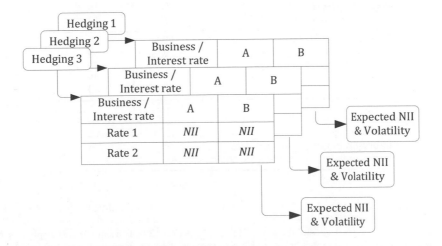

FIGURE 24.4   Mean and volatility of NII with hedge

24.4.3 Implementing the Matrix Approach

When using two scenarios, there are only two columns and two rows. It is possible to summarize each business scenario by a gap value. The gap used here is the variable interest rate gap after financing the balance sheet. All gaps and calculations refer to a future time point and the NII is calculated over a single period. Since rates are annual, we use a one-year period. The interest rate scenarios are defined by a single flat rate. None of these assumptions are restrictive. Using the entire term structure of rates is feasible, but the calculations would be more complex. The same calculations would apply to more interest rate references with the corresponding interest rate gaps.

Referring to the example detailed in the previous chapter (Chapter 23), we use two gap values of –4 and –8 cross-tabulated with two interest rate scenarios, with + 8% and +11% as single flat rates. As a reminder, the example with variable interest rate gap –4 is in the first column. The commercial spreads were set at +3% for assets and –3% for liabilities (Table 24.6).

The original value of the NII with rate at 8% is 1.80[1] with a gap equal to –4, and it becomes 1.68 with interest rate equal to 11%, or a variation equal to –4 × 3% = –0.12, according to the gap model. When rates vary, it is easy to derive the new NII value within each column, since the gap is constant along a column. The second business scenario results in a variable interest rate gap of –8 post-financing. The corresponding NII is again 1.80 originally since the interest rates are derived from the same 8% market rate, same volumes of assets and liabilities, and same commercial spreads. Because the gap is now –8, the NII declines by –8 × 3% = –0.24, and becomes 1.56 with this new gap value. All NII calculations are conducted with no hedging.

The variation of the NII results from the interest rate gap, and gaps depend on the hedging solution. The initial matrix is as follows in this simple case (Table 24.7), with the corresponding expectation and volatility in the right-hand table, for a single time point one year from now, and no hedging.

TABLE 24.6 Two business scenarios

Projected balance sheet	Scenario A	Scenario B
Fixed rate assets	19	19
Interest sensitive assets	17	17
Fixed rate resources	15	11
Interest sensitive resources	9	13
Total assets	36	36
Total liabilities	24	24
Gaps		
Liquidity gap	12	12
Interest rate gap – banking portfolio	8	4
Interest rate gap – total balance sheet	–4	–8

---

1   The average asset rate is 8% + 3% = 11% and the average cost of liabilities is 8% – 3% = 5%. The calculation of the NII is: 36 × 11% – 24 × 5% – 8% × 12 = 1.80. If the interest rate shifts up to 11%, the NII variation is –4 × 3% = –0.12, and the new NII is 1.80 – 0.12 = 1.68. The same inputs apply to scenario B, resulting in same NII when interest rate is 8% and the variation when interest rate shifts upward is –8 × 3% = –0.24, with corresponding NII = 1.80 – 0.24 = 1.56.

TABLE 24.7 Matrix of NII with two interest rate scenarios and two business scenarios

	Scenarios		Risk–return profile	
Rate	Gap = –4	Gap = –8		
8%	+1.80	1.80	E(IM)	1.7100
11%	+1.68	1.56	σ(IM)	0.1149

From the two business scenarios, with net gaps of –4 and –8, and two interest rate scenarios, +8% and +11%, we find the expectation and volatility of the NII across the matrix. The expected NII and its volatility across the four cells are respectively 1.7100 and 0.1149[2]. In the range of scenarios considered, the worst-case value of the NII is 1.56.

By multiplying the number of scenarios, we could get many more NII values, and find a wider distribution than the three above values. Sticking to the (2×2) matrix, if we hedge the gaps, we obtain a new matrix. There are as many (2×2) matrixes as there are hedging solutions.

24.4.4 Hedging both Interest Rate and Business Risks

For any given scenario, there is a unique hedging solution immunizing the NII against changes in interest rates. This hedging solution is the one that offsets the variable interest rate gap.

A first implication is that, with several scenarios, it is not possible to lock in the NII for all scenarios by hedging, because gaps differ from one business scenario to the other. We can consider as hedging solutions those who close the variable interest rate gaps under business scenarios A and B. The issue is to find the best hedging solution among these two. By modifying the hedge, we change the entire matrix of values. With two hedging scenarios, there are eight combinations with equal probabilities resulting from two matrices and each hedging solution is summarized by a couple of values, the average NII and the NII volatility.

The first hedging scenario locks in the interest rate for a debt of 4. The remaining debt, 12 – 4 = 8, required to bridge the liquidity gap, is a floating rate debt. The second solution locks in the interest rate for an amount of 8, the remaining 4 being floating rate debt. Those are the H1 and H2 hedging solutions, summarized in Table 24.8. The hedges simply change the mix of variable rate/fixed rate financing of the same liquidity gap of 12.

Since the first hedge makes the NII constant under business scenario A, the variable rate gap is zero with A. With an initial variable rate gap of –4, the hedge offsets this gap with a payer swap (paying the fixed rate) of notional 4, making the financing fixed rate for an amount of 4. The variable rate gap after hedge is increased by 4 for both scenarios A and B. The variable rate gap for A is zero. The variable rate gap with B is initially –8 and becomes –4. The same rationale applies when fully hedging the NII under scenario B. For B, the swap closes the variable rate gap and, for A, it results in a positive variable rate gap of +4.

---

2 The standard deviation uses the formula for a sample, not over the entire population of outcomes (i.e. it divides the squared deviations from the mean by 3, not 4).

TABLE 24.8 Funding scenarios

Scenarios	A	B
Interest rate gap (banking portfolio)	+8	+8
Liquidity gap	−12	−12
Hedging[a]		
Hedging H1	8 vr + 4 fr	
Hedging H2	4 vr + 8 fr	
Interest rate gap after hedging[b]		
Hedging H1	0	+4
Hedging H2	+4	0

[a]The hedging solution is the fraction of total funding of which rate is locked in. "fr" and "vr" designate respectively the fractions of debt with fixed rate and variable rate.
[b]The interest rate gap is that of the banking portfolio less the floating rate debt.

24.4.5 The Matrices of Net Interest Income

When the interest rate is 8%, the NII is the same, equal to 1.80, with scenarios A and B. Starting from the same initial NII for both A and B when interest rate is 8%, we derive the NII variation with the gap formula and the new values of NII for both business scenarios when interest rate increases. The NII variation with a change in interest rates of $\Delta i = +3\%$ is $\Delta NII = gap \times \Delta i$. For example, with scenario A, the initial NII is 1.80, and the variable rate gaps are 0 with hedge H1 and +4 with hedge H2. With H1, the NII is unchanged and, with H2, it increases by $+4 \times 3\% = 0.12$, becoming 1.92. The same method provides the values of the NII with scenario B: NII is constant with scenario B and it declines by $-4 \times 3\% = -0.12$, or down from 1.80 to 1.68 for scenario A. This provides the two matrices shown in Table 24.9, one for the first hedging solution and another for the second hedging solution.

TABLE 24.9 Optimization of hedge

Hedging H1				
NII	A	B		
			Mean m	1.770
8.0%	1.800	1.800	σ (NII)	0.060
11.0%	1.800	1.680	m / σ	29.500
Hedging H2				
NII	A	B		
			Mean m	1.830
8.0%	1.800	1.800	σ (NII)	0.060
11.0%	1.920	1.800	m / σ	30.500

For each matrix, the average value of the margins and the volatility[3] across the cells of each matrix are calculated. The Sharpe ratio, the ratio of the expected NII to the NII volatility, is also calculated. This ratio is a risk-adjusted measure of profitability[4]. The first solution generates a lower average NII with the same risk. The second generates a higher average NII, with the same risk. Hence, the second hedge is better.

In general, a large number of hedging solutions are considered, combined with several business scenarios and several interest rate scenarios. When graphed in the risk–return space, they generate a cloud of points[5]. Each dot summarizes a matrix combining all target variables values corresponding to each combination of interest rate scenarios, business scenarios and hedging scenarios. In spite of the high number of simulations, changing hedging scenarios simply moves the "summary" dots in the risk–return space.

"Inefficient" solutions are those with an expected NII lower than others, at the same risk level or, alternatively, those with the same expected NII than others, but with a higher risk. The only solutions to consider are those that dominate others. The set of those solutions is called the "efficient frontier." In this particular case, we are only considering two business scenarios and a simple hedge over one period. The gap varies linearly with the notional of the swap used for hedging. The variations of NII are a linear function of this gap. But the variance of such variation depends on the square of the magnitude of the hedge if the variation of rates is given. Hence the relationship with the size of hedge is parabolic, as shown in Figure 24.5. Figure 24.6 is more representative of what happens when using multiple scenarios and several periods.

A risk–return combination is efficient if there is no other better solution at any given level of risk or of return. The efficiency criterion leads to several combinations rather than a single one. The optimization problem is as follows:

- minimize the volatility of the margin subject to the constraint of a constant return

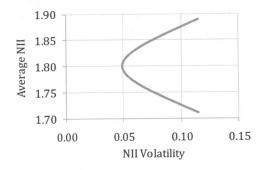

FIGURE 24.5   Risk–return combinations

---

3   The volatility is the square root of the sum of the squared deviations of the margin from the mean. All values in the matrix have the same probability. The expected value is the arithmetic mean.

4   The Sharpe ratio is a convenient measure of the risk-adjusted performance of a portfolio. It also serves when modeling the credit risk of the portfolio.

5   The graph shows the risk–return profiles in a general case. In the example, the only variable that changes the risk–return combination is the gap after funding. When this gap varies continuously, the risk–return combinations move along a curve. The upper "leg" of this curve is the efficient frontier of this example.

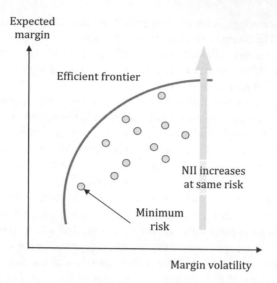

FIGURE 24.6   Risk–return combinations

- maximize the expected margin subject to the constraint of a constant risk.

For each level of profitability, or of return, there is an optimal solution. When the risk, or the return, varies, the optimum solution moves along the efficient frontier. In order to choose a solution, a risk level has to be set first. For instance, the minimum risk leads to the combination that is located at the left-hand side close to the efficient frontier. When both interest rate and business risks interact, solutions neutralizing the margin risk do not exist. However, a minimum risk solution does still exist. Generally, a bank might prefer other solutions to the extent that they increase substantially the expected NII and the Sharpe ratio.

25

Implicit Options Risk

This chapter explains the nature of embedded, or implicit, options, and details their payoff, in the event of exercise for the individual borrower. Embedded options in banking balance sheets raise a number of issues.

- What is the cost for the lender and the pricing mark-up that would compensate this cost?
- What is the portfolio risk due to options or "convexity risk?"
- How can banks hedge such risks?

This chapter assesses the benefit for the borrower, calculated as the payoff of the option under various interest rate levels. For a long-term fixed rate loan, the option payoff is the time profile of the differential savings (annuities) after and before exercising the renegotiation option. Alternatively, it is the present value of these cash savings at the date of renegotiation. The payoff increases with the differential between the initial and the new interest rates and the residual maturity of the loan. The payoffs under immediate exercise differ from the value of the option. The value of the option is higher than the payoff as long as there is a chance that future payoffs increase beyond their current value if rates drift further away.

Section 25.1 details the nature of options embedded in various banking lending contracts. The subsequent sections address renegotiation of rates by borrowers or prepayment risk. Some prepayment models are statistically based and serve for modeling the fraction of renegotiated rates or prepayment as a function of the time elapsed after origination of loans. The principle is summarized in Section 25.2. The other sections address the valuation of such renegotiations or prepayment. Section 25.3 calculates the payoff of such options. The final sections value the embedded option using the lattice tree method and translate such value in an additional markup for pricing the option.

Contents

25.1 OPTIONAL RISK

The gap model is very attractive because it is very intuitive and simple. But gaps are no more defined when embedded options in banking products allow fixed rate to become variable, or vice versa. Embedded options can be explicit or implicit.

25.1.1 Optional Risk is Always Adverse to the Bank

There are explicit options, such as a variable rate embedding a cap on the interest rate. This is a simple option. There are other explicit options which are quite complex to handle in some hybrid products.

The case of complex options is illustrated by some regulated saving accounts that allow borrowing after the saving phase. Such saving accounts combine a saving phase followed by a lending phase for financing residential property acquisitions. For both phases, rates are contractually fixed from the origination of the contract. The saving phase is at least 4 years and can extend up to 10 years. The client has several options. The client can shorten the saving period if the regulated rate is lower than other rates of alternate investments. If the client maintains the saving plan, he has the options for contracting a loan at a preset rate at dates spread from 4 to 10 years. At the end of the saving phase, the client compares the contractual rate at which it is possible to borrow for acquiring a home with prevailing mortgage rates. If the contractual lending rate, set at inception of the contract many years before, is lower than prevailing rates, the client will opt for the contractual rate rather than the prevailing rate. With such long horizons, assessing the value of such options is hardly feasible.

The most well-known implicit options are the renegotiation of interest rates or the prepayment options embedded in mortgage loans. Such renegotiation or prepayments occur when interest rates decline and fixed rate borrowers who borrowed earlier wish to benefit from lower rates. In many instances, it is difficult for banks not to renegotiate rates and accept a lower rate. If they do not, they risk losing the client who prepays the loan and borrows elsewhere at a lower rate. Since banks sell multiple products to their clients, such as credit card and consumer lending, they are reluctant to lose revenues from these products and prefer to adjust the fixed rate at a lower level. The implicit prepayment option makes the loan "callable," at the initiative of the clients, as opposed to a straight "non-callable" loan.

The renegotiation might generate a cost to the borrower, but the cost can be lower than the expected gain from exercise. For instance, a prepayment penalty of 3% of the outstanding balance might be imposed on the borrower, usually if the client leaves the bank. Even with a penalty for renegotiation, the cost does not offset the gain of borrowing at a lower rate if the interest rate declines substantially and/or if the mortgage residual maturity is long enough. Renegotiations are an issue for the lender because customers substitute a new lower rate for the old one, while the debt stays there at the same rate, thereby deteriorating the margin.

There are many other common implicit options embedded in banking products. Clients may decide to transfer their demand deposits to money market funds for earning a higher return. This does not imply necessarily a loss of liquidity if the bank also provides money market funds, but it entails a higher cost of funds.

A general rule applies to all embedded options: they are always adverse to the bank, since the client will always pick up the most profitable opportunity. Embedded options have an adverse effect on the net interest income as well as on the economic value of the bank's balance sheet (Chapter 26).

25.1.2 Optional Risk and Hedging

Implicit or embedded options generate the risk of adverse variations of the NII. Wide shifts of interest rates will trigger such options since individual clients are slow to react to small changes.

Hedging the adverse effects of embedded options can be done in various ways. The first way is to charge to the customer the value of the option, which implies valuing the option. Hedging through pricing the option to customer is feasible only when competition allows doing so. A drawback is the potential adverse effect on market shares if other banks do not price the option to customers for fear of losing clients. The alternate choice is to hedge the optional risk. The bank then pays the cost of hedging. A natural protection against renegotiation of fixed rates when rates decline is a floor. For caps embedded in variable rate loans, the natural hedge consists of buying caps on the debt backing the loan. For minimizing the cost, it is advisable to buy caps and floors out-of-the-money.

When it is feasible to price options to customers, the issue is the valuation of the options. When caps and floors are being used, the issue is monitoring the "optional" gap, the gap between options sold to clients and those acquired by the bank to hedge their risk. Determining the size of exposure to optional risks is also an issue. How many and when will renegotiations of rates and prepayments occur? Without some projection of the renegotiated volume of loans potentially subject to renegotiation, we do not know how much should be hedged and when.

25.2 MODELING PREPAYMENTS

Considering prepayments which follow economic rules, they depend on the fixed rate of the loan, the new rate, the residual life of the loan and any penalty to be paid. The new rate could be fixed or variable depending on the behavior of clients. Also, there are behavioral thresholds that generate a lag between the time when it becomes economical to prepay and the actual time of prepayment.

Modeling the economics of prepayment consists of determining the payoff for the borrower, which is the loss for the lender. The size of potential renegotiations at any point in time is that of those loans that generate a potential positive payoff for the borrower.

The point in time payoff is lower than the value of the prepayment option because renegotiating the interest rate at a later date might be more beneficial than today. This is the time value of the option. The expected value of those payoffs at all time points until maturity is the value of the option. Calculating the point-in-time payoff is a necessary step for valuing the option. It provides the exposure to optional risk, which is required for hedging. It is an intermediate step for assessing the value of the option, a value either sold or given away by the bank. If given away to borrowers because of competition, the value of the loan should be reduced by the value of the option.

The simplest prepayments models measure the fraction of loans subject to renegotiation as a function of the age of the loan, using historical data. More comprehensive models should factor in the interest rate differential between loans and prevailing rates and such demographic variables as geographic mobility or any factor that triggers prepayment. Historical data is not necessarily shared by banks, although mortgage institutions (the mortgage agencies in the US) pool large amounts of data on which full-blown models of client behavior are based. Retail pools of mortgages have been securitized for a long time. All relevant data for the pool have to be made available for securitization purposes, since the notes issued by securitizations vehicles are backed by the cash flows, which include prepayments, interest rate renegotiations, seasoning effects (aging of loans) on prepayments, default rates and recovery rates.

The simplest model is the constant prepayment rate (CPR) model that simply states that the prepayment at any date is the product of a prepayment rate with the outstanding balances of loans. In fact the prepayment rate depends upon the age of the loans. Renegotiation does not occur in the early stage of a loan because the rates do not drift suddenly away and because the rate negotiation is still recent. When the loan gets closer to maturity, the renegotiation has fewer benefits for the borrower because the payoff is reduced by the residual time to maturity. Therefore, renegotiation rates increases steadily, reach a level stage, then stay there for some time and normally level off when getting closer to maturity. Prepayments and renegotiations normally peak in between inception and maturity since there are no payoffs close to origination or when residual maturity is too short. Seasoning effects also apply to default rates, since the incentives to default are also small with new loans and when the residual life is short.

Because renegotiations, prepayments and defaults depend on aging of loans, as well as on interest rates, it is necessary to isolate generations of loans, defined by period of origination, for capturing the "seasoning effect," or "aging effect," as well as the rate differential, which varies across cohorts.

Note that the time path of interest rates is relevant for options. If the rates decline substantially at the early stage of a loan, they trigger an early prepayment. If the decline occurs later, the prepayment might also occur later. The current level of interest rates is not sufficient to capture timing effects. The entire path of interest rates is relevant. Hence the prepayment rate does not relate only to the current interest level.

25.3 PAYOFF OF PREPAYMENT

This section determines the borrower's payoff at a point in time, which is also the loss for the lender. The gain is valued under immediate exercise if the option is in-the-money. The option value differs from point-in-time payoff because of the time value of American options.

Consider a fixed rate amortizing loan, repaid with constant annuities including interest and capital (Table 25.1). The customer renews the loan at a new fixed rate if he exercises the renegotiation option. The loan might be representative of a generation of loans of a portfolio. It is assumed that the new loan has a maturity equal to the residual maturity of the original loan

TABLE 25.1 Characteristics of original loan

Original loan	1000
Original maturity (years)	5
Original fixed rate	12.00%
Original annuity	277.41

TABLE 25.2 Repayment schedule of the original loan

Dates	1	2	3	4	5
Annuity before prepayment	−277.4	−277.4	−277.4	−277.4	−277.4
Principal repayment	157.4	176.3	197.5	221.1	247.7
Outstanding amount (end of period)	842.6	666.3	468.8	247.7	0.0

at the exercise date. If the borrower repays the loan, subject to a penalty cost, for instance 3% of the outstanding balance, the penalty cumulates with the outstanding balance of the original loan to make up the new debt. The payoff of prepayment is the present value at the new rate of the differential annuity between the original loan and the new loan. Table 25.2 details the repayment schedule of the loan. The present value of all annuities at the loan rate, 12%, is equal to the amount borrowed, or 1000.

Consider a prepayment at end of period 2, once the annuity due has been paid. The new interest rate decreases to 8%. The amount of the new loan is the outstanding balance of the old loan plus a 3% penalty. The new annuity corresponds to the value of the new loan, for a residual maturity of 3 years. The characteristics of the new loan are shown in Table 25.3. The new loan is the residual principal plus 3%, or 666.29 × (1 + 3%) = 686.28.

The periodical cash savings for the borrower are the differences between the old and new annuities, or 277.41 − 266.30 = 11.11. The present value at the new rate of this differential gain for the borrower is 28.63 (Table 25.4). The payoff from renegotiation, for the borrower, as of the date of renegotiation (*t*), is equal to the difference between the values of the old and the new debts, calculated at the new loan rate:

$$\text{value}(t, \text{ new rate}) \text{ original loan} - \text{value}(t, \text{ new rate}) \text{ new loan}$$
$$= \text{value}(t, \text{ new rate}) \text{ original loan} - \text{outstanding balance } (1 + \text{penalty } \%)$$

The second part of the equation shows that the renegotiation option has a payoff equal to the value of the original loan calculated at the new fixed rate minus a strike equal to the outstand-

TABLE 25.3 Example of a fixed rate loan

Prepayment date (end of period)	2
Principal outstanding	666.29
Residual maturity (years)	3
Penalty (% of outstanding principal)	3%
New debt after prepayment	686.28
New rate of new debt	8%
New annuity	−266.30

TABLE 25.4   Calculation of payoff of renegotiation

New loan	686.28		
New loan dates	3	4	5
Annuity new loan	−266.30	−266.30	−266.30
Principal repayment	211.40	228.31	246.57
Outstanding principal	474.88	246.57	0.00
Cash savings: new annuity − old annuity	11.11	11.11	11.11
V(new loan) − V(original loan)	28.63		

ing principal plus penalty. The underlying of the implicit option is the value of the original loan calculated at the current customer rate. The breakeven value of the new rate making the borrower's payoff positive is around 10.3%. At this new rate, the net gain for the borrower is zero. The payoff for the borrower is also the cost for the lender. This cost increases when the decline in rates is significant. If the rate moves down to 8%, the present value of the loss for the bank reaches 28.63. This is 4.30% of the original capital outstanding in the example (28.63/666.29). The payoff is not the value of the option. The next section provides an example of the valuation of a prepayment option.

25.4 THE VALUE OF IMPLICIT OPTIONS

The value of an option combines its liquidation value, or the payoff under exercise, plus the value of waiting further for larger payoffs. Valuing an option requires simulating all future outcomes for interest rates, at various periods, for determining when the option is in-the-money and what are the gains under exercise. The option value discounts the expected future gains, using the simulated rates as discount rates. The purpose of the next sections is to illustrate how to use the simple binomial model[1] of interest rates for valuing prepayment options. The value of prepayment options depends on the entire time path of the interest rates from origination to maturity, because interest rate changes can trigger early or late exercise of the option, depending on when the changes occur.

Note that this is a significant departure from classical ALM models, which uses in general a small number of discrete scenarios instead of referring to full-blown simulations of rates, representative of all outcomes. The interest simulation technique applies because it is necessary to generate the entire spectrum of payoffs of the option up to the loan maturity, including all intermediate values. Because renegotiation or prepayment occur before maturity, it is likely that the option will be exercised by the borrower at intermediate dates. Such embedded options are American options. From a pricing prospective, the value of the option represents an asset for the borrower and an expected cost for the bank, which the bank should charge to borrowers.

Assume that the option is valued. The ALM has to hedge the risk of receiving a lower rate in the future in the case of fixed rate mortgage loans. The discussion of optional hedges is deferred to the Chapter 27, which discusses hedging optional risk. Pricing the value of the option to the

---

1   As presented in Chapter 14.

borrower from inception of the loan would simply offset the expected loss of the bank, but not hedge the option payoffs if it becomes in-the-money.

Assuming that the value of the option is known, pricing optional risk to borrowers requires converting the today's value of the option into a percentage mark-up. The mark-up reflects the difference of values between a straight fixed-rate debt, which the borrower cannot repay, and a "callable debt," which is a straight debt combined with the prepayment or renegotiation option. The callable loan has a lower value than the straight debt for the bank, the difference being the option value. The percentage mark-up is the "option-adjusted spread" (OAS). The OAS is the spread added to the loan rate making the value of the "callable" loan identical to the value of a straight loan. The callable debt has a lower value than the straight debt for the lender, the difference being the value of option given away to the borrower. For bringing the value of the straight debt in line with the value of the debt plus the option, it is necessary to increase the discount rates applied to the future cash flows of the callable debt. The additional spread is the OAS. For pricing the option, banks include the OAS into the customer rate, if competition allows.

The first step is to value the prepayment/renegotiation option. The methodology expanded here is the simulation of interest rates using a binomial tree. Next, the payoffs of the option at each step, allowing early exercise when optimum for the borrower, are derived. Finally, the option-adjusted spread is determined from the option value.

25.5 THE SIMPLE "BINOMIAL TREE" TECHNIQUE APPLIED TO INTEREST RATES

The principles and rules for deriving lattice trees were detailed in Chapter 14. They are applied here to short-term risk-free rates. We use the risk-neutral valuation method, and a lattice tree of short-term rates. Because the risk-free rate is not constant, the discounting applies to sub-periods of the tree over which the rate is constant.

25.5.1 The Binomial Tree for Interest Rate

Each "step" is a small interval of time between two consecutive dates, t and $t + 1$[2]. Given a value of the short-term rate at date t, there are only two possible values at $t + 1$. The rate can only move up or down by a fixed amount at each step. The magnitudes of these movements are u and d, which are percentage coefficients applied to the starting value of the rate to obtain the final values after one step. If i_t is the interest rate at date t, the up and down movements are $i_{t+1} = u \times i_t$ and $d \times i_t$. It is convenient to choose $d = 1/u$ for minimizing the number of nodes. The binomial tree is shown in Figure 25.1. In addition to u and d, the probabilities of an up move and of a down move are set to 50%. The values of u and d matching the volatility of short-term rates are derived from the formulas:

$$u = \exp(\sigma\sqrt{\Delta t})$$

$$d = \exp(-\sigma\sqrt{\Delta t})$$

---

2 The literature uses a small interval Δt, which tends towards zero.

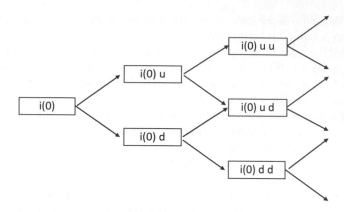

FIGURE 25.1   The binomial tree of rates

TABLE 25.5   The binomial tree of numerical values

Dates	0	1	2
	10.00%	11.62%	13.50%
Rates		8.61%	10.00%
			7.41%

In the example used in this section, the yearly volatility is 15%, and the steps correspond to a one-year period. The numerical values selected for u and d are:

$$u = \exp(15\%) = 1.1618$$

$$d = \exp(-15\%) = 0.8607$$

Finally, we assume that there are only three years to maturity. There are two steps in the tree, which is the minimum to obtain uncertain rates in the second step, since the rates at current dates are known. In practice, one should use shorter time steps for more accuracy. The short-term interest rates are not an asset. As an intermediate step, the value of a zero-coupon bond, a simple asset, is derived from such a binomial tree (Table 25.5).

25.5.2 Valuation of a Bond

In a no-uncertainty world, the time path of rates would be unique. When rates are stochastic, the volatility is positive, and there are numerous interest rate paths diverging from each other. Each sequence of rates is a realization of uncertain paths of rates over time. For each sequence of rates, there is a discounted value of the stream of flows generated by an asset. Discounting uses the risk-free rate in a risk-neutral world. There are as many discounted values as there are time paths of interest rate values. The value of the asset is the average of these values assuming that all time paths of rates are equally probable[3].

With the simple zero-coupon bond, the terminal flow of 100 is certain. The value of the bond, when considering only one step, is the discounted value of the first short-term rate, which is known and equal to 10%. Uncertain rates appear after step 1. The present value as of date 1 uses the unknown rate at period 2. There are only two possible sequences of rates in this example, hence two possible values of the same asset as of date 0:

$$100/[(1 + 10.00\%) (1 + 11.62\%)] = 81.445$$

$$100/[(1 + 10.00\%) (1 + 8.61\%)] = 83.702$$

The average value is $(81.445 + 83.702)/2 = 82.574$, which is the expected value given the uncertainty on interest rates (Table 25.6). The two-period interest rate is a geometric average of the two short-term rates, the first one being known.

Another equivalent technique for calculating the value serves later. At date 2, the value of the flow is 100 for all time paths of rates. However, this flow has two possible values at date 1 corresponding to the two possible values of the rate between dates 1 and 2: $100/(1 + 11.62\%)$ $= 89.590$ and $100/(1 + 8.61\%) = 92.073$. The current value results from discounting the average value at date 1, using the current rate, which gives $[(89.590 + 92.073)/2]/(1 + 10.00\%) =$ 82.574. The result is the same as above. In the former case, the value as of date 0 is obtained by discounting twice the final value 100 and averaging after. The second method calculates two values as of date 1 by discounting once, 89.950 and 92.073, averages them into a single value at 1, or $(89.590 + 92.073)/2 = 90.8315$, and then discounts this single averaged value to the present $(90.8315) (1 + 10\%) = 82.574$. Mathematically, the final formula is identical.

But the second method calculates the current value using a recursive process starting from the end, and moving backward to date 0. The process can be generalized. Starting from final values, we derive values at the immediately preceding date and proceed until the current date. The only difference with options is that the discounted flows change with rates, since they become the payoffs of the option, instead of being independent of interest rate scenarios. Since it is possible to use flows defined conditional upon the value of the interest rates, the model applies to American options.

TABLE 25.6   Values of the bond at various dates

Dates	0	1	2
Values	82.574	89.590	100
		92.073	100
			100

3   The maximum number of time paths is 2^n where n is the number of periods, since, at each date, there are twice as many nodes than at the preceding date.

25.5.3 The Global Calibration of the Binomial Tree

The value of listed assets, calculated with all the time paths of interest rates, should replicate those observed on the market. In order to link observed prices and calculated prices, the rates of each node of the tree need an adjustment, which is another piece of the calibration process.

The binomial tree in Figure 25.1 does not yet include all the available information. The rate volatility sets the upward and the downward moves at each step. However, this unique adjustment does not capture the trend of rates, any liquidity premium or credit spread observed in markets. All factors should show up in simulated rates for mimicking the actual prices. A global calibration will capture all missing factors in the model.

In the above example, the value of the zero-coupon is 82.574. Its actual price might diverge from this one. For instance, let us assume that its observed price is 81.5. The simulated rates need adjustments to reconcile the two values. In this example, the simulated rates should be higher, so that the simulated price decreases until it reaches the observed price. The volatility should not be changed, since the up and down moves already replicate the market volatility. In the case of the zero-coupon maturing at date 2, the initial value of the interest rate is 10% and is fixed. Hence, only rates as of date 1 need an adjustment. The easiest way to modify them is to add a common constant to both rates at date 1. The constant has an empirical value such that it makes the calculated and the observed prices identical. This constant is the "drift." In the example, the drift should be positive to increase the interest rates and decrease the discounted value. The numerical calculation shows that the required drift is around 1.40% to obtain a value of 81.5. The calibrated rates at 1 become: $i_{1u} = 11.62\% + 1.40\% = 13.02\%$ and $i_{1d} = 8.61\% + 1.40\% = 10.01\%$.

Once the rates at date 1 are adjusted, the calibration extends to subsequent periods using the prices of listed assets having longer maturity. It is necessary to repeat this process for extending the adjustment of the whole tree. This technique enforces the "external" consistency with market data.

25.5.4 The Valuation of American Options

The same process used for valuing a bond applies for an American option. In order to obtain an option value, we start from its terminal values given the interest rate values simulated at this date. Once all possible terminal values are determined from the terminal values of rates, the recursive process serves for deriving the values at other dates. For American options, whose exercise is feasible at any time between now and maturity, there is a choice at any date when the option is in-the-money. Exercising the option depends upon whether the borrower is willing to wait for opportunities that are more profitable or not. An American option has two values at each node (date t) of the tree: a value under no exercise and the exercise value. If exercise is deferred to later periods, the value is the average of the two possible values at the next date $t + 1$. If exercised, the value is the difference between the strike price and the gain. The calculation rule is to use the maximum of those two values. With this additional rule, the value of the options results from the backward process along the tree, starting from terminal values which are known.

25.5.5 The Current Value of the Prepayment Option

This methodology applies to a loan amortized with constant annuities, of which maturity is 5 years and fixed rate is 10%. The current rate is also 10%. The yearly volatility of rates is 20% (in percentage of interest rate). The borrower considers a renegotiation when the decline in interest rates generates future savings whose present value exceeds the penalty of 3%. However, being in-the-money does not necessarily trigger exercise, since immediate renegotiation may be less profitable than a deferred exercise. The borrower makes the optimal decision by comparing the immediate gain with the expected gains of later periods. The expected payoff is the expected value of all discounted gains one period later, while the immediate payoff is the exercise value.

The first step of the process consists of simulating the interest rate values at all dates. Equal annual periods divide the horizon. The values of u and d correspond to a yearly volatility of 20%. The binomial tree is the same as above, and extends over five periods. Dates are as of end of year (Eoy), so that date 1 is the end of period 1. The binomial tree simulates short-term rates, which are valid from one date to the next. The interest rate is not a market rate since it is a client's rate. If the bank's spread remains constant, the fixed rate follows the same process as a market rate. The strike price is 1.03 times the outstanding principal of the original loan. The payoff under immediate exercise is the difference between the value of the original loan and the strike price. Finally, the optimum payoff is determined at each node. The present value of these optimum payoffs is the option value.

We need some assumptions for making the calculations simple. Consider that the original and the new loan are fully amortized at the same date. The relevant rate for calculating the payoff for the client is the fixed rate of the loan for its remaining maturity, which declines over time.

25.5.6 The Original Loan

Since dates refer to the end of each year, we need to specify when the annuity flow occurs. At any date, end of period, the borrower immediately pays the annuity after the date. Hence, the outstanding debt at any date includes the next annuity without discounting. The date 0 is the date of origination. The terminal date 5 is the end of the last period, the date of the last annuity, 263.80, completing the amortization. Hence, the last flow, 263.80, occurs at date 5. The value of existing debt is exactly 263.80 before the annuity is paid. Table 25.7 shows the original repayment schedule of the loan. The constant annuity is 263.80 with an original rate of 12%.

The present value of all annuities at a discount rate of 10% is exactly 1000[4].

TABLE 25.7   Repayment schedule of loan

Dates	0	1	2	3	4	5
Loan	1000					
Annuities		263.80	263.80	263.80	263.80	263.80
Capital repayment		163.80	180.18	198.19	218.01	239.82
Outstanding balance		836.20	656.03	457.83	239.82	0.00

---

4   The 1000 value discounts all annuities of 263.8, starting at end of period 1, so that:

$$1000 = \sum_{t=1,5} 263.8 / (1+i)^t$$

25.5.7 Binomial Tree of Interest Rates

When using equal probabilities of up and down movements and $u = \exp(\sigma\sqrt{t}) = 1/d$, plugging in $\sigma = 20\%$ and $t = 1$, we have $u = 1.2214$ and $d = 0.8187$. The binomial tree of rates is shown in Table 25.8.

TABLE 25.8   Binomial tree of interest rates

Date	0	1	2	3	4	5
1	10.00%	12.21%	14.92%	18.22%	22.26%	27.18%
2		8.19%	10.00%	12.21%	14.92%	18.22%
3			6.70%	8.19%	10.00%	12.21%
4				5.49%	6.70%	8.19%
5					4.49%	5.49%

Using an original rate starting at 10% results in a value of the debt at date 0 higher than 1000 because we average debt values which are not a linear function of rates. In order to find exactly the value of 1000 when moving along the "tree" of rates, it is necessary to adjust all rates by deducting a constant drift of −0.171% (Table 25.9). Instead of starting at 10% we start at 10% − 0.171% = 9.83%. The same drift applies to all rates of the tree.

TABLE 25.9   Binomial tree of rates after calibration

Dates	0	1	2	3	4	5
Drift	−0.171%	−0.171%	−0.171%	−0.171%	−0.171%	−0.171%
Calibrated rates	9.83%	12.04%	14.75%	18.05%	22.08%	27.01%
		8.02%	9.83%	12.04%	14.75%	18.05%
			6.53%	8.02%	9.83%	12.04%
				5.32%	6.53%	8.02%
					4.32%	5.32%
						3.51%

Using this tree of short-term rates, proceeding backward to initial date, the value of the loan is exactly 1000. Because we need to obtain the initial value of loan before any annuity payment, all values are calculated before annuity payment, supposed to be paid immediately after current date.

25.5.8 The Market Value of Loan

At any intermediate date, the value of the debt discounts future annuities. At maturity, the value of debt at date 6 would be zero under all scenarios and equals the constant annuity at date 5 (Table 25.10).

25.5.9 The Exercise Price and the Payoff of the Option

The market value of the original loan varies with interest rates and is the underlying of the prepayment option. It is the present value of all subsequent annuities, given the market rate. The

TABLE 25.10   Market value of loan[a]

Dates	0	1	2	3	4	5
Flows	0.00	263.80	263.80	263.80	263.80	263.80
	1000.00	1061.72	867.37	676.15	479.88	263.80
		1134.86	920.66	709.02	493.69	263.80
			961.11	733.82	503.99	263.80
				751.89	511.42	263.80
					516.67	263.80
						263.80

[a]Values include the annuity paid immediately after each date.

rate values of each node served above to calculate the time paths of the value of the loan. The gain from renegotiation is the difference between the current value of the loan and the current strike price. The strike price of the debt is the amount of outstanding loan plus the penalty. The strike price of the option derives from the repayment schedule of the debt and adding 3% to outstanding capital due (Table 25.11).

Once we have all values of the loans and the strike price, the immediate payoff of the option is the positive difference between the value of loan and the strike price, without considering further opportunities of exercise. For making the calculation consistent, the value of loan should be net of principal repayment as well, whether it was calculated above before such repayment. The immediate payoff at any date is equal to the market value of loan minus principal times $(1 + 3\%)$ (Table 25.12).

The payoff at date 1, after a downward move of interest rate is, $1134.86 - 861.29 = 9.77$, and so for other dates. There is no positive payoff at inception, because the strike price is above the value of the loan at those dates.

TABLE 25.11   Outstanding capital due and penalty for early repayment

Dates	0	1	2	3	4
Outstanding capital	1000.00	836.20	656.03	457.83	239.82
Capital (1 + 3%)	1030.00	861.29	675.71	471.57	247.01

TABLE 25.12   Payoff of options under immediate exercise

Dates	0	1	2	3	4	5
	0.00	0.00	0.00	0.00	0.00	0.00
		9.77	0.00	0.00	0.00	0.00
			21.60	0.00	0.00	0.00
				16.52	0.61	0.00
					5.86	0.00
						0.00

Payoff = loan value – principal (1 + 3%).

25.5.10 Payoffs of the Option under Differed Exercise

The optimum behavior rule applies. The expected value of deferred gains at the next period is the average of their present values. The payoff of the option at t is the maximum between immediate exercise payoff and the present value of expected payoff of the next period, or zero. This behavioral rule changes the time profile of gains. The rounded present value of the option as of today is 12.85 (Table 25.13).

TABLE 25.13 Expected payoffs from the prepayment option[a]

Dates	0	1	2	3	4	5
	4.61	0.06	0.00	0.00	0.00	0.00
		10.06	0.13	0.00	0.00	0.00
			21.60	0.28	0.00	0.00
				16.52	0.61	0.00
					5.86	0.00
						0.00

[a]Option value = max (exercise value at t; expected exercise values of $t + 1$ discounted to t en t; 0).

The value of the prepayment option is 4.61 for a loan of 1000, or 0.461% of the original value of the loan. Accordingly, the actual value of the loan is $1000 - 4.61 = 995.39$. An additional markup should be added to the loan rate for making the value equal to the original value of the loan. This markup is the option-adjusted spread that account for the lower value of the loan due to the option given away from the bank to the borrower.

25.5.11 Option-adjusted Spread

For the lender, the loan is an asset whose value is less than that of a straight debt of 1000 at 10%, the difference being the value of the prepayment option. For the borrower, the loan is a liability whose value is also lower than the 1000 at 10%. In both cases, the differential value compared to a straight non-callable loan is 4.61.

This cost is 0.461% of the current loan principal in current value. This decline of the loan value by the amount of the option value should appear under "fair value" in the balance sheet. It represents the economic value of the debt, lower than the book value by that of the option given away by the bank. Fair value is a better image than the book value because it makes losses due to prepayments visible immediately rather accruing losses later on when borrowers actually repay or renegotiate their loans.

Pricing this prepayment risk necessitates a markup over the straight debt price. This periodical markup is an additional margin equivalent to the value of the option. The spread required to make the value of the non-callable debt identical to that of the debt with the option is the option-adjusted spread (OAS). For determining the OAS, we need to find an additional drift of all rates bringing back the value of the loan bundled with option to 1000. For increasing the value of the loan, we need to add a negative drift, which will decrease all discounting rates. We find that the drift is –0.29%. This drift is equivalent to the loss for the lender due to the option. For compensating such a loss, the lender should price the loan at a higher rate that compensates this percentage loss. The 0.29% drift is the OAS spread that should be added to the loan rate for pricing the option to the borrower (Table 25.14).

TABLE 25.14 Summary of characteristics of the loan

A: loan without prepayment option

Debt	Maturity	Rate	Annuity
1000	5	10.00%	263.80

B: loan with prepayment option

Current rate	Value of the option	Value of loan without option	Value of debt with option[a]	OAS
10.00%	4.61	1000	995.39	0.29%

[a]The difference between the loan without options and the option value is rounded.

The methodology used to determine the OAS is similar to that of calibration. However, the goal differs. The calibration serves for linking the model to the market. The OAS serves for determining the cost of the option embedded in a loan and the required markup for pricing it to the borrower.

26

Economic Value of the Balance Sheet

This chapter defines economic value (EV) and its properties that make it a target variable of ALM. In essence, the economic value is the net present value of the asset cash flows and the liability cash flows. Economic value considers the value of explicit and implicit options embedded in assets and liabilities, while gaps do not. Moreover, a general property of economic value is that it relates very simply to the present value of the entire stream on net interest income (NII) of the bank up to the longest maturity. Therefore economic value captures profitability over the long run, whether NII refers to a short run period (one or two years). Both views of profitability are required and both target variables are subject to risk, a risk that should be controlled by banks. The relationship between EV and future NII is demonstrated by decomposing all-in flows generated by the balance sheet into capital flows and interest flows.

We present the economic value calculation in Section 26.1. For the economic value to have the above properties, we need to use as discount rate the risk-free rate, which allows valuing the risky spreads between loan rates and the spreads for deposits rates that are earned by the bank. The next step is conducted with an example using a simplified balance sheet and calculating the economic values from the cash flows and the periodical NII from the spreads with the risk-free rate. The cash flows are independent from the prevailing rates when considering fixed-rate assets and liabilities. The NII calculation is dependent on interest rates whenever we extend the horizon beyond the maturity of assets or liabilities. The process allows comparing the present values of cash flows with the present values of the periodical NII projected up to the longest horizon (discounting both at the same rate). The final step consists of generalizing the finding, by picking up any horizon and proceeding as above. In both cases, we find that the economic value is identical to that of the streams of NII eventually adjusted for changes of interest rates. Section 26.4 demonstrates why such identity prevails in general.

The next chapter (Chapter 27) deals with the interest rate risk management of EV, rather than interest income as the target variable of ALM. Duration gaps substitute for the classical interest rate gaps for this purpose.

Contents

26.1 ECONOMIC VALUE (EV)

The economic value of the banking balance sheet is the mark-to-market value of assets minus the mark-to-market values of liabilities. As such, it discounts at market rates all cash flows from assets and liabilities. Economic value is mentioned under Pillar 2 of the Basel 2 Accord which deals with ALM issues. Since amortizing flows are summarized by liquidity gaps, economic value is identical to the present value for all liquidity gaps plus all interest flows.

NII and book values have drawbacks. The net interest income is a popular target of interest rate risk management because it is a simple measure of current profitability that shows up directly in the accounting reports. But, because it is periodical, it characterizes only particular periods, ignoring any income beyond the horizon. Book values are not risk-adjusted, whether mark-to-market values are to the extent that any spread from a risky loan, for example, appears as a mark-to-market value higher than face value, provided that we use as discount rates the risk-free rates. Moreover, embedded options, common in retail banking, do not appear in book values, but would be valued in "economic values."

The economic value is, in fact, a mark-to-model value because loans are not tradable[1]. The calculation of an EV does not imply any assumption about liquidity of loans. It is an "economic" value calculation, based on the DCF model, not the price at which assets could trade. The EV has other distinctive features. It differs from the "fair values" of assets by the value of credit risk of borrowers, because it uses risk-free rates[2], without differentiating them according to the risk of individual borrowers. The credit risk of borrowers is in the spread over risk-free rate that they pay to the bank.

EV and market value of equity are not at all identical. EV can be negative, whereas equity value is always positive. In addition, equity is not a fixed income liability. Since equity investors take on all risks of the bank, the required rate of return should be above the cost of debt. Therefore, it does not make sense to consider the equity investor as a "pure net lender," who would be long with bank's loans and short with bank's liabilities. The market value of equity is the discounted value of the flows that compensate equity, with a risk-adjusted rate equal to the required return on equity, given the risk of equity measured by the β of the bank's stock. Moreover, the EV can be negative, when stock prices cannot, since it is a difference.

Several discount rates can be considered. Fair value should use risk-adjusted market rates inclusive of credit spreads applying to the credit grade of borrowers. The cost of financing of the bank also makes sense because any spread of assets above this cost of financing would show up as an excess spread. The cost of financing of the bank is the weighted average of all sources of funds, equity and debts, or weighted average cost of capital (Wacc) of the bank.

---

1 Mark-to-model differs from mark-to-market in that the latter would use all market parameters that should be embedded in market prices, in order to replicate those prices. Mark-to-model can be seen as a partial mark-to-market.
2 The subsequent paragraph discusses the choice of a proper discount rate.

In fact, we will show that the risk-free rate and the DCF are relevant for highlighting major properties of EV.

Economic value, or EV, is a target variable for ALM because it can be shown that it measures the present value of all net interest incomes over all future periods. When focusing on short-term horizon, say up to 2 years, ALM's natural target is the NII and the gap model remains appropriate, except for options. When focusing over the long-term, the EV becomes appropriate and it becomes necessary to derive risk measures for this new target variable.

In this section, we look at different "views" on the EV. The present value of the stream of future flows F_t is:

$$V = \frac{\sum_t F_t}{(1+r_t)^t}$$

The market rates are the risk-free zero-coupon rates r_t derived from yield curves. The formula provides a value of any asset that generates contractual flows. The EV is the net value of a portfolio long in assets and short in liabilities. It can be positive or negative. The change in EV depends entirely upon the sensitivities of these two portfolios. The next chapter, Chapter 27, discusses the behavior of EV when market rates change.

26.2 ECONOMIC VALUE AND NET INTEREST INCOME FOR A BANK WITHOUT CAPITAL

The EV is an economic measure of performance. If the value of assets is above face value, it means that their return is above the market rates, a normal situation if loans generate a spread above market rates. If the bank pays term deposits at a rate lower than market rates, such deposits cost less than market rates. Their market value gets below their face value. This results in a positive EV, because assets are valued above face values and liabilities are below face value. Accordingly, the EV increases when spreads between customer rates and market rates widen, and the NII also improves. We now expand the relationship between economic value and NII through the use of an example.

26.2.1 Sample Bank Balance Sheet

The current market risk-free rate is 5%. The bank funding is a one-year debt at the current rate of 6%, with a spread of 100 basis points over the risk-free rate, 5%. This rate is fixed for one period and is reset after. The asset has a longer maturity than the debt. It is a single bullet loan, with 3 years maturity, with a contractual fixed rate of 8%. The bank charges to customers the current market rate plus a 3% spread and pays a 1% spread above risk-free rate. Note that we include a credit spread for the bank financing, assuming that the bank has only financial debt and no deposits. For simplicity, we use a flat interest rate curve, which is not restrictive. The net interest income is immune to interest rate changes for the first year only, since the debt rate reset occurs only after one year. The balance sheet is shown in Table 26.1. The bank's equity is zero, an assumption relaxed subsequently.

The stream of cash flows from assets and liabilities is fixed from these data (Table 26.2).

TABLE 26.1   Example of a simplified balance sheet

	Assets	Liabilities
Amount	1000	1000
Fixed rate	8%	6%
Maturity	3 years	1 year

TABLE 26.2   Stream of cash flows generated by assets and liabilities

Dates	0	1	2	3
Assets	1000	80	80	1080
Liabilities	1000	1060	0	0

The cash flows are not identical to the NII. The differences are the principal repayments. For instance, at year 1, two cash flows occur: the interest revenue of 80 from the asset and the repayment of the bank's debt plus interest cost, or 1060. The net interest income depends only upon interest revenues and costs. It is equal to $80 - 60 = 20$. For subsequent years, the projection of NII requires assumptions, since the debt for years 2 and 3 has to be renewed. NII beyond the first period depends upon the cost of debt, which might change after the first year.

The horizon is the longest maturity, or 3 years. For projecting NII beyond one year, we have to roll over the debt at the market rate prevailing at renewal dates and project NII changes with interest rates. The contractual cash flows of assets do not change. The debt has to be renewed until the longest maturity, given the prevailing rate starting from period 2 and up to 3. Keeping the risk-free rate at 5% after the first year, the NII is projected using again 5%. Table 26.3 shows the cash flows and the NII over the 3 years.

26.2.2   EV and Projected Interest Income at Risk-free Rate

For calculating the economic value, we use the risk-free rate, 5%. Expanding the calculations, the formulas are:

$$PV(asset) = 80/(1 + 5\%) + 80/(1 + 5\%)^2 + 1080/(1 + 5\%)^3 = 1053.5$$

$$PV(debt) = 60/(1 + 5\%) + 60/(1 + 5\%)^2 + 1060/(1 + 5\%)^3 = 1027.5$$

TABLE 26.3   The asset and liability cash flows

Dates	0	1	2	3
Assets	1000	80	80	1080
Liabilities	1000	60	60	1060
Revenues	—	80	80	80
Costs	—	60	60	60
NII	—	20	20	20

The economic value is the difference:

$$EV = PV(asset) - PV(debt) = 54.5$$

Because we used the risk-free rate, the economic value of the debt is above the par value since it costs more than the risk-free rate. The asset value is also above the par value for the same reason. Next, we calculate the present value of all future interest incomes at the prevailing market rate 5%:

$$20/(1 + 5\%) + 10/(1 + 5\%)^2 + 10/(1 + 5\%)^3 = 54.5$$

The two calculations provide exactly the same value, showing that EV from cash flows is exactly equal to the present value of interest incomes at the same rate:

$$EV = \text{present value of NII} = 54.5$$

We can now change the discount rate, taking an extreme example with a sudden large jump of the risk-free interest rate up to 15% – we have a negative EV. The cash flows of assets do not change. The debt, when renewed at the new rate costs much more, 15% + 1% = 16%. Table 26.4 shows the cash flows and the NII, and the present values of both cash flows and NII at the risk-free rate of 15% are shown in Table 26.5. We now find that both present values are equal to –95.7 and are negative. The present values of assets and of debt are now below par because we discount at a rate higher than the initial rate.

We can understand why the economic value is negative, and equal to –95.7. This is because the EV discounts highly negative NIIs, which result from mismatch risk combined with a high increase of short-term rates.

TABLE 26.4   Using 15% as cost of debt for the bank

Dates	0	1	2	3
Assets	1000	80	80	1080
Liabilities	1000	60	160	1160

Interest revenues and costs: Debt rolled over at current rate

Revenues	—	80	80	80
Costs	—	60	160	160
NII	—	20	–80	–80

TABLE 26.5   Present values of cash flows and of NII at the risk-free rate

Dates	0	1	2	3
PV (assets)	840.2	69.6	60.5	710.1
PV (liabilities)	935.9	52.2	121.0	762.7
EV (balance sheet)	–95.7			
PV (NII)	–95.7	17.4	–60.5	–52.6

Note that changes of EV result from the different variations of asset values and liability values when we change the discount rate. The magnitude of their changes is different because they do not have the same sensitivity to a change of interest rate. Should we need to control the risk of the economic values, we would need to adjust their sensitivities to interest rates. This is the purpose of the next chapter. The choice of discount rates equal to risk-free rates becomes clear at this stage. This choice allows valuing any spread between customers' rates or market rates, that would show up in banks' NII.

26.3 NII AND EV

The above results obtain with a balance sheet without equity. Similar results exist when equity differs from zero, but they require an adjustment for the equity term. We will see in the next section that this is a specific case of a more general formula.

With capital, the debt is lower than assets and the interest income increases because of the smaller volume of debt. In the example below, equity is 100, debt is 900 and assets are 1000 (Table 26.6). All other assumptions are unchanged. The first year cost of debt at 6% is now 6% × 900 = 54. After the first year, it becomes indexed to whatever risk-free rate prevails. Using the same spreads above risk-free rate for loans and for the bank's debt, the cash flows, the NII and economic value change (Table 26.7).

Duplicating the same calculations as above with the new set of data, and discounting cash flows at 6%, we find new values of EV and the present value of NIIs:

$$EV = 157.2$$

$$PV (NII) = 70.8$$

TABLE 26.6   Simplified balance sheet with equity

	Assets	Liabilities
Loans at 8%	1000	
Capital		100
Debt at 6%		900

TABLE 26.7   Cash flows and NII

Dates	0	1	2	3
Assets	1000	80	80	1080
Liabilities	900	54	54	954

Interest revenues and costs: Debt rolled over at current rate

Revenues	—	80	80	80
Costs	—	54	54	54
NII	—	26	26	26

The difference is 86.4. This difference is due to equity. We observe that $86.4 = 100/(1 + 6\%)^3$, in other words, that the difference is the present value of equity positioned as the longest maturity. In fact, if we cut off the horizon at the end of period 3, we should pay back the equity amount to shareholders and deduct it from the EV. The economic value should be calculated by adding an additional flow of 100, as a liability due at final horizon, and discounted at 6%. Then the identity between economic value and present value of NIIs is preserved. The EV equals the discounted value of future NIIs if we deduct the present value of equity positioned at the latest date of the calculation:

$$EV = 157.2 - 86.4 = 70.8 = PV \text{ (NII)}$$

We now show why this is a general rule that applies whatever the discount rate used, and that the equality between EV and discounted NII applies to any horizon as long as we plug-in the liquidity gap of assets and liabilities at the horizon.

26.4 IDENTITY BETWEEN EV AND "ALL-IN" CASH FLOWS (CAPITAL AND INTEREST)

The reason why EV and the present value of NIIs remain equal is that the EV discounts all-in flows, interest and capital. The relationship between the two calculations stems from the relation between all-in cash flows and interest flows.

26.4.1 Separating All-in Flows into Capital and Interest Flows

By definition, the EV discounts the all-in cash flows, capital plus interest. We can split the two types of cash flows by sub-period. Consider $t - 1$ to t:

all-in (capital + interest) flows $(t - 1, t)$ = capital flows $(t - 1, t)$ + interest flows $(t - 1, t)$

Net capital flows over periods are amortizations of assets and liabilities and equal to the variations of the liquidity gaps. Net interest flows over the same periods are the NII. The EV is the present value of all-in cash flows:

$$EV = PV \text{ (future interest margins)} + PV \text{ (Δ liquidity gaps)}$$

Present values are calculated at market rates corresponding to each maturity of each cash flow generated by assets and liabilities, whether interest or capital. From the previous example of a simplified balance sheet with equity, we see that the liquidity gap is equal to equity at date 3. Therefore, the EV should be the present value of such liquidity gap -100 (with the sign convention asset – liability) as of 3 plus that of NIIs for all three periods. It is easy to see that the identity works for any horizon and any liquidity gap profile. A final example illustrates the general above property of economic value and NII.

26.4.2 Economic Value and NII: General Example

Taking the same balance sheet as before but allowing assets and liabilities to amortize progressively, we show that the identity applies to all horizons. We stick to the same values of assets and liabilities, the same spreads, and the same original risk-free rate, but we remove the assumption of full amortization at horizon 3. Instead assets and liabilities amortize progressively and there is a liquidity gap at the cut-off horizon 3.

The rates and spreads are identical to the previous example (Table 26.8). For generality, we now assume that there is an increase of the risk-free rate from 5% to 6% after the first period. Assets are fixed rate as well as debts. The equity is 100. The asset interest rate is fixed for all three periods, and is 8%, 3% above the initial risk-free rate of 5%. The debt interest rate is fixed at 6% for all non-amortized balances. Subsequently, the risk-free rate increases to 6%. All discount factors use the new risk-free rate of 6%.

Consider the projected balance sheet with amortizing assets and liabilities. Note that the capital flows measures the variations of the liquidity gaps and are marginal liquidity gaps. With sign conventions, the amortization of assets is an inflow and the amortization of liabilities is an outflow. The capital flows are the net values of such inflows and outflows. They are identical to the variations of liquidity gaps (Table 26.9). The interest revenues and costs of period t are calculated from the outstanding balances of assets and liabilities as of $t-1$ using the fixed rates applicable to assets and debt (Table 26.10).

TABLE 26.8   Interest rate data

	Spread	Initial rates	Projected rates
Asset rate	3%	8%	8%
Debt rate	1%	6%	7%
Market rate		5%	6%

TABLE 26.9   Balance sheet amortization up to a fixed horizon

Dates	0	1	2	3
Assets	1000	900	800	600
Liabilities	900	800	600	500
Liquidity gaps		100	200	100
Asset flows		100	100	200
Liability flows		−100	−200	−100
Net capital flows		0	−100	100

TABLE 26.10   Interest revenues and costs

Interest revenues and costs at t (using balances of A&L as of t − 1)			
Revenues	80.0	72.0	64.0
Costs	54.0	48.0	36.0
NII	26.0	24.0	28.0

TABLE 26.11   Discount factors

Dates	0	1	2	3
Discount factors at 6%		0.943	0.890	0.840

TABLE 26.12   Present values of all-in flows, capital and interest flows

PV(capital flows)		0.0	−89.0	84.0
Σ PV(capital flows)	−5.0			
PV(NII)		24.5	21.4	23.5
Σ PV(NII)	69.4			
All-in flows		26.0	−76.0	128.0
PV(all-in flows)		24.5	−67.6	107.5
Σ PV(all-in flows)	64.4			
Economic value	64.4			

From capital flows and NII flows, we derive the present value of each. The economic value is the sum of the present values of capital flows and of NIIs. The discount factors use the final risk-free rate of 6% (Table 26.11). Finally, the present value of all-in flows provides the economic value and is identical to the present value of all NIIs and capital flows up to the cut-off horizon (Table 26.12).

The present value of NIIs is the economic value minus the present value of capital flows over any horizon:

$$PV \ (NII) = \text{economic value} - PV \ (\text{capital flows})$$

$$PV \ (NIIs) = 64.4 - (-5) = 69.4$$

These identities hold for all horizons. When extending the horizon to the longest horizon, we see that the present value of all NIIs over sub-periods is simply the economic value minus the final liquidity gap, which becomes then equal to equity in absolute value.

Economic value is a target variable of ALM because it summarizes in a single value the present value of the entire stream of net interest income up to any cut-off horizon. This corrects a major drawback of gaps, which is that they are periodical. Gaps are fine for hedging the NII of particular periods, if there are no options in the balance sheet, but the economic value it is better to measure is the entire stream of NIIs up to a cut-off horizon. Managing the risk of EV should be conducted simultaneously with gap management because it targets a longer horizon. The next chapter explains how EV risk can be hedged or controlled.

27

Economic Value and Convexity Risk

The techniques for managing the risk of economic values rely on the duration and the convexity of assets and liabilities. The duration is the sensitivity, or the slope of the curve, linking the relationship between economic value and discount rate. Convexity is the change of duration when interest rates change significantly, and measures the curvature of the relation. Since economic value depends on the asset and on the liability values, it depends also on the shapes of the curves representing how asset value and liability value change when interest rates vary, hence on their relative durations and convexities. Moreover, convexity increases in the presence of options. This suggests measuring the optional risk through differentials between embedded options and optional hedges. It is common to designate duration risk as "delta" risk and convexity risk as "gamma" risk following the generic terminology used for options.

The first part of the this chapter addresses, sequentially, duration properties, the condition on the duration gaps that make economic value immune to small variations of interest rates, and how to meet such conditions with derivative instruments. In the presence of significant volatility of interest rates, convexity effects become non-negligible. Accordingly, the second part of this chapter addresses, sequentially, the properties of convexity, the conditions on convexities of assets and liabilities that serves for protecting the economic value in presence of volatility of interest rates, and how to achieve such a result through a proper usage of derivatives. Convexity effects exist whenever interest rates are subject to large shocks. They also appear in the presence of options because these magnify convexity. The part of this chapter addresses optional risk and the related optional gap. Once all effects are covered, it becomes clear that interest rate gaps are not enough for managing interest rate risk. They should be supplemented by duration gaps, by convexity gaps and by optional gaps to avoid adverse effect on the economic value of the balance sheet.

Contents

27.1 DURATION PROPERTIES

For fixed-rate assets, the economic value varies inversely with interest rates because the value discounts future cash flows with market interest rates that vary. The relationship is not linear. The market value is the DCF of all contractual cash flows and is inversely related to the parallel shift of interest rates. The curvature of the shape looks upward (Figure 27.1). For floating rate assets, the relationship becomes flat and the duration is zero.

In what follows, we use the generic term "duration" for designating the sensitivity. The general formula for sensitivity to a rate y is:

$$\Delta V/V = -D\Delta y$$

The relative change in value, as a percentage, is equal to the modified duration[1] multiplied by the absolute percentage interest rate change. The sensitivity in value is the change of value of the asset generated by a unit change in interest rate. This value is equal to the market value of the asset multiplied by the modified duration and by the change in interest rate:

$$\Delta V = -[D/(1+y)]V\Delta y$$

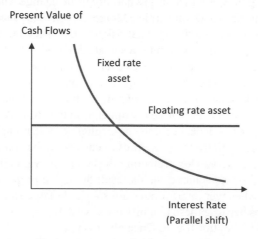

FIGURE 27.1   Market value/interest rate profile

---

1 Modified duration is $D/(1+y)$. This is the first derivative of value with respect to a shift Δy of all rates. In Chapter 15 on sensitivities, we did not make any distinction, implying that we used D as modified duration.

The duration of a portfolio is the average of the durations of assets weighted by their market values. This property is convenient to derive the durations of the portfolios of assets and liabilities as a simple function of the durations of its individual components.

The duration has several important properties[2]. The duration is a "local" measure. When the interest rate changes, the duration drifts as well. This makes it less convenient to use whenever there are important shocks on interest rates because it is not acceptable anymore to consider duration to be constant. The duration also changes when time passes. It increases with maturity, but less than proportionately. When time passes, from t to $t + 1$, the residual life of the asset decreases by 1. Nevertheless, the duration decreases by less than 1 because of convexity. If the duration is 2 years today, it will be more than 1 year after one year, because it diminishes less than residual maturity. This is the "duration drift" over time. Due to duration drift, any constraint on duration holding at a given date does not hold any more after a while, due to both interest rate changes and time drift.

The return of an asset calculated over a horizon equal to its duration is immune to any interest rate variation. With fixed-rate assets, obtaining the yield-to-maturity requires holding the asset until maturity. When selling the asset before maturity, the return is uncertain because the price at the date of sale is unknown. This price depends upon the prevailing interest rate at this date. If the interest rates increase, the prices decrease and vice versa. The holding period return combines the current yield (the interest paid) and the capital gain or loss at the end of the period.

The total return from holding an asset depends upon the usage of intermediate interest flows. The return, over any intermediate horizon, results from the capital gain or loss, plus the interest payments, and plus the proceeds of the reinvestments of the intermediate flows up to this horizon. If the interest rate increases during the holding period, there is a capital loss due to the decline of the price. At the same time, intermediate flows benefit from a higher reinvestment rate up to the horizon at a higher rate. If the interest rate decreases, there is a capital gain at the horizon. At the same time, all intermediate reinvestment rates get lower. These two effects tend to offset each other. There is a horizon such that the net effects of the reinvestment of the intermediate flows, plus the capital gain or loss, cancel out. When this happens, the future value at the horizon is immune to interest rate changes. This horizon is the duration of the asset[3].

27.2 SENSITIVITY OF ECONOMIC VALUE AND DURATION GAPS

Since economic value is the difference between asset value and liability value, its sensitivity depends on their differential durations, which is the duration gap. The duration gap is the equivalent of the interest rate gap for controlling the variations of the net interest income.

27.2.1 Duration Gap

For neutralizing the sensitivity of the economic value, the variations of the values of assets and of liabilities should be identical. This condition implies a relationship between the values

---

2 The book of Bierwag (1987, [11]) is entirely dedicated to duration definitions and properties.
3 This is demonstrated in [11].

and the durations of assets and liabilities. With a parallel shift of the yield curve equal to Δi, the condition is:

$$\Delta EV/\Delta i = \Delta(V_A - V_L)/\Delta i$$

V_A and V_L are the market values of assets and liabilities. The changes in these values result from their durations, D_A and D_L. They are $(-D_A V_A \Delta i)$ and $(-D_L V_L \Delta i)$. If we divide by Δi, we obtain:

$$\frac{\Delta EV}{\Delta i} = \frac{[-D_A V_A + D_L V_L]}{(1+i)}$$

The immunization condition is:

$$V_A D_A = V_L D_L$$

This condition states that the changes in the market values of assets and liabilities are equal. Note that this duration gap is in value, not in years. When adjusting durations, it is more convenient to manipulate durations in years without the value weights. The immunization condition is:

$$\frac{D_A}{D_L} = \frac{V_L}{V_A}$$

The formula stipulates that the ratio of the duration and liabilities should be equal to the ratio of market values of liabilities to assets.

The EV sensitivity is the sensitivity of the net portfolio of assets minus liabilities. Its duration is a linear function of these, using market value weights:

$$\Delta EV = \frac{[-D_A V_A + D_L V_L]}{(1+i)} \Delta i$$

The sensitivity of the EV has a duration equal to the term in brackets. The term in brackets is the duration gap. The duration gap is the gap of durations of assets and liabilities weighted by the market values of assets and liabilities.

$$\text{duration gap} = -D_A V_A + D_L V_L$$

An alternate designation for the duration of EV is the "duration of equity." It implies dividing the duration gap in value by the EV. This formula expresses the duration of EV in years rather than in value.

$$\frac{\Delta EV}{EV} = \frac{[-D_A V_A + D_L V_L]}{(1+i)} \frac{\Delta i}{EV}$$

The EV sensitivity is much higher than those of assets or liabilities since we divide by EV, whose value is much lower than that of assets and liabilities.

For instance, using as orders of magnitudes book values, we consider approximately that $V_L = 96\% \times V_A$ when equity is 4% of assets (weighted according to regulatory forfeits). EV represents also around 4% of the balance sheet. If we have $D_L = 1$ and $D_A = 2$, the weighted duration gap is around:

$$-2 \times 100\% + 1 \times 96\% = -1.04$$

The "equity" or "EV" duration is $-1.04/4\% = -26$.

These conditions are extremely simple. Note that the duration gap is weighted by market values. One could wonder what represents the unweighted duration gap, or setting equal durations of assets and liabilities ($D_A = D_L$). When durations match, any change of rates generates the same percentage change for assets and for debts. Since the change in the debt to asset ratio is the difference of those two percentage changes, it becomes zero[4]. If the debt to asset ratio is constant, the debt to equity ratio of a bank is also constant. Hence, matching durations means that market value leverage is immune to changes of interest rates.

Such a condition would apply for example to a fund which uses a constant leverage in term of market values. Typically, a fund has asset and debt complying with the constraint that asset value remain above that of debt, the asset to value ratio. Maintaining such ratio would imply equal duration of assets and of debt pledged by those assets.

27.2.2 Controlling Duration with Derivatives

The adjustment of duration necessitates changing the weights of durations of the various items in the balance sheet. Unfortunately, customers determine what they want, which sets the duration values. Hence, modifying directly the durations of assets and liabilities on-balance sheet is not the proper way to adjust the portfolio duration.

An alternate method is to use derivatives. Hedges, such as interest rate swaps, modify duration to the extent that they modify the interest flows. When converting a fixed-rate asset into a variable rate asset though an interest rate swap, the value becomes insensitive to interest rates since it behaves as the value of a floater, with zero duration and constant value.

Future contracts have durations identical to the underlying asset because they track its value. We discussed forward contracts, which are not traded in organized exchanges. Since forward contracts on interest rate lock in a forward rate, for example for a forward loan, the forward loan market value becomes sensitive to interest rate changes. This amounts to increasing the sensitivity. Hence, forward and futures, which are similar[5] to traded forwards, also provide a flexible way to adjust durations through off-balance sheet transactions rather than on-balance sheet adjustments.

27.2.3 Duration Gap and Sensitivity of EV

The value-interest profiles of EV have various shapes depending upon the relative durations of the assets and the liabilities. The duration gap measures such sensitivity. When equal to zero, the EV is immune to variations of interest rates as long as they are not too big. A

---

4 Simply note that: $\Delta(V_A/V_L) = (\Delta V_A)/V_A - (\Delta V_L)V_L$. Since the difference is that of the durations of A and L, equal durations imply a constant ratio V_A/V_L. Using $V_A = V_L + VE$, with V_E being economic value, it is easy to show that V_L/V_E is also constant.

5 Futures are not identical to forward contracts, since the value of entering into a futures contract is the mark-to-market value of the forward loan and triggers daily margin calls.

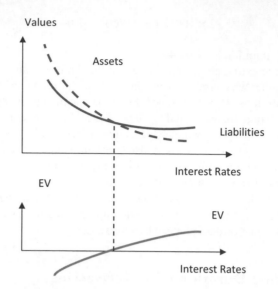

FIGURE 27.2   EV and duration mismatch

duration mismatch – weighted by asset and liability values – between assets and liabilities makes the EV sensitive to rates. The change in EV is proportional to the change of interest rates since the values of assets and liabilities are approximately linear functions of the rate change. Figure 27.2 shows the sensitivity of the EV under duration mismatch. There is a value of interest rates such that EV is zero. If the interest rate changes, the EV becomes positive or negative.

Mismatch risk implies mismatch of durations, thereby creating duration gaps. By modifying and neutralizing the duration gap, it is possible to have a more favorable case. In Figure 27.3, the convexities of the curves are not very important, and the durations of assets and liabilities match. Small variations of interest rates do not affect the EV much. Matching the weighted durations of assets and liabilities makes the EV immune to small variations of interest rates. This is a "local" (context-dependent) rule.

Sensitivities of both assets and liabilities, and, therefore, of the EV, depend upon the level of interest rates. But for larger changes, the EV becomes sensitive due to the different convexities of the profiles of assets and liabilities. In Figure 27.3, the two profiles, for assets and liabilities, have the usual shape with an upward-looking convexity. In Figure 27.3, the EV is positive, and the slope of the curves representing assets and liabilities are identical because their durations match. The EV is almost insensitive to interest rate variations, except when significant variations of interest rates occur.

27.3 ECONOMIC VALUE, DURATION AND CONVEXITY

Duration captures the first-order effect of a change of interest rates and convexity measures second-order effects. If convexity is important, matching durations does not make the EV immune to rate changes and the duration gaps are not a reliable measure of sensitivity.

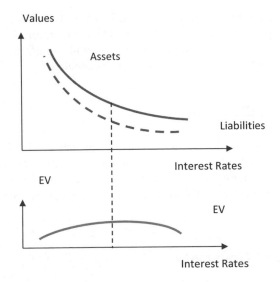

FIGURE 27.3 EV–interest rate profile

27.3.1 Convexity

The difference, the EV, has a shape that depends upon the relative curvatures of the profiles of assets and liabilities. Convexity risk arises from the different convexities of the curves representing the relationship between asset and liability values to interest rates. When there are significant differences between the curvatures, or "convexities," of the asset/interest rate and liability/interest rate profiles, significant variations of the EV might occur, even when slopes are similar at the current rate. This is "convexity risk."

Graphically, the slope of the "market value/interest rate" profile relates to duration. When the interest rate moves, so does the duration. The curvature of the profile shows how the slope changes (Figure 27.4). The curvature means that the sensitivity to downward moves of the

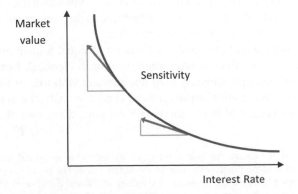

FIGURE 27.4 Sensitivity and interest rates

interest rate is higher than the sensitivity to upward moves. The effect of a decrease in rates, from 9% to 8%, is bigger than the change generated by a move from 4% to 3%. "Convexity" measures the change in duration when the rates move. With significant variations of interest rates, the second-order effect, or convexity, should be considered.

27.3.2 Sources of Convexity

The first source of convexity is the non-linear relationship between market value and discount rates, due to discount factors, such as $(1 + i)^t$. A fraction of convexity comes from this mathematical formula. Wide variations of interest rates make the convexity become non-negligible. Convexity also relates to options embedded in banks' balance sheets beause of their "kinked" payoffs.

27.3.3 Measure of Convexity

Mathematically, convexity results, as does duration, from the formula that gives the price as the discounted value of future cash flows or from the formula pricing an option. In both cases, it is a second derivative. The mathematical formula for referring to sensitivities and convexity is the Taylor expansion formula introduced in the sensitivity chapter (Chapter 15).

Financially, convexity increases with the time dispersion of flows. This can be illustrated by comparing two assets – a zero coupon bond and a portfolio of two zero-coupons bonds. A zero-coupon bond has duration equal to maturity. A portfolio of two zero-coupon bonds can have value and weights such that value-weighted maturity is equal to the maturity of the single zero bond. Because we can change both the nominal and maturity of each zero bond within the portfolio, we can make the portfolio duration and the portfolio value equal to that of the single bond[6]. Shifting the interest rate by varying amounts, we can see that the portfolio has more convexity that the single zero bond. This illustrates the fact that convexity is higher when the dispersion of flows along time is higher. Figure 27.5 shows the portfolio (continuous lines) and the single bond. They have equal duration when the interest rate is 6%. But the portfolio has a stronger convexity than the single bond.

Convexity is relevant because it has value in the market and provides an additional return when the volatility of interest rates becomes significant. The intuition results from Figure 27.6. The convexity of the asset value/interest rate relation makes the average value of assets between two distant interest rates higher than the current value.

Assume that the interest rate can have two values with equal probability, at equal distance from the current value of the interest rate, when duration is identical. Compare the expected value of an asset with an approximately constant duration with that of the convex portfolio with same duration and same initial value. If there is no convexity, the expected value would be on the straight line tangential to the curve with the same duration at the average rate. The

---

6   We have a system of two equations: one is for equating the value-weighted duration, and one is for equating the sum of value of the portfolio to that of the single bond. The portfolio used in the example is made of two zero-coupon bonds with, respectively, values 35.71 and 8.10, rates 1% and 4%, and same maturity 30 years. The same duration zero-coupon bond has a maturity of 15 years, a 5% rate and a value 43.81, equal to the value of the portfolio of the two zero bonds.

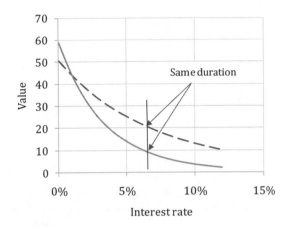

FIGURE 27.5   Convexity and dispersion of cash flows across time

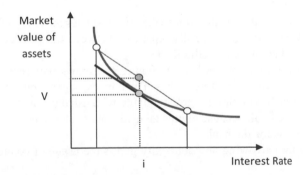

FIGURE 27.6   Value of convexity

convex portfolio has higher values when the interest rate shifts upward and downward by the same amount. The average value of the convex portfolio is on the higher straight line joining the portfolio values matching the two interest rates. Interest rate volatility increases the expected value of convex assets. The higher the volatility of interest rates, the higher the value of convexity.

The implication is that it is better to have a higher convexity of assets when the interest rate volatility increases, because this would increase the EV. Conversely, a lower convexity of liabilities would make their value lower under the same interest rate variations.

27.3.4 Economic Value and Convexity Gaps

Closing the duration gaps makes the EV immune to variations of interest rates as long as they are small. But discrepancies of convexities between assets and liabilities, or convexity gaps,

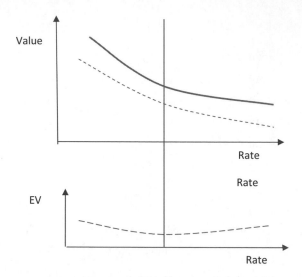

FIGURE 27.7   Convexities and EV sensitivity to interest rate optimization

weaken the protection of matching durations when interest rates move significantly away from the current value. Convexity gaps are discrepancies between the convexities of assets and liabilities. Sometimes they have a small effect.

In theory, they could also benefit the bank, as Figure 27.7 shows, with economic value increasing on both sides of variations of interest rates. The convexity gap would be favorable.

Unfortunately, such convexities are not attainable with usual products, and convexity risk is always adverse to the bank because clients take advantage of any positive payoff for them, and such payoff is a loss for the bank.

The easiest way for narrowing any convexity gap is the usage of convex instruments, or options.

27.4 CONVEXITY GAPS AND OPTIONS

A second source of convexity gap is optionality. The relationship between the market value of an option and the underlying parameter is highly convex when the option is at-the-money, and the payoff of an option, as a function of the underlying asset, has a "kink." Options create "kinks" in duration and create convexity risk. When the option is out-of-the money, the sensitivity, or delta, is very low, and conversely, when the option is in-the-money, the delta is close to one. Hence, all options, including embedded options in the balance sheet of banks, have a high convexity effect when close to at-the-money.

Options are a major source of convexity in a balance sheet, and the main source of errors when using local measures of sensitivity to measure risk. Embedded options cap the value of assets and impose floors to the value of liabilities.

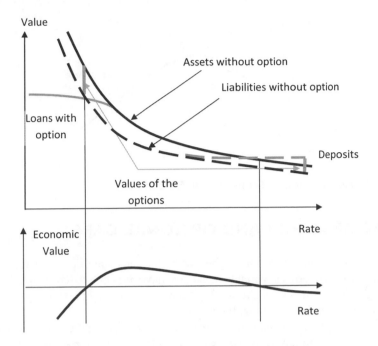

FIGURE 27.8 **"Scissors Effect" on EV due to embedded options**

For instance, the value of a loan with a renegotiation option cannot go above some maximum value, since the borrower can renegotiate the loan interest rate. A decline in interest rate normally increases the value of the asset, until we reach the point when renegotiation occurs. When we reach the cap, the loan behaves as if it were variable, at least at the time of renegotiation. The difference between the maximum loan value and the value of the straight loan is the value of the option.

On the liability side, options generate a floor for the value of some liabilities when the interest rates rise. Beyond some upper level of market rates, depositors shift their funds from deposits that earn no return at all, or earn a low fixed rate, towards interest-bearing assets. The value of the liability hits a floor instead of decreasing with the rise of interest rates. Even if resources stay within the bank, they become variable rate liabilities and have a constant minimum value when rates increase.

Beyond some variations of interest rates, fixed-rate assets and liabilities tend to behave as variable rates assets and liabilities. The shape of the "value/interest rate profile" of assets and liabilities flattens and becomes horizontal when hitting some upper bounds when interest rates decline and lower bounds when interest rates increase, as shown in Figure 27.8.

Figure 27.9 shows that, whatever the direction of the interest rate movement, the effect on economic value is always adverse to the bank. This is sometimes called "the scissors effect" on economic value. When interest rates remain in a narrow range, the EV remains positive. However, if they deviate beyond upper and lower bounds that triggers the embedded caps or floors, options gain values and generate a negative EV. This is the general case. Remember that EV is the present value of all NIIs. When interest rate volatility grows higher, it has always an adverse effect on both EV and NII.

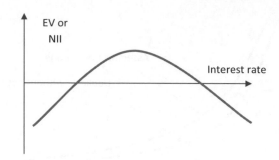

FIGURE 27.9   Adverse effect of convexity on EV and NII

27.5 OPTIONAL RISK AND OPTIONAL GAPS

Optional risk results in interest revenues given up by the bank when options to renegotiate fixed rates, or when caps embedded in variable rate loans, have been granted to clients. Closing down the duration gap limits the EV sensitivity. The convexity gap might remain open, however. As any optional gap, it can be hedged with options.

The hedge for variable rate loans with caps consists of capping the cost of financing by the bank though the acquisition of caps. The hedge against renegotiation of fixed rates consists of buying floors for protecting interest revenues when interest rates decline. The "optional gap" is the gap between options given away to clients and options used for hedging by the bank. Optional gaps can be calculated as the difference between the amount of options given away (or sold) and the notional of options acquired by the bank. Such difference provides only a view of the magnitudes of the optional exposures. For considering the value effect, the payoff of options sold and bought is more relevant. The net payoff for the bank is the payoff of the optional gap, which depends on interest rate scenarios.

We consider separately the cases of caps sold to clients when interest rates increase and that of implicit options to renegotiate fixed rates when interest rates decline.

27.5.1 Hedging Caps Sold to Clients

Considering the pool of variable rate loans with a contractual cap on rates, the amount and strikes of caps held by clients are both known. The amount subject to caps with different strikes is the optional exposure. It should be broken down by range of values of strikes. The point-in-time payoff for the clients can be calculated assuming immediate exercise for those caps that have a positive payoff for the borrowers. At future dates, the payoff depends on scenarios of interest rates. The payoff for clients will increase when projected interest rates increase and conversely.

The hedge for the banks against such increases is made of caps acquired by the bank that set a guaranteed borrowing rate. The payoff from immediate exercise can also be derived from amounts and strikes of this hedging portfolio of caps. It depends on scenarios of interest rates for future dates.

The optional gap is the gap between options held by clients and options acquired by the bank. The optional gap serves for monitoring optional risk. The difference between capped amounts

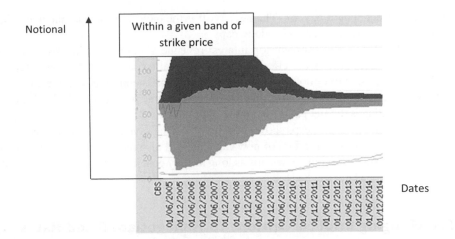

FIGURE 27.10   Sample optional gap report

of loans and the notional of hedging caps is a "gap of caps" or optional gap. It is a difference between the notional of caps held by clients and caps held by the bank. Such an optional gap should be broken down by range of values of strikes, and for each strike band, there would be a different optional gap of caps. In the graph of "gap of caps" (Figure 27.10), the top line shows the caps sold and the bottom line the caps bought by the bank. The difference is the gap of caps. The size of both exposures diminishes with time as a result of amortization.

The net payoff equals the gain from caps acquired for hedging minus the losses from caps of clients for various interest rate scenarios. The losses from caps given to clients are the differential between rates and the cap rate times the notional matching each range of values of the strike of the caps. The gains from hedging caps are also the differentials between strikes and interest rates, times the amounts hedged. For a given period, putting together the interest revenues given away to clients and the interest savings for the bank from hedging caps, we

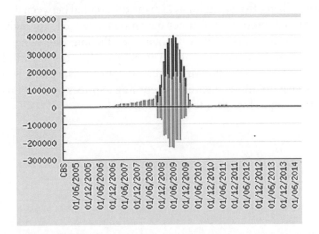

FIGURE 27.11   Interest revenue given up minus interest income from caps

obtain the net effect of both payoffs. The net payoff is the payoff of the optional gap, which is commonly seen as a variation of NII due to caps.

In Figure 27.11, the bars show on top interest revenue given up and interest payoff from bank's caps. The net value is the effect on NII. Such values are dependent on interest rate scenarios. The exposure to optional risk is the "gap of caps" combined with the gap between interest revenues given up by the bank, and the interest income received by the bank from caps acquired for hedging is the net payoff from the optional gap.

The NII effect of the gap of caps shows how much can be saved by additional hedges. Such new hedges would cost the premium of new caps but will also reduce the interest given up to clients. It makes sense to acquire new caps as long as they cost less than the fraction of interest revenues given up and not yet hedged.

27.5.2 Hedging Implicit Options to Renegotiate Fixed Rates

For fixed rates loans, the strikes of options are not contractual as they are for variable rates capped. However, it is also feasible to find out the benefits from immediate exercise, or payoff, of options to renegotiate fixed-rate loans.

Considering a point in time, the economic payoff of exercising the option can be calculated for each fixed-rate loan. The payoff increases with the differential between the original fixed rate, the new prevailing fixed rate for mortgages, and with the residual maturity. The larger the immediate payoff, the larger is the likelihood of renegotiation. It is feasible to break down the portfolio of loans into segments matching ranges of values of the economic gain from renegotiations for borrowers. A proxy of such breakdown would pool together loans according to the level of fixed rate and the residual maturity. Such breakdowns provide the amount of subject to optional risk. As with caps, this breakdown is the exposure to optional risk on the loan side. A symmetrical treatment for optional hedges acquired by the bank provides the optional gap, to be broken down according to bands of strike prices.

The net payoff of the optional gap depends on interest rates. Given an interest rate scenario, it equals the gain from floors acquired for hedging minus the losses from the renegotiation option of clients. The losses from options held by clients are the payoff of renegotiation of the fixed rate. The payoff for the bank from hedging is also the differential between the strikes of the floor acquired by the bank and interest rates, times the amounts hedged. For a given period, putting together the interest revenues given away to clients and the interest savings for the banks from hedging with floors provides the net payoffs. The net payoff is the payoff of the optional gap, which is commonly seen as a variation of NII due to options. The graph is similar to those for gaps of caps. The net payoff allows deciding, according to prices of additional hedges, whether or not they provide an additional gain for the bank.

SECTION 8
Funds Transfer Pricing Systems

Beyond global balance sheet management, ALM contributions to bank-wide risk management is the definition of economic transfer prices, the internal cost of funds, through the "funds transfer pricing" (FTP) scheme. The FTP system serves primarily for transferring funds from excess cash units to deficit cash units through pool of funds, which is the treasury or ALM. The FTP is also an income-allocating system, breaking down the global earnings from the banking portfolio into earnings allocated to each business line. FTP schemes are relatively simple and are as well relatively rarely addressed in the literature, although the following remarks show that it is critical.

The FTP scheme serves for allocating income and risk-based pricing. Two main tools for global bank-wide risk management are the FTP system and the capital allocation system. The capital allocation system aims at allocating risks within the bank and is dealt with in Section 13. FTP systems are another necessary building block of risk management systems. Without such systems, independently of which unit is in charge, allocating income to transactions and sub-portfolios would not be feasible, thereby making both capital allocation and risk-adjusted performance measures useless in bank-wide management.

Because they serve for allocating performance, transfer prices are most important. Should their credibility be at stake, such flaws would contaminate all performance measures in commercial banking. Non-economic benchmarks of transfer prices would entail improper arbitrages by business units and customers as well. Because these are so critical, "economic transfer prices" should be based on objective and meaningful criteria.

This section contains two chapters. The basic purpose and organization of funds transfer pricing is addressed in Chapter 28:

1 allocating funds within the banks
2 calculating the performance margins of a transaction or any sub-portfolio of transactions and its contributions to the overall margin of the bank (revenue allocation)
3 providing incentives or penalties, differentiating the transfer prices to allow their consistent use with the commercial policy.

A second set of contributions relates more to the economics of transfer prices is in Chapter 29.

1 Defining economic benchmarks for pricing and performance measurement purposes. This implies choosing the right references for economic transfer prices. The "all-in" cost of funds of the bank provides this reference.
2 Defining pricing policies. Risk-based pricing is the pricing that would compensate the risks of the bank in line with the target overall profitability target of the banks.
3 Providing mis-pricing reports, making explicit the differences between the effective prices and what they should be, i.e. target risk-based prices.
4 Transferring liquidity and interest rate risk to the ALM unit, making the performance of business lines independent of market movements that are beyond their control.

Both lists demonstrate that the FTP system is a strategic tool, and that it is a main interface between the commercial sphere and the financial sphere of the bank. Any malfunctioning or inconsistency in the system interferes with commercial and financial management, and might create a gap between global policies and operations management, in addition to impairing bank-wide risk management.

Chapter 28 specifies how the system should be designed, i.e. which funds should be transferred and how to make sure that performances of all business units actually sum up to the bank's earnings. Chapter 29 discusses the definition of economic and fair transfer prices.

28

Funds Transfer Pricing Systems

All the business units of a financial institution share a common resource: liquidity. The first function of the funds transfer pricing (FTP) system is to exchange funds between business units and ALM since business units do not have balanced uses and resources. The FTP system nets the balances of sources and uses of funds within the bank.

The exchange of funds between units and with ALM requires a pricing system. Transfer prices serve to calculate revenues as spreads between customers' prices and internal references. Without such prices there would be no way to calculate internal spreads of transactions, product lines, customers or market segments, and business units. Transfer prices provide a major link between the global bank earnings and the earnings of individual sub-portfolios or individual transactions.

Section 28.1 discusses the organization of FTP systems and the definition of which funds should transit through the central pool. It is easy to show that, for allocating income to all transactions, the entire outstanding balances of assets and liabilities of each business unit should transit through the pool. Section 28.2 illustrates the mechanism of income allocation and shows how such an allocation is made consistent with the bank's overall net interest income. The condition for achieving this goal is that all funds transit through ALM and that transfer prices serve for determining the income statements of both business units and the ALM unit.

Contents

28.1 THE ORGANIZATION OF FTP SYSTEMS

Since uses and resources of funds are generally unbalanced for business units, the FTP system allows netting the differences and allocating funds to those having liquidity deficits, or purchasing excesses of funds where they appear.

The Treasury is the unit, which, in the end, raises debt or invests excesses of funds in the market. Its role consists of compensating in the capital market any net excess of deficit of funds. Since internal prices also serve to monitor commercial spreads, management control is also involved. Since ALM is the unit in charge of managing the liquidity and interest rate exposures of the bank, the internal prices should be consistent which the choices of ALM. The price of internal funds, if improperly defined, can create biases and incentives which are not economical. If they are too low, they make it easier for business units to generate a higher income and create an incentive for business development. The converse holds if they are too high. Market-related business units might also arbitrage internal prices whenever they see a discrepancy. For example, it becomes easier to hold assets guaranteeing a spread above transfer prices if those are lower than market rates. There are apparently numerous instances when such non-economical incentives might appear. One example is in the UBS Shareholder Report [75], which notes that lower than market rates allowed piling up excessive amounts of pools of loans intended to be securitized later.

In this chapter, we consider that ALM is in charge of the system, and that other management units are end-users of the system. Pools of funds are virtual locations where all funds, excesses and deficits, are centralized. There are several solutions for organizing the system. An important choice is to decide which balances are "netted" and how.

28.1.1 Exchanging Net Balances of Funds between Units

A first possibility is that the FTP nets the excesses of some business units with the deficits of others. The central pool of resources offsets the excesses and deficits of funds of the different units. It sounds simple to exchange only the net balances of business units through a central pool. Transfer price applies only to net balances. Such a system is "passive" and simply records excesses and deficits and nets them (Figure 28.1). Some systems use several pools of funds, for instance by grouping them according to maturity and setting prices by maturity.

Since assets and liabilities are netted before transfer to the central pool, all assets and liabilities of A and B do not transit through the system. The drawback of this version is that transfer prices do not apply to all assets and liabilities. Because they do not, the scheme is not an income allocation system. For example, consider a loan that is not subject to any exchange with the central pool simply because it is not grouped within the net balance that transits through the pool. There is no price attached to the financing of that loan and it is impossible to calculate a spread for this loan. Furthermore, there is no way to decide which loan should be exchanged though the pool and which one does not belong to the net balances that are exchanged. This is enough to rule out such a simple scheme.[1]

---

1 To that extent, banks cannot use liquidity netting as implemented in non-financial firms. For example, a group with several subsidiaries, in the same currency, and with centralized funding, should care about netting all accounts of all subsidiaries in a central account every day. Only the netted balance will be managed centrally, easing funds when needed and investing excesses of funds. Liquidity netting avoids having excess funds in one company's accounts and a deficit in another company simultaneously.

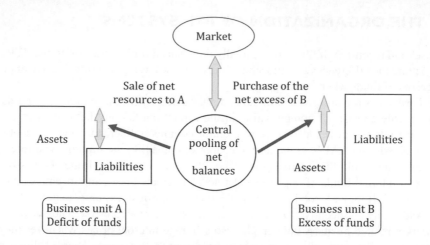

FIGURE 28.1   Transfers of net balances only

28.1.2 Exchanging all Outstanding Balances

Instead of exchanging and pricing only the net excesses or deficits, the alternate solution is that the ALM purchases all resources and sells all funds financing all assets, without prior local netting of assets and liabilities. The full amounts of assets and liabilities transit through the central pool, which is the ALM unit. This scheme creates an internal capital market with internal prices. After all transfers, the ALM invests any global excess of funds, or finances any global deficit, in the capital markets (Figure 28.2).

The major difference, with the system exchanging net local balances only, is that the internal prices hit all assets and liabilities of each business unit and allow allocating income to business units as well as to transactions. Note that setting transfer prices creates a powerful leverage on business units. All business unit incomes become dependent upon transfer prices. Transfer prices should be economical for avoiding biases with market prices.

Markdowns might be deducted from such economic prices for creating incentives to the commercial development of some products lines or markup added to penalize some other products lines, for pure commercial purposes. When such commercial markups or markdowns are allowed, care should be taken to record the economic transfer prices, for isolating the effect of the commercial policy.

This system serves as reference in what follows because it fully allocates earnings to products and business lines.

28.2 CALCULATING INCOME WITHIN A FTP SYSTEM

The commercial margin is the spread between customer prices and the internal prices. The financial margin is the NII of ALM, which results from the volumes exchanged combined with the spreads between internal prices and the market prices used for borrowing and lending in the capital markets. In the FTP system, the banking portfolio is the mirror image of the ALM portfolio, since ALM buys all liabilities and sells all assets. The sum of the NIIs generated by

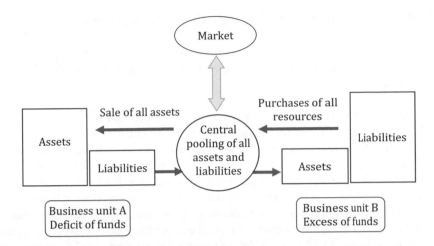

FIGURE 28.2 **Central pool of all assets and liabilities**

the business units and those generated by the ALM balance sheet should be equal to the actual NII of the bank, since internal exchanges, between commercial units and the central ALM unit, cancel out (Figure 28.3). For reconciling the commercial margins with that of the bank, we need to include the ALM earnings resulting from internal exchanges.

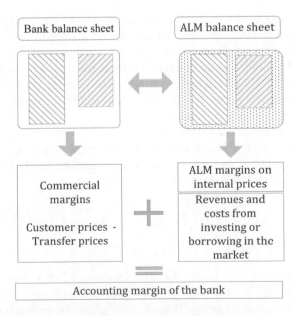

FIGURE 28.3 **Bank's balance sheet and the ALM balance sheet**

28.2.1 Allocating Income through the FTP System

The calculations use a simple example. The commercial margin calculation scope is the entire balance sheet of all business units. Operating costs are not considered in what follows, only interest revenues and costs.

- For the bank, we simply sum up all revenues from lending and borrowing to customers, including any revenue or cost for lending and borrowing in the market.
- For the lending units, revenues result from the spread between customer prices and the cost of internal purchase of resources at transfer prices from the central unit (ALM).
- For units collecting resources from depositors, costs result from the interest paid to customers (depositors) and the revenues from selling these resources to the ALM at transfer prices.
- For the ALM unit, the revenues result from charging the lending units the cost of their funds, and the costs result from the purchase of resources from those units that collect customers' deposits. In addition, ALM faces an interest cost when funding a deficit and gets market revenue from investing any global excess of funds.

The income calculations use a simplified balance sheet. After calculating the bank's accounting margin, we proceed by breaking it down across business units and ALM using the transfer prices. The system can accommodate operating cost allocations for completing the analytical income statements, and any differentiation of multiple transfer prices, down to individual transactions. As long as the ALM records internal transactions properly, the overall NII of the bank can be reconciled with the allocated NII to business lines and transactions.

28.2.2 The Accounting NII of the Bank

The business balance sheet generates a deficit funded by ALM. The average customer price for borrowers is 12% and the average customer rate paid to depositors is 6%. The ALM borrows in the market at the 9% current market rate. There is a unique transfer price. It applies to both assets sold by ALM to business units and to resources purchased by ALM from business units. This unique value is 9.20%. Note that this value differs from the market rate deliberately. There could be several transfer prices, but the principle would be the same. Table 28.1 shows the balance sheet and the averaged customers' rates.

The transfer price mechanism insures the consistency of all analytical income statements of the business units with the bank's NII. If transfer prices change, they simply transfer income from ALM to business units, but they do not change the overall bank NII. For illustrating the process, we subdivide the banks into three business units:

- collecting resources
- originating loans
- ALM, managing financial risks.

The aggregated balance sheet is in Table 28.1. The volumes of loans, deposits and external funding are under the control of each of the three business units.

The direct calculation of the accounting margin is straightforward since it depends only on customer's rates and the funding cost by the ALM:

$$2000 \times 12\% - 1200 \times 6\% - 800 \times 9\% = 96$$

TABLE 28.1 Bank's balance sheet

	Volume	Rate
Assets		
Loans	2000	12.00%
Total	2000	
Resources		
Deposits	1200	6.00%
Funding	800	9.00%
Total	2000	

28.2.3 Breaking Down the Bank Margin into Contributions of Business Units

From the average customer rates and the transfer price set by the ALM unit (assuming a flat yield curve), we calculate the NII of each commercial unit purchasing or selling funds to the ALM (Table 28.2). The ALM unit buys and sells funds internally and funds externally the bank's deficit.

With a unique internal price set at 9.20%, the commercial margin in percentage terms is 12% − 9.20% = 3.20% for loans, and 6% − 9.20% = −2.80% for deposits. Note the sign convention for collecting resources: The negative sign simply means that the bank pays less to depositors than the ALM pays. But the 3.20% is a positive spread from the deposit collection unit.

The total commercial NII is 94.4, and is lower than the bank accounting NII. This total commercial NII adds up the contributions of the lending activity and of the collection of resources. The lending activity generates a margin of 56.0, while the collection of resources generates 38.4. The system allocates the NII to the different business units. The ALM has symmetrical revenues and costs, plus the cost of funding the deficit of 800 in the market. Summing up business NIIs with the ALM NII, we find the bank's NII. The ALM NII is positive because ALM actually overcharges the business units with a transfer price of 9.20%, higher than the market rate (9%).

TABLE 28.2 Calculation of NII

Market rate	9.00%
Transfer price	9.20%

Margin	Calculation	Value
Direct calculation of NII		
Accounting NII	2000 × 12% − 1200 × 6.00% − 800 × 9.00%	96.0
Commercial NII		
Loans	2000 × (12% − 9.20%)	56.0
Deposits	1200 × (9.20% − 6.00%)	38.4
Total commercial NII	2000 × (12% − 9.20%) + 1200 × (9.20% − 6.00%)	94.4
ALM NII		
ALM NII	2000 × 9.20% − 1200 × 9.20% − 800 × 9.00%	1.6
Bank NII	Commercial NII + ALM NII	96.0

TABLE 28.3 Calculation of NII

| Market rate | 9.00% | |
| Transfer price | 9.00% | |

Margin	Calculation	Value
Direct Calculation of NII		
Accounting margin	$2000 \times 12\% - 1200 \times 6\% - 800 \times 9\%$	96.0
Commercial NII		
Loans	$2000 \times (12.00\% - 9.00\%)$	60.0
Deposits	$1200 \times (9.00\% - 6.00\%)$	36.0
Total commercial NII	$2000 \times (12\% - 9.00\%) + 1200 \times (9.00\% - 6.00\%)$	96.0
ALM NII		
ALM NII	$2000 \times 9.20\% - 1200 \times 9.20\% - 800 \times 9.00\%$	0.0
Bank margin	Commercial margin + ALM margin	96.0

If the ALM NII is zero, the entire bank margin becomes equal to the commercial NII. This is the reference case. The ALM is neutral and generates neither profit nor loss. Then the entire bank NII is "in" the commercial units, as in the calculations of Table 28.3. Note that we keep the customers' rates constant, so that the internal spreads between customers' rates and transfer prices change. They become 9% – 8% = 1% for lending and 8% – 3% = 5% for collecting deposits. Evidently, since all customers' rates are constant, as is the cost of market funds, the bank's NII remains 96 (Table 28.3). Nevertheless, the allocation of this global NII between business units and ALM differs.

The above examples show that:

- transfer prices allocate the bank NII between the business units and ALM
- the overall NII is always equal to the sum of the commercial interest margin and of the ALM interest margin.

The next chapter shows how internal prices should reflect the "true" cost of funding. Setting economic benchmarks for these prices is addressed in the next chapter. Note that transfer prices are also used as commercial signals for developing markets and products while restricting business on others through markups and markdowns. As long as we record the transfer prices and their gaps with economic prices, we know the costs/benefits of the commercial policy.

29

Economic Transfer Prices

Transfer prices are internal reference interest rates that serve for transferring funds internally and for allocating income. They also serve for setting pricing benchmarks. The FTP should provide economic benchmarks for the cost of financing over which mark-ups or mark-downs are set to meet the bank target profitability. Because banks do not want their commercial spreads to move up and down with interest rates, the FTP system has to transfer the interest rate risk and the liquidity risk to this ALM central unit, which is in charge of managing these risks.

Section 29.1 shows that correct transfer prices should be market based to avoid internal arbitrage by business units and external arbitrage by borrowers. A distinction is made between "pure transfer prices," whose sole purpose is to exchange funds across units, and the all-in cost of funds, which includes operating cost plus any mark-up for the cost of risk, whose purpose is to define risk-based prices for customers. Section 29.2 defines economic benchmarks for transfer prices for lending activities. Section 29.3 addresses the same issue for collecting resources units. Section 29.4 makes explicit the conditions for ensuring effective transfer of interest rate risk to the ALM unit. Finally, Section 29.5 addresses risk-based pricing for lending.

Contents

29.1 COMMERCIAL SPREADS AND MATURITY SPREAD

The basic principle for defining such "economic" transfer prices is to refer to market prices because of arbitrage opportunities between bank rates and market rates whenever discrepancies appear. Economic benchmarks derive from market prices. Mark-ups or mark-downs over the economic benchmarks serve for pricing in relation to the banks' target profitability. In this and subsequent sections, we ignore commercial markups or markdowns, and the last paragraph of this chapter discusses what could be done with such "pure commercial" markups and mark-downs, which are independent of banks' overall target profitability

Discrepancies between banks' customers' prices with market interest rates would lead to arbitrage by customers as well as by business units. In order to ensure that banks make a positive margin whatever the rates, it is necessary to relate transfer prices to maturity because the term structure of rates is generally not flat. The case of bullet transactions with customers is the simplest to discuss. Bullet loan prices should be above market rates of the same maturity. Term deposits rates should be below the market rate of the same maturity. Demand deposits rates should be below the short-term rate. When lending above the market rate, the bank can borrow the money on the market and have a positive spread whatever the maturity. When collecting resources below market rates, the bank can invest them in the market and makes a profit. Figure 29.1 illustrates this simple pricing scheme, which applies only to bullet loans and deposits.

If the business units buy resources at a lower price than market, they can dump client lending price, or trading units can carry portfolios of market assets at lower price than market. If the Treasury or ALM charges to commercial units a higher than market rate, it makes an easy spread by borrowing on the market and creates disincentives for development. For the banking portfolio, the issue for determining economic references is finding what is the exact cost of lending and the revenue from collecting deposits. For market activities, the issue is to use a price of funds in line with markets for avoiding internal arbitrage by business units.

Transfer prices address two issues.

- What should be the cost of transferring resources from excess funds units to units with deficit of funds?
- For the lending portfolio, what is the benchmark cost of financing for pricing?

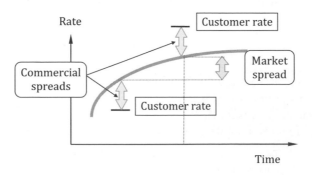

FIGURE 29.1   Commercial and market spreads

In the first case, transfer prices should be neutral and not penalize nor subsidize business units. Economic transfer prices serve for transferring funds and allocating earnings. The transfer prices also serve to track mis-pricing, which is the gap between effective prices and target risk-based prices, for reporting purposes and taking corrective actions.

There are several pricing rationales in practice, mixing economic criteria and commercial criteria. It is possible to make them fully distinct before assembling them in a consistent framework.

- Risk-based pricing is the benchmark, and should be purely economic. It implies two basic ingredients: the cost of funds and mark-ups. The mark-ups for credit risk should differentiate the interest rate charged to the borrower. It is based on the credit risk allocation system, which allocates a capital charge to each transaction, based on regulatory rules or economic model of credit economic capital. We consider such capital allocations as given here and concentrate of the economic costs of funds.
- Commercial pricing refers to markups and markdowns over economic benchmarks for pure business policies purposes, providing incentives and penalties for promoting some products and penalizing others. Such markups and markdowns are purely business driven rather than driven by target profitability.

Transfer prices serves as the basis for exchanging funds internally and also serve for determining the "all-in" cost of funds. Operating costs, when feasible, should be included, so that the contribution margin is high enough to absorb operating costs. Risk-based prices should also add on top the cost of risk when lending.

For making a distinction between the all-in cost of funds and the transfer prices used for exchanging funds across units, we call the latter "pure transfer prices." The all-in cost of funds serves for pricing purpose, not for transferring funds internally.

29.2 ECONOMIC TRANSFER PRICES FOR LOANS

Transfer prices depend upon the definition of the funds backing the assets. One view would be to refer to existing assets and resources. The underlying assumption is that existing resources exactly match assets. The second view consists of defining a reference financing solution that mirrors exactly the funded assets, and to use the cost of this funding solution as the transfer price.

29.2.1 The Cost of Existing Resources

Using the existing resources sounds intuitively appealing. Those resources actually fund assets, so that their cost has to be relevant. However, this solution raises conceptual inconsistencies. There are several types of assets and liabilities with different characteristics. Each type of resource has a different cost. Therefore, we could use either the Wacc (weighted average cost of capital), the average cost of resources or several costs. Another solution could be to match assets and resources based on their similar characteristics. For instance, we can try to match long-term resources with long-term assets, and so on for other maturities. This is the rationale for multiple pools of funds based on maturity buckets. This principle also raises several issues. Since the volumes of assets and resources of a given category, for instance long-term items, are in general different, the match cannot be exact. If long-term assets have a larger volume than long-term resources, other resources have to fill up the deficit. Rules are required to define which other resources will fund the mismatch, and the resulting cost of funds becomes dependent on such conventions.

Moreover, using the cost of existing resources might be "unfair" for resources collected from customers. Any cheap resource, such as deposits, subsidizes the profitability of assets. Matching a long-term loan with the core fraction of demand deposits might be acceptable in terms of maturity. However, such a match actually transfers the low cost of deposits to the margin allocated to loans. Moreover, this assumes implicitly that new deposits fund each new dollar of loans, which is unrealistic.

Given inconsistencies and unrealistic assumptions, matching of assets with existing resources is not economic. Transfer prices require other benchmarks.

29.2.2 The "Notional" Funding of Loans

The unique funding solution that neutralizes both liquidity and interest rate risks of a specific asset is the funding that "mirrors" the time profile of flows and the interest rate. For a fixed-rate term loan, the funding should replicate exactly the amortization profile and carry a fixed rate. Such a funding is "notional" rather than material. It does not depend on the existing resources. It does not imply either that ALM actually decides to implement full cash flow matching. It serves as a benchmark for determining the cost of funds backing any given asset.

In some cases, the replication is obvious and the cost of funds is easily defined. A bullet debt matches a bullet loan. The relevant rate is the market rate corresponding to the maturity of the transaction. In general, the notional funding is different. For an amortizing loan, the outstanding balance varies over time until maturity. Using the market rate of this maturity would mean that we fund an amortizing loan with a bullet debt, which would be inconsistent. The funding that replicates the time profile of the loan is the mirror image of the loan, which is an amortizing debt with exactly the same repayment schedule.

The transfer price is the cost of such debt. It is a combination of debts of various maturities. In the example below, a loan of 100 amortizes in two years, the repayments of capital being 40 and 60. Figure 29.2 shows the profile of the reference debt. The funding solution combines two spot bullet debts, of maturities 1 and 2 years, contracted at the market rates[1].

The solution is simpler with floating rates than with fixed rates. For floating rate transactions, the replicating funding is a floating-rate debt with reset dates matching those of the assets. The amortization profile should mirror that of the floating-rate asset.

---

1 There is another solution for backing the loan. For instance, a spot debt for one year could be contracted for the full amount of the loan that is 100 for one year at the spot market rate, followed by another one year debt, for an amount of 60, starting one year from now. Nevertheless, such funding does not replicate the loan, since a fraction of debt needs renewal for another year at a rate unknown today.

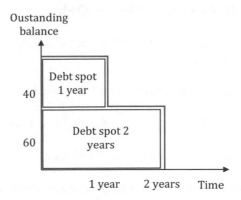

FIGURE 29.2   A two-year amortizing loan

29.2.3 The Cost of the Mirror Debt

The cost of the "mirror" debt is its yield. For a fixed-rate loan, the mirror debt can be decomposed in several zero-coupon debts, with volumes and maturities matching the time profile of the amortizing debt. The yield can be expressed as a function of zero-coupon rates. In the above example, there are two layers of debt: 60 for 2 years, and 40 for 1 year. The relevant rates are the spot rates for these maturities. However, there should be a unique transfer price for a given loan. It is the average cost of funds of the two debts. Its exact definition is that of a yield, or the discount rate making the present value of the future flows generated by the two debts equal to the amount borrowed.

The future outflows are the capital repayments and interests. The interest flows cumulate those of the one-year and the two-year market rates. If the debts are zero-coupon, the interest payments are at maturity. The flows are $40(1 + r_1)$ in one year and $60(1 + r_2)^2$ in two years. The yield y of this composite funding is a discount rate y such that:

$$100 = 40(1 + r_1)/(1 + y) + 60(1 + r_2)^2/(1 + y)^2$$

The discount rate is somewhere between the two market rates. An approximate solution uses a linear approximation of the exact formula:

$$100 = 40(1 + r_1 - y) + 60(1 + 2r_2 - 2y)$$

$$y = (40r_1 + 60 \times 2 \times r_2)/(40 + 2 \times 60)$$

The rate y is the weighted average of the spot rates for one and two years, using weights combining the size of each debt and its maturity. With rates r_1 and r_2 equal to 8% and 9%, $r = 8.75\%$. The rate is closer to 9%, because the two-year debt is the one whose amount and maturity are the highest.

In practice, transfer prices tables provide immediately the yield of the mirroring debt, which is a composite of market rates, given the time profile of loans and the current market rates.

29.2.4 The Benefits from the Mirror Debt

Using the cost of funds of a debt that fully replicates the assets offers numerous economic benefits. Perfect matching implies that:

- the margin of the asset is immune to interest rate movements
- there is no need of conventions for assigning existing resources to usages of funds
- there is no transfer of income generated by collecting resources to the income of lending activities
- the calculation of a transfer prices is mechanical and easy.

Using the yield of this notional funding mimicking the loan as the transfer price complies with all consistency requirements.

The replicating debt is defined for a loan which has a maturity schedule. However, contractual maturities are not effective maturities, due to prepayments of mortgage loan for example. In such cases, we have to plug in the option cost in the pricing, adding the option-adjusted spread in the all-in cost of funding. Most other credit lines are floating rates, such as committed lines of credit. The financing replicates the time profile of the drawn fraction using floating rates and reset dates matching the reference index used for the line of credit. However, the issue of lines without maturity is even more important with deposits.

The ALM unit does not have to use a funding policy that actually immunizes the interest margin of the bank. The debt replicating the asset characteristics is a "notional debt." The ALM policy generally deviates from perfect matching of the flows, simply because it wishes to keep an open position, for example, due to the existence of demand deposits which do not require raising financial debt in the market.

29.3 ECONOMIC TRANSFER PRICES FOR RESOURCES

For deposits, the same principle applies. It implies defining the "mirror" asset replicating the maturity schedule of deposits. The transfer price reflects the market rates on alternate investing opportunities to lending. Their rates are the "opportunity costs" of deposits. They make sense as transfer prices because they represent the returns that the bank would give up if it invested instead of lending. Deposits considered short-term earn the short-term market rate and long-term core deposits earn long-term rates.

Based on this principle, the transfer price for deposits depends on how the bank models the time profile of deposits. Using the short-term rate is relevant for the volatile fraction of deposits. Using long-term rates is applicable to the core base of deposits. Both fractions can be defined with time series models, for example.

More elaborate solutions can serve as reference. The opportunity cost of excess deposits becomes the average rate of such investments. The investment depends on the hypothesis for amortizing deposits. With 10 years' amortization, there are 10 such layers invested from 1 to 10 years. The "ladder" policy averages the time series of annual term structures of interest rates when such investments roll over (see Chapter 22 on liquidity management).

29.4 TRANSFERRING LIQUIDITY AND INTEREST RATE RISK TO ALM THROUGH THE FTP SYSTEM

The principle of the replicating debt for loans and the replicating investment for resources fits the full hedging principle. For loans, it sets the cost of financing to that of the debt that eliminates any interest rate risk and liquidity risk. For deposits, the replication is approximate but follows the same principle. Looking at individual loans, such mirroring debt would remove both interest rate and liquidity risk. Hence transfer prices transfers the risks to ALM, which complies with the principle of removing those risks from commercial net interest income. However, guaranteeing this risk transfer requires another addition to the FTP system.

For instance, if a fixed-rate asset generates 11% over a transfer price of 9%, the margin is 2%. Recalculating the margin of the same asset with a new rate at the next period would result in a change. Resetting the transfer price after origination at 10%, because of an upward shift of 1% of interest rate, would result in a decrease of the margin to 1%. The commercial NII would be again at risk.

For removing the risk, transfer prices cannot be modified once assigned to a transaction. The transfer price assigned to a transaction over successive periods should be the historical transfer price, dating from the date when the loan was contracted. Doing so would effectively lock in the commercial spread over the life of the transaction. Spreads calculated over moving transfer prices are only apparent spreads that are not immune to interest rate risk because they change with interest rates. One should note, however, that using such historical prices for each transaction puts an additional burden on the information system.

Table 29.1 shows the time profile of both apparent spreads, calculated over market rates and spreads effectively immune to interest rates because they are calculated over guaranteed historical transfer prices. The pricing remains in line with a target margin of 2% over the transfer

TABLE 29.1 Apparent margin and margins on historical transfer prices

	Period		
Transactions	1	2	3
A	100	100	100
B		100	100
C			100
Current rate	10%	11%	12%
Target % margin	2%	2%	2%
Customer rate	12%	13%	14%
Apparent margin over current rate	$100 \times (12 - 10)$	$100 \times (12 - 11)$ $+ 100 \times (13 - 11)$	$100 \times (12 - 12)$ $+ 100 \times (13 - 12)$ $+ 100 \times (14 - 12)$
Apparent margin in value	2	3	3
Apparent margin in %	$2/100 = 2\%$	$3/200 = 1.5\%$	$3/300 = 1\%$
Margin over guaranteed historical price	$100 \times (12 - 10)$	$100 \times (12 - 10)$ $+ 100 \times (13 - 11)$	$100 \times (12 - 10)$ $+ 100 \times (13 - 11)$ $+ 100 \times (14 - 12)$
Margin over guaranteed price (value)	2	4	6
Margin over guaranteed price (%)	2%	2%	2%

price. Only the margin over guaranteed prices remains constant when time passes. This last addition makes the transfer price system comprehensive and consistent.

29.5 PRICING FOR LENDING

Pure transfer prices are the cost of financing a loan. Other components of pricing should include:

- all operating costs are expressed in % of total loans
- the cost of credit risk when lending
- plus a mark-up (lending) or a mark-down (deposits) that should be in line with the target profitability of the bank.

Target profitability is commonly defined as a target return on capital ("ROC") or return on equity ("ROE"). Risk-based pricing requires moving from the global target ROC to target commercial spreads (customer rate – transfer price) and target clients' rates.

29.5.1 The All-in Cost of Funds of the Mirror Debt

The pure economic benchmark is the notional economic cost of funds, described above, which is the cost of funding that mirrors exactly the loan. We assume here that this cost of funds is 7%.

The "all-in" funding cost of the loan adds up the operating costs. We use here an add-on of 0.5% to obtain an "all-in" cost of funds of 7.5%. Other commercial mark-ups or mark-downs might add up to the all-in cost of funds to move to the customer price. Ignoring the commercial items, the all-in cost sums up the cost of funding plus operating costs. The minimum client's rate to absorb these costs would be 7.50% (Table 29.2). We consider all costs as a percentage of the loan balance.

Note that revenues from borrowers include interest rate charged plus some non-recurring fees, or upfront fees, plus some recurring fees. Non-recurring fees create distortion of revenues across time. The common solution to correct such a distortion is to use an annualized all-in-revenue, which averages all revenues, recurring and non-recurring, over the life of the transaction. Similarly, the "all-in-spread" is the annualized spread above the cost of debt calculated as an annual average over the life of the transaction. In what follows, the rate charged to borrower is an "all-in rate," or inclusive of fees.

However, using operating plus funding cost would not absorb the cost of credit risk, which is borrower- and transaction-specific. Since pricing to client is before tax, we use the before

TABLE 29.2   All-in cost of funds

Components	%
Cost of debt	7.00%
Operating costs	0.50%
= Transfer price	7.50%

tax cost of capital. Taking $k\% = 25\%$ as target ROC before tax, we need to find the additional margin compensating this target ROC.

29.5.2 The Cost of Credit Risk and the Risk Premium

The cost of risk includes two components: the statistical loss, or average loss due to defaults ("expected loss"), and the cost of losses in excess of the average loss. The statistical loss is the average loss due to defaults (or "expected loss"), as a percentage of the balance of the loan. Expected loss depends on the borrower's credit risk. It is equal to the loss rate of $DP \times EAD$.

The cost of losses in excess of average loss is measured by capital, either regulatory (Basel 2) or economic "risk-based capital" from models. Both can serve as reference. The cost of (equity) capital is the target return on capital (ROC) or of equity (ROE). If the loan were risk-free, there would be no capital charge and both the statistical loss from default and the loss in excess of this average would be zero. The cost of risk would be zero.

If there is credit risk, capital is required, in addition to expected loss. The percentage cost of the capital allocated to the transaction is the cost of equity for the bank, k. The overall financing combines debt and capital. The cost of credit risk capital is the cost of substituting capital K to debt D, as shown in Figure 29.3. All costs or mark-up for cost of risk should be expressed as a percentage of the asset since we look for a target rate. Furthermore, since such rate is pre-tax, all costs should be pre-tax, including the cost of equity capital. Assume that the cost of capital is 25% pre-tax and that the cost of debt pre-tax is 7%.

The cost of funding or transfer price is $i = 7\%$. The additional cost of substituting capital to debt is:

$$K(k - i) = K \times (25\% - 7\%)$$

This additional "cost" is called the risk premium due to credit risk. If regulatory capital is 4% of loan 1000 (the former Cooke ratio), or 40, the risk premium in € is:

$$40(25\% - 7\%) = 7.2€$$

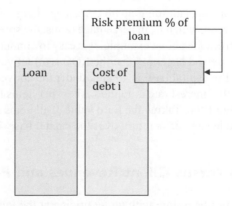

FIGURE 29.3   Risk premium

TABLE 29.3   Components of risk-based prices

Components	%
Transfer price	7.00%
Operating costs	0.50%
= All-in cost of funds	7.50%
Expected losses	0.50%
+ Risk-based premium	0.72%
= Target risk based price	8.72%
+ Commercial incentives	0
= Target customer rate	8.72%

For moving from the required return on capital to the target margin of the loan, we find the required mark-up in percentage of loan balance over all-in cost. This percentage is the ratio of risk premium to loan. The ratio uses the ratio of capital to loan, which is fixed (4% for Cooke ratio):

$$(k - i) \, (K/\text{loan}) \text{ in } \% \text{ of loan} = 4\% \times (25\% - 7\%) = 0.72\%$$

The risk premium, $(k - i)K/A$, is proportional to capital and to the excess of cost of capital over debt. The risk premium is also dependent on the target return on capital.

Note that, in this calculation, we ignored the fact that capital should be reinvested risk-free. Otherwise, if capital funds loans or any risky asset, it would bear an additional credit risk, which would require additional capital. This adjustment for reinvesting capital at the risk-free rate is fully detailed in the risk-adjusted performance chapter, Chapter 55. It assumes that the loan is entirely funded by debt and that capital has a return, in addition to the loan return that is the risk-free rate.

Starting from the pure transfer price, the cost of debt mirroring the loan, we add operating cost. Next we add the cost of risk, with its two components, the expected loss and the risk premium for using up capital. Finally, we could add any commercial incentives, negative or positive, for obtaining the final price. This final price is not the risk-based price which is the all-in cost of funds plus the cost of risk, unless commercial incentives are zero, as in the example (Table 29.3).

This calculation is bottom-up, summing up all percentage items, for finding the target customer rate and the target spread, which is, in percentage terms, the spread over the transfer price or 8.72% − 7% = 1.72%. From the above example, it is easy to conduct a top-down calculation starting from interest revenue and checking that the ROC is effectively 25% before tax (Table 29.4). For a loan of 1000, the capital base is 40 and, under the above assumptions, the debt is 1000 − 40 = 960, to which the interest rate is applied. The other items follow by applying above percentages to the loan value 1000. Taking the Euro value of all items results in earnings before tax of 10, a value that matches the 25% return over the capital base 40.

29.5.3 Transaction Versus Client Revenues and Pricing

Risk-based pricing might not be in line with target pricing at the individual transaction level because of competition or because market spreads are not high enough to price all costs to a

TABLE 29.4 Top-down calculation of the return on capital (ROC)

Loan	1000
Capital base	40
Debt	960
Transfer price	67.2
Operating costs	5.0
= All-in cost	72.2
Expected losses	5.0
Total cost	77.2
= Interest revenue	87.2
Interest revenues	87.2
– Total cost	–77.2
NII	10.0
Capital base	40.0
ROC	25.0%

large corporate that has access to markets directly. Such discrepancy is called "mispricing" and might not be avoidable.

However, this does not imply that the overall client revenue cannot meet the bank's target profitability. Banks provide products and services and obtain as compensations interest spreads and fees. The overall client revenue is a more relevant measure for calculating profitability, and comparing it to target profitability, because it groups all forms of revenues from all transactions, plus all services resulting from the bank's relationship with the clients. Loans and services are a bundle. The client is a better base for assessing profitability than standalone transactions. This is a strong argument for developing economic income statements at the client level.

29.5.4 Economic and Commercial Transfer Prices

Using two sets of internal prices makes sense. One set of transfer prices should refer to economic benchmarks, such as market rates. The other set of transfer prices serves as commercial signals. Any discrepancy between the two prices is the cost of the commercial policy. These discrepancies are the penalties (mark-up) or subsidies (mark-down) decided by the commercial department. Note that as long as we know economic transfer prices, any discrepancies due to commercial incentives or penalties can be isolated. Cumulating such discrepancies multiplied by the amount lent or collected provides the net contribution, positive or negative, due to such commercial incentives and penalties. This scheme reconciles diverging functions of the transfer prices and makes explicit the cost of enforcing commercial policies that are not in line with economic references.

SECTION 9

Dependencies and Portfolio Risk

The modeling of portfolio risk is a core building block in risk management. The issue is to measure and quantify the diversification effect. The higher the dependency between positions, the lower the diversification is. Furthermore, quantification of portfolio risk requires the distribution of the portfolio values, which is highly sensitive to dependencies.

Contents

DEPENDENCIES MODELING AS A KEY BUILDING BLOCK FOR RISK MODELING

Diversification of risk has been the key principle that allows financial institutions to bear a much lower risk than the sum of individual risks. Combining risks does not follow the usual arithmetic rules, unlike income. The summation of two risks, each equal to 1, is not 2. It is usually lower because of diversification. Individual risks are said to be "sub-additive." Measuring dependencies with correlations shows that the sum of two individual risks of same size is in the range of 0 to 2. This is the essence of diversification.

Standalone risk is the risk of a single position. For example, it can be measured by the volatility of returns of a single market instrument, or as the probability weighted loss under default of a single loan. For market risk, adding the adverse effects of individual transactions does not make sense because it would assume that all transactions would move adversely jointly. When the market moves, some positions gain while others lose value, and only the net effect after offsetting gains and losses makes sense. For credit risk, the dependencies across firms are generally positive because all firms are generally adversely affected when economic conditions deteriorate. But not all firms will default together. The positive dependency between the credit standing of all firms determines how likely joint defaults are. Again, summing up all standalone risks of loans or bonds within a portfolio assume that all positions default together and ignore diversification effects.

When the position belongs to a portfolio, some of its risk is diversified away by other assets held within the portfolio. Under a risk prospective, summing the standalone risks of each position, whatever the measure used, does not make sense. The diversification effect is the difference between the (arithmetic) sum of individual transaction risks and the risk of the sum. Portfolio risk results from individual risks and from how dependent these risks are. Dependencies are critical for assessing risk of portfolios, both trading and banking portfolios, because they allow measuring the diversification effect. There are multiple measures of dependencies: correlation, factor models, joint and conditional probabilities, and copula functions.

MEASURES OF DEPENDENCIES

A correlation is a measure of linear association between random variables, such as random returns and values of individual positions. It is linear in that it is more reliable when the relationship of return is a close to a straight line. Conversely, it is less reliable when the relation is a curve. Then the correlation would capture the straight line that best fits the curve. The traditional example of the drawback of correlation is the association between the random variable X and its square X^2. If we consider only positive values of X, the correlation would capture the increase of X^2 with X, although the relation is a curve, because they both increase simultaneously. If we consider both positive and negative values, there would be no correlation at all between X and X^2.

Correlation is the most common measure of dependency in spite of its drawbacks. The theory of portfolio diversification relies on correlations. The common linear regression analysis also relies on correlation. The coefficients of a regression, a relation between an "explained" variable and one or several "explaining" variables, are related to correlation measures. Many financial models rely on linear relations between variables, used as a proxy of the actual relations. Portfolio risk is typically measured by the volatility of its return. Modeling such portfolio volatility relies on variance–covariance matrices and correlation matrices. The variance–covariance matrix assemble in a square table the covariances between pairs of variables, usually returns on assets, plus the variances along the diagonal of the table. Such matrices remain the most common tool for modeling portfolio risk.

Rank correlation is a non-linear measure because it focuses on ranks, or ordinal values, rather than cardinal values. Assuming that two variables move along a monotonously increasing curve, the rank correlation would simply capture the fact that both variables are higher or lower than their original values: they have a perfect rank correlation. Consider the previous example of a variable and its square when the values are positive. A rank correlation would capture a better dependency than a standard correlation, because the matching of ranks between X and X^2 would be perfect for positive values. Rank correlation has been used for a long time for capturing relations that are not linear as well as for simulating values of variables that are dependent.

Factor models measure the linear dependencies of factors returns. Factor models relate one or several return or risk variables to common factors. The variables are the returns of individual positions, the market risk or the credit risk of individual positions. The dependency on common factors makes them co-vary when the factors change. The dependency on a common set of risk factors is a very convenient feature. Because there are many more individual positions in a portfolio than there are risk factors, it is much easier to capture dependencies across risk factors than using pair correlations. Factor models relate the return on a position to its risk factors that influence its return. Because they relate positions to a common set of risk factors, the dependency across risk factors create dependencies across position returns.

Joint and conditional probabilities are another measure of dependencies. A joint probability of two events is the probability that two events occur together. The joint probability is simply the product of the probabilities of each event if they are independent. But it is higher if the events tend to occur simultaneously and it is much lower if the likelihood of one event varies inversely with the likelihood of the other. Joint probability and conditional probability are two sides of the same coin. A conditional probability is the probability conditional on some event. There are many examples of conditioning. For example, defaults within an industry depend on how well or badly the industry is doing. Conditional probabilities are higher than unconditional probabilities, when the conditioning event increases the likelihood of the conditional event. If this is the case, there is a positive dependency between the two events. Conversely, a conditional probability is lower than the unconditional probability if the conditioning scenario, making the probability of observing the event lower.

Copula functions are the current best practice for capturing dependencies. Unlike correlations, they are not linear measures. To that extent, they are similar to rank correlations. In fact, it can be shown that a copula function has a direct relation with rank correlations. Copula functions capture the probability of joint events, such as joint probabilities of moving up and down. Consider again two random variables X and Y. The copula function is the joint probability that X is lower or equal to a particular value x and that Y is also lower and equal to a particular value of y. In probability notations, a copula function is simply written as: $P(X \leq x, Y \leq y)$. Joint probabilities provide an intuitive view of the more elaborated copula function discussed next. A copula density function, not to be confused with the copula function itself, is simply the ratio of the joint probability of two events if they were independent to the joint probability if they are dependent. A copula density is similar to a relative measure of dependence using independency as the benchmark case.

In most applications of portfolio return and risk modeling, traditional approaches rely on the normal distribution because of its attractive properties. But normal distributions do not fit the distribution of returns. A copula function would allow the use of other distributions or returns, such as the Pareto distribution, which has fatter tails as observed in the markets. Some random variables simply do not follow normal or symmetric distribution. For example, default intensity models measure the time elapsed until the first default. The corresponding distribution is the exponential distribution. Measuring dependencies across exponential distributions is a simple exercise with copula functions. In essence, copula distributions allow modeling dependencies separately from the univariate underlying distributions of variables.

SIMULATIONS

Simulations are widely used in finance and other fields as "what-if" analysis. In finance, simulations are used as a pricing tool for assets for which no closed-form pricing formula exists. Under a risk prospective, they serve for exploring the effects of multiple scenarios, from a few scenarios for investigating the effect of pre-determined market conditions that are of interest, for stress-testing purposes for example, up to thousands of simulations to generate distributions of portfolio returns and measure VaR. Simulation is a simple exercise with a single variable with a known distribution. It becomes more involved when considering multiple variables which are interdependent. The challenge of simulations is to generate scenarios that are consistent with the dependencies observed in the market.

There are two methods for generating large sets of values of dependent variables: using factor models or using the copula approach. The second one is more general since it plugs in the dependency structure independently of the distribution of variables of interest. Simulating the values of correlated risk factors relies on the variance–covariance matrix and their "Cholesky" decomposition[1], applicable for normal variables. Factor models that explain returns with a set of common factors simplify the issue because they rely on variance–covariance matrix of the factors, with much smaller dimensions than the individual positions of a portfolio. But the factor model approach requires using normal variables. The copula functions, in spite of their apparent

---

1 The Cholesky decomposition is introduced in Chapter 34 when expanding the algorithm used for simulating correlated normal variables.

mathematical complexity, provide another simple way of generating dependent variables, using various distribution functions, other than normal. The last chapter of this section illustrates the implementation of both approaches to simulations of dependent variables, normal or not.

SECTION ORGANIZATION

This section gradually moves from basic correlation definitions to the more elaborated copula approach in five chapters:

- correlation and variance–covariance matrices (Chapter 30)
- the conditional probability approach to dependencies (Chapter 31)
- factor models, which are very commonly used for modeling dependencies (Chapter 32)
- the modern copula approach that allows addressing dependency between non-normal distributions (Chapter 33)
- the simulation algorithms that apply to random variables, through the factor model approach and the copula approach (Chapter 34).

30

Correlations and Covariances

The classical method for modeling dependencies relies on correlations and variance–covariance matrices. Section 30.1 defines correlations, variance and covariances. The characteristics of variance–covariance matrices are summarized in Section 30.2.

The classical application of modeling portfolio return with correlated asset returns is used as an example in Section 30.3. The calculation of the portfolio return uses both standard algebra and matrix formulas, which are more compact and general.

The example of portfolio return is a very classical example. But in many important instances, we are interested in the volatility of different target variables. The volatility of the P & L of a trading portfolio is a measure of market risk. The volatility of losses across a credit portfolio is a measure of credit risk. In all cases, whether the target variable is the market return of a portfolio, or the P & L of a trading portfolio, or credit loss volatility, correlations are critical for assessing the diversification effect on risk.

Contents

30.1 CORRELATIONS AND COVARIANCES

This section uses the classical concepts of expectations, variance, covariance and correlation, applied to a portfolio made of two assets only. We provide here only a reminder of basic definitions. Asset values and asset returns are random variables. In this section, we do not consider the weights assigned to each asset and consider their values, or their returns, as two un-weighted random variables.

30.1.1 Correlations, Variances, and Covariances

Correlation measures the extent to which random variables change together or not, in the same direction or in opposite directions. Two statistics characterize this association: The correlation coefficient or the covariance for pairs of random variables. The covariance is the weighted sum of the products of the deviations from the mean of two variables X and Y, the weights being the joint probabilities of occurrence of each pair of values. The coefficient of correlation is simpler to interpret because it is in the range -1 to $+1$. It is calculated as the ratio of the covariance by the product of the variances of X and Y. The value $+1$ means that the two variables change together. The correlation -1 means that they always vary in opposite ways. Zero correlation means that they are independent.

The notations and formulas are as follows in this section. The covariance between two random variables X and Y is σ_{xy}. It is related to the correlation coefficient between those two variables through the relation:

$$\sigma_{xy} = \rho_{xy}\sigma_x\sigma_y,$$

The correlation between variables X and Y is ρ_{xy} and σ_x and σ_y are the standard deviations, or volatilities, of variables X and Y.

30.1.2 Correlation and Volatility of a Sum of Random Variables

The volatility of a sum depends upon the correlations between variables. It is the square root of the variance. The variance of a sum is the sum of the variances of each random variable plus all covariance terms for each couple of variables. Starting with the simple case of a pair of random variables, the formula of variance of the sum is as follows:

$$V(X + Y) = \sigma^2(X + Y) = V(X) + V(Y) + 2\text{Cov}(X, Y)$$

$$V(X + Y) = \sigma^2(X) + \sigma^2(Y) + 2\rho_{xy}\sigma(X)\sigma(Y)$$

The covariance between X and Y is $\text{Cov}(X, Y)$, $V(X)$ is the variance of X, equal to $\sigma^2(X)$, $\sigma(X)$ is the standard deviation, and ρ_{xy} the correlation coefficient. The volatility is the square root of the variance. Since the covariance is a function of the correlation coefficient, the two above formulas are identical. If the covariances are not zero, the variance of the (unweighted) sum differs from the sum of variances. The correlation term drops to zero only if the two variables are independent and the above formulas simplify.

$$V(X + Y) = \sigma^2(X) + \sigma^2(Y)$$

$$\sigma(X + Y) = \sqrt{[\sigma^2(X) + \sigma^2(Y)]}$$

The variance of the sum becomes the sum of variances only when all covariances are equal to zero, when the variables are independent.

As an example, consider a portfolio of two stocks. The equity returns are X and Y. The volatilities of the two equity returns are 2.601% and 1.826%, and the correlation between returns is 27.901%. The sum of volatilities is 2.601% + 1.826% = 4.427%. The variance of the sum is:

$$V(X+Y) = 2.601\%^2 + 1.826\%^2 + 2 \times 37.901\% \times 1.826\% \times 2.601\% = 0.137\%$$

The volatility is:

$$\sigma(X+Y) = \sqrt{0.137\%} = 3.7014\% < 4.427\%$$

This value is lower than the sum of volatilities. The difference measures the diversification effect. Risks do not add arithmetically, except in the extreme case where correlation is perfect (its value is 1).

30.1.3 Visual Representation of the Diversification Effect

The diversification effect is the gap between the sum of volatilities and the volatility of a sum. A simple image visualizes the formula of the standard deviation of a sum of two variables (Figure 30.1). The visualization shows the impact of correlation on the volatility of a sum. A vector whose length is the volatility represents each variable. The angle between the vectors varies in line with correlation. The vectors are parallel whenever the correlation is zero, and they are opposed when the correlation is –1. With such conventions, the vector equal to the summation of the two vectors representing each variable represents the overall risk. The length of this vector is identical to the volatility of the sum of the two variables[1]. The geometric visualization shows how the volatility of a sum changes when the correlation changes.

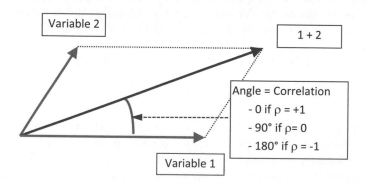

Length of vectors is equal to volatility

FIGURE 30.1 **Geometric representation of the volatility of the sum of two random variables**

---

1 This result uses the formula for the variance of a sum, and by expressing the length of the diagonal as a function of the sides of the rectangle of which it is a diagonal.

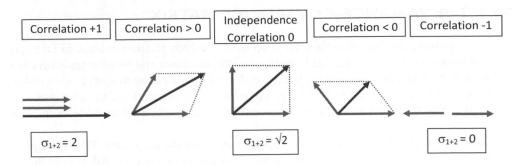

FIGURE 30.2 Volatility of a sum when correlation changes

Figure 30.2 shows different cases. The volatilities of the two variables are set to 1 and the correlation only changes. The volatility of the sum is the length of the geometric summation of vectors 1 and 2. It varies between 0, when the correlation is −1, up to 2 when the correlation is +1. The intermediate case, when correlation is zero, shows that the volatility is √2. We extend now the formulas to the general case of a portfolio with many assets.

30.1.4 Extension to any Number of Variables

This formula extends the calculation of the variance and of the volatility to any number N of variables X_i. This is the single most important formula for calculating the portfolio returns or value volatility, expanded later on using weights of assets within the portfolio. The formula also illustrates why the sum of individual risks is not the risk of the sum, due to the covariance terms. The general formula is:

$$\sigma^2\left(\sum_{i=1}^{m} X_i\right) = \sum_{i=j=1}^{m} \sigma_{ii}^2 + \sum_{i=1,m,j=1,m}^{i \neq j} \sigma_{ij}$$

$$\sigma^2\left(\sum_{i=1}^{m} X_i\right) = \sum_{i=j=1}^{m} \sigma_i^2 + \sum_{i=1,m,j=1,m}^{ij} \rho_{ij}\sigma_i\sigma$$

In this formula, σ_i^2 is the variance of variable X_i, equal to the square of the standard deviation σ_i, and σ_{ij} is the covariance between variables X_i and X_j. The sign Σ corresponds to a generalized summation over all couples of random variables X_i and X_j. A similar, and more compact, notation writes that the variance of the random variables summing m random variables is the summation of all σ_{ij} with, whenever $i = j$, we obtain the variance $\sigma_i^2 = \sigma_j^2$.

$$\sigma^2\left(\sum_{i=1}^{m} X_i\right) = \sum_{i=1,j=1}^{m} \sigma_{ij}$$

30.2 THE VARIANCE–COVARIANCE MATRIX

There are as many covariances as there are couples of variables. But the covariance or the correlation between any pair of variables is identical to the covariance and the correlation between the same pair of variables in reverse order. The above formula shows that, with m variables, we have m variances terms and only $(m - 1)^2$ covariances and correlations, a total of $m(m - 1) + m = m^2$ terms. If we arrange these variances and covariances into a square table, the table is also symmetric.

The variance–covariance table has $m \times m$ terms: it is square and symmetric. The off-diagonal terms above and below the diagonal are identical. Such table is a matrix with m rows and m columns. All matrices in the text are designated by bold letters. The current matrix is a variance–covariance matrix and is shown here.

$$\Sigma = \begin{vmatrix} \sigma_1^2 & \sigma_{12} & & \sigma_{1m} \\ \sigma_{21} & \sigma_2^2 & & \sigma_{2m} \\ \sigma_{31} & \sigma_{32} & & \sigma_{3m} \\ & & & \\ \sigma_{m1} & \sigma_{m2} & & \sigma_{m^2} \end{vmatrix}$$

In the above example of two random variables, the variance–covariance matrix is as shown here.

$$\Sigma = \begin{vmatrix} 0.0677\% & 0.0180\% \\ 0.0180\% & 0.0333\% \end{vmatrix}$$

30.2.1 Matrix Notations[2]

The conventions are that bold letters designate matrices and vectors. The essentials of matrix algebra are reminded in the text. For any matrix, we specify the number of rows and the number of columns. For example, a matrix $\mathbf{M}$ with n rows and m columns is a $(n \times m)$ matrix. The first number is always number of rows and the second number is always the number of columns. Unless otherwise specified, a vector is a set of m terms in a column: It is a matrix of 1 column and m rows, or a $(1 \times m)$ matrix. We add an additional notation, $\mathbf{M}^T$, which is the transpose of $\mathbf{M}$, where the transpose of an $n \times m$ matrix is obtained by swapping rows and columns.

30.2.2 Variance–Covariance Matrix of Portfolio Returns

A variance–covariance matrix is a square symmetric matrix of variances and covariances of m variables, such as stock returns. The asset return is y_i. We use the subscript i for asset i and there are m such assets. The variances are along the diagonal and the covariances are off-diagonal

---

2 See appendix for some common matrix definitions and formulas.

terms. The relation between variances, covariances and correlation coefficients hold. Next, we specify the notations for variances and covariances for all m assets:

σ_i: standard deviation of asset i return
σ_j: standard deviation of asset j return
$\text{Cov}(y_i, y_j)$: covariance between two asset returns, equal to $\rho_{ij}\sigma_i\sigma_j = \sigma_{ij}$
$V(y_i) = \sigma_i^2$: variance of asset i return.

For all $i \neq j$, $\text{Cov}(y_i, y_j) = \rho_{ij}\sigma_i\sigma_j = \sigma_{ij} = \text{Cov}(y_j, y_i) = \rho_{ji}\sigma_j\sigma_i = \sigma_{ij}$ since the variance–covariance and correlation matrices are symmetric. The variance–covariance matrix is an $(m \times m)$ matrix Σ:

$$\Sigma = \begin{array}{|c|c|c|c|}
\hline
\sigma_1^2 & \sigma_{12} & & \sigma_{1m} \\
\hline
\sigma_{21} & \sigma_2^2 & & \sigma_{2m} \\
\hline
\sigma_{31} & \sigma_{32} & & \sigma_{3m} \\
\hline
 & & & \\
\hline
\sigma_{m1} & \sigma_{m2} & & \sigma_m^2 \\
\hline
\end{array}$$

An alternate form, using correlation coefficients, is another $m \times m$ matrix, identical to above, but specifying covariances as a function of correlation coefficients and variances:

$$\Sigma = \begin{array}{|c|c|c|c|}
\hline
\sigma_1^2 & \rho_{12}\sigma_1\sigma_2 & & \rho_{1m}\sigma_1\sigma_m \\
\hline
\rho_{21}\sigma_{21} & \sigma_2^2 & & \rho_{2m}\sigma_2\sigma_m \\
\hline
\rho_{31}\sigma_3\sigma_1 & \rho_{32}\sigma_2\sigma_3 & & \rho_{3m}\sigma_3\sigma_m \\
\hline
 & & & \\
\hline
\rho_{m1}\sigma_m\sigma_1 & \rho_{m2}\sigma_m\sigma_2 & & \sigma_m^2 \\
\hline
\end{array}$$

Consider the above example of two stocks. Their correlation matrix is simple.

$$\Sigma = \begin{array}{|c|c|}
\hline
1 & 37.901\% \\
\hline
37.901\% & 1 \\
\hline
\end{array}$$

Their variance–covariance matrix can be written as the product:

$$\begin{array}{|c|c|}
\hline
2.601\% & 0 \\
\hline
0 & 1.826\% \\
\hline
\end{array} \times \begin{array}{|c|c|}
\hline
1 & 37.901\% \\
\hline
37.901\% & 1 \\
\hline
\end{array} \times \begin{array}{|c|c|}
\hline
2.601\% & 0 \\
\hline
0 & 1.826\% \\
\hline
\end{array}$$

$$= \begin{array}{|c|c|}
\hline
0.0677\% & 0.0180\% \\
\hline
0.0180\% & 0.0333\% \\
\hline
\end{array}$$

Next, we move to more realistic examples that apply to real portfolios, for calculating the volatility of a weighted portfolio of assets, such as stocks. The difference with that above, where we used unweighted data, is that we need to explicitly introduce the weights of each asset within the portfolio.

30.2.3 The Variance–Covariance Matrix of Portfolio Return

Any portfolio is characterized by a column vector **w** of weights, which are initial weights known as of current date 0. Weights are w_i. The weights are the ratio of each asset value at the original date 0 to the portfolio value P at the same date $w_i = X_i/P$. The portfolio P includes m assets X_i, and its value is a linear function of asset values and weights. For convenience, we omit the initial date 0.

$$P = \sum_{i=1,m} w_i X_i$$

We use generally returns rather than values. The portfolio return Y_P, over a discrete period, omitted in notations, is the weighted average of all asset returns y_i, between the same dates, using the original weights w_i. The weights are constant, and characterize a "crystallized portfolio" with constant asset weights. The portfolio return is:

$$Y_P = \sum_{i=1,m} w_i y_i$$

The portfolio return variance follows. Using abbreviated notations:

$$\sigma_i^2 = \sigma^2(y_i) \text{ and } \sigma_{ij} = \text{Cov}(y_i, y_i) = \rho_{ij}\sigma_i\sigma_i$$

The variance of the portfolio return is, remembering that the weights w_i are constant:

$$\sigma^2\left(P = \sum_{i=1,m} w_i y_i\right) = \sum_{i=j=1,m} w_i^2\sigma_i^2 + \sum_{i\neq j} w_i w_j \sigma_{ij} = \sum_{i=j=1,m} w_i^2\sigma_i^2 + \sum_{i\neq j} \rho_{ij} w_i w_j \sigma_i\sigma_j$$

In matrix notations, this expression becomes much simpler:

$$\sigma^2(Y_P) = \mathbf{w}^\mathsf{T}\Sigma\,\mathbf{w}$$

The variance of the portfolio return is a scalar, a real positive number, equal to the variance of P. Accordingly, the volatility of Y_P is:

$$\sigma(Y_P) = \sqrt{\mathbf{w}^\mathsf{T}\Sigma\mathbf{w}}$$

These results are now used to illustrate the diversification effect of a weighted portfolio. In this book, the above formula also serves, notably, in the calculation of delta-normal VaR (Chapter 41), where the weights are replaced by the sensitivities of each portfolio position to risk factors.

For the variance to be positive, the variance–covariance matrix has to be semi-definite positive. This condition implies that not all symmetric matrices can be considered as a variance–

covariance matrix. The condition for the matrix to have the desired property derives from matrix algebra and is not defined here[3].

30.2.4 Portfolio Return Volatility

The example uses the two-asset portfolio above. A second example shows the effect of portfolio diversification when the number of assets increases.

Instead of using an unweighted portfolio we now assign weights to the above portfolio of two stocks. The weight of the first asset is 30% and the weight of the second asset is 70%, both weights totaling 100%. The volatility of the portfolio is given by the matrix formula:

$$\sigma(Y_P) = \sqrt{\mathbf{w}^T \Sigma \mathbf{w}}$$

In an expanded format, we have the portfolio variance and volatility shown in Table 30.1. The same calculation can be performed using the explicit algebra:

$$\sigma^2 \left(P = \sum_{i=1,2} w_i y_i \right)$$

$$= w_1^2 \sigma_1^2 + w_2^2 \sigma_2^2 + 2\rho_{ij} w_1 w_2 \sigma_1 \sigma_2$$

$$= 30\%^2 \times 0.0677\%^2 + 70\%^2 \times 0.0333\%^2 + 2 \times 30\% \times 70\% \times 2.601\% \times 1.826\%$$

$$= 0.0300\%$$

The volatility is the square root of variance. By varying the weights we would find the set of weights minimizing volatility and we would obtain the traditional curve representing volatility of all combinations of weights of the two stocks. The benefit of the matrix calculation of variance is that it can be extended to any number of assets, using the same compact matrix formula, and that calculations are easier. The same formula will be applied for calculating the volatility of the P & L of a trading portfolio, or the volatility of credit losses in a credit portfolio, using as vector inputs, respectively, sensitivities and exposures.

TABLE 30.1   Portfolio variance and volatility

		0.0677%	0.0180%	30%
		0.0180%	0.0333%	70%
30%	70%	0.0329%	0.0287%	0.0300%
		Portfolio variance of return		0.0300%
		Portfolio volatility of return		1.7317%

---

3 As a reminder, the condition implies that the Eigen values of a matrix are positive or equal to zero.

30.3 PORTFOLIO RETURN RISK AND CORRELATION

The standard representation of the diversification effect applies to portfolio and asset returns. The principles date from Markowitz principles[4]. The portfolio return varies with the equity index as risk factor. The specific risk of each asset is independent of this common factor.

Extending the number of assets creates diversification because the specific risks of individual asset returns offset each other. The undiversifiable risk is the general risk common to all assets. This well-known result applies notably to stock returns and to asset returns in the structural model of default, and is the basis for modeling diversification effect for credit risk.

When looking at values rather than returns, the same basic mechanisms of diversification apply. Nevertheless, unlike return volatility that tends to decline down to a floor corresponding from general risk, the volatility of the value increases with each new asset. The portfolio value volatility increases with the number of assets and portfolio average return correlation.

A simple way of illustrating the mechanism of diversification effect is to refer to a simple uniform portfolio, and see what happens when the number of assets increases. A uniform portfolio is such that all assets have the same weights, with same return volatility and same pair correlation between returns. All values V_i and all weights w_i are now equal: $V_{i0} = V_0$. The portfolio value is $V_{P0} = NV_0$. The value of each asset is €1. The common weight is $w = 1/n$. All variances, covariances and correlations of returns are equal as well. The volatility of each asset return is $\sigma(R_i) = 30\%$. The correlation between pairs of assets is $\rho = 30\%$.

The notations are now simpler:

$$\sigma(R_i)^2 = \sigma^2$$

$$\mathrm{Cov}(R_i, R_j) = \rho_{ij}\sigma_i\sigma_j = \rho\sigma^2$$

The portfolio return volatility sums up n variance terms weighted by the constant weights $1/n^2$ and $n(n-1)$ covariance terms equally weighted by $1/n^2$. The variance of the portfolio return is:

$$\sigma(R_P)^2 = \frac{\sigma^2}{n} + \frac{(n-1)}{n}\rho\sigma^2$$

The portfolio return variance and volatility now simplify to:

$$\sigma(R_P)^2 = \frac{\sigma^2}{n}[1+\rho(n-1)]$$

$$\sigma(R_P) = \frac{\sigma\sqrt{1+r(n-1)}}{\sqrt{n}}$$

Sample calculations are shown below for the portfolio return volatility and its changes when n increases (Table 30.2).

With the above inputs, we observe the decrease of portfolio return risk due to diversification when the number of assets increases. The above relations also show that with small values of n, the portfolio return volatility increases with n and with the uniform volatility. It is also proportional to the uniform correlation. When the uniform correlation increases, the portfolio

---

4 See Markowitz, H. M. (1952), Portfolio selection, *Journal of Finance*, 7, 77–91. Also the textbook of Bodie, Kane and Marcus is an excellent reference on "Investments" and portfolio management [14].

TABLE 30.2 Variance and volatility of the uniform portfolio

$\sigma(R_i)$	30%
ρ	30%
V	1

n	$\sigma^2(RP)$	$\sigma(RP)$	Marginal $\sigma(RP)^2$
1	9.00%	30.00%	30.00%
2	5.85%	22.15%	−7.85%
3	4.80%	18.81%	−3.33%
4	4.28%	16.90%	−1.91%
5	3.96%	15.65%	−1.26%
6	3.75%	14.75%	−0.90%
7	3.60%	14.07%	−0.68%
8	3.49%	13.54%	−0.53%
9	3.40%	13.11%	−0.43%
10	3.33%	12.76%	−0.35%
11	3.27%	12.47%	−0.30%

return volatility also increases, as well as the minimum value of portfolio return volatility when n increases (Figure 30.3).

Note that this example, using as target variable the portfolio return, is very classical. But the same basic formulas apply in other contexts, when the variable of interest changes. The volatility of the P & L of a trading portfolio P & L is a critical parameter for market VaR determination. For credit VaR, the target variable is the portfolio loss volatility due to credit risk and its variation when adding a facility or expanding the exposure to any one obligor.

The portfolio return volatility decreases quickly from the initial 30% to a minimum value equal to systematic risk, which, in this example, is around 10%. The threshold is approximately reached around 30 assets, a well-known result in portfolio theory. This implies that maximum diversification is almost reached with around 30 assets in the portfolio.

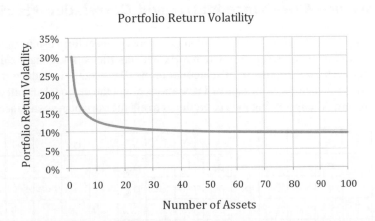

FIGURE 30.3 Variation of the portfolio return volatility with the number of assets

30.4 APPENDIX: MATRIX NOTATIONS AND FORMULAS

30.4.1 Transpose Matrix

Consider any square matrix **M**.

$$
\mathbf{M} =
\begin{array}{|c|c|c|}
\hline
2 & 3 & 4 \\
\hline
5 & 6 & 7 \\
\hline
8 & 9 & 10 \\
\hline
\end{array}
$$

The transposed matrix is $\mathbf{M}^{\mathrm{T}}$:

$$
\mathbf{M}^{\mathrm{T}} =
\begin{array}{|c|c|c|}
\hline
2 & 5 & 8 \\
\hline
3 & 6 & 9 \\
\hline
4 & 7 & 10 \\
\hline
\end{array}
$$

Consider the column vector:

$$
\mathbf{V} =
\begin{array}{|c|}
\hline
2 \\
\hline
5 \\
\hline
8 \\
\hline
\end{array}
$$

The transpose $\mathbf{V}^{\mathrm{T}}$ is a row vector of which terms are that in rows in the same order:

$$
\mathbf{V}^{\mathrm{T}} =
\begin{array}{|c|c|c|}
\hline
2 & 5 & 8 \\
\hline
\end{array}
$$

30.4.2 Variance–Covariance Matrix and Correlation Matrix

This form is fully expanded, but it can be written in a more compact form using matrix notations and using the correlation matrix, ρ, a square matrix with coefficients 1 along the diagonal and correlations between asset returns in off-diagonal terms. We need to introduce σ, a diagonal matrix of standard deviations, with standard deviations along the diagonal and all off-diagonal terms equal to zero. The following matrix product equals the variance–covariance Σ matrix.

$$
\Sigma =
\begin{array}{|c|c|c|c|c|}
\hline
\sigma_1 & & & & \\
\hline
 & \sigma_2 & & & \\
\hline
 & & & & \\
\hline
 & & \cdots & & \\
\hline
 & & & & \sigma_m \\
\hline
\end{array}
\times
\begin{array}{|c|c|c|c|}
\hline
1 & \rho_{12} & \cdots & \rho_{1m} \\
\hline
\rho_{12} & 1 & \cdots & \rho_{2m} \\
\hline
\rho_{13} & \rho_{32} & \cdots & \rho_{3m} \\
\hline
\cdots & \cdots & \cdots & \cdots \\
\hline
\rho_{1m} & \rho_{2m} & \cdots & 1 \\
\hline
\end{array}
\times
\begin{array}{|c|c|c|c|c|}
\hline
\sigma_1 & & & & \\
\hline
 & \sigma_2 & & & \\
\hline
 & & & & \\
\hline
 & & & & \\
\hline
 & & & & \sigma_m \\
\hline
\end{array}
$$

The variance–covariance matrix can also be expressed, noting that the transpose σ^T of the diagonal matrix σ is identical to σ:

$$\Sigma = \sigma^T \rho \sigma$$

30.4.3 Variance Formula and Correlation Matrix

Note that we can replace the $(m \times m)$ variance–covariance matrix Σ by the $(m \times m)$ correlation matrix ρ using:

$$\Sigma = \sigma^T \rho \sigma$$

Since the transpose of the product $\mathbf{w}\sigma$, or $(\mathbf{w}\sigma)^T$ is the product of the transpose in reverse order, $(\mathbf{w}\,\sigma)^T = \sigma^T \mathbf{w}^T$, the variance of a weighted asset portfolio is:

$$\sigma^2(Y_p) = \mathbf{w}^T \sigma^T \rho \mathbf{w} \sigma$$

31

Conditional Probabilities

Unconditional probabilities of a random variable are "normal" probabilities when we have no information on any other event that influences the random variable. Conditional probabilities, on the other hand, embed the information related with some random event that influences the original variable. Conditional probabilities involve two variables – the conditioning variable and the conditioned variable. Conditional probabilities differ from unconditional probabilities only when there is dependence between the random variable and the conditioning random event or variable. Conditional probabilities apply directly to random discrete events such as defaults[1]. Accordingly, all examples apply to default events dependent on another variable.

Section 31.1 explains how conditional probabilities and the joint probabilities of occurrence of two events that are dependent are defined and calculated. This section introduces the basic formulas that apply to conditional probabilities. The next sections present two applications. The first application, in Section 31.2, shows how default probabilities can be made dependent on a variable representing the state of the economy. The conditional probabilities on the state of the economy are the inputs and we derive the unconditional default probability using the above rules. The same principle applies for conditioning the entire distribution of defaults within a portfolio. The other application, in Section 31.3, derives the joint default probability of two obligors. Dependency between defaults is obtained by assigning a value to the probability of default of one obligor conditional on the default of the other obligor. This application is again used several times later on, for example for determining the joint probability of default of a guarantor and a direct borrower (Chapter 51).

Contents

---

1 See for example [35] for an intermediate text on probabilities.

31.1 DEFINITION OF CONDITIONAL AND JOINT PROBABILITIES

The purpose of this section is to introduce the properties of joint and conditional probabilities, and the basic formulas for calculating conditional and joint probabilities.

31.1.1 Conditional Probabilities

Conditional probabilities are probabilities conditional on some information that influences this probability. If X is a random event of which probability of occurrence depends upon some random scenario S, then the probability of X occurring given S is the conditional probability $P(X|s)$, with s being a particular value of the random variable S representing the state of the economy.

The conditional probability framework is adapted to default events, which we use as an example. We characterize default events by a random variable X taking only two values, default or non-default, or 1 and 0 respectively for these two states. The unconditional default probability of X taking the default value 1 is $P(X)$. This is an unconditional default probability that applies when we have no particular information on whatever influences this probability. The random state of the economy S influences the likelihood of X values. The probability of X defaulting once S is known, or $P(X|S)$, is the conditional default probability of default of X given S.

The conditional probability depends on the correlation between the two events. For example, if economic conditions worsen, the default probability of all firms increases. In such a case, there is a correlation between the default event X and the occurrence of worsening economic conditions, a value of S. If there is no relation, the conditional probability $P(X|S)$ collapses to the unconditional probability $P(X)$. If there is a positive relation, the conditional probability increases above the unconditional probability, and if there is a negative correlation, it is lower.

We have already used the concept when addressing some risk models. For example, the GARCH $(1, 1)$ model determines the current volatility depending on lagged estimates of variance and of squared returns. This variance is conditional on those two explaining variables. By contrast, the unconditional variance is the long-term variance in the GARCH model, which is estimated by fitting the model to time series of variances. The conditioning principle is applied in numerous instances.

31.1.2 Conditional and Joint Probabilities

A joint probability is the probability that two events occur simultaneously. It applies to both continuous and discrete variables. The two random events are X and Y. The basic relationship that relates joint probabilities and conditional probabilities is given below. The relationship between the joint probability that both events X and Y occur and the conditional probabilities of X given occurrence of Y, or Y given occurrence of X, is:

$$P(X, Y) = P(X) \, P(Y|X) = P(Y) \, P(X|Y)$$

Consider a bivariate normal distribution. It is the distribution applying to two normal correlated variables. The bivariate normal distribution assigns a probability of observing a pair of values for each of the normally distributed variables. This probability is a joint probability. When one of these two variables is fixed, the other variable follows a normal distribution, of which parameters are determined by the first variable. The first variable is the conditioned variable and the second variable is the conditioning variable. Because we are dealing with normal distributions entirely defined by two parameters, expectations and variance, the conditioned variable distribution is entirely determined by those parameters.

When X and Y are independent, the joint probability collapses to the product of their standard probabilities, and the conditional probabilities are equal to the standard unconditional probabilities.

$$P(X, Y) = P(X) \, P(Y)$$

$$P(X|Y) = P(X)$$

31.2 DEFAULT PROBABILITY OF A FIRM DEPENDENT ON THE STATE OF THE ECONOMY

A first example relates the default probability to the state of the economy. A firm has an "unconditional" default probability of 1.15%. The random value X, taking the values "default" and "non-default," characterizing the status of the firm. The firm's unconditional default probability $P(X = \text{default}) = 1.15\%$. The unconditional probability represents the average across all possible states of the economy.

Let us now consider three discrete states of the economy. The three possible values of S are $s = $ base, $s = $ best case and $s = $ worst case. The probability of observing the worst-case state is 20%. Let us assume that the corresponding default probability increases up to 2%. This probability is conditional on S value. The formula is:

$$P(X = \text{default} \mid S = \text{worst case}) = 2\%$$

The joint probability of having simultaneously a default of the firm and a worst-case state of the economy is, by definition:

$$P(X = \text{default}, s = \text{worst case}) = P(s = \text{worst case}) \, P(X = \text{default} \mid s = \text{worst case})$$
$$= 20\% \times 2\% = 0.4\%$$

As a summary:

$$P(X = \text{default} \mid s = \text{best case}) = 0.4\%$$

$$P(X = \text{default} \mid s = \text{base case}) = 1\%$$

$$P(X = \text{default} \mid s = \text{worst case}) = 2\%$$

If the state of the economy does not influence the credit standing of the firm, the conditional probability of default is equal to the unconditional default probability, or 1%. This implies that $P(X = \text{default}| s = \text{worst case}) = P(X = \text{default}) = 1\%$. The joint probability of having a worst case situation plus default drops down to $P(X = \text{default}, s = \text{worst case}) = 1\% \times 20\% = 0.2\% <$ 0.4%. Under independence, the joint probability is lower than the conditional probability.

With correlated variables X and S, the joint probability depends on the correlation. If the correlation is positive, the joint probability increases above the product of the unconditional probabilities. This implies that $P(X|Y) > P(X)$ and $P(Y|X) > P(Y)$. With positive correlation between X and Y, conditional probabilities are higher than unconditional probabilities. This is consistent with $P(X, Y)$ being higher than the product of the unconditional probabilities $P(X)$ and $P(Y)$ since $P(Y|X) = P(X, Y)/P(X)$ and $P(X|Y) = P(X, Y)/P(Y)$.

Consider again a single firm whose default probability is conditional on the state of the economy. When inferring probabilities, the rule for averaging conditional probabilities is helpful. Let us assume that there are three (or more) possible states for the economy S, with s representing the state of the economy. The default probabilities of firm X varies with the state of the economy. If it worsens, the default probabilities increase and vice versa, with only three states of the economy possible with unconditional probabilities $P(S = s_1)$, $P(S = s_2)$ and $P(S = s_3)$ respectively equal to 50%, 30% and 20%. The three states represent, respectively, the best, the base, and the worst case of the state of the economy. The probabilities sum up to one since there are no other possible states.

The averaging rule stipulates that the unconditional default probability of the firm X is such that:

$$P(X) = P(X|s_1) \, P(S = s_1) + P(X|s_2) \, P(S = s_2) + P(X|s_3) \, P(S = s_3)$$

The default probability varies with S, representing the state of the economy. Taking 2.0%, 1%, and 0.5% as conditional default probabilities of X for each the three states respectively, the unconditional default probability has to be:

$$P(X) = 2.0\% \times 30\% + 1\% \times 40\% + 0.5\% \times 30\% = 1.15\%$$

The unconditional default probability is the weighted average of the conditional default probabilities under various states of the economy, the weights being the probabilities of occurrence of each state. In general, the unconditional probability is the weighted average of all conditional probabilities over all possible states k of the economy[2].

$$P(X) = \sum_{i=1,k} P(X \mid s_i) P(s_i)$$

The same example serves for conditioning the entire distribution and models the distribution of the number of defaults within a portfolio.

When the defaults are independent, the number of defaults within a portfolio follows a binomial distribution, with parameters equal to the number n of obligors and their unique default probability. Unfortunately, the binomial distribution only counts defaults, not losses, and uses a

---

2 Should S be a continuous variable, we would transform the summation symbol by and integration symbol over all values of S using $P(S)$ as the probability of S being in the small interval ds: $P(X) = \int_s P(X \mid s) \, P(s) \, ds$.

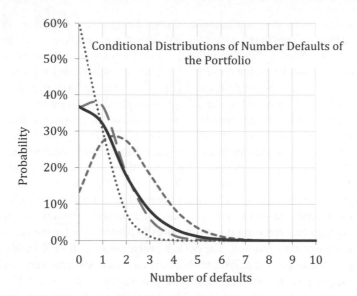

FIGURE 31.1   Conditional distributions of defaults on the state of the economy

common default probability. However, it can serve for illustrating how conditioning can model the effect of correlations on defaults. Since it is entirely defined by the common default probability, it is sufficient for conditioning the loss to make this probability conditional of the state of the economy, as above. We obtain as many binomial distributions as there are states of the economy, plus the weighted average, which is the unconditional distribution of the number of defaults. Figure 31.1 shows the three binomial distributions, and how they shift when the state of the economy changes. The mode of the distribution shifts to the right when the state of the economy deteriorates. The unconditional distribution is the continuous line.

This simple case illustrates the principle. Conditioning probability distribution is used several times in this text. Under the copula approach, the distribution conditional on the value of another variable is the principle that allows making variables dependent. The so-called limit distribution for a granular uniform portfolio developed in Chapter 49 is another useful example.

31.3 THE TWO-OBLIGOR PORTFOLIO AND CONDITIONAL PROBABILITIES

The two-obligor portfolio is the simplest of all portfolios. We use this simple portfolio to demonstrate that joint probability and conditional probabilities are related. The probabilities of default conditional on the default or non-default of the second obligor characterize the dependence. Increasing the default probability of an obligor conditional on default of the other implies a higher correlation between defaults.

We consider two cases for clarity: the case where default events are independent and the case where defaults are dependent. In both cases, we derive the conditional probabilities and show that they relate directly to the joint default probability. The starting point uses only three inputs:

- the default probability of Y conditional on X default
- the two standalone default probabilities of X and Y.

The remaining probabilities follow.

31.3.1 The Independence Case

In the independence case, all joint probabilities of any couple of credit states of X and Y are simply the products of the unconditional probabilities of X and Y having the corresponding credit states (Table 31.1).

The calculation of above probabilities is straightforward since the joint probabilities of two events are the products of the unconditional probabilities of each obligor defaulting or surviving. The basic relationship serving for constructing the table is:

$$P(Y|X) = P(X, Y)/P(X)$$

The joint default probability is $3\% \times 2\% = 0.06\%$. The joint probability that X defaults and Y does not is, similarly, $3\% \times 98\% = 2.94\%$. In addition, the conditional probability $P(X|Y)$ or $P(Y|X)$ are identical to the unconditional probabilities in the independent case because $P(X, Y) = P(X) P(Y)$. Their values, in Table 31.1, serve for subsequent comparisons with the positive correlation case.

The example shows that standalone probabilities of obligors' defaults and non-default in a portfolio context differ from the unconditional probabilities of default. For example, the probability that Y only defaults is $1.94\% = 97\% \times 2\%$, which differs from its standalone default probability of 2%.

How can we explain the paradox of differing single default probabilities of X out of a portfolio and within a portfolio? The essence of the explanation is that X defaulting alone, in a portfolio context, is conditional on others not defaulting, and is not any more an unconditional probability of default. It is the joint probability of default of X and of others non-defaulting. This is a non-intuitive result illustrating the difference of a standalone view of X and of a view of the same X in a portfolio context. This result holds even when conditional probabilities are equal to unconditional probabilities, due to independence, as illustrated in Table 31.1.

TABLE 31.1   Calculation of joint default probabilities of two independent obligors

Unconditional probability X		Unconditional probabilities Y		Conditional P(Y | X) P(Y | X)	Joint probabilities
D	3.00%	D	2.00%	2.00%	0.06%
		ND	98.00%	98.00%	2.94%
				100.00%	3.00%
ND	97.00%	D	2.00%	2.00%	1.94%
		ND	98.00%	98.00%	95.06%
				100.00%	97.00%

31.3.2 The Dependent Case

We proceed with the same portfolio as with the independence case. The conditional probabilities now differ from the unconditional default probabilities. The framework of calculations is the same as above.

The process for calculating all the joint probabilities starts from the conditional probability $P(Y = D|X = D)$. The probability that X defaults is $P(X = D)$, and $P(X = ND)$ is the probability that X does not default, with similar notations for Y. The "tree" of unconditional and conditional probabilities serves for demonstrating that a single conditional probability, plus the unconditional probabilities, is sufficient to derive all other conditional probabilities (Table 31.2).

The first line provides the joint default probability 0.60%, given the conditional $P(Y|X) = 20\%$. The calculation is:

$$P(Y = D|X = D) = P(X = D)\, P(Y = D|X = D) = 3\% \times 20\% = 0.60\%$$

Since Y has only two credit states, default or no default, given X credit state, the conditional probabilities given X credit state have to sum up to 1. The conditional survival probability of Y if X defaults is simply 1 minus the above probability:

$$P(Y = ND|X = D) = 1 - 20\% = 80\%$$

Next, the joint survival probability is $1 - P(X = D) - P(Y = D) - P(X, Y) = 1 - 3\% - 2\% - 0.60\% = 95.60\%$. The joint survival probability equals the product of the unconditional survival probability of Y times the conditional survival probability of Y upon survival of X. The equality defines the conditional survival probability of Y, $P(Y = ND|X = ND) = P(Y = ND|X = ND)\, P(X = ND)$.

$$P(Y = ND|X = ND) = 95.60\%/P(X = ND) = 95.60\%/97\% = 98.56\%$$

Once the survival probability conditional on X survival is calculated, the default probability of Y conditional on X survival is the complement to 1, or 1.44%.

The sum of conditional probabilities of B defaulting weighted by the probabilities of the conditioning event, X defaulting or not defaulting, is the unconditional default probability of Y. The formula below makes this dependence explicit:

TABLE 31.2   Unconditional default probabilities, conditional probabilities

Unconditional probability		Unconditional probabilities		Conditional P(Y | X)	Joint probabilities
X		Y		P(Y | X)	
D	3.00%	D	2.00%	20.00%	0.60%
		ND	98.00%	80.00%	2.40%
				100.00%	3.00%
ND	97.00%	D	2.00%	1.44%	1.40%
		ND	98.00%	98.56%	95.60%
				100.00%	97.00%

TABLE 31.3   Matrix of joint probabilities

		Y		
		D	ND	
X	D	0.60%	2.40%	3.00%
	ND	1.40%	95.60%	97.00%
		2.00%	98.00%	100.00%

$$P(Y = D) = P(Y = D|X = D) \, P(X = D) + P(Y = D|X = ND) \, P(X = ND)$$

$$P(Y = D) = 20\% \times 3\% + 1.44\% \times 97\% = 2\%$$

The same results are summarized in the matrix of joint probabilities of the four combinations of joint events, default or survival (Table 31.3). The sum of the elements, by row and by column, of the matrix cross-tabulating the outcomes for X and Y are identical to standalone default probabilities and survival probabilities of X and Y. The probabilities in rows or columns sum up to 100%.

Note that the joint probability of defaults is 0.60%, well below the standalone default probability of each obligor. Basel 2 proposes an approach allowing using the double default in presence of a third party providing a guarantee to the direct borrower. In general, this approach allows using a much lower probability of default than the "substitution approach" which simply takes the lower probability of default of the guarantor as probability of default when there is a third party guarantee.

31.4 APPENDIX: CONDITIONING, EXPECTATION AND VARIANCE

Some additional formulas serve in applications. The conditional probability distribution of X subject to Y is the probability distribution of X given a value of Y. The conditional expectation of X results from setting Y first, then cumulating ("integrating") over all values of X.

$$E(X) = E[E(X|Y)]$$

$E(X|Y) = E(X)$ implies that X does not depend upon Y. The expectation of a variable can be calculated by taking the expectation of X when Y is set, then taking the expectation of all expected values of X given Y when Y changes. Conditional expectations are additive as unconditional expectations are. These formulas serve for defining the expectation when a distribution of a variable is conditional on the value of some external factors, such as the state of the economy.

The variance of a random event X depending on another event Y results from both the variance of X given Y and of the variance of the conditioning factor Y:

$$V(X) = V[E(X|Y)] + E[V(X|Y)]$$

It is convenient to use this formula in conjunction with: $V(X) = E(X^2) - [E(X)]^2$. This formula allows the decomposition of the variance into the fraction of variance due to the conditioning factor Y and the variance due to the event X.

32

Factor Models

Portfolio models are used for determining the portfolio risk, given diversification effects. The diversification effect depends on dependency across individual assets. Portfolio models traditionally rely on factor models for modeling the dependency between individual assets. This chapter is an overview of factor models, and of their contribution to the determination of portfolio risk from common factors explaining the asset returns[1].

The main properties of factor models and of their contributions to modeling dependencies are summarized in Section 32.1, before expanding the details in subsequent sections. Section 32.2 details the generic forms and properties of factor models. All subsequent sections address portfolio risk using factor models, using as an example two-asset portfolios, which facilitate the detailed presentations of numerical examples.

Section 32.3 addresses portfolio risk using an example of a two-asset portfolio with one-factor model, as an intermediate step. The derivation of the variance–covariance matrix, of the correlation between asset returns, and the decomposition of portfolio risk into general risk related to the single factor and specific risk are all conducted with this example. Many applications used in this text rely on one-factor models.

Section 32.4 generalizes the rules with multiple-factor models. The generic form of the multiple-factor model applied to several assets is introduced as a preliminary to subsequent examples. The major convenient property of factor models for modeling systematic risk, using the variance–covariance matrix of the factors (instead of the matrix of asset returns), is that they are much less numerous than the number of assets; this is introduced at this stage and illustrated in all subsequent examples.

Section 32.5 uses, as first its example, a one-factor model for explaining the risk of a two-asset portfolio. The section details how portfolio return risk is decomposed in general and specific risks, with formulas detailed at each step using both standard algebra and matrix formats

---

1 The book of Carol Alexander (2008) [2] provides in the first two chapters the essentials on factor models. The RiskMetrics and CreditMetrics documents of JP Morgan provide insights on factor models.

compact formulas. Systematic risk modeling is based on the variance–covariance matrix of factors rather than on the matrix of asset returns.

The formulas for a two-asset portfolio and two-factor models are expanded, through an example, in Section 32.6. It is shown that portfolio risk uses the same basic formulas as a single asset provided that portfolio return is expressed as a single linear function of weighted exposures of each asset within the portfolio, detailing general risk, specific risk and portfolio return variance and volatility. The core building block for assessing general risk is the variance–covariance matrix of factors and portfolio general risk uses as inputs the weighted exposures of each asset. The general matrix formulas with portfolio weights apply to any portfolio whatever the number of assets and the number of factors. The specific risk is made explicit without any restriction to the residuals of each factor model applied to each asset of the portfolio.

Section 32.7 introduces orthogonal factor models, using principal components analysis (PCA) which is much simpler to manipulate because the factor model relies on independent factors rather than on factors that have a complete variance–covariance matrix. The principles of PCA are summarized in an appendix (Section 32.9).

In Section 32.8 we summarize the generic formulas of portfolio general and specific risks as reference for subsequent developments. The simulation technique using factor models is exposed in the last chapter of this section (Chapter 34) together with simulation techniques using the copula approach which follows in the next chapter (Chapter 33).

Contents

32.1 FACTOR MODELS

A factor model is a linear relation between asset or portfolio returns, and explaining variables called factors. The coefficients of the relation are called factor loadings. They measure the sensitivity of the target returns to be linked to each factor, or the response of asset returns to a standard change of the factor. Factor models are estimated using traditional regression analysis, which provides the factors that affect the target variable significantly, their coefficients, and how significant they are, plus the residual, called the error term due to variations unrelated to the explained variable, and its standard deviation, called standard error, which is the residual risk unaccounted for by the factors.

Factor models serve for modeling portfolio risk. Usually, the variable of interest is the portfolio return and the risk metrics used is the volatility of portfolio return. Factor models serve for modeling dependency because they relate each asset return to a set of common factors. When factors vary, they generate co-movements between asset returns that allow accounting for diversification. The general risk is the risk explained by factors. Its magnitude depends on factor volatilities and on coefficients of the factor model. Hence, general risk captures both volatilities of asset returns as a combined result of their sensitivities and the volatilities of factors.

Factor models are used for modeling asset and portfolio returns. They extend to any asset, as long as the asset return is a linear function of factors. They are applied for market VaR and credit VaR models because they allow modeling dependencies, and hence diversification effects. The factor models allow decomposing the risk into general risk, which depends on factors, and specific risk. Only specific risk can be diversified away since general risk depends on the same common factors. However, the general risk does capture the effect of diversification within the portfolio.

In general, dependencies within portfolios are characterized by a variance–covariance matrix of asset returns. With portfolios, there are a large number of assets and the matrices become unmanageable. One benefit of factor models is that general risk depends on common factors that explain variations of asset returns. This allows the modeling of the dependence structure within portfolios by relying only on the variance–covariance matrix of factors rather than assets. Since there are many fewer factors than assets, the matrix has much lower dimensions and is much easier to manage.

Factor models are used for modeling portfolio risk and for conducting simulations using the dependence between asset returns and factors. All that needs to be done is generating random factor variables that comply with the dependency structure of factors. Because simulation can only be explained with a minimum background on factor models, the usage for simulations is deferred to the next chapter.

Factor models apply to all assets and portfolios of assets. For example, the return of a fund is related to variables that characterize the management style of the fund manager. Traditional variables characterizing styles are "value," "growth," "large cap," "mid cap."

- "Value" refers to stock of which value that is estimated from fundamental analysis.
- "Growth" applies to stocks having a higher than average potential for price growth.
- "Small cap," "mid cap" and "large cap" refer to the size of the company whose stock is traded, "cap" being the shortcut for market capitalization, or market value of equity.

In general, there are a large number of variables that can help explaining the return of stocks or portfolios. Most fund managers and analyst firms perform such statistical techniques to explain relative excess of deficit return compared to benchmark returns.

32.2 THE GENERIC FORM OF FACTOR MODELS

This section provides a reminder of the Capital Asset Pricing Model (CAPM) as an example of a one-factor model designed for explaining individual stock returns. Next, we introduce the generic expressions of single-factor models and of multiple-factor models.

32.2.1 Example of a One-factor Model

A traditional example of a single-factor model is the Sharpe's CAPM, where the return of a single stock is explained by the return on the stock index. Under the CAPM, stock returns are driven by the equity index return. The coefficient of the equity index is the β, which measures the relative sensitivity of the stock return to the index return. The expected return of a stock should be related to the expected equity index return and the coefficient is the β which depends on the particular stock. The conceptual equation of the CAPM for a single stock "i" is:

$$E(r_i) = r_f + \beta_i[E(r_m) - y_f]$$

The equation says that the expected stock return should be equal to the risk-free rate plus a "risk premium," that is the difference between the expected index return and the risk-free rate, times β_i, which is specific to the stock of interest. The β_i is the sensitivity of the stock return to the stock index return. For the index itself, the β has to be equal to 1. Some stocks have high β and others low β. The response to a standard shock on the equity index return, for example +1%, is the $\beta \times 1\%$. If β is higher than 1, for example 2, the stock return should, on average, respond with an increase of +2%. If the β is 0.5, the response to the same shock on equity index would be, on average, +0.5%.

The statistical version of the theoretical equation is a one-factor model:

$$r_i = \beta_0 + \beta_1 r_m + \varepsilon$$

Since a factor model is based on a regression analysis, in all factor models, all cross covariances between the factors and the residual are zero and the expectation of the residual term is zero. According to the theory, the constant should be $\beta_0 = r_f(1 - \beta_i)$ and the factor coefficient should be $\beta_i = \beta_{1i}$. The residual in the linear statistical relation is the random variation of the stock return that is independent of the equity index return. Both the residual and the coefficient depend on the stock.

This single-factor model does not fully explain the variations of the stock return. The volatility of the first term is the general or "systematic risk." The volatility of the residual is the specific risk of the individual stock. The systematic risk cannot be diversified away in portfolios since all stocks are more or less sensitive to index return, meaning that they all move with the Index, although with various sensitivities. The total risk of the stock return sums up the specific and the general risk. Statistically, since the residual is independent of the common factor, the variance of the return is the sum of the variance of the first term and of the variance of the residual. Such a model has been extended, notably with Ross's APT [65], to several variables. Extending the number of factors allows one to explain a grater fraction of the total risk with factors.

32.2.2 The Single-factor Model

Moving to the general form of the one-factor model, we explain Y by X, according to the regression equation, where we drop the subscript "i" designating the asset:

$$Y = \beta_0 + \beta_1 X + \varepsilon$$

Because the residual and the factor are independent, the variance is:

$$V(Y) = \beta_1^2 V(X) + V(\varepsilon)$$

$$\sigma^2(Y) = \beta_1^2 \sigma^2(X) + \sigma^2(\varepsilon)$$

The standard technique for estimating a factor model is the regression technique, which provides estimates of β_0 and β_1, as well as standard statistics, which tell us whether those coefficients are significantly different from zero. The standard deviation of the residual is called the standard error. The expectation of the error term is zero. The covariance between the error term and X is zero. The ratio of the explained variance by X to the total variance indicates how much variance of the explained variable is due to the "explaining" variable X. This ratio is called the R square, or R^2, of the regression. It is desirable to have high R^2.

The formulas for the coefficient depend on all historical observations Y_i and X_i of Y and X and on the size of the sample of data, made of a time series of values of X and Y. The ordinary least square regression technique provides the best fit to the actual relation, defined as the fit that minimizes the squared deviations from the mean of the estimated return of the stock and actual observations over the sample of observations. The significance of the coefficients depends on the sample size. It is possible to have low R^2 and still have significant coefficients at some confidence level, such as 5% or 1%.

Using the independence between the factor and the residual, the total risk decomposition of the single asset into general and specific risk is given by the equation:

$$\sigma_Y^2 = \beta^2 \sigma_X^2 + \sigma_\varepsilon^2$$

From the regression analysis, the formula of the coefficient β is:

$$\beta = \frac{\text{cov}(Y,X)}{\sigma_X^2}$$

The covariance between X and Y, $\text{cov}(Y, X)$, results from the independence between the residual and the factor:

$$\text{cov}(Y, X) = \text{cov}(\alpha + \beta X + \varepsilon, X) = 0 + \beta \text{cov}(X, X) + \text{cov}(X, \varepsilon) = \beta_1^2 \sigma^2(X)$$

By definition of the correlation coefficient, it is:

$$\rho_{XY} = \frac{\text{cov}(X,Y)}{\sigma_x \sigma_Y}$$

Using the covariance $\text{cov}(Y, X)$, the coefficient of the factor model becomes:

$$\beta = \rho \frac{\sigma_Y}{\sigma_X}$$

32.2.3 The Generic Form of Multiple-factor Models

In general, we use K risk factors X_k, with $k = 1$ to K, and express the return Y of each asset in terms of a linear function of factors, the factor weights being β_k, plus a residual ε specific to each asset. Starting with a single asset, we have the linear equation:

$$Y = \beta_0 + \beta_1 X_1 + \beta_2 X_2 + \dots + \beta_k X_k + \varepsilon$$

With several assets, each with subscript "i," with $i = 1$ to N, the equations relating each asset return to several common factors use double subscripts. The first subscript relates to the factor and the second subscript to the asset. With N assets and K factors, the general equation becomes a function of the same K common factors, but the coefficients and the residual now depend on the asset:

$$Y_i = \beta_{0i} + \beta_{1i} X_1 + \beta_{2i} X_2 + \dots + \beta_{ki} X_k + \varepsilon_i$$

For deriving the variance–covariance matrix of several assets whose returns depend on several factors, we progress in steps. The first step consists of considering a single asset and multiple factors. The second step consists of using two assets, forming a portfolio, and two factors. We will see that the equation explaining the portfolio return with the factors is similar to the single-asset equation after some simple manipulations. For tractability, we use numerical examples.

The entire process of writing multiple-factor models for several assets, deriving the portfolio return model, the variance–covariance matrix of assets as a function of the variance–covariance matrix of factors, and the risk decomposition into general risk and specific risk, can all be expressed in matrix format. The matrix format is very convenient because it is quite compact, although it looks abstract. For demonstrating the equivalence between algebra formulas and matrix formulas, all calculations in the subsequent numerical examples use the two notations.

With several assets and multiple factors, two variance–covariance matrices are used. One matrix applies to asset returns and the other one applies to factors. The first one has much larger dimensions than the second one because there are many more assets than factors. This is one of the major benefits of factor models because they allow modeling the variance–covariance matrix of individual assets using the factor variance–covariance matrix, which is much easier to handle because it has much smaller dimensions. All examples used a two-asset portfolio. The generalization with matrix formulas, which are provided in all examples, is straightforward.

32.3 RISK OF A TWO-STOCK PORTFOLIO WITH THE ONE-FACTOR MODEL

Both total risk of a portfolio and its decomposition into general risk (systematic risk) and specific risk (residual risk), are simpler with a single asset. For portfolios, it is easy to show that similar formulas to those of a single asset apply, providing that we plug-in the weights of each asset in the formula, so the presentation of a two-asset and one-factor model is helpful as an intermediate step. A subsequent intermediate step uses a two-factor model for asset returns. From there, we can generalize with a two-asset portfolio and several factors.

For stock returns, used as an example, the single common factor is the equity index. Returns are measured by the relative variations of the stock price and of the index of $\Delta S/S$ and $\Delta I/I$, where S and I are the values of the stock price and of the index. Logarithmic returns, which are $\ln(\Delta S/S)$ and $\ln(\Delta I/I)$, measured over small time intervals, such as one day, can be used equivalently.

32.3.1 The One-factor Model

Using a set of daily returns for equity index, $\Delta I/I$, r_m and two stocks, we obtain several statistics: the volatilities of the time series, or standard deviations, and the variances and covariances, plus the correlation, between the asset returns r_1 and r_2 (Table 32.1).

The equations of the model to be fitted to a data sample now use the subscript "i," for the asset, where $i = 1$ and 2.

$$r_i = \beta_{0i} + \beta_{1i} r_m + \varepsilon_i$$

The above data is obtained using the linear regression technique. With the sample set of data used, of around 400 daily observations, all coefficients are significant at more than 0.1%. This confidence level means that we can reject the hypothesis that the coefficients differ from 0 with a probability higher than 99.9%, and there is only a 0.1% chance that they equal zero. The standard error of the residual is its volatility, $\sigma(\varepsilon_i)$, and is obtained from the fit. The two one-factor models are, using a sample:

$$r_1 = 0.169 + 0.404 r_m + \varepsilon_1$$

$$r_2 = 0.287 + 0.946 r_m + \varepsilon_2$$

The relevant statistics for these two models are in Table 32.2. The cross correlation between residuals is not significantly different from 0. The correlations between the explaining variable r_m and the residuals, within each model, are exactly 0, for the pairs (r_m, ε_2) and (r_m, ε_2). The models outputs for each asset (with $i = 1, 2$) are summarized in Table 32.2. For each stock, we have the systematic risk and the specific risk, of which variances are additive (Table 32.3).

TABLE 32.1   Basic statistics for the return data sample

Volatility			
$\sigma(r_m)$	0.940		
$\sigma(r_1)$	0.793		
$\sigma(r_2)$	1.278		

	r_m	r_1	r_2
r_m	1		
r_1	0.479	1	
r_2	0.696	0.384	1

TABLE 32.2   Main outputs of the two one-factor models

	β_{0i}	β_{1i}	$\sigma(\varepsilon_i)$	R^2
r_1	0.169	0.404	0.696	22.9%
r_2	0.287	0.946	0.918	48.4%

TABLE 32.3   Total risk and risk decomposition for the two-asset portfolio

Risk	Systematic	Specific	Total	R2
Stock 1	0.144	0.484	0.629	0.229
Stock 2	0.791	0.843	1.633	0.484

The R^2 measure of variance is explained by the equity index and is the ratio of systematic risk to total risk. The coefficients, β_i, are the sensitivities of asset returns to the index return. They result from the correlation between the explaining variable r_m (the factor) and the explained stock return r_i times the ratio of their volatilities, or $\rho_{im}\sigma(r_m)/\sigma(r_i)$.

32.3.2 The Variance–Covariance Matrix

By definition of the regression model, the random equity index return is independent of the residual ε_i. The covariance between any pair of equity returns depends only on the variance of the single factor and the β_{21} and β_{22} coefficients[2] and the cross-covariance between residuals of each model.

$$\text{cov}(r_1, r_2) = \text{cov}(\beta_{01} + \beta_{11}r_m + \varepsilon_1, \beta_{02} + \beta_{12}r_m + \varepsilon_2)$$

$$= \beta_{11}\, \beta_{22}\, \text{cov}\,(r_m, r_m) + \text{cov}\,(\varepsilon_1, \varepsilon_2)$$

$$= \beta_{11}\, \beta_{22}\, \sigma^2(r_m) + \text{cov}\,(\varepsilon_1, \varepsilon_2)$$

The cross-covariance terms between the index return and the residuals, $\text{cov}(r_1, \varepsilon_1)$ and $\text{cov}(r_2, \varepsilon_2)$, are zero. The cross-covariance between residuals is not significantly different from zero in this example. However, this is not a general result. The covariance and the correlations between any pair of equity returns r_1 and r_2 collapses are derived from above relations.

$$\text{cov}(r_1, r_2) = \beta_1\beta_2\sigma^2(r_m)$$

The correlation coefficient follows:

$$\rho_{ij} = \text{cov}(r_i, r_j)/\sigma(r_i)\sigma(r_j) = \beta_i\beta_j\sigma^2(r_m)/\sigma(r_i)\sigma(r_j)$$

---

2 Since the constant does not contribute either to variance or covariances.

Moreover, the variance of each individual asset return is:

$$\sigma^2(r_i) = \beta_i^2 \sigma^2(r_m) + \sigma^2(\varepsilon_i)$$

The total risk is the sum of the "general" or "systematic" risk, due to the common factor, plus the specific risk of the stock due to the residual.

We found an interesting property of single-factor models. The covariance between the asset returns $\text{cov}(r_1, r_2)$ depends only on the single-factor variance and the coefficients of factors. It is equal to $\beta_{11} \beta_{22} \sigma^2(r_m)$, if we ignore the cross-covariance $\text{cov}(\varepsilon_1, \varepsilon_2)$ between residuals. Note that the latter is a restrictive assumption in general.

32.3.3 Variance–Covariance Matrices of Asset Returns and of Factors

If we extend the model to N stocks, the covariances between pairs of stocks would only depend on the variance of the index return and the factor coefficients for each stock.

When dealing with portfolios, we have a large number, N, of assets. There are as many covariances and correlations as there are pairs of stocks. The direct measures of the variances and covariances of stock returns would imply measuring N^2 terms (the variance–covariance matrix is squared with dimensions $N \times N$). Since the matrix is symmetric, we have $N(N-1)/2$ covariance terms plus N variance terms, the total being $N + N(N-1)/2 = N(N+1)/2$ different terms. Under the single-factor model, and subject to assuming zero cross-covariances between residuals, we need only N coefficients, plus the single-factor variance for general risk, or $N + 1$ terms. This is much less than the number of items required using pair correlations. Using a factor model allows a considerable reduction in the number of items for determining the variance–covariance matrix applying to individual stocks.

In general, pecific risk depends on cross-covariances and variances of residuals. It is a square symmetric $(N \times N)$ matrix. The matrix has also $N(N-1)/2$ covariance terms plus N variance terms, the total being $N + N(N-1)/2 = N(N+1)/2$ different terms.

32.4 PORTFOLIO RISK WITH MULTIPLE-FACTOR MODELS

When considering several assets, the benefits of calculating risk from factors only is that there are many less factors than assets in a portfolio. The variance–covariance matrix of all assets would be huge, while that of common factors would be of lesser dimensions. Since asset returns depend on common factors, their correlations, the variances and covariances also depend only on the number of factors, which is much less than the number of assets.

A general portfolio has N assets, of which returns can be modeled with K factors. The variance–covariance matrix of the risk factors is Σ with dimensions $(K \times K)$. The factor coefficients are the β_{ij}, where the factor subscript, i, varies from 1 to K and the asset subscript, j, varies from 1 to N.

The factors are selected according to the nature of assets. It is convenient to pick up all risk factors that have a relation with any of the asset returns. This will increase the number of factors. Some factors might be not significant for some assets and their coefficients would be zero, but, on the other hand, we have a common set of factors for all assets. Once selected, the factors do not change across assets, but their coefficients, the constant and the residual, do change when we move from one asset to another. For each asset, the same form of linear relation is used, with the common set of K factors.

The constant β_{0i} and the residual ε_i of the model depend only on the asset and have a single subscript "i," referring to each asset of the N assets, with $i = 1, N$. Since we use common factors for all assets, factors have only one index k, the subscript $k = 1, K$. As above, all factor coefficients, β_{ki} of each of the K factors, now have a double index, the first being the factor index, k, the second being the asset index, i. The corresponding N equations, one for each asset, i, becomes:

$$Y_i = \beta_{0i} + \beta_{1i}X_1 + \beta_{2i}X_2 + \ldots + \beta_{Ki}X_K + \varepsilon_i = \beta_0 + \Sigma_{k=1,K}\beta_{ki}X_k + \varepsilon_i$$

Portfolios require consideration of the weights w_i of each asset within the portfolio, the sum of the weights being 1. Weights w_i are given and maintained constant because this makes the portfolio return a weighted average of asset returns, the weights being initial weights within the portfolio[3].

Finally, note that it might be convenient to use standardized values of factors, with zero expectation and variance 1. This simply involves scaling the coefficients of the models, since a non-standard variable is transformed into a standardized variable $X_s = (X - m)/\sigma$, where m and σ are the mean and the standard deviation of the non-standardized variable. We do not use this rule below, except when mentioned.

For highlighting the basic rules for modeling portfolio risk, it is sufficient to use two assets only for deriving the variance–covariance matrix of assets from the one of factors, and for decomposition of the total risk into general and specific risks.

Correlations and variances of individual asset returns and risk factors are derived from the variance–covariance matrix of factors and from the covariance of residuals. A first technique for obtaining the variance–covariance matrix is to measure it through a sample of direct observations of individual asset returns, usually on an historical basis.

Consider, in general, N assets and K factors. With N assets, the square symmetric variance–covariance matrix includes a total of $N(N + 1)/2$ terms. Using covariances for pairs of assets directly raises several difficulties. First, the high number of assets makes it unpractical to create a matrix with all pair covariances between individual asset returns. Second, the observed variances and covariances might not comply with the basic properties of variance–covariance matrices, such as being semi-definite positive. This happens because some observed parameters might correlate strongly[4] or because the estimates of covariances are not significant.

Using a multi-factor model, we reduce the problem of determining its systematic risk to the determination of a square $(K \times K)$ variance–covariance matrix for the K factors. The number of terms for systematic risk is considerably reduced by using a factor model because the systematic risk depends only on the variance–covariance matrix of the factors, which is common to all assets, and the K coefficients (other than the constant), instead of calculating each covariance between all pairs of assets.

---

3   When time passes, each asset value changes. Therefore the weights of assets within the portfolio change. But it can easily be shown that the portfolio return is the weighted average of asset returns provided that we use as weights the initial weights.
4   When two variables have a correlation of 1, the matrix has not the desired property. Highly correlated variables might result in a similar result.

We illustrate this general methodology in two cases: single-asset portfolio, and a portfolio of two assets and using a two-factor model. We show that the two-asset portfolio case can be formulated as a single asset case, provided that we use as single asset a weighted average of the two assets. From these simple examples, we derive generic matrix formulas. Besides being extremely compact, the matrix formulas are general whatever the number of assets and of factors, for N assets and K factors.

The formulas are easily tractable when considering only a single asset or two assets with two factors. They can be written in standard format and in matrix format. We provide both throughout the example.

32.5 RISK FOR A SINGLE ASSET AND TWO-FACTOR MODELS

The risk calculations for a single asset have no other objective that providing the formulas, which, later, are applied to a portfolio by plugging-in the weights of each asset within a portfolio.

Assume that each single asset depends now on two risk factors. With a single asset, the sensitivities to each factor are 0.5 and 1. We derive the systematic and specific risks from the model for the single asset. The model for the single asset is:

$$Y = \beta_{0i} + 0.5X_1 + 1X_2 + \varepsilon$$

The variance–covariance matrix Σ for factor returns is given in Table 32.4. The risk does not depend on the constant β_0. There is no subscript for the asset since we consider a single asset. We use subscripts, with values 1 or 2, for the factors. The variances σ_i^2 of factor returns X_i are σ_{ii}, where $i = j$, and the σ_{ij}, for $i \neq j$, are the covariances of factor returns X_1 and X_2.

The analytical formula of the systematic variance $V_{sys}(Y)$, when we ignore the variance of the residual term, is, for the single asset, with factor coefficients β_1 and β_2:

$$V_{sys}(Y) = (\beta_1 \sigma_{11})^2 + (\beta_2 \sigma_{22})^2 + 2 \beta_2 \beta_1 \sigma_{12}$$

Replacing β_1 and β_1 by their respective values, 0.5 and 1:

$$V_{sys}(Y) = 0.5 \times 0.25 + 12 \times 0.04 + 2 \times 0.5 \times 1 \times (-0.01) \times 0.04 = 0.1081$$

$$\sigma_{sys}(Y) = \sqrt{[V_{sys}(Y)]} = 0.3288$$

The correlation coefficient between the two factors is given by $\rho\sigma(X_1)\sigma(X_2) = \text{cov}(X_1, X_2)$.

The same result would be obtained from the matrix formula (Table 32.5), where the bottom right-hand cell contains the general variance, already calculated above.

TABLE 32.4 Variance–covariance matrix with a two-factor model

	σ_{11}	σ_{21}		0.25	−0.01
$\Sigma =$	σ_{12}	σ_{22}	=	−0.01	0.04

TABLE 32.5   Matrix formula for general variance of a single asset and a two-factor model

0.25	−0.01
−0.01	0.04

0.5
1.2

0.5	1.2

0.113	0.043

0.1081

In this matrix formula, we multiply the (1×2) transposed vector of coefficients $\boldsymbol{\beta}^{\mathrm{T}}$ by the square (2×2) variance–covariance matrix of factors $\boldsymbol{\Sigma}$, and we multiply the row vector obtained by the (2×1) vector $\boldsymbol{\beta}$ of coefficients. The matrix formula for systematic variance is:

$$V_{\mathrm{sys}}(Y) = \boldsymbol{\beta}^{\mathrm{T}}\boldsymbol{\Sigma}\boldsymbol{\beta}$$

The specific risk in the case of a single asset is the variance of the single residual and the total risk, measured by the variance of the asset return, sums up the systematic and the specific risks:

$$V(Y) = \boldsymbol{\beta}^{\mathrm{T}}\boldsymbol{\Sigma}\boldsymbol{\beta} + \sigma^2(\varepsilon)$$

32.6 A TWO-ASSET PORTFOLIO WITH TWO-FACTOR MODELS

The core of the factor models is the variance–covariance matrix of the risk factors, $\boldsymbol{\Sigma}$, and the factor loadings of each factor, plus the constants and the residuals. The variance–covariance matrix of factors is common to all assets. The residuals of each model have a mean of zero and a variance that depends on the model and the risk decomposition varies accordingly with each asset. Residuals, for each asset, have no correlation with the factors, but they might have cross-correlations between themselves differing from zero. Accordingly, we make explicit the variance–covariance matrix of residuals. In this sub-section, we show that the portfolio can be dealt with as a single asset by using asset weights within the portfolio.

32.6.1 The Two-factor Model Applied to a Two-asset Portfolio

As above, we use double subscripts for variances and covariances of factors. The σ_{ii}, where $i = j$, are the variances σ_i^2 of factor return X_i, and the σ_{ij}, for $i \neq j$, in this case a single value, σ_{12}, represents the covariance of factor returns X_k, where k takes the values 1 and 2. The variance–covariance matrix of factors $\boldsymbol{\Sigma}$ is:

$\boldsymbol{\Sigma} =$	σ_{11}	σ_{21}	$=$	0.25	−0.01
	σ_{12}	σ_{22}		−0.01	0.04

Note that in the above matrix, the double index refers to factors only, unlike the double index used in the two-factor model, where the first subscript refers to the factor and the second one to the asset.

We have two models, one for each of the two assets. There are two sets of sensitivities with same factors, plus residuals attached to each of the two assets. The factor models for each asset return are:

$$Y_1 = \beta_{01} + 0.5X_1 + 1.0X_2 + \varepsilon_1$$

$$Y_2 = \beta_{02} + 1.2X_1 + 0.8X_2 + \varepsilon_2$$

The coefficients of the two models have double subscripts, one for the asset and another for the factor. The first subscript refers to the factor and the second subscript refers to the asset. Note that the double subscripts are different for the variance–covariance matrix of factors, where they refer to factors only, and for the coefficients of the models, where they refer to factor (first subscript) and to asset (second subscript).

The constant of each model, are, respectively, $\beta_{01} = 0.1$ and $\beta_{02} = 0.05$. They do not contribute to variances and covariances, but they contribute to the expected return of the portfolio. The matrix of coefficients of the two models is as follows, ignoring the two constants because they do not contribute to risk.

$$\beta = \begin{array}{|c|c|} \hline \beta_{11} & \beta_{21} \\ \hline \beta_{11} & \beta_{22} \\ \hline \end{array} = \begin{array}{|c|c|} \hline 0.5 & 1.0 \\ \hline 1.2 & 0.8 \\ \hline \end{array}$$

We first derive the portfolio return and show that it has the same generic format as the single-asset two-factor model, although we need to input the weights of each asset in the formulas. The rest follows as in the single-asset model: variance–covariance matrix of asset returns and risk decomposition.

32.6.2 The Two-asset Portfolio Return

The risk of the portfolio depends on weights applied to each asset. The weights are indexed by the asset index "i" and sum up to 1. Weights are the ratios of initial value of each asset to portfolio value, and they are constant, and equal to their initial values. The portfolio return, Y_P, is the weighted average of each asset return.

$$Y_P = w_1 Y_1 + w_2 Y_2$$

The portfolio return is now that of a sum of weighted asset returns, weights being constant.

$$Y_P = w_1[\beta_{01} + 0.5X_1 + 1.0X_2 + \varepsilon_1] + w_2[\beta_{02} + 1.2X_1 + 0.8X_2 + \varepsilon_2]$$

$$Y_P = (w_1\beta_{01} + w_2\beta_{02}) + (w_1 0.5 + w_2 1.0)X_1 + (w_1 1.2X_2 + w_2 0.8)X_2 + (w_1\varepsilon_1 + w_2\varepsilon_2)$$

The portfolio return is a linear model of the two factors. The coefficients are the weighted values of the sensitivities of the two assets. The constant is the weighted value of the constants of the two assets. The residual is the sum of weighted values of the two standalone (single-asset) residuals. This shows that we can proceed as if we had one standalone single asset with the constant, the coefficients of factors, the constant and the residual being the weighted values of the single asset model for the coefficients, constant and residual. The portfolio return is explained by a linear two-factor model.

For calculating the coefficients of this set of two models of each asset return, we need the set of weights and the constants. The weights are 0.7 and 0.3 for assets 1 and 2, or, in vector notation $\mathbf{w}^T = (0.7, 0.3)^T$. The constants are 0.1 and 0.05, for assets 1 and 2, or (0.1, 0.05).

The weighted constant is calculated as above: $0.7 \times 0.1 + 0.3 \times 0.05 = 0.085$. It can also be written as a vector product. The (1×2) row vector of constants $\boldsymbol{\beta_0}^T$ multiplied by the column (2×1) vector of weights $\mathbf{w}$ is the constant of the portfolio return model, or $\boldsymbol{\beta_0}^T\mathbf{w}$:

	Weights
	0.7
	0.3

Constants		
0.1	0.05	0.085

The column (2×1) vector of weighted coefficients of factors X_1 and X_2 is obtained as above as weighted averages of factor coefficients. They are:

$$\text{For } X_1: w_1 0.5 + w_2 1.0 = 0.680$$

$$\text{For } X_2: w_1 1.2 + w_2 0.8 = 1.080$$

They can also be calculated as the product of the square matrix of coefficients by the column vector of weights, or $\boldsymbol{\beta}\mathbf{w}$:

	Weights
	0.7
Matrix of factor	0.3
coefficients	

0.5	1.1	0.680
1.2	0.8	1.080

Similarly, the linear function of residuals is the product of the row (1×2) vector of residuals by the column (2×1) vector of weights, or $\boldsymbol{\varepsilon}^T\mathbf{w}$:

$$w_1\varepsilon_1 + w_2\varepsilon_2 = 0.7\varepsilon_1 + 0.3\varepsilon_2$$

The global model for the weighted portfolio return, or Y_p, is:

$$Y_P = 0.085 + 0.680X_1 + 1.080X_2 + 0.7\varepsilon_1 + 0.3\varepsilon_2$$

We end up with a single linear function of the same risk factors that relate to each asset return. But we added a linear function of the residuals of each model. The set of two-factor models, one for each asset, simplifies to a single two-factor model of the portfolio return, with two weighted coefficients, a single weighted constant, and a single weighted residual.

The expected portfolio return is the sum of expectations, whatever the covariances, except that we need to introduce the asset weights within the portfolio. The equation representing Y_P as a two-factor model has weighted constants, weighted coefficients and weighted residuals. Applying the expectation operator to the single two-factor model of the portfolio return, and using the zero expectation of residuals, the expectation of the portfolio return is:

$$E(Y_P) = 0.085 + 0.680E(X_1) + 1.080E(X_2)$$

The expectation of the portfolio return depends on the constants of each of the factor models. If we use standardized normal factors, return expectations then collapse to zero. It collapses to the weighted constant because each factor has a zero expectation.

32.6.3 Portfolio Systematic Risk: Two-factor Models

The calculation of systematic risk follows the same matrix formula as above, except that we need to replace the vector coefficients by their weighted averages using the asset weights in the portfolio. When proceeding in this way, we use the rule that the transpose of a product is the product of the transposed in reverse order:

$$(\boldsymbol{\beta}\mathbf{w})^T = \mathbf{w}^T\boldsymbol{\beta}^T$$

The expanded form of the matrix calculation is as shown in Table 32.6.

TABLE 32.6 Calculation of the portfolio systematic risk with two-factor models

	X1	X2		
	0.25	-0.01		0.680
	-0.01	0.04		1.080
0.680	1.080		0.1592	0.0364	0.148

The systematic variance of the portfolio is 0.148 and the volatility is 0.384. The compact formula for this matrix is:

$$V_{Sys} = \mathbf{w}^T \boldsymbol{\beta}^T \boldsymbol{\Sigma} \boldsymbol{\beta} \mathbf{w}$$

Note again that systematic risk becomes of a function of the variance–covariance matrix of factors, instead of assets.

At this point, it is worth remembering the financial interpretation of the coefficients of factor models in these calculations. The coefficients β measure the sensitivity of each asset to a factor. Within the market universe, those sensitivities are simply the response of the market value to a shock applied to factors. It is common to designate such sensitivities as positions within a portfolio because they are the starting points of all calculations, which describes the portfolio. When addressing market risk VaR, we will use exactly the same formulas, except that the basic inputs will be sensitivities to risk factors. The point remains valid when plugging in weights within portfolios. The positions are entirely defined by their weighted sensitivities to each risk factor, as the next section shows. In general, sensitivities are used in monetary values, which equal the weighted coefficients used above.

32.6.4 Portfolio Systematic Risk Decomposition into Additive Items

Risks do not add up arithmetically, due to diversification effects. However, the above calculations allow determining additive "risk contributions" by decomposition of the variance into additive items.

The intermediate result obtained with the above first matrix product, or $\mathbf{w}^T \boldsymbol{\beta}^T \boldsymbol{\Sigma}$, can be interpreted. The first term of the first matrix product is $w_1\beta_1\sigma_{11} + w_2\beta_2\sigma_{12}$ and the second term is $w_1\beta_1\sigma_{12} + w_2\beta_2\sigma_{22}$. The first term of the first matrix product represents the covariance between Y_p and X_1, or $cov(Y_p, X_1)$:

$$cov(w_1\beta_1 X_1 + w_2\beta_2 X_2, X_1) = cov(w_1\beta_1 X_1, X_1) + cov(w_2\beta_2 X_1, X_2) = 0.1592$$

Conversely, the second term represents the covariance between Y_p and X_1. This second term of the first matrix product is $w_1\beta_1\sigma_{12} + w_2\beta_2\sigma_{22}$ and represents the covariance between Y_p and X_2, $cov(Y_p, X_2)$, or 0.0364. The general variance of the portfolio return is the weighted sum of these covariances by β_1 and β_2:

$$V(Y_p) = w_1\beta_1 Cov(Y_p, X_1) + w_2\beta_2 Cov(Y_p, X_2) = 0.1592 \times 0.680 + 0.0364 \times 1.080 = 0.148$$

The general variance is the weighted sum of the covariances of Y_p with each of the two factors. The weights are the factor coefficients times the asset weights. The general variance is decomposed into a sum of weighted covariances between Y_p and each of the factors. This decomposition allows breaking down the total general variance 0.148 into additive contributions to the total general risk. The risk contributions are the weighted covariances between the asset and each factor, respectively $0.1592 \times 0.680 = 0.1083$ and $0.0364 \times 1.080 = 0.0393$. The sum is the total systematic variance, or $0.1083 + 0.0393 = 0.1476$, rounded to 0.148 above.

At this stage, it is worth mentioning important applications in risk management. One major issue is that risks do not add up algebraically. But the variance is additive in that the sum of the weighted covariances equals the general variance. Such weighted covariances are called risk contributions, which add up algebraically. They provide a methodology for allocating systematic risk to each factor with additive contributions. This is the foundation of risk allocation using the contribution to variance. Such risk contributions are simply the terms that add up to total variance. The methodology is used in the risk allocation chapters (section 13) for credit risk.

32.6.5 Two-asset Portfolio and Two-factor Model: Specific Risk

The specific risk results from the residuals. The residuals and the risk factors are independent for each factor model. Using the zero cross-correlations between factors and residuals, we have again a variance–covariance of the linear combination of residuals: $0.7\varepsilon_1 + 0.3\varepsilon_2$. The matrix formula of the variance applies, using as weights for each residual the asset weights. We need the covariance matrix of residuals, noted $\mathbf{E}$, which is a square symmetric matrix:

$$\mathbf{E} = \begin{array}{|c|c|} \hline \sigma_{\varepsilon 11} & \sigma_{\varepsilon 12} \\ \hline \sigma_{\varepsilon 21} & \sigma_{\varepsilon 22} \\ \hline \end{array}$$

We can assign numerical values to $\mathbf{E}$:

$$\mathbf{E} = \begin{array}{|c|c|} \hline 0.002 & 0.015 \\ \hline 0.015 & 0.003 \\ \hline \end{array}$$

The next step for specific risk consists of proceeding exactly like with systematic risk, using the covariance matrix of residuals and using the portfolio weights of assets (Table 32.7). The specific risk is 0.005. The process is identical to the one used for deriving systematic risk, except that we use the variance–covariance matrix of the residuals instead of the variance–covariance matrix of the factors. In matrix format, the above expression is:

$$V_{\text{Spe}} = \mathbf{w}^T \boldsymbol{\beta}^T \mathbf{E} \boldsymbol{\beta} \mathbf{w}$$

TABLE 32.7 Portfolio specific risk and two-factor models

		ε1	ε2		
		0.0020	0.0150		0.700
		0.0015	0.0030		0.300
0.700	0.300	0.00185	0.0114		0.005

32.6.6 Portfolio Total Risk and Two-factor Model

The total risk for the two-asset portfolio is: $0.148 + 0.005 = 0.153$. This can be summarized by the compact matrix format expression:

$$\text{Variance (portfolio return)} = V_{\text{Sys}} + V_{\text{Spe}} = \mathbf{w}^\mathsf{T}\boldsymbol{\beta}^\mathsf{T}\mathbf{E}\boldsymbol{\beta}\mathbf{w} + \mathbf{w}^\mathsf{T}\boldsymbol{\beta}^\mathsf{T}\mathbf{E}\boldsymbol{\beta}\mathbf{w}$$

32.7 ORTHOGONAL MULTIPLE FACTOR MODELS AND PCA

Orthogonal factor models have the same linear form as the general factor model, but they are such that the cross-covariances across factors are zero. This simplifies the formulas considerably. The new factors are obtained using "principal component analysis" (PCA). They are called "principal components" (P_k) and the coefficients are the factor loadings. Any factor model can be transformed into an orthogonal factor model with the same number of factors. The principal components are linear combinations of standard factors. The main principles of PCA analysis are expanded in the appendix (Section 32.9).

The main characteristic of PCA is that factors, or principal components, are independent of each other. The conceptual foundations of PCA are derived in the appendix (Section 32.9). Because we now use orthogonal factors, the coefficients of the new factor model now differ from the previous β_k. We name them η_k.

PCA applies best when we have highly correlated data, because a large fraction of the total general variance is explained by the first few principal components. This is why a major application of PCA is the modeling of the term structure of interest rates, since all of them are highly correlated. We will apply PCA for simulating interest rates in market VaR analysis, and for simulating scenarios of interest rates in ALM (Chapter 37).

In general, PCA is more convenient because, even though we keep all principal components as in standard factor models, independent factors considerably simplify the variance–covariance matrix of factors. The matrix collapses to a diagonal matrix with principal components variances[5], $\sigma^2(P_K)$, along the diagonal and all off-diagonal terms are zero.

32.7.1 Using PCA for Single Assets

The simplification is illustrated by an example. The models for two-asset returns and two independent factors are:

$$Y_1 = \eta_{01} + 1.0P_1 + 1.2P_2 + \varepsilon_1$$

$$Y_2 = \eta_{02} + 0.8P_1 + 0.5P_2 + \varepsilon_2$$

The variance of the explained variable is the variance of a sum of independent variables weighted by the factor loadings, plus the residual variance. It is the summation of general risk

---

5 The variances of the principal components are called λ_k.

variance plus the specific risk variance of the residual. The formula for the variance of each asset return is:

$$\sigma^2(Y_i) = \text{cov}(\eta_{1i}P_1 + \eta_{1i}P_2 + \varepsilon_i, \eta_{1i}P_1 + \eta_{2i}P_2 + \varepsilon_i)$$

$$\sigma^2(Y_i) = (\eta_{1i})^2\sigma^2(P_1) + (\eta_{2i})^2\sigma^2(P_2) + \sigma^2(\varepsilon_i)$$

We can use standardized factors with variance 1 by scaling them, which simplifies again the formulas. The variances of each asset return are:

$$\sigma^2(Y_1) = (1)^2 \times 1 + (1.2)^2 \times 1 = 2.44$$

$$\sigma^2(Y_2) = + (0.8)^2 \times 1 + (0.5)^2 \times 1 = 0.89$$

The total risk adds the specific risk, which depends on variances of residuals. Assume that they equal to 1.5 and 1.0 for the first and the second assets, respectively.

$$\sigma^2(Y_1) = (1)^2 \times 1 + (1.2)^2 \times 1 + 1.5 = 3.94 = 1.985^2$$

$$\sigma^2(Y_2) = + (0.8)^2 \times 1 + (0.5)^2 \times 1 + 1 = 0.64 + 0.25 + 1 = 1.89 = 1.375^2$$

32.7.2 Two-asset Portfolio and Two Orthogonal Factors

Assume that we form a portfolio with these two assets, using weights 0.7 and 0.3. Then we would use the weighted sensitivities to each factor for each asset. The two models are:

$$Y_1 = \eta_{01} + 1.0P_1 + 1.2P_2 + \varepsilon_1$$

$$Y_2 = \eta_{02} + 0.8P_1 + 0.5P_2 + \varepsilon_2$$

The portfolio return model is also a two-factor model, with the constant, the coefficients of factors, and the residuals being the weighted values of each single-asset coefficients, constant and residual.

$$Y_P = w_1[\eta_{01} + 0.5X_2 + 1.0X_2 + \varepsilon_1] + w_2[\eta_{02} + 1.2X_1 + 0.8X_2 + \varepsilon_2]$$

$$Y_P = (w_1\eta_{01} + w_2\eta_{02}) + (w_10.5 + w_21.0)X_1 + (w_11.2X_2 + w_20.8)X_2 + (w_1\varepsilon_1 + w_2\varepsilon_2)$$

We focus on the systematic variance, the methodology being the same as for standard factor models for residuals or specific risk. The column (2×1) vector of weighted coefficients of factors P_1 and P_2 is obtained as before as weighted averages of factor coefficients, calculated as the product of the square matrix of coefficients by the column vectors of weights, or $\boldsymbol{\eta}\mathbf{w}$:

Weights
0.7
0.3

Matrix of factor coefficients

1	1.2	1.060
0.8	0.5	0.710

The global portfolio return is an orthogonal two-factor model:

$$Y_P = (w_1\eta_{01} + w_2\eta_{02}) + 1.060 P_1 + 0.710 P_2 + (w_1\varepsilon_1 + w_2\varepsilon_2)$$

The variance–covariance matrix Σ for principal components is a diagonal matrix with variances σ_i^2 of factor return P_i with numerical values as follows:

$$\Sigma = \begin{vmatrix} \sigma_{11} & 0 \\ 0 & \sigma_{22} \end{vmatrix} = \begin{vmatrix} 0.20 & 0 \\ 0 & 0.10 \end{vmatrix}$$

The compact formula for the general variance matrix is the product of row vector of weights by the diagonal variance matrix of factors and the column vector of weights:

$$V_{Sys} = \mathbf{w}^T \mathbf{\eta}^T \Sigma \mathbf{\eta} \mathbf{w}$$

The matrix calculation of the general risk now uses a diagonal factor matrix. The individual positions of assets within the portfolio now differ because the factor loadings in PCA differ from those of standard factor models (Table 32.8).

The systematic variance of the portfolio is 0.275 and the volatility is 0.525. Note that the systematic variance term for the portfolio sums up the squared weighted sensitivities times the factor variances.

$$V(Y_P) = 0.2^2 \times 1.060^2 + 0.1^2 \times 0.710^2 = 0.275$$

TABLE 32.8   Portfolio general risk with PCA

	PI	P2	
	0.2	0.0	1.060
	0.0	0.1	0.710
1.060	0.710		
	0.212	0.071	0.275

32.8 PORTFOLIO RISK: SUMMARY OF MATRIX FORMAT CALCULATIONS

In the general case, we have N assets and a common set of K factors. The total risk of the portfolio is a matrix formula, using two covariances matrices, the one of factors and the one of residuals.

The expectation is:

$$E(Y_P) = \boldsymbol{\beta}_0{}^\mathrm{T}\mathbf{w} + E(\mathbf{X}^\mathrm{T}\mathbf{w})$$

The total variance sums up the systematic variance and the specific variance:

$$V(Y_P) = \mathbf{w}^\mathrm{T}\boldsymbol{\beta}^\mathrm{T}\boldsymbol{\Sigma}\boldsymbol{\beta}\mathbf{w} + \mathbf{w}^\mathrm{T}\mathbf{E}\mathbf{w}$$

The standard deviations, or volatilities, of the portfolio returns, are the square roots of variances, systematic variance, specific variance and total variance:

$$\sigma_P = \sqrt{\mathbf{w}^\mathrm{T}\boldsymbol{\beta}^\mathrm{T}\boldsymbol{\Sigma}\boldsymbol{\beta}\mathbf{w} + \mathbf{w}^\mathrm{T}\mathbf{E}\mathbf{w}}$$

Systematic volatility is the square root of the first term under the radical and specific volatility is the square root of the second term under the radical.

32.9 APPENDIX 1: THE CONCEPTUAL FOUNDATIONS OF PCA

The principle of PCA is to start with the same factors and to transform them into new factors which are independent called principal components. The transformation is linear. It is based on the properties of square symmetric variance–covariance matrices.

We introduce the principles of such transformation starting from the variance–covariance matrix of factors $\mathbf{X}$, $\boldsymbol{\Sigma}$, without detailing the demonstrations. $\boldsymbol{\Sigma}$ can be written $\mathbf{X}^\mathrm{T}\mathbf{X}$ if we use factors $\mathbf{X}$ with zero expectations. As a reminder, $\mathbf{X}$ is the $(T \times K)$ matrix of all observations of all X_k factors. Each column of $\mathbf{X}$ is the set of T observations of the values of each column $(T \times 1)$ X_k factor.

Principal components are new explaining variables, P_k, $k = 1$, K, ordered in a new $(T \times K)$ matrix $\mathbf{P}$. Each $(T \times 1)$ column vector made of all T values of the new factor P_k. The relation between $\mathbf{X}$ and $\mathbf{P}$ is $\mathbf{P} = \mathbf{X}\mathbf{W}$, where $\mathbf{W}$ is a matrix defined as the matrix of Eigen vectors of $\boldsymbol{\Sigma}$. Eigen vectors of a square symmetric matrix are special vectors $\mathbf{w}$ such that $\boldsymbol{\Sigma}\mathbf{w} = \lambda\mathbf{w}$. In plain words, $\mathbf{w}$ is a vector which is such that, multiplied by the original matrix, it becomes the same vector scaled by the constant λ. The scalar λ is called an Eigen value of $\boldsymbol{\Sigma}$. There are K Eigen vectors, as many as the initial factors $\mathbf{X}$.

Furthermore, the Eigen vectors $\mathbf{w}$ are orthogonal in matrix algebra, meaning independent in statistical words. Then, matrix algebra shows that the variance–covariance matrix $\mathbf{P}^\mathrm{T}\mathbf{P}$ becomes a diagonal matrix named $\boldsymbol{\Lambda}$. A diagonal matrix is such that the non-zero elements are on the diagonal and that all off-diagonal elements are zero. The on-diagonal elements are the Eigen values of the original matrix $\boldsymbol{\Sigma}$. By ordering the Eigen vectors in $\mathbf{W}$, we can find a diagonal matrix such that these Eigen values are decreasing when moving down along the diagonal.

The final result is that the variance–covariance matrix of the factors $\mathbf{P}$ collapses to the diagonal matrix Λ, meaning that the new factors have zero covariances, or are independent.

Reverting to standard linear functions, we drop the time dimension and use X_k and P_k as factors. Each principal component P_k is a linear combination of the original X_k. Finally, we have a new factor model with P_k as factors, and all factors are now independent. We use as coefficients of the principal components η_k, since these sensitivities are not the same as the original sensitivities:

$$Y = \Sigma_{k=1,K}\eta_k P_k + \varepsilon$$

The general variance using the principal components becomes simply the sum of all diagonal elements λ_k, or Eigen values, of the diagonal matrix Λ, which are the variances of each component ordered in decreasing values. In statistical terms, we simply write that the variance of independent principal components is the sum of their variances. The fraction of total variance explained by the m first P_k is the sum of the first largest λ_k, with $k = 1, m$. In many instances, the first m terms make up most of the total general variances. In other instances, we might want to use all terms for taking advantage of the simplified formula of the total systematic variance.

32.10 APPENDIX 2: PORTFOLIO GENERAL RISK, ORTHOGONAL FACTORS

Generalizing to K factors, and using the weighted sensitivities, η_{2P}, the general variance simply sums up the factor variances weighted with the new factor loadings:

$$\sigma^2(Y_P) = \Sigma_{k=1,K}(\eta_{kP})^2\sigma^2(P_k)$$

The systematic variance is a simple vector product. The first vector is the row $(1 \times N)$ vector of all N squared coefficients, $(\eta_{ki})^2$, and the second vector has all factor variances in column.

			$\sigma^2(P_1)$
			$\sigma^2(P_2)$
			...
			$\sigma^2(P_K)$

| $(\eta_{k1})^2$ | $(\eta_{k2})^2$ | ... | $(\eta_{kN})^2$ | | $\Sigma_{k=1,K}(\eta_{ki})^2\sigma^2(P_k)$ |

The formula can be written in matrix format: $(\mathbf{\eta}^2)^T\mathbf{\sigma}^2(\mathbf{P})$. The specific risk should be calculated from the variance–covariance matrix of residuals.

33

Dependencies and Copula Functions

Numerous applications of dependencies include portfolio models and diversification effects, and VaR for market risk and credit risk. Diversification effects of portfolio are highly sensitive to dependencies between values, instruments or credit events. The correlation methodology is widely implemented. The copula methodology is more powerful in that it models dependencies of variables independently of the nature of their distributions, and allows the use of different distribution functions than normal functions. The methodology therefore allows dealing with distribution with fat tails and asymmetrical distributions such as credit risk losses.

The copula methodology is not easy to grasp intuitively. Helpful publications, not excessively mathematical, include [18] and [2]. We address the methodology here with a light weight on the mathematical side and try to provide intuitions of what the method achieves. We illustrate the methodology with the classical bivariate case and the Gaussian copula throughout the chapter because it relies on familiar Gaussian formulas, although other copulas are more useful in some cases, for example for capturing correlation in fat tails and skewness of distributions. In this chapter, we focus on the case of two variables, which is sufficient to understand the basic principles and we reduce the mathematical formulation to well-known normal distributions, without loss of generality.

Section 33.1 summarizes the key benefits of the copula approach. Section 33.2 describes the general notations used in this chapter. Section 33.3 provides definitions of copula functions using bivariate functions. The copula function $C(x, y)$ of two variables X and Y is a joint cumulative probability function defined by:

$$C(x, y) = P[(X \leq x) \text{ and } (Y \leq y)]$$

which is often defined as a function of two uniform standard variables U and V representing the cumulative distribution of X and Y, respectively. Depending on notations used, there are various forms of the same copula functions that are listed here for convenience. A major important property appears when changing notations: the problem of simulating of dependent variables following some univariate functions, which can be normal but need not be, becomes the problem of simulating as many uniform standard variables, following $U(0, 1)$, with the same dependency. The copula density function is then defined as the ratio of the joint probability of two variables that are dependent to the ratio of the joint probability of the same two variables if they were independent. The definition is possibly one of the most intuitive ways of understanding copula functions. The ratio is higher than one as long as variables are positively dependent on each other. The conceptual generalization to any number of variables is straightforward, although the implementation gets more complex, and we stick in all subsequent sections to the bivariate case.

Section 33.4 discusses extensively the bivariate Gaussian copula function, whose main attractive property is that the explicit form of the copula or the copula densities are based on the familiar Gaussian distribution. The choice is made for convenience only since the Gaussian copula is not necessarily the one that adds more value to the copula approach. The copula density function has an explicit form.

Section 33.5 addresses conditional normal distributions derived from the copula function. When one variable is defined, the conditional distribution of the second variable is determined. The properties of the conditional normal distribution are extensively used in subsequent chapters and all details of such distributions are expanded here. Moreover, they provide the entry point for conducting simulations under the copula approach. The idea is that it allows one to define a second uniform variable conditional on the value of another uniform standard variable. The process provides the closed-form formula that makes two uniform variables dependent. Once we know how to embed dependency between two uniform standard variables, U and V, it is easy to move back to any univariate function by taking the inverse function of such uniform variables, using the distribution functions that are of interest, normal or not. The principles for simulation of dependent pairs of variables follows, starting from the simulation of two independent standard uniform variables and making them dependent through the formula that embed dependency.

The simulation techniques based on the copula approach follows in the next chapter, which deals with simulations using the various methods to model dependencies.

Contents

33.1 KEY BENEFITS OF COPULA DEPENDENCY

Copula functions have some distinctive features that make them essential when dealing with portfolio risk. Copula functions are the most general method for dealing with dependency between variables. They allow modeling dependency between variables that do not follow the same distributions, inclusive of non-normal distributions. The copula functions can be used with different distributions of variables, and those distributions are called univariate marginal distributions. When considering only two variables once the copula function is defined and the first distribution is defined, the second distribution is determined and is conditional on the first distribution.

The key benefit of copula functions resides in the separation between the dependence structure and the univariate distributions of the variables. This property allows copula functions to model dependencies for any type of distribution functions. Copula functions separate the dependency structure from the standalone distribution functions followed by each variable. They are used when we need to model dependencies with non-normal distributions, although the copula methodology also works for normal distributions. It is worth remembering that the Cholevsky decomposition applies only to normal variables. (See Chapter 34.)

A major theoretical result that allows separating dependency from marginal distributions is the Sklar's theorem[1], which states, in plain words, that, for any couple of distribution functions, normal or not normal, there is a unique copula function. The theorem restricts the choice of copula functions once marginal (univariate) distribution functions defined. However, several copula functions can be used depending on the nature of the distribution functions. There are many examples of dependency which cannot be dealt with by the usual normal distributions.

- Dependency between times to default of two different obligors, since they follow an exponential distribution.
- Dependency between with extreme events. The normal distribution fails to capture such rare events, and their dependency for extreme values. Fat tails are better modeled with student distributions.
- Asymmetric dependency for extreme events. The dependence between some variables is not symmetric, meaning that it differs depending on whether we have up co-movements or down co-movements. When equity returns are down, they tend to be more dependent than when they are up. Some copula functions allow dealing with such asymmetric co-movements.
- Copula functions correct the deficiencies of correlations, which have drawbacks due to the linear dependency that they measure.

Copula functions apply wherever the classical covariances or correlation matrices apply: portfolio return volatility, portfolio VaR, plus any case when we deal with correlated variables and factors. For example, the issue is identical when pricing a derivative depending on two or more dependent variables, such as a digital option triggered when two market variables together reach threshold values (strikes). In credit risk, the issue is the same with the structural model of default, since the joint default of two obligors occurs when the asset values of the two firms become, together, equal or lower than their default points.

---

1 See [18].

A major application of copula function is the simulation of dependent variables. We will see that simulations of dependent variables, normal or non-normal, follow a simple principle. The problem of simulating of N dependent variables following the univariate F, which can be normal but need not be, becomes the problem of simulating N uniform standard variables, following $U(0, 1)$, with the same dependency. Simulations are deferred to the next chapter on simulations.

33.2 REMINDERS AND NOTATIONS

For random variables, the following conventions, used in the chapter on probability distributions, are used.

- Capital letter X: random variable.
- Normal letter x: a particular value x of the random variable X.
- P is a probability. For example the α percentile, α being a given number between 0 and 1, is such that $P(X \leq \underline{x}) = \alpha$. $P(X = x)$ is the probability that the random variable falls in the infinitesimal range $[x, x + dx]$ or that a discrete variable takes one of its possible values. The upper bound of X matching the α percentile is often called $x(\alpha)$.

The cumulative probability function, CDF, provides $P(X \leq x) = u$, or the probability that a random variable is less than or equal to a threshold. By definition $P(X > x) = 1 - P(X \leq x) = 1 - u$. For univariate distributions, we use $F(x)$ as identical to the CDF, or $P(X \leq x) = u$.

The probability density function, PDF, is the probability that a continuous variable falls within a infinitesimally small range $[x$ to $x + dx]$, or that a discrete variable takes one of its possible values. For univariate distributions, we use $f(x)$ as the density function, or $f(x) = P(x \leq X < dx)$, with dx being a very small interval. The density functions are $f(x) = F'(x)$, where F' is the derivative of the cumulative distribution functions dF/dx. For some specific distributions, some alternate notations might be used. The normal distribution is $N(\mu, \sigma)$ where the mean of the random variable X is μ and the standard deviation is σ. The corresponding notations for a standard normal distribution are $\Phi(x) = P(X \leq x)$ and $\varphi(x)$.

Joint distribution functions provide the probability that events occur jointly. When considering two random variables, with PDFs $f(x)$ and $f(y)$ respectively, there is a joint probability that $X = x$ and $Y = y$. The joint probability is $P(X = x$ and $Y = y)$. It is designated by the joint PDF($X = x, Y = y$), or, in a more compact form, by $f(x, y)$. Similarly, with CDFs $F(X)$ and $F(Y)$, there is a joint probability that X and Y are such that $X \leq x$ and $Y \leq y$, or $P(X \leq x$ and $Y \leq y)$. This joint probability is cumulative, designated as joint CDF(x, y), or, in compact form, $F(x, y)$. Note that joint probabilities, cumulative or not, depend on the dependency between X and Y. For example, for independent variables, $f(x, y) = f(x)f(y)$. When the variables are not independent, $f(x, y)$ differs from the product $f(x)f(y)$.

33.3 DEFINITION OF COPULA FUNCTIONS

A copula function is a joint cumulative distribution of two or more variables. We start with the definition of bivariate functions X and Y.

33.3.1 Bivariate Copula

We consider two random variables X and Y. When considering each variable X or Y in isolation, we ignore any dependence of X or Y on the other variable. Their univariate distributions are called unconditional distributions. The distribution of one variable, conditioned by a given value of the other variable, is the conditional or marginal distribution. The two random variables X and Y follow the unconditional CDFs $F_1(X)$ and $F_2(Y)$ and their PDFs are $f_1(X)$ and $f_2(X)$. There are no restrictions on F_1 and F_2, which are univariate distribution functions. The functions can be normal but they do not need to be.

The usual properties of unconditional univariate distributions apply. The cumulative density functions are $P(X \leq x) = F_1(x)$ and $P(Y \leq y) = F_2(y)$. The joint probability that two variables X and Y are, respectively, less than the threshold values x and y is expressed as joint $P[(X \leq x)$ and $(Y \leq y)]$, or equivalently joint $CDF(x, y)$. We use $F(x, y)$ to represent this joint probability.

$$\text{joint } P[(X \leq x) \text{ and } (Y \leq y)] = F(x, y)$$

The copula function $C(x, y)$ is defined as this joint probability:

$$C(x, y) = F(x, y) = P[(X \leq x) \text{ and } (Y \leq y)]$$

There are various types of copula functions. An obvious example of a copula function is that of independent variables. It collapses to a simple product of the two marginal CDF F_1 and F_2 or densities f_1 and f_2. For independent variables, the joint probability $F(x, y)$ is simply the product of the cumulative distribution functions $F_1(x)$ and $F_2(y)$. The copula function is:

$$C(x, y) = F(x, y) = F_1(x)F_2(y)$$

The notation for conditional distributions is $F(X \mid Y)$ for cumulative functions or $f(X \mid Y)$ for density functions. If the variables are dependent, the conditional probability of Y given X, or $P(X \leq x \mid y) \neq F_1(x)$, follows the rule of conditional probabilities:

$$P(X = x \mid Y = y) = P(X \leq x \text{ and } Y = y)/P(Y = y)$$

The joint probability density (JDP) is assigned to the simultaneous event $(X \leq x$ and $Y \leq y)$. When X and Y are independent, the JDP collapses to the product of the two probabilities that $X = x$ and $Y = y$. Otherwise, it differs from the product, and can be higher, when X and Y tend to co-vary, or lower when they tend to vary inversely.

33.3.2 Properties of Copula Functions

A copula function depends on the cumulative density functions, or cumulative probabilities that $X \leq x$ and $Y \leq y$. For continuous functions, those summations are integrals of the joint distribution densities, and for discrete variables, they are sums with countable elements. This makes them difficult to manipulate, which is why most of the time we use the so-called "copula density functions," as explained subsequently. Copula functions have some simple properties.

- The maximum value of the copula is 1 since it is a joint probability.
- The copula value is zero whenever one of the arguments is zero. If the cumulative probability attached to the value x of variable X is zero, the variable cannot take any value up to x. Since the joint probability is $F(X, Y) = P(X \leq x) P(Y \leq y \mid X \leq x)$, the first term is zero, and the second being always bounded by 1, the product is zero.
- Hence, copula functions take values between 0 and 1, like any probability.
- When the value of one of the arguments is 1, such as $P(X \leq x) = 1$, the joint probability simplifies to $F(X, Y) = P(Y \leq y)$, and the copula takes the value of the other argument.

33.3.3 Distribution Functions and Percentiles

For a continuous distribution of a variable with upper and lower bounds being minus infinity and plus infinity, the CDF $F(x)$ is S-shaped and the cumulative distribution $u = F(x)$ monotonously increases when u moves from 0 to 1 (Figure 33.1). Therefore, there is a unique relation between u and x. If we start from a value x of the random variable, we obtain u from $u = F(x)$, which is the "u percentile" of x, such that the probability $P(X \leq x) = u$. Accordingly, the probability $P(X > x) = 1 - u$. If we start from a standard uniform number u, or the u percentile of the random variable X, then $x = F^{-1}(u)$. The value x represents a particular value of the random variable X and u represents a cumulative probability $P(X \leq x) = u$, or the u percentile of X.

Summarizing the essentials, the value of any cumulative probability $F(x)$ can be seen as the value u of a uniform standard distribution $U(0, 1)$. Any value of the probability u, from $U(0, 1)$, matches a value x of X such that $u = F(x)$. The reciprocal is also true. Each value of a random variable x can be written as the inverse of the percentile u: $x = F^{-1}(u)$ since $F(X)$ is increasing and monotonous with the values x of X. In these notations, u is always a probability, or percentile, while x is always the value of the random variable. Mapping any univariate cumulative distribution of X to a value u following $U(0, 1)$ is a procedure used repeatedly. For simulating any random variable whose distribution is known, the first step is to simulate a standard uniform variable u and determine x as $x = F^{-1}(u)$.

For copula functions, we need to use two variables at least for modeling dependencies. Any pair of values, $U = u$ or $V = v$, matches a pair of values of the variables x or y with values

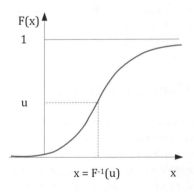

FIGURE 33.1 Relation between $F(x)$ and $F^{-1}(u)$

u and v within $(0, 1)$, or $x = F^{-1}(u)$ and $y = F^{-1}(v)$. The values u and v are percentiles of each distribution $F_1(x)$ and $F_2(y)$.

There are alternate forms of a copula function depending on which arguments we use. The same generic bivariate copula above takes the form:

$$C(x, y) = F(x, y) = F[F_1^{-1}(u), F_2^{-1}(v)]$$

The percentiles are used extensively in risk models where we use a risk metric that is associated with a confidence level, u, such as VaR models. The confidence level is the percentile, or the probability that the random variable is lower or equal to a threshold point $x(u)$ with a given probability, or $P(X \leq x) = u$. In VaR models, u is the small probability such that the variable falls below the threshold x. The value x is the potential loss not exceeded except with a small probability $\alpha = u$. The complement to 1 of the confidence level, $1 - u$, is the probability that the random variable exceeds a threshold with a given probability $P(X > x) = 1 - u$.

33.3.4 Various Forms of Bivariate Copula Functions

A copula function can be written in various ways, using either the values of the original univariate distributions (x and y) or the cumulative probabilities themselves (u and v). The following notations for the copula function $C(x, y)$ are identical:

- As a function of the values of the variables following such distributions, $X = x$ and $Y = y$, the copula is $C(x, y)$.
- As a function of the cumulative distributions, $C(x, y) = C[F_1(x), F_2(y)]$.
- As a function of the values of the percentiles, u and v of x and y, both within the interval $(0, 1)$, such that $u = F_1^{-1}(x)$ and $v = F_2^{-1}(y)$, $C(x, y) = C(u, v)$.
- As a function of the inverse of the probabilities $F_1(x), F_2(y)$, $C(x, y) = C[F_1^{-1}(x), F_2^{-1}(y)]$.

The four forms are equivalent:

$$C(x, y) = C[F_1(x), F_2(y)] = C(u, v) = C[F_1^{-1}(x), F_2^{-1}(y)]$$

When using uniform standard variables, u and v always represent probabilities within 0 and 1 whether x and y are always values of random variables following univariate distribution functions.

The important result is that the problem of simulating N dependent variables following the univariate F, which can be normal but need not be, becomes the problem of simulating N uniform standard variables, following $U(0, 1)$, with the same dependency.

33.3.5 The Bivariate Copula Function: Expanded Form

Starting from the definition of a copula function, various forms of copula functions are used: the expanded form, the compact form based on standard uniform functions, and the copula density function.

In general, the copula function has arguments CDF functions $F_1(X)$ and $F_2(Y)$ and is equal to $C[F_1(x), F_2(y)]$. The arguments are functions. Expanding the notations helps to make the function more explicit, but involves integrals. Dealing with the integral of density functions is quite complex. Hence, we move next to the copula density function, which avoids such integral forms.

With continuous univariate distribution functions, the arguments involve integrals from the lower bounds of X and of Y up to values x and y, respectively:

$$F_2(y) = \int_{lowerbound}^{y} f_2(s)\,ds, \; F_2(x) = \int_{lowerbound}^{x} f_2(s)\,ds$$

F_1 and F_2 are, respectively, distribution functions of x and y. When moving to joint probabilities, the expanded form of the copula function $C[x, y]$ is the joint CDFs $F_1(X)$ and $F_2(Y)$, or $F(X, Y)$, given the dependency between the two variables.

$$C[x, y] = \int_{lowerbound}^{x} \int_{lowerbound}^{y} f(s,t)\,ds\,dt$$

The variable s and t are intermediate variables that serve for integration. The JDF $f(s, t)$ is the joint density function of the pair of values of $X = s$ and $Y = t$.

33.3.6 The Copula Density Function

The copula density function is the joint density function of X and Y, $f(x, y)$. For independent variables, the joint density function is the product of the densities of the marginal distribution functions, using $X = x$ and $Y = y$: $F(x, y) = f(x)f(y)$. For dependent variables, it increases with the positive dependency between those variables. The copula density is the ratio of the joint density to the product of the two densities[2].

$$c[F_1(x), F_2(y)] = \frac{f(x, y)}{f_1(x) f_2(y)}$$

The copula density provides an intuitive view of copula functions. Whenever the variables are independent it is equal to 1. When the joint $f(x, y)$ is higher than the product, which happens when X and Y co-vary together, it is higher than 1. When the opposite holds, X and Y vary inversely, and the copula density is lower than 1.

The next paragraphs deal with the Gaussian copula example and detail all its forms, expanded or compact, starting with remainders of the bivariate normal distribution.

---

2 In general, it is shown, in the appendix, that the joint density function $f(x, y)$ is the product of the two density functions multiplied by the second derivative of the copula C with respect to F_1 and F_2:

$$f(x, y) = f_1(x)f_2(y)\frac{\partial^2 C[F_1, F_2]}{\partial F_1 \, \partial F_2}$$

33.3.7 Generalization to Several Variables

When extending copula to more than two variables, it is convenient to designate variables using subscripts i, with i varying from 1 to N, N being the number of variables. If we use the values of the variables $X_i = x_i$, each following $F_i(X_i)$:

$$C(x_1, x_2, \ldots, x_N) = F(x_1, x_2, \ldots, x_N)$$

The same copula is also expressed as a function of the percentiles u_i of each variable:

$$C(x_1, x_2, \ldots, x_N) = F(x_1, x_2, \ldots, x_N) = F[F_1^{-1}(u_1), F_2^{-1}(u_2), \ldots, F_2^{-1}(u_N)]$$

Throughout this chapter we deal with bivariate copula functions, and avoid subscripting the variables, using different letters for the two variables (u and v and x and y). However, we keep subscripts for the cumulative distribution functions and the probability density functions, respectively $F_1(X)$ and $F_2(Y)$ and $f_1(x)$ and $f_2(y)$, because they can be other than normal distributions.

The easiest copula function to handle is the Gaussian copula because it takes the same familiar form of an integral of jointly normal functions. The Gaussian copula is detailed hereafter. It leads to formulas similar to those used to correlate normal distributions and serves as an example throughout this chapter. Alternative copula functions deal with student distributed variables or exponentially distributed variables. For convenience, we stick in this chapter to the Gaussian copula.

33.4 BIVARIATE NORMAL STANDARD DISTRIBUTIONS

For the Gaussian copula, it is easier to use standard normal function, with density φ and cumulative function Φ. Standard normal variables have a cumulative distribution noted $\Phi(0, 1)$, where Φ is the normal standard distribution, with mean zero and standard deviation 1. For non-standard normal distributions, we use $N(m, \sigma)$ as CDF, where the arguments are, respectively, the mean and standard deviation.

The normal copula function $C[F_1(x), F_2(y)]$ matches the bivariate normal standard distribution with a defined correlation, using as arguments x and y. A prerequisite is to define the univariate and bivariate normal standard functions. As a reminder we provide below the definitions of the standard normal joint CDF Φ and of the joint PDF φ. We also provide the formula of the bivariate standard normal distribution, with CDF $\Phi(x, y, \varrho)$ and with density $\varphi(x, y, \rho)$, where ρ is the correlation coefficient.

33.4.1 Univariate and Bivariate Normal Distributions

Note that PDF are integral functions, such as for the normal standard distribution:

$$\Phi(x) = \int_{-\infty}^{x} -\frac{1}{\sqrt{2\pi}} \exp\left(-\frac{x^2}{2}\right) dx$$

It is much easier to work with the density of the normal distribution because it has a closed form, which is the argument under the integral summation. The density at x of the normal standard variable is:

$$\varphi(x) = \frac{1}{\sqrt{2\pi}} \exp\left(-\frac{x^2}{2}\right)$$

The density $N(x)$ of a non-standard normal distribution is:

$$N(x) = \frac{1}{\sigma\sqrt{2\pi}} \exp\left[-\frac{(x-\mu)^2}{2^2}\right]$$

Any standard normal variable X_s is related to a non-standard normal variable X through the relation $X_s = (X - m)/\sigma$ or $X = m + \sigma X_s$, where m and σ are, respectively, the mean and standard deviation of the non-standard normal variable X.

Moving to bivariate normal standard distributions, we need to add a correlation coefficient ρ between the two variables and focus on joint distributions, either cumulative or density. Joint distributions depend on mean and expectation plus the correlation ρ. With two variables, the joint distribution is the distribution of any pair of values of x and y. The joint probability density function (joint PDF) of the pair (x, y), or $F(x, y)$ and the joint cumulative distribution functions (joint PCF), or $f(x, y)$, are defined as follows:

$$F(x, y) = P[(X \leq x) \text{ and } (Y \leq y)] = \Phi(x, y, \rho) = \int_{-\infty}^{x} \int_{-\infty}^{y} \varphi(x, y, \rho)\, dx\, dy$$

$$F(x, y) = P[(X = x) \text{ and } (Y = y)] = \text{joint PDF}(x, y) = \varphi(x, y, \varrho)$$

33.4.2 Bivariate Normal Standard Density

The bivariate normal standard density distribution (JDF, normal standard) has an explicit form. It depends on the correlation ρ, with mean 0 and standard deviation 1 for standard normal variables X and Y. It provides the joint probability of having standard normal variables $X = x$ and $Y = y$:

$$\varphi(x, y, \rho) = \left(\frac{1}{2\pi\sqrt{1-\rho^2}}\right) \exp\left[-\frac{x^2 + y^2 - 2\rho xy}{2(1-\rho^2)}\right]$$

Setting the correlation $\rho = 0$, the formula collapses to a simpler form:

$$\varphi(x, y, 0) = \left(\frac{1}{2\pi}\right) \exp\left[-\frac{x^2 + y^2}{2}\right]$$

This expression is simply the product of the two probabilities of $X = x$ and $Y = y$, as is the case with any pair of independent variables.

The graphs in Figures 33.2 and 33.3 show the bivariate normal standard densities with correlation 0 and 0.5. On the two horizontal axes, we have the variables x and y. When the correlation is zero, the horizontal tranches are circles. When the correlation is positive, they become ellipses. Horizontal tranches correspond to a given joint probability. The ellipses (or

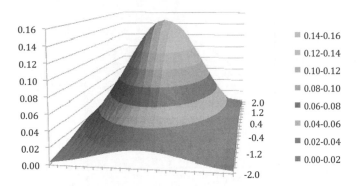

FIGURE 33.2   Bivariate standard normal density, two independent variables

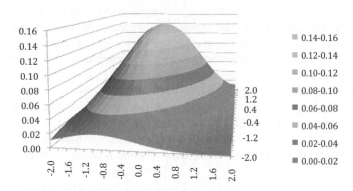

FIGURE 33.3   Bivariate standard normal density, two variables with correlation 0.5

circles when variables are independent) correspond to all pairs of values of which the joint probability of occurrence is identical. Figure 33.3 corresponds to ellipses, elongated from left to right, because the correlation is positive.

33.4.3 The Bivariate Normal Copula

The normal copula is a cumulative distribution that involves an integral for calculating the joint $P[(X \leq x) \text{ and } (Y \leq y)]$. Its form is that of the cumulative bivariate standard normal distribution.

Following the above presentation of the bivariate distribution, the copula density is the joint probability distribution of two normal variables. When such copula density has a fixed value, the pairs of values having such joint probability of occurrence form an ellipse. The copula function is a cumulative distribution and is the probability that both variables are lower than thresholds sets for each of the two variables. If we project the ellipses on the horizontal plane formed by the two variables, we have a projected image of the ellipses on the (x, y) horizontal plane. The copula function can be seen as the rectangle area between the two threshold points of x and y

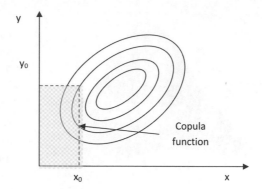

FIGURE 33.4   Representation of a normal copula function

and the lower bounds of these values. Such lower bounds are not represented since both x and y can have negative infinite values. The higher the correlation between the two variables, the more elongated are the ellipses. The copula function increases with positive correlation, since the joint probability that we have couples of values falling within the rectangle increases.

We use this representation for introducing the modeling of joint default probability under the structural model of default[3] (Figure 33.4). Because the ellipses are elongated under positive correlation, the joint frequency increases with the correlation. The same representation serves for representing the probability of a digital option, which takes the value 1 when the two underlying market variables are below the two strike prices, is "in-the-money."

The fully expanded form of the normal copula function is the joint CDF(x, y, ρ):

$$C(x,y,\rho) \equiv (x,y,\rho) = \int_{-\infty}^{x} \int_{-\infty}^{y} \left(\frac{1}{2\pi\sqrt{1-\rho^2}} \right) \exp\left[-\frac{x^2 - 2\rho xy + y^2}{2(1-\rho^2)} \right] dx\, dy$$

In this expression, x and y are values of the standard normal density function, within the interval (support) from $-\infty$ to $+\infty$. The normal copula function, as any other, involves integrals. The joint normal standard density is a closed form formula much easier to deal with.

33.4.4 Forms of the Gaussian Copula

This expanded form can be simplified using the mapping of any CDF function to a standard uniform $U(0, 1)$ function. The second form of the same copula function uses as argument the uniform standard variables U and V, following $U(0, 1)$. Any standard uniform function value, $U = u$ or $V = v$, matches a pair of values, x of X and y of Y:

$$\Phi(x) = u \text{ and } \Phi(y) = v$$

By definition, $u = \Phi^{-1}(x)$ and $v = \Phi^{-1}(y)$, where u and v are values of the uniform standard distributions. They represent the probabilities that the values of the standard normal variables

---

3 In Chapter 52.

X and Y are lower or equal to upper bounds, respectively, x and y. The compact form of the same Gaussian copula is:

$$C(x, y, \rho) = C[\Phi^{-1}(x), \Phi^{-1}(y)] = C[u, v]$$

The analytical expanded formula for the Gaussian copula becomes:

$$C(x,y,\rho) \equiv (x,y,\rho) = \int_{-\infty}^{\Phi_x^{-1}} \int_{-\infty}^{\Phi_y^{-1}} \left(\frac{1}{2\pi\sqrt{1-\rho^2}} \right) \exp\left[-\frac{x^2 - 2\rho xy + y^2}{2(1-\rho^2)} \right] dx\, dy$$

In subsequent applications, we use the compact form of the Gaussian copula function:

$$C(u,v,\rho) = \Phi_2 \left[\Phi^{-1}(u), \Phi^{-1}(v) \right]$$

In this equation, the bivariate normal is called Φ_2 and is identical to $\Phi(x, y, \rho)$. This form can be generalized to N variables, in which case we use N uniform standard variables, and use Φ_N for designating the multivariate Gaussian distribution for n variables.

33.4.5 The Normal Standard Copula Density and the Joint Density of Two Variables

The joint density of two variables provides an intuitive view of copula functions. By definition, the copula density c, using as univariate unconditional normal standard variables X and Y, with the same standard normal density $\varphi(x)$ and $\varphi(y)$, is:

$$c\left[\Phi(x), \Phi(y) \right] = \frac{\varphi(x,y)}{\varphi(x)\varphi(y)}$$

The copula density is the ratio of the joint probability that two normal standard dependent variables X and Y take two values x and y to the joint probability that two normal standard independent variables X and Y take the same values $X = x$ and $Y = y$. The joint probability density of x and y is:

$$\varphi(x, y, \rho) = \varphi(x)\, \varphi(y)\, c[\Phi(x), \Phi(y)]$$

We can find the joint density of x and y from the copula density function multiplied by the univariate standard normal densities of x and y. Replacing the copula density function by its form and each univariate density by their normal standard density, adding up the arguments under the exponential functions and simplifying, we find the joint density of the bivariate standard normal function.

$$\varphi(x,y,\rho) = \left(\frac{1}{2\pi\sqrt{1-\rho^2}} \right) \exp\left[-\frac{x^2 + y^2 - 2\rho xy}{2(1-\rho^2)} \right]$$

The details are expanded in the appendix. Making explicit the difference between the numerator and the denominator of the copula density, we can also write the copula density as:

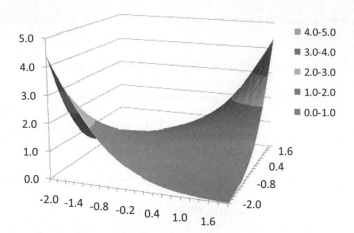

FIGURE 33.5   **Bivariate Gaussian density: correlation 0.5**

$$c\left[\Phi(X=x),\Phi(Y=y)\right]=\frac{\varphi(x,y)}{\varphi(x)\varphi(y)}=\frac{F(X=x,Y=y,0)}{F(X=x,Y=y,\rho)}$$

Note the difference in the last term, where the denominator uses a zero dependency, while the numerator uses the dependency measured by the correlation coefficient between the two normal distributions. The copula density looks inverted compared to the original bivariate density with same positive correlation 0.5 (Figure 33.5).

The maximum values are reached when both variables have high values or when both have low values. The minimum values are reached when one variable reaches its maximum value and the other reaches its minimum value. The maximum values of the copula density can be interpreted as the ratio of the joint density to the product of the univariate marginal densities. When the ratio is close to one, there is almost independence, which occurs in the center of the distribution when both x and y are close to zero, the mean of the two variables. The joint probability of being in this area gets close to the product of the standalone probabilities of each variable.

On the other hand, when the ratio is much higher, the joint density is much higher than the product of the two densities, because of the positive correlation. Joint co-movements are more likely and joint inverse movements less likely than under independence, with positive correlation.

Note that, with correlation zero, the copula density collapses the value 1 since the joint distribution is exactly the product of the two standard normal densities and the copula density is the ratio of these two densities (ratio of joint density to product of marginal densities). Then: $\varphi(X=x)\varphi(Y=y)=\varphi(X=x,\ Y=y)$ and the ratio is 1 (Figure 33.6).

$$c\left[\Phi(X=x),\Phi(Y=y)\right]=\frac{\varphi(x,y)}{\varphi(x)\varphi(y)}=\frac{JDF(X=x,Y=y,0)}{JDF(X=x,Y=y,0)}$$

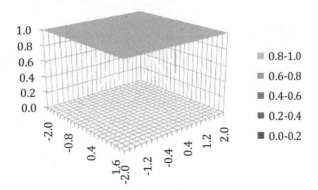

FIGURE 33.6 Copula density equal to 1 under independence

33.5 CONDITIONAL PROBABILITY FROM THE COPULA DENSITY

In this section, we use the letters Y and Z for the two random variables because they fit the notations of factor models, and because they make it easier to compare the one-factor model, the factor being Z, to the following expressions. The two variables Y and Z follow the joint density of the bivariate standard normal function. We know the joint density of a bivariate normal distribution expressed as its closed form function and using the copula density function. The joint density of a bivariate normal standard distribution is:

$$\varphi(Y,Z,\rho) = \left(\frac{1}{2\pi\sqrt{1-\rho^2}}\right) \exp\left[-\frac{Y^2 + Z^2 - 2\rho YZ}{2(1-\rho^2)}\right]$$

The copula density function is:

$$\varphi(Y, Z, \rho) = \varphi(Y)\,\varphi(Z)\,c[\Phi(Y), \Phi(yZ)]$$

The conditional densities are obtained by setting a particular value to the conditioning variable Z.

33.5.1 Conditional Density of Normal Bivariate

Conditional densities are obtained by setting a value to the conditioning variable Z. They result in conditional normal distributions of Y. Those can be seen as vertical tranches of the bell shape of the bivariate normal distribution, each tranche being defined by a value of Z. The other variable Y follows a normal distribution conditioned by the value of Z. Each of these conditional curves is a normal distribution, which is not standard. The conditional distributions of Y are shown in Figure 33.7 as vertical tranches for different values of Z. They have different means, increasing with $Z = z$, and a constant variance depending on the correlation, as explained below.

It is useful to remember that Y and Z follow a standard bivariate distribution with correlation ρ if and only if both variables, X and Z, are normal standard:[4]

---

4 See also the Cholesky decomposition in Chapter 34.

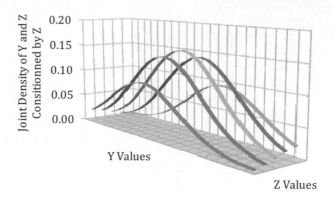

FIGURE 33.7 **Conditional distribution function of** *Y* **when** *Z* **is given**

$$Y = \rho Z + \sqrt{(1 - \rho^2)}X$$

Assigning a value z to Z, the mean of Y conditioned by Z is $E(Y \mid Z) = \rho z$ since $E(X) = 0$. The variance of Y conditional by Z is $V(Y \mid Z) = V[\rho z + \sqrt{(1 - \rho^2)}X] = 1 - \rho^2$ when $Z = z$ is fixed[5]. The conditional variable $(Y \mid Z)$ is non-standard and normal with mean ρz and standard deviation equal to $\sqrt{(1 - \rho^2)}X$ when $Z = z$ is fixed.

Note that the relation, $Y = \rho Z + \sqrt{(1 - \rho^2)}X$, is the same as the one obtained using the one factor model. It is also identical to the form of the Cholevsky decomposition for generating correlated normal variables Y and Z (Chapter 34). This relation is the conditional distribution of Y conditioned by Z. All three approaches converge to the same conditional form for the conditional distribution of Y.

When the conditioning variable $Z = z$ increases, the mean of $(Y \mid Z)$ increases if the correlation is positive, and the variance is unchanged. The variance of $(Y \mid Z)$ declines when the absolute value of correlation increases. When the correlation is 1, the two variables are perfectly correlated and Z determines Y.

We use $N(m, \sigma)$ for the cumulative PDF of a non-standard variable with mean m and standard deviation σ and Φ for the cumulative PDF of a normal standard variable. Y follows N and Y_s follows Φ. Y_s is a monotonous increasing linear function of Y. Therefore, for each value y_s of Y_s such that $P(Y_s \leq y_s) = \alpha$, where α is a percentile of the normal standard variable Y_s, conditional on a value z of Z, there is a value of y of Y such that $P(Y \leq y) = \alpha$.

33.5.2 Conditional Distributions and Simulations

The essential property of copula functions implemented for simulations is that we transform the problem of simulating dependent variables following normal or non-normal distributions into a problem of simulating dependent uniform variables. This results from the equality:

$$P(Y \leq y, Z \leq z) = C[F(y), F(z)] = C(u, v)$$

In this equation, F is the distribution of Y and Z, and u and v are uniform standard values representing percentiles. The central building block for simulation becomes the simulation of dependent uniform standard variables.

---

5 The variance of the constant ρz is fixed when z is fixed. The variance of X is 1.

The process always starts from the simulation of a first uniform standard variable U. A second uniform standard variable V should comply with the dependency embedded in the copula function, with distribution conditional on the value of the first one. The conditional percentile of V given $U = u$ is: $P(V \le v \mid U = u)$. This conditional probability is the conditional copula function $C(V \mid U = u)$. The conditional copula, $P(V \le v \mid U = u) = C(V \mid U = u)$, can be expressed as a function of V and $U = u$.

For proceeding, it is necessary to revert to the variables Y and Z, and consider the copula function in its alternate form: $P(Y \le y, Z \le z) = C[F(y), F(z)]$. The conditional copula function is $C(V \mid V = v) = C(Y, Z \mid Z = z)$. The conditional distribution of Y on Z is standard and not normal. Under the bivariate Gaussian copula, the variable Y is normal standard:

$$Y = \frac{X - \rho z}{\sqrt{1 - \rho^2}}$$

According to the above, Z is the conditioning variable and Y is conditional on Z. The variable $Y = (X - \rho z)/\sqrt{(1 - \rho^2)}$ is the copula conditional on $Z = z$. Consider X and Z, normal standard and independent variables: $Z = \Phi^{-1}(u)$ and $X = \Phi^{-1}(v)$, where u and v are independent uniform standard variables. The issue is to find the conditional distribution of V given U.

The dependency between Y and Z is materialized by the above relation between Y, X and Z. It is the conditional copula on $U = u$. It can be written as follows because X and Z are normal standard:

$$C(V \mid U = u) = \alpha(z) = \Phi \left\{ \frac{\Phi^{-1}(v) - \rho \Phi^{-1}(u)}{\sqrt{1 - \rho^2}} \right\}$$

This equation represents a percentile $C(V \mid U = u) = P(V \le v \mid U = u)$. The conditional copula is a percentile:

$$C(V \mid U = u) = C(Y \mid Z = z) = \alpha$$

The conditional percentile is also called the conditional Gaussian copula.

$$\alpha = \Phi \left\{ \frac{\left[\Phi^{-1}(v) - \rho \, \Phi^{-1}(u) \right]}{\sqrt{1 - \rho^2}} \right\}$$

In this equation, the percentile α is given and is equal to the normal standard cumulative function of the argument within brackets in the right-hand term of the equation. For extracting the value of V conditional on U, we write that $\Phi^{-1}(\alpha)$ equals the argument within brackets on the right-hand side. From $\Phi^{-1}(\alpha)$, we isolate $\Phi^{-1}(v)$:

$$\Phi^{-1}(v) = \rho \Phi^{-1}(u) + \sqrt{(1 - \rho^2)} \Phi^{-1}(\alpha)$$

This relation determines V conditional on U, for the given percentile α. Taking the inverse, the value v is the cumulative normal standard function:

$$v = \Phi \left[\rho \Phi^{-1}(u) + \sqrt{(1 - \rho^2)} \Phi^{-1}(\alpha) \right]$$

Solving for $\Phi^{-1}(u)$:

$$\Phi^{-1}(u) = \frac{\Phi^{-1}(v) - \sqrt{(1-\rho^2)}\,\Phi^{-1}(\alpha)}{\rho}$$

Note that the two inverse functions, $\Phi^{-1}(v)$ and $\Phi^{-1}(v)$, now depend on $\Phi^{-1}(\alpha)$, making them dependent. These equations resolve the issue and the value of v of V is now dependent on U.

Originally, we need to simulate independent uniform variables U and V. Starting with a value of $U = u$, we search the value v of V conditional on U. The variable $(V \mid U)$ and U are dependent, the dependency being embedded in the copula function.

This could be done by reverting to Y and Z, but Y is not standard normal. By sticking to U and V, we can use the normal standard function and its inverse. Note that $X = \Phi^{-1}(v)$ and $Z = \Phi^{-1}(v)$. The input for calculating u and v is the percentile α, distributed as a uniform standard variable. The percentile α is an intermediate variable, which is standard uniform.

Moving to the simulation problem of dependent U and V, the algorithm is as follows. First, we generate random values of U. Then we simulate random values of a second uniform variable, which is called U_2 in subsequent applications. U_2 is an intermediate variable representing the random percentile α. From these two values, we find $V = V(U, U_2)$, where $V = v$ is a percentile of the cumulative standard normal. The uniform variables U and V are dependent. Next we show an example of simulation of two standard uniform variables.

33.5.3 Application: Simulating Two Uniform Standard Variables with Conditional Copula

Before proceeding, we need to be reminded that simulating two uniform standard variables that are dependent allows the generation of dependent variables Y and Z following any distribution, normal or not, by looking at those two dependent uniform variables as percentiles of the distribution function F of the two "targets" Y and Z. The process for simulating non-normal dependent variables starts with the above building block and proceeds by deriving the simulated values of Z and Y, writing that $F(Z) = U$ and $F(Y) = V$. The two "target" dependent variables are $Z = F^{-1}(U)$ and $Y = F^{-1}(V)$.

The core building block consists of simulating the dependent uniform standard variables, U and V. The process can be decomposed as follows. We start by simulating $U = U_1$, a random uniform standard number within $(0, 1)$ using a random number generator (such as the one in Excel™). Say that $u = u_1 = 0.525$. Next, we simulate a second random uniform standard number, which represents the percentile α, using a random number generator. We find $U_2 = u_2 = 0.810$. This simulation provides only independent variables U_1 and U_2. U_2 is an intermediate variable. The third step calculates the argument of the cumulative standard normal function of which percentile is v since:

$$\Phi^{-1}(v) = \rho\,\Phi^{-1}(u_1) + \sqrt{(1-\rho^2)}\,\Phi^{-1}(u_2)$$

In this equation, $u_1 = 0.525$ and $u_2 = 0.810$. We need to input the correlation of the Gaussian copula. Let us use $\rho = 70\%$. The numerical calculation becomes:

$$70\%\,\Phi^{-1}(0.525) + \sqrt{(1-70\%^2)}\,\Phi^{-1}(0.810)$$

Replacing:

$$\Phi^{-1}(0.525) = 0.06334$$

$$\Phi^{-1}(0.810) = 0.87809$$

$$70\%\Phi^{-1}(0.525) + \sqrt{(1 - 70\%^2)}\,\Phi^{-1}(0.810) = 0.88868$$

Finally, the second dependent uniform variable V is:

$$v = \Phi\left[70\%\Phi^{-1}(0.525) + \sqrt{(1 - 70\%^2)}\,\Phi^{-1}(0.810)\right] = 0.53533$$

The algorithm is summarized below.

ρ	70%
$U = U_1$	0.52525
U_2	0.81005
$\Phi^{-1}(U_1)$	0.06334
$\Phi^{-1}(U_2)$	0.87809
$\rho\,\Phi^{-1}(U_1) + \sqrt{(1 - \rho^2)}\,\Phi^{-1}(U_2)$	0.65901
V	0.74505

By running simulations several times, for example 200 times, it is possible to check that the random uniform variables U and V are dependent. The scatter plot of U and V is elongated along the first diagonal, illustrating graphically the positive dependence (Figure 33.8).

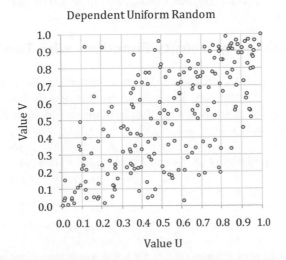

Dependent Uniform Random

FIGURE 33.8   Scatter plot of the simulated random uniform variables

33.6 APPENDIX: COPULA FUNCTION AND COPULA DENSITY

33.6.1 Deriving the Copula Density from Copula Function

Since the copula function C is a joint CDF taking as arguments the CDF functions derivatives with respect to x and y, implies using the chain rule for derivatives: Taking first the derivative with respect to arguments of C, F_1 and F_2, which are functions of x and y, and multiplying each by the derivatives of $F_1(x)$, $F_2(y)$ with respect to their arguments x and y.

The chain rule for derivatives using two functions g and h of x, such that $k(x) = g[h(x)]$ implies that:

$$\partial k(x)/\ \partial x = (\partial g/\partial h)(\partial h/\partial x)$$

In the joint CDF, the copula function C is the equivalent of g and the joint CDF $F_i(x)$ is the equivalent of $h(x)$. Hence with a single function of x, we would write:

$$\partial C(x)/\partial x = (\partial C/\partial F_i)(\partial F_i/\partial x)$$

The rule applies as well to two functions:

$$\text{joint PDF}(x, y) = \{\partial^2 C[F_1(x), F_2(y)]/\partial F_1 \partial F_2\}\ \{[\partial F_1(x)/\partial x]\ [\partial F_2(y)/y]\}$$

$$\text{joint PDF}(x, y) = F_1{}'(x)\ F_2{}'(y)\ \partial^2 C\ [F_1(x), F_2(y)]/\partial F_1(x)\ \partial F_2(y)$$

It should be kept in mind that the CDFs F are themselves functions of x and y, so that the expanded expression of C is:

$$C[F_1(x), F_2(y)] = \partial^2 C[F_1(x), F_2(y)]/\ \partial F_1(x)\ \partial F_2(y)$$

33.6.2 Joint Probability Density Functions with Two Variables

The copula function is a joint CDF, equal to the probabilities that the two variables are lower than or equal to x and y, respectively. The joint probability density function, or joint PDF, is the probability that two variables following the distributions functions $F_1(x_1)$ and $F_2(x_2)$ take the joint pair of values x and y.

$$\text{probability } (X = x \text{ and } Y = y) = \text{joint PDF}(x, y)$$

Starting from the copula function:

$$\text{joint CDF}(x, y) = C[F_1(x), F_2(y)]$$

Because it cumulates the probabilities of X and Y being lower than x and y, it sums up all joint probabilities of couples of values of X and Y lower than x and y. The copula, being a cumulative function, is the integral of the corresponding joint density function that applies to a couple of values x and y. This joint PDF, or joint probability applicable to the pair (x, y), is derived from the copula function by taking the derivatives with respect to the two values x and y, or the second derivatives with respect to x and y respectively:

$$\text{joint PDF}(x, y) = f(x, y) = \partial^2 \text{ joint CDF}(x, y)/\partial x\, \partial y$$

The derivation of this expression is expanded in the next section.

When the CDF of x is $F(x)$, the PDF of x is $f(x) = F'(x)$. Moreover, for two variables, the joint PDF is simply $f(x, y)$. This makes the notations a bit easier to follow. The two univariate density functions are $f_1(x) = F_1'(x)$ and $f_2(y) = F_2'(y)$. Putting those notations together, we get the joint density function as the product of the two density functions multiplied by the second derivatives of the copula C with respect to the CDFs F_1 and F_2:

$$f(x, y) = f_1(x) f_2(y)\, \partial^2\, C[F_1, F_2]/\, \partial F_1\, \partial F_2$$

It is convenient to use as abbreviation for this second derivative of the copula C, the small letter c, defined as:

$$c(F_1, F_2) = \partial^2 C(F_1, F_2)/\partial F_1\, \partial F_2$$

$c(F_1, F_2)$ is the copula density. The copula density provides the joint density function of variables X and Y as the copula density multiplied by the marginal (unconditional and univariate) densities (or probabilities) of X and Y, $F_1(x)$, $F_2(y)$. The copula density is a function of the joint density of two variables and their unconditional (marginal) densities.

$$f_1(x) f_2(y)\, c\, [F_1(x), F_2(y)] = f(x, y)$$

The copula density is:

$$c[F_1(x), F_2(y)] = f(x, y)/f_1(x) f_2(y)$$

This provides the intuitive understanding of the copula density, as the ratio of the joint probability density to the product of the probabilities that $X = x$ and $Y = y$. The product is equal to the joint probability of x and y occurring only when X and Y are independent.

- When X and Y are independent, the copula density takes the value 1.
- When X and Y are positively correlated, the copula density is higher than 1 because the joint probability $f(x, y) > f_1(x) f_2(y)$.
- When X and Y are inversely related, the copula density is lower than 1 because $f(x, y) < f_1(x) f_2(y)$.

33.6.3 Derivation of the Normal Copula Density

The expression of using the above expression of joint normal standard density $f(x, y)$ and of univariate standard normal density $f(x)$ and $f(y)$, is:

$$c\big[F_1(x), F_2(y)\big] = \frac{\left(\dfrac{1}{2\pi\sqrt{1-\rho^2}}\right)\exp\left[-\dfrac{x^2-2\rho\,xy+y^2}{2(1-\rho^2)}\right]}{\left[\dfrac{1}{\sqrt{2\pi}}\exp\left(-\dfrac{x^2}{2}\right)\right]\left[\dfrac{1}{\sqrt{2\pi}}\exp\left(-\dfrac{y^2}{2}\right)\right]}$$

The common factor 2π appears in both numerator and denominator, and can be eliminated. Next, we use the properties of exponential functions:

$$c\big[F_1(x), F_2(y)\big] = \left(\frac{1}{\sqrt{1-\rho^2}}\right)\frac{\exp\left[-\dfrac{x^2-2\rho\,xy+y^2}{2(1-\rho^2)}\right]}{\left[\exp\left(-\dfrac{x^2}{2}\right)\right]\left[\exp\left(-\dfrac{y^2}{2}\right)\right]}$$

$$c\big[F_1(x), F_2(y)\big] = \left(\frac{1}{\sqrt{1-\rho^2}}\right)\exp\left[\frac{-x^2+2\rho\,xy-y^2+x^2(1-\rho^2)+y^2(1-\rho^2)}{2(1-\rho^2)}\right]$$

$$c\big[F_1(x), F_2(y)\big] = \left(\frac{1}{\sqrt{1-\rho^2}}\right)\exp\left[\frac{2\rho xy - x^2\rho^2 - y^2\rho^2}{2(1-\rho^2)}\right]$$

In both cases, once a variable has a fixed value, it is easy to see from the above formulas that the second variable follows a normal distribution. This conditional distribution depends on the assigned value to the first variable and, in the example, on the correlation, which now appears in the bivariate PDF $f(x, y)$.

For moving from density distributions to cumulative distributions, we cumulate the probabilities over the range defined by the lower bound $-\infty$ and the upper bounds of each variable x and y respectively.

33.6.4 Joint Density of a Bivariate Normal Distribution and the Copula Density Function

The copula density function stipulates a joint density of two dependent variables of which we know the unconditional distribution. We apply the formula using two standard normal functions. The formula for the joint density of these variables X and Y, derived from the general copula density formula, is:

$$\varphi(x, y, \rho) = \varphi(x)\,\varphi(y)\,c[\Phi(x), \Phi(y)]$$

We know each function of this product with normal densities. The copula density function is derived in the previous appendix. The densities of standard normal variables follow the usual formulas. We replace all three terms above by these known functions.

$$c\big[\Phi(x), \Phi(y)\big] = \left(\frac{1}{\sqrt{1-\rho^2}}\right)\exp\left[-\frac{(x^2+y^2)\rho^2 - 2\rho\,xy}{2(1-\rho^2)}\right]$$

$$\varphi(x) = \frac{1}{\sqrt{2\pi}} \exp\left(-\frac{x^2}{2}\right)$$

$$\varphi(y) = \frac{1}{\sqrt{2\pi}} \exp\left(-\frac{y^2}{2}\right)$$

Adding up the arguments of the exponential functions, and simplifying, we find the joint density of a bivariate normal standard distribution.

$$\varphi(x, y, \rho) = \left(\frac{1}{2\pi\sqrt{1-\rho^2}}\right) \exp\left[-\frac{x^2 + y^2 - 2\rho xy}{2(1-\rho^2)}\right]$$

33.6.5 Conditional Distributions and Copula

For moving to conditional distributions, we need to set a value for one variable. For example $Y = y$. The conditional density of $(X | y)$ is:

$$P(X = x | Y = y) = f(x | y)$$

Starting from the copula function, we have the cumulative joint distribution:

$$F(x, y) = C[F_1(x), F_2(y)]$$

For conditional cumulative function of X given $Y = y$, all we need to do is to take the derivatives with respect to y. For doing that, we apply the first derivative with respect to x only:

$$F(x | y) = \partial F(x, y)/\partial x = \partial C[F_1(x), F_2(y)]/\partial x$$

34

Simulations with Factor Models or the Copula Approach

This chapter addresses classical simulation techniques based on factor models and explains the simulation of dependent variables using the copula approach. The prerequisite, in both cases, is the simulation of a random variable following a predefined distribution. This module is a common block to all simulation techniques.

Generating correlated random variables can be straightforward with factor models. The dependency of the simulated variables results from the common dependence to factors. The process relies on a linear relation between the explained variables, the factors and the residual. The relation allows generating correlated random factors and random residuals, and deriving the correlated explained variables, using the coefficient of the factor. This is straightforward for a single factor.

For several factors, we need to generate correlated factor values in addition to the residual. The technique is based on the Cholesky decomposition method. The method applies to any number of dependent variables complying with a variance-covariance matrix, provided that they are normally distributed. The Cholesky decomposition allows deriving from independent variables, simulated in a first step, the dependent variables as a linear function of such independent variables. The simulation process collapses to generating as many independent normal variables as necessary and deriving the dependent variables from the former independent normal variables, the coefficients of the linear relation resulting from the decomposition technique.

We apply the principle to the bivariate case using the Gaussian copula to pairs of variables. We consider various cases. The case of two uniform standard variables is a common building block for all other variables. We also implement the copula approach to normal variables, which is a parallel example to the former classical methodologies (factor models and Cholesky methodology). The case with most interest is that of the simulation of dependent times to default, since they follow a non-normal distribution, namely an exponential distribution.

Section 34.1 describes the common module for simulating a random variable using the inverse function and inputting standard uniform random number.

Section 34.2 deals with single one-factor models for generating simulations of a correlated pair of normally distributed variables. The principles for simulating variables from factor models consist of simulating random variables for each factor and another variable that represents the residual of the factor model. If we ignore cross-correlations across residuals, each residual is an independent normal variable. The process is extremely simple with a single factor, used as an example in a first step. If we need to generate correlated normal variables, the Cholesky methodology applies. It starts from as many independent normal variables as necessary and transforms them into dependent variables complying with variance-covariance matrix by making them linear functions of the independent variables. The coefficients depend on the Cholesky methodology. The technique is implemented in this section with two variables first, when the coefficients are easily derived, and to a larger number of variable. The Cholesky methodology principle is the main text, while the details are provided in the appendix (Section 34.7). A summary of the methodology for factor model-based simulations is provided.

Section 34.3 deals with simulation based on the copula approach. The basic principle is simple: the problem of simulating N dependent variables following the univariate F, which can be normal but need not be, becomes the problem of simulating N uniform standard variables, following $U(0, 1)$, with the same dependency. Once this principle is revisited, the simulation algorithm follows. It is based on simulating random independent uniform variables, then plugging in the dependency relation for finding a third uniform standard dependent variable. Once we have two dependent uniform standard variables, we revert to the target variables by inverting the simulated values of the two dependent uniform standard variables.

Subsequent sections provide examples. Section 34.4 deals with the common module to simulations, which consists of generating two dependent uniform variables. Section 34.5 uses the methodology for normal variables for the simple purpose of comparing the procedure with the above Cholesky classical methodology. The final section (Section 34.6) uses the copula approach for simulated dependent times to default. All steps are the same in all three approaches, but only the last example shows the complete set of steps making up the simulation algorithm. Section 34.6 applies to non-normal distributions, using the case of exponentially distributed times to defaults. This last case is used subsequently for modeling default for credit portfolio models.

Contents

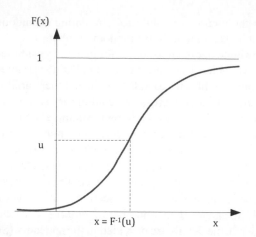

FIGURE 34.1   Relationship between a random variable X and its percentile $u = P(X \leq x)$

34.1 SIMULATIONS AND INVERSE FUNCTIONS

With any distribution $F(x)$, the CDF, or $f(x)$, the PDF, of the random variables X distribution, the CDF is S-shaped and monotonously increasing with the random normal variable (Figure 34.1). Upper and lower bounds of $F(x)$ are 0 and 1 for any X. For any particular value x of X, $x = F^{-1}(u)$ and $u = F(x)$. The variable U is a standard uniform variable. It is the cumulative probability, or u percentile, of X. When starting from x, $u = F(x)$, and is a probability, or the u percentile of X and $x = F^{-1}(u)$. When staring from u within [0, 1], the relationship between the percentile u and x is the inverse cumulative function, or $x = F^{-1}(u)$. There is a unique relation between u and x.

The properties of inverse functions are used for simulating random variables following any distribution function. The process consists of generating random numbers between 0 and 1, all intermediate values having an equal probability. The random numbers follow a standard uniform distribution, when picking up numbers within the interval [0, 1]. Each random value between 0 and 1 is a percentile. Then, for each random uniform value simulated, the matching value of the variable, or u percentile, with a specified distribution function $F(x)$ follows.

These basic relationships allow the generation of any random variable defined by $F(X)$ using random number generator of $U(0, 1)$.

In many instances, we need to generate random variables complying with a variance-covariance matrix. The variables are generally risk factors, such as the asset values of firms or economic factors influencing the default rates of segments.

34.2 SIMULATION OF CORRELATED NORMAL VARIABLES WITH FACTOR MODELS

There are two classical techniques, which are equivalent, for simulating variables with factor models. The first one is based on factor models and the second one uses the Cholevsky decomposition of the variance-covariance matrix. Both techniques serve for generating, through multiple simulations, correlated normal standard variables, complying with a variance-covariance matrix.

This section shows how to run simulations of two correlated variables, with a given correlation coefficient. The correlation coefficient ρ_{ij} between pairs of variables is given. An example of single factor models of two random variables is that of stock returns depending on a common factor, the stock index. All random returns are dependent through this common factor.

We first show how to generate two random normal variables complying with a correlation. A similar procedure can be used for a large number of variables. This is a specific extension of the two-variable case.

34.2.1 Standardizing the Single-factor Model

Each random variable Y_i is a function of a common factor Z and of a specific factor ε_i. The specific factor is independent of the common factor. There is a unique common factor. The factor model states that a variable Y_i is a linear function of the common factor, with a constant and a residual uncorrelated to the common factor.

The factor model equation for a single variable and a single factor is:

$$Y = \beta_0 + \beta Z + e$$

The model is non-standardized. None of the variables are normal standard; the error term has volatility equal to its standard error. General formulas for non-standard normal returns X and Y are:

$$E(Y) = \beta_0 + \beta E(Z) + E(e) = \beta_0 + \beta E(X)$$

$$\sigma_Y^2 = \beta^2 \sigma_X^2 + \sigma_e^2$$

$$\rho_{XZ} = \frac{\text{cov}(X,Z)}{\sigma_x \sigma_Z}$$

$$\rho_{Y\varepsilon} \sigma_x \sigma_e = \text{cov}(X,e) = 0$$

It is easier to work with standard normal variables. The transformation involves a change of variable for each of them. In general, if a variable X follows $N(m, \sigma)$, then the standardized variable of V is $V_S = (V - m)/\sigma$, and $V = V_S \sigma + m$. It is easy to show that we end with a model with same form except that the coefficients are changed[1].

From now on, we use standardized models. We keep the same notations, but the variables Y and X are now standardized. The same equation as above now applies to standardized variables.

$$Y = \beta_0 + \beta X + e$$

---

1 Replacing each non-standard variable, X, Y, using the transformation $V = V_S \sigma + m$, results in a new relation where the coefficients depend on the means and standard deviations of the initial variables. Standard regression packages provide the transformation routinely.

From the expectation equation:

$$E(Y) = E(\beta_0 + \beta X + e) = \beta_0 + \beta E(X) = 0$$

Since $E(X) = 0$, $E(Y) = \beta_0 = 0$, and $\beta_0 = 0$. The variance of Y does not depend on the constant β_0 and is $\sigma_Y^2\ 1 = \beta^2 + \sigma_e^2$. Hence: $\sigma_e^2 = 1 - \beta^2$. The new coefficient β becomes equal to the correlation coefficient ρ since $\beta = \rho\ (\sigma_Y/\sigma_X)$ and $\sigma_X = \sigma_Y = 1$. Since X and Y have variance 1, $\mathrm{cov}(Y, X) = \rho$. Summarizing, given that $\beta_0 = 0$, $\beta = \rho$, the model becomes $Y = \rho X + e$.

The model uses standard normal variables X and Y, but the residual has variance $\sigma(e)^2 = (1 - \rho^2)$ and is not standard. If the variable e follows $N(0, \sigma)$, then $(e - 0)/\sigma$ is the standard normal. Consequently, the new variable, $\varepsilon = e/\surd(1 - \rho^2)$, is standard. The final form of the model with standard normal variables is:

$$Y = \rho X + \surd(1 - \rho^2)\varepsilon$$

For generating two correlated random variables, it is sufficient to start from two independent standard normal variables X and ε and to generate Y according to the above equation. This is a special simple case of the application of the Cholesky decomposition technique.

34.2.2 The Simulation Algorithm for Standardized Normal Variables using Single-factor Models

The simulations of these standard normal variables are normal standard inverse of uniform variables following $U(0, 1)$. With standardized variables, the models take more familiar forms, with Y_i being the standardized stock returns, Z being the standardized index return, and the new residuals X_i being both the same independent standard normal variable.

$$Y_1 = \rho Z + \surd(1 - \rho^2)X_1$$

$$Y_2 = \rho Z + \surd(1 - \rho^2)X_2$$

In these equations, all variables are now normal standard. The issue is to generate random correlated standard normal variables using the standardized factor model. We know that the factor and the residual are normal independent. For generating random returns for a single stock, we simply generate random standard normal variable for the factor and the residual.

The algorithm for generating correlated normal standardized variables Y_1 and Y_2 dependent on a common factor Z collapses to the generation of two normal standard variables with correlation coefficient ρ. The algorithm is the following:

- generate three uniform independent variables following $U(0, 1)$, u_1, u_2, u_3
- take the normal inverse of u_1 for generating a normal standard variable Z
- take the normal inverse of u_2 for generating a normal standard variable X_1
- take the normal inverse of u_3 for generating a normal standard variable X_2

For each set of three values of Z, X_1, X_2, calculate Y_1 and Y_2, using the same standardized equation. The values of Y_1 and Y_2 have correlation ρ. Table 34.1 shows the first 10 simulations.

TABLE 34.1   Sample simulations of two correlated variables depending on a single factor

u_1	u_2	u_3	$\Phi^{-1}(u_1)$ Z_s	$\Phi^{-1}(u_2)$ X_{1s}	$\Phi^{-1}(u_3)$ X_{2s}	Y_{1s} $\rho Z_s+\sqrt{(1-\rho^2)}X_{1s}$	Y_{2s} $\rho Z_s+\sqrt{(1-\rho^2)}X_{2s}$
0.376	0.455	0.725	−0.316	−0.113	0.598	−0.152	0.209
0.984	0.379	0.300	−0.308	−0.525	−0.525	−0.148	−0.592
0.279	0.826	0.757	0.940	0.698	0.698	0.450	1.155
0.024	0.039	0.760	−1.757	0.706	0.706	−0.841	−0.716
0.924	0.731	0.612	0.617	0.283	0.283	0.296	0.633
0.482	0.492	0.056	−0.020	−1.593	−1.593	−0.010	−1.158
0.849	0.437	0.386	−0.158	−0.289	−0.289	−0.076	−0.318
0.476	0.474	0.817	−0.066	0.906	0.906	−0.032	0.604
0.638	0.209	0.842	−0.810	1.002	1.002	−0.388	0.156
0.518	0.034	0.025	−1.829	−1.961	−1.961	−0.876	−2.681

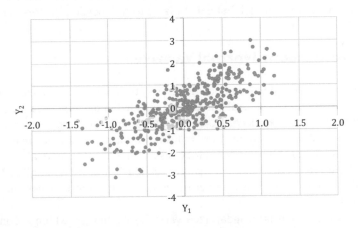

FIGURE 34.2   Simulation of two dependent standardized returns

The first simulations in the case of a single factor are shown in Table 34.1.

Figure 34.2 plots the results of 400 simulations for the pair of standardized returns.

For moving back to non-standard returns, we need to revert from standard to non-standard variables. Since all variables are normal standard, they can be expressed directly as a function of the independent uniform $U(0, 1)$ variables.

$$Y_1 = \rho\Phi^{-1}(u_1) + \sqrt{(1-\rho^2)}\Phi^{-1}(u_2)$$

$$Y_2 = \rho\Phi^{-1}(u_1) + \sqrt{(1-\rho^2)}\Phi^{-1}(u_3)$$

These formulas bridge the gap between the forthcoming copula approach and the classical approach.

The procedure would be similar with several factors since the residual is always independent from the factors. It is even simpler with independent factors because we can proceed exactly as above by generating as many independent normal factors as needed. If the factors are not independent, we need to use the Cholesky technique for generating random values of factors complying with their variance-covariance matrices. The procedure is described below.

34.2.3 The Cholesky Decomposition Method: Two Variables

Cholesky decomposition allows imposing a variance-covariance structure on N random normal standard variables[2]. The process consists of generating N independent variables X_i, standard normal. N other random variables, Y_i, complying with the given variance-covariance structure, are then calculated as linear functions of the independent variables. The dependent variables represent the factors and the X_i serve as intermediate independent standard normal variables.

The Cholevsky decomposition provides the coefficients of these linear combinations. It is expanded in the appendix (Section 34.7). We illustrate the simple case of two variables and show how the coefficients are found in a second step. In this case, we find a form of equation similar to the above single factor model, but generalizing to N dependent factors is much easier.

34.2.4 Two Random Normal Variables

The rationale of the Cholesky decomposition is easy to demonstrate in the case of two variables, and makes the extension to several variables, expanded in the appendix, easier to follow. The starting point of the Cholesky decomposition is the variance-covariance matrix of the dependent variables. The Cholesky decomposition writes the variance-covariance matrix as a product of two triangular matrices. A triangular matrix is such that the off-diagonal terms on one side of the diagonal are zeros. The triangular matrix is called "lower triangular," or $\mathbf{L}$, when the zero terms are above the diagonal. It is upper triangular, with name $\mathbf{U}$, when the zeros are below the diagonal.

Next, we use two normal standardized variables X_1 and X_2, which are independent. The standard normal dependent variables Y_1 and Y_2 complying with the given correlation are linear functions of the independent normal variables. The variance-covariance matrix of two standard normal variables with correlation ρ is:

1	ρ
ρ	1

The elements of the lower triangular matrix $\mathbf{L}$ should be such that $\mathbf{Z} = \mathbf{LX}$, where $\mathbf{X}$ and $\mathbf{Y}$ are the two column vectors (2×1) representing the two sets of variables. The X_i are independent variables and the Z_k are dependent variables. The $\mathbf{L}$ matrix is written with coefficients α_{ij} with the double subscript i (column) and j (row) as:

$$\mathbf{L} = \begin{array}{|c|c|} \hline \alpha_{11} & 0 \\ \hline \alpha_{12} & \alpha_{22} \\ \hline \end{array}$$

---

2 If all variables are normal standardized, the variance–covariance matrix collapses to the correlation matrix, with correlation coefficients varying for each pair of variables and all diagonal terms are equal to 1.

The issue is how to determine the corresponding coefficients α_{ij} such that two new variables, Z_1 and Z_2, are dependent with correlation ρ. The linear relations derived from $\mathbf{Y} = \mathbf{L}\mathbf{X}$ are:

$$Y_1 = \alpha_{11}X_1$$

$$Y_2 = \alpha_{12}X_1 + \alpha_{22}X_2$$

The first equation should comply with the unit variance of the new variable:

$$V(Y_1) = \alpha_{11}^2 = 1$$

This requires $\alpha_{11} = 1$, and $Y_1 = X_1$. Next, the covariance of the new variables is given. Moreover, Y_2, a linear function of the two X_1 and X_2, should have a unit variance, given that the original variables X_1 and X_2 are independent and standardized. These conditions result in two simple equations:

$$\mathrm{Cov}(Y_1, Y_2) = \mathrm{Cov}(\alpha_{11}X_1, \alpha_{12}X_1 + \alpha_{22}X_2) = \alpha_{11}\alpha_{12} = \rho_{12}$$

$$V(Y_2) = \alpha_{12}^2 + \alpha_{22}^2 = 1$$

Since $\alpha_{11} = 1$, we have two unknown α_{12} and α_{22}. The correlation equation imposes that $\alpha_{11}\alpha_{12} = \rho$, therefore $\alpha_{12} = \rho$. The last condition is:

$$\alpha_{12}^2 + \alpha_{22}^2 = 1$$

$$\alpha_{22} = \sqrt{(1 - \rho^2)}$$

We found the lower matrix $\mathbf{L}$ of the Cholesky decomposition:

$$\mathbf{L} = \begin{array}{|c|c|} \hline 1 & 0 \\ \hline \rho & \sqrt{(1 - \rho^2)} \\ \hline \end{array}$$

For finding the dependent variables, we write that:

$$\begin{array}{|c|} \hline Z_1 \\ \hline Z_2 \\ \hline \end{array} = \begin{array}{|c|c|} \hline 1 & 0 \\ \hline \rho & \sqrt{(1 - \rho^2)} \\ \hline \end{array} \times \begin{array}{|c|} \hline X_1 \\ \hline X_2 \\ \hline \end{array}$$

The matrix equation $\mathbf{Y} = \mathbf{L}\mathbf{X}$, with $\mathbf{L}$ being the lower triangular matrix with above coefficients, $\mathbf{X}$ being the column vector of X_i variables, and $\mathbf{Z}$ being also a column vector of Z_j variables defines the two variables Y_1, Y_2, as linear functions of standardized independent normal variables X_1, X_2 according to:

$$Y_1 = X_1$$

$$Y_2 = \rho X_1 + \sqrt{(1 - \rho^2)}X_2$$

It is easy to check that the Y_k have correlation ρ, using $Cov(X_1, X_1) = V(X_1) = 1$:

$$Cov(Y_1, Y_2) = Cov(X_1, \rho X_1 + \sqrt{(1 - \rho^2)}X_2) = \rho Cov(X_1, X_1) = \rho$$

Hence, the variance-covariance matrix Σ of Y_1 and Y_2 is:

1	ρ
ρ	1

It is easy to check that this simple variance-covariance matrix is the product **LU** where **U** is the transpose of **L**:

1	ρ		1	0		1	ρ
ρ	1	=	ρ	$\sqrt{(1 - \rho^2)}$	×	0	$\sqrt{(1 - \rho^2)}$

The appendix provides general formulas with N variables.

34.2.5 Application of Cholesky Decomposition

The subsequent example uses four variables. The starting point is the original variance-covariance matrix Σ. The Cholesky decomposition is such that $\Sigma = \mathbf{LU}$. The appendix shows how to calculate the coefficients of the lower matrix in the general case where we have N variables. The (4×4) variance-covariance matrix Σ becomes a simple correlation matrix with standard normal variables.

Correlation matrix

1.000	0.200	0.300	0.400
0.200	1.000	0.500	0.600
0.300	0.500	1.000	0.700
0.400	0.600	0.700	1.000

Next, we determine the Cholesky lower matrix and we check that it is such that $\mathbf{LU} = \Sigma$ (Table 34.2).

The **LU** matrix is identical to the original correlation matrix.

If **Y** is the column vector of the correlated normal Y_j, and **X** is the column vector of the independent normal X_i variables, **Y** derives from the **X** vector of independent variables through:

$$\mathbf{Y} = \mathbf{LX}$$

If we proceed for all Y_j, we find k values for each Y_j, and the values comply with the correlation structure. We use the above decomposition. We start by generating a large number of values of the four independent normal standard variables. The process consists of generating large

TABLE 34.2 Cholesky distribution

Upper			
1.0000	0.2000	0.3000	0.4000
0.0000	0.9798	0.4491	0.5307
0.0000	0.0000	0.8416	0.4060
0.0000	0.0000	0.0000	0.6273

Lower				L U			
1.0000	0.0000	0.0000	0.0000	1.000	0.200	0.300	0.400
0.2000	0.9798	0.0000	0.0000	0.200	1.000	0.500	0.600
0.3000	0.4491	0.8416	0.0000	0.300	0.500	1.000	0.700
0.4000	0.5307	0.4060	0.6273	0.400	0.600	0.700	1.000

TABLE 34.3 Generating independent normal variables

	1	2	3	4	5
U_1	0.604	0.179	0.965	0.930	0.521
U_2	0.089	0.789	0.622	0.147	0.589
U_3	0.456	0.714	0.964	0.836	0.692
U_4	0.119	0.854	0.910	0.607	0.354
X_1	0.263	−0.918	1.809	1.475	0.052
X_2	−1.349	0.803	0.311	−1.051	0.226
X_3	−0.112	0.566	1.796	0.979	0.502
X_4	−1.179	1.054	1.342	0.272	−0.376

number of values (u_i) of four uniform standard variables, and finding the values of the independent normal variables by writing that $x_i = \Phi^{-1}(u_i)$. The first five values of uniform and normal variables are in rows. The uniform variables are random numbers within $(0, 1)$. For each value of a uniform variable, we find the normal standardized variable as above. For example, taking the first cell on up and left-hand tables $U_1 = u_1 = 0.604$ and $\Phi^{-1}(u_1) = 0.263$ (after rounding both values to 3 decimals) (Table 34.3).

For finding the correlated normal standard variables, we multiply the (4×4) lower matrix **L** by the $(4 \times N)$ **X** matrix (second lower block in Table 34.3). N can be as large as necessary, and the matrices are truncated to the first five values. The first five values in rows are obtained by making the product **LX**. The number of values in rows for the X_i and the Y_i is as large as necessary (Table 34.4).

The right-hand lower block shows the values of the correlated normal standard variables. Each line shows the value of a normal standard variable Y_j. Since we simulate four correlated normal variables, we have a table with correlated values in rows. The full table has four rows and N columns. Each cell, from any column, is a value of the standard normal variable in the corresponding row. The entire set of simulated correlated normal standard normal variables makes up a matrix $(4, N)$, where N is the number of simulations.

We can check that the two first variables, for example, Y_1 and Y_2 are correlated by plotting their values (Figure 34.3). The number of simulations is $N = 200$.

We can also check the correlations, and we find, for example, the correlations of the first variable with the three others, using all simulated values (Table 34.5).

TABLE 34.4   Generating dependent variables as linear functions of independent variables

X_1	0.263	-0.918	1.809	1.475	0.052	...
X_2	-1.349	0.803	0.311	-1.051	0.226	...
X_3	-0.112	0.566	1.796	0.979	0.502	...
X_4	-1.179	1.054	1.342	0.272	-0.376	...

Lower matrix

1.000	0.000	0.000	0.000		Y_1	0.263	-0.918	1.809	1.475	0.052	...
0.200	0.980	0.000	0.000		Y_2	-1.269	0.603	0.667	-0.735	0.232	...
0.300	0.449	0.842	0.000		Y_3	-0.621	0.561	2.194	0.794	0.539	...
0.400	0.531	0.406	0.627		Y_4	-1.396	0.950	2.459	0.600	0.109	...

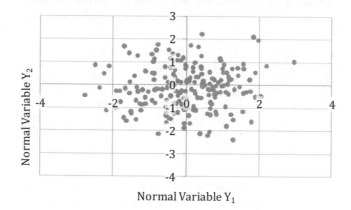

FIGURE 34.3   Scatter plot of two simulated correlated normal standard variables

TABLE 34.5   Correlations between simulated values of dependent variables

$\rho 11$	$\rho 12$	$\rho 13$	$\rho 14$
1.000	0.218	0.320	0.416

Comparing with the first line of the correlation matrix, we find that simulated variables have correlations reasonably close to the preset correlations of the first variables, for a small set of 200 simulations.

Generalizing, we can generate as many N values as we have variables complying with a correlation matrix. The simulation is usually done with matrix formulas, as above. This is the standard procedure for simulating normal standard dependent variables and risk factors.

34.2.6 Classical Methodology: Summary

We summarize here the classical methodology for simulating dependent normal variables. First, for generating a single independent normal variable, we use the inverse function, after having generated K values of the uniform $U(0, 1)$ variable. For generating N normal variables that are independent, it is sufficient to generate as many uniform variables and derive the normal variables using the inverse functions.

Now assuming that we need to simulate a number of dependent variables, we can use directly the standardized form of the factor models. The common methodology starts with the variance-covariance matrix and uses the Cholesky decomposition. The process consists of generating as many independent normal variables as necessary, then deriving the dependent variables complying with such matrix as linear combinations of the independent variables and using coefficients derived from the Cholesky decomposition of the variance-covariance matrix.

The copula methodology allows one to perform the same tasks, but it allows separating the dependence structure from the specifications of the univariate distributions of the dependent variables, which can be normal but need not be.

34.3 SIMULATION OF DEPENDENT VARIABLES WITH THE COPULA APPROACH

Under the copula approach, the dependency between variables is modeled by the copula function and its density. The mechanism for generating dependent variables is illustrated with two variables and the Gaussian distribution. The main difference with the Cholesky distribution is that we can generate dependent variables following any distribution, not only normal distributions.

The first subsection here is a reminder of the basic principle of copula simulations. The second sub-section describes the algorithm used in the examples.

34.3.1 Main Principle

The basic methodology follows a simple principle. Any joint CDF of any univariate distributions of random variables X_1 and X_2 can be expressed as the same copula function applied to uniform standard variables U_1 and U_2. The problem of simulating N dependent variables X_i following the univariate CDFs $F_i(X_i)$ becomes the problem of simulating N uniform standard variables U_i, following $U(0, 1)$, with the same dependency.

34.3.2 Simulation Algorithm

For simulating values of two variables X_1 and X_2 following univariate distributions $F(X_1)$ and $F(X_2)$, not necessarily normal, dependent, the above principle applies. The starting point is a set of uniform standard variables which embed the dependency relation through the conditional copula function. The next step consists of taking the inverse of the dependent uniform variables for finding dependent variables following any distribution function F.

The first step generates two uniform standard dependent variables, the dependency being embedded in the bivariate Gaussian copula. We start with two independent uniform standard variables. Next, we embed the copula dependency in a normal variable. The Cholesky method is used to generate this third normal standard variable. The normal standard variable is an intermediate variable. Its inverse is a uniform standard variable, which is dependent on the first uniform variable. The final result is a set of two dependent uniform variables, the first one and the third one. The steps of the algorithm are as follows.

- Generate two independent uniform standard variables U_1 and U_2.
- Generate a third variable N_3, standard normal, derived from the Gaussian copula. We use Φ as notation for the normal standard definition. Looking at the two independent uniform standard variables as cumulative standard normal distribution functions F, it is a simple matter to generate the standard normal variable dependent on the two uniform standard variables:

$$N_3 = \rho \Phi^{-1}(U_1) + \sqrt{1-\rho^2}\ \Phi^{-1}(U_2)$$

This normal standard variable N_3 is an intermediate variable.
- Finally, transform this normal standard N_3 into a uniform standard by applying the cumulative standard normal function to obtain a uniform standard V correlated to $U = U_1$. This new standard uniform variable V is the normal inverse of N_3, $V = \Phi(N_3)$. V is a cumulative normal standard function and represents a probability.
- We end up with two uniform dependent variables, U and V.

The last step consists of reverting from the two dependent uniform variables to dependent variables following a specified distribution, which can be normal, but need not be. We call this distribution F. F can be normal, or exponential for example. We equate the values u_1 and u_3 of U and V with the CDFs of the two variables of interest X_1 and X_2, writing $F(X_1) = u$ and $F(X_2) = v$. For doing so, calculate $x_1 = F^{-1}(u)$ and $x_2 = F^{-1}(v)$ by taking the normal inverses of U and V: $X_1 = F^{-1}(U)$ and $X_2 = F^{-1}(V)$ are dependent variables with distribution F. We find:

$$X_1 = \Phi^{-1}(U)$$

$$X_2 = \Phi^{-1}\left[\rho F^{-1}(U) + \sqrt{(1-\rho^2)}F^{-1}(V)\right]$$

In X_2, we take the normal inverse of the term within brackets because it represents V and is a cumulative normal standard probability. But, within brackets, we use the inverses of a distribution function F for reverting from the cumulative probabilities represented by the dependent uniform standard variables to the distribution of interest for the final dependent variables, which is normal or not normal. We now apply the simple formulas above to various cases of non-normal variables.

34.4 SIMULATION OF TWO DEPENDENT UNIFORM STANDARD VARIABLES

This is the common building block for other cases. There are two methods for generating two dependent uniform standard variables. The first one uses the traditional Cholesky decomposition to generate correlated normal standard variables. Then, taking the inverse of each normal standard variable, we obtain the dependent uniform variables. Or we can use the Gaussian copula method, which is equivalent.

The starting point uses two independent uniform standard variables using a random real number generator: $U = U_1 = u$ and $U_2 = u_2$. For generating two uniform standard dependent variables U and V, one method uses two normal standard variables, correlated with the Cholesky decomposition as above.

Starting from two independent standard uniform variables, the two independent normal standard variables can be written as $X_1 = \Phi^{-1}(U_1)$ and $X_2 = \Phi^{-1}(U_2)$. The second independent normal variable is an intermediate variable. The first dependent normal standard normal variable is $Y_1 = X_1$. The second dependent normal standard normal is Y_2, dependent on Y_1, as a linear function of the two independent standard normal variables with Cholesky coefficients. The equations defining Y_1 and Y_2 as a function of the independent normal variables X_1 and X_2 are:

$$Y_1 = X_1$$

$$Y_2 = \rho X_1 + \sqrt{1-\rho^2}\, X_2$$

These two normal standard variables can be expressed as functions of uniform variables. Writing $U_1 = U$, they are equivalent to:

$$Y_1 = X_1 = \Phi^{-1}(U_1)$$

$$Y_2 = \rho \Phi^{-1}(U_1) + \sqrt{1-\rho^2}\, \Phi^{-1}(U_2)$$

The cumulative probability of Y_2 is a uniform standard variable V that is dependent on $U = U_1$, using $V = \Phi(Y_2)$. We end up with two dependent uniform variables U and V. The first two independent uniform variables are $U = U_1$ and U_2. The third uniform variable is V. The uniform standard variables U and V are dependent. The dependence relation between U_1 and U_2 is the Y_2 relationship above. In all examples, we use this dependence relation for obtaining the second dependent uniform variable.

The example mimics the core building block of generating dependent uniform standard variables. The correlation ρ of the Gaussian copula is $\rho = 70\%$. We ran 100 simulations and we show the first simulations in Table 34.6. The normal standard variable used as intermediate variable is N, with $Z_2 = N(U_1, U_2, \rho)$, from above equation for Y_2. The dependence function is embedded in $N(U_1, U_2, \rho)$, or $\rho \Phi^{-1}(U_1) + \sqrt{1-\rho^2}\, \Phi^{-1}(U_2)$ (Table 34.6).

The scatter plot of the two dependent uniform standard variables U and V is shown in Figure 34.4.

In the general case, we would use U and V and invert term using $U = F^{-1}(Y_1)$ and $V = F^{-1}(Y_2)$ for obtaining the dependent variables Y_1 and Y_2 following the non-normal distribution F. When only two dependent uniform standard variables are required, the function is U and the inverse functions collapse to $U^{-1}(u) = u$.

TABLE 34.6   Generating two dependent random variables U and V

$U = U_1$	U_2	$N(U, U_2 \, \rho)$	$V = \Phi(N)$
0.525	0.810	0.671	0.749
0.357	0.711	0.141	0.556
0.907	0.283	0.515	0.697
0.723	0.829	1.092	0.863
0.371	0.860	0.542	0.706
0.465	0.821	0.596	0.724
0.507	0.977	1.431	0.924
0.483	0.687	0.318	0.625
0.740	0.662	0.748	0.773
0.680	0.452	0.240	0.595

Dependent Uniform Random

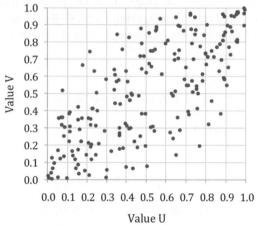

Value U

FIGURE 34.4   Scatter plot of two dependent uniform variables

34.5 SIMULATION OF TWO DEPENDENT NORMAL STANDARD VARIABLES

Using the methodology for normal standard variables has no other use than showing why we necessarily obtain correlated variables using the copula function, since we can easily correlate standard normal variables using the Cholesky methodology. The distinctive feature of the copula approach is that we go through uniform variables rather than working directly with the normal variables.

For illustrating why we find the same results as in the classical approach, we do not need to conduct simulations. Instead, we revert to the algorithm. As usual, the starting point is two independent uniform standard variables U_1 and U_2. The uniform variables are converted into standard uniform variables, which can be correlated with the Cholesky distribution for obtaining a correlated normal variable with the first one. The standard normal variable used as intermediate variable is the inverse of the uniform standard V:

$$\Phi^{-1}(V) = \Phi^{-1}(U_1, U_2, \rho) = \rho\Phi^{-1}(U_1) + \sqrt{(1 - \rho^2)}\Phi^{-1}(U_2)$$

The copula approach transforms this variable into a third uniform standard by taking the inverse function of $\Phi^{-1}(V)$, which is V itself. As above, U and V are now dependent.

The next step is reverting to the target distribution F, which is now normal standard, by taking the inverses of U and V. The first normal standard variable is N_1 and equals $\Phi^{-1}(U)$. The second normal standard variable N_2 is the normal standard inverse of V:

$$N_2 = \Phi^{-1}(V) = \Phi^{-1}(U_1, U_2, \rho) = \rho\Phi^{-1}(U_1) + \sqrt{(1 - \rho^2)}\Phi^{-1}(U_2)$$

This equation is the dependency relation applying in general. In this case, the univariate distribution function is normal and $\Phi^{-1}(V) = V$ is normal. In other cases, we would use $F^{-1}(U)$ and $F^{-1}(V)$ instead for finding Y_1 and Y_2. The benefit of the copula distribution is that we do not need to use normal variables. Starting with uniform variables, we obtain two dependent uniform variables and we revert to non-normal variables by taking the inverses of U and V.

Note that this final equation collapses in the case of normal variables to the equation of Cholesky decomposition, a function of two standard normal variables that are independent. Since we have embedded the dependency between U and V, we have the same dependency between N_1 and N_2. The next example uses the exponential time to default distribution.

34.6 SIMULATION OF TWO DEPENDENT TIMES TO DEFAULT

In this paragraph, we use the copula methodology for simulating dependent times to default. The first sub-section shows how to simulate times to default for a single obligor. The second sub-section uses the copula methodology for simulating dependent times to default for two obligors.

34.6.1 Simulation of Time to Default for a Single Obligor

The distribution of times to default in credit risk is an exponential distribution, as shown in the credit risk models. In such a case, the probability that the time to default is less than or equal to t is an exponential distribution. We briefly summarize here the parameters and the function.

The intensity of default λ measures the probability that a discrete event, a default, occurs during a small time interval dt, or:

$$P(t \leq \text{default time} < t + dt) = \lambda dt$$

Taking a small interval:

$$P(\text{default}) = \lambda dt$$

The probability of survival until t is $\lambda \exp(-\lambda t)$ and the probability that time to default is less than or equal to t is, by integration from 0 to t, the exponential function:

$$F(t) = 1 - \lambda \exp(-\lambda t)$$

TABLE 34.7 Simulating first time to default for a single obligor

U(0,1)	Time to default
0.39460	10.037
0.19907	4.440
0.36490	9.079
0.72696	25.963
0.62970	19.869
0.17176	3.769
0.05818	1.199
0.71579	25.161
0.45865	12.274
...	...
...	...

The first random time to default is T_1. The simulation of a single series of time to default values uses a first $U_1(0, 1)$ uniform standard variable and derives the values obtained for $F(T_1)$, the survival exponential distribution, with $F(t_1) = u_1$. Each value t_1 of T_1 is the inverse function of F, the exponential distribution:

$$t = F^{-1}(u) = -\ln[(1 - u)/\lambda]$$

This procedure allows the construction of the frequency distribution of times to default for a single obligor. The example uses $\lambda = 5\%$ for 1 year, from the default frequency attached to the rating of this first single obligor (Table 34.7).

For example, the first time to default is obtained as:

$$t = -\ln[(1 - u)/\lambda] = -\ln[(1 - 0.3946)/5\%] = 10.037 \text{ years}$$

Extending the series to 100 simulations, we find the cumulative probability, $F(T_1)$, between 0 and 1, along the horizontal axis, that the time to default is inferior or equal to any value of the time to default (between 0 and 140 years along the vertical axis) (Figure 34.5). Taking a frequency distribution, we have the density of time to defaults, as simulated above. Both tables can be generated with Excel™.

The frequency distribution is a proxy of the density of time to defaults, as simulated above. Both tables are generated with Excel™. For constructing this frequency distribution, we need to choose the constant interval between values of times to default, here five years. Hence, we have many fewer dots than in the above $F(T_1)$. Figure 34.6 shows the time to default in years along the horizontal axis and the frequency for each interval of the values simulated.

We have simulated a series of 100 values of times to default for a single obligor. Next we take the example of a second obligor and proceed to make its time to default dependent on that of the first obligor.

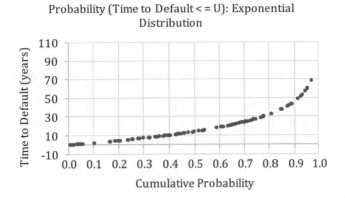

FIGURE 34.5   Cumulative distribution of the first time to default of a single obligor

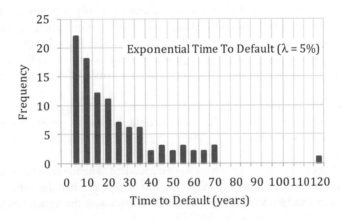

FIGURE 34.6   Frequency distribution of simulated first time to default for a single obligor

34.6.2 Simulation of Two Exponentially Distributed Dependent Times to Default

For making dependent the times to default of two obligors, T_1 and T_2, the copula methodology is implemented, still using here the Gaussian copula. T_1 and T_2 represent a special case of more general variables X_1 and X_2 following distribution functions than the exponential distribution.

The first phase of the process is to obtain two dependent uniform standard variables. We start from two uniform standard dependent variables, $U = U_1$ and U_2. The second one is an intermediate variable for determining the third uniform standard variable $V = U_3$, correlated with U_1. U and V are uniform standard variables dependent through the copula function. The second phase consists of reverting from the two dependent uniform standard variables, U and V, to the random times to default. Since each value of U and V matches the times to default T_1 and T_2, the inverse function $F(t) = 1 - \exp(\lambda t)$ provides t using:

$$u = u_1 = F(t_1) \text{ and } t_1 = F^{-1}(u)$$

$$v = u_3 = F(t_2) \text{ and } t_2 = F^{-1}(v)$$

To find the inverse of the function $F(t) = 1 - \lambda \exp(\lambda t)$, we write that $\exp(\lambda t) = 1 - F(t)$, take the logarithm and obtain $\lambda t = \ln[1 - F(t)]$ or $t = \ln[1 - F(t)]/\lambda$. Replacing $F(t)$ by the values of either u_1 or u_3, we find the matching values of t_1 and t_2. Recall that $F(t) = u < 1$, and that the logarithm of a positive number is positive, hence t is positive. The two times to default, t_1 and t_2, are obtained by replacing $F(t)$ by, respectively, u_1 and u_3.

$$t_1 = F^{-1}(u_1) = \ln[1 - F(t_1)]/\lambda) = \ln(1 - u)/\lambda$$

$$t_2 = F^{-1}(u_3) = \ln[1 - F(t_2)]/\lambda) = \ln(1 - v)/\lambda$$

The series of values of t_1 and t_2 are dependent.

The first step consists of simulating a series of exponentially distributed times to default starting from a random number. This is the standard method for generating any random variable starting from a single series of uniform standard variable. The second step uses the Gaussian copula to generate two series of values of dependent times to default, as described above.

The correlation coefficient equals 70%. The same intensity of default for the two variables is 5%.

First, generate the random standard uniform variable u for generating a first series of values which represent the CDF of the first time to default t_1. Next, generate a second series of independent uniform standard values u_2. Then, correlate these two series of uniform standard random numbers.

We proceed as above to find u and v which are dependent. The intermediate steps are: generating an intermediate independent uniform standard variable u_2; then deriving from $u = u_1$ and u_2 the third uniform standard variable V correlated with u using the dependency relationship:

$$V = [\rho\Phi^{-1}(U_1) + \sqrt{(1 - \rho^2)}\Phi^{-1}(U_2)] = \Phi(N)$$

The first time to default t_1 is associated to u_1 by inverting the survival function. The second one t_2 is associated with $v = u_3$. The two times to default are:

$$t_1 = -\ln[(1 - u)/\lambda] \text{ and } t_2 = -\ln[(1 - v)/\lambda]$$

In Table 34.8, the first two columns are values of the two independent standard uniform variables. The third column calculates the dependent normal distribution resulting from the two standard normal distributions derived from the two independent standard uniform variables. The third variable V is uniform standard and dependent on U. Finally, the two times to default are the inverse function of U and V.

We check that the two uniform variables U and V are dependent by plotting the simulated values (Figure 34.7).

Next we cross-tabulate the two times to default, T_1 and T_2, and see an elongated scatter plot, which results from the positive correlation imposed.

Figure 34.8 shows how to generate dependent variables which are not normal using the Gaussian copula, the dependency relation being generally of the form $[\rho\Phi^{-1}(U_1) + \sqrt{(1 - \rho^2)}$

TABLE 34.8 Simulated two dependent times to default from the Gaussian copula function

$U = U_1$	U_2	$N(U, U_2\, \rho)$	$V = \Phi(N)$	$T_1 = \Phi^{-1}(U_1)$	$T_2 = \Phi^{-1}(V)$
0.944	0.477	1.073	0.858	57.752	39.086
0.402	0.966	1.130	0.871	10.274	40.914
0.054	0.355	−1.393	0.082	1.104	1.708
0.434	0.205	−0.705	0.240	11.386	5.499
0.798	0.599	0.763	0.777	31.983	30.028
0.646	0.396	0.074	0.529	20.747	15.071
0.142	0.661	−0.453	0.325	3.062	7.864
0.321	0.021	−1.781	0.037	7.735	0.763
0.316	0.618	−0.121	0.452	7.603	12.023
0.660	0.562	0.400	0.655	21.576	21.303

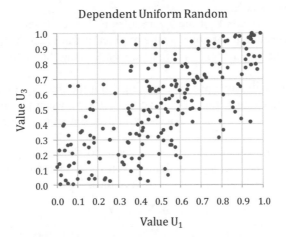

Dependent Uniform Random

FIGURE 34.7 Scatter plot of the dependent uniform variables

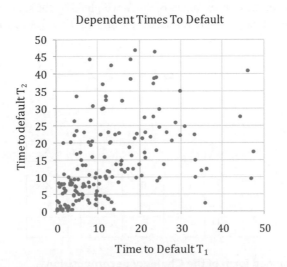

Dependent Times To Default

FIGURE 34.8 Scatter plot of the dependent times to default

$\Phi^{-1}(U_2)$, from which we derive the second dependent uniform variable V. Then, as above, we invert the function F, F being other than the exponential function, for obtaining the dependent variables having the same dependence structure as U and V.

The correlation between the two series of simulated times to default is 71.8% in this sample simulation.

34.7 APPENDIX: THE CHOLESKY DECOMPOSITION METHOD

Generalizing to N variables requires a N-dimension squared variance-covariance matrix Σ. **L** and **U** stand respectively for "lower" triangular matrix and "upper" triangular matrix. The **U** matrix is the transpose of the **L** matrix: $\mathbf{U} = \mathbf{L}^T$. By construction, $\mathbf{LU} = \mathbf{LL}^T$ is the original variance-covariance matrix Σ.

The column $(N \times 1)$ vector **Y** of the Y_i variables is derived from the vector column $(N \times 1)$ vector **X** of X_i independent variables by the product in that order: $\mathbf{Y} = \mathbf{L}\,\mathbf{X}$. **L** is the lower triangular matrix of the α_{ij} coefficients (Figure 34.9). Solving the matrix equation $\mathbf{Z}^T = \mathbf{L}\,\mathbf{X}^T$ determines **L**.

The solution uses an iterative process, starting from the first equation imposing $\alpha_{11} = 1$, and proceeding by imposing iteratively the correlations, between the first pair of variables, the next correlation between the next pair of variables, and so on. We add the unit variance equation for each Y_i.

The Cholesky decomposition determines the set of coefficients, α_{ij}, of the linear combinations of the X_j such that the Y_j comply with the given variance-covariance structure. We have N independent X_i variables and N Y_j correlated variables.

$$Y_j = \sum_{m=1,j} \alpha_{im} X_i$$

This set of coefficients transforms the independent variables X_i into correlated variables Y_j. The coefficients result from two sets of equations. The first set of equations imposes a unit variance of Y_j, equal to the sum of the unit variances of the X_i weighted by the squares of α_{ij}, for i varying from 1 to j. We have j equations, one for each Y_j, with j varying from 1 to N:

$$V\left(Z_j\right) = V\left(\sum_{m=1,j} \alpha_{im} X_i\right) = \sum_{m=1,j} \alpha_{im}^2 = 1$$

Y_j	=	L			×	X_i

Y_1	=	α_{11}	0	...	×	X_1
Y_2	=	α_{12}	α_{22}	...	×	X_2
...		...	...	...		...

FIGURE 34.9   **Expanded form of the Cholesky decomposition**

The index m varies from 1 to j, j being the number of independent variables of which Y_j is a linear combination. The index j of Y_j varies from 1 to N because there are as many correlated variables as there are independent variables X_i.

The second set of equations imposes the correlation structure ρ_{ij} for all i different from j. The covariance of Y_j and Y_k is:

$$\mathrm{cov}\left(Z_j, Z_k\right) = \mathrm{cov}\left(\sum_{m=1,j} \alpha_{mj} X, \sum_{j=1,k} \alpha_{jm} X\right) = \rho_{ij}$$

This imposes a constraint on the coefficients:

$$\sum_{j \neq m} \alpha_{jm} \alpha_{jk} = \rho_{ij}$$

The problem is to find the set of α_{jm} for each pair of different values of j and m. Using the two sets of equations provides the coefficient of $\mathbf{L}$.

SECTION 10
Market Risk

Market risk is the risk of adverse deviations of the market value transactions due to market moves during the time required to liquidate positions.

Market risk applies to the trading portfolio. This section essentially deals with the VaR models. For market risk, the positions are measured as sensitivities to risk factors. A number of techniques have been implemented for modeling VaR. The horizon for modeling the daily P & L is always relatively short since it is limited to the liquidation period.

The "value-at-risk" (VaR) methodology[1] aims at valuing potential losses resulting from current risks. Market risk VaR is a measure of the potential losses during the time needed to effectively liquidate exposures. It is the "worst-case" potential adverse move of the trading portfolio value. The potential loss is the loss not exceeded in more than a predetermined small fraction of all possible situations, or a loss percentile. Market risk is now subject to capital constraint regulations imposed on banks. Market risk VaR requires measuring the low likelihood of large losses for the trading portfolio, based on price observations in the market and the likelihood of their deviations. Since risk-based capital, or economic capital, is precisely the capital level that matches potential losses generated by all risks, the VaR methodology applies. It is developed in a first stage for measuring market risk in this section, and is extended in the next section to different credit risk.

All market VaR techniques have some common building blocks. They all require mapping positions to risk factors and revaluation of instruments. The valuation is based only on sensitivities in the delta-normal VaR, or it is a full revaluation of each position using closed-form formulas whenever possible, when they exist, or simulations when they do not exist. The horizon for modeling the daily P & L is always relatively short since it is limited to the liquidation period.

The delta-normal VaR model relies on restrictive assumptions of normal returns over the period of liquidation and constant sensitivities. It requires inputting the dependencies of risk factors through a variance-covariance matrix, which is frequently updated. The delta-VaR model is used for so-called "linear" instruments, which essentially excludes optional instruments because of convexity (variable sensitivities) or "gamma risk." The delta-VaR allows highlighting all intermediate steps required for modeling VaR.

The historical VaR is a fairly common practice that applies to all instruments. It is based on capturing the daily P & L of the current portfolio, looking backwards at variations of risk factors. The historical variations of risk factors embed the dependencies, which allow bypassing the variance-covariance matrix. Historical VaR relies on a valuation either based on sensitivities, or, better, on full revaluation of instruments, which allows dealing with convexity risk. Historical VaR also bypasses the normal assumption for returns, since it provides an empirical distribution of daily P & L, from which loss percentiles are derived. Hence it relies on a nonparametric distribution, as opposed to the normal distribution, which depends on its first two moments only.

Monte Carlo VaR, hypothetical VaR, relies on full-blown simulations, and it is similar except that it looks forward by simulating the random dependent processes of risk factors, which is both complex and time intensive. Modeling dependent processes implies modeling dependencies, and simulations of all risk factors. Simulation techniques are unavoidable anyway for exotic instruments whose valuation cannot rely on closed-form formulas. The full simulation

---

1 There are numerous references on VaR, notably the book of Jorion [43]. Note that VaR is a measure of risk which is not always "consistent", as defined and explained in [4].

technique is the "brute force" technique since it implies modeling all risk factor processes, and all revaluations at horizon.

Both historical VaR and hypothetical VaR are presented together because they share some common features, although the first technique is more widely implemented because it is simple and applies to all instruments, linear or non-linear. Some VaR extensions are detailed. They include notably the expected shortfall, or E-VaR, which was introduced previously when the general VaR concept was introduced. E-VaR is commonly used, because it is additive across segments. All techniques that allow deriving VaR, and already presented at this stage, also allow determining the E-VaR.

The simulation of interest rates is important for both VaR and ALM. The principal components analysis is common because it reduces the number of risk factors in general to three principal components, instead of all interest rates of the term structure of rates. Because of such transversal features, it is presented in a distinct chapter, after having discussed the VaR modeling approaches.

This section covers market risk VaR in four chapters.

- Chapter 35: delta-normal VaR, which applies to linear instruments – following the basic steps already identified in Chapter 18 on risk models.
- Chapter 36: historical and hypothetical VAR, with notably the first one being embedding dependencies through historical simulations and being the most commonly used.
- Chapter 37: simulations of interest rates, which serves for both ALM modeling and market VaR modeling, deferred here because it requires as a pre-requisite defining dependency modeling.
- Chapter 38: back-testing, stress-testing, and benchmarking, which are transversal techniques applying to both market risk and credit risk models.

35

Delta-normal VaR

This chapter explains in details the steps and assumptions for the determination of the "delta-normal VaR." The salient features of such VaR methodology is that is applies to portfolios that are linear functions of risk factors and that it derives VaR as percentile of a normal distribution P & L.

Section 35.1 details the sequence of steps for determining VaR and illustrates the process with the simple case of a portfolio of two elementary positions. Section 35.2 addresses the mapping issues. A VaR calculation relies on mapping each exposure to risk factors. Since not all risk factors can be considered in practice, mapping to a subset of all risk factors raises issues for preserving value and volatility of an original position. For explaining how the methodology applies to a portfolio, we use the example of a forward contract, which, like a portfolio, depends on several risk factors in a nonlinear fashion. The example of a forward foreign exchange contract is fully developed. The forward exchange contract is a non-linear function of three risk factors. The mark-to-market value of the contract is detailed in Section 35.3[1]. For moving from the contract value to VaR, the pre-requisite is to decompose such a contract in a linear function of elementary positions, one for each factor, the coefficients being the sensitivities of the contract value to each of the three risk factors. Section 35.4 shows how such decomposition is performed, using various techniques. Once this decomposition is achieved the contract behaves like a portfolio of three elementary positions. At this stage, the derivation of the portfolio variance and volatility uses the standard matrix formulas, and inputting the sensitivities as weights of each position. Section 35.5 is a straight application of formulas derived in section 9 on dependencies, completed by the VaR calculation using the loss percentiles of the normal distribution.

All critical assumptions are summarized in the last section (Section 35.6), many of them to be relaxed for non-linear portfolios, and expanded in the next chapters.

---

1   The example replicates the example of Chapter 7 on foreign exchange derivatives.

Contents

35.1 PORTFOLIO DELTA-NORMAL VAR

The VaR – value-at-risk – is the value of potential losses, over a given horizon, which will not be exceeded in more than a given fraction of all possible events. The delta-normal VaR applies to linear instruments in that it relies on the constant sensitivity to risk factor assumptions. Furthermore, it assumes a normal distribution of the portfolio value. Such assumptions should be relaxed with non-linear portfolios, such as those with optional instruments.

35.1.1 Steps for Determining VaR

The process for detraining portfolio VaR requires several steps:

1 The first step is to map the positions to the risk factors influencing their values.
2 Mapping of each position to risk factors allows defining their sensitivities with respect to each risk factor. Sensitivities are the "deltas" of the delta-VaR.
3 The variations of the portfolio value become a linear function of the variations of each risk factor, if we assume that sensitivities are constant.
4 The volatility of the portfolio becomes the volatility of a linear function of random variables. Volatility is defined for a given horizon, for example daily.
5 Moving from volatility to VaR implies an assumption about the distribution of the changes of value. The delta-normal VaR relies on the normal distribution assumption.
6 Since confidence levels and multiples of volatility are related in normal distributions, the VaR at given confidence level follows.

As a preliminary to a more complex example, we use a simple example with two simple assets.

35.1.2 A Simple Portfolio of Two Zero-coupon Bonds

It is easier to illustrate the process and highlight dependencies effect on a simple two-asset portfolio in a first step (Table 35.1). The portfolio is made of two zero-coupon bonds with the following characteristics.

The four steps for deriving delta-VaR are:

TABLE 35.1   Portfolio of two zero bonds

Portfolio	Bond A	Bond B
Value	1000	500
Duration	2	5
Interest rate volatility (annually)	2%	1%

- mapping to market parameters
- deriving sensitivities to these risk factors
- deriving the volatility of the portfolio value
- deriving the VaR under the normal distribution assumption.

35.1.2.1 Mapping to Risk Factors

A zero-coupon bond has only one flow at maturity, hence it depends on a single interest rate, the one observed on the yield curve for this maturity. The values of each of the two zero-coupon bonds B_a and B_b depend on interest rates i_a and i_b. These two interest rates are the risk factors.

35.1.2.2 Sensitivities to Selected Market Parameters

The portfolio value of two bonds is $B_a + B_b$. The random changes of value of the portfolio depend on the sensitivities, or durations, of each bond:

$$\Delta(\text{portfolio value}) = -D_a B_a \Delta i_a + -D_b B_b \Delta i_b$$

If sensitivities and initial values of each bond are constant, the random changes of value of the portfolio are a linear function of the changes of the random market parameters

$$\Delta(\text{portfolio value}) = -2 \times 1000 \times \Delta i_a - 5 \times 500 \times \Delta i_b$$

The volatility of the portfolio value is the volatility of a linear function of two random variables, Δi_a and Δi_b, as long as we can consider current values of bonds and durations constant. The initial data on the portfolio is in the table below. The portfolio value is $B_a + B_b = 1500$. The random changes of the portfolio value are:

$$\Delta(\text{portfolio value}) = -2 \times 1000 \times \Delta i_a + -5 \times 500 \times \Delta i_b$$

The volatility of the portfolio value is the volatility of a linear function of two random variables as long as we can consider current values and durations constant.

35.1.2.3 Volatility of the Portfolio Value

The volatility of the portfolio value is the volatility of a linear function of two random variables, Δi_a and Δi_b, as long as we can consider current values of bonds and durations constant. The two interest rates, to which each position is mapped, do not deviate by the same amount at the same time, which implies inputting their correlations.

The standard formula for the volatility of two variables uses the volatilities of each random variable and their correlation. Volatilities and correlations are derived from historical time series. The standard formula starts from variance "σ^2" and derives volatility "σ" (standard deviation) as the square root of variance:

$$\sigma^2(aX + bY) = a^2\sigma^2(X) + b^2\sigma^2(Y) + 2\rho_{xy}ab\sigma(X)\sigma(Y)$$

In this general equation, a and b are constants, X and Y are random, ρ_{xy} is their correlation (between -1 to $+1$), σ is the standard deviation. Using this formula with the random variations of portfolio value, we have:

$$\sigma^2(\text{portfolio value}) = 2^2 \times 1000^2\sigma^2(\Delta i_a) + 5^2 \times 500^2\sigma^2(\Delta i_b) + 2\rho_{ab}(-2) \times (-5)1000 \times 500 \times \sigma(\Delta i_a)\sigma(\Delta i_b)$$

Using annual volatilities in this example: $\sigma(\Delta i_a) = 2\%$ and $\sigma(\Delta i_b) = 1\%$, we need to input the correlation ρ_{ab}, for example 30% for finding the portfolio value variance and volatility.

35.1.2.4 VaR under the Delta-normal Assumptions

Finally, we use the normal distribution multiples for determining the variance of the portfolio value, then its volatility and its VaR as a loss percentile.

The example in Table 35.2 shows that using simple assumptions, the VaR is easily calculated when there are dependencies. The VaR is proportional to the horizon used for volatilities. For varying the horizon, we use the scale root of time rule for adjusting volatilities and calculating the VaR. If we need a daily volatility, we scale down the annual volatilities by the factor $1/\sqrt{250}$. The portfolio daily volatility is $53.15/\sqrt{250} = 53.15/15.811 = 3.362$ and the daily VaR becomes 26.33.

A more elaborate example, calculating the VaR for a single forward contract on foreign exchange, illustrates more comprehensively the VaR calculation process. Before that, we address some general issues.

35.2 MAPPING AN INSTRUMENT TO RISK FACTORS

Modeling all individual asset returns within a portfolio is overly complex to handle. Since the number of market indexes is much smaller than that of individual assets, it is more efficient to

TABLE 35.2

Correlation 30%	Portfolio A + B
Variance	2825.00
Volatility	53.15
VaR at 1%: 2.33 Volatility	123.84

**TABLE 35.3   Data for mapping a position
to two positions**

| Position | 1,000,000 |
| Maturity (years) | 1.250 |

	1-year	2-year
Zero rate (%)	5.200	5.400
Bond price volatility	8.00%	10.00%

Correlation matrix	1-year	2-year
1-year	1.000	0.900
2-year	0.900	1.000

derive asset returns from a reduced set of market parameters that influence their values. The mapping process results from pricing models in order to identify the main value drivers of asset values. In general, not all risk factors can be selected. Mapping individual asset returns to a subset of all market parameters is simpler but requires adjustments.

For example, if interest rate references do not correspond to exact maturities, it is possible to interpolate a proxy of the corresponding rate using the references. The exclusion of some value drivers results in "basis risk," since the modeled values do not track exactly the actual asset prices any more. There are as many interest rates as there are maturities for example. Mapping a position to selected risk factors transforms a single position into a weighted set of positions. The value and volatility of this set of positions should match those of the original instrument.

Instead of using bonds whose interest rates match exactly those that drive the bond value, consider a single zero bond of maturity 1.25 years, while using as selected risk factors the 1-year and 2-year maturities. The risk factor driving this bond value is the 1.25 year interest rate. The selected risk factors are the 1-year rate and the 2-year rate. The original position is a €1000,000 zero bond of maturity 1-year plus 3 months (1.25 years).

With the two 1-year and 2-year positions, it is necessary to replicate the original position. The interest rates and the bond volatilities for 1 and 2 years and the correlations between the 1- and 2-year rates are known (Table 35.3). Since we have two risk factors distinct from the exact risk factor matching this position, we need to decompose this position into two positions that map to the two selected risk factors. The combined position of the bonds should match the value and the volatility of the original instrument in VaR calculations.

For doing so we have to select weights such that we preserve the value and volatility of the initial positions.

35.2.1 Interpolation of Interest Rate from Selected Risk Factors

Since the 1.25-year interest rate is not usable directly, we need to allocate the position to the time points retained as risk factors. How much value should we allocate to the 1-year time point and how much to the 2-year time point?

The first step is finding the value of the 1.25-year position, from interpolation of the 1.25-year interest rate from the 1-year and the 2-year interest rates. In order to find the appropriate interest rate applicable to the 1.25 years position, a linear interpolation provides a proxy of the 1.25 years interest rate:

$$i(1.25 \text{ year}) = i(1 \text{ year}) \times [i(2 \text{ year}) - i(1 \text{ year})] \times 0.25$$

$$i(1.25 \text{ year}) = 5.20\% + (5.40\% - 5.20\%) \times 0.25 = 5.25\%$$

With this rate, the value of the initial position is calculated.

35.2.2 Value Preservation

The value for the position using the proxy of the 1.25-year interest rate (i) is €1000,000/(1 + i)$^{1.25}$, where i is the above interpolated rate from the two rates. The value is:

$$1000,000/(1 + i)^{1.25} = 938,052$$

Next we need to define the volatility of this position.

35.2.3 Volatility Preservation

The mapping process should preserve volatility. We know only the volatilities for the 1-year and 2-year bonds as percentages of their values. Using available 1-year and 2-year volatilities, we find the interpolated 1.25-year volatility.

$$\sigma(1.25 \text{ year}) = \sigma(1 \text{ year}) + [\sigma(2 \text{ year}) - \sigma(1 \text{ year})] \times 0.25$$

$$\sigma(1.25 \text{ year}) = 8\% + (10\% - 8\%) \times 0.25 = 8.5\%$$

The variance of the 1.25-year bond is $8.5\%^2 = 0.723\%$.

35.2.4 Mapping and Allocation

The final step is to determine the allocations of the initial position to the two equivalent 1-year and 2-year positions.

We could use the distance to the time points as the allocation rule, or allocate $0.25 \times (1.25 - 1)$ to 1 year and $0.75 \times (2 - 1.25)$ to 2 years. But the variance of such a portfolio will not match the interpolated volatility of the 1.25-year position. The correct process consists of finding the allocation percentages that make the variance of the replicating portfolio of two positions identical to the interpolated volatility. If we allocate w to the 1-year bond and $1 - w$ to the 2-year bond, the resulting variance is that of a portfolio of these two positions. The formula of portfolio variance is:

TABLE 35.4 Allocating weights and values to each reference position

Allocation to 1-year bond w	64.10%
Allocation to 2-year bond $1 - w$	35.90%
Total	100.000%
Portfolio variance	0.723%
Value	938,042
Allocation 1-year bond	601,285
Allocation 2-year bond	336,757

$$\text{portfolio variance} = w^2\sigma_1^2 + (1 - w)^2\sigma_2^2 + 2\rho_{12}w(1 - w)\sigma_1\sigma_2$$

Matching this variance with the interpolated variance implies that the coefficient w, with the volatilities of the bonds and the correlation coefficient of 90%, is such that this variance matches exactly the interpolated variance 0.723% (Table 35.4).

The allocation is $w = 64.1\%$ for the 1-year bond and $1 - w = 35.9\%$ for the 2-year bond. Such an allocation applied to the interpolated value of the 1.25-year position, 938,042, provides the values of each of the two 1-year and 2-year positions.

The initial position is equivalent to these two equivalent positions. In the VaR calculation, the initial position will be replaced by the two equivalent positions, which depend on retained risk factors only, not on the 1.25-year interest rate which is not selected. Such allocation preserves value (interest rate interpolation) and volatility (volatility interpolation). The replicating portfolio is:

$$1.25\text{-year bond} = 64.1\% \times 1\text{-year bond} + 35.9\% \times 2\text{-year bond}$$

Since we have the percentage allocations, we can proceed with risk factors 1-year and 2-year. The sensitivities with respect to each interest rate are the percentage allocations multiplied by the sensitivities of the two elementary positions. The volatilities of each position are expressed as percentage allocations multiplied by the volatilities of the two elementary positions.

Next we proceed to a more general example of delta-VaR using as an example a forward contract on foreign exchange. The example shows the methodology for decomposition of a contract that depends on a non-linear relation with several risk factors.

35.3 THE EXAMPLE OF A FORWARD FOREIGN EXCHANGE RATE

The general delta-normal VaR methodology can be illustrated with a simple instrument, such as a forward exchange contract. The forward is replicated by three transactions.

- Borrowing in \$ at $i\$\%$ (5%) for 1 year such, in 1 year, we get exactly 1\$ to pay, paid by the expected inflow.
- Converting the proceeds of borrowing in USD into EUR at the spot prevailing exchange rate S €/\$: S = 0.769231 €/\$ or exactly 1/1.3 \$/€.

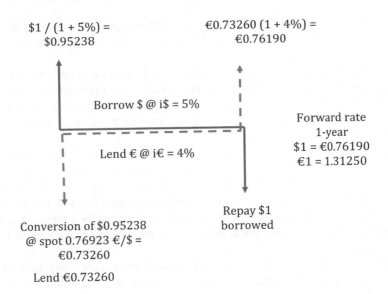

$1 / (1 + 5%) =
$0.95238

€0.73260 (1 + 4%) =
€0.76190

Borrow $ @ i$ = 5%

Forward rate
1-year
$1 = €0.76190
€1 = 1.31250

Lend € @ i€ = 4%

Conversion of $0.95238
@ spot 0.76923 €/$ =
€0.73260

Repay $1
borrowed

Lend €0.73260

FIGURE 35.1　Borrowing/lending in two currencies

- Lending the proceeds in EUR at $i€$% (4%) for 1 year, which results in 0.769231 € × (1 + $i€$) = 0.76190 € in 1 year

The forward contract combines a long position in EUR and a short position in USD, of which amounts in a common currency are identical with the current spot rate, with same maturity (Figure 35.1).

The implied forward exchange rate is such that: $1= 0.76190 € or €1 = $1.3125.

The replicating portfolio of the forward embeds constant contractual flows. Say the forward pays $10,000,000 and receives €12,380,952 million 1 year from now. These terms are set today at the forward exchange rate of 0.76190 €/$ or 1.31250 $/€.

The forward contract depends on the following three "risk factors":

- spot rate "S": 1.30 €/$ or 0.76923 €/$
- "$i €$" = 4.00% annually
- "$i $$" = 5.00% annually.

The value of the forward F_t, as of current date t, in EUR is equal to the present value of its long leg (lending in €) at the € rate minus the present value of the short leg (borrowing in $) in USD at $ rate plus. Using a point in time t, subsequent to the original date of the contract (0), the mark-to-market value of the forward contract depends, after date 0, on the prevailing values of the risk factors. The discounting is from current date t up to maturity $T - t$, with T being 1 year in this example.

$$F_t(€) = -S_t€/\$ \times \$10,000,000/(1 + i_\$)^{T-t} + €7,619,048/(1 + i_€)^{T-t}$$

The value of the contract at inception date 0 is zero. Subsequently, its value fluctuates with the values of the three risk factors according to the above formula, and given the contractual fixed cash flows in the two currencies.

This dependency on multiple risk factors is a general feature of most instruments. Coupon bonds depend on all interest rates of each coupon date. Forward interest rate contracts depend on two interest rates. The foreign exchange contract $F_t(€)$ is an exact non-linear function of three risk factors. It is necessary, in general, to move from the exact relationship between value and risk factors to a proxy linear relation.

The example illustrates what happens with several risk factors not linearly related to the value of the instrument. Any instrument depending on several risk factors requires the decomposition in elementary positions, each depending on one single risk factor. This is the general case of portfolios. Portfolios combining several instruments also depend on several risk factors. The number of risk factors for a portfolio will be much higher than for a single instrument. The decomposition process in a linear portfolio of elementary positions also applies to portfolios of several assets.

Note that the example is not representative of optional instruments. The relationship between value and risk factors is stable because the replicating portfolio of a forward contract is static – it does not change with time. This is not so with options, because the replicating portfolio of an option changes with time. The sensitivities with respect to the underlying risk factor might change significantly even in small time intervals. The case of options is expanded after the forward example.

For implementing calculations with the forward, we need the volatilities and the correlation across risk factors, or the variance-covariance matrix of risk factors. Those are determined historically, and sample values are provided in Table 35.5. The variance-covariance matrix results from annual volatilities of the risk factors and their correlations, using $\sigma_{ij} = \rho_{ij}\sigma_i\sigma_j$.

For proceeding, it is necessary to decompose the forward contract into a linear set of elementary positions, using the sensitivities to each risk factor.

TABLE 35.5   Correlation and variance-covariance matrix between risk factors

Market parameter	Yearly volatilities
1-year € i	0.61%
1-year $ i	0.58%
S €/$	0.35

Historical correlations		
1-year € interest rate	1-year $ interest rate	Spot €/$ forex
100%	10%	20%
10%	100%	10%
20%	10%	100%

Variance-covariance matrix		
1-year € interest rate	1-year $ interest rate	Spot €/$ forex
0.00372%	0.00035%	0.04270%
0.00035%	0.00336%	0.02030%
0.04270%	0.02030%	12.25000%

35.4 THE CONCEPTUAL FRAMEWORK OF DELTA-NORMAL VAR

The conceptual framework for decomposing the variations of value of an instrument into a linear function of elementary positions is the Taylor expansion formula[2]. The Taylor expansion formula states that any function of multiple variables can be approximated, for small variations, by a linear function of the changes of value of each argument, the coefficients being the first derivatives of the function with respect to each argument. This is the first-order approximation. There is no need to consider the second-order terms of the expansion.

The value of an instrument that depends on several arguments, which are risk factors, is a function of which variations are approximated. Using the Taylor expansion, a small change of value ΔV of an instrument is a linear function of the small changes of random market parameters, the coefficients being the first derivatives of the value with respect to each risk factor. The first-order Taylor expansion for the forward contract value is:

$$\Delta V = (\partial V/\partial S)\Delta S + (\partial V/\partial i_s)\Delta i_s + (\partial V/\partial i_e)\Delta i_e$$

The forward can be approximately replicated by a portfolio of three positions combined in a linear fashion. The sensitivities with respect to each factor are the first derivatives of the forward value with respect to each risk factor. The formula replicates the variation of value by a linear decomposition into as many positions as there are risk factors. This allows considering the contract as a linear portfolio of elementary positions.

For moving to VaR, we need two other steps. The first next step consists in determining the volatility of the random variations of value of the contract as a function of those of risk factors. Whenever a random variable is a linear function of random risk factors, its volatility is determined by the variance-covariance matrix of the risk factors. The second step for finding the VaR consists in defining the distribution of the random variations of value of the contract. The normal distribution is convenient. If all risk factors follow a normal distribution, the linear combination of elementary positions replicating the contract also follows a normal distribution.

The delta-normal VaR is based on two critical assumptions:

- sensitivities, or first-order derivatives, are constant, so that portfolio changes are a proxy linear function of market parameter changes
- assume normal distribution for deriving VaR from volatility.

We now apply the methodology to the forward contract.

35.4.1 Deriving Sensitivities

Sensitivities can be derived analytically, as first derivatives of the contract with respect to the risk factors, or numerically by changing slightly the value of each risk factor and recalculating the contract value. It is feasible in this example to calculate analytically the first derivative with respect to each risk factor using the function relating the value of the contract to risk factors.

---

2 The Taylor expansion formula is introduced in Chapter 15 on sensitivities.

TABLE 35.6 Initial values of risk factors

Risk factor	Value	Change
Spot rate	0.7692 €/$	0.01
"i $" (annual rate)	5.00%	0.010%
"i €" (annual rate)	4.00%	0.010%

The alternate numerical methodology is applicable to any such function and when values are calculated numerically when there is no closed form formula.

With a residual maturity of one year, the analytical formula is:

$$F(€) = -S€/\$ \times \$10,000,000/(1 + i_s) + €7,619,048/(1 + i_e)$$

The initial values and changes of risk factors are shown in Table 35.6.

The formula can be used for deriving analytical sensitivities or for determining them by applying the small changes of values considered for the risk factors and revaluing the contract with the new value. Value and value changes are calculated at inception of the contract, when its initial value is zero.

35.4.2 Mathematical Sensitivities

Sensitivities $S(m)$ with respect to each market parameter (risk factor) "m" are the first derivatives for the forward with respect to each factor. The sensitivity values are the product of these derivatives with the change considered for the risk factor.

$$S(s) = \delta V/\delta S = -9523,810/(1 + i_e)$$

$$S(i€) = \delta V/\delta i_e = S \times 10,000,000/(1 + i_e) \times [-1/(1 + i_e)^2]$$

$$S(i\$) = \delta V/\delta i_s = 10,000,000/(1 + i_s) \times [-1/(1 + i_s)^2]$$

The forward is equivalent to three positions, each one of them depending on one risk driver only, the other risk drivers being held constant. Numerical values are derived from closed form formulae above, where LP is the long position (in €) and SP is the short position (in $). Plugging in the initial values of the parameters, we find the numerical values of the derivatives (Table 35.7).

The sensitivities apply to a unit change of the risk factor. For small changes, they are multiplied by the changes considered above.

TABLE 35.7 Sensitivities in € value

Sensitivities: first derivatives (in €)	Mathematical values
$S(i€) = dF / di€ = LP€ \times [-1/(1 + i€)^2]$	-7,044,238
$S(i\$) = dF / di\$ = -(s \times SP\$) \times [-1/(1 + i\$)^2]$	6,977,150
$S(s) = dF / ds = -SP\$ / (1 + i\$)$	-9,523,810

TABLE 35.8 Calculation of the initial value of the contract

Short position SP $ – 1 year	10,000,000	$
Long position LP € – 1 year	7,619,048	€
Spot rate "s" €/$	0.7692	€/$
"i $" annually	5.0%	
"i €" annually	4.0%	
Forward value €	0.00	€

35.4.3 Numerical Sensitivities

Initially, the forward value is zero because we lend and borrow exactly the same amounts valued in a single currency. After initiating the contract, all market parameters move, but the final values are exchanged at the forward exchange rate: $10,000,000 and €7619,048.

The initial value of the forward contract is zero because the present values of the long and short legs of the forward are identical in a common currency: $10,000,000/(1 + i\$) =$ $952,380.95, with $i\$ = 5\%$. At the initial spot rate this is identical to the value of the long leg in €, or €7619,048/(1 + 4%) (Table 35.8).

For calculating the sensitivities numerically, we start from initial values of risk factors, and we change the values of each one of them, one at a time, by a small amount. With the new set of values, there is a new value of the forward contract derived with the analytical formula. Instead of deriving the changes of values using the constant sensitivity assumption, the variation of value is obtained by revaluation of the contract with the new values of the risk factors. The difference with the initial value zero is the sensitivity with respect to the modified risk factor. Revaluation and differences are calculated numerically starting from the initial value as of the initial date of the contract.

Sensitivities of the forward contract are variations of its value in € when each one of the market parameters changes by a small amount; they are summarized in Table 35.9, where both initial and final values of the contract are shown.

The numerical sensitivities are derived from revaluation of the forward contract when each factor changes by an arbitrary and small amount. The variation of each factor appears in bold in Table 35.10.

The numerical values are identical to the mathematical values derived above. Note that the calculation of sensitivities is entirely different depending if we use the formulas for sensitivities directly or when revaluing the contract, as done above. In the first case, sensitivities are calculated analytically directly, while on the second case, the variations of the value of the contract for a given change of market parameters derives from the initial value of zero and a final value using as inputs their initial values plus a small change. The sensitivities become inputs for further calculations.

TABLE 35.9 Numerical sensitivities in Euro value

Variation of spot exchange rate: 0.01 €/$	$–95,238
Variation of i$ by 1 basis point (0.01%)	€+698
Variation of i€ by 1 basis point (0.01%)	€–704

TABLE 35.10   Detailed calculations of the forward sensitivities

Initial forward value			0.000

Risk factors, initial values	Variation of risk factors	Initial values	Final values
Spot rate "S": €/$	**0.010**	0.7692	0.7792
"i $" annually	0.000%	5.000%	5.000%
"i €" annually	0.000%	4.000%	4.000%

Forward value			−95,238
Variation of forward value			−95,238

Risk factors, initial values	Variation of risk factors	Initial values	Final values
Spot rate "S": €/$	0.000	0.7692	0.7692
"i $" annually	**0.010%**	5.000%	5.010%
"i €" annually	0.000%	4.000%	4.000%

Forward value			698
Variation of forward value			698

Risk factors, initial values	Variation of risk factors	Initial values	Final values
Spot rate "S": €/$	0.000	0.7692	0.7692
"i $" annually	0.000%	5.000%	5.000%
"i €" annually	**0.010%**	4.000%	4.010%

Forward value			−704
Variation of forward value			−704

The usage of full revaluation of the contract is the unique method used in the simulations methodology, developed in the next chapter, when we cannot consider sensitivities as constant, which is the case for options. The difference with the above full revaluation used for calculating the sensitivities only once is that we need to revalue the contract for all hypothetical scenarios in simulations.

35.4.4 Decomposition of the Forward as a Linear Function of Elementary Positions

The variation of the forward value as of date zero is a linear function of the small changes of each risk factor:

$$\Delta(\text{forward value}) = -95{,}238\$ \times \Delta S \ €/\$ - 698€ \times \Delta i€ - 704€ \times \Delta i\$$$

The forward is equivalent to three simple positions of which variations of values are proportional to the random changes of each of the three risk factors, expressed in units consistent with the numerical values of the sensitivities.

35.5 VOLATILITY AND DELTA-NORMAL VAR OF THE FORWARD VALUE

The variance of a linear sum of three random variables weighted by sensitivities results from elementary statistical formulas, using the cross-correlations of the three risk factors.

$$\sigma^2(\Delta V) = \sigma^2(S_s \Delta s + S_{i\epsilon} \times \Delta i_\epsilon + S_{i\$} \times \Delta i_\$)$$

The general formula with the correlations $\rho_{S,i\epsilon}$, $\rho_{S,i\$}$, $\rho_{i\$,i\epsilon}$, of which historical values are known, is:

$$\sigma^2(\Delta V) = S_s^2\sigma^2(S) + S_{i\epsilon}^2\sigma^2(i\epsilon) + S_{i\$}^2\sigma^2(i_\$) + 2\rho_{S,i\epsilon}S_s\sigma(S)S_{i\epsilon}\sigma(i_\epsilon) + 2\rho_{S,i\$}S_s\sigma(S)S_{i\$}\sigma(i_\$) + 2\rho_{i\$,i\epsilon}S_{i\epsilon}\sigma(i\epsilon)S_{i\$}\sigma(i_\$)$$

The volatility is the square root of the variance: $\sigma(\Delta V) = \sqrt{\sigma^2(\Delta V)}$. The variance formula can also be expressed in matrix format. The inputs are the sensitivities grouped into a single row vector with three elements S^T. The variance-covariance matrix is Σ. The variance of the portfolio characterized by the vector of sensitivities is $S^T \Sigma S$, where S^T is the row vector of sensitivities, transpose of the column vector S (Table 35.11).

The contract value is in € and so is its volatility. The VaR is a multiple of volatility matching the confidence level. The multiple is 2.33 for a 1% one-tailed confidence level under the normal distribution assumption. The variance and volatility are annual in above calculations. For calculating the daily VaR, we use the square root of time rule for obtaining the daily volatil-

TABLE 35.11 Calculation of the variance and volatility of the forward contract

	Variance-covariance matrix				
	1-year € *interest* *rate*	*1-year $* *interest* *rate*	*Spot €/$*		
	0.00372%	0.00035%	0.04270%	−7,044,238	S(i€)
	0.00035%	0.00336%	0.02030%	6,977,150	S(i$)
	0.04270%	0.02030%	12.25000%	−9,523,810	S(S)

S(i€)	S(i$)	S(S)				Variance
−7,044,238	6,977,150	−9,523,810	−4,304.1	−1,723.5	−1,168,258.2	11,144,562,180,531
						Volatility
						3,338,347
						Daily volatility
						211,136

TABLE 35.12 Annual and daily VaR of the forward contract

Confidence level	1%
Multiple	2.330
Annual VaR	7,777,337
Daily VaR	211,110

ity of the value of the forward contract as the annual volatility scaled down by the coefficient $1/\sqrt{250}$ (Table 35.12).

35.6 THE DELTA-VAR OF THE FORWARD CONTRACT: SUMMARY

The calculation of the delta-normal VaR for the forward contract was conducted step by step, and relies on some critical assumptions. The steps are as follows.

• Map the forward contract to risk factors. In this case, we started from a closed-form formula and used directly the risk factors as they appear in the value of the contract.
• Determine the sensitivities with respect to each factor. We used two methods. The first one is usable only with closed-form formulas since it calculates sensitivities as first derivatives with respect to each risk factor. The second method is numerical and derives sensitivities by applying small variations to each input and revaluing the contract. The last method is applicable when there is no closed form for the price.
• Decompose the forward contract in a linear portfolio of three positions, each corresponding to a single risk factor.
• Calculate the variance and volatility of the portfolio of three positions.
• Apply a multiple matching the confidence level using a normal distribution for finding the daily VaR and scale it up according to the horizon.

The critical assumptions are as follows.

• Constant sensitivities to risk factors, and valid for both upside and downside movements of value.
• Normal distribution of the variations of values. The normal distribution is applicable here because the contract is transformed into a linear decomposition of elementary positions. Since the sum of normal variables is also normal, the volatility of the portfolio is the correct parameter for the distribution of values of the contract.

For a portfolio, the steps and assumptions would be identical as for the forward contract. It is often used for portfolios with no optional instruments because the assumption of constant sensitivity is not acceptable for those.

The delta-VaR methodology has several drawbacks. It relies on the normal distribution assumption, which might differ from real distributions. Notably, it undervalues extreme events as the normal distribution generally does. In some cases, the normal assumptions might lead to negative values for assets or risk factors that cannot be negative (stock prices, interest rates, for example).

The historical VaR is often used as a substitute in such cases, using the full revaluation method to avoid the restrictive assumptions of constant sensitivities. The Monte Carlo simulation, or hypothetical simulation methodology, also deals with the general case using full-blown valuations of the risk factors.

36

Historical and Hypothetical Simulations

The delta-VaR methodology suffers from restrictive assumptions, the main one being the constant delta assumption. Moreover, it involves variance-covariance matrices. For such reasons, two alternative methods can complement or substitute delta-VaR.

The historical VaR is commonly used[1] because it relies on past data for capturing correlations and volatilities of risk factors without making any assumption on their distributions. The process consists of deriving variations of risk factors from historical time series, applying them to the current portfolio and, finally, revaluing the portfolio accordingly. The output is a P & L distribution that is empirical rather than parametric, as the normal distribution is.

The hypothetical scenarios methodology is more involved. It implies simulating future risk factors values, complying with their dependency structure and revaluation for a large number of simulations the portfolio. Such full-blown simulations can be calculation intensive. Furthermore, it relies, as the delta-VaR technique, on variance-covariance matrices of risk factors.

Both historical VaR and hypothetical VaR use full revaluation of asset values in order to bypass the linear assumption of the delta-VaR technique. As such they apply to convex instruments.

Section 36.1 addresses historical simulations. It shows how to apply historical daily variations of risk factors to the current portfolio. The methodology is applied to a forward contract example. Section 36.2 addresses hypothetical simulations, using Monte Carlo simulations. It mentions the grid simulations methodology used for simplifying the process in some cases, and simply reminds how simulations of risk factors can be conducted. As an example, we provide

---

1   In a review of 25 bank annual reports for 2006, we found that historical VaR was mentioned 19 times, delta-VaR 8 times and Monte Carlo simulations 4 times. In all cases, delta-VaR was used in conjunction with another methodology for non-linear instruments, which explains why the total exceeds 25.

simulation for an option contract, by simulating the underlying asset distribution and deriving the option value using the closed-form formula for pricing options.

The last section (Section 36.3) addresses common extensions of the VaR methodology, notably the E-VaR method which is attractive because the measure is additive unlike the VaR. It provides an estimate of the E-VaR of the forward contract.

Contents

36.1 HISTORICAL SIMULATIONS

Historical VaR is a common methodology for deriving VaR. It does not rely on correlation and volatility measures but rather uses historical time series of risk factors which embed correlations and volatilities of risk factors. Both the principles and implementation are relatively simple and do not rely on restrictive assumptions, other than assuming that the historical data, on a time window that can be adjusted, is representative of the current market conditions. This is presumably why it is so commonly used. Finally, note that there are some common features to historical and hypothetical simulations, the main difference being how series of values of risk factors are generated.

36.1.1 Principles

Say we observe 250 daily values of the three risk factors driving the value of the forward contract. We could obtain 250 values of the contract. The historical risk factor values are not identical to those that result in the current value of the contract. Since relevant deviations are from the current value, these historical observations should be converted into daily changes applicable to the current values of these risk factors. Applying these percentage changes to the current values, we obtain what would be the 250 values of risk factors starting from their current values. The new set of risk factor values mimics the historical changes starting from today's values. There is no need to rely on the normal assumption for deriving VaR. Since we have an empirical distribution of values, we can derive directly from this distribution the percentiles.

The major benefits of historical simulations are:

- there is no need to derive correlations and volatilities because they are embedded in historical data
- there is no need either to rely on the unrealistic assumption of normal distributions.

The delta-VaR and the historical VaR differ in the sequence of calculations and in the number of calculations. Under delta-VaR, sensitivities are calculated only once. The deviations of risk factors from their current values are derived and the deviations of value of the instrument, using these sensitivities, follow directly. This is a "partial revaluation" method because the new values result from applying constant sensitivities to initial values. Under the full revaluation method, the simulated values of risk factors serve, first, for revaluing the instrument for all multiple scenarios. Second, the changes of value of the instrument from its current value are derived. The sequence of calculations is the reverse of the partial revaluation method.

In historical simulations, the partial revaluation of instruments is still feasible, but has the major drawback of relying on the assumption of constant sensitivities, an assumption which collapses, notably for optional instruments. In both historical and hypothetical simulations, the full revaluation method bypasses this assumption. In both cases, we have a set of values of risk factors for each historical or hypothetical scenario.

The full revaluation methodology implies recalculating values of instruments for a very large number of scenarios. This is easy when closed-form formulas are available for pricing, such as with the forward contract or plain vanilla options. When no such formulas are available, we need to rely on numerical simulations for pricing instruments for each of those multiple scenarios. This leads to "simulations within simulations," which becomes much more calculation intensive. Partial revaluation and full valuation can be used in conjunction for simplifying the calculations, as long as partial revaluations apply to linear instruments.

The process involves the following steps:

- determine the series of historical values of risk factors
- transform this series into percentage changes
- apply the percentage variations to the current risk factor values to mimic the historical changes starting from today's values of risk factors
- derive for each historical change of each risk factor the value of the forward, either using the constant sensitivities assumption or by revaluing the instrument with each of the 250 sets of risk factor values
- for each daily variation of risk factor values, we obtain a daily variation of the value of the instrument – such a daily variation is the daily P & L (daily change of value) of the forward
- construct the distribution of daily P & L
- find the loss percentile not exceeded in more than the confidence level one-tailed, such as 1%, 2.5%, 5%, from this empirical (non-parametric) distribution.

36.1.2 Historical VaR: Forward Contract Example

Table 36.1 shows the current values of the three risk factors, followed by the time series of values for four consecutive days. The second block of the table shows the percentage variations. Those are variations from one day to the next. There is no value for the first day. For example the "Day 2" percentage variation of the spot rate is $(0.81132 - 0.81251)/0.81251 = -0.146\%$. The third block of the table applies these percentage variations to the current values of the risk factor. For example, the simulated "Value 2" of the spot rate is $-0.146\% \times 0.76923 = 0.7681$.

Using the set of 250 simulated values of risk factors, derived from current values to which daily percentage changes are applied, the forward values are recalculated using either the partial revaluation method, or using the exact formula for pricing the contract for each set of daily simulated values of the three risk factors.

TABLE 36.1 Deriving historical percentage changes of risk factors

	Spot rate S €/$	"i $" annually	"i €" annually
Current values	0.76923	0.05000	0.04000
Historical values			
Day 1	0.8125	0.049800	0.038520
Day 2	0.8113	0.049720	0.039521
Day 3	0.8126	0.049102	0.039871
Day 4	0.7925	0.050100	0.040150
...	...	...	...
Daily variations of historical values			
Day 1			
Day 2	−0.146%	−0.161%	2.599%
Day 3	0.153%	−1.243%	0.886%
Day 4	−2.472%	2.033%	0.700%
...	...	...	...
Daily simulations of values			
Value 1	0.7692	0.05000	0.04000
Value 2	0.7681	0.04992	0.04104
Value 3	0.7704	0.04938	0.04035
Value 4	0.7502	0.05102	0.04028
...	...	...	...

In both cases, we obtain 250 simulated daily variations, or daily P & L, of the contract from which the empirical distribution of P & L is constructed, with 250 points. From the distribution, the loss percentiles, or losses not exceeded in more than the confidence interval one-tailed, such as 1%, 2.5%, 5%, are directly derived. The loss value exceeded in 2 to 3 times, out of 250, corresponds to a percentile of 1%, etc.

The drawback of historical VaR with full revaluation is that the technique is backward looking. It also averages observations of market parameters independently of how representative they are of current conditions. In some cases, it is conservative, because historical observations capture market shocks of large magnitude. In others, it averages so much the past values that it misses the current market conditions, which might be an outlier compared to historical scenarios. Finally, historical VaR cannot serve for stress-testing the VaR since the nature of scenarios is predetermined by past data.

Historical VaR serves for back-testing alternate VaR methodologies, by making sure that the portfolio values include those that would have appeared if the past is replicated on the current portfolio structure.

The Monte Carlo simulation method is similar to historical VaR with full revaluation except that it uses simulations to generate hypothetical scenarios.

36.2 MONTE CARLO SIMULATIONS

Monte Carlo simulations are hypothetical simulations complying with the dependency structure of risk factors. The hypothetical simulation method consists of simulating the random values of risk factors and revalues accordingly the instruments from such multiple simulations. The methodology is identical to Monte Carlo simulations. Each simulation of the set of risk factor values is a hypothetical scenario. The methodology still relies on the variance-covariance matrix for conducting such simulations. The methodologies for simulating dependent variables are expanded in the dependencies chapters. When the linear approximation collapses, as for options, we need to revert to full valuation technique. The full revaluation method avoids the drawback of relying on the constant sensitivity assumption, as with historical simulations.

The main drawback of Monte Carlo simulation is that it is calculation intensive. This drawback is magnified when dealing with instruments for which no closed formula exists, such as look-back options valued with simulations. In such cases, revaluation of derivatives requires simulations within each hypothetical scenario, or "simulations within simulations," making the process overly complex.

Because of these complexities, several techniques help simplifying the process. Historical simulation with full revaluation is a first technique that reduces the calculations to historical data and avoids dealing explicitly with dependencies embedded in past data. It is discussed above. Another way to address the calculation intensive process is to minimize the number of simulations. There are variations around these common principles. The simplest ones include:

- grid simulations
- full Monte Carlo simulations.

36.2.1 Grid Simulations

Before generating a very large number of scenarios, it is tempting, for limiting the calculations, to restrict the approach to a small number of scenarios. The grid Monte Carlo approach uses an exact valuation for each grid point and uses a linear interpolation between points. Grid simulation consists of using a limited number of simulated values. The selected values should cover the maximum range of values of each parameter. The process is less calculation intensive than full Monte Carlo simulations because we limit the number of simulations and we use the interpolation technique between grid point simulations.

36.2.2 Full Monte Carlo Simulations

Under full Monte Carlo simulations, the process starts with modeling the stochastic processes of market parameters, doing the best to ensure that they capture recent worst-case situations. It is similar to historical simulations except that we look forward using simulated values rather than historical values. Modeling the inputs is a crucial issue. Inputs include volatilities and correlations whose measures raise issues with respect to their volatilities over time.

The next stage is the generation of random values of risk factors complying with this input structure. The last stage is portfolio revaluation for each set of values generated. Since the simulations capture all forward-looking information, as well as past information embedded in modeling inputs, we have the best of both worlds. The main drawback of the full-blown simulations is that it is calculation intensive. All instruments should be valued for all sets of markets parameter values and the number of runs has to be high enough to provide a sufficient accuracy for the portfolio value distribution.

By contrast, the correlation (delta-VaR) methodology uses the same variance-covariance matrix for all portfolios and the calculation requires only a product of matrices to obtain the portfolio volatility.

36.2.3 Example: Option Contract

To illustrate the process, we use a simplified example of a single option contract: a call option on stock. Options raise many issues beyond the variations of the sensitivity (delta), which can vary from 0 to 1. Option values also depend on the interest rate and non-constant volatilities. The purpose of the example is only to isolate the effect of the "kink" of the delta of the option. Accordingly, we use a simple simulation with, as a single risk factor, the underlying asset.

The formula for a call option C on stock is the Black-Scholes formula:

$$C = S_0 N(d_1) - K \exp(-rt) N(d_2)$$

$$d_1 = [\ln(S_0/K) + (r + \sigma^2/2)t]/\sigma\sqrt{t}$$

$$d_2 = [\ln(S_0/K) + (r - \sigma^2/2)t]/\sigma\sqrt{t} = d_1 - \sigma\sqrt{t}$$

The formula allows calculating the price of the option with inputs:

- continuous risk-free rate[2], $r = 4.879\%$ (which matches a discrete annual return of 5%)
- current stock price, $S_0 = 100$
- strike price, $K = 90$
- maturity, $t = 1$ year
- volatility of stock price return (annualized) = 30%.

For the above inputs, the value of the call option is 19.6308. The parameter and values are:

$$d_1 = [\ln(100/90) + (4.879\% + 30\%^2/2) \times 1]/30\% \times \sqrt{1} = 0.6638$$

$$d_2 = 0.6638 - 30\% \times \sqrt{1} = 0.3638$$

$$N(d_1) = 0.7466$$

$$N(d_2) = 0.6420$$

$$C = 100 \; 0.7466 - 90 \exp(-4.879\% \times 1) \times 0.6420 = 19.6308$$

The stock price follows a log/normal distribution, meaning that the Napierian logarithm of the stock price follows a normal distribution. The stock price distribution depends on the continuous return of the stock price. The Napierian logarithm of the stock price follows a normal distribution with mean and standard deviation:

---

2 The continuous return r is derived from the discrete return using $r = \ln(1 + R)$ for one year.

TABLE 36.2   Simulation of the stock and call value

u	ln(S)	Stock value	Option value
0.7714	4.969	143.82	58.67
0.6086	4.828	124.98	40.80
0.0758	4.315	74.84	5.09
0.9898	5.441	230.73	145.02
0.4528	4.710	111.04	28.45

- mean $= \ln(S_0) + (\mu + \sigma^2/2)t$
- standard deviation $= \sigma\sqrt{t}$

With the current inputs and horizon $t = 1$, the numerical values are:

- mean $= \ln(S_0) + (y + \sigma^2/2)t = \ln(100) + (9.531\% + 30\%^2) \times 1 = 4.75$
- standard deviation $= \sigma\sqrt{t} = 30\% \times \sqrt{1} = 30\%$

For simulating the logarithm of the stock price, we simulate the values of a random uniform distribution $U(0, 1)$. The logarithm of the stock price, $\ln(S)$, is the normal inverse of the uniform values, using as normal distribution the one with mean and standard deviation as above. It follows that:

$$\ln(S) = N^{-1}[\ln(S_0) + (y + \sigma^2/2)t, \sigma\sqrt{t}] = N^{-1}[4.75, 30\%]$$

We are interested in simulating the distribution of the call option value when the underlying equity price varies randomly. The simulation of 500 values of the stock price and of the option price proceeds as follows in Table 36.2, where we have shown the first 5 lines, out of 500.

Using 500 simulations, we find the distribution of the stock price and the distribution of the option price. The distribution of the stock price is log/normal and skewed to the right (Figure 36.1). The distribution of the option value is highly skewed to the right because the option value gets near zero when the option is far out-of-the-money. The high skewness shows that

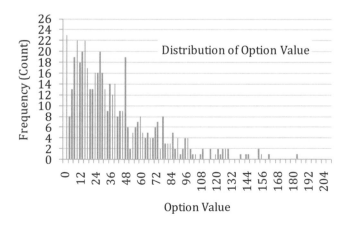

FIGURE 36.1   Distribution of the call option payoffs

the normal distribution would collapse in capturing the truncated left-hand tail and the large right-hand fat tail.

The values matching high percentiles are 10 times higher than the current value (19.6308) of the option. Such percentiles would be relevant for the VaR of the seller of the option, if the option sold is not hedged. When using the Monte Carlo simulation, the procedure for determining percentiles is the same. The distribution is empirical and not parametric. Percentiles are count of cumulative frequencies for the different values, and are derived empirically from the distribution.

36.3 EXTENSIONS OF THE MARKET VAR METHODOLOGY

There are several extensions of the VaR methodologies. The E-VaR is the expectation of VaR conditional on exceeding the threshold at the preset confidence level. It is easy to derive under the normal assumptions but can be derived from historical or hypothetical simulations as well. Hypothetical scenarios allow also stress-testing the VaR to see what happens in extreme conditions.

36.3.1 E-VaR or Expected Shortfall

The E-VaR, also named expected shortfall or expected tail loss, is the expected loss conditional on loss being lower or equal to VaR. We call the random loss L and the threshold point matching the percentile α, or VaR, $L(\alpha)$. The VaR is the loss percentile $P[(L \leq L(\alpha)] = F(\alpha)$. The cumulative distribution function F of losses is empirical under historical VaR and normal under the delta-normal VaR. The E-VaR is the probability weighted average of losses exceeding the VaR.

Using Bayes' rule, considering a value x of the random portfolio loss:

$$P[(L \leq x) \mid L \leq L(\alpha)] = P[(L \leq x)]/P[L \leq L(\alpha)]$$

By definition, $P[L \leq L(\alpha)] = \alpha$. The probability $P(L = x)$ that the random loss L is lower than or equal to value x conditional on being lower than or equal to $L(\alpha)$ is the unconditional probability that the loss is lower than or equal to x divided by the unconditional probability that the loss is lower than or equal to $L(\alpha)$, or $F(\alpha)$. By definition, the summation of all probabilities $P(L \leq x)$ from the lower bound of L up to the loss percentile $L(\alpha)$ is $F(\alpha)$:

$$\int_{\text{lowerbound}(L)}^{L(\alpha)} p(l)\mathrm{d}l = F(\alpha)$$

For example, if we select the percentile $\alpha = 1\%$, and $F(\alpha) = F(1\%)$, and the cumulative probability of exceeding the VaR threshold is 1%. The conditional probabilities attached to any value of loss, x, lower than VaR are $P(l)/\alpha = p(l)/1\%$. The sum of all probabilities conditional on $L \leq L(\alpha)$ is equal to 1%.

The expected shortfall is the probability weighted average loss conditional on loss lower than or equal to $L(\alpha)$. This formula requires the calculation of the expectation of the truncated distribution $F(L)$, from the lower bound of L and up to the truncation occurring at $L(\alpha)$. In the case of a normal distribution, the E-VaR can be derived from the probability density function of the normal distribution. In this case, $F(\alpha) = \Phi(\alpha)$ and $L(\alpha) = \Phi^{-1}(\alpha)$. Using $\varphi(L)$ as the probability density function of the standard normal distribution, with y being the standardized variable of loss:

$$\text{E-VaR} = \frac{1}{\alpha} \int_{-\infty}^{\Phi^{-1}(\alpha)} y\,\varphi(y)\mathrm{d}y = \frac{\varphi\left[\Phi^{-1}(\alpha)\right]}{\alpha}$$

It is proportional to the normal density of $\Phi^{-1}(\alpha)$ since the value of the density of the lower bound is zero[3]. Since this applies to a standardized variable of portfolio loss, this value should be multiplied by the volatility of the portfolio loss, neglecting the expectation of the P & L variation of very a short period.

In practice, we can find the E-VaR from any parametric or non-parametric distributions, by taking the average value of all adverse deviations of the daily P & L. Say we have n values of losses strictly lower than the loss matching the VaR at 99%, each with frequency in percentage equal to p_i. The E-VaR is:

$$\text{E-VaR} = \frac{\displaystyle\sum_{i=1,n} p_i l_i}{\displaystyle\sum_{i=1,n} p_i}$$

Figure 36.2 shows the tail of the distribution of the historical VaR of the forward contract. The full distribution of loss values was obtained by running 1000 simulations of the risk factors.

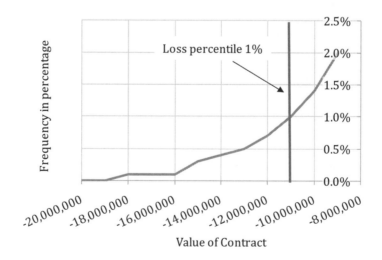

FIGURE 36.2   Tail of the distribution of values of the forward contract

---

3 Writing the density of the normal distribution, and making a change of variable:

$$\int_u^v \frac{1}{\sqrt{2\pi}} y\exp\left(-\frac{y^2}{2}\right)\mathrm{d}y = \frac{1}{\sqrt{2\pi}} \int_u^v \exp\left(-\frac{y^2}{2}\right)\mathrm{d}\left(\frac{y^2}{2}\right) = \frac{1}{\sqrt{2\pi}}\left[\exp\left(-\frac{v^2}{2}\right) - \exp\left(-\frac{u^2}{2}\right)\right]$$

The integral collapses to $\dfrac{1}{\sqrt{2\pi}}\exp\left(-\dfrac{v^2}{2}\right)$ when u is minus infinity, while the density of the upper bound v, equal to $\Phi^{-1}(\alpha)$.

TABLE 36.3 Calculation of E-VaR

Frequency count	Loss value	Weighted loss value	Cumulative frequency (%)
3	−11,000,000	−33,000,000	1.0%
2	−12,000,000	−24,000,000	0.7%
1	−13,000,000	−13,000,000	0.5%
1	−14,000,000	−14,000,000	0.4%
2	−15,000,000	−30,000,000	0.3%
0			0.1%
0			0.1%
1	−18,000,000	−18,000,000	0.1%
0			0.0%
0			0.0%
7		−19,800,000	0.70%

The tail losses and their frequencies are shown in Table 36.3. The VaR at 1% is exactly 11,000,000. The frequency count shows the number of times a loss value is observed. The loss value is the next column. The next column shows the weighted loss value by the frequency count. The last column shows the cumulative frequencies in percentage. The loss percentile 1%, 11,000,000, can be obtained by summing all frequency counts of loss occurrences across rows, which totals 10 or 1% out of 1000 simulations. The first row shows the loss value matching the percentile 1%.

The E-VaR is the average of loss occurrences beyond the VaR. The same loss can occur several times, as Table 36.3 shows in the first column, and should be counted as many times as it occurs. The E-VaR is the average of the weighted losses by the number of occurrences of the each loss value. In other words we observe the loss values beyond the VaR and we take the weighted average, ignoring blank values. Blank cells correspond to loss values that do not appear in the distribution. The E-VaR is 19,800,000. In the calculation, only those losses in excess of VaR are used, ignoring the first row.

The E-VaR is above the VaR since is a weighted average of loss values by number of occurrences beyond the VaR on the graph.

36.3.2 Hypothetical Scenarios, Stress-tests and Extreme VaR

Note that hypothetical simulations allow stress testing those factors to which the portfolio is highly sensitive. Extreme VaR measures involve extreme scenarios. Such scenarios might be judgmental and selective, as explained in Chapter 38 on stress tests. For instance, if the management fears wide variations of risk factors selected according to the high sensitivity of the portfolio to such factors, assigning shocks to these factors would results in high adverse deviations of the P & L. This is the "factor-push" methodology, of which a pre-requisite is the identification of those factors to which portfolio sensitivity is higher. The magnitude of adverse effects would make explicit the responses to stressing one or more factors. Using the extreme conditions that prevailed historically over a long period is a common way to stress test portfolios.

Extreme VaR techniques differ in that they attempt to model extreme situations, using the fat tail distribution. A common technique is to fit a distribution with fat tails to selected highest loss values. The extreme value distribution, or the Pareto distribution family, serves for fitting the tail, separately from the rest of the distribution. The technique involves "smoothing the tail" to obtain better estimates of the value percentiles. It allows using a known distribution instead of the modeled or the simulated ones, for determining loss percentiles at low confidence levels without requiring to calculation intensive simulations. By definition, it relies on a small number of observations and smoothing the tail ignores ranges of "blank values" and jumps, which can be a drawback.

37

Simulation of Interest Rates

The simulation of the term structure of interest rates is a common issue for ALM simulations and optimization as well as for fixed income portfolios market VaR. A first possibility is to select few interest rates and risk factors and correlate them. But it would be better to model several rates and simulate a "consistent" term structure of interest rates.

Under an ALM perspective, the issue is to explore what could happen with simple scenarios other than standard shifts of all interest rates or increasing the long-term and short-term spread. ALM simulations of the term structure interest rates provide the faculty of testing, bask-testing and stress-testing what would happen with a large number of simulations of the term structures of interest rates. In ALM, the target variables are the NII and the economic value. Under a market VaR perspective the horizon is shorter and limited to current conditions, and the target variable is the P & L of the market portfolio. Any methodology relying on factor models, notably the delta-VaR methodology, requires simulating consistent term structure of interest rates.

Interest rate models used for pricing purposes are not so helpful for such simulations. The statistical methodology based on principal component analysis is adequate since a few principal components summarize fairly well the set of highly correlated interest rates[1].

This chapter explains simulations based on PCA and its applications to ALM policies and market VaR. Section 37.1 is a reminder of the basics of principal component analysis and properties of the factors, or principal components. Section 37.2 details the process of fitting a PCA model to interest rates. A fit of the model to Euro interest rates, using daily observations over a period of around 3.5 years until July 2007 is described. The results from this fit of the PCA model is used for simulations in Section 37.3. As usual in such a case, it is found that a very few factors explain the variance of interest rates. In general, three factors are sufficient and represent parallel shift of the curve, changes in steepness of the curve and a bump of the

---

1 The reference paper is that of Frye [30]. Note that the Vasicek model presented in Chapter 13 allows simulations, but the version limited to a single factor does not allow comprehensive simulations on the long-end of the term structure.

curve (if any). Section 37.3 uses the fit to conduct simulation of the entire curve by generating random normal standard values of the factors. The last two sections address applications to market VaR (Section 37.4) and ALM (Section 37.5). For market VaR, the simulations of the curve provide the distribution of the daily P & L using given portfolio sensitivities to some selected rates, and converting them into sensitivities to principal components that drive the interest rates. The same process is implemented for ALM simulations of the net interest income using sensitivities with a bank with significant mismatch risk.

Contents

37.1 INTEREST RATES AND FACTOR MODELS

The correlation between interest rates varies across maturities. But very short-term rates might not be correlated with short-term and longer-term rates. The convenient methodology for simulating interest rate variations is to use the principal components analysis, or PCA. The reader should refer to the factor model chapter (Chapter 32) for the conceptual framework. As a reminder, PCA serves for explaining a set of variables using orthogonal factors, which are much easier to handle than usual (correlated) factors. The factors are called principal components. The number of factors that contribute significantly to the variance explained decreases with the correlations between variables. Hence PCA allows explaining the variance of multiple correlated variables with a smaller number of factors. It is notably successful for interest rates because they are highly correlated.

Let Y_i be the set of variables to be explained, interest rates, the generic form of factor model is a linear relation between the explained variables and the factors X_k:

$$Y_i = \beta_0 + \beta_{1i}X_1 + \beta_{2i}X_2 + \beta_{3i}X_3 + \ldots + \varepsilon_i$$

The notations are those of Chapter 32 on factor models. The PCA uses independent variables as factors. The independent variables are constructed as linear functions of the observable factors used in the standard regression technique. The concepts behind PCA are detailed in Appendix 1 of Chapter 32. The generic form of the PCA models is:

$$Y_i = \eta_{0i} + \eta_{1i}P_1 + \eta_{2i}P_2 + \ldots + \varepsilon_i$$

A major application of PCA is the modeling of the term structure, because it was observed that very few factors, usually no more than three, suffice for explaining most of the variance of interest rates. The technique is commonly used in market VaR, but serves as well for providing interest rate simulations in ALM with other than simple interest rate scenarios, such as parallel shifts or standard changes of the steepness of the term structure of rates.

Because PCA uses as independent factors combinations of standard regression variables, one can wonder what principal components mean. In the case of interest rates, the interpretation, as we will illustrate, is fairly simple.

37.2 PRINCIPAL COMPONENT ANALYSIS AND THE TERM STRUCTURE OF INTEREST RATES

As usual for factor models, we need to start with historical observations. The data window should be selected according to the goal. For market VaR, recent periods are most relevant. For ALM applications, it might make sense to uses various periods with different behaviors of the term structure of rates, for stress-testing purposes, for example.

The data set comprises 911 daily observations of Euro interest rates for 1 month, 2 months, 6 months, 9 months, and 1, 3, 5, 7, 10, 15, 20 and 30 years. These rates zero rates. The rates designated as E_m1, E_m2, E_m3, E_m6, E_m12, E_y1, E_y3, E_y5, etc., where "m" stands for month, "y" for year, and "E" represents the Euro currency. Observations are from January 2, 2004 until July 12, 2007, a period of roughly 3.5 years. Over the period, the yield curve was upward sloping at the beginning of the period and progressively flattened out in the later years. The period is characterized by a high volatility of short-term rates and a flattening of the yield curve. The last observations for the Euribor 3-month and 10-year rate are, respectively 4.226% and 4.844%. For the first observation date, the same Euribor 3-month was only 2.099% and the 10-year rate 4.438%. Therefore we do not expect to have any "bumps" in the curve, but we should capture the variations of level and steepness of the curve for the observation period.

The correlations between the interest rates and the short-term rate E_m1 are higher than 0.9 up to the 3-year maturity, with longer term rates having a declining correlation with E_m1, declining from 0.847 for E_y5 down to 0.064 for E_y30. The correlations are high with the 1-month rate up to 5 years and fall down near zero for the 30-year rate. Long-term rates vary almost independently of the short-term rate, while intermediate interest rates co-vary strongly with it.

For implementing PCA analysis, standard statistical techniques provide the coefficients of the model, or factor loadings, for normal standard factors:

$$Y_i = \eta_{0i} + \eta_{1i}P_1 + \eta_{2i}P_2 + \ldots + \varepsilon_i$$

The Y_i are the 11 interest rates selected. The PCA analysis provides a total of 11 factors, but, in this example, only the first two contribute significantly to explaining the variance. The factors are numbered 1 to 11 and ranked according to the percentage of variance explained. Table 37.1 shows the first five factors, with the two first factors only explaining most of the variance of interest rates (99.3%). The two main principal components explain cumulatively 99.31% of the variance of the interest rates. P_1 explains 81.39%, and P_2 17.91% of the total variance.

The interpretation of principal components is based on the correlations between the factors and the various interest rates, provided in Table 37.2. There are as many correlations as there are interest rates, for each factor. Table 37.2 isolates the first two factors. The coefficients, or factor loadings, of each one of the two main principal components are shown in the two columns of Table 37.2.

TABLE 37.1   Applying PCA to the term structure of interest rates

Factor	% of variance	Cumulative %
1	81.392	81.392
2	17.914	99.306
3	0.632	99.938
4	0.044	99.983
5	0.012	99.994

TABLE 37.2   Factor loadings in the PCA analysis

Factor	1	2
E_m1	0.1840	−0.0872
E_m3	0.2079	−0.1065
E_m6	0.2343	−0.1220
E_m12	0.2492	−0.1102
E_y3	0.1186	0.0709
E_y5	0.0431	0.1449
E_y7	0.0060	0.1721
E_y10	−0.0195	0.1866
E_y15	−0.0377	0.2016
E_y20	−0.0489	0.2155
E_y30	−0.0590	0.2272

We observe that the first factor is positively correlated with all interest rates. A shift of this factor would increase all interest rates, creating a more or less parallel shift of all rates. This suggests that the first factor represents a shift of the entire term structure. The second factor has negative correlations with the short-term rates and positive correlation with long-term rates. Hence a positive shift of that factor would increase the slope of the curve, making short-term rates lower and long-term rates higher. The factor represents the slope of the term structure.

These are general findings. When using long periods with changes of shapes of the term structure, three factors accounts for the variance of rates. The first two represent a shift of the curve and a change of its slope. The third factor, when it appears as a significant contributor to the variance, represents "bumps" of the term structure of the curve, in that it correlates positively with intermediate maturity interest rates and correlates negatively with the short-end and the long-end of the curve. In our example, the yield curve was upward sloping, initially, and progressively flattened out. With this sample, there was no "bump" in the curve, which is why we have only two contributing factors that explain the variance almost entirely.

The mean and standard deviations of the two factors, P_1 and P_2, are obtained by fitting the model to observed historical data. Note that all variables are standardized, both the factors and the interest rates. For example, the 3-month standardized interest rate value is 0.2079 times the standardized P_1 and −0.1065 times the standardized P_2 (second row of the table). These factor loadings allow determining the variations of each standardized rate as a function of the factor variations. The same process applies with all rates, making them a function of only two principal components.

37.3 INTEREST RATE SIMULATIONS WITH PCA

The PCA allows simulating the values of interest rates. Assume that there is a small variation of the factors ΔP_1 and ΔP_2. We calculate the variations of all interest rates as linear functions of the variations of the two first factors, ignoring residuals since they have very small influences on interest rates. For example, considering the Euribor 3-month, E_m3, its standardized value is a linear function of the factors:

$$E\_m3(\text{standardized}) = 0.2079P_1 - 0.1065P_2$$

Generating random variations of P_1 and P_2 generates random variations of the standardized interest rate. Applying similar relationships between each interest rate and the same common two factors, all standardized interest rates are linear functions of P_1 and P_2, with coefficients given in Table 37.2. If we generate random values of those two factors, we generate values of all 11 interest rates. They are dependent because they derive from the same factors, with different sensitivities. This principle allows generating entire term structures of the 11 interest rates by varying the two factors randomly.

Generating random values of P_1 and P_2 is extremely simple since those two factors are independent and standardized principal components. All we need to do is generate two series of random values of a uniform standard function $U(0, 1)$ and take the normal standard inverse function of these random values. The two uniform standard values of U_1 and U_2, and the random values of P_1 and P_2 are:

$$P_1 = \Phi^{-1}(U_1)$$

$$P_2 = \Phi^{-1}(U_2)$$

For simulation k, the values of P_1 and P_2 are $p_{1k} = \Phi^{-1}(u_{1k})$ and $p_{2k} = \Phi^{-1}(u_{2k})$

For moving back from factor values to interest rates, we have to revert from the standardized value of interest rates to non-standardized values. The statistics of the interest rates provide the historical estimates of mean and standard deviation of each rate. The standardized variable derived from the non-standard variable X is $X_S = (X - \mu)/\sigma$ since X_S has mean zero and σ equal to 1. Reversing the equation, we obtain the non-standard variable $X = X_S\sigma + \mu$. Since the Euribor 3-month is non-standard, and since we simulate its standardized value, the simulated values are obtained by the above transformation. The historical mean and standard deviations of each rate are required for converting standardized values to non-standardized values. Both the mean and the standard deviation of each interest rate are in Table 37.3. For the principal components, there is no need to transform them, since they serve for modeling standardized values of interest rates.

The algorithm uses the following steps, illustrated for the first simulations of the Euribor 3-month. The first step generates random values of the independent P_1 and P_2, for example 0.340 and −1.313 in the first simulation run. Table 37.4 reproduces the first five simulations[2]. The standardized value of Euribor 3-month results from the linear function with principal components, where the second subscript "i" of the coefficients refers to the Euribor 3-month:

---

2 As usual, two independent uniform standard variables are generated and converted into standard normal variables using the normal standard inverse function.

TABLE 37.3 Mean and standard deviation
of interest rates

	μ	σ
E_m1	2.612	0.678
E_m3	2.687	0.714
E_m6	2.776	0.756
E_m12	2.922	0.790
E_y3	3.306	0.639
E_y5	3.554	0.521
E_y7	3.751	0.454
E_y10	3.974	0.410
E_y15	4.200	0.395
E_y20	4.320	0.397
E_y30	4.384	0.401

TABLE 37.4 Simulations of the principal components

Simulations	U_1	U_2	$P_1 = \Phi(0,1)$	$P_2 = \Phi(0,1)$
1	0.633	0.095	0.340	−1.313
2	0.127	0.134	−1.142	−1.108
3	0.948	0.786	1.629	0.792
4	0.961	0.719	1.764	0.581
5	0.188	0.203	-0.885	−0.831

$$\eta_{1i}P_1 + \eta_{2i}P_2 = 0.2079P_1 - 0.1065P_2$$

The value obtained with the first couple of simulated values of P_1 and P_2 is a standardized value of the Euribor 3-month. The non-standardized value of any one of the interest rates is $i = i_s\sigma(i) + \mu(i)$, where $\sigma(i)$ and $\mu(i)$ are the standard deviation and mean of interest rates, and i_s is the standardized value of i. The first simulated value of the Euribor 3-month is:

$$i(\text{E\_m3}) = (\eta_{1i}P_1 + \eta_{2i}P_2)\sigma[i(\text{E\_m3})] + \mu[i(\text{E\_m3})]$$

The numerical values are:

$$i(\text{E\_m3}) = (0.2079P_1 - 0.1065P_2) \times (0.714) + 2.687$$

The simulation of P_1 and P_2 are in Table 37.5.

Replacing P_1 and P_2 by the simulated values, respectively, 0.340 and −1.313, we find a simulated value of the Euribor 3-month "i," in percentage:

$$i(\text{E\_m3}) = [(0.2079 \times (0.340) - 0.1065 \times (-1.313)] \times 0.714 + 2.687 = 2.838$$

The five first simulations of all eleven rates are in rows in Table 37.5. The simulated factor values are in the first two columns of the table and the 3-month interest rate is the column labeled "EU_m3." The equations ensure that the interest rates are equal to their long-term mean values

TABLE 37.5 Simulations of interest rates from PCA

	P1	P2	E_m1	E_m3	E_m6	E_m12	E_y3	E_y5	E_y7	E_y10	E_y15	E_y20	E_y30
1	0.340	−1.313	2.732	2.838	2.957	3.103	3.272	3.462	3.649	3.871	4.091	4.201	4.257
2	0.126	−0.334	2.647	2.731	2.829	2.976	3.300	3.531	3.725	3.948	4.172	4.289	4.351
3	0.625	0.336	2.670	2.754	2.856	3.016	3.369	3.593	3.779	3.995	4.218	4.337	4.400
4	−0.233	2.076	2.461	2.494	2.543	2.696	3.382	3.706	3.912	4.135	4.370	4.502	4.579
5	−0.475	−0.352	2.574	2.643	2.724	2.859	3.254	3.517	3.722	3.951	4.180	4.299	4.364

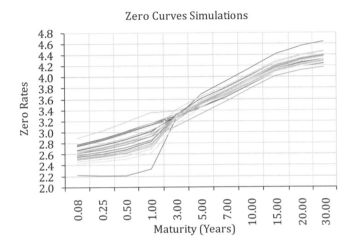

FIGURE 37.1 Simulation of zero interest rates

plus a random element obtained as the linear combination of the random factor values, using factor loadings as coefficients, multiplied by the standard deviation of the 3-month rate.

Using the same algorithm, for example 100 times, we obtain 100 randomly generated term structures of rates. Figure 37.1 shows the first 20 random term structures of interest rates. The graph provides a partial image of interest rate scenarios matching the fitting period used for determining the factor loadings.

37.4 APPLICATION TO MARKET VAR

Dependent variations of interest rates are required for calculating the P & L of a portfolio of positions depending on the interest rates as risk factors. This is the VaR calculation for these positions, as illustrated in the next example, using the factor model.

We map the position to the selected interest rates and assign sensitivities to the 3-month rate, the 5-year rate and the 10-year rate. The sensitivities, or deltas, are those of the market portfolio positions on interest rates in monetary values. By definition, each delta represents the change of the position value due to a unit shock of the interest rate.

These sensitivities have to be converted into sensitivities to each principal component. The conversion requires using the volatility of the interest rate because the coefficients of the principal components provide the response to a change of this factor to the standardized rate.

The sensitivity of a position to principal components, in monetary value, is the product of each position delta by the factor loading and the volatility of the interest rate. From the vector of market sensitivities of the portfolio, we calculate weighted sensitivities to factors, the weights being the products of factor loadings and interest rate volatility.

For daily VaR, volatilities of interest rates need to be daily. In our sample, the reference period is 911 days, and observations are daily. Therefore we have a long-term estimate of the daily volatility, which does not require any scaling.

The portfolio is characterized by its sensitivities to each interest rate. In the example, only three sensitivities are non zeros. Then, the volatility of each position with sensitivity S is obtained as: $S\sigma_1(i)\eta_1$ and $S\sigma_1(i)\eta_2$. The weighted sensitivities to principal components are shown in the two last columns in Table 37.6. They are calculated in the same way for all interest rates, with factor loadings and interest rate volatility varying from one rate to the other. Table 37.6 shows the factor loadings of each interest rate, the sensitivity measured by the size of the bank's position (named S) to each selected interest rate, and the last two columns show the weighted sensitivities of these positions to the principal components as the product of exposure size multiplied by the interest rate volatility multiplied by the factor loadings η_{1i} of each factor with respect to the interest rate i.

The sensitivities to individual interest rates become sensitivities to each principal component, which are additive algebraically since they refer to same factor. The portfolio sensitivities to principal components are summarized by two sensitivities to two principal components, instead of the three interest rates. The algebraic summation provides the sensitivities of the entire portfolio as S_{P1} and S_{P2}, respectively equal to –977 and 1312. The same would happen if the positions were mapped to more interest rates. The principal components still summarize the interest rates and the weighted sensitivities serve for calculating the variations of the P & L according to the unique linear equation:

$$\Delta(P \& L) = S_{P1} \times \Delta P_1 + S_{P2} \times \Delta P_2$$

$$\Delta(P \& L) = -977 \times \Delta P_1 + 1312 \times \Delta P_2$$

TABLE 37.6   Portfolio sensitivities to interest rates

	P_1	P_2	Sensitivity S	$\sigma_1(i)$	$S\,\eta_1\,\sigma(i)$	$S\,\eta_2\,\sigma(i)$
E_m1	0.184	−0.087	0	0.6777	0	0
E_m3	0.208	−0.107	−10000	0.7140	−1485	764
E_m6	0.234	−0.122	0	0.7562	0	0
E_m12	0.249	−0.110	0	0.7900	0	0
E_y3	0.119	0.071	7000	0.6389	532	318
E_y5	0.043	0.145	0	0.5210	0	0
E_y7	0.006	0.172	0	0.4542	0	0
E_y10	−0.020	0.187	3000	0.4102	−25	230
E_y15	−0.038	0.202	0	0.3947	0	0
E_y20	−0.049	0.215	0	0.3969	0	0
E_y30	−0.059	0.227	0	0.4015	0	0
		Weighted portfolio sensitivities			−977	1312

Note that the PCA analysis relies on normal distributions, which could result in negative interest rates, notably if interest rates are too low, especially at the short-end of the curve, which has been upward sloping over a large fraction of the period. Such values should be eliminated by setting a floor to zero, although this is an ad hoc method.

The next step is to simulate the variation of values of the portfolio, which is its daily P & L. The variation of the portfolio is the portfolio P & L, is equal to:

$$\Delta(\text{P \& L}) = S_{P1} \times \Delta P_1 + S_{P2} \times \Delta P_2$$

First we generate random standard normal factors. We simulate independent uniform standard variables U_1 and U_2 and take their normal standard inverse to obtain factor values distributed normally. For each simulated couple of values of P_1 and P_2, we derive the P & L. Then we transform these values into P & L variations for a large number of simulations using the linear decomposition of the portfolio into positions with respect to the principal components. We run 100 such simulations. The first five simulations are shown in Table 37.7. Running 100 simulations, we obtain the daily P & L distribution. The distribution should be normal with a larger number of simulations (Figure 37.2).

The expected value of the P & L is positive because the portfolio receives the long-term rates and pays the short-term interest rate, initially lower. The dispersion of values illustrates the risk of the portfolio. The theoretical distribution should be normal. It is not here because of the small number of simulations (100). The frequency distribution of the P& L is the basis for deriving mean, standard deviation and loss percentiles. Note that it is extremely simple to

TABLE 37.7   Simulations of the portfolio P & L

Simulations	U_1	U_2	$P_1 = \Phi^{-1}(U_1)$	$P_2 = \Phi^{-1}(U_1)$	P & L
1	0.514	0.754	0.035	0.686	864.5
2	0.950	0.409	1.645	−0.229	−1908.7
3	0.387	0.245	−0.287	−0.690	−624.0
4	0.379	0.820	−0.308	0.914	1500.5
5	0.130	0.974	−1.127	1.950	3659.3

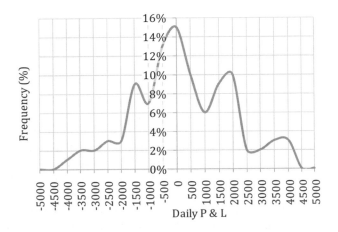

FIGURE 37.2   Distribution of the portfolio P & L

calculate the standard deviation of the P & L, using the above equation making the variations of P & L a linear function of the two principal components:

$$\Delta(P \& L) = S_{P1} \times \Delta P_1 + S_{P2} \times \Delta P_2$$

Since the principal components are independent, the variance is the sum of the variance of each term and the daily volatility of P & L is the square root of this sum:

$$\sigma(P \& L) = \sqrt{[S_{P1}^2 \sigma^2(\Delta P_1) + S_{P2}^2 \sigma^2(\Delta P_2)]}$$

$$\sigma(P \& L) = 1636$$

The portfolio delta-normal VaR at confidence level 1% would be $-2.33 \times 1636 = -3811$, ignoring the positive mean of the daily P & L. Using percentiles of the above simulated distribution, we find that the 1% loss percentile equals exactly -4000, which is pretty close to the theoretical value.

37.5 ALM APPLICATIONS

For ALM purposes, such simulations allow capturing long-term movements and simulating what the net interest income of the economic value would be. They allow generating distributions of these key target variables. They also serve for simulating ALM policies by plugging in gaps or duration gaps and various hedging solutions or policies. Such simulations allow assessing the effect of historical scenarios on:

- NII and EV, with various conventions on deposit amortizations, which drive the rolling over of investments of deposits, at the long-term interest rates
- back-testing various hedges against historical movements
- isolating certain periods of unstable interest rate conditions to see what would happen today with the current balance sheet
- stress-testing certain policies, conventions, hedges
- etc.

The benefit is that decision makers can use both short-term and long-term scenarios by selecting a reference historical period that matches current conditions, or selecting a longer period for capturing a much wider range of scenarios, or selecting one or several reference period(s) of highly unstable rates for stress-testing purposes. For each reference period, the PCA analysis needs to be fitted to the historical data for obtaining all related statistics.

Note that the methodology is analogous to the historical VaR methodology. The difference is the purpose of the analysis. Instead of deriving a current VaR, or a distribution of NII in ALM, for current conditions only, shown by, for example, a single year of historical observations, we use various reference periods according to what needs to be investigated.

The methodology allows simulating the target variable NII in a straightforward manner. Consider a balance sheet with exposures, or gaps, on the short-term Euribor 3-month, the 3-year interest rate and the 10-year interest rate. The positions mapped to these rates are negative for the short-term rate, assuming that the compensation for short-term deposits is the 3-month rate, and positive with the 5-year and the 10-year rate. Such positions would arise for example when there are excess deposits and when the entire deposit base serves for financing lending and investing.

The deposits are amortized over 10 years, which allows rolling over investments over 10 years for smoothing out variations of interest rates. For simplification purposes, in the example, the 10-year lending is not rolled over, and it is lent one-shot. The rest of lending activities is made of loans to corporations for example. We merge all loans in the example and assume that average maturity is 5 years. None of these assumptions are restrictive. We can map all positions of the balance sheet to as many interest rates as needed. Note that such positions are not netted positions. Rather, they represent the balance sheet exposures, without considering gaps. The example is representative of a bank having a structural position, lending long with short-term resources for taking advantage of the long-term/short-term spread of rates that prevailed in the early years of the period. The mismatch risk for interest rate is fairly high in the period retained for observation. The positions are mapped to the selected interest rates and assign sensitivities to the 3-month rate, the 5-year rate and the 10-year rate. The sensitivities represent the size of positions from lending and borrowing, since they are the base for the calculation of interest rate income. Once the portfolio is mapped to each rate, we need to plug-in the factor loadings multiplied by the interest rates volatilities (because the PCA provides here standardized interest rates).

Note that we used the same numerical values for NII sensitivities to each interest rate as the deltas of the previous market portfolio to the same interest rates. We can use any relevant value. Because we target the annual NII of the bank, we use annualized volatilities. We start from daily volatilities measured over 911 days. Daily volatilities should be scaled up to one year[3], the scaling factor being $\sqrt{250} = 15.811$. Once this done, we can derive the pairs of weighted sensitivities to each principal component as the product of the sensitivity of each position to interest rates multiplied by the factor loading and multiplied by the annualized interest rate volatility. We have three such sensitivities to each factor P_1 and P_2. By summing up algebraically the sensitivities of each column across rows, for the last two rows, we obtain the bank's balance sheet NII sensitivities to each principal component (Table 37.8). We have only two factors, whatever the number of selected interest rates used as risk factors.

The balance sheet annual NII varies with principal components according to the relation:

$$\Delta(\text{NII}) = S_{P1} \times \Delta P_1 + S_{P2} \times \Delta P_2$$

The numerical relation is $\Delta(\text{NII}) = -15\ 455\Delta P_1 + 20\ 738\Delta P_2$

TABLE 37.8   Sensitivities of the ALM portfolio

	P_1	P_2	Sensitivity S	$\sigma_1(i)$	$S\,\eta_1\,\sigma(i)$	$S\,\eta_2\,\sigma(i)$
E_m1	0.184	−0.087	0	10.7151	0	0
E_m3	0.208	−0.107	−10000	11.2889	−23481	12079
E_m6	0.234	−0.122	0	11.9570	0	0
E_m12	0.249	−0.110	0	12.4902	0	0
E_y3	0.119	0.071	7000	10.1018	8415	5021
E_y5	0.043	0.145	0	8.2371	0	0
E_y7	0.006	0.172	0	7.1815	0	0
E_y10	−0.020	0.187	3000	6.4853	−389	3638
E_y15	−0.038	0.202	0	6.2408	0	0
E_y20	−0.049	0.215	0	6.2763	0	0
E_y30	−0.059	0.227	0	6.3482	0	0
		Weighted portfolio sensitivities			−15455	20738

---

3 Therefore, in Table 37.8, the column labelled $\sigma_1(i)$ is different from the previous table, since "1" now refers to one year instead of one day, as in Table 37.6.

Next, we proceed as above for simulations, by generating independent normal standard principal components and deriving the annual NII values for each simulation using the above relation. This allows obtaining the distribution of the NII. The standard deviation of the NII is derived, as above, using:

$$\sigma(\text{NII}) = \sqrt{[S_{P1}^{2}\sigma^{2}(\Delta P_{1}) + S_{P2}^{2}\sigma^{2}(\Delta P_{2})]} = 25\ 864$$

The distribution of annual NII is shown in Figure 37.3.

Because the bank lends longer than it borrows, the expected value of the NII is positive. But the mismatch risk appears in the dispersion of the distribution, which is notably large because the short-end of the term structure of interest rates went up over the period. It is possible to define the NII at risk using loss percentiles. For example, the value-at-risk of the NII at the 1% confidence level would be $-2.33 \times 856.9 = -60,262$. The cumulative probability that the NII is negative is around 41%. Presumably, the bank would have hedged the mismatch risk to avoid extreme negative values of the NII. The 1% loss percentile from the above distribution is between 50,000 and 60,000, gain fairly close to theoretical value.

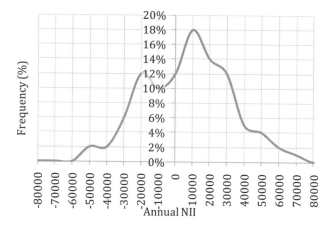

FIGURE 37.3 **Distribution of ALM NII**

38

Back Tests, Benchmarks and Stress Tests

Back tests serve for checking that the risk measures effectively capture actual observed variations. Stress tests serve for assessing what would happen under stressed conditions. Benchmarking aims at comparing how different models perform the same tasks. Back testing has not much to do either with stress tests, or with benchmarking. Back testing is part of model calibration (or "fitting") whether stress tests are designed to see what happens under stressed conditions. Benchmarking compares outputs of various models to alternate models serving as benchmarks.

Because they all serve for assessing the reliability of models and measure their effects on target variables, they can be addressed in a single chapter. The principles of back tests, benchmarking and stress tests are simple. However, technicalities and processes involved have become more critical. This has been highlighted by the financial crisis of 2007–2008, which demonstrated that reliability and compliance to sound best practices remained a persistent technical and organizational challenge.

A back test compares "before the fact" measures with "after the fact" measures. A stress test, in its simplest form, is a sensitivity analysis with a focus on critical variables. Benchmarking is essentially a comparison of models. They all require technical expertise and judgmental approaches. Stress testing does not simplify to inputting stressed values in risk factors. Its main challenge is in assessing the "second level" indirect effects, as explained in this chapter. Traceability of those effects makes stress testing a difficult issue.

Back testing is dealt with in Section 38.1. Benchmarking is briefly discussed in Section 38.2. Stress testing, sensitivity analyses and scenario-based factor-push techniques are discussed in Section 38.3. Finally, some validation issues are discussed briefly in Section 38.4. Note that in this chapter we address both market risk and credit risk. For credit risk, we do not need other concepts than those already defined. Moving from market risk to credit risk and vice versa can be easily inferred with examples provided.

Contents

38.1 BACK TESTING

Back testing aims at checking that any risk measure is in line with after-the-fact observations of whatever was measured. It implies comparing "after-the-fact" values with "before-the-fact" measures. Back testing is based on historical data. It is subject to sampling error since any pool of historical data is only a sample of the entire set of data.

The back test for market VaR is relatively to perform. It is analogous to historical VaR. Once VaR is modeled, it should be checked that P & L deviations does not exceed the VaR with a percentage fraction higher than the confidence level. The process involves modeling the VaR and, then, calculating historical deviations of the P & L over a reference historical period. If the VaR is the 1% percentile, it implies that daily P & L variations would not exceed 2 to 3 times the VaR over a year (2.5 times is 1% of 250 trading days in a year). Back testing of VaR commonly uses an annual window with daily observations[1]. For market VaR, back testing should compare the actual portfolio variations of value, given historical data, with the modeled VaR. Such comparison requires the usage of a crystallized portfolio.

In the case of market VaR, historical VaR is actually a back test since it is based on actual variations of value using the "crystallized" structure of the portfolio. To a certain extent Historical VaR is "self back tested," although it could be further back tested by using longer historical time series.

VaR estimates are by definition procyclical. VaR should move in line with current conditions for being relevant. Using longer windows or different methodologies for estimating volatility would result in different estimates of VaR because it is highly sensitive to the behavior of volatility. Using a moving average of volatility or a GARCH model would result in very different VaRs. The choice of methodology for modeling volatility depends on the relevance of the calculations. Using longer windows of observations might make it smoother, except that when the window moves through time, some historical shocks might disappear, resulting in abrupt movements of VaR. Whatever the method, the VaR should pass simple back tests. Going beyond simple back tests is more like stress testing, or calculating a VaR under stressed conditions.

Let's consider default risk in anticipation of Chapter 41. Note that back testing is a process integrated with any model calibration to the extent that such calibration require "in-the-sample" and "out-of-the-sample" estimate for checking resiliency of the model. In and out of the sample data might refer to different periods, as above, or to the same time period. The scoring tech-

---

1 Note that there is a sampling error when using a past sample. The back test should provide evidence that the historical deviations of values are within a tight confidence level. In standard statistics, the sampling error is inversely related to the number of observations. A volatility estimate is within upper and lower bounds that get narrower when the number of observations increases. If the VaR is calculated on equally weighted observations for calculating volatility, the estimation error of VaR is proportional to that of volatility. A conservative estimate should take the upper bound of the sampling error interval for volatility.

nique applies for modeling borrowers' defaults and is explained in Chapter 41. The scoring technique in retail banking is back tested with the CAP profile. Standard techniques for scoring include comparing the results of the same models applied to different samples of data. Scoring techniques rely on statistical analysis for model fitting. Such standard methods include the "in-the-sample" and "out-of-the-sample" methodology. A model is fitted to a sample. Then, a check should show that it provides a reasonable fit in another sample. This is similar to a back test integrated to the model calibration technique. However, in- and out-of-the-sample fits refer to the same period of observation, where a back test would compare modeled scores, and derived default probabilities, to past default frequencies.

Back testing techniques do not apply well when data is scarce as it is for low default portfolios. The credit risk data pool being progressively built will improve the situation. Note that recovery risk can be back tested relatively easily, as default probabilities are in retail banking. Alternative sources can be used for credit risk such the historical data on EDF© as modeled by Moody's-KMV Credit Monitor. However, EDFs© are point in time probabilities that barely compare with the Basel 2 "through-the-cycle" default probabilities.

38.2 BENCHMARKING

An alternative technique differs from back testing but serves the same purpose of insuring the reliability of the data. Benchmarking consists of comparing the outputs of some models to the outputs of alternative models that could be applied. For example, several "pricers," or valuation models, of market instruments apply to the same instrument. Alternatively, a single model applies to several instruments. This allows benchmarking the outputs of various models that apply to the same instrument or comparing which models fit better the calibration of a single instrument family.

Benchmarking is feasible only when there are alternative models. Some simpler models than those actually used might be less accurate but can serve at least for checking the orders of magnitude of outputs. Since there are several modeling options, it is generally feasible to design simple models that can serve as a benchmark. For credit risk, there are in-house models and vendors' models of economic capital. This allows benchmarking. For Basel 2 calculations, in-house models serve in "production mode," meaning for recurring calculations bank-wide. But Basel 2 calculations are easy to replicate for single transactions. This makes benchmarking feasible by sampling some transactions and comparing the outputs of the "production" model to the sample calculations. If outputs are similar, there is no issue. If not, the issue is to trace why there are discrepancies. Benchmarking implies traceability of calculations.

38.3 STRESS TESTING, HYPOTHETICAL SCENARIOS AND SENSITIVITY ANALYSES

Stress testing aims at investigating the possibility of exceptional losses by stressing the value of the risk factors. It is essentially the combination of a sensitivity analysis and of a "factor-push" technique, by stressing the factors that influence most portfolio values. The technique requires ranking the risk factors according to the portfolio sensitivity to each one of them. Since main risk factors might vary through time, the ranking changes.

Any stress test requires sensitivity analysis and is scenario based. For example, Basel 2 requires stress tests based on discrete scenarios in ALM, for the interest income and for the economic value. The benefit of scenarios is that they are not black boxes, as the VaR is. Selected "factor-pushes" are judgmental, based on either extreme values observed at certain periods and on judgment of how far the deviations could be. With a portfolio, it is not simple to identify which deviations of which parameters result in extreme losses because asset value changes offset within the portfolio.

We take the example of a credit portfolio. Various sensitivity analyses apply to portfolios. To proceed on an orderly basis, we need to refer to a unique base case, and change only one variable at a time and use a "factor-push" technique, or equivalently, a "what-if" technique.

38.3.1 Direct Effects or "Factor-push" Techniques

Consider any credit portfolio or sub-portfolios, such as the low risk sub-portfolio (segment A) and a high-risk portfolio (segment B). For instance, we can change exposure from, say 100 to 110, an increase of 10%, then revert to the 100 value of exposure. We can then change another factor, such as the default correlation between obligors by 10%, then revert again to the base case. We can then change another variable. Several variables are of interest, such as the default probabilities or recovery rates.

A sensitivity analysis requires focusing on some relevant target variables, such as the portfolio loss volatility, VaR and capital. Changing values of inputs changes the values of the output variables. Since there are several risk factors to consider, the number of runs can increase quickly. It is necessary to restrict the number of "what-if" simulations for easily interpreting them. Second, the influence on the target variable can be large or small. Ranking inputs according to the change on the target variables is a standard practice for limiting the number of inputs to critical ones that have the most important changes on the target variables.

A convenient representation of this type of analysis is the "so-called" "tornado" graph (Figure 38.1). A "tornado" graph visualizes, for a given target variable, such as the portfolio loss volatility, the influences of given variations of the inputs. Once a range of variations of an input is given, the variations of the target variable appear ranked from largest to smallest. On top of the "tornado," large bars represent the largest changes generated by the input variations to which the calculated variable is the most sensitive. Moving down, the sensitivity decreases and the bars get shorter, resulting in the "tornado" shape. Critical inputs are on top. In Figure 38.1, the portfolio loss volatility is sensitive to the exposure, to the default probabilities, and to the default correlation, the other variables being less critical (given the ranges of variations considered). The illustration can be readily implemented to any risk measures. The number of factors can increase substantially. Then, it becomes even more essential to isolate factors that have the most important effect.

Sensitivity analyses provide only first-level direct effects. Stress testing should be more comprehensive. Moreover, the factor-push technique tends to be used by stressing one factor at a time. When risk factors are dependent, it is more relevant to stress a bunch of factors together.

38.3.2 Indirect Effects and Factor-push Scenarios

Stress tests are not as simple as it seems from the example. For any "what-if" analysis, there are direct and indirect effects. Consider the example of ratings, which can be downgraded

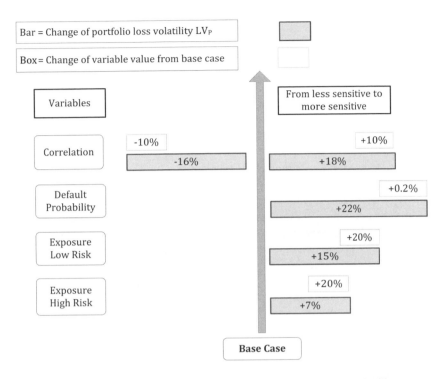

FIGURE 38.1 Tornado graph and sensitivity analysis of portfolio loss volatility

by 1 or more notches. The direct effect would be an increased default probability and higher required credit capital for example. But indirect effects include margin calls, or precluding doing business with some counterparties, or a shortage of liquidity because solvency is impaired in stress tests.

The same would happen with market VaR. Downgrading ratings might trigger increased collateral requirements and collateral values directly influence the VaR. First-level stress tests are easy to design, but tracing their indirect effects is far from trivial, if feasible at all, since tracing all indirect effects might not be within specifications of risk systems.

However, using the easier first-level direct effects falls below standards of stress testing. Traceability of effects throughout key variables is the main challenge. The crisis revealed that tracing indirect effects would have provided a much better view of what happened than simple factor-push techniques. One way of conducting full stress tests would be to rely on scenarios rather than factor-push techniques. Scenarios bundle together factors that tends to be associated under stress conditions. Historical crisis might help in identifying the bunch of factors that need to be stressed together for a more comprehensive stress test. For being usable, such scenarios should be transformed into factor variations that move together. The set of factors to be stressed does not depend anymore on dependencies between factors. Rather, it depends on the dependency between global scenarios and all factors that are affected by such scenarios. The transformation of global crisis scenarios requires mapping the global scenarios to all factors that are scenario dependent. Once such mapping is conducted, it becomes feasible to apply the factor-push technique to all scenario-related factors.

38.4 VALIDATION

Validation is the process aiming at insuring consistency and compliance with basic principles of modeling and risk management. The validation methodology is not easy to design, notably given the variety of tools used within banks and the complexity of risk regulations.

All three topics of this chapter serve for validation, whoever is in charge. Models are supposed to be back tested, benchmarked and stress tested. All techniques serve the purposes of assessing the reliability and consistency of risk measures.

Other principles should be implemented for a sound validation process. For being feasible, all tools should be properly documented, which might sound obvious, but is not in practice. The validation unit(s) should be independent from business and empowered with the necessary authority to give recommendations to be followed by business lines and research teams. They should define adequate auditing methodologies, for which due diligence does not exist everywhere. They should have access to models and be able to develop their own models. Their own models might be downgraded to a certain extent, since there is no point is obtaining perfect accuracy, but rather checking that orders of magnitudes are in line with what can reasonably be expected.

All three techniques, back testing, benchmarking and stress testing, are essentially validation techniques that serve for internal and external supervisors who face the challenge of making sure that models are consistent. They should be performed by an independent validation unit. Such a principle might not be used as widely as it should, possibly because it would require duplicating expert resources in the front-office and in a validation unit. "Embedded" validation units suffer from the same drawback as "embedded" risk managers. The benefit of being embedded is to have access to details, data, processes and tools. The drawback is that the third party independence might become theoretical rather than effective.

We tend to consider that a "four eyes" view principle should prevail. The "four-eye" principle refers to two independent views of the same risk models, risk metrics, or exposures. In general, the "four-eye" principle applies within the first line of defense of banks, when back and middle office systems check the front-office treatment of deals. But implementing a "four-eye" view between the front office and the central risk unit is not as common. Technically, central risk systems exist, and would allow organizing such a double view. Such central risk systems ensure consistency between what the risk department can see and what the business lines record and report.

SECTION 11

Credit Risk: Standalone

Credit risk is the risk of incurring losses due to the deterioration of the creditworthiness of counterparties. Credit risk is the oldest and the most important risk for banks. Nevertheless, it remained far from easy to measure. This section addresses credit risk of single transactions, out of any portfolio context, that would otherwise diversify away some of their risk. The building blocks of standalone credit risk provide the foundations of the next two sections addressing credit portfolio risk.

The assessment of credit risk is usually judgmental, because of its multiple dimensions, and closely related to the "fundamentals" approach. "Fundamentals" refer to any factor important for understanding strengths and weaknesses of a borrower or a counterparty in market transactions. This extends from to the ability of facing debt obligations with the firm's cash flows to the management track record. The core business of ratings agencies, for example, Moody's, Standard & Poors, Fitch, to mention only the "global" ones, is to assign ratings, or "coded letter-grades" ranking the level of credit risk of a debt issue relative to others. Ratings convey major information on the market, allowing investors to rely on rating agency assessments of credit risk.

The quantitative assessment of credit risk results from the mandatory capital adequacy directives. Risk components designate the basic ingredients of credit risk. They include "default probability," "exposure at default," and "loss under default" (after all recoveries). Credit risk quantification lagged behind measures of other risks because such information is hardly available and needs to be modeled.

An elegant approach to this challenge emerged in the 1990s, building on earlier theoretical contribution of Merton (1973 [51]). Since credit event information is scarce, it is possible to turn around the difficulty by modeling unobservable credit events. Still, at some point, one has to make sure that modeled credit risk is in line with actual credit losses. Data restrictions limit the empirical validation of models. It is no surprise that the New Basel Accord puts a lot of emphasis on enhancing risk data.

In all chapters of this section, credit risk is standalone, or assessed independently of any diversifying portfolio context. The section on standalone credit risk is divided in eight chapters:

- credit risk data covering the main credit risk components – default probabilities, exposure at default, recoveries – plus historical migration data (Chapter 39).
- rating systems, for both rating agencies and internal credit rating systems (Chapter 40)
- scoring systems, which mostly apply to the retail banking portfolio (Chapter 41)
- the "structural default model," originally from Merton, and implemented in the Moody's-KMV Credit Monitor model, which models a default event as a deficiency of asset value compared to debt payment obligation (Chapter 42)
- the hazard model, or "reduced model," which models default as a rare event process, calibrated on observed default frequencies, based on the well-known paper of Li (2000 [48]) (Chapter 43)
- the potential future exposure model, which addresses uncertainty of exposure and two-way risk for derivatives (Chapter 44)
- the modeling of recoveries, for collateral-based lending and borrowing, which transforms credit risk in a collateral value risk, and third-party guarantees which transform credit risk through default probabilities (Chapter 45)
- standalone credit risk models, based on full reevaluation at horizon using migrations between initial and final dates, modeled using standard transition matrices or the structural model which provides a continuous distribution of asset values (Chapter 46).

39

Credit Risk Data

This chapter provides an overview of credit risk data that is available publicly. The credit risk data are default statistics, recovery statistics and transition statistics, all based on historical data. Long-term averages are usually available for rated entities. Defaults occur when a borrower fails to comply with an obligation payment. A migration, or a "transition," is a change of risk class. Recoveries are measured by the ratio of a bond value after default to its par value.

When considering public statistics from rating agencies, care should be taken that such statistics apply to rated entities only, generally large and very large corporations, banks and sovereigns. Applying such statistics to the pool of loans of banks is necessary only when there are no other alternatives, since the same data presumably change with the size of the entities. Internal rating systems are supposed to take care of that. In addition, Basel 2 provided major incentives for developing internal data pool within banks and stimulating data sharing across banks for those counterparties for which external data is scarce, such as specialized lending and public sector entities.

The three sections address default data (Section 39.1), recovery data (Section 39.2) and migration data (Section 39.3).

Contents

39.1 DEFAULT STATISTICS

Most statistics rely on public statistics of credit rating agencies. However, there are also valuable studies that provide useful information, even if they are older. They include Asarnow's review on loan defaults over 24 years [5], the review of Carty and Lieberman [17], or the works of Altman [3]. In this chapter we rely on rating agency data that are publicly available and relatively recent.

The external ratings map to yearly and cumulated default rates, as shown below (Table 39.1). Historical data report risk statistics as frequencies, as numbers or as percentages of a reference population sample. The percentages are either arithmetic or weighted, notably for default rates, by size of defaulting bonds. We use here rates based on numbers of firms, rather than value-weighted rates. When calculating a default rate, it is necessary to refer to the number of surviving firms at the beginning of the period. The process implies the following steps.

- Aggregating default data for a given population of firms defined by those firms rated at the beginning of a period and which are still rated at the end of the period.
- Breaking down the population into sub-portfolios by rating class.
- Calculating the default rate as the ratio of the number of defaults over the period over the total of surviving firms at the beginning of the period.

In practice, when starting from external rating agencies data, these include rating withdrawals, which implies that the firm does not exist in the database at end of periods. If we select a particular year starting at t, there will be differences in the number of rated firms existing at the initial date when the population was defined and the population of firms at date t due to withdrawn ratings and mergers, which should be isolated for defining historical default frequencies and migrations. Tables from rating agencies provide cumulative default probabilities for a population defined at an initial date and up to any future date. Averages over several years also use "cohorts" of firms defined at various dates and averages data by rating class across cohorts. Table 39.1 shows the Moody's ratings and default frequencies from Moody's Investors Service.

TABLE 39.1   Ratings and default statistics: average default frequencies in percentage for the first year (average 1983–2005)

Rating	Year 1
Aaa	0.000
Aa	0.010
A	0.022
Baa	0.213
Ba	1.307
B	5.693
Caa–C	20.982
Investment-grade	0.075
Speculative-grade	5.145
All corporates	1.737

Source: Moody's Investors Service, 2007.

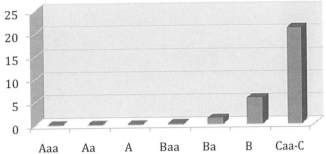

First year Default rates

FIGURE 39.1   Annual default rates and ratings (souce: Moody's: Average 1983–2000)

39.1.1 Annual Default Rates

Annual default rates are ratios of defaulted firms to surviving firms at the beginning of the year. There are arithmetic default rates based on the number of issuers. Figure 39.1 shows the magnitude of yearly default rates for the six rating classes in the Moody's simplified rating scale. Actual values vary every year. The default rates are close to zero for the best risk qualities. They increase to around 21% a year for the lowest rating class (in the six-class simplified rating scale). The top three ratings characterize investment grade borrowers. The three other classes are speculative grade. For investment-grade borrowers, the yearly default rate is below 0.1%. For speculative-grade borrowers, it ranges from 0.2% to 21% a year. Plotting these figures, we observe the typical approximately "exponential-like" shape of the increase of default frequency when the credit ratings move along the simplified scale. The first-year default rates are averaged across all years of observations.

Ratings drive the cost of borrowing for banks and their eligibility for participating in certain activities. Improving the rating of a bank is therefore of major importance. The required capital increase required for gaining one rating class, measured in gain of default rate, is much higher in the lower grades of the scale than in the upper grades. Since economic capital calculation uses a confidence level that represents the default risk of the bank, Figure 39.1 shows that targeting investment grade ratings implies very tight confidence levels, way below 0.1%. The importance of modeling the fat tail of the loss distribution follows.

39.1.2 Cumulative Default Rates

Default rates cumulate over time. Figure 39.2 shows the characteristic shapes of the default frequencies time profiles by rating for the period 1983 to 2005. The figure shows cumulative default rates for investment grades, all grades and speculative grades, in that order, the highest curve being for speculative grades. The default rates increase with the horizon. The longer the period, the higher are the chances of observing a default. The growth of default rates with horizon is not proportional. For high ratings, or low default rates, the increase is more than proportional. For low ratings and high default rates, it is less than proportional. High-risk bor-

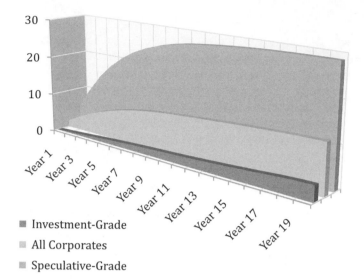

FIGURE 39.2 Average cumulative default rates by letter rating from 1 to 20 years (%). (Source: Moody's 1983–2005)

rowers improve their risk, when they survive, over long horizons. Low-risk borrowers face risk deterioration when time passes.

Figure 39.3 provides the same figure by broad rating class. Annualized rates are derived from such figures. They are cumulative default frequencies divided by the number of years. Due to the shape of the cumulative default rates, annualized rates are higher than the annual first-year rate when default rates increase less than proportionally to horizon. The opposite holds when rates increase less than proportionally with time. For Basel 2 purposes, the first-year default rate is relevant because ratings are supposed to be reviewed annually.

39.2 RECOVERY STATISTICS

Available recovery statistics are mainly based on the prices of defaulted bonds and loans, calculated as the ratio of the value of the defaulted issue to its par value. Recovery rates vary by seniority levels, as shown in Table 39.2. There is a wide variation around the mean, so that the actual ranges across types of debts widely overlap. The last column shows the average 1982–2005. Another empirical fact pointed out by Moody's is that recovery rates seem correlated with economic conditions. Hence, when these worsen, chances are that recoveries also do. Most models using recoveries as an input do not account for such correlations. The R square of the regression of recovery rates on default rates is 64%, with a negative coefficient for default rates (Moody's, 2007).

Recoveries are a major determinant of losses under default. Therefore, it is not surprising that the New Accord focuses on building up recovery data. Recovery data by seniority level, types of products and nature of guarantees would help differentiate the average recoveries for these sub-classes more significantly. Note that for asset classes such as specialized finance, recovery data is scarcer than for corporates. Initiatives for pooling data across banks are ongoing.

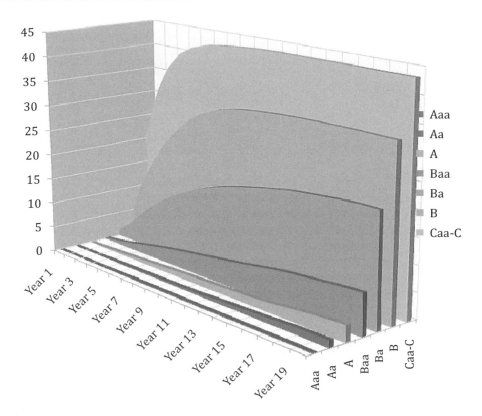

FIGURE 39.3 Average cumulative default rates by letter rating from 1 to 20 years (%). (Source: Moody's 1983–2005)

TABLE 39.2 Recovery rates by seniority level of debt

	2005	2004	1982–2005
Bank loans			
Senior secured	81.6	86.1	70
Senior unsecured			57.6
Bonds			
Senior secured	77.9	78.7	51.9
Senior unsecured	55.2	53.2	36
Senior subordinated	33.6	47.5	32.4
Subordinated			31.8
Junior subordinated			23.9
All bonds	55.9	59.9	35.9
All debt instruments	54.5	63.3	37.7

Source: Moody's Investors Service, 2007.

39.3 TRANSITION MATRICES

When time drifts, the risk either improves or deteriorates, as illustrated by the cumulative default rates. These shifts are captured by the transition frequencies between risk classes. Within a given period, transition rates between classes are transition frequencies divided by the number of original firms in each risk class.

A transition matrix looks like Table 39.3. Since the higher transition frequencies occur mostly in the neighboring classes of ratings, there is a concentration along the first diagonal of the matrix. Each row and each column is a rating class. The next to the last row provides the frequency of defaulting per risk class. The last row shows the percentage of withdrawn ratings within the period, for which no final state can be assigned. All transition probabilities, plus the percentage of withdrawn ratings, sum up to one across rows because each row lists all possible final states. Transition matrices are subject to constraints:

- all sums across rows sum to one because they group, together with the default state, all possible migrations
- all migration probabilities are positive and lower than one.

Migrations, other than long-term averages, are conditional on prevailing economic conditions. When modeling variations of default rates, all migrations rates have to shift for preserving consistency of the matrix. Such modeling exists in credit portfolio view, an econometric model of credit portfolio[1].

It is possible to map ratings classes with observed credit spreads in the market. With such mapping, it is possible to assign different credit spreads to the final credit state, and value a loan or a bond accordingly. This allows the generation of a distribution of values at a forward horizon for any asset with a given original rating class. This is a common technique for valuing migration risk in credit risk models. However, credit spreads do not depend on rating class only. Statistical analyses on credit spreads show that they depend mainly on rating class, industry and geographic region, for a given asset class, such as corporates[2].

TABLE 39.3 Average 1-year whole letter rating transition rates, 1983–2005 (% of issuers)

Beginning of year rating	End of year rating									Total
	Aaa	Aa	A	Baa	Ba	B	Caa-C	Default	WR*	
Aaa	94.65	5.21	0.00	0.00	0.00	0.00	0.00	0.00	0.15	100
Aa	4.43	92.28	1.38	0.00	0.00	0.00	0.00	0.00	1.90	100
A	0.00	2.90	91.73	3.19	0.52	0.00	0.00	0.00	1.66	100
Baa	0.00	0.00	8.88	79.02	6.85	0.85	0.00	0.00	4.40	100
Ba	0.00	0.00	0.00	4.28	85.93	8.29	0.73	0.62	0.15	100
B	0.00	0.00	0.00	0.00	3.50	87.18	2.09	3.89	3.34	100
Caa-C	0.00	0.00	0.00	0.00	0.52	28.18	53.12	18.18	0.00	100

*WR, withdrawn rating
Source: Moody's 2007.

---

1 See Chapter 51 on credit portfolio models.
2 As found by the author and other proprietary statistics.

40

Rating Systems

Credit ratings are assessments of the credit standing of borrowers and guarantors. Credit ratings usually apply to large corporations, banks, insurance companies, sovereign or public sector entities. In retail banking, the large volume of statistics allows assessing the risk from statistical models or scores, which are addressed in the next chapter (Chapter 41). The major difference is that ratings include a judgmental component while scores result from a mechanical statistical fit of default events and observable variables.

Ratings rank the credit standing of debt issues using ordinal measures materialized by coded letter-grades for the ratings from agencies. Ranks are "ordinal numbers," not absolute values of the level of risk, by contrast with default probabilities which quantify the likelihood of default over a given horizon. Internal ratings refer to ratings assigned by banks to their borrowers. Unlike agency ratings, which use public scales, internal ratings use proprietary scales that vary across banks.

Credit ratings serve as the foundation for the "internal rating-based" approach of the New Accord and play a major role for differentiating credit risk of loans. Note that external ratings apply to debt issues, not of issuers. Ratings assigned to senior unsecured debt are close to issuer ratings since the debt defaults only if the issuer does. Basel 2 internal ratings should be issuer ratings.

Practices range along the entire spectrum of implementation of statistical models to "expert" judgment, with the intermediate solution blending some judgmental view with model outputs. Rating schemes use various criteria, from qualitative factors, such as strengths or weaknesses of firms, as well as the financials of corporate borrowers. The broad definitions are by credit rating agencies, even though the proprietary methodologies are much more detailed and structured. We provide in an appendix (Section 40.7) a sample of such broad descriptions of letter-grade credit ratings.

This chapter provides details about the philosophy underlying credit ratings and how they help in quantifying risks. Section 40.1 contrasts the philosophies of credit ratings for external rating agencies and for Basel 2 internal credit ratings from banks. Section 40.2 explains why the hierarchies of counterparties are of major importance for rating systems. Section 40.3 provides examples of common business rules for assigning credit ratings. Section 40.4 provides an overview of the main building blocks of internal credit ratings, which serve for making the rating system consistent and comprehensive. Section 40.5 provides sample rating grids for corporations and for banks. Section 40.6 explains how to move from internal ratings to default probabilities – one of the major credit risk components in risk models.

Contents

40.1 CREDIT RATINGS

The philosophy underlying credit ratings differs for external rating agencies and for the regulators.

Rating agencies rate debt issues rather than issuers because lenders' and investors' views look at the risk of the debt that they consider buying or holding. Issuer ratings characterize the credit standing of the issuer. The same issuer usually has several debt issues, not all of them having the same risk. Debt issues differ by seniority levels and guarantees. Subordinated debt might default before senior debt, and secured debts have a risk mitigated by various guarantees, so that their ratings differ from the issuer's credit standing. Senior unsecured ratings are very close to issuer ratings because they benefit from first priority repayments in the event of default.

The regulators' philosophy differs since internal credit ratings serve for assessing the default probability of an issuer, through an issuer rating. The severity of loss in the event of default is transaction specific because it depends on collateral or guarantees that are generally facility specific. The case of specialized lending, as defined under Basel 2, is the extreme case where the credit risk is almost entirely dependent on the transaction rather than on the counterparty that sponsors the financing. In the case of project financing, for example, the credit risk is mitigated essentially by the project cash flows and by the series of covenants that impose constraints on participants to the project. When the transaction-specific risk is the dominant risk, ratings characterize facilities rather than issuers. Some samples of credit risk criteria are provided in the Basel 2 Accord in Appendix 6 of reference [7] as a guide for banks for assigning ratings to such transactions.

Under both philosophies, credit ratings should be based on the long-term fundamentals of a firm and do not change frequently under normal conditions. Both banks and agencies are supposed to continuously review their ratings on a periodical basis or following contingent events that affect the credit standing of an issuer. An example is a merger or an acquisition, which changes significantly the risk profile of a corporate borrower. It is often mentioned that credit ratings from agencies are "sticky" and do not adjust as frequently as they should. The waves of downgrades that characterized the financial crisis in 2007 and 2008 provide some support to the excessive "stickiness" of ratings.

External ratings from agencies exist only for issues of large listed companies. When internal ratings rely on external ratings for assessing default probabilities, there is a bias in default statistics because the sample of counterparties rated by agencies is usually not representative of the banks' portfolios. Banks operating in the middle and small business markets face credit risks entirely different than those of large corporates or banks that make up the lion's share of agencies' ratings. Banks need to rely on their own internal rating schemes for differentiating the risk of their exposures to these counterparties.

Internal rating scales have a varying number of levels, typically from 10 and up to 30, like the rating agency scales, simplified or detailed. Moody's simplified rating scale uses three levels for investment grade ratings and the next three levels are "speculative" grade. Detailed scales include around 20 levels, excluding the near default states, for Moody's, S & P and Fitch. The issue of mapping ratings with default frequencies illustrates how wide the differences of mapped default probabilities can be, especially in the speculative grade zone. This is addressed in the last section.

The appendix describes a typical rating scale of rating agencies. In general, the qualifications of various levels are broad and do not specify how ratings are assigned. There is a wide variety of criteria influencing the credit standing of a borrower, differing across types of borrowers, and their weights change according to the nature of obligors.

40.2 CREDIT RATINGS AND LINKS BETWEEN COUNTERPARTIES

Internal ratings are counterparty ratings, or issuers' ratings, not facility ratings. In several instances, ratings should extend to counterparties other than the direct borrower. One common case is that of third-party guarantees or collateral, because it is possible to substitute the collateral or the guarantor rating to the direct borrower's rating. This implies extending ratings beyond that of the direct borrowers to guarantors and issuers of securities posted as collateral.

Legal links between the direct borrower and another entity such as, typically, the subsidiary/holding company relationship, should be recorded and risk assessed. Whenever the direct borrower depends on another entity such as a group, credit risk depends on the potential support of the group and there is also an implicit indirect exposure to the group's risk. Without considering support, a small and medium-sized enterprise (SME) belonging to a group would be assessed in the same way as a standalone SME that does not belong to any group.

A critical piece of credit risk measurement and internal ratings is the internal database of counterparties, which should record those links. Managing the hierarchy of counterparties is critical, otherwise the lender might not effectively identify with who it is at risk. Credit risk transfer rules specify when the exposure to a direct borrower is in effect an exposure to the head of the hierarchy, because there is a strong support from the head of group. Credit risk transfers also apply when the substitution rule is implemented for CRM under Basel 2. Whenever credit risk transfers apply, both direct borrower's rating and the rating of the entity towards risk transfer occurs should be recorded.

Monitoring hierarchies of entities is not a trivial task. Groups keep merging and making acquisitions and such links should be monitored. Modern information technology systems embed a full module for managing such hierarchies of entities and helping analysts to make sure with whom the bank is at risk.

Another critical piece of the system is the management of identifiers of counterparties. Names are not adequate. For example, Continental could apply to an airline with that name or to a manufacturer of automobile products. Similarly, IBM and International Business Machines are the same entity. Names are not sufficient to identify a specific counterparty. Commonly used identifiers include the CUSIP and ISIN codes and tickers for example. The counterparty management system should include a permanently monitored mapping between internal identifiers of the bank's counterparties and those multiple external identifiers.

Many direct exposures are in effect indirect exposure to several obligors. Exposures to securitizations or funds are exposures to the underlying issuers of assets within the portfolio. A "look through" policy identifying the indirect exposure to the underlying obligors raises difficulties, either because the information is not disclosed or because it is overly complex to manage.

40.3 INTERNAL CREDIT RATINGS AND BUSINESS RULES

Rating systems require business rules for implementation. A common and important example is the rule relating sovereign risk to corporate or banking borrowers. When country risk materializes as transfer risk, it becomes unfeasible to recover cash from a local borrower. This is the rationale for capping an intrinsic borrower's rating by the country rating. If the latter materializes, the lender faces a default due to transfer risk, even though the borrower's credit standing remains unaffected.

Other rules apply to risk transfer from one member of a hierarchy to the head of hierarchy, or to a third party guarantee. The exposure is then automatically transferred internally to the entity that the bank considers as most adequate for allocating the amount at risk.

A third type of rule relates to contagion effects across counterparties. For example, the default of a group might trigger internally the default of all or some subsidiaries, even though there is no effective default of those. Contagions are not legally based and follow internal rules. The bank that has a relationship with the group might judge that the likelihood of default within the hierarchy is actually dependent on default events occurring within the hierarchy and triggers contagion to the direct borrower. Legal contagion effects exist when the obligor's debt is subject to covenants that trigger defaults when other debts within a group of counterparties default.

40.4 BUILDING BLOCKS OF THE INTERNAL CREDIT RATING SYSTEM

Internal credit ratings grids typically have several components synthesized in the final rating assigned to a direct counterparty.

The intrinsic rating assesses borrower's risk as a standalone entity. But the coverage of credit ratings should extend to all counterparties that are linked to the direct borrower or to the facility. Note that support is not a legal guarantee but rather results from an implicit commitment, that is effective or not, of the group for supporting a subsidiary. Since the group is usually much larger than its subsidiaries, ignoring the potential support of the group would be misleading. For assessing support, it is necessary to assess the credit standing of the borrower, that of the supporting entity and the "strength" of the support. Combining support assessment with intrinsic rating provides the borrower's overall rating.

Internal ratings of banks should include:

- the intrinsic rating of the borrower
- in presence of a supporting entity
- the rating of the supporting entity
- an assessment of the "intensity" of support of a parent company if any.

The overall borrower's rating combines all three elements. Credit ratings extend also to guarantors or issuers of securities used as collateral. But such ratings do not alter the credit standing of the direct borrowers since when they are facility specific, and affect rather the facility recovery rate.

40.5 RATING GRIDS

Issuers' rating criteria include a qualitative assessment of the counterparty's credit standing plus quantitative variables, many of them being financial variables. Rating a corporate entity always involves a judgmental component simply because there are so many factors that influence the credit standing of the counterparty. What follows cannot be comprehensive, but provides an overview of the nature of rating criteria.

40.5.1 Judgmental Ratings versus "Rating Models"

The two main blocks are the qualitative assessment and the financial criteria. A major feature of a rating grid is that criteria and their weights vary across industries and across counterparty types, such as corporations versus financial institutions. Moreover, the rating "model" is not compensating. Some criteria might be critical and drive the rating, independently of other criteria. For example, the legal support of a sovereign entity might be enough to assign the sovereign rating rather than the standalone rating of the direct borrower. In other cases, criteria might compensate within the rating grid, meaning that favorable and adverse items offset to a certain extent. This is a major difference from a scoring system which relates the risk assessment to a number of variables and allows offsetting effects across criteria of the scoring model.

From a statistical standpoint, "rating models" might be fit to the data when trying to explain ratings by various observable variables[1]. Empirical findings show that external ratings are sensitive to operating profitability, measured as ROA, size and financial leverage (debt to equity ratio), and market to book value, when available, which presumably captures the efficiency of capital markets in assessing the strengths and weaknesses of firms. Note also that many of these variables are correlated, i.e. that highly profitable firms have relatively low leverage and so on.

In general, such rating models, which make ratings look like scores, are not suitable for rating assessment whenever a judgmental component is necessary for refining credit ratings.

---

1 See for example Altman, [1] and [3].

The criteria for credit risk assessment are weighted by credit analysts, and both the criteria and the weights vary across industries. Simplified ratings grids for corporations and for banks are provided as examples.

40.5.2 Corporate Sample Rating Grid

The intrinsic rating grid sub-divides into qualitative analysis and financial profile. The intrinsic analysis is followed by support assessment. The final rating is the synthesis of both intrinsic ratings and support when it exists.

The "support" block is assessed and its effect on credit risk depends on the legal framework. One would think that support has a positive effect, which reduces credit risk. This is so as long as the group has a better credit rating than the subsidiary, that the support is effective and that it is positive. In some instances, support can be negative. That would happen when the holding company is legally authorized to use the assets of the subsidiaries if it needs to, which is authorized in some countries, or when there is a dependency between the credit standing of the head of hierarchy and the borrower. In such cases, a difficulty in the holding company might lead to liquidating assets of the subsidiary for enhancing the credit standing of the holding company. This ambiguous effect of support has a direct effect on the computation of the default probability of a subsidiary which is subject to positive or negative support.

In the example of corporations, the three building blocks that make up the final rating assemble a number of pieces of information, as illustrated in Tables 40.1–40.3. In these tables, the last lines show a fictitious letter-grade rating in bold letters.

TABLE 40.1 Intrinsic rating criteria

1. Intrinsic rating	Corporations	Weight?
Fundamentals		
Industry	Growth potential, cyclicality, technology, capital, competition, regulations, regional dynamics, barriers to entry.	
Position and market share, business model	Size and market share, diversity and stability of revenues (flow business), business model, reputation, alliances.	
Management and governance	Experience and track record, achievement of goals, efficiency.	
Financials		
Financials	Key ratios: debt – equity; management ratios; profitability (return on equity, return on assets).	
Financing	Access to various sources of financing, committed lines of credit exists.	
Repayment ability	Cash flow and revenue generation, flexibility of costs, debt cover ratios (DCR).	
Intrinsic rating		100% **C**

TABLE 40.2   Support assessment criteria

2. Support	
Existence of a supporting entity (holding company):"Support" does not imply any legal guarantee	
Core business of holding company	Yes
Track record of support	Good
Economic and technology links	Some
Support is financial	No
Assessment of support	**Strong**
Supporting entity	
Rating supporting entity	**B**

TABLE 40.3   Final rating assessment

3. Synthesis	
Intrinsic rating	C
Rating of supporting entity	B
Quality of support	Strong
Existence of a country cap rating	No
Final rating	**B**

40.5.3 Banks: Sample Rating Grid

The standard credit rating grids vary across counterparty types. In the case of banks, there are some common factors, such as strategy, management and competitive advantage, but the financial nature of assets and liabilities and the associated risk makes the analysis radically different. We concentrate on intrinsic rating, the others building blocks being similar (support, rating of support and synthesis) (Table 40.4).

40.6 MAPPING RATINGS TO DEFAULT PROBABILITIES

The "IRB" approaches to capital of the Basel 2 Accord makes the internal ratings a critical building block. Under Basel 2, both internal ratings and scores should map to a master scale showing the default probability attached to each rating or score. The mapping implies that the rank correlation between ratings and the default probabilities of the master scale be one, or that default probabilities of the master scale are monotonous functions of ratings. In general, when scoring is not used, ratings rely on expert judgment to a certain extent, and the corresponding portfolios are generally "low default portfolios," implying that internal statistics cannot be used for deriving default probabilities from internal ratings.

The simplest technique is mapping internal ratings with external ratings and using the correspondence between external ratings with default probabilities to obtain the missing link from internal ratings to default probabilities. This sounds simple in theory, but there are practical

TABLE 40.4   Banks rating assessment

1. Intrinsic rating	Banks	Weight?
Fundamentals		
Regulations and regulators	The regulators and their capability of enforcing rules. The economic context under its financial aspects: Leverage of firms, of individuals and how sensitive banks are to economic conditions.	
Position and market share, business model	The competitive position, as for corporates: Some specializations could isolate the bank from competition, even if it is small, such as a regional influence and close links with municipalities and strong local industries.	
The risk profile and diversification	Banks can offer a limited range of products or be universal, have a narrow range business lines or a wide range of business lines. For example a bank with an important M & A business line is riskier than a universal bank.	
Strategy	Strategy is driven by risk appetite in addition to other standard elements.	
Management and governance	Experience and track record, achievement of goals, effectiveness.	
Financials		
Profitability	Key ratios: return on equity, return on assets.	
Capital base	Capital base is the foundation of bank's solvency since it absorbs unexpected losses beyond statistical losses and economic provisions.	
Credit quality of bank's portfolio	Diversification of financial assets and liabilities across risk classes (traded assets versus lending, deposit base); loan portfolio risk, which depends on its concentration or diversification across industries and regions; risk policy and control of the bank. Loan loss reserves can vary with the bank's policy and regulations.	
Financing and liquidity	The deposit base is a stable source of financing which might not depend from the credit standing of the bank; whereas debt issues and interbank borrowings depend on the credit rating. The liquid asset base and the repo financing base are key factors for stable financing. Diversification across financing sources is beneficial, although the core deposit base remains a major factor for financing stability.	
Intrinsic rating		100% C

difficulties. There should be a minimum convergence of methodologies that ensure that internal ratings are consistent with external ratings. Discrepancies are made explicit by cross-tabulating internal ratings with external ratings, and making sure, as a pre-requisite, that date differences between internal and external ratings are not too distant in time. Normally, there should be a concentration along the diagonal, and outliers should be reviewed.

Considering external ratings first, the curve showing annual default frequencies by rating class is not monotonously increasing, at least when using a detailed rating scale with 20 to 30 rating notches. The ranking of ratings does not match the ranking of default frequencies, even when taking long-term averages of such annual default frequencies. Smoothing the curve is an ad hoc necessary methodology.

We illustrate this fact with three charts (Figure 40.1–40.3). We assign a rank to each rating class: "1" is the highest rating (AAA for Standard & Poor's and Fitch Ratings and Aaa for Moody's) and "17" is the lowest grade considered (CCC/C for the first two rating agencies and Caa/C for Moody's). Then, we plot along ranks the historical 1-year default frequencies as averaged from 1983 until 2004. Figure 40.1 shows the curves, which look pretty smooth. But zooming in the highest grades shows that default frequencies are not any more a monotonous increasing function of the ranks (Figure 40.2).

Second, historical default frequencies from agencies are generally not representative of the portfolio of banks. There are around 5000 corporations listed and rated. Considering the portfolio of large corporations as representative of the bank's portfolio is generally not true except for the "low default portfolios" of the investment banking pole of banks dealing with large corporations. Moreover, lower size corporations have on the average a higher chance of default than very large corporations.

The assumption for using default frequencies attached to external ratings for internal rating is that rating methodologies are comparable, and therefore that an internal rating is similar to an external senior unsecured rating. Then corporates not belonging within the universe of listed and rated corporations should be assigned a rating consistent with external ratings.

In fact, they are internal biases of internal ratings compared to external ratings. For example, analysts might assign internal ratings systematically above external ratings, for some rating classes. Such biases should be corrected. Otherwise assigning external rating default frequencies to internal ratings would be inconsistent. The process requires mapping internal ratings to external ratings, with eventual adjustment for the bias, before attaching an external default frequency to an internal rating.

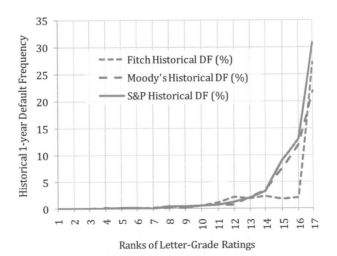

FIGURE 40.1 **Letter-grade ratings and historical default frequencies**

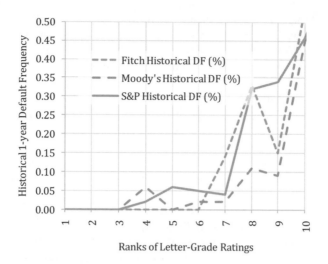

FIGURE 40.2   Letter-grade ratings and historical default frequencies: zooming on investment grade ratings

Finally, the principle stating that any given external rating matches a certain credit standing across corporations, banks and other financial entities looks like wishful thinking. Most existing statistics of default apply to rated corporations. Considering that banks having the same rating also have the same default probability is simply inconsistent with historical data. Considering that municipalities default as corporations do, when they are assigned the same rating, is equally inconsistent with available data. Default data is scarce for municipalities and any convergence of historical default frequencies would be subject to wide confidence intervals. The unique rationale for using this principle is simply that default events are more frequent for corporations than other entities, and, because they are the main source of default frequencies, they tend to be used for all types of counterparty.

The standard argument for considering that an equal rating for different types of counterparties measures the same credit risk is that expert judgments from credit analysts provide ratings that are comparable in terms of credit standing, therefore in terms of default probability. For example, SMEs are riskier than large corporates and should, on average, have lower credit ratings. A better solution than postulating that equal ratings measure equal risks would be to shift to default probabilities directly rather using ratings as an intermediate step.

It is easy to see that default frequencies within an external rating class overlap over default frequencies of other different rating classes. The evidence stems from the distribution of defaults within each rating class. The aggregated default rate is an average. Alternate analyses of such overlaps use default probability models, which provides point-in-time default probabilities as derived from equity prices, as explained in the structural model of default chapter (Chapter 42). The most common model is Moody's-KMV Credit Monitor, of which principles are explained in the same chapter. The output of the model is called "EDF©," for "Expected Default Frequency," because such default probabilities are derived from stock prices, supposed to be forward looking. When using such individual default probabilities, it can be seen that the distributions of the EDF© within ratings classes significantly overlap, notably between adjacent rating classes.

FIGURE 40.3 **From internal ratings to external ratings and default statistics**

The mapping process is common in spite of such limitations, with the two usual steps for low default portfolios, from internal to external ratings and from external ratings to historical default frequencies (Figure 40.3).

In any case, it is highly recommended to set up confidence intervals around smoothed function of default frequencies against ratings. Such confidence intervals can be assigned using standard regression techniques. A preliminary is to convert letter-grade ratings into rank and to use such numbers instead of codes. A simple regression analysis of default frequencies on ratings ranks provides both the coefficients and their confidence intervals as outputs.

40.7 APPENDIX: RATING SCALES OF RATING AGENCIES

Table 40.5 gives the rating scales of rating agencies.

TABLE 40.5 **The rating scales of rating agencies**

S&P			Moody's	
AAA	Highest	A1	Aaa	Highest
AA	Strong	A2	Aa	High grade
A	Still strong	A3	A	Upper grade with some risks
BBB	Adequate but sensitive adverse conditions	B	Baa	Medium grade. Not outstanding; speculative
BB	Major uncertainties	C	Ba	Speculative elements. Risk exists
B	Strong uncertainty	D	B	Small insurance of making payments
CCC	Vulnerable		Caa	Poor standing. Possibly, some issues defaulted
CC	Highly vulnerable		Ca	Speculative to a high degree
C	Still facing obligation despite bankruptcy or like action		C	Extremely poor prospects
D	D is non-performing. Default materialized.			

41

Statistical and Scoring Models

There are several generations of models of credit risk and default probabilities, starting from the early statistical models linking ratings to financial characteristics of firms and up to elaborate econometric techniques and neural network models.

This chapter focuses on statistical scoring techniques. Credit scoring allows one to model credit risk using techniques for discriminating between defaulters and non-defaulters. Scoring does not rely on conceptual models, but on statistical fits of "scoring functions." It applies when a large volume of default data is available, which is the case for the retail portfolio. For larger entities, credit ratings are used. A "scoring function" provides a score from observable attributes, which is a number. Score ranges should map on a one-to-one basis to default frequencies.[1]

Section 41.1 explains the principles of scoring. Section 41.2 discusses the economics of scoring models, or the costs of making errors. The core of scoring models is the Logit models, detailed in Section 41.3. Section 41.5 describes the implementation process of fitting a scoring model to retail data. A preliminary distinction is made in Section 41.4 between behavioral models, used for existing clients, and origination models that apply for new clients or for new transactions. The process for developing scores requires several sequential steps: Identifying relevant observable attributes, dealing with non-linear relationships between scores and explaining variables, before proceeding to the statistical fit. Section 41.6 explains how "cumulative accuracy profiles" serve for measuring the accuracy of default models, comparing them and back testing scoring models. The last section (Section 41.7) addresses the mapping issue between scores and default probabilities.

---

1 This chapter focuses on implementation of score and Logit model. The reference [47], from Kleinbaum, provides technical details of logistical regressions.

Contents

41.1 SCORING

The principle of scoring is to use a metric for dividing "good" and "bad" credits into distinct groups, using observable characteristics, or attributes, of borrowers. For firms, the technique uses current and past values of observable attributes such as financial ratios. Such variables include profitability, leverage, size and others. For individuals, income, age and professional activities relate to their credit standing.

The technique forms a linear combination of all discriminating variables to obtain a discriminant function. The discriminant function values are the scores. The functions are such that they maximize the likelihood of separating the population into defaulters and non-defaulters. For every individual, a numerical value of the score results from observed attributes and scores. If the value is high, the credit is good, and the higher the score, the higher is the quality for the credit. A bad score indicates a lower quality credit. Scores allow separating defaulters from the rest of the population and serve to rank all scored entities according the level of credit risk.

Among outputs of the procedure are the coefficients of the classification function that help in interpreting which coefficients best explain the classification, and the posterior probabilities of belonging to a given group. Posterior probabilities are conditional default probabilities given score. Let us assume that high scores relate to bad credit standing. When the company attributes result in a high score value, the posterior probability is higher and vice versa.

Scoring does not use a conceptual framework, such as KMV Credit Monitor, which implements the Merton model[2]. It simply fits a function that best discriminates between high-risk and low-risk populations. The fit might necessitate repeated calibration to account for changing conditions, although the attributes might also capture the changing conditions.

Therefore, scoring potentially discriminates firms according to their credit standing, and can serve both as default predictors and as a rating device. For firms, scoring models based on a small number of indicators, such as accounting ratios, have been successful. There are a number of classical studies explaining scoring systems and providing numerical results. A famous, and continuously updated score, is Altman's Z-score model (Altman 1977, [1] the first contribution being 1968) for corporations. This is a multivariate model built on the values of selected ratios and categorical measures. The Z-score models have been applied to a large variety of borrowers, from small to medium-sized firms, non-manufacturing and manufacturing firms, and even emerging markets firms.

---

2 See Chapter 42.

The basic Z-score model is public. It uses five variables for discriminating between obligors. These are:

- working capital/total assets
- retained earnings/total assets
- EBIT/total assets
- market value of equity/book value of liabilities
- sales/total assets.

The discriminant function is linear. All ratios have a statistical coefficient in the function:

$$Z = F(X_1, X_2, X_3, X_4, X_5)$$

The value of the Z-score measures the likelihood to default. High scores indicate low likelihood of failure and conversely. The implementation implies to define ranges of values of the Z to make a decision. A typical utilization of such a model requires defining cut-off values for Z such that:

- below a lower bound, the firm's likelihood to fail is high
- above an upper bound, the firm's likelihood to fail is low
- in between the upper and lower bounds, we do not know, because the model does not discriminate well the two categories. In this "grey zone," scores assess the intermediate credit standing.

These cut-off values of scores serve for classifying obligors into "good" or "bad" categories, or in between. The benefit of scoring is to speed up the credit decisions and the rating process. There are drawbacks.

- Some critical characteristics, other than ratios, might be relevant and not be included in the discriminant function. For example, management quality for small firms is critical.
- There are no conceptual foundations to scoring, except that the effects of variables are in line with intuition. This is not a drawback as long as the issue is the end-result, not the conceptual foundations of the fitting process.

Scoring is mainly used for large numbers of very small entities. Retail banking is defined under Basel 2 as granular portfolios, with a cap on the size of individual loans, both in monetary units and in percentage of the portfolio size.

Scoring is widely used for consumers' lending. Scoring allows automation of the credit process because there is no real need to examine the profile of individuals in detail. There are plenty of reliable portfolio loss statistics, given the large number of individuals. The relevant criteria combine the potential revenues, the value added for the bank, and the risks. Income per dependent in the family, renting or owning home, marital status and occupation are examples of "attributes" for assessing the credit standing. Information on other credit cards and other loans by other institutions, when available, provide information on the exposure to other competitors and the level of debt. Years spent in the same address and years spent in the same job provide information on the mobility to be expected and the length of the financial services provided by the bank.

41.2 THE ECONOMICS OF SCORING SYSTEMS

The usage of scoring has economic implications, which are the relative costs of rejecting a good credit and of accepting a bad credit.

Scoring is a statistical technique that might fail to make the right predictions, as all techniques do. Beyond some value, the likelihood of failing is negligible, and beyond another lower value, the likelihood of default is close to one. In between, a relationship between default probability and the value of the score is modeled by scores. Used in this way, we have both a default predictive tool and a rating device. Types of errors for score-based decisions are:

- type I error – accept bad credits
- type II error – reject good credits.

Since the costs of the two types of errors are widely different, the economics of errors has an influence on the cut-off values of the score for lending decisions. For individual decisions, type I errors result in a full loss of principal and interest should the risk materialize. Type II error costs are opportunity costs of not lending to a wealthy borrower. The opportunity cost is the lost income. Hence, the cost of a type II error is much lower than that of a type I error. Based on these simple economics, type II errors are more acceptable than type I errors, because the unit loss is lower. Since the cut-off values of scoring models drive the probabilities of types I and II errors, choosing them depends on both the quality of predictions and the differential cost of errors.

Accordingly, scoring does not apply only to credit risk measurement. It extends to attributes representative of the potential "richness" of a customer to the bank. Richness relates to future revenues and "intensity of services," such as the number of accounts and services with a customer, and future transactions expected with the customer, such as new loans and credit cards loans. "Service intensity" and expected profitability are criteria correlated to the personal profile of individuals, and overlap with criteria for assessing default probability. Banks might require from the potential client historical data of other accounts held for reviewing the flows of the accounts and their balances across time for both purposes.

41.3 LOGIT MODELS

There are models dedicated for predicting binary events, such as default or non-default, or for scaling the probabilities that such events will occur. These models include the linear probability models and the more adequate Logit and Probit models. In what follows, "individual" means individual observation, an observation relating to any type of borrowers, consumers or corporates. These models use the multivariate regression technique. The explanatory variables are the attributes X_i. These techniques also apply to model a categorical dependent variable from observable attributes, and assigning individuals to several categories based on observable attributes. In that case, they serve to define a typology of clients under a commercial view, rather than a risk view.

41.3.1 The "Basic" Linear Model Drawbacks

The simple linear probability model illustrates the principle. The linear probability model makes the probability P of the event a linear function of several attributes X_i. The purpose is to relate the Bernoulli variable, default or no default, Y, taking values 0 for non-default or 1 for default, using the observable attributes. The essentials are easy to explain with a single attribute, X, but would be the same using several observable characteristics. The model is:

$$Y = \alpha + \beta X + \varepsilon$$

Y is either 0 or 1. Taking the expectation of Y, and using a zero expectation for the error term ε of the regression:

$$E(Y) = 1 \times P(Y = 1) + 0 \times [1 - P(Y = 0)]$$

$$P(Y) = 1 = \alpha + \beta E(X)$$

The model provides the value of the probability of Y equal to 1, or the default probability. All observed values of Y within the sample are either 0 or 1. But the linear regression provides coefficients such that Y can take values which are not necessarily within the 0 to 1 range. This implies truncation to avoid such outliers. The Logit models avoid this drawback.

41.3.2 Logit Model Family

The Logit models address the problem of translating the values of attributes X_i, whatever they are, into a number Y that ranges between 0 and 1, which represents the default probability. Moreover, the function Y should vary monotonously with the default probability.

Individual observations fall into either one of the two categories, default and non-default. The attributes are observable characteristics of individuals. The first step is to express Y as a function of the attributes X_i. The general formula would replace X a vector of n attributes X_i to model their influences on the credit state, default or no default:

$$Y = \beta_0 + \sum_{i=1,n} \beta_i X_i + \varepsilon$$

For simplicity, we write the equation with a single X. The basic linear model moves directly from Y to a probability. Instead, the Logit model transforms the Y using a cumulated distribution function, or CDF(Y). A cumulative distribution function assigns one value, and only one, between 0 and 1, to any value of the random variable Y that it models. Any predicted value of Y, without any boundary, corresponds to a probability (within the 0 to 1 range) using a known distribution function. The predicted probability depends on the particular distribution used to define the cumulated distribution CDF(Y).

The Logit model uses the cumulative logistic probability distribution for the CDF. Let's use $X = \sum_{i=1,n} \beta_i X_i$. The model fits the model $Y = \alpha + X + \varepsilon$ and calculates $P(Y)$ as:

$$P(Y) = \frac{1}{\left[1 + \exp(-Y)\right]} = \frac{1}{\left\{1 + \exp\left[-(\alpha + X + \varepsilon)\right]\right\}}$$

When Y gets very high, the exponential becomes close to zero and $P(Y)$ tends towards 1. When Y gets very negative, the exponential becomes very high and $P(Y)$ tends towards 0. Therefore, any value of $P(Y)$ is within the boundary values of probabilities and $P(Y)$ can be seen as a probability, which is a monotonous function of Y. Since $P(Y)$ declines monotonously from 1 to 0 when Y increases from negative values to positive values, $P(Y)$ can also be seen as a number that characterizes the credit standing of the borrower and can serve to assign ratings along the default probability scale.

In order to show that, we use a simple transformation of the Logit model:

$$\exp(Y) = P(Y)/[1 - P(Y)]$$

Taking the natural logarithm, we get:

$$\ln\left[\frac{P(Y)}{1-P(Y)}\right] = Y = a + X + \varepsilon$$

This allows an easy interpretation of the model (Figure 41.1). The argument of the logarithm, $P(Y)/[1 - P(Y)]$, is called the odd ratio, also equal to $\exp(-Y)$. The odd ratio is the ratio of the probability of belonging to a group to the probability of not belonging to that group. The logarithm of the odd ratio is the "Logit." $P(Y)$ is a monotonously increasing function of Y, and so is the odd ratio. We show below the relationship between Y and $P(Y)$. When $Y = 0$, the logarithm is 1, the odd ratio is 1, meaning that there are as many chances to belonging to one group as they are to belong to the other, implying a common value $P(Y = 0) = \frac{1}{2}$. One attractive feature of the Logit model is that it transforms the issue of predicting probabilities into a linear model predicting the logarithm of the odds of a credit event. Once the model fitted to data, we have the coefficients. The value $Y = \beta_0 + \sum_{i=1,n} \beta_i X_i + \varepsilon$ is simply the logarithm of the odds ratio, and its exponential is the odds ratio itself.

The Logit model has some drawbacks. When $P(Y) = 0$ or 1, the logarithm is undefined, making the regression inadequate. The remedy is to use grouped observations where we can observe the fraction of observations belonging to one group. This ensures that values will not

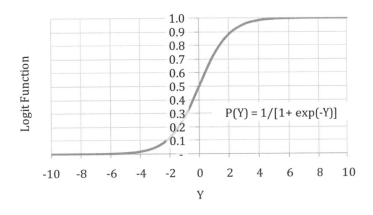

FIGURE 41.1   Function P(Y)

reach extremes. The Logit model is widely used for scoring purposes. It is also used in Credit Portfolio View, a credit portfolio model[3].

The Probit model performs similar functions than the Logit model, but uses the normal distribution instead of the logistic distribution. Because the normal distribution CDF is more complex than the logistic distribution, the model looks more complex. The Logit and the Probit models give very close results. The only difference is that the Logit form is easier to handle.

41.4 SCORING IN RETAIL BANKING: BEHAVIORAL VERSUS ORIGINATION MODELS

Statistical scoring models (usually Logit models) relate the status "default"/"no default" of individuals with observable variables, such as revenues, age of accounts, etc. There are several types of models according to the details of the "credit history" that is available to measure attributes predictors of the client's credit standing.

"Behavioral models" attempt to model the behavior of existing clients, when there is no new event that would change the debt level, given historical data of account and loan behavior. They apply to existing clients for whom there is historical data, for, say, at least 6 months. It makes it easier to deal with existing clients than for new clients for which there is no credit history.

"Origination models" aim at describing the credit standing for new clients or when new products are originated for existing clients. There are two types of origination models. For new clients, there is less information, although all banks would collect a minimum set of data on the client, such as revenue, wealth and, eventually, historical behavior of other existing accounts in other banks. Therefore, we cannot use the same attributes for modeling their risk as with existing clients. Consider an existing client that requests a new loan. A second type of origination model is required, because we already have historical data on the client. In this case, we have a different origination model, which applies to a known client whose credit standing might be affected by a new loan. It is also an origination model because "originating" to this existing client a new loan is considered.

41.5 IMPLEMENTATION OF SCORING IN RETAIL BANKING

We give below an example of implementing a scoring model. The variables that can be used as attributes for discriminating the credit standing of individuals or small entities in retail banking depend on whether we use a behavioral or an origination model.

41.5.1 Discriminating Variables

For behavioral models, a history of 6 months is a good compromise for measuring attributes. Those include, for example:

---

3   See Chapter 51 on credit portfolio models.

- time series of flows, measured by the absolute value of flows, both negative and positive and averaged over a period, over the past 6 months
- number of debit days, measured by the maximum of debit days the over the past 6 months
- number of transactions suspended by credit officer because they would have triggered an excess overdraft
- count of incidents over the past 6 months
- amount of liquid savings – a measure of wealth often known by the bank, with some average calculated from the end of month average of balances over the past 6 months
- leverage ratio – monthly payments due/credit flows
- age since origination of the account
- other personal wealth characteristics.

In the function Y of the Logit model, $Y = \beta_0 + \Sigma_{i=1,n} \beta_i X_i$, the above variables are the attributes X_i. For fitting the model, we use historical data for explaining the binary variable Y (default, no default). Using historical data, we have the values of Y. We derive the coefficients of the model by fitting the model to the data. Once we have the coefficients, we obtain as outputs for Y and $P(Y)$, which is interpreted as a score.

41.5.2 Identification of Potentially Significant Attributes

Obviously, it is interesting to compare the mean values of discriminating variables between defaulters and non-defaulters. A large difference between, for example, the number of debit days in the last 6 months, suggests that the variable should be considered in the Logit model. As usual in statistics, large differences do not mean much unless we relate them to the number of observations. The difference has to be statistically significant, using standard statistical tests for comparing means across sample populations, based on the sample variance of the observed variable. In retail banking, the volume of observations is usually high, as well as the number of defaults, which is much lower. In a sample population of 1000,000 individuals, with 1% defaulted, we already have a sub-population of defaulters which is 10,000.

Assume that we find that the number of debit days is 5 over 6 months for non-defaulted individuals, while it is 20 for defaulted individuals and that the difference is statistically significant. The difference suggests including the variable as an attribute for predicting defaults. Similarly, the mean of the age of defaulted accounts would be considered as a relevant attribute if it is, for example, 81 months versus 123 months for non-defaulters. However, means across the entire population might be similar even though the attributes do discriminate, which implies that comparing means only might not provide convincing results. We illustrate the identification process with these two variables.

41.5.3 Non-linear Relationship between Selected Attributes and Credit State

The graphs in Figures 41.2 and 41.3 are frequency distributions of attributes selected for discriminating defaulters and non-defaulters over a 6-month period. There are two frequency distributions: one for non-defaulted individuals and another for defaulted individuals. The two variables considered for discriminating between "good" and "bad" credit standings are the number of debit days over 6 months and the age of the account (the time elapsed since the account was opened). The lines represent the frequencies over the two sub-populations of defaulters and non-defaulters. We could add confidence intervals around each of those lines to check whether the confidence intervals at, say 5%, overlap or not.

Considering the number of debit days, the frequency of low numbers of debit days is much higher for non-defaulters. The opposite occurs for large numbers of debit days, beyond 25 days: the frequency of defaulters is much higher than that of non-defaulters. In the interval from around 3 debit days and up to 20 debit days over 6 months, the frequency is almost identical with the two groups (Figure 41.2). Overall, defaulters have higher frequencies of high numbers of debit days and a lower frequency of small numbers of debit days. This is in line with intuition. Note that considering the mean of the variable over the entire distribution might not produce significant differences, because the differential values appear only for the two end segments of the distributions.

The striking feature of this relation between means of the two sub-populations is that the relation between the number of debit days and the frequency of defaults is not linear. Hence, a linear relation such as $Y = \alpha + \beta X + \varepsilon$, where Y is a binary variable of default and X is the number of debit days over 6 months will not work too well.

Similar characteristics appear when we construct the frequency distributions of the age of the account for defaulted individuals and non-defaulted individuals (Figure 41.3). Non-defaulters have a higher age of account than defaulters. When the age of accounts is lower than 100 months, default frequency is higher for defaulters. When the age extends beyond 100 months, the default frequency gets much higher for non-defaulters. Young accounts default more frequently than old accounts. Again, we ignore here confidence bands around those

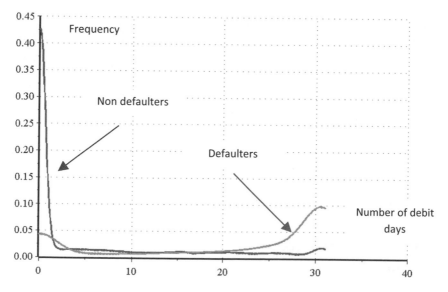

FIGURE 41.2   **Distribution of the number of debit days over 6 months for defaulters and non-defaulters**

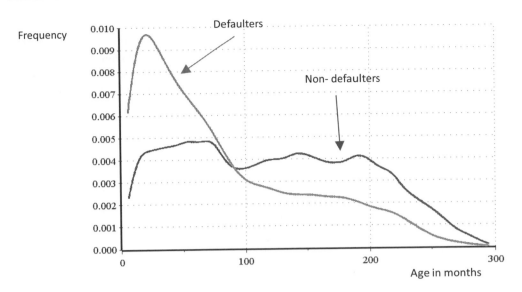

FIGURE 41.3 Frequency distribution of age of account for defaulters and non-defaulters

curves. But a linear relationship will not fit very well the relation between age of account and probability of default.

The next step consists of dealing with such non-linear relations within the Logit model where Y is a linear function of attributes. The variables have to be transformed for using a linear function.

41.5.4 Constructing Attributes from Observed Characteristics

The standard correction for fitting a non-linear relationship between two variables is to breakdown the continuous variables, such as the number of debit days or the age of accounts, into several discretized variables. An example of discretization is shown in Table 41.1. The intervals are selected empirically according to the gap between frequencies of defaulters and non-defaulters.

Table 41.1 shows that the number of debit days above 22 days over a 6-month period corresponds to 11% of all accounts and to 61% of all defaults, with an average default frequency of 6.36%. Conversely, 63% of all accounts have zero debit days over the same reference period

TABLE 41.1 Discretization of continuous variables

Number of debit days	% of all accounts	% of all defaults	Default frequency %
0	62.83	19.31	0.36
> 0 and ≤ 12	15.64	8.11	0.60
> 12 and ≤ 22	10.39	11.27	1.25
> 22	11.14	61.31	6.36
Total	100	100	1.16

and corresponds to 19% of all defaults, but with a much lower default frequency of 0.36%. The optimum discretization is determined empirically. In this case, the optimum discretization is shown in Table 41.1. It consists of dividing the number of debit days into four binary variables taking the values 0 or 1 according to whether the number of debit days is within the above intervals. In other words, each of these four binary variables is defined as indicator functions:

$$N_1 = 1 \text{ if } n = 0$$
$$N_1 = 0 \text{ if } n \neq 0$$

The indicator function means that N_1 is equal to 1 when $n = 0$ and zero otherwise. The three other intervals allow defining the remaining variables, using the indicator function (noted $\mathbb{1}$):

$$N_2 = \mathbb{1} \ (n > 0 \text{ and } n \leq 12)$$

$$N_3 = \mathbb{1} \ (n > 12 \text{ and } n \leq 22)$$

$$N_4 = \mathbb{1} \ (n > 22)$$

Using such variables, we can now construct the Logit model using:

$$Y = \alpha + \beta_1 N_1 + \beta_2 N_2 + \beta_3 N_3 + \beta_4 N_4 + \varepsilon$$

The Logit model becomes $P(Y) = 1/[1 + \exp(-Y)]$ where Y is the linear function of discretized variables as above.

41.5.5 Fitting and Back Testing Scoring Models

The model should be fitted to various samples of the population. A first sample provides a first fit. Then, an "out-of-the-sample" fit, using another sample of the population, serves for checking that the same model provides similar results. In- and out-of-the-sample fits are conducted over the same reference period.

They differ from back tests that compare what the model predicts with what has happened in reality, from historical data on defaults, or making a comparison "before and after." Any scoring model will predict $P(Y)$. When performing a back test, we should compare the finding of the models for sub-groups of the population with historical default frequencies. In theory, there should be a good match, in terms of ranks, between the score and such historical frequencies of defaults. In practice this is not always the case.

The process for mapping scores to default probabilities involves several steps. First, the population is divided in sub-groups according to ranges of values of $P(Y)$ ranked in ascending order. Then, for each group, an historical default frequency is calculated. For calculating a default frequency, a starting date is defined. At this date, we have only sound individuals. The default frequency DF over a period, T, is the ratio of counts of defaults to the initial number of individuals as of the starting date 0, or DF(0, T). For having 1-year default frequency, T should be set to one year.

$$DF(0, T) = \text{number of defaults within } [0, T] \text{ / initial number of individuals}$$

Assigning default frequencies to scores requires a "mapping" of scores and default frequencies to a master scale valid across segments. This master scale is simply a scale of range of default probabilities. The mapping process should ensure that the default frequency derived from scores increases monotonously when moving along the scale from low-risk obligors to high-risk obligors. The mapping issue is discussed in the last section of this chapter.

41.6 ACCURACY OF SCORING MODELS: THE "CAP"

A standard technique for visualizing and quantifying the accuracy of any credit risk measure is the usage of "power curves," also called "cumulative accuracy profile" or CAP. This is a back testing methodology. It applies to any credit risk quality measure, whether from scoring or more involved modeling such as the Moody's-KMV Credit Monitor EDFs©[4], or agency ratings predictive ability.

The cumulative accuracy profile plots the fraction of defaulted individuals as predicted by the model with fractions of population ranked by decreasing risk. Plotting a "CAP" requires ordering obligors by risk score, from riskiest to safest. The horizontal axis measures the fraction of population ranked by decreasing risk (measured by a score Y or the probability of default). The vertical axis measures the fraction of the population actually defaulted, as a percentage of the total population, observed historically, over a given period such as one year. Note that the vertical axis is expressed as a percentage of the defaulted population, or the fraction of defaulted individuals over the total population of defaulted individuals. Hence, 100% means that 10% of the population defaulted.

Assume, for example, that the default frequency of the population sample is 10% and the size of the sample is 1000 individuals. When moving up along the horizontal axis, the fraction of defaulted population also increases but it cannot exceed 100%, which is equivalent to 10% of the entire population. When moving to the right on the horizontal axis, the risk declines, and is highest on the left-hand side. For example, 10% on the horizontal axis represents the 10% worst ranked in terms of credit standing of the entire population; 20% represents the 20% most poorly rated, etc. The maximum value is 100% of the entire population rated by the score.

If the scoring model were perfect, the first 10% of individuals of the entire population would be those who actually defaulted. The 10% value on the horizontal axis would match exactly the 10% of actual defaults along the vertical axis. In this case, when reaching 10% of the worst ranked population, we also hit the 10% of the entire population on the vertical axis. Moving beyond 10% along the horizontal axis, the fraction of defaulted population measured along the vertical axis remains 100%, or, equivalently, the total fraction of entire population that defaulted.

The upper bound of the CAP from 0% to 10%, along the horizontal axis, is the straight line representing the fraction of individuals that actually defaulted. The upper bound beyond 10% measured along the horizontal axis is 100% of the defaulted population. It is the horizontal line, at 100% on the vertical axis, starting from the value of 10% on the horizontal axis. The overall upper bound for the CAP is a made of those two lines.

No model is perfect. Let us assume that the score does not provide any information on defaulters. If the score were independent of actual defaults, the score would not discriminate between defaulted and non-defaulted individuals. Whatever its value, there would be a 50%:50%

---

4 The Credit Monitor model is detailed in Chapter 42.

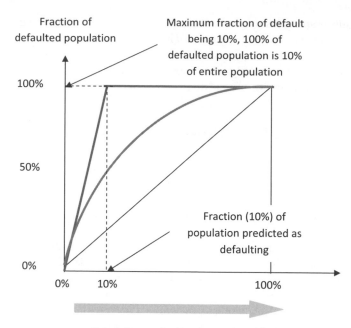

FIGURE 41.4   The CAP and accuracy of default models

chance of default or not default. The fraction of the defaulted population will be the same as the fraction of the entire population ranked according to the model. This is the first diagonal in Figure 41.4. It is the lower bound of the CAP.

If the model does provide information on who defaults and who does not, we move above the diagonal. Since no model can be perfect, among the 10% riskiest persons, some will not have defaulted, and the fraction of defaulted individuals will remain below the line. This implies that individuals who did not default were rejected, a type II error of rejecting "good" individuals. Conversely, some of the individuals ranked as less risky than the first 10% did default. The model predicted no default while there was a default. This is the second case, accepting individuals as "good" while they prove to be "bad," or the type I error of accepting "bad" individuals that should have been rejected.

Once we have the CAP profile, a common measure of accuracy is how close is the actual CAP to the upper boundary lines. A simple measure is the Gini coefficient, which is the ratio of the area between the actual CAP line and the first diagonal to the area below the upper bound and the same first diagonal.

accuracy measure = area below upper bound of CAP / area below actual CAP profile

The area below the actual CAP profile is obtained from the actual curved CAP line, which has a continuous shape, and monotonously increasing when moving to the right. This area is purely empirical, while the area under the upper bound made of the two straight lines can be calculated easily. Using as a lower bound the first diagonal, the accuracy measure has a minimum value of 0, meaning that the model does not discriminate the risk. The maximum value is 100%. The higher the Gini coefficient, the better the model is. Acceptable values start at 60% and can go up to values much closer to 100%.

41.7 MAPPING SCORING MODELS TO A MASTER SCALE OF DEFAULT PROBABILITIES

Default probabilities are derived from scores, by mapping the scores of subsets of the entire population defined by a range of score values to historical default frequencies. We would like the default frequencies to increase with the average risk of each sub-group, the groups being defined by ranking individuals according to score value. However, ranking and grouping by scores does not ensure that the average default frequency of groups varies monotonously with the average score of each group, even though individuals are being ranked by score values before grouping.

Consider two groups A and B. A is supposed to be less risky than B in term of scores. All individuals of A have a higher score than those of B. Accordingly, the historical default frequency of A should be higher than the historical default frequency of B. But mismatch of ranks between scores and historical default frequencies might occur, even though the model has been back tested with several samples of the population.

An algorithm is required to segregate groups, by varying the size of each group until the risk actually increases both in terms of scores and in terms of historical default frequency. When varying the size, each group should have a significant number of individuals. The sampling error must be small enough for groups to differ significantly in terms of default frequency. Merging sub-groups might be necessary for meeting this condition. Each sub-group is then mapped to default frequencies. The mapping provides the final default probabilities assigned to each sub-group, defined by their historical default frequencies.

This difficulty is compounded by the necessity of dividing the retail portfolio in segments according to the type of counterparty: individuals, very small enterprises, etc. The models differ across segments since the attributes relevant for credit risk differ according to the type of counterparty. For each segment, the same process as above is conducted.

Once the exercise performed across segments, the scores of each segment can be mapped to a master default scale of default probabilities. Usually, some segments of the retail portfolio have higher default frequencies than others, and might not have default frequency values spread equally over the entire range of default frequencies of the master scale. The entire mapping process has several phases:

1 Within each portfolio segment defined by nature of counterparty, individuals are grouped by score making sure that the historical default frequency varies monotonously from one group to the next one.
2 All portfolio segments, with segments being defined by the nature of the counterparty, are processed using the same algorithm.
3 Finally, all groups of all segments are mapped to a common master scale which extends over all default frequencies resulting from this process.

42

The Option Approach to Defaults and Migrations

The option theoretic approach to default modeling follows the simple principles set up by R. Merton in his seminal paper of 1973. In short, the option theoretic approach views default as an "economic" event triggered by a market value of assets lower than debt payment obligation. This approach views the default as a put option, held by equity holders, to sell assets to lenders with a strike price equal to debt face value. The foundation of this framework is the limited liability of shareholders. The option model of default is also called the "structural model" of default.

The Credit Monitor Model of Moody's-KMV Corporation makes the Merton model instrumental. Credit Monitor uses public equity prices for inferring asset values and traces back the implied default probability embedded in equity prices and debt. The output is the well-known "EDF"©[1]. The structural model looks forward because it relies on market data, which embeds market expectations. It also relies on a conceptual framework, unlike empirical statistical models using historical data, or unlike the reduced form model of default intensity, which sees default events as a stochastic process.

Section 42.1 defines economic default, as opposed to actual default and shows why the asset value is the most relevant criteria for modeling default. Section 42.2 presents the "structural model of default," where default is viewed as an "option to default" given by lenders to borrowers. In this framework, shareholders have both a call on asset value and a put on the same asset value. These relations allow one to derive the unobservable asset value and volatility from observable equity returns and volatilities. Section 42.3 builds on this framework for explaining the implementation of the model, by Moody's-KMV Credit Monitor model, and determining the default probability called EDF©. Sections 42.4–42.7 expand the derivation of the theoretical value, with sample calculations of the value of the "option to default," of the

---

1 The contributions of Kealohfer in [47] and [48] provide details on the Credit Monitor model.

EDF© and of the percentile attached to the asset value at a given horizon when debt payment is due. Section 42.8 briefly summarizes some extensions of the original Merton model. The last section (Section 42.9) provides the simplified version of the model, which summarizes all inputs of the lognormal distribution of assets value by a single input, which is the default probability. The simplified version is used for conducting simple simulations of correlated defaults in several subsequent instances.

Contents

42.1 HOW FIRMS DEFAULT

The most common view on default is that a firm defaults if it does not generate enough free cash flow to repay the debt obligation. The cash flow generated by a firm is its "free cash flow," or FCF. The FCF is by definition generated by operations, and after necessary investments for continuing operations. The exact definition of the FCF is as follows:

$$FCF(\text{after tax}) = NoPaT + \text{depreciation} - \Delta OWC - \text{investment}$$

In this equation, NoPaT is the net operating profit after tax, that does not include, notably, any interest revenue or expense. The OWC is the operating working capital:

$$OWC = \text{receivables} + \text{inventories} - \text{payables} + \text{other assets related to operations} - \text{other liabilities related to operations}$$

Finally, the investment is the minimum value required to maintain the firm in good conditions for continuing operations. The FCF can be positive or negative and is the available cash flow that remains for lenders and equity holders. A negative FCF does not imply default even for a firm that uses leverage. It implies that the firm needs to raise more debt or equity over the period.

A cash flow view of default is not sufficient for modeling default. If the cash flow is not high enough to repay debt over a certain period, or is negative, new debt or equity can be raised. Moreover, future FCF might become high enough to repay both current and additional debts. The point is that the cash flow model of default is flawed because it does not consider the entire stream of cash flows and has a limited horizon. Cash flows are not a relevant criterion for solvency because a temporary shortage of cash does not trigger default as long as there are chances of improvement in the future. Persistent cash flow deficiencies make default highly likely; temporary deficiencies do not.

The economic value of the firm, or, equivalently, the firm's asset value, is the present value of future free cash flows at the cost of capital. Under corporate finance theory, the firm value is the discounted values of all future FCF at weighted average cost of capital (Wacc). The foundations were laid down by the famous 1958 Modigliani–Miller paper. Extensions included bankruptcy costs and other factors such as agency cost (the cost of having an agent taking care of the firm on behalf of stockholders), etc. Therefore, the following equation is an identity:

$$\text{firm value} = \text{asset value} = \text{equity value} + \text{debt value}$$

Merton (1973) introduced the concept of economic default [51]. Default occurs when a firm's value, which sums up the entire future stream of FCFs, discounted to present, gets lower than face value of debt payments. This view sounds like a paradox since by definition, asset value is equal to equity value plus debt value, hence cannot be below debt value. The paradox is resolved by pointing out that the face value of debt, the amount to be repaid, and the economic value of debt are distinct. Both equity value and debt value move down when risk increases, but the debt repayment at some horizon does not change. Hence, the face value of the risky debt, not its economic value, is the trigger to default.

42.2 THE OPTION THEORETIC FRAMEWORK OF VALUATION OF EQUITY AND DEBT

The rationale of economic default is that, if the asset value falls below the debt payment obligation, the equity holders are better off by giving up the assets to the lenders rather than repaying the debt. Therefore, the equity holders have an option to sell assets to the lenders at a strike value equal to debt obligation. Equity holders are long on the put option, and the lenders have sold this option to equity holders. The underlying of the option is the firm's asset value. In short, default is viewed as an option to default, which exists because of the limited liability feature of equity.

For a full understanding of the option to default, the view of equity and credit risky debt should be expanded further. Some horizon has to be defined. At that horizon, the debt has a certain value, and the debt obligation implies a contractual cash outflow. Debt value and debt obligation at some future date are not identical. Next, equity can be seen as a call option on asset value. The shareholders are long on both the call and the put option to default. If the asset value is well above the debt due, the call option is in-the-money and asset value far exceeds debt value, and the put option is far out-of-the-money and has no value. The limited liability feature of equity is seen as a put option on assets. Credit risky debt is seen as a risk-free debt minus the value of the option to default sold by lenders to equity holders.

The next graphs show what happens depending on the asset value at some future horizon. Equity is a call on asset value with strike equal to face value of debt (Figure 42.1). When asset value declines below face value of debt, equity declines to zero and lenders take over. When asset value is well above debt obligation, the call value is near asset value, plus a time value, the value of chances that it gets even higher.

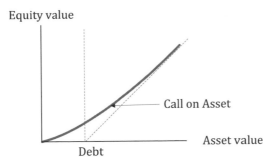

FIGURE 42.1   Equity as a call on asset value

Debt has a credit risk-free component and a credit risky component, which is the put option to default. Conversely, lenders have given away this "put option to default" and they hold a loan adjusted for the put option to default.

value of debt = value of credit risk-free debt − value of put option

Risk-free debt is constant as long as we ignore interest rate movements. It is a horizontal line in a graph showing risk-free debt as a function of asset value.

credit risky debt = risk-free debt − put option to default

When asset value increases well above debt payment, debt value tends towards risk-free debt. When asset value declines, and gets closer to debt obligation, the put option gains value. The risky debt value can decline down to zero, net of the put value, when asset value tends towards zero. This is summarized in Figure 42.2.

The value of equity remains equal to asset value minus debt. When asset value declines, the value of equity gets lower, down to zero at the limit. Debt value declines as well, and asset value also tends towards zero. Summarizing, equity is a call on asset value and credit risky debt is a risk-free debt minus the put option to default. When summing up equity value and debt value at horizon, we always get asset value because of call and put parity, sharing the same

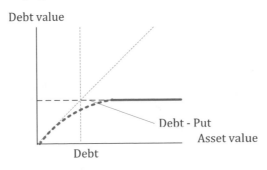

FIGURE 42.2   Debt value equals risk-free debt minus the put option to default

underlying asset value and strike. Asset value is obtained by adding up vertically the risky debt value and the equity value (Figure 42.3):

$$\text{put} + \text{call} = \text{asset value (straight line)}$$

The payoffs of the call and put options on assets are also shown (Figure 42.4).

For defining default, we need to make a distinction between economic value of debt and its face value. Under the original Merton model, the horizon is the maturity of debt. Then, default occurs when asset value gets lower than the face value of debt. The model implies that default likelihood increases when asset value gets close to debt repayment (face value). The lower the asset value, the higher the default probability. At some point, the "default point," the asset value gets lower than face value of debt and "economic default" occurs. Note that economic default is not a legal default. It is defined based on an economic view of equity and debt values given the limited liability of equity.

The Merton model is a model of default probability. The closer the random asset value is to debt obligation at maturity, the higher the default probability. Modeling the behavior of asset

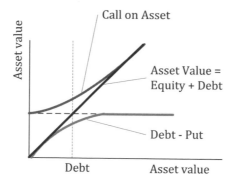

FIGURE 42.3 **Asset value as the summation of a call on asset value and risk-free debt minus option to default**

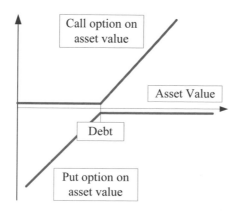

FIGURE 42.4 **Call and put option payoffs of stockholders and lenders**

value and of debt through time allows to model default. The original Merton model used a fixed amount of debt. Later extensions extended the framework to random debt values driven by the interest rate. The current implementation of the Merton model by Moody's-KMV assumes debt payment at horizon given.

42.3 IMPLEMENTING THE STRUCTURAL MODEL OF DEFAULT

Moody's-KMV Corporation made this framework very popular. This basic scheme extracts from equity prices the default probability of the firm. Moody's-KMV model defaults as the probability that the assets get under the debt obligation (or the cash outflow required for repaying debt at horizon). Moody's-KMV calls "default point" the value of asset equal to debt obligation at horizon. The probability of this event results from the random asset value distribution and from the debt value. It is an implied default probability that Moody's-KMV Corporation names "EDF,"© for "Expected Default Frequency." The EDF© is forward looking, unlike historical data, because equity prices are forward looking. The Moody's-KMV Credit Monitor model implements this framework to extract the EDF© from observable equity price data.

Implementing this framework raises difficulties and needs simplification. Moody's-KMV models default at a given horizon. The debt value combines short-term debt plus a fraction of long-term debt. The main difficulty, however, is to extract the asset value and distribution at horizon from observable data. Asset value is not observable; only equity value is. The starting point has to be the observable equity prices, returns, and their volatility. Since equity value is a call option on asset value, equity value and equity volatility are both a function of the underlying asset value and asset volatility. Asset value and asset volatility are extracted from those two relations.

From Moody's-KMV public documentation, two equations serve for extracting implied asset value and asset volatility from equity values and volatilities.

equity value = f(book value of debt, asset value, asset volatility, horizon T)

volatility of equity value = g(book value of debt, asset value, asset volatility, horizon T)

In compact notations:

$$E = f[D_T, A, \sigma(A), T]$$

$$\sigma(E) = g[D_T, A, \sigma(A), T]$$

In these equations:

- T is the horizon
- D_T is the certain book value of debt at horizon
- E is the random market value of equity
- A is the unobservable random market value of assets
- $\sigma(A)$ is the volatility of the random asset return
- $\sigma(E)$ is the volatility of the random equity return.

For equity, viewed as a call on asset value, with exercise price equal to book value of debt and maturity T, the Black-Scholes formula is:

$$E_0 = A_0 N(d_1) - D_T \exp(-rT)N(d_2)$$

- D_T = debt value, or exercise price of the call on the random asset value
- r is the risk-free rate
- $N(d_1)$ and $N(d_2)$ are the Black-Scholes formula coefficients, which depend on asset volatility.

The formula for the call on asset value provides a first equation. But we need the asset value A and its volatility $\sigma(A)$. A second equation is required for finding both values. There is a second relation between the volatility of equity $\sigma(E)$ and that of the underlying asset value $\sigma(A)$. The relationship results from the Black-Scholes formula[2]:

$$\sigma(E) = A\sigma(A)N(d_1)/E_0$$

The asset volatility derives from this new equation:

$$\sigma(A) = \frac{E_0 \sigma(E)}{A_0 N(d_1)}$$

With two equations, it is possible to obtain the implied asset value and volatility into the equity price and volatility. Moody's-KMV also uses a calibration process with actual default data.

42.4 MODELING DEFAULT PROBABILITY AND CREDIT STANDING AT HORIZON

When looking forward at a future date, economic default occurs when the asset value drops below debt. The debt level triggering default is unclear since debt amortizes according to some schedule by fractions. Moody's-KMV uses a debt value combining short-term debt at horizon plus a fraction of the long-term debt. The issue is to determine the chances that the asset value will fall below that level.

Asset future values are random. The asset return follows a stochastic process with drift, just as stock prices do. The asset value at horizon follows a lognormal distribution. We need to find out the probability that asset value goes under debt value at horizon, which is the theoretical EDF©. The asset volatility allows using the approximations for finding this probability.

Figure 42.5 shows what happens at horizon, given that the time path of asset values follows a stochastic process starting from the known value as of today. The "distance to default," or DD, is the gap between expected asset value and default point to the asset standard deviation. The DD is the downside drop, measured in standard deviation units, required for defaulting.

---

2 In order to derive this second equation, we can use Ito Lemma, which provides the drift and the volatility of the stochastic process of a function $A = f(E)$, both A and E following stochastic processes, that of equity E being the usual generalized geometric Wiener process.

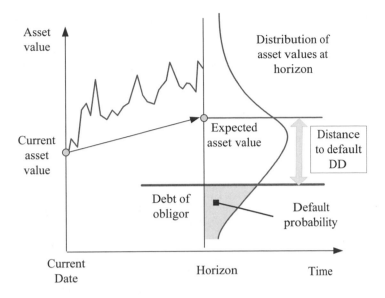

FIGURE 42.5 **Moody's KMV modeling of EDF©**

The higher is the DD, the better is the credit standing at horizon and conversely. Hence DD is a measure of the credit standing of the firm at horizon.

As an example, using the simple normal distribution, instead of the lognormal distribution at horizon[3], it is very straightforward to define the intermediate values. Assuming an expected asset value is 100 at horizon, a debt value at horizon is 50, and that asset volatility is 21.46[4], with the normal distribution assumption, the probability of economic default is that the asset value drops by $50/21.46 = 2.33$ standard deviations, or 1% in this case. This is the EDF©. The actual calculation should use the lognormal distribution for asset value (as in Chapter 17).

42.5 IMPLEMENTING THE EDF© MODEL

A number of corrections are necessary to actually mimic the actual default behavior. The value of debt obligation at horizon is the default point. This is a theoretical value. In fact, the actual value might differ, so that the calibration of the model requires mapping the distances to default to these observed default frequencies. With this mapping, the model replicates the actual default frequencies. The commercial version of that model is "Credit Monitor." The calibration process relies on proprietary default databases. It is necessary to have a sufficient number of defaulted companies for mapping distances to default to actual default frequencies. Periodical fits are necessary to make sure that the model actually fits the data.

The time path of the asset value is stochastic. There are multiple time paths, each one reaching a specific value along the distribution at horizon. Modeling the time paths as a stochastic process is not necessary as long we care only at what happens at horizon. Note, however, that

---

3   The subsequent numerical example uses the lognormal distribution.
4   The numerical value 21.46 makes the multiple of the standard deviation exactly 2.33.

it is possible that the time path of asset value crosses the default point before horizon. Then, default would occur before horizon. In Credit Monitor, default occurs either at maturity of the facility if is it shorter than horizon, or at horizon.

The Credit Monitor EDF© could approximately match default probabilities mapped to rating. In fact, average EDFs© and average default probabilities by rating class might differ significantly. The market-based EDF© fluctuate continuously, and in spite of recalibration of the Moody's-KMV proprietary model, there are significant discrepancies with default probabilities mapped to ratings. This is not an inconsistency. Point-in-time EDF© and long-term default probability have no reason to coincide. Market-based EDF© should anticipate rating changes. Ratings tend to lag somewhat the changes in credit standing of issues, simply because they are long-term oriented.

Casual observations of Credit Monitor EDF© support this view that market-based measures lead ratings changes to a significant extent. Moody's-KMV Credit Monitor provides all information to make such comparisons: the EDF©, the underlying values of the EDF© drivers, and the rating equivalent. Looking at time profiles of these values shows that EDF© can be used as an early-warning system of adverse rating migrations and defaults.

Several studies compare the Moody's-KMV EDF© with similar results obtained with other techniques, such as scoring and using credit ratings. They rely on the CAP to show how well the model discriminates between defaulters and non-defaulters. They suggest that Credit Monitor provides at least a comparable accuracy.

A limitation of Credit Monitor is that it applies to public companies since it uses equity prices. To address the issue of equivalent default risk measures for private companies, Moody's-KMV Corporation provides another model "EDF© Calculator," or the "Private Firm Model," which necessitates minimal information on private company to model default risk. The basic information is in financial statements. In addition, the usage of the EDF© calculator requires documenting the industry and region of the firm. The principle is to proxy, through this information, the actual EDF© of an "equivalent" public company.

42.6 THEORETICAL VALUES OF THE OPTION TO DEFAULT AND THE EDF©

We calculate below the various variables determining distance to default. The calculation of the theoretical EDF© is relatively easy. The process requires the formulas of the put option to default plus the usual assumptions on the asset value stochastic process leading to the lognormal distribution of the asset value at horizon. We summarize the basic formulas, before making a sample calculation.

Both the call option on asset and the put option to default held by equity holders are European: they allow exercise only at horizon T. When the default probability gets higher, the put value increases, and the debt value declines by the gain in the put value.

42.6.1 Valuation of the Put Option to Default

The standard Black-Scholes formula applies for valuing the call on asset or the put of equity holders. These are:

$$C_0 = A_0 N(d_1) - D_T \exp(-rT)N(d_2) = E_0$$

$$P_0 = D_T \exp(-rT)N(-d_2) - A_0 N(-d_1)$$

The current date is 0 and $T = 1$ for horizon. The call represents also the value of equity. The put-call parity is such that, at horizon[5]:

$$C_0 + D_0 = P_0 + A_0$$

and

$$P_0 = C_0 + D_0 - A_0$$

The strike price is the debt at 1, and the value of debt at date 0 is:

$$D_0 = \exp(-rT)$$

The values of the options are:

$$C = A_0 N(d_1) - D_1 \exp(-rT)N(d_2)$$

$$P = D_1 \exp(-rT)N(-d_2) - A_0 N(-d_1)$$

According to the Black-Scholes formula:

$$d_1 = [\ln(A_0/D_T) + (r + \sigma^2/2)T]/\sigma\sqrt{T}$$

$$d_2 = [\ln(A_0/D_T) + (r - \sigma^2/2)T]/\sigma\sqrt{T} = d_1 - \sigma\sqrt{T}$$

In these formulas, $N(X)$ stands for the standard normal distribution, ln is the Neperian logarithm, and r is the risk-free rate. The volatility σ is the volatility of the random asset return. It is useful to note that $N(d_1) = 1 - N(1 - d_1)$ and that $N(d_2) = 1 - N(1 - d_2)$. The standard formulas for sensitivities show that the delta of the call is $\Delta(\text{call})/\Delta A = N(d_1)$ and that of the put is $\Delta(\text{put})/\Delta A = N(d_1) - 1 = N(-d_1)$.

In the example below, we choose an expected asset value of 100 and a debt at date 0 of 50, resulting in a leverage ratio (debt/equity) of 1, or a ratio debt to asset of 0.5. The risk-free rate is 10%. There is a continuous rate equivalent to this discrete rate, which is 9.53102%. With this value, we check that the date 1 year from now is:

$$D_T = D_0 \exp(-rT) = 50 \exp(9.53102\% \times 1) = 55$$

The value of D_1, 55, is the strike price of both options. However, the option formula requires using the current debt value, 50, and the current asset value because they provide the present value of the options.

---

5 There is no need to discount to present date 0 if we are at horizon.

42.6.2 Determination of the Default Probability

The firm's asset value follows a standard geometric Brownian motion, starting from the value A_0 at date 0 until date $T = 1$. The firm's asset value is the underlying random asset. Under risk-neutral valuation, the asset provides the risk-free return r. The asset value follows a lognormal distribution at the horizon:

$$A = A_0 \exp\{(r - \tfrac{1}{2}\sigma^2)T + \sigma\sqrt{T}\,Z\}$$

Since A/A_0 follows a lognormal distribution, the logarithm follows a normal distribution with mean $(r - \tfrac{1}{2}\sigma^2)T$ and standard deviation $\sigma\sqrt{T}$. Using a normal standard variable Z[6], the logarithm of final to initial asset value can be written as:

$$\ln(A/A_0) = (r - \tfrac{1}{2}\sigma^2)T + \sigma\sqrt{T}\,Z$$

The default point occurs when $A = D_1$, which is when:

$$\ln(D_1/A_0) = (r - \tfrac{1}{2}\sigma^2)T + \sigma\sqrt{T}\,Z$$

or when:

$$Z = \frac{\ln\left(D_1 / A_0\right) - (r - \tfrac{1}{2}\sigma^2)T}{\sigma\sqrt{T}}$$

Since Z follows $N(0, 1)$, the value of the normalized distance to default is:

$$DD = \frac{\ln\left(D_1 / A_0\right) - (r - \tfrac{1}{2}\sigma^2)T}{\sigma\sqrt{T}} = d_2$$

Hence, the distance to default is simply d_2. The probability of hitting that point is:

$$P\{Z \le -[\ln(A_0/D_1) - (r - \tfrac{1}{2}\sigma^2)T]/\sigma\sqrt{T}\} = P\{Z \le DD\} = N(-d_2)$$

Therefore, the EDF© is $N(-d_2)$, which is the value of the area under the lognormal curve below default point. Because $N(-d_2)$ depends only on leverage, it is insensitive to the size of asset and debt. This shows that the value of the put is:

$$P_0 = [D_0 - A_0 N(-d_1)/N(-d_2)]N(-d_2)$$

The put is the present value of the cost of default for lenders. It is the product of the default probability $N(-d_2)$ multiplied by a value of debt lower than the book value at 0, D_0. The difference is the expected loss under default, and is equal to the second term of the equation above. The expected loss is the expected value of asset, conditional on default[7]. Since the asset value

---

6 Given that Z is standard normal, this expression follows a normal distribution with the desired mean and standard deviation.
7 It is similar to the E-VaR or the expected value of loss conditional on asset value lower than debt.

triggering default is equal to the debt at date 1, it is still positive, so that lenders recover the expected value of assets conditional on default.

42.6.3 Determining the Percentile of the Final Asset Value

The above formulas model the lognormal distribution of asset value and derive the default point by making the final value equal to the debt at horizon. The process determines the EDF© as the value percentile of final value such that the ratio of final to initial value equals (D_1/A_0). The problem can be reversed by determining the α percentile matching a final asset value when the expected asset return is μ. With more general notations, the α percentile of final asset value is $V(\alpha)$ and the initial asset value is V_0. The formula uses the ratio of final to initial value $V(\alpha)/V_0$. The formula for the α percentile of this ratio derives from the same formula as above:

$$\ln\left[\frac{V(\alpha)}{V_0}\right] = \{\Phi^{-1}(\alpha)\sigma\sqrt{T} + (\mu - \tfrac{1}{2}\sigma^2)T$$

$$\frac{V(\alpha)}{V_0} = \exp\left[\Phi^{-1}(\alpha)\sigma\sqrt{T} + (\mu - \tfrac{1}{2}\sigma^2)T\right]$$

When using an expected return of 10%, a volatility of asset return of 30% and a horizon T of 1 year, the ratio is:

$$V(\alpha)/V_0 = \exp\{\Phi^{-1}(1\%) \times 30\%\sqrt{1} + (10\% - \tfrac{1}{2} \times 30\%^2) \times 1\} = 40.7\%$$

This implies that the downside variation of value is: $1 - 40.7\% = 59.3\%$. This downside variation is the loss not exceeded in more than 1% of all cases. Therefore, the VaR at 1% confidence level is 59.3%, or $59.3\% \times V_0$, if initial value is not one.

42.7 SAMPLE CALCULATIONS OF EDF© AND OF THE PUT AND CALL VALUES

The process starts from asset value and volatility as inputs, which derive from the equity value and its volatility. When moving from equity data to asset value and volatility, we need to solve the basic equations through an iterative numerical process.

Starting from the basic inputs, r, σ, t and A_0 and D_T, the EDF© is $N(-d_2)$, which is the value of the area under the lognormal curve below default point. The values of the call and the put options result from the Black-Scholes formula. The volatility of the equity is the volatility of the call option on asset. The relationship between the volatility of the call and that of the asset is as specified above:

$$\sigma(E) = A_0\sigma(A)N(d_1)/E_0$$

The book value of debt is 50 and the value of assets is 100 at date 0, and the strike price is 55 at $T = 1$ if the risk-free rate is 10%. The volatility of equity is 28.099%. This value results

TABLE 42.1   Equity value as a call option on assets value and default put

$\ln(A_0/D_1)$	0.59784
$(r + \sigma^2/2) \times T$	0.13479
$(r - \sigma^2/2) \times T$	0.05583
$d_1 = [\ln(A_0/D_1) + (r + \sigma^2/2)T]/\sigma T^{0.5}$	2.607333
$d_2 = [\ln(A_0/D_1) + (r - \sigma^2/2)T]/\sigma T^{0.5}$	2.32635
$N(d_1)$	0.99544
$N(d_2)$	0.99000
Call on asset $= A_0 N(d_1) - D_1 \exp(-rT)$	50.04374
Put $= D_1 \exp(-rT)N(-d_2) - A_0 N(-d_1)$	0.04374

(*) Values rounded to the sixth decimal digit

in an EDF© of 1%, once the calculations are done. This is sufficient to derive all the above values (Table 42.1).

The theoretical value of equity E_0, valued as a call option with the above inputs, is 50.04374. It is higher than the equity value without the put, or $50 = 100 - 50$, because of the upside on asset value. The gain for stockholders equals the expected loss from debt holders, or the value of the put 0.04374. The distance to default is $d_2 = 2.32635$. The EDF© is $N(-d_2)$, or 1%, using $N(-x) = 1 - N(x)$. The expected loss is the value of the put. The expected recovery is the second term of the put value, or $A_0 N(-d_1)/N(-d_2)$. The expected loss given default is the difference with the debt, 50, or 4.3744. The expected loss is the loss given default multiplied by the default probability and is 1% (Table 42.2). The debt value is the book value at 0 minus the put value at date 0, $50 - 0.04374 = 49.95625$.

The implied equity value results from the relationship:

$$\sigma(E) = A_0 \sigma(A)N(d_1)/E_0 = (100 \times 28.099\% \times 0.99544)/50 = 55.9408\%$$

TABLE 42.2   EDF© and loss on debt

Distance to default $= d_2$	2.32635
Probability of default EDF© $= N(-d_2)$	1.000005%
Expected recovery on debt	45.62565
Loss given default (LGD $= 50 -$ recovery)	4.37435
Expected loss: $N(-d_2) \times 45.625651$	0.04374

The equity volatility is much higher than the asset volatility. This is due to the leverage effect. Leveraged firms have asset volatility lower than equity volatility. This calculation also shows how to work backward from equity value and volatility back to asset value and asset volatility. There is only one couple of values of these parameters that complies with the structure of all equations.

The Merton model also provides the risky debt value, which is lower than the risk-free value by the amount of the put. This allows one to determine the theoretical credit spread that applies to the risky debt. Since the debt value is the face value minus the put value, it is lower than 50. There is a discount rate that makes the present value of 55 at date equal to the present value 49.95626, lower than the initial 50. The gap between the higher discount rate and the original discount rate is the credit spread. The risky yield making the 55 equal to debt value, using continuous discounting, is such that:

$$49.95626 = 55 \exp(-yT)$$

The risky yield is $y = 9.6185\%$. This rate is higher than the risk-free continuous rate, equivalent to the 10% discrete rate 9.5310%. The gap is the credit spread, or 0.0875% in continuous compounding, or 8.7 basis points.

42.8 VARIATIONS ON THE MERTON'S MODEL

Some variations of the Merton's model, implying default when asset value goes under a preset value of debt exist, date before 1973, and others are extensions, progressively extending the scope of the model to other variables. Beyond Merton's model, variations exist, mentioned by Duffie and Singleton in [28].

One benefit of the Merton model is that it looks forward. Another is that asset value captures the present value of the entire stream of future free cash flows. Hence, a single negative cash flow cannot fail the firm, and cumulated cash drains cannot either as long as the firm has sufficient upside potential. This is what happens when high growth firm have negative profit and are "cash-eating" machines until they finally reach the stage where cash flows become positive.

Moody's-KMV implementation has several obvious limitations. Default occurs only at a given horizon, where asset value is above or below the debt value. Real situations are more complex than considering debt as a bullet bond with exercise at horizon. In fact, both the asset value and the debt value, linked to interest rates and to the default risk, follow a stochastic process. In addition, the value of debt is a combination of short-term debt and a fraction of long-term debt. This is only a proxy of the actual time structure of debt repayments. Moreover, if the time path of asset value crosses the default point before horizon, default could occur before horizon.

42.9 MAPPING DEFAULT PROBABILITY TO THE STANDARDIZED NORMAL DISTANCE TO DEFAULT

A simplified version of the Merton model assumes that the default probability embeds all relevant information about the underlying asset value and use a normal standardized asset value. The simplified version is commonly used for modeling correlated defaults because it is extremely simple to correlate standardized normal asset values.

Since the asset value follows a standardized normal distribution, the default points corresponding to a given default probability derive from the tables of the standardized normal distribution. If the default probability is 2.5%, the corresponding standardized asset value is −1.96; if the probability of default is 1%, it becomes −2.33. If the asset value falls in between

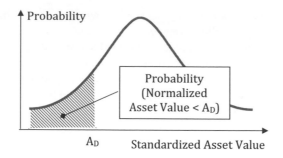

FIGURE 42.6   Asset value and default probability

two threshold values, we are in the risk class bounded by the upper and lower default probability. There is a one to one correspondence between the asset value A_D triggering the default and the default probability DP, resulting from: P (asset value $<= A_D$) = DP (Figure 42.6).

The α percentile matches the default probability DP. The probability that the asset value falls below the default point $A(\alpha)$ is $\Phi[A(\alpha)] = DP = \alpha$ and implies that $A(\alpha) = \Phi^{-1}(\alpha)$. The absolute values of $A(\alpha)$ and the corresponding default probabilities are shown in Figure 42.7.

If an obligor has a 1% default probability, the standardized distance to default is 2.33 under the simplified standardized default model. The standardized asset value should move down by −2.33 for triggering default, or, equivalently, the default threshold for the obligor's asset value is $A(1\%) = -2.33$. The financial interpretation is that the debt value is lower than the asset value by 2.33 standard deviation units.

Note that using the lognormal distribution, the percentile of the ratio $V(\alpha)/V_0$ would depend on asset return and volatility according to the formula:

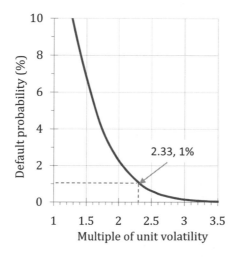

FIGURE 42.7   Multiples of volatility and default frequency (standardized normal distribution)

$$\frac{V(\alpha)}{V_0} = \exp\left[\Phi^{-1}(\alpha)\sigma\sqrt{T} + (\mu - \tfrac{1}{2}\sigma^2)T\right]$$

The standardized model bundle all required inputs into a single one, which is the default probability d.

43

Default Probability and Default Intensity

Starting from any set of annualized default and survival probabilities, annual probabilities can be derived for a first year as well between two future dates. The latter are called "marginal" or forward probabilities. They serve whenever default risk has to be calculated at a period starting at future dates. The time profiles of cumulative probabilities over several years embed migrations across risk classes that serve for revaluing at horizon any facility that migrates thorough times, and those migrations are materialized by migration matrices. Default intensity models embed a hazard rate that has to be calibrated with the entire time term structure of default probabilities, since they generally break down any future horizon in, typically, annual periods[1].

This chapter presents the term structure of default probabilities and forward default probabilities in discrete time, starting from cumulative default rates, such as those provided by rating agencies (Section 43.1). Next, forward default probabilities are seen as conditional probabilities on survival over preceding periods (Section 43.2). Migration matrices serve for revaluation of facilities at a future horizon, according to their final credit states, in most full valuation models of credit risk. Their properties are detailed in Section 43.3. Default intensity models are presented in Section 43.4, assuming that the set of spot and forward default probabilities across time periods is given, for calibrating such models over several periods. The default intensity models rely on continuous time intensity of defaults over sub-periods that replicate the term structure of probabilities and are commonly used to model time to defaults.

---

1 The Li model uses the intensity of default framework together with the copula approach [48].

Contents

43.1 CUMULATIVE DEFAULT AND SURVIVAL PROBABILITIES

Default frequencies and default probabilities vary when the horizon changes. If we use the discrete form of default probability, it is common to consider a 1-year period for reference. Cumulative default frequencies apply from as of one date to longer horizons measured in years. The term structure of default probabilities and of historical default frequencies refers to forward or marginal default probabilities. These are default probabilities between two future dates, or default probabilities conditional on no default prior to the first date of the future period considered. For discrete periods, default probabilities are noted DP, with two dates, written as $DP(t_1, t_2)$, t_1 being the beginning of the period and t_2 the date of the end of the period. This is a simplification, since forward DPs are like forward rates, meaning that they are defined by current date t and the two future dates. Notations simplify by setting current date as 0 and omitting the first argument, t. It is assumed that all firms having a rating at date 0 still have one at the current date, which is not restrictive, because any data set will be adjusted for such withdrawn ratings. The focus is on the calculation of marginal and cumulative default rates over a given population of firms existing at initial date, or zero. Default frequencies and probabilities are always based on counts of defaults between two dates.

For the generation created at date 0, counting a number $N(0)$ firms, we observe defaults every year. For default probabilities referring to the original population formed at date 0, the arithmetic default rate or default probability at any year t, beginning at date t and ending at date $t + 1$, compares the count of defaults between t and $t + 1$ to the number of firms, within the generation formed at date 0, to the surviving firms of this cohort at t. Hence all calculations apply to a single generation of firms.

We use the following notations:

- capital letters designate numbers
- lower case letters are rates, or ratios in percentages
- $N(0)$ is the original number of firms at the time 0 when the generation is formed
- $D(0, t)$ is the cumulative number of defaulted firms among the original population defined at zero, up to t
- $S(0, t)$ is the number of firms surviving at date t, and, by definition $S(0, 0) = N(0)$ is the original number of firms of the generation.

From these definitions, we derive the cumulative count of defaults from 0 up to t and the corresponding cumulative default rate $d(0, t)$, as well as the cumulative number of surviving firms at t, or $S(0, t)$ and the survival rate $s(0, t)$. The corresponding formulas for default and surviving rates determined for the "date 0" generation are:

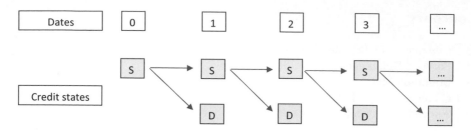

FIGURE 43.1   **Transitions of credit states through time**

$$d(0, t) = D(0, t)/N(0) = [N(0) - S(0, t)]/N(0) = 1 - s(0, t)$$

$$d(0, t) = S(0, t)/N(0) = [N(0) - D(0, t)]/N(0) = 1 - d(0, t)$$

Such counts or percentages are cumulative.

We can visualize the default process in discrete periods as follows. At the end of each period, firms either survived or defaulted. This is a binomial tree, because there are only two possibilities at each end of period (Figure 43.1). The default state is an absorbing state, meaning that once a firm defaulted, it cannot revive again. This is a simplification as well. Firms that default, under bankruptcy law, can go under Chapter 11 in the US and become economically viable after a while. Individuals who default in one period can be back to the non-default credit state if they finally succeed in making up for delayed payments.

43.2 FORWARD DEFAULT AND SURVIVAL PROBABILITIES

Consider two dates posterior to date 0 for defining forward-looking defaults and survival probabilities. We omit the original date 0 since the formulas are for this single generation formed at date 0.

43.2.1 Basic Formulas

$D(t - k, t)$ is the number of defaults between dates $t - k$ and t. It is a forward count of defaults. For $k = 1$, $D(t - 1, t)$ is the number of defaults within the year starting at date $t - 1$ and ending at t. The number of surviving firms at t is $S(0, t) = N(0) - D(0, t)$. The marginal default rate between $t - 1$ and t, or $d(t - 1, t)$, is the number of firms defaulting between $t - 1$ and t, or $D(t - 1, t)$, to the number of surviving firms at t, $S(0, t - 1)$. The forward, or marginal, default percentage (or rate) at $t - 1$ up to t is the ratio:

$$d(t-1,t) = \frac{D(t-1,t)}{S(0,t-1)} = \frac{D(t-1,t)}{N(0)-D(0,t-1)}$$

The mechanism is generalized using more compact notations, with subscripts rather than arguments:

$$\text{number of defaults in } 0, 1: D_{01}$$

$$\text{number of survivals in } 0, 1: S_{01} = 1 - D_{01}$$

We first start with 2 periods and 3 dates: 0, 1, 2. The cumulative default and survival probabilities are calculated from 0 to 1 and from 0 to 2. The forward, or marginal, default probabilities from 1 to 2, as seen from 0, are related to the cumulative probabilities. In subsequent formulas, we use probabilities, in normal letters for percentages. The cumulative survival probabilities from 0 to 2 are the probabilities of not defaulting between dates 0 and 1 and between 1 and 2:

$$s_{02} = (1 - d_{12})(1 - d_{01}) = s_{01}(1 - d_{12})$$

Therefore, the forward or marginal default probability D_{12} is conditional on survival between 0 and 1:

$$d_{12} = 1 - (s_{02}/s_{01})$$

This can be generalized to any single period $t - 1$ to t. The survival from 0 to t depends on survival from 0 to $t - 1$ and default probability from $t - 1$ to t:

$$s_{0t} = (1 - d_{01})(1 - d_{12}) \dots (1 - d_{t-1,t}) = s_{0,t-1}(1 - d_{t-1,t})$$

Forward default probabilities are derived from cumulative survival probabilities:

$$d_{t-1,t} = 1 - \frac{s_{0,t}}{s_{0,t-1}}$$

Forward default probabilities depend only on cumulated survival probabilities. Survival probabilities are simpler to use, for defining the forward default probabilities, than default probabilities.

43.2.2 Calculating Marginal Default Probabilities

A numerical application serves for illustrating the mechanism. Consider the numerical example below, where we start from cumulative default probabilities for deriving marginal default probabilities. The data is as follows:

$$d_{01} = 5.00\%; d_{02} = 10.70\%; d_{03} = 16.95\%$$

From this data we can calculate:

1 the marginal d_{12} from cumulative default probabilities between 0 and 1, and 0 and 2, d_{01} and d_{02}
2 the forward d_{23}, given cumulative d_{03} (and s_{03})
3 inversely, starting from the two first marginal probabilities d_{01} and d_{12}, it is possible to find again the cumulative default and survival probabilities d_{02} and s_{02}.

Using conditional probabilities, the probability of defaulting between dates 1 and 2 is the probability of defaulting between 1 and 2 conditional on having survived up to 1. For finding the marginal, or forward, d_{12} as seen from 0, the starting point is the general formula:

$$d_{12} = 1 - s_{02}/s_{01}$$

By definition, survival between 0 and 1 is 1 minus the probability of defaulting between 0 and 1, or:

$$s_{01} = 1 - d_{01} = 1 - 5\% = 95\%$$

Similarly, since we start from cumulative probabilities:

$$s_{02} = 1 - d_{02} = 1 - 10.7\% = 89.3\%$$

Then

$$d_{12} = 1 - (s_{02}/s_{01}) = 1 - (89.3\%/1 - 5\%) = 6\%$$

We could think intuitively that, since the firm defaults either in 0, 1 or 1, 2, d_{02} would be d_{01} + d_{12} and $d_{12} = d_{02} - d_{01} = 10.7\% - 5\% = 5.7\%$. This latter calculation is wrong because d_{12} is conditional on survival up to 1. The unconditional probability of defaulting between 1 and 2 is effectively $d_{02} - d_{01} = 5.7\%$. But d_{12} is conditional upon survival up to 1. Hence $d_{02} - d_{01}$ assumes that the firm defaults either in 0, 1 or in 1, 2 and ignores the condition of having survived up to 1. The correct value is $d_{12} = 6\%$.

For calculating d_{23}, conditional on survival up to 2, the simple difference $d_{03} - d_{02} = 16.95\%$ $- 10.70\% = 6.25\%$ is the unconditional probability of defaulting between 2 and 3. The correct calculation is:

$$d_{23} = 1 - s_{03}/s_{02}$$

S_{02} is the probability of not defaulting between dates 0 and 2, or $1 - d_{02} = 1 - 10.7\% = 89.3\%$. Similarly, $s_{03} = 1 - d_{03} = 1 - 16.95\% = 83.05\%$. Finally:

$$d_{23} = 1 - s_{03}/s_{02} = 1 - (83.05\%/89.3\%) = 1 - 0.93\% = 7\%$$

The alternative calculation for d_{23} starts from the unconditional default probability between 2 and 3, which is $d_{03} - d_{02} = 16.95\% - 10.7\% = 6.25\%$. The default probability between 2 and 3 is conditional upon survival up to 2, which is $s_{02} = 89.3\%$. Then $d_{23} = 6.25\%/89.3\% = 7\%$.

Those examples show that it is much easier to use survival probabilities to calculate forward default probabilities, using $d_{t-1,t} = 1 - (s_t/s_{t-1})$. Dropping the subscript 0, which serves as the common original date, the survival probability s_t can be expressed as $1 - d_t$, as long as we use cumulative probabilities for s and d, starting from 0 and up to t and $t - 1$.

The example can be reversed, starting from marginal default probabilities and finding cumulative probabilities. We take only one example. We found the marginal default probabilities from the above calculations:

$$d_{01} = 5\%; \, d_{12} = 6\%; \, d_{23} = 7\%$$

The cumulative default probability from 0 to 2 is $d_{02} = 1 - s_{02}$ and $s_{02} = s_{01} \times s_{12} = (1 - d_{01}) \, (1 - d_{03}) = (1 - 5\%) \, (1 - 6\%) = 95\% \times 94\% = 89.3\%$ identical to the previous s_{02}. Once we have the cumulative survival probability, we derive the cumulative default probability $d_{02} = 1 - s_{02} = 10.7\%$. This is the same default probability as given above. This calculation shows how to move back from marginal default probabilities to cumulative default probabilities.

43.3 MIGRATION MATRICES

Migration matrices provide discrete transition probabilities across rating classes, as illustrated in Chapter 39 on historical credit risk data. Migrations are relevant for modeling risk under full valuation mode. They are used for projecting the structure of a portfolio by rating class and they have a direct relationship with cumulative probabilities. Furthermore, they serve for valuing credit VaR. This calculation is expanded in Chapter 46 for calculating the standalone credit VaR of a single facility using full valuation mode, using the "matrix valuation" process, which consists of mapping credit spreads to the final credit ratings for revaluation at horizon. We address here the relationship between cumulative default probabilities and migration probabilities considering a standalone obligor.

43.3.1 Migration Matrices and Cumulative Default Probabilities

A migration matrix is a squared matrix with initial credit state, or rating, in rows and final credit state in columns. There is usually an additional column, called "WR," for firms existing at the beginning of the period and whose rating was withdrawn within the period. We ignore the "WR" column in the example. The default state is a particular credit state among several. However, the default state is considered as an absorbing state. In plain words, it means that once the firm migrates to the default state, it does not get out of this special state.

Consider the simplified square transition matrix with annual transition probabilities. The basic assumption used here is that the matrix is stable through time. This assumption is restrictive. For multi-period models, one should use transition probabilities conditional on the state of the economy. This approach is used in one credit portfolio model, "Credit Portfolio View," described in the credit portfolio models section 12.

The example uses only three credit states, named A, B and D, inclusive of the default state (D), since this enough to highlight the essential properties of those matrices (Table 43.1).

TABLE 43.1

	A	B	D	Total
A	0.80	0.15	0.05	100%
B	0.10	0.80	0.10	100%
Default	0	0	1	100%

The matrix is squared and not symmetric. The highest transition probabilities are along the diagonal. A transition probability has two subscripts, the first one for the initial state and the second for the final credit state. The transition probability from initial credit state i to the final credit state j is t_{ij}. The migration probabilities out of the default state are zero, because it is an absorbing state. The matrix has the Markov properties which imply time invariance and that T_{ij} depends only on the credit states and does not change with time. Such transition probabilities are by definition unconditional.

43.3.2 Direct Calculation of Default Probability over Two Periods

For highlighting the relation between cumulative default probabilities and transition matrices, we consider the default probability over two years, periods 1 and 2. The tree of successive credit states is summarized in Table 43.2.

The default probability DP at year 1 is 0.05. The probability of default over 2 years could be thought of summing up the default probability in period 1 with the same DP conditional on survival until 2. According to such rule, the default probability over the total 2-year period would be the over year 1 plus the DP over year 2 weighted by the survival probability in year 1:

$$0.05 + 0.05 \times (1 - 0.05) = 0.0975 = 9.75\%$$

But the risk migrates to A or B if the firms survives in period 1, which requires considering default over the second period for both credit states. At the end of period 2, there are three possibilities: State A, state B, default state. If the firm stays in state A, the default probability is again 0.05 but it becomes 0.15 if the firm migrates to state B in period 1. The default probability in period 2, conditional on survival in period 1, is the weighted average of these default probabilities, using the transition probabilities as weights. Over the two periods, the firm defaults either in period 1 or in period 2. Since the events are exclusive, we sum up the default probability in year 1 with the weighted default probabilities in year 2. The result is the actual default probability over the two years, given migrations:

$$0.80 \times 0.05 + 0.15 \times 0.10 + 0.05 \times 1 = 10.5\%$$

It is higher than the naïve calculation assuming no migration, which was 9.75%, because we now consider correctly the increase of default risk if the firm migrates to the B state. Note that we weight the default probability in period 1 with 1, since this is the probability of staying in the default state, once migrating there at period 1.

TABLE 43.2 Sequence of credit events

Initial state 0	Event period 1	Event | S	Event probability		Weighted DP period 2
A	Survive S	Migrates A	0.80	0.80×0.05	0.040
		Migrates B	0.15	0.15×0.10	0.015
	Default D		0.050	Default in 1	0.050
				Total =	**0.105**

43.3.3 General Calculation of Default Probability over Two Periods

Decomposing the calculation, we can write the default probability over the two periods, when initial state is A as:

$$DP(A) = t_{AA} \times t_{AD} + t_{AB} \times t_{BD} + t_{AD} \times t_{DD} = 10.5\%$$

Similar equations can be written for DP(B) and DP(D). Notably, the latter probability simplifies to 1 because all transition probabilities out of the default state are zero and the probability of staying there is one:

$$DP(D) = t_{DA} \times t_{AD} + t_{DB} \times t_{BD} + t_{DD} \times t_{DD} = 0 + 0 + 1$$

These default probabilities are the elements of the matrix product **M D**, where **M** is the square (3×3) migration matrix, and **D** is the (1×3) column vector of default probabilities of A, B and D, identical to the last column of the matrix. The default probabilities over two years are the elements of the (1×3) column vector **M D** (Table 43.3).

The argument can be generalized. We can do the same with vectors **A** and **B**, using the two first columns of the matrix. Starting in A, the probability of ending in B is:

$$t_{AA} \times t_{AB} + t_{AB} \times t_{BB} + t_{AD} \times t_{DB}$$

A similar calculation provides the probability of ending in A. This process shows that the transition matrix over two periods is simply the matrix product **M M** = **M²**, as shown in Table 43.4. Generalizing this result, the transitions over N periods are simply given by the matrix **M^N**.

43.3.4 Generator Matrices

It is easy to calculate N-year transition frequencies (assuming that they are constant). But it is difficult to find, for example, a 6-month set of transition probabilities. Generator matrices

TABLE 43.3 Migration probabilities over two periods

			Vector **D**
			0.05
			0.1
Transition matrix	**M**		1
0.8	0.15	0.05	0.105
0.1	0.8	0.1	0.185
0	0	1	1

TABLE 43.4   Cumulative probabilities from migration matrices

A	B	D
0.8	0.15	0.05
0.1	0.8	0.1
0	0	1

	A	B	D
A	0.8	0.15	0.05
B	0.1	0.8	0.1
D	0	0	1

0.655	0.24	0.105
0.16	0.655	0.185
0	0	1

TABLE 43.5   Diagonalization of a migration matrix

Matrix **E**		
0.577	0.775	-0.775
0.577	0.632	0.632
0.577	0.000	0.000

D = E^{-1} M E		
1.000	0.000	0.000
0.000	0.922	0.000
0.000	0.000	0.678

are used to find transition frequencies over any time interval T, including fractions of years. Generator matrices use simple matrix algebra shortcuts.

The technique relies on matrix diagonalization, explained in the appendix (Section 43.5). Using the properties of diagonalization, starting from a square matrix **M**, it is shown that there exists a matrix **E** such that the product **E M E^{-1} = D** is a diagonal matrix. Using the above migration matrix, we find the matrix **E** and the diagonal matrix **D** (Table 43.5). The power N of matrix **M** is **M^N**, such that:

$$M^N = E \ D^N \ E^{-1}$$

The power matrix **D^N** is made of the diagonal matrix with the diagonal elements being the power N of the diagonal elements of **D**. The technique provides a simple way for generating **M^N**. For example, we find the above square matrix of transitions over two years using these formulas (Table 43.6).

TABLE 43.6   Generating the two-year migration matrix

M² = E D² E⁻¹		
0.655	0.240	0.105
0.160	0.655	0.185
0.000	0.000	1.000

TABLE 43.7   Generating the 6-month migration matrix

Mᵗ = E D⁰·⁵ E⁻¹		
0.892	0.084	0.024
0.056	0.892	0.052
0.000	0.000	1.000

The generator matrix can serve for any horizon, once we have **E** and **D**. The calculation involves simply taking the power of the diagonal elements of **D**. For example, the transition matrix over 6 months is shown in Table 43.7.

43.4   CREDIT INTENSITY MODELS

Credit intensity models serves for modeling times to default or times to migration events. Used for default, they are known as the reduced form model, since they do not rely on conceptual foundations, as the "structural model of default," described in Chapter 42, does. The intensity model serves for modeling time elapsed between rare events. They have been implemented for market pricing for capturing "jumps" in market prices, and they apply as well both to defaults and migrations in the credit risk universe.

43.4.1   Default Intensity Models

Credit intensity, or hazard, models are continuous time models. Over the small interval Δt, the intensity is the probability of default over the period, conditional on no prior default:

$$DP(t, t + \Delta t) = \lambda(t)\Delta t$$

The default intensity per unit of time is $\lambda(t)$. In continuous time the small interval Δt tends towards zero and is replaced by the infinitesimal dt. The model is identical to the so-called "rare event process" or "jump process." Remember that the number of "jumps" or rare events is a count of discrete occurrences taking place during a given time interval. The number of rare events follows a Poisson distribution using λ as the time intensity of rare events.

In pricing theory, jumps in asset prices are modeled by using stochastic processes for the asset return that depend both a diffusion term of variance dt and a Poisson process for adding "jumps," which are large variations that occur discretely. In credit risk, such model of rare events serves for modeling time to default rather that a discrete default probability. The default intensity is the number of defaults per unit of time. It is measured consistently with the time unit. For example, if the unit is one year, the time intensity should be measured accordingly. Default intensity models are also the foundation of the pricing of credit default swaps. The fixed leg of a CDS is made of a recurring premium, whether the variable leg is contingent on the first default event, making credit insurers pay the loss under default to the buyer of protection.

In order to demonstrate the connection between the jump model and the time to default, we can use as a first proxy a constant time intensity of default. In practice, the $\lambda(t)$ are piece-wise linear, that is constant over discrete time periods but variable across time periods. The time to default follows an exponential distribution. If λ is a constant default rate, the probability of survival or of no default from 0 to t is $(1 - \lambda \Delta t)^n$ over n time intervals of length $\Delta t = t/n$. The survival probability is then compounded over the n small intervals.

$$\text{survival probability} = (1 - \lambda \times \Delta t)^n = [1 - \lambda \times (t/n)]^n$$

When n increases, the expression $(1 + x/n)^n$ tends towards $\exp(x)$:

$$[1 - \lambda t/n)]^n \rightarrow \exp(-\lambda t)$$

Accordingly, the survival probability is an exponential function of time t:

$$\text{survival } (0, t) = s(0, t) = \exp(-\lambda t)$$

43.4.2 Forward Default Intensity

The forward default probability at t is the probability of default during Δt conditional on survival until t. Its probability is the product of the probability of defaulting during Δt conditional on survival until t, which is the above exponential distribution.

$$P[\text{default over } (t, t + \Delta t) \mid \text{survival until } t] = \lambda \Delta t \exp(-\lambda t)$$

This is the equivalent over very small intervals of the discrete forward default probability in discrete intervals. When moving from small intervals Δt to longer intervals between two distant dates, we need to calculate the integral of the exponential function. Because it is easy to integrate and differentiate derivatives, the probability of defaulting between two distant dates a and b is[2]:

$$P(a < T \le b) = \int_a^b \lambda \exp(-\lambda t) \, dt = -\exp(-\lambda t) \, |_a^b = \exp(-\lambda a) - \exp(-\lambda b)$$

---

2 The integration between two dates of the instantaneous forward probability uses the variable change $u = -\lambda t$. We find that $du/dt = -\lambda$, $du = d(-\lambda t) = -\lambda dt$. This allows writing: $\int_a^b \lambda \exp(-\lambda t) dt = \int_a^b [-\exp(-\lambda t)] d(-\lambda t)$. Using the same variable change, we know that the integral of $\exp(u)$ is also $\exp(u)$. However, the bounds of the integral change when we replace u by $-\lambda t$ and become for $t = a$: $u = -\lambda a$ and for $t = b$: $u = -\lambda b$. Substituting in the integral, we find: $\exp(-\lambda a) - \exp(-\lambda b)$.

43.4.3 Time to Default

For finding the probability of a default occurring between 0 and T, we replace $a = T$ and $b = \infty$:

$$P(t < T \leq \infty) = \exp(-\lambda T) - 0$$

The time to default t is exponentially distributed, or, equivalently, the probability of survival until a date T is:

$$P(t < T \leq \infty) = \exp(-\lambda T)$$

It is easy to check that default occurs between now and infinity by setting $a = 0$ and $b = \infty$:

$$P(0 < T \leq \infty) = 1 - 0 = 1$$

Finally, the expectation of the time to default is simply $1/\lambda$. Using the expression of expectation for a continuous variable:

$$E\left[t \exp(-\lambda t)\right] = \int_0^\infty t \exp(-\lambda t)\, dt = \frac{1}{\lambda} \int_0^\infty \lambda t \exp(-\lambda t)\, d(\lambda t)$$

The next step is, as above, the same change of variable $u = \lambda t$. But the integration between 0 and infinity with respect to u is $-\exp\left(u\right)\big|_0^\infty$ [3]. The expectation of the time to default is $1/\lambda$ and is equal to its standard deviation $\sigma(t) = 1/\lambda$. This last result follows from simple calculations, as above. The shape of the distribution of the time to default is shown in Figure 43.2.

Examples are useful. First, we show how to calibrate the default intensity from the observed discrete default frequency. We need to find the default intensity when we know that the 1-year default probability is 4%. This means that the survival probability over 1-year in continuous time is $s(0, 1) = \exp(-\lambda \times 1) = \exp(-0.04) = 96.1\%$. The default probability in continuous time is $1 - 96.1\% = 3.9\%$. The slight discrepancy between the discrete default probability 4% and the continuously default intensity 3.9%, with unit 1-year, comes from the continuous compounding

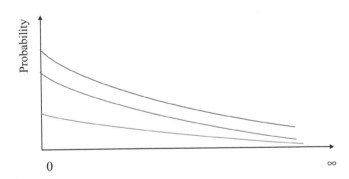

FIGURE 43.2 Exponential distributions of time to default

---

3 Use variable change $u = \lambda t$. With $t = 0$, $u = 0$; with $t = \infty$, $u = \infty$. Write: $\int_0^\infty \lambda t \exp(-\lambda t)\, d(\lambda t) = \int_0^\infty u \exp(-u)\, d(u) = -\exp(u)\big|_0^\infty$. Then: $\int_0^\infty u \times \exp(-u)\, d(-u) = -\exp(-u)\big|_0^\infty = \exp(0) - \exp(-\infty) = 1$ and, finally: $E[t \exp(-\lambda t)] = 1/\lambda \times 1 = 1/\lambda$, which shows that expectation(time to default) $= 1/\lambda$

between 0 and 1 year of the default intensity 3.9%. If we change the figures, we find that the default intensity matching a discrete default probability of 10% is: $1 - s(0, 1) = 90\% = \exp(-\lambda \times 1)$ which implies $\lambda = 10.54\%$.

In general, for calibrating a default intensity to a given default probability $DP(0, t)$, we write that $1 - DP(0, t) = \exp(-\lambda t)$, and take the logarithm to find the default intensity calibrated to $DP(0, t)$:

$$-\lambda t = \ln[1 - DP(0, t)] \text{ and } \lambda = -\ln[1 - DP(0, t)]/t$$

With the last example, where $DP(0, 1) = 10\%$, $\lambda = -\ln[1 - DP(0, t)]/t = -\ln(0.9)/1 = 0.1054$.

Conversely, we can take the default intensity equal to exactly 4% and find the corresponding discrete default probability. The continuous survival probability over 1-year when $\lambda = 4\%$ is $s(0, 1) = \exp(-\lambda \times 1) = \exp(-0.04) = 96.1\%$, which matches a discrete default probability of 3.9%. The expectation of the time to default is $1/\lambda = 1/0.04 = 25$ years, which is also the standard deviation of the time to default.

Finally, we can infer from the expectation of the time to default the continuous default probability over any time period. Assume that the average lifetime of a transistor is 100 working hours. What is the probability that the transistor will work for 50 hours? Since we know that the average life is equal to the inverse of intensity of defaulting, $\lambda = 1/100 = 1\%$. Then the survival probability over 50 hours will be $\exp(-\lambda \times 50) = \exp(-0.5) = 1.65\%$.

As a final remark, we used the intensity model for default. Intensity models also apply to migrations. We used a constant intensity, which is a restrictive assumption. Piece-wise intensity models make the intensity variable across time periods, t to t_1 and t_1 to t_2, the intensity being constant within a period. Consider the case of two periods, which could be 1 and 2 years, with marginal time intensities over each periods being constant and equal to λ_1 and λ_2. The time to default over the two periods is the sum of the probability of default between 0 and t_1 and the marginal probability of defaulting between t_1 and t_2 (which is conditional upon no default over the first period). Both probabilities are survival times, hence:

$$P(0 < T \leq t_2) = P(0 < t \leq t_1) + P(t_1 < t \leq t_2) = \exp(-\lambda_1 t_1) + \exp(-\lambda_2 t_2)$$

$$P(0 < T \leq t_2) = \exp(-\lambda_1 t_1 - \lambda_2 t_2)$$

The probabilities are additive and apply to the total period. Piece-wise intensity models are sufficient since they can be calibrated over the corresponding marginal default intensity.

43.5 APPENDIX: MATRIX DIAGONALIZATION

Any square matrix can be diagonalized using Eigen values and Eigen vectors. Given a matrix, **M**, there are real numbers, called Eigen values λ, and Eigen vectors **V** such that

$$\mathbf{M} \mathbf{V} = \lambda \mathbf{V}$$

The matrix made of column Eigen vectors **V**, **M**, serves for diagonalizing **M**. **D** is a diagonal matrix with Eigen values along the diagonal and zero for all off-diagonal terms. Taking the example of a square (3×3) matrix, **M**, the diagonal matrix **D** is:

$$\mathbf{E\,M\,E^{-1} = D}$$

As numerical example, we use the simple square matrix:

	A	B	D
A	0.80	0.15	0.05
B	0.10	0.80	0.10
Default	0.00	0.00	1.00

The Eigen values are 3, 2 and 1. The diagonal matrix of Eigen values is:

3	0	0
0	2	0
0	0	1

The (3×3) matrix of the 3 Eigen vectors $\mathbf{V}_i$, in columns, is called $\mathbf{E}$:

V_1	V_2	V_3
-1	0	-1
-1	0	0
2	1	2

The inverse of $\mathbf{E}$ is $\mathbf{E^{-1}}$:

0	-1	0
2	0	1
-1	1	0

Taking the product $\mathbf{E\,M\,E^{-1}}$, we find the diagonal matrix of Eigen values:

$$\mathbf{E^{-1}\,M\,E}$$

3	0	0
0	2	0
0	0	1

For diagonalization, we need matrix algebra formulas providing the Eigen values and the Eigen vectors.

44

Credit Risk Potential Exposure

The Basel 2 Accord stipulates that exposure at default ("EAD") is a key input to the regulatory capital assessment process. Exposure risk relates the uncertainty of future exposures arising from contingent events for the banking portfolio and from market movements for the trading portfolio. Sources are Coopers and Mello [20] and the BCBS guidelines [9].

This chapter starts with a reminder of exposure uncertainty for banking and market instruments (Section 44.1). Section 44.2 defines counterparty risk and potential future exposures ("PFE") for derivatives. Section 44.3 is a remainder of the simplified rules defining regulatory add-ons to exposures for banks that do not use simulation of such random exposures. Section 44.4 defines the methodology used for modeling PFEs, which is based on the distribution of the main risk factors that drives the derivative value, and on upper or lower bounds of such risk factors at a given confidence level. The upper bound of the derivative has a time profile and is generally considered as a "loan equivalent." The PFE time profile until maturity of the instrument is recalculated daily. Section 44.5 expands a simplified example of an interest rate swap. The last section (Section 44.6) discusses the case of portfolios, which like the market VaR, requires simulations for deriving the PFE, combined with netting for sub-portfolios of instruments belonging to a netting agreement.

Contents

44.1 BANKING PORTFOLIO EXPOSURES

There are many contractual exposures because term loans do represent a large fraction of outstanding loans. For most other products, the amount at risk is unknown in advance. The "hard" data for banking exposures are:

- the amount and maturity of committed lines
- the amortization schedule for term loans
- the maturity of the authorizations
- the dates of reviewing the authorizations
- the current usage of committed lines.

Note that, because of economic measures of exposures, there is a mismatch between these and the basis for calculating revenues based on current exposure.

44.1.1 On Balance Sheet

In general, exposure differs from the current exposure because the amount at risk at future dates is uncertain. The notable exception is term loans. Their amortization profile is a proxy for the future exposures. Still, contractual repayments are subject to prepayments, and the effective maturity is a substitute. Effective maturity results from experience or models for mortgages.

Exposure risk exists in general because we do not know the future usage of a banking line. For many credit lines, there is a commitment of the bank to let the borrower draw on the line up to a maximum limit at the initiative of the borrower. Committed lines of credit are on the balance sheet for the used fraction and off balance sheet for the unused portion of the line. Overdrafts, consumers' loans and credit cards balances are subject to renewal and borrowers can make new drawings at their initiative. Project financing is subject to exposure uncertainty both for the construction phase and for the subsequent operation phase when the repayments occur. Uncertain exposures are the rule more than the exception. Since current usages differ from future usages, it is necessary to define expected exposures time profiles plus exposure under default. EAD presumably increases when credit risk deteriorates because firms need cash when they face difficulties.

A facility has two characteristics bounding the exposure: maturity and authorization. For non-committed lines of credit, authorization can be revised at any time. For committed lines, authorizations have a fixed maturity. In both cases, the authorization caps the exposure.

44.1.2 Off Balance Sheet Commitments

Off balance sheet exposures can move up on balance sheet at any time. The regulatory Basel 1 treatment of off balance sheet exposures is to use a CCF of 50% factor. Basel 2 focuses on expected usage and EAD.

For committed lines of credit, it makes sense to set the exposure at 100% of the commitment since the bank is contractually at risk for this total amount, even if current usage is zero. Regulations allow using a lower percentage because the likelihood of maximum usage remains remote in many cases. However, a borrower getting close to default is likely to fully draw the line. Under the Basel 2 advanced approach, banks can model the EAD conservatively.

Third-party guarantees given have only a remote possibility of exercise, contingent on borrower's default. However, they are similar to direct exposures since the borrower's default triggers the guarantee as if there was a direct exposure. The regulatory view guarantees given as equivalent to a direct exposure. However, there is a wide spectrum of third-party guarantees given, ranging from simple letters of comfort to first recourse "full" guarantees. The former do not carry any real risk because there is no legal commitment. Legal commitments are equivalent to lending directly. Credit derivatives sold by the bank have the same treatment.

Other commitments, such as back-up lines of liquidity for issuing commercial paper, look more like financial services than "true" exposures. What triggers drawing is not the default of the client. Hence, there is a case for differentiating them from guarantees, but the likelihood of materialization of the risk remains judgmental. Back-up lines of credit have been the source of liquidity issues during the crisis because many were triggered leading to a massive amount of involuntary lending.

44.2 MARKET INSTRUMENTS AND POTENTIAL FUTURE EXPOSURES (PFES)

Traded instruments are subject to market risk only. For "buy and hold" portfolios, such as "spread books" of bonds (earning the spread between the bonds and the cost of repo financing of these bonds), there is a random credit risk exposure driven by market risk factors. Credit risk results from a change of credit standing over the holding period and depends on the random size of exposure at default. OTC instruments are a case in point. Because the exposure is market driven, both expected exposure and potential exposure have to be modeled.

Market instruments are subject to "counterparty risk," because the risk is both ways, depending on whether the exposure is positive or negative. Swaps fall under this category. Derivatives include currency and interest swaps, options, and any combination of these building blocks. Swaps exchange interests flows based on different rates, or flows in different currencies. Options allow buying or selling an asset at a stated price. The credit risk of derivatives results from the buy and hold view applicable to over-the-counter instruments since they are not traded in organized markets.

Trading in organized markets would make the issue less critical because daily margin calls limit the risk to daily variations, since any gain or loss of value has to be posted with the clearing-house. In OTC markets, the risk prevails up to maturity. For derivatives, the "originate and hold" view prevails, and the risk is the potential positive liquidation value of instruments until maturity. However, counterparty risk is often mitigated by collateral posted by both parties and is subject to margin calls. In such instances, only the exposure net of risk-adjusted collateral is at risk[1].

The credit risk of derivatives has specific features:

- it is a two-way credit risk, which shifts from one counterparty to the other depending on whom owns the positive liquidation value
- options are a one-way risk, since only the option buyer is at risk whilst the seller has no risk since it does not have to pay anything to a defaulted buyer

---

1 OTC derivatives are contracted under master agreements between parties. The Credit Support Annex (CSA) provides provisions agreed upon for posting collateral.

- it depends on market risk factors since the amount at risk is the liquidation value, if it is positive.

We look at three different examples: interest rate swaps, foreign exchange swaps and options.

44.2.1 Interest Rate Swaps

Say a bank holds a swap, receiving a fixed interest rate and paying a variable rate. If the variable rate declines enough, the value of fixed interest rate flows exceeds that of variable rate flows paid. The swap has a positive mark-to-market value. The bank is a net receiver of interest flows and the swap is similar to an asset. The bank receiving the positive net interest flow is at risk with the counterparty, because, should the latter fail, the bank would lose this positive value. Conversely, when the variable rate increases above the fixed rate, the bank is a net payer of interest flows and the swap is similar to liability. The value of the swap is negative for the bank. The bank does not have to pay such liability if the counterparty defaults, and has no credit risk. But its counterparty is a net receiver of positive flow and becomes at risk with the bank.

The situation is symmetrical for the bank and its counterparty. When a swap has a positive value for the bank, the bank is at risk with the counterparty and the bank's counterparty has no risk. The converse holds if the swaps held by the bank has negative value. Because variable rates are random, the credit risk might shift from the bank to its counterparty. A credit risk is said to be "two-way" when it can shift from one party to the other.

Whoever is at risk has a random and market-driven exposure. The current risk is the current liquidation value, which changes over time and might be positive or negative. But it could become positive in the future if the variable rate declines sufficiently. The issue is to assess potential positive values of the swap, which depends on scenarios of interest rates.

For addressing this issue, the potential future exposure (PFE) has been defined. The PFE is the time profile of the upper bounds of positive exposures, at a given confidence level, obtained by generating distributions of potential derivative values at all future time points until maturity. From a risk standpoint, we take a conservative view assuming that the drift of rates is adverse, the one that maximizes the swap value for the bank. The counterparty should do the same. For a swap receiving the variable rate, sold by one party, the value becomes positive when variable rates decline. For the other party, exposure becomes positive when interest rates move up. As usual, we need to define an upper bound or a lower bound by a confidence level. For swaps, the common practice is to use a 2.5% confidence level.

Interest rate swaps are amortizing. Therefore the final value tends towards zero. Hence deviations of interest rates can increase the swap value between now and maturity. Since we end up with zero at maturity, the maximum value PFE should be reached somewhere between today and maturity. To illustrate the mechanism, we provide a sample calculation (44.5) of the upper bounds of the value of an interest rate swap under very simple assumptions, for making the essentials clear.

44.2.2 Foreign Exchange Swaps

The same principle applies to other derivatives. A currency swap exchanges USD 1 million (the notional) against the equivalent in Euros. The original exchange rate of the swap is 0.9

EUR/USD, and the USD 1 million is valued at EUR 0.9 million at inception. However, if the exchange rate fluctuates, the differential flow changes. If the USD reaches EUR 1, the buyer of EUR is entitled to a gain of EUR 0.1 million. This is the amount of the loss if the counterparty defaults. If the exchange rate varies in the opposite direction, the buyer of EUR has no risk since it owns a "negative" liquidation value. The credit risk remains with the counterparty that owns the positive liquidation value.

For assessing credit risk, the PFE should be defined. It would be based on adverse deviation of the foreign exchange, those that maximize the positive value of the swap for the party. Again, the upper bound of those variations requires a confidence level. Note that in this case, there is a single exchange of flows at maturity. Therefore, since the drift of exchange rates increases with time and the maximum value of the positive exposure is reached at maturity.

44.2.3 Options

For options, the risk differs according to whether the bank is the seller or the buyer of the option. Only the buyer is at risk because the counterparty might default on its obligation to pay if the buyer exercises the option. When time passes, there are always some chances that the option gets "in-the-money" and has a positive value. The PFE of the option should be constructed, starting from current value and assuming that the underlying varies in the direction making the option more valuable. The time profile of the upper bounds of the options bought is derived from scenarios that maximize the buyer's option value, within a preset confidence level. For a European option, there would be a single exchange of flows at maturity and the maximum PFE would be reached at maturity.

44.3 REGULATORY ADD-ONS FOR DERIVATIVES

All derivative transactions have a notional amount that measures the size of the transaction. The notional is the base which, combined with market parameters, determines the interest flows or the currency flows of swaps, or the value of an optional transaction in terms of the underlying. Measuring exposures using notional is meaningless. At inception of swaps, the value is zero, whatever the size of notional. Moreover, only positive values are meaningful in terms of credit risk.

The standard regulatory add-ons, in percentage of notional, have been defined for assessing such potential upward drifts of derivative values, depending on the nature of the underlying and on maturity. These percentages apply to the notional of derivatives in order to get some proxy of potential positive values.

But regulatory add-ons to current values pile up arithmetically. They ignore offsetting effects within a portfolio. Values can change in opposite ways within portfolios. Moreover, netting allows to net positive and negative values within an ISDA (International Swap Dealer Association) master agreement. Netting within an ISDA agreement is allowed on the same underlying instrument. Nevertheless, piling up add-ons across netting agreements falls short from capturing portfolio effects. Modeling the PFE, using both netting effects and dependencies across risk factors, is generally beneficial in terms of exposure and regulatory capital.

44.4 CREDIT RISK FOR DERIVATIVES: METHODOLOGY

The future potential exposure is made of the upper bounds of liquidation values, at each time point until maturity, given a confidence level[2].

For finding future worst-case exposures given market risk factors, the principle is to assess the values of these instruments, at all future dates until maturity. These are "mark-to-future" values, since the potential values are derived at all intermediate dates between today and maturity. The methodology generates time profiles of liquidation values, whose shapes depend upon the nature of the instrument.

For interest rate swaps, the numbers of cash flows decreases when the time to maturity decreases. For currency swaps, a single flow occurs at maturity. Interest rate swaps have bell-shaped exposures, while foreign exchange swaps have an ever-increasing exposure with time.

According to standard terminology, the current value is the "current risk," and the possible upward changes of the value generate an additional "potential risk." The overall risk at any point in time is the sum of the current and the potential risks. The expected potential exposure (EPE) is the average value of all positive exposures at all time points.

Sometimes, PFEs are considered as loan equivalents. Whatever its shape, we consider the PFE as the time profile of exposure as if it was a loan. Loan equivalents simplify the management of exposure and the definition of limits. This is conservative because the likelihood of reaching continuously an upper bound recalculated when time passes, is fairly remote.

The potential risk should capture the upward deviations of market values, since only upside moves, up to positive values, increase credit risk exposure. There are as many future values, at any future date, as there are possible values for market parameters at those dates. The upper bounds for the mark-to-market value of the swap are defined by the volatility of risk factors, risk factors correlations, and a distribution of value for defining bounds at a given confidence level. The mechanism is easier to illustrate when considering an individual transaction, and ignoring correlation effects across transactions. The upper and lower bound values of the derivative, at the given same confidence level, are obtained from revaluation of the derivative using upper or lower bound values of market parameters.

Note that there is usually a single main risk factor, but that the value depends on many risk factors. For example, a foreign exchange swap is more sensitive to foreign exchange rates. But its value also depends on interest rates. We deal with a foreign exchange swaps as if its value were driven by the single exchange rate, or as if it were an elementary position, ignoring the secondary effects of interest rates.

A foreign exchange swap has notional of USD 1 million and exchanges EUR and USD at the preset rate of 0.09 EUR/USD in one year. The volatility of the exchange rate of the USD against the Euro is 10%, for instance, with a current exchange rate of 0.9 EUR/USD. The volatility is therefore 0.09 EUR/USD. Let us use a normal distribution of exchange rate for illustration purposes. The deviation of the exchange rate will not exceed 1.96 times the volatility of 0.9 in more than 2.5% of all cases. The upper bound of the exchange rate is the current rate plus 1.96 standard deviations, or 1.0764 EUR/USD. With this upper bound for the exchange rate, the upper bound for the currency swap is $(1.0764 - 0.9)$ EUR/USD $\times$ 1 million USD =

---

2 The guidelines were defined by the Group of 30 (1993) and reused by the BCBS in [9]

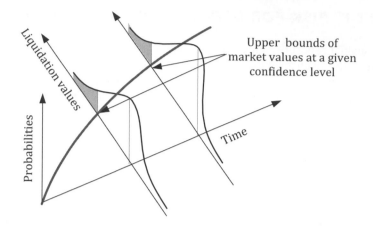

FIGURE 44.1   Upper bounds of mark to market values of a foreign exchange swap

0.1764 million EUR. This value is the PFE at the 1-year time point at the 2.5% (one-tailed) confidence level.

The resulting PFE can be calculated as an add-on in dollar value or as a fraction in percentage of the notional. For instance, the 0.1764 million EUR deviation of liquidation value is 17.64% of the notional value of the swap. For obtaining a time profile of exposures, such add-ons should be calculated for all future dates until maturity. The market volatility increases with horizon, following the square root of time formula: $\sigma_t = \sigma_1 \sqrt{t}$, where t is in years and σ_1 is the annualized volatility. Note that over long horizons, the rule does not apply, notably for interest rates which are mean reverting. Nevertheless, the general methodology does not change (see Figure 44.1.).

The calculation raises an apparent paradox. The probability of continuously hitting all maximum exposures at all time points is much lower than the confidence level, so that the approach sounds too conservative. On the other hand, if we hit the highest potential exposure at date 1, chances are that we go beyond this exposure later, making the approach appear not conservative enough. This is not exact since such distribution curves are obtained as time paths of the random values starting as of current date. Moreover, the PFE should be updated when moving forward in time. Hence, whatever the current value, close or not from the previous day's upper bound, it is recalculated and the future distributions of value always make sense and should not be interpreted as a once for all profile of values (Figure 44.2).

At time point 0, the value of the swap is zero and the PFE reaches the maximum value at maturity. In Figure 44.2, the other curves show what happens at time point 1. The upper curve went up because the value became positive at that date. The PFE uses this positive value as new starting point for reevaluation of the time profile of future exposures. The lower curve starts at a negative value at time point 1. There is no credit risk for negative values. But adding a drift proportional to the square root of time, the new PFE curve might still end up positive at maturity. Only the fraction of this lower curve with positive PFE generates credit risk. The revaluation at intermediate time points takes care of the continuous drifts of values.

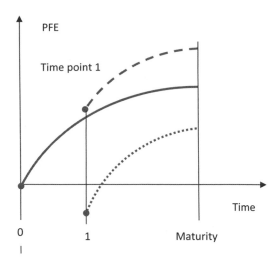

FIGURE 44.2   Recalculation of the PFE as time passes

Worst-case exposures serve for measuring worst-case losses. When looking at expected loss, the expected exposure is a best measure. The expected exposure results from the distribution at any time point, except that positive values only are relevant. Hence, the expected exposure at this time point is the expected value of the truncated distribution at any date[3]. We now illustrate the process with an interest rate swap under simplifying assumptions.

44.5 CALCULATING THE PFE FOR AN INTEREST RATE SWAP

A bank contracted a swap with another bank at date 0. The swap is a 4-year interest rate swap, notional 1000, receiving the fixed rate and paying the floating. The yield curve is flat so that all forward rates are equal to spot rates. The fixed rate is 10% and equal to the floating rate at date 0. The value of the IRS at inception was zero. Dates refer to end of year, date 1 being the end of year 1, and so on. We are at date 1 (end of year 1). Such simplifying assumptions are not restrictive.

The current floating rate is 8%. Its annual volatility is 1.0%. The value of the swap is the discounted value of all future flows. Interest is paid at every end of year. The discount rate to be used is the prevailing unique market rate (flat curve). The primary source of uncertainty is the interest rate indexed to the floating rate. Our convention for calculating present values of each leg is that the interest flows at the current date have been paid, and we discount only subsequent flows. In reality, the curve increases before the interest payment and has a downside jump, equal to interests exchanged, immediately after.

Under these assumptions, the value of the IRS at different dates is the present value calculated with the prevailing (flat) rate. Note that the present value of the variable leg is always equal to nominal. We can simply discount the interest flows, rather than adding two opposite

---

3   The expected value of a normally distributed exposure is $\sigma/\sqrt{2\pi}$. We need to multiply this value by the notional and to add any positive current value to get the expected value exposure.

flows representing the principal at maturity. We started at date zero. The IRS value is zero at origination. Then we move to date 1, assuming that the flat yield curve moved down from 10% to 8%. The IRS gains value when the floating rate declines. Starting at date 1, we need to plug-in an annualized volatility of interest rate and use the square root of time volatility $\sigma_t = \sigma_1 \sqrt{t}$ for finding the lower bounds of the interest rate at all subsequent dates at confidence level 2.5%. Again, for simplifying purpose, we use the confidence intervals of a normal curve. Such lower bounds are simply the initial interest rate minus a drift equal to $1.96\sigma_1\sqrt{t}$. The variations of the value of the IRS are entirely due to its fixed-rate leg, since the floating rate leg has a constant value. Therefore upward variations result from declining interest rates for a receiver swap. However, we show both legs for clarity (Table 44.1).

The value as of date zero is not relevant any more. The IRS has a positive value equal to 51.54 as of date 1. When we move further in time, we have the new current risk time profile of the value of the IRS. It declines because the swap amortizes, meaning that there are fewer flows when getting closer to maturity. This curve is the current risk, not the potential exposure, since we are at date 1, and we use the current rate 8%. For determining the potential exposure we make the interest rate shift downward starting from date 2, and using $1.96\sigma_1\sqrt{t}$.

Table 44.2 shows the time profile of such lower bounds of interest rates using annualized volatility 1%. The calculation is approximated because we use a normal distribution for the variations of interest rates. We recalculate the interest flows by multiplying the lower bounds of interest rates by the notional and the IRS upper bound values are the netted values of the fixed leg minus the floating rate leg (Table 44.3). The last line is the PFE of the swap. It cumulates the current risk and the drift of interest rate. The time profile of the potential risk of the IRS is shown in Figure 44.3, starting as of date 1, when the swap has gained value. The potential risk

TABLE 44.1   Time profile of the IRS value at current rate

Dates	0	1	2	3	4
Fixed interest	10%	10%	10%	10%	10%
Floating interest	10%	8%	8%	8%	8%
Fixed leg (receiver)	100.00	100.00	100.00	100.00	100.00
Floating leg (payer)	100.00	80.00	80.00	80.00	80.00
Liquidation value time profile at date 1					
Fixed leg	316.99	257.71	178.33	92.59	0.00
Floating leg	−316.99	−206.17	−142.66	−74.07	0.00
Swap current risk time profile at date 1	0.00	51.54	35.67	18.52	0.00

TABLE 44.2   Time profile of lower bound of interest rates (approximated)

Dates	0	1	2	3	4
Square root of time (as of 1)	0.00	0.00	1.00	1.41	1.73
Volatility			1.00%	1.41%	1.73%
Lower bound of interest (1 s)	10.0%	8.0%	7.0%	6.6%	6.3%
Lower bound of interest (1.96 s)	10.0%	8.0%	6.0%	5.2%	4.6%

TABLE 44.3 PFE of the IRS as of date 1

Dates	0	1	2	3	4
Fixed leg	100.00	100.00	100.00	100.00	100.00
Floating leg @ upper bound of rate	100.00	80.00	60.40	52.28	46.05
Swap potential value	0.00				
Fixed leg	316.99	257.71	178.33	92.59	0.00
Floating leg	−316.99	−206.17	−107.71	−48.41	0.00
Swap potential risk	0.00	51.54	70.62	44.18	0.00

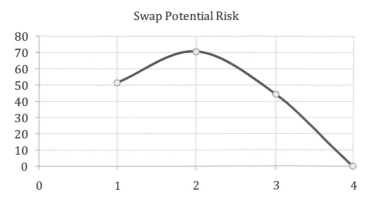

Swap Potential Risk

FIGURE 44.3   Time profile of the IRS PFE

has the typical shape of an IRS. It starts increasing then declines down to zero when there are no flows to be paid at maturity (after interest flows exchanged).

Note the simplifying assumptions used in the example. Actual simulations would require determining the entire yield curve at different time points and rely on interest rate models. The distribution of interest rates would not be normal when using adequate processes for simulating the interest rates, because those tend to be mean-reverting, rather than normally distributed. The normal assumption used above allows interest rates to become negative. Actual simulations would use the mean-reverting process of short-term rates, after calibration of the mean-reversion parameter λ.

The time profiles of add-ons for swaps have different shapes. When the last flows are the most important, the risk increases with time because of the effect of increased volatility of this last flow. This is the usual profile of foreign exchange swaps. The increasing drift over time of risk factors is the "diffusion effect." The "amortizing effect" refers to the decreasing number of remaining flows with time. Those two factors have offsetting effects on the deviations of the liquidation value. When amortization is negligible, the increase in volatility results in increased deviations of liquidation value with time. When the amortization effect dominates, the liquidation values obtained from the bounds of market parameters declines. Hence, there is a maximum for the deviations of the liquidation value of the swap somewhere between now and maturity. Actually, potential risk of IRS usually peaks between one-third and half of the residual life (Figure 44.4).

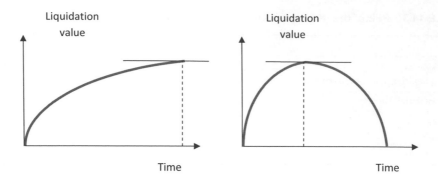

FIGURE 44.4   **Time profiles of credit risk of swaps**

44.6 CREDIT RISK EXPOSURE FOR PORTFOLIOS OF DERIVATIVES

With derivative portfolios, the total liquidation value is the sum of individual liquidation values. With "netting" agreements, positive deviations net against negative deviations. In addition, individual deviations depend on each other, since they are market driven and market parameter variations comply with a correlation structure.

With netting agreements, banks exchange only the netted value of instruments. For instance, if A has two transactions with B whose liquidation values are 50 and –20, the risk exposure is the netted value, or +30. Without a netting agreement, only positive liquidation values are at risk. In the above example, the risk will be +50 and zero for the second transaction. Within netting agreements, the risk is lower because we add up algebraically the values of each instrument. The liquidation value of the portfolio at any future date should net the liquidation values of individual instruments and net collateral values as well. This requires direct measures of the current and potential risks for the entire sub-portfolio subject to netting. The evaluation of offsetting effects within portfolios depends on correlation between risk factors.

The adequate methodology requires simulations plus full revaluation of non-linear instruments, such as options bought. The methodology is the same as that used to value the VaR for market risk for portfolios. The technique generates a distribution of the values of the portfolio

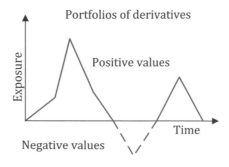

FIGURE 44.5   **Time profiles of credit risk exposure: example**

for each future date (Figure 44.5)[4]. The upper bound at a given confidence level results from this distribution. Note that the distribution is empirical and non-parametric with portfolios. The composition of the portfolio changes over time. Some derivatives reach maturity and their liquidation value vanishes at that time. The portfolio value will decline if the liquidation value of the instruments was positive. Discrepancies of maturities results in non-monotonous time profiles with ups and downs. There is no typical shape because the portfolio amortization combined with netting effects can generate any shape.

---

4 Straight lines are proxies of actual profiles, which are usually curved.

45

Modeling Recoveries

Modeling facility recoveries remains a challenge of risk management, either because of the scarcity of data or because the sources of recoveries remain too difficult to assess economically. There are some exceptions, however. In all cases, there is always a residual credit risk even a comprehensive protection is provided, as demonstrated by modeling the risk when feasible, as in the examples provided. Collateral transforms the credit risk into a price risk of securities posted. Third-party guarantees and credit derivative protection, and support, mitigate the credit risk through default probability assigned to the facility. Statistical data also provide some support for modeling the distribution of recoveries with the "beta" distribution. Covenants can be seen as options contingent on credit events, but assessing their value remains subject to practical ad hoc shortcuts.

This chapter addresses first credit risk mitigation that is collateral based (Section 45.1). An example of the calculation of economic haircuts shows why a residual risk always remains, due to the price risk of collateral. The section also refers to the Basel 2 haircuts under the treatment of eligible collateral. Next (Section 45.2), third-party guarantees or credit derivative protections are addressed through the joint default model, which depends on risk correlation between a guarantor and borrower (as shown in Chapter 31). Section 45.3 addresses the algebra of probabilities that applies to support of a direct borrower by a group for determination of the default probability of the borrower. The variety of legal frameworks and the uncertainty of support mitigates somewhat the straightforwardness of the probability modeling. Section 45.4 presents the characteristics of the beta distribution which is often used to model recovery risk and for fitting the distribution to recovery statistics when available. Finally, the last section (Section 45.5) briefly mentions some economic views that could apply to covenants, which are no substitute for judgmental assessment.

Contents

45.1 COLLATERALIZED SECURITIES LENDING/BORROWING

In collateral agreements, the borrower is committed to post a value of securities such that the debt remains below a certain agreed percentage, lower than 100%, of the value of pledged assets. The difference is the haircut. For all other collateral-based financing, the loan to value ratio should be lower than 1 as well, by a varying amount depending on the transaction (for example mortgage loans). The residual risk is the risk that the collateral value falls below the value of debt.

45.1.1 Economic Derivation of Minimum Over-collateralization

For securities posted as collateral, the principle of haircuts is to minimize such deficiency although there cannot be a zero risk. With a single haircut relative to a single risk factor, the economic calculation of collateral is fairly simple, but requires setting the minimum risk acceptable. Consider 100% as the debt amount, with posted collateral as above 100%. The excess amount of collateral above debt depends upon worst-case calculations of the deviation of its value between collateral. Usually, additional collateral is called when there is a deficiency of collateral and minimal haircuts imposed.

For instance, with a debt of 1 million € collateralized at 120%, the collateral value is 1,000,000 €. Should the collateral value fall below 1,000,000 €, the lender is required to post additional securities or repay a fraction of the debt, otherwise the collateral is liquidated and proceeds serve for repaying the debt. The point is that we do not know whether such a 20% haircut is sufficient for making sure the collateral value after liquidation will be above debt value (100%). A minimum time elapses between the initial deficiency and completing the liquidation. During this lapse of time, the collateral value might decline further. Hence the issue is to determine the level of collateralization that makes the probability that the liquidation proceeds are below debt equal to a very low probability. The starting point is the debt value (100%) and the probability of final deficiency is set to 1%. Proceeding from there, it becomes feasible to determine the appropriate level of over-collateralization, although the process requires several assumptions.

The first assumption relates to the minimum time required between the initial deficiency and the final time when liquidation is complete. The elapsed time combines various periods. The example data is fictitious, but the calculation follows general principles.

- The notification period, necessary to notify the lender of a collateral deficiency. We consider here that it equals zero. The notification date is t_0.

- The period T_1 is allowed, as a grace period, for the borrower to respond to a margin call (a small number of days, such as 2). At the end of period T_1, either additional collateral is posted or existing collateral is liquidated. The end date after the grace period is $t_1 = t_0 + T_1$.
- The length of time required for liquidating the collateral. It is constrained by the market liquidity and the volume of securities. Assume that the liquidation period is 3 days. At date $t_2 = t_0 + T_1 + T_2$, the liquidation is complete.
- The total amount of time T that elapses before selling the collateral sums up the grace period T_1 and the liquidation period T_2: $T = T_1 + T_2$.

In addition to timing assumptions, the market volatilities and the sensitivity of the pool of securities pledged are also required. The collateral has a percentage sensitivity s to the underlying risk factor, which we assume unique. The daily volatility of the risk factor is σ_m. The daily volatility of the collateral value for a given time period T in days is $s\sigma_m\sqrt{T}$. If the collateral value follows a simple normal distribution, the loss at the 1% percentile, or potential downward deviation of the collateral value, is $-2.33s\sigma_m\sqrt{T}$.

This formula provides the haircut, which is $2.33s\sigma_m\sqrt{T}$. The required level of collateral follows since it adds the haircut to the debt value D: $(2.33s\sigma_m\sqrt{T} + 1)D$.

The calculation starts with the volatility. If the annual volatility of the risk factor is 25%, the daily volatility is 1.58%, or $25\%/\sqrt{250}$. The 5-day volatility is 7.91%, or daily volatility times $\sqrt{5}$. For the final value after liquidation to be equal to debt, the minimum collateral is 107.91%. The margin call for additional collateral should occur at 107.91% for having less than 1% chance of having a loss if the borrower fails to post collateral.

The calculation relies on many assumptions, including the time assumptions, the sensitivity and the volatility of the risk factors. Note that during the liquidation period, the securities price keeps falling down, but remains above the debt value. At the end of the liquidation period, the average proceeds from liquidation are actually higher than assumed above. The calculation assumes that the price of collateral was the final price at the end of the liquidation period. In reality it will be between the price at the start of liquidation and the price when liquidation is complete[1]. Hence, the probability of lower proceeds from liquidation than debt is lower than 1% (Figure 45.1).

45.1.2 Basel 2 Treatment of Collateralized Transactions

The comprehensive approach under Basel 2 for eligible collaterals determines the net value of exposure as a function of several haircuts for, respectively, exposure value, collateral value and currency mismatches[2]:

$$E^* = \max\{0, [E(1 + H_e) - C(1 - H_c - H_{fx})]\}$$

The exposure subject to capital charge is the difference between exposure value and collateral value to which add-ons are applied, assuming that the exposure value can grow by the amount

---

1 In the above liquidation, we could assume, for example, that the effective price of liquidated collateral is the average between the starting price and the final price. This would reduce collateral required given the final deficiency probability of 1%.
2 See the chapter on Basel 2 regulations.

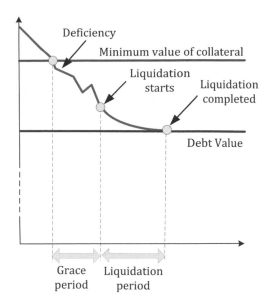

FIGURE 45.1 Determination of the minimum collateral value

of the haircuts and that the collateral value can decrease by the amount of the haircuts. The formula is conservative to the extent that it assumes that all risk factors affecting the exposure value and the collateral value vary simultaneously in adverse directions.

The full calculation for an economic haircut with three risk factors, respectively for the exposure, collateral value and foreign exchange risk, if there is a currency mismatch, should embed the correlations between the risk factors[3]. Basel 2 allows the use of a VaR model for the calculation of required economic haircuts. The VaR of the collateral value at percentile 1% would embed all parameters, sensitivities and volatilities of the three risk factors and their correlations. If several securities are posted as collateral, the VaR calculation would apply to this portfolio of securities. The haircut should be equal to this VaR since the debt is fixed. Note in both the single factor case expanded above and VaR determination of haircuts, there is always a residual risk.

45.2 VALUATION OF CREDIT RISK GUARANTEES, INSURANCE OR CREDIT DERIVATIVES

The valuation of insurance, guarantee, or credit derivatives depends on the correlation between the credit risk of the two parties, the risk seller or buyer of a protection, and the risk buyer, or seller of the protection. The issue, for a proper valuation of the guarantee, is to determine the joint default probability of the buyer of protection and the seller of protection. In general, it decreases far below the default probability of the borrower, which is the key to valuing third-party protection.

---

3   This assumes that each position depends on a single risk factor.

In Basel 2, the recognition of a third-party guarantee is treated, under the first Basel 2 sub-approach to third-party guarantees, as a risk transfer. Under risk transfer, the credit risk is transferred to the guarantor, provided that the guarantor has a better credit standing than the direct borrower and that the guarantee is readily enforceable by the guarantor. This is consistent with the practice of assigning to the direct borrower the credit rating of the guarantor. This is also consistent with the common practice of assigning the risk, in the bank's risk system, to the guarantor. Under this rule, the lender is at risk with the indirect exposure on the insurer rather than on the primary borrower.

This is a conservative principle because the actual default probability is neither that of the direct borrower nor that of the guarantor, but is the joint default probability, which is significantly lower. The second sub-approach of third-party guarantees, under Basel 2, recognizes the joint default probability, or "double default," subject to eligibility conditions, such as enforceability of the guarantee and a higher credit standing of the guarantor. This section is a reminder of the joint default probabilities and on correlations that influence this probability. It does not address the legal risk, assuming that the guarantee is readily enforceable.

The calculation of the joint default probability of a direct borrower B and a guarantor G is explained in Chapter 31 on conditional probabilities. The formula providing the default probability of a primary borrower B benefiting from a fully enforceable guarantee from the guarantor G is:

$$P(B,G) = bg + \rho\sqrt{b(1-b)g(1-g)}$$

In the formula, b is the unconditional default probability of the direct borrower, g is that of the guarantor and ρ is the correlation between the two discrete default events.

When the correlation is 0, when the default events are independent, the joint probability $P(B, G)$ collapses to $b \times g$, and the conditional default probabilities become identical to the standalone default probabilities. With standalone default probabilities being, for example, 2% for the guarantor and 3% for the direct borrower, under independence, the joint default probability is $2\% \times 3\% = 0.06\%$. The gain in default probability of B, compared with no guarantee, is $3\% - 0.06\% = 2.94\%$. The guarantee turns a speculative grade rating into an equivalent Aa rating. This result holds even though the guarantor has a 2% default probability, equivalent to a speculative grade rating. An important conclusion is that a poor rating guarantor actually enhances significantly the default probability of the borrower under independence.

When the correlation becomes positive, the joint default probability increases with the correlation coefficient. The correlation between default events is generally much lower than the correlation of the equity values of two firms. Tables 45.1 and 45.2 calculate the joint default probabilities of two obligors when they are independent and when the correlation between credit events is 3%. The default probabilities of each obligor are in rows and columns. The joint default probability is in each cell. The comparison shows that the joint default probability is highly sensitive to the correlation. In the case of independence, the joint default probability is simply the product of the two default probabilities. Under dependence, the term $\rho\sqrt{[b(1-b)}$ $g(1-g)]$ is added to the product. In order to convert the joint default probability into a rating, it is possible to use the rating that matches a range of default probabilities within which this joint default probability is.

The treatment of joint defaults adjusts the default probability of the guaranteed exposure, not its recovery rate. If the exposure guarantee is so strong that the joint probability of default drops to zero, the guaranteed exposure becomes risk free. It makes also sense to consider the

TABLE 45.1   Joint default probability between two obligors (X and Y) under independence

DP(Y)	DP(X)						
	0.1%	0.5%	1.0%	2.0%	3.0%	4.0%	10.0%
0.1%	0.000%	0.001%	0.001%	0.002%	0.003%	0.004%	0.010%
0.5%	0.001%	0.003%	0.005%	0.010%	0.015%	0.020%	0.050%
1.0%	0.001%	0.005%	0.010%	0.020%	0.030%	0.040%	0.100%
2.0%	0.002%	0.010%	0.020%	0.040%	0.060%	0.080%	0.200%
3.0%	0.003%	0.015%	0.030%	0.060%	0.090%	0.120%	0.300%
4.0%	0.004%	0.020%	0.040%	0.080%	0.120%	0.160%	0.400%
10.0%	0.010%	0.050%	0.100%	0.200%	0.300%	0.400%	1.000%

TABLE 45.2   Joint default probability between two obligors (X and Y) under independence (default correlation: 3%)

DP(Y)	DP(X)						
	0.1%	0.5%	1.0%	2.0%	3.0%	4.0%	10.0%
0.1%	0.134%	0.232%	0.314%	0.433%	0.523%	0.599%	0.915%
0.5%	0.232%	0.302%	0.371%	0.480%	0.569%	0.645%	0.975%
1.0%	0.314%	0.371%	0.432%	0.535%	0.622%	0.699%	1.048%
2.0%	0.433%	0.480%	0.535%	0.634%	0.722%	0.802%	1.193%
3.0%	0.523%	0.569%	0.622%	0.722%	0.814%	0.899%	1.335%
4.0%	0.599%	0.645%	0.699%	0.802%	0.899%	0.991%	1.475%
10.0%	0.915%	0.975%	1.048%	1.193%	1.335%	1.475%	2.273%

exposure netted from the guaranteed fraction, which is equivalent to a recovery rate equal to the guaranteed exposure. This applies for government guarantees, for instance for government-owned guarantors of export/import finance.

A third-party guarantee does not transfer risk to the guarantor to the extent that the joint default probability is much lower than the guarantor's default probability. The risk transfer towards the guarantor overestimates the true risk. Note that if the guarantor default probability is used, it implies that the joint default probability be equal to that of the guarantor. This cannot be true unless both borrower and guarantor have the same default probability, in addition to perfect correlation.

45.3 SUPPORT

Support is not identical to third-party protection because it is implicit. A positive support is similar to a guarantee. The value depends on the joint default probability of the borrower and the supporting entity. Support also differs from a guarantee because it can be negative, and its effect becomes adverse, i.e. increases the default probability assigned to the exposure to the direct borrower.

Negative support occurs in various instances. For example, the supporting entity default triggers the default of the borrower, perhaps because a subsidiary is highly dependent on the holding company business, or because the holding company has access to the assets of the subsidiary if it faces difficulties. The latter case depends on the legal framework, which might not allow a holding company to "pump up" the assets of the subsidiary. Another case is that of a supporting entity dependent on the borrower's default, because the subsidiary's survival is critical for the core business of the holding company. The borrower's default would then trigger default of the supporting entity.

These are extreme cases, since the relations are not deterministic. Negative support seems similar to a high correlation between defaults. Formally, it is not. With negative support, the risk is more an "either/or" risk than an "and" risk. Either the borrower defaults or the supporting entity's default triggers default of the borrower, the reverse effect being possible as well. "Either/or" events follow different rules than "and" rules for combining default probabilities. The probability that either entity defaults, the borrower or the supporting entity, is equal to the sum of their default probabilities minus the probability that both occur. The general corresponding formula is:

$$P(\text{borrower default or supporting entity default}) =$$
$$P(\text{borrower default}) + P(\text{supporting entity default}) - \text{joint default probability (both default)}$$

Let B be the direct borrower and S be the supporting entity. The correlation still influences the risk through the joint default probability. The formula is consistent with the intuition that the lender is exposed to both risks. The default probability is approximately equal to the sum of the standalone probabilities of the borrower and the guarantor. The following calculation illustrates the mechanism of negative support:

$$P(B) = 2\%$$

$$P(S) = 3\%$$

$$P(B, S) = 1\%$$

$$P(B \text{ or } S) = 3\% + 2\% - 1\% = 4\%$$

The default probability under negative support is much higher than any one of the standalone default probabilities unless the joint default probability is very high.

The usage of the above relationship is subtle. If we consider that a single default, either that of B or of S, deterministically triggers the default of the other, the correlation is one. If the correlation is one, consistency constraints imply that both default probabilities are equal and that their value is equal to the joint default probability. When either B or S mechanically triggers the default of the other, it becomes impossible that the standalone probabilities differ from each other.

This is a limit case. In practice, this need not be the case because the relationship is neither deterministic nor necessarily symmetrical. It is possible that the supporting entity default triggers that of the borrower while the reverse is not true. The correlation coefficient does not reflect this asymmetry in any other way that being different from one.

45.4 DISTRIBUTION OF RANDOM RECOVERIES

Since recovery uncertainty results from a number of sources of risk, modeling some of them is not sufficient to capture the overall recovery risk. Recovery rates might follow some predetermined distributions fitting historical data. The statistics provide both mean and volatility around the mean by debt category. It is possible to fit a distribution to both moments, so that the fitted distribution has the same average and volatility as the empirical distributions observed.

The beta distribution has the attractive property of being representative of any shape of recoveries and of being fitted to observable mean and volatility. Recovery distributions can be U-shaped, representative of the fact that "either we recover something or not." They can also be bell-shaped or highly skewed. For example, in some cases, there no reason why recovery should be significant, as with with unsecured transactions. The mode then gets close to zero.

The beta distribution depends upon two parameters, n and r. The formula of the beta density is:

$$F(RR) = [(n-1)!/(r-1)!(n-r-1)!] RR^{r-1} (1-RR)^{n-r-1}$$

In this formula, F designates the density, and RR is the random recovery rate value, between 0 and 1. The expectations and the variance of the beta distribution are:

$$E(RR) = r/n$$

$$V(RR) = r(n-r)/n^2 (n+1)$$

The mean and variance formulas depend on two variables, r and n, making it possible to fit a beta distribution using these two values only. The shape depends upon the combination of r and n. The ratio $k = r/n$ is the expected value of the distribution. This ratio is used as a control parameter when we have the average recovery from empirical observations. If $k = r/n$, the variance is also a function of k, since $r = n \times k$:

$$V(RR) = \frac{r(n-r)}{n^2(n+1)} = \frac{nk(n-nk)}{n^2(n+1)} = \frac{k(1-k)}{(n+1)}$$

The variance gets closer to zero when n becomes large, which implies that recoveries are nearly certain. For smaller n, the distribution can have all desired shapes (Figure 45.2). If $r = 1/2$, the distribution is symmetric. If r/n is lower than 1/2, the distribution is skewed, with a long tail to the right. In this case, the highest probability is that of low recoveries, but there is still some chance of having significant recoveries. If r/n is higher than 1/2, the long tail is on the left. This is the case where recoveries are expected to be high, because we have guarantees or some collateral. As long as $r > 1$ and $n - r > 1$, the distribution has a single mode equal to $(r-1)/(n-2)$. When $r \leq 1$ or $n - r \leq 1$, the distribution can have two modes, with modes equal to either 0 or 1, or be U-shaped with the modes at 0 and 1. When $r = 1$ and $n = 2$, it becomes the uniform distribution.

One simple rule is to use the best guess value of recovery as the mode of the distribution $(r-1)/(n-2)$. Then, n is set so that the recovery volatility is in line with observation. Because of these properties, the beta distribution is widely used in modeling recoveries with some uncertainty.

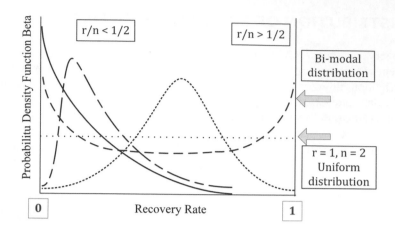

FIGURE 45.2 **Various shapes of the beta distribution**

45.5 COVENANTS

Covenants allow for preventive action. They are efficient when risk management is active, with a permanent monitoring of risk. The effect is very different from that of collateral and guarantees because these look more like insurance policies activated only when default occurs. To that extent, covenants are like options. On the other hand, covenants enhance the effect of proactive credit risk management. However, covenants have no mechanical effect on risk. Their effectiveness depends on how loose or tight they are. Their protection potential depends also on the bank's attitude for monitoring risk. Some banks might impose corrective actions when there is a breach of a covenant, others might grant a waiver, and others might not monitor the risk.

Looking at covenants as tools for avoiding larger losses, their value would be the difference between the asset value of the borrower net of recovery costs when a breach occurs, and the value without covenants, when a default event occurs. The sooner the breach occurs, the higher should be the asset value and the recoveries. Moreover, covenants and collateral increase the cost of default of the borrower since they make it an obligation to give up their projects or their collaterals when they still have a significant value.

Hence, one path for valuing covenants would be increasing the recovery. Looking at covenants as options for restructuring before default, their economic values would be that of a cap on the default risk of the borrower. Unfortunately, modeling the value of covenants is not easy, because there is no available price that would allow doing so, such as for default options once modeled the asset value. Hence, it is difficult to go beyond floors on recovery rates and/ or floors on default probabilities.

46

Credit Risk Valuation and Credit Spreads

Credit risk losses (or gains) depend on events, default and migrations, between the current dates and horizon that affect the value of facilities. Future valuation at horizon is required to assess all credit loss statistics, expected loss, unexpected loss and loss distribution for credit risk VaR. For default-only models, the distribution of values for each facility collapses to two states, default and non-default. For full valuation models, migrations to a different risk class than the original risk class results in a change of value because the credit states changes.

When considering a single facility or a single obligor, it is possible to define its standalone credit risk and measure it as a credit VaR. The risk results from migrations between today and horizon. Valuation provides credit risk-adjusted values over the entire spectrum of possible credit states at a future time point. The credit risk adjustment uses default probabilities and credit spreads of various terminal risk classes. The distribution of credit states results in a distribution of values, because the credit spreads differ across credit states, from which credit risk VaR and other statistics can be derived. The differential credit spreads are the source of these variations. The credit spreads are related to the default probability and the percentage loss given default, as shown as a preliminary.

The first section (Section 46.1) shows that credit spreads are the product of the intensity of default and loss given default, as shown by equating the valuation under risk-neutral probabilities and valuation using the risky rate, in a simplified continuous time setting. Section 46.2 explains how a credit VaR can be derived from migrations, for a single facility, by revaluing the facility for all final credit states at horizon using the credit spread matching each credit states. Section 46.3 provides an example of numerical calculations. Section 46.4 shows how the structural model can serve for modeling migrations, using the horizon distribution of asset values, and deriving a standalone credit VaR for asset value. The last section (Section 46.5) discusses the valuation effect due to excess spreads, or gaps between the facility return and market required return, given the credit risk of the facility.

Contents

46.1 CREDIT SPREAD, IMPLIED DEFAULT INTENSITY AND RECOVERY RATE

Credit spreads are related to default probabilities and loss given default. The relationship results from the two alternate methods for valuing a risky bond:

- discounting at the risk-free rate the expected payoff
- discounting at the risky rate the contractual payoffs.

The discount factor, in continuous time, applying to a future date t for calculating a present value as of today is:

$$D(t) = \exp(-yt)$$

where y is the discount rate. The bond value discounts the promised payoffs at the risky yield to maturity y as:

$$V = \int_0^T F_t \exp(-yt)\,dt$$

In this summation, t is any intermediate date, when a payoff occurs, between now and maturity T.

For using risk-neutral valuation, it is necessary to derive the probabilities of default and survival over each time interval, and to discount at the risk-free rate such expected payoffs. The risk-neutral intensity of default is $\lambda(t)$ and the recovery rate is R in percentage of amount due. For simplification purposes, we assume that both are constant. In practice, we can also use discrete time intervals over which they can be assumed constant.

Rather than using integrals for valuing the bond, we consider valuation over a small time interval in a continuous time setting[1]. The small period of time Δt is defined by two time points, t and $t + \Delta t$, such that Δt tends towards zero. The default probability from t to $t + \Delta t$ is $\lambda\Delta t$. The cumulative survival probability until t viewed from today is the exponential function $\exp(-\lambda t)$. The expected payoff at any intermediate date t is F_t under no default, with probability $\exp(-\lambda t)$. The payoff under default is R with a probability equal to the probability of default conditional on survival until t. This probability is equal to the product of the probability of survival until t multiplied by the probability of default in the interval t to $t + \Delta t$, or $\exp(-\lambda t)\lambda\Delta t$.

Over a small interval of time Δt, using the risk-neutral valuation, the value of the bond at the beginning of the interval $[t, t + \Delta t]$ discounts the payoffs under survival and recoveries under default:

---

1 This is inspired by the simple presentation by Duffie and Singleton [28].

$$V(\text{bond}) = F_{t+\Delta t} \exp(-y_f \Delta t)[(1 - \lambda \Delta t) + \lambda \Delta t R]$$

Since the argument of the exponential is small, its first-order approximation is $\exp(-u) \sim 1 - u$:

$$\exp(-y_f \Delta t) \sim (1 - y_f \Delta t)$$

The value of the bond at the beginning of the interval, t, is the discounted value of the payoff at the end of the interval, or $F_{t+\Delta t}$. The value using the risky yield y, equal to the risk-free rate plus the credit spread s, is:

$$V(\text{bond}) = \exp[-(y_f + s)]\Delta t = 1 - \Delta t(y_f + s)$$

The value of the bond using risk neutral valuation discounts its expected payoff at the risk-free rate:

$$V(\text{bond}) \sim F_{t+\Delta t}(1 - y_f \Delta t)[(1 - \lambda \Delta t) + \lambda \Delta t R]$$

From this formula we can factor out the payoff because the recovery rate is a percentage of the payoff. Expanding the bracket terms, we obtain:

$$(1 - y_f \Delta t)[(1 - \lambda \Delta t) + \lambda \Delta t R] = [(1 - \lambda \Delta t) + \lambda \Delta t R] - y_f \Delta t + y_f \lambda \Delta t^2 - y_f \lambda R \Delta t^2$$

We ignore the second-order terms (Δt^2) when the small interval Δt tends towards zero, and simplify the second expression to:

$$[(1 - \lambda \Delta t) + \lambda \Delta t R] - y_f \Delta t = 1 - \Delta t [(y_f + \lambda(1 - R)]$$

We obtain two alternative valuations of the bond value:

$$\text{risk-neutral valuation: } V(\text{bond}) \sim F_{t+\Delta t} \{1 - \Delta t [(y_f + \lambda(1 - R)]\}$$

$$\text{risky yield valuation: } V(\text{bond}) \sim F_{t+\Delta t} \{1 - \Delta t (y_f + s)\}$$

Eliminating the contractual payoff and equating those two values, we extract the credit spread s:

$$s = \lambda(1 - R) = \lambda \text{ LGD}$$

The credit spread is the product of the risk-neutral default intensity and loss given default (LGD). This shows that the credit spread equals expected loss under risk-neutral probabilities.

46.2 CREDIT VAR AND MATRIX VALUATION

Credit risk losses (or gains) depend on events, default and migrations between the current date and horizon that affect the value of facilities. Future valuation at horizon is required to assess all credit loss statistics, expected loss, unexpected loss and loss distribution for credit risk VaR.

The "matrix valuation" methodology, introduced originally by CreditMetrics[2], considers a discrete number of credit states at horizon, matching rating classes, for assigning a final value to a facility. The probabilities of reaching each of the final states, including the default state, result from transition matrices. For each credit state, different credit spreads apply, which allows calculating the value of any facility or bond at this future time point from the contractual cash flows up to maturity. From the distribution, we derive the expected values at the future date, value volatility and VaR as percentiles of value changes. The methodology relies on migrations and ratings, plus a credit spread attached to each rating. Because the credit spreads vary with rating and residual maturity, they are tabulated in a matrix cross-tabulating ratings and maturities. This revaluation technique is sometimes referred as "matrix valuation" and is a common building block for several credit portfolio models.

When looking at forward valuation at horizon, there are as many possible credit states as there are migrations, inclusive of the default state. When the facility defaults, the value of the facility is the loss under default. When the facility migrates to another credit state, it is revalued at horizon using the credit spreads mapped to each credit state or rating. There are as many values at horizon as there are risk classes, including default. The distribution of values allows deriving credit risk measures and credit risk VaR.

CreditMetrics uses the migration matrix technique. Applied to a single facility, as illustrated in Figure 46.1, the technique provides only a small number of final values. When applied to a portfolio of facilities, the migrations results in a much higher number of values. Using the forward credit spreads to discount contractual flows beyond horizon provides the values at horizon for all credit states.

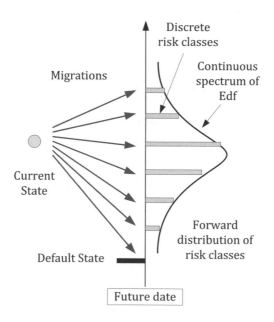

FIGURE 46.1   **Migration risk and distribution of future values**

---

2 The CreditMetrics technique is developed in the J.P. Morgan technical document [37].

The valuation formulas of an asset for a forward date are similar to those providing valuation as of the current date. The current date is zero and the horizon for modeling credit risk is one year (date 1).

Forward valuation should use the forward rates and credit spreads for the horizon as seen from today. Since we isolate credit risk, there is no need to consider changes of interest rates. The valuation discounts future payoffs prior to the future date 1. Discount factors applying to the payoffs after the future date 1 are based on forward rates. The forward risky rates are $y(0, 1, t)$, with 0 being the current date, 1 the horizon for future valuation and t the dates of future payoffs prior to date 1 and up to maturity T. Forward credit spreads are derived from forward rates between two future dates. Forward default probabilities from the horizon of the future valuation up to the maturity of a facility are the marginal default probabilities applicable between two future dates, conditional upon no prior default.

The migrations are considered between now and horizon, using, for example, published transition matrices matching that period. The formula for forward valuations as of date 1 is as follows:

$$V(1) = \frac{\sum_{t>1,T} F_t}{\left[1 + y(0,1,T)\right]^t}$$

The discount rate is the forward risky yield to maturity T starting at one, as seen from today, and up to the maturity of the asset.

A maturity of the asset, T, larger than 1 year is explicit in the above formula. In practice, for shorter maturities than horizon, we consider the final payoff under the two states, default or no default, discounted to today. Gains and losses due to credit risk result from comparing forward values at horizon with the current value. The following example illustrates the technique.

46.3 CREDIT VAR AND MATRIX VALUATION: APPLICATION

We consider a facility of maturity 2 years, with face value 1000, a periodical return of 6.5%, and a recovery rate of 50% under default, with repayment at maturity. Recoveries under default are 50% of the contractual amount due, inclusive of interest earned 65 (at end of year), or 532.5. We assume a flat yield curve, which makes all rates flat, and forward rates identical to spot rates. The facility is assigned a borrower's rating "B," with credit spread 1%. The risk-free rate is 5% and the current risky market rate applicable for valuation of the facility is 6%. The facility has an excess spread of 0.5%. We apply the valuation technique at date 1, when residual maturity is 1 year. The transition matrix, starting from rating B is given in Table 46.1, along with the corresponding credit spreads.

The current value of the facility is the present value of the next two cash flows, 65 and 1065, at the credit risk adjusted market rate 6%. It is above par because of the positive excess spread:

$$65/(1 + 6\%) + 1065/(1 + 6\%)^2 = 1009.2$$

We proceed to the valuation as of end of year 1 for all credit states, as given in the matrix in Table 46.1. For each credit state at 1, we discount the remaining flow at the credit risk-adjusted market rate assuming that the intermediate payoff of 65 is paid, except for the default state

TABLE 46.1   Migrations, final credit states and credit spreads

	Transition probabilities	Spread	Risky rate at date 1
Rating A	10.0%	0.1%	5.1%
Rating B	75.0%	1.0%	6.0%
Rating C	7.0%	2.0%	7.0%
Rating D	5.0%	4.0%	9.0%
Rating E	2.0%	8.0%	13.0%
Default	1.0%		
	100.0%		

where the payoff is 532.5 (assuming that default occurs at end of the first year since we take the total annual accrued interest). Valuation at end of year 1, under survival up to date 1, is obtained by discounting the final flow at end of year 2, 1065, at the risky yield matching the final rating at end of year 1: $V_1 = 1065/(1 + y_i)$ where i is the rating A to E. Under default we use the 532.5 value (Table 46.2).

Note that the final value when the rating B does not change, or 1004.7, is lower than the current value, due to a roll-down effect combined with a positive excess spread (Table 46.3). This roll-down effect is discussed in the next section. The value distribution as of date 1 is obtained using the transition probabilities.

The distribution of gains and losses is graphed in Figure 46.2. The horizontal axis is truncated at –80 and does not show the largest loss equal to –476.7 (= 1009.2 – 532.5). The distribution is highly skewed to the left. We can derive loss percentiles from Table 46.3. For example, the credit loss at the 97% confidence level is –22.9 and it is –57.5 at the 99% percentile.

TABLE 46.2   Gains and losses at horizon

	Transition probabilities	Rate	Value at date 1	Gain (+), loss (−)
Rating A	10.0%	5.1%	1,013.3	13.3
Rating B	75.0%	6.0%	1,004.7	4.7
Rating C	7.0%	7.0%	995.3	−4.7
Rating D	5.0%	9.0%	977.1	−22.9
Rating E	2.0%	13.0%	942.5	−57.5
Default	1.0%	Recovery	532.5	−467.5

TABLE 46.3   Distribution of gains and losses at horizon

Rating	Value at date 1	Gain (+), loss (−)	Transition probability	Cumulated probability
A	1013.3	13.3	10.0%	10.0%
B	1004.7	4.7	75.0%	85.0%
C	995.3	−4.7	7.0%	92.0%
D	977.1	−22.9	5.0%	97.0%
E	942.5	−57.5	2.0%	99.0%
Default	532.5	−476.7	1.0%	100.0%

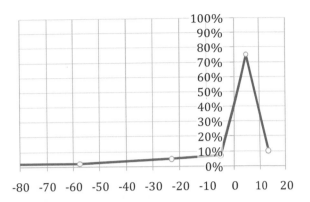

FIGURE 46.2   Distribution of gains and losses at horizon

46.4 MIGRATIONS AND VAR UNDER THE STRUCTURAL MODEL

The matrix approach uses discrete final credit states. The structural model of default provides a continuous distribution of credit states at horizon, which depends on the distance to default. Migration matrices group historical frequencies of transitions across risk classes over a specified horizon, for example one year. The final states include all risk classes plus the default state. The default option model also applies to migrations since it models the default probabilities that map with risk classes. The difference is that the distribution of migrations is continuous rather than discrete.

Each final asset value corresponds to a distance to default and a default probability. The distribution of asset values is a continuous distribution of migrations. For mapping asset values, or final distance to default, to discrete ratings, the continuous distribution has to be discretized. The process consists of defining ranges of asset values and distances to default that map to the default probabilities of ratings.

When considering a future horizon, the asset value distribution is lognormal. Each asset value has a probability and corresponds to a distance to default and a default probability. The mapping can use the EDF© for defining ranges of asset values that map to the default frequencies assigned to ratings. For example, given such default frequency, we can define a range of asset values such that the probability-weighted EDFs© in the range equals the default frequency. Each final credit rating can be assigned a range of asset values (Figure 46.3).

When modeling migrations by asset values, note that the migration probabilities from initial EDF© to all final EDFs© is lognormal, as is the distribution of asset values. It is embedded in the model simulations. The migrations observed historically are not lognormal. This does not matter if we match ranges of final asset values to ratings through the EDFs©.

The lognormal distribution was used for deriving the default probability, given the debt obligation at horizon. But the same distribution can be used as above for deriving a standalone VaR. The VaR is the negative variation of value matching a percentile. It is defined as the negative difference between $A(\alpha)$ and A_0 at confidence level α. For obtaining such VaR under the structural model, it is sufficient to substitute to the debt value a value percentile (Figure 46.4).

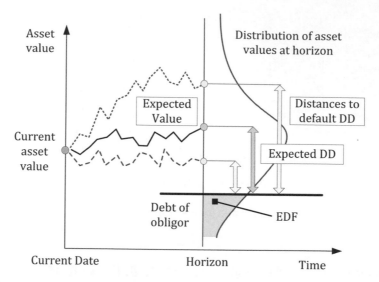

FIGURE 46.3   Asset values and migrations

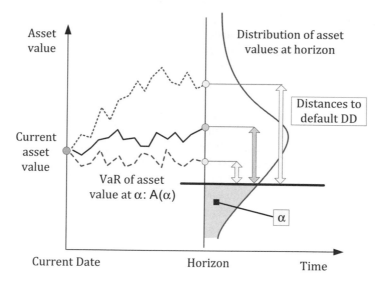

FIGURE 46.4   VaR of asset value

In Chapter 42 describing the structural model, value percentiles were defined for the ratio $V(\alpha)/V_0$ of final to initial value. The formula for the α percentile of this ratio was:

$$\frac{V(\alpha)}{V_0} = \exp\left[\Phi^{-1}(\alpha)\sigma\sqrt{T} + (\mu - \tfrac{1}{2}\sigma^2)T\right]$$

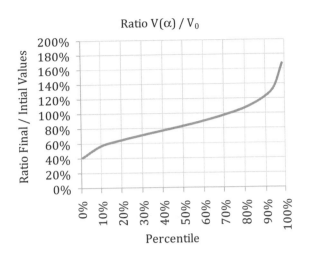

FIGURE 46.5 **Percentiles of the ratio of final asset value to initial asset value (expected return 10%, volatility 30%, horizon 1 year)**

Replicating the example, when using an expected return of 10%, a volatility of asset return of 30% and a horizon T of one year, we find that the 1% percentile of the ratio $V(\alpha)/V_0$ is 40.7%. This result is summarized by:

$$P[V(\alpha)/V_0 \leq 40.7\%] = 1\%$$

The downside deviation of value matching the 1% percentile is the complement to 1, or 59.3%. This value, 59.3% $\times$ V_0 is the VaR at 1% confidence level. The graph showing the ratio value, with the same data as the above example, and the percentiles is shown in Figure 46.5. It depends on the inputs used above. Figure 46.5 is a summary of migrations. Higher than 1 values of the ratio correspond to upward migrations, and lower than 1 values corresponds to adverse deviations. The graph is dependent on all inputs.

Note that with the standardized model using a standard normal distribution, the VaR at 1% confidence level matches a decline of value of -2.3263σ, or 0.7. The decline of value is 70%, much higher than with the lognormal distribution because the downside tail of the normal distribution is more extended than the truncated at 0 left-hand tail of the lognormal distribution (Figure 46.5).

46.5 FORWARD VALUATION AND EXCESS SPREADS

Excess spreads are the excesses of the asset rate r over the required risky yield y, or $r - y$. Excess spreads exists notably for loans, whose return can be higher or lower than the credit risk adjusted spread for a given maturity. The excess spread can be positive or negative. Excess spreads relate to the relative "richness" or "poorness" of facilities. When excess spread is positive, the value of the assets is above par, and the reverse occurs when the excess spread is negative. A "rich" asset provides a higher return than the market requires given risk. A "poor" asset pays less than the required market return. A "rich" facility is more valuable than a "poor" one. These properties apply for all risky assets, except that, for each risk class, we need to refer to market rates corresponding to this specific risk class. Note that these definitions and calculations apply to any asset, traded or not in the market. Hence, a loan has a mark-to-model value, but we cannot compare it with an actual price

To make this explicit, let consider a zero coupon maturing at T, with a unit face value, providing the fixed yield r to the lender, and a risk such that the risky discount rate is y, including the credit spread.

$$V = \frac{(1+r)^T}{(1+y)^T}$$

The excess spread is $r - y$. It is obvious that $V > 1$ and $V \leq 1$ depending on whether $r > y$ or $r \leq y$. Two loans with identical book values and amortization schedules and same risk can have different economic values if they have different excess spreads. Mark-to-model valuation reflects both risk and excess revenues compared to the market benchmarks for risky returns.

For a given migration scenario, the forward value specific to a migration path differs from the current value because of several effects. Moving forward in time implies:

- the specifics of the facility, notably excess spread, or yield minus the market required yield, its maturity, and its amortizing schedule
- an amortization effect, or roll-down effect, refers to the lower number of remaining payoffs at horizon compared to today and the residual maturity is lower at horizon than today
- the usage of forward parameters rather than their current values such as the forward yields, both risk-free and risky, and the corresponding credit spreads.

When looking at their future values, everything other than excess spread being equal including same risk (no migration), the rich facility loses value and the poor facility gains value. The rich facility loses value, at constant risk, because it generates less high interest flows. The reverse applies to the poor facility. It "looks like" the risk is higher for the rich facility. Rather it is a pure valuation effect. Consider a facility at a given time point. The market risky yield is y, the facility has nominal N, provides a periodical return r, with bullet repayment at maturity. Its economic value V discounts at the market risky yield y all future interest payments plus the final repayment of nominal. It is a function of residual maturity T:

$$\frac{V}{N} = \left(1 - \frac{r}{y}\right)\frac{1}{(1+y)^T} + \frac{r}{y}$$

- If $r = y$, there is no excess spread and the value is constant and equal to initial nominal K.
- If $r < y$, or a positive excess spread, the ratio V/N increases when residual maturity T declines.
- If $r > y$, or a negative excess spread, the ratio V/N declines when the residual maturity T declines.

The following example illustrates the excess spread effect. The returns of the "rich" and "poor" facilities are, respectively, 12% and 8%. The market risky yield is the same 10%. The nominal N is the same and equals 1. Both facilities are coupon bonds, with annual payment of interest. The above formula applies. Table 46.4 shows the variation of values when residual maturity declines from 10 years to 1 year, the risk remaining constant and the market yield is constant[3]. The variations of values have the same absolute values when residual maturity T declines[4]. The value of the poor facility is always below nominal and increases when maturity declines. The reverse happens with the rich facility. It is above par, but the variations of values are all negative. Hence, the rich facility loses value while the poor facility gains value. This is not a risk effect but a valuation effect. Moreover, the value variations have higher amplitudes with short residual maturities.

TABLE 46.4 Variation of value of two loans with different excess spreads when residual maturity declines

T	Poor value	Rich value	Poor Δ value	Rich Δ value
10	87.7%	112.3%		
9	88.5%	111.5%	0.8%	−0.8%
8	89.3%	110.7%	0.8%	−0.8%
7	90.3%	109.7%	0.9%	−0.9%
6	91.3%	108.7%	1.0%	−1.0%
5	92.4%	107.6%	1.1%	−1.1%
4	93.7%	106.3%	1.2%	−1.2%
3	95.0%	105.0%	1.4%	−1.4%
2	96.5%	103.5%	1.5%	−1.5%
1	98.2%	101.8%	1.7%	−1.7%

3 This implies a flat yield curve and a flat market spread.
4 The first derivative with respect to T depends only the variation of $1/(1 + y)^T$, which is the same term for both facilities.

SECTION 12

Credit Portfolio Risk

Credit risk for portfolios applies to the banking portfolio and all buy-and-hold positions in market instruments, such as OTC derivatives. The challenge of portfolio risk modeling is to address dependencies between credit events. It is easy to show that credit portfolio losses are highly sensitive to dependencies. The typical loss distribution for credit risk has a single mode, the peak of most frequent small losses, and a long fat tail with large losses with low probability. When dependencies increase, the fat tail grows longer and the peak loss increases. Credit loss distributions are asymmetric and highly skewed and leptokurtic.

Credit portfolio models share some common building blocks. Because we look forward, an horizon is selected for obtaining the credit loss distribution. The valuation block uses either the "default mode" or the "full valuation" mode. Under default mode, only default and survival are considered. Under full valuation, all migrations states in addition to the default state are considered. The full valuation mode relies either on matrix valuation, using credit spreads of the final credit classes for reevaluating risky date, or risk-neutral valuation whereby the value is the expected value at horizon using risk-free rates for discounting payoffs from horizon until maturity of each facility.

Dependency modeling is the key building block because of highly sensitive loss (or value) distributions at horizon. Traditional approaches rely on factor models to generate dependency between risk factors that drive credit events. For models based on the structural model, the primary risk factors are asset values of obligors, while "second-levels" risk factors include all financial and economic indexes, plus country-industry factors, that make asset values dependent. When using the reduced form model of default, dependencies are plugged into hazard models applying to each obligor. Dependencies are also tracked by indices affecting the default intensities applying to each obligor. Reduced form models require the copula approach for dealing with non-normal distributions of times to default, such as the Li model [49]. Note that such models impose inputting dependencies, whether other portfolio models embed a module generating dependencies from factor models.

The main output of credit portfolio models is a value distributions of all facilities, from which loss percentiles, expected loss and credit risk economic capital – or Credit VaR – are derived. The section covers the building blocks of credit portfolio models in five chapters.

- The various approaches to credit event dependencies are addressed first. The dependency modeling under the structural model of default is detailed here (Chapter 47).
- Assuming dependencies given, a very simple case of a two-obligor portfolio serves only as an illustration of the effect of dependencies (Chapter 48).
- Analytical distributions of portfolio values, which rely on some restrictive assumptions, are covered in Chapter 49.
- The simulation algorithms shared by most credit portfolio models is addressed in Chapter 50.
- This section concludes with an overview of most well-known models, detailing their main building blocks. They include Moody's-KMV Portfolio Manager, Credit Metrics, Credit Risk+ and Credit Portfolio View (Chapter 51).

47

Credit Event Dependencies

Joint defaults are rarely observed and dependencies between these events have to be modeled rather than observed.

The asset value of the firm is the main risk factor that drives dependencies. Since they are not observable, asset values use either the equity value as proxy, or they are modeled from equity prices under the conceptual framework of the option model of default. Dependencies of default events result from asset value or equity value correlations. The basic idea is to model joint defaults, or joint migrations, from these correlations.

There are alternative approaches for modeling dependencies of default. They require inputting a correlation between credit events, which brings us back to the issue of assessing them first. Considering default and survival as discrete events, the joint default embeds the correlation of defaults events. For a pair of obligors, this joint default probability was expanded in the chapter on recoveries (Chapter 45). Another approach uses conditional default probability on the credit events of another obligor. In both cases we directly input a correlation first. This explains why most credit portfolio models rely on simulations of asset values or their proxy, equity values and returns.

Section 47.1 relies on the structural model of default for modeling joint defaults. The same technique applies for modeling dependent migrations, although migrations are subject to specific constraints, which is that they sum up to one. Hence changing the default probabilities implies shifting the migration probabilities. Finally, we conclude that simulations of asset values are the best method to address dependencies of default. Most models make the asset values dependent using factor models.

Contents

47.1 MODELING JOINT MIGRATIONS AND DEFAULTS WITH THE STRUCTURAL MODEL

Unlike market prices, observations of credit risk events are not frequent enough. In retail banking, the high volume of statistics helps for modeling migrations and defaults using econometrical techniques. For medium-sized firms and large firms, joint defaults are rarely, or never, observed. The case of "low default portfolios" illustrates the difficulty of some investment banks dealing with large corporates or other banks. Unlike market risk, which relies on risk factors that are readily observable in most cases, joint defaults have to be modeled. The structural model of default provides an instrumental framework for deriving default or migration correlations. The principle is to model the joint probability of the assets of two obligors of falling under thresholds triggering either default (or migration) events.

47.1.1 Dependency and Joint Default Probability

Default events occur whenever asset value gets lower than debt. When considering two obligors, we are looking for the joint probability of their asset values both falling below the levels of their respective debts. This joint probability embeds the correlation of default events. To explain the joint default phenomenon, it is convenient to show visually how joint default occurs.

The asset value distributions are lognormal since asset returns are normally distributed in a continuous time framework. Figure 47.1 shows the distributions of the asset values of two firms, the asset value of firm X being on the horizontal axis and the asset value of firm Y being on the vertical axis. Accordingly, for firm X, the distribution shows the probability vertically, whether for the firm Y, the probability is measured horizontally[1]. Two straight lines represent the debt levels of each firm at some preset horizon. The vertical line refers to the debt of X and the horizontal line to the debt of Y.

The joint probability of default is the area under the left lower rectangle between the origin of the axes and the two lines representing the debt levels of two obligors X and Y. Both default

---

1 The graph is simplified. There should be two horizontal axes and two vertical axes, one for the asset value and the other for the probability. For this intuitive visual representation, we omit the two probability axes. This is inspired from the documents of Credit Portfolio Manager.

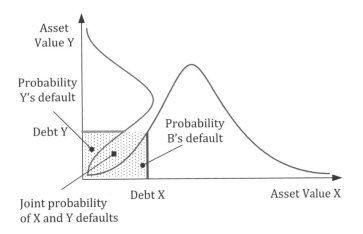

FIGURE 47.1   Joint default probabilities of two obligors and assets correlation

when the asset value of X falls below its debt and when the same happens simultaneously to Y. The area under the distribution curves visualizes these probabilities for X or for Y.

The correlation effect on the joint default probability appears in Figure 47.2. The chart plots the asset values of two obligors on two axes. The "cloud" of values is more or less round according to correlation. With a zero correlation, the cloud of dots is a circle. When correlation increases, the cloud of dots tends to extend along the first diagonal. The density of dots in the rectangle represents the joint default probability. With an elongated cloud of dots, the number of dots inside the rectangle changes, and this number represents the frequency of joint defaults. Both Figures 47.1 and 47.2 illustrate the effect of a positive dependency. If the dependency is positive, as shown in the Figure 47.2, the joint default frequency increases.

Correlations across pairs are available in KMV Portfolio Manager and in Credit Metrics, from different sources: modeled assets returns for KMV, and equity return correlations for Credit Metrics.

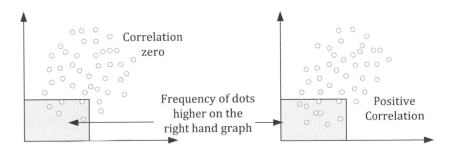

FIGURE 47.2   Effect of assets' correlation on the joint default probability

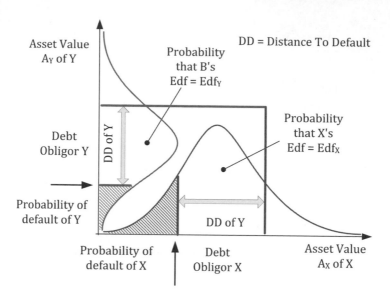

FIGURE 47.3   Joint migration probabilities of two obligors and asset correlation

47.1.2 Dependency and Joint Migration Probabilities

The same model applies to migrations derived from asset values. Using two obligors, we have a larger number of migration events than default events. Migrations are modeled as the distance to default in the structural model. The distance to default is the distance between the expected asset value and the debt threshold that triggers default. Higher distances to default result in lower default probabilities. Migration events are defined as asset values falling in the range of two distances to defaults.

   The same model of default correlation extends to correlations between migrations of two obligors. The only difference is that the distances to default of the final expected credit state are positive rather than zero or negative, as is the case for default events. Migration thresholds are above the default thresholds. Asset correlations generate joint migration probabilities for migrations as they do for defaults. Figure 47.3 uses a similar presentation to that of defaults. Each positive distance to default matches a credit state other than default. The rectangle between straight lines represents the joint probability that X and Y's distances to default are lower or equal to those threshold values.

   Credit Metrics models migrations using various threshold levels to define bands of asset values at horizon defining the final risk classes matching final ratings. The model was introduced earlier by defining the various credit states other than default, matching confidence levels representing expected default probabilities.

47.2 JOINT DEFAULT PROBABILITY USING DISCRETE VARIABLES

There is no need to use the methodology for deriving the joint probability that both asset values are below their default points, provided that we start from the correlation between discrete default events, ρ(default X, Y), rather than the correlation between asset values.

Correlation relates to conditional probabilities. It is equivalent to say that there is a correlation between default events of X and Y, and to consider that the probability that X's default occurs gets higher if X's default occurs than Y's "unconditional" default probability. For instance, the unconditional probabilities of default of X and Y are 1% and 2% respectively. If the probability that Y defaults when X's default probability becomes 10%, the conditional default probability of Y given X's defaults is $P(X \mid Y) = 10\%$, which is much higher than the unconditional probability of Y's default, which is $P(Y) = 2\%$. This implies a strong correlation between X and Y's default events. Then, the joint default probability becomes:

$$\mathrm{JDP}(X, Y) = P(X \mid Y) \times P(Y) = 10\% \times 1\% = 0.1\%$$

This is much higher than 0.02%, the joint default probability if the defaults were independent.

Correlation implies that conditional probabilities differ from unconditional probabilities, and the converse is true. Correlation and conditional probabilities relate to each other, but they are not identical. Conditional probabilities are within the (0, 1) range, while correlations are within the (−1, +1) range.

The modeling is the one presented in the chapter of recoveries for modeling the joint default of guarantor and borrower (Chapter 45). There is no need to replicate the model here. We consider a pair of obligors, X and Y, and the derivation of the joint default probability follows, after having defined the default correlation.

In a first step, we calculate the joint default probability of two obligors. The notations use the following rules, with D and S representing default and survival:

$$P(X = D) = P(X) = x \text{ and } P(X = S) = 1 - P(X) = 1 - x$$

$$P(Y = D) = P(Y) = Y \text{ and } P(Y = S) = 1 - P(Y) = 1 - y$$

The joint default probability is $P(X, Y) = \sigma_{XY} + x\,y$, or:

$$P(X,Y) = x\,y + \rho\sqrt{x(1-x)\,y(1-y)}$$

The joint default probability increases with a positive correlation between default events. However, there are boundary values for correlations and for unconditional default probabilities. Intuitively, a perfect correlation of +1 would imply that X and Y default together. This is possible only to the extent that the default probabilities are identical. Different unconditional probabilities are inconsistent with such perfect correlation. This is one of the limits of the correlation measure. In this case, the correlation cannot take all values in the range −1 to +1.

Figure 47.4 shows the relationship between the joint default probability of two obligors and the correlation. Their unconditional default probabilities are respectively 3% and 2%. The correlation increases the joint default probability, thereby decreasing the value of the guarantee.

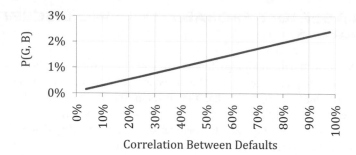

FIGURE 47.4 Joint default probability of borrower and guarantor (unconditional probabilities are respectively 3% and 2%)

This relation is linear, according to the above formulas. Note finally that the correlation between asset values differs from the correlation of discrete default events.

47.3 CONDITIONAL PROBABILITIES AND CORRELATION

This section applies to any credit state, default or migrations. From a practical standpoint, it might be easier to define conditional probabilities than specifying a correlation value between default events. The numerical example below was used in Chapter 31 on conditional probabilities. It is reproduced as Table 47.1 for convenience.

This choice has an intuitive interpretation, since it means that the default probability of Y jumps to 20% if X defaults. For making explicit conditional probabilities, we need to refer to the conditioning credit states. The credit states "D" and "ND" refer, respectively to default and no default.

TABLE 47.1 Joint default probabilities and conditional probabilities

Standalone probability		Standalone probabilities		Conditional probabilities	Joint probabilities
X		Y		P(Y | X)	
D	3.00%	D	2.00%	20.00%	0.60%
		ND	98.00%	80.00%	2.40%
				Total	3.00%
ND	97.00%	D	2.00%	1.44%	1.40%
		ND	98.00%	98.56%	95.60%
				Total	97.00%

It is not possible to assign default probabilities and correlation independently. There are internal consistency constraints because the conditional probabilities have to be within the [0, 1] range and because there are relationships between conditional probabilities, and between conditional probabilities and default correlation.

$$P(Y = D \mid X = D) = JDP(X, Y)/P(X = D) = y + (\rho/x)\sqrt{[x(1 - x) \times y(1 - y)]}$$

$$P(X = D \mid Y = D) = JDP(X, Y)/P(Y = D) = x + (\rho/y)\sqrt{[x(1 - x) \times y(1 - y)]}$$

These relationships derive from the arithmetic of conditional probabilities. Therefore defining, for example, $P(Y = D \mid X = D)$, given unconditional default probabilities, implies a value for correlation. The implied correlation is bounded. The upper bound is reached when the conditional probability reaches 100%. An implication is that a correlation coefficient between default events of any pair of obligors, or a conditional probability, cannot be "picked up" like that. Permissible values depend upon the standalone default probabilities of the two obligors[2]. Although this is not intuitive, it becomes obvious in certain cases. For example, if a counterparty never defaults (zero default probability) such as an Aaa guarantor, there is no correlation at all with any other risky counterparty. This implies that both the correlation and the joint default probability collapse to zero.

47.4 JOINT MIGRATION MATRICES

The transition matrices of rating agency data over long periods are unconditional on the state of the economy and reflect historical data. They provide the probabilities than an obligor in risk class i moves to risk class j during a certain period. Joint transition matrices provide the probability that a pair of obligors moves from one pair of credit states to another pair of credit states. Credit Metrics [37] derives the probability of joint migrations from the correlated asset returns of firms. This requires only the correlation structure of asset values, which Credit Metrics proxies by the correlations between equity returns. Joint migration matrices tabulate the final states of two obligors and assign probabilities to them. Because there are more final credit states when dealing with migration than default only, the construction of a joint migration matrix involves larger tables than default models. The principle is the same.

However, dealing with several credit states implies consistency constraints. When adjusting a transition probability within a transition matrix, all transitions still have to sum up to 1 along rows. If we shift a transition probability upward within a row due to correlation, some other transition probabilities will decline to comply with the same 100% total of transition probabilities along a same row. This implies that the correlation between migration probabilities varies along a single row.

This makes the usage of joint transition matrices more difficult to handle. One credit portfolio model, Credit Portfolio View, resolves the problem by making shift of conditional migration

---

2   It is easier to deal with correlations between continuous variables such as assets values or equity values, because they are observable, and because these constraints disappear. Whatever the values are, the correlation coefficient can take any value within the [−1, +1] range. Here, there are permissible ranges $[\rho_{min}(x, y), \rho_{max}(x, y)]$ of which boundary values depend upon the unconditional default probabilities of the two obligors (x and y).

probabilities proportional to the shift of the default probability from its standalone, or uncondi-tional value. The model refines the adjustment by making speculative grade firms more sensitive to the general factors that affect the default probabilities and the investment grade firms less sensitive. The interpretation of such a shift is that the specific risk, unrelated to general condi-tions, is higher for investment grade firms and lower for speculative grade firms.

These difficulties are expanded in the presentation of Credit Portfolio View in Section 12 dealing with Credit Portfolio Models. By contrast, the structural model of default provides both joint default probabilities and joint migration probabilities in a single step. Once the distribu-tion of asset value at horizon is constructed, we have all the probabilities of migrating to the default state and all probabilities of the values of the distance to default, which is a metric of the default probability, hence of the final credit states.

47.5 SIMULATION OF JOINT DEFAULTS AND MIGRATIONS

For implementation purposes, portfolio models revert to the simulation of asset values, as explained in the chapter on Monte Carlo simulations (Chapter 50), since correlations between asset values are either observed or modeled.

The vendors' models are described in a dedicated chapter (Chapter 51). Credit Metrics derives the correlations from those of equity returns, using a multifactor model of equity returns. By contrast, Moody's-KMV Portfolio Manager extracts the correlations from the modeled assets values under the option theoretic approach and uses a multifactor model with orthogonal factors for making modeled asset values dependent. Credit Portfolio View uses a different approach based on migration matrices and making them dependent on common fac-tors using lagged variables.

48

Example of Portfolio Loss Distribution

The purpose of this chapter is to determine a loss distribution for a simple portfolio of two obligors. This shows how correlations alter the loss distribution of portfolios. The measures of risk are the expected loss (EL), the loss volatility (LV), and VaR, which is the loss percentile value $L(\alpha)$ at confidence level α.

After providing the example data, Section 48.2 details the loss distribution with a two-obligor portfolio with independent individual risks. In Section 48.3, the defaults are dependent. The correlation between the individual credit risks of the two obligors is modeled by defining standalone default probability and one conditional probability in this example. In both cases, the loss statistics characteristics are the expected loss, the loss volatility loss percentiles and compared. The comparison follows in Section 48.4.

The next chapters model the dependency effect in the general case, using the techniques of the main credit portfolio models. The example in this chapter is used in the subsequent chapters on risk allocation (Chapters 53 and 54).

Contents

TABLE 48.1   Portfolio of two obligors

	Default probability	Exposure
A	7.00%	100
B	5.00%	50
ρ_{AB}	0% or 10.00%	

48.1 PORTFOLIO OF TWO OBLIGORS

The next sections develop the case of a simple portfolio with two obligors A and B subject to default risk. Table 48.1 describes the portfolio, with the unconditional (or standalone) default probabilities and the exposures of each. The loss given default is 100% of exposure. The loss distribution includes four points[1]. The tables provide the intermediate calculations of the corresponding probabilities using the "tree" form used previously for modeling joint probabilities (Chapter 31). Correlation implies that conditional default probabilities differ from the unconditional default probabilities. In order to calculate the probabilities of the four possible loss values, we use the structure of conditional loss probabilities. We consider two cases: the simple case of independency between credit events and the case where there is a positive correlation. The case of independence serves for comparing loss statistics under independence and dependence.

48.2 PORTFOLIO OF TWO INDEPENDENT OBLIGORS

The methodology for deriving the combinations of credit events and the loss distribution use the "tree" of credit events, and follows the same sequence of calculations as the example provided in the conditional probability chapter (Chapter 31), based on three inputs: the two standalone default probabilities and one conditional probability.

48.2.1 The Loss Distribution

The next tables (Tables 48.2–48.4) provide the joint probabilities of the four possible combinations of default and survival for two obligors. Note that this model is in default mode, which does not deal with migrations others than to the default state. Hence, there are losses if any of the two obligors default. In this reference case, the unconditional probabilities are equal to the unconditional probabilities. The matrix (Table 48.3) synthesizes all probabilities of the four possible cases.

For moving from probabilities assigned to each pair of credit events to loss distributions, we need to plug-in the loss under default, L, of each firm and calculate the loss for each of the four combinations of the possible credit states of the two firms.

Plotting the probabilities along the loss horizontal axis shows the loss distribution (Figure 48.1). It has the characteristic credit loss distribution elongated tail towards higher losses.

---

1 The four cases are: A only defaults, B only defaults, neither defaults, and both A and B default.

TABLE 48.2   Calculation of joint default probabilities of two independent obligors

Unconditional probabilities		Unconditional probabilities		Conditional P(B | A)		Joint probabilities
A		B				
D	7.00%	D	5.00%	5.00%		0.35%
		ND	95.00%	95.00%		6.65%
				100%	P(A)	
						7.00%
ND	93.00%	D	5.00%	5.00%		4.65%
		ND	95.00%	95.00%		88.35%
				100%	P(B)	
						93.00%

TABLE 48.3   Joint probability matrix: independent defaults

		A		
		Default	No default	
B	Default	0.35%	6.65%	7.00%
	No Default	4.65%	88.35%	93.00%
		5.00%	95.00%	100.00%

TABLE 48.4   Joint probability matrix: independent defaults

	Loss	Total probabilities	Cumulated probabilities
A & B default	150	0.350%	100.000%
A defaults	100	6.650%	99.650%
B defaults	50	4.650%	93.000%
None default	0	88.350%	88.350%

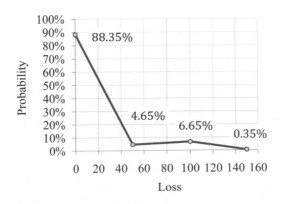

FIGURE 48.1   Loss distribution: independence case

48.2.2 The Loss Statistics

The calculation of the expected loss EL and of the loss volatility follows directly from the probabilities of all joint events and the corresponding values of portfolio loss. The EL is the weighted average of losses, using probabilities as weights. The loss volatility is the square root of the loss variance, which is the weighted average of the squares of deviation from EL, using joint probabilities as weights. Table 48.5 provides all the intermediate calculations.

Finally, the loss percentiles are cumulative probabilities. For instance, the loss percentile of 99.65% is such that $P(L \le 99.65\%)$. It matches a value of loss $L(99.65\%) = 100$. The maximum loss is 150.

TABLE 48.5   Loss statistics: independence case

	Loss (L)	Joint probabilities	Cumulative probabilities	Expected loss	Loss volatility of obligor i
A & B default	150	0.350%	100.000%	0.53	69.09
A defaults	100	6.650%	99.650%	6.65	544.65
B defaults	50	4.650%	93.000%	2.33	76.27
None default	0	88.350%	88.350%	0.00	79.74

EL	9.50
Loss volatility	27.74
Loss variance	769.75

48.3 DEPENDENT DEFAULT EVENTS

We proceed with the same portfolio as with the independence case, except that the correlation between default events is 10%. The conditional probabilities now differ from the unconditional default probabilities. It is possible to derive all joint event probabilities from the joint default probability as a starting point. Correlation increases the joint default probability, the loss volatility and makes the "fat tail" of the distribution thicker. The framework of calculations is the same as above. In addition, we extend them to show the relationships between standalone risk, measured by expected loss and loss volatility of each obligor, and the portfolio risk.

48.3.1 Calculation of Joint Default and Conditional Probabilities

Under dependence, the three inputs (the standalone default probabilities plus the default probability of B conditional on A defaulting), are sufficient for determining all other probabilities and the correlation between defaults (Table 48.6). Instead of assigning a value to $P(A = D \mid B = D)$, we can also start with the joint default probability of the correlated A and B default events as a function of a given correlation, for example 10%. The joint default probability $P(A, B)$ results from the general formula:

TABLE 48.6 Unconditional default probabilities, conditional probabilities and default correlation

	Unconditional probabilities		Unconditional probabilities		Conditional probabilities		Joint probabilities
A		B		P (B | A)			
D	7.00%	D	5.00%	12.9440%		0.9061%
		ND	95.00%	87.0560%		6.0939%
				100%	P(A)	7.0000%
ND	93.00%	D	5.00%	4.4021%		4.0939%
		ND	95.00%	95.5979%		88.9061%
				100%	P(B)	93.0000%

P(A, B) correlated	0.9061%
P(A, B) independent	0.3500%

D = default; ND = no default

$$P(A,B) = ab + \rho_{AB}\sqrt{a(1-a)\,b(1-b)}$$

$$P(A, B) = 7\% \times 5\% + 10\% \sqrt{[5\% \times (1 - 5\%) \times 7\% \times (1 - 7\%)]} = 0.9061\%$$

48.3.2 Loss Distribution

The process above results in the matrix cross-tabulating both entities' credit states, showing the joint probabilities (Table 48.7). The matrix margins summarize the column probabilities and the row probabilities, which equal the unconditional probabilities.

The same observation on single defaults applies to the independent and the correlation cases (Table 48.8). For instance, the default of A alone has a probability of 6.094%, whereas its unconditional default probability is 7%. Inputing the loss gives default of each exposure, the loss distribution, with cumulated probabilities (Figure 48.2).

TABLE 48.7 Joint probability matrix: default correlation = 10%

		A		
		Default	No default	Total
B	Default	0.9061%	4.0939%	5.0000%
	No default	6.0939%	88.9061%	95.0000%
	Total	7.0000%	93.0000%	100.00%

TABLE 48.8   Loss distribution: default correlation = 10%

	Probabilities	Cumulated probabilities
A & B default	0.906%	100.000%
A defaults	6.094%	99.094%
B defaults	4.094%	93.000%
None default	88.906%	88.906%

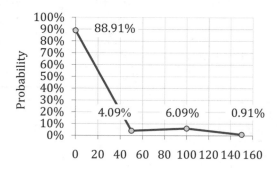

FIGURE 48.2   Loss distribution: default correlation = 10%

48.3.3 Loss Statistics

The calculations show that the expected loss EL remains the same as with the independence case, as expected since expectation is independent of correlation (Table 48.9). Loss volatility and loss percentiles, matching the same loss values, increase with the correlation. These calculations allow us to relate the portfolio loss statistics with standalone risk measures, such as individual expected loss and loss volatility, and to show the effect of diversification on these.

TABLE 48.9   Loss statistics: default correlation = 10%

	Loss	Total probabilities	Cumulated probabilities	Expected loss	Probability × (loss − EL)²
A & B default	150	0.906%	100.000%	1.36	178.86
A defaults	100	6.094%	99.094%	6.09	499.11
B defaults	50	4.094%	93.000%	2.05	67.15
None default	0	88.906%	88.906%	0.00	80.24

EL	9.50
Loss volatility	28.73
Loss variance	825.36

48.3.3.1 Expected Portfolio Loss and Standalone Expected Losses

The EL of the portfolio results directly from the distribution of losses for the entire portfolio made of two facilities:

$$EL = 150 \times 0.35\% + 100 \times 6.65\% + 50 \times 93\% + 0 \times 88.35\% = 9.50$$

It is easy to check that this is the sum of the standalone expected losses of each facility or:

$$EL(A) = 0 \times 100 + 7\% \times 100 = 7.00$$

$$EL(B) = 0 \times 50 + 5\% \times 50 = 2.50$$

$$EL(A + B) = 7.00 + 2.50 = 9.50$$

It is identical to the figure resulting from the direct calculation based on the loss distribution (Table 48.9). This value does not depend on the correlation.

48.3.3.2 Portfolio Loss Volatility and Standalone Loss Volatility

The portfolio loss volatility σ_p is:

$$\sigma_p^2 = (150 - 9.50)^2 \times 0.906\% + (100 - 9.50)^2 \times 6.094\% + (50 - 9.50)^2 \times 4.094\% + (0 - 9.50)^2 \times 88.906\% = 825.36$$

$$\sigma_p = 28.729$$

This value depends on loss correlation. If losses were independent, the portfolio loss variance would be the sum of individual facilities variances. The individual loss variance rate $\sigma = X\sqrt{[d1 - d)]}$, where X is the exposure, and d is the default probability and l the loss underdefault. Hence:

$$\sigma(A) = 100 \times \sqrt{[7\% \times (1 - 7\%)]} = 100 \times \sqrt{0.0651} = 25.515$$

$$\sigma(B) = 50 \times \sqrt{[5\% \times (1 - 5\%)]} = 50 \times \sqrt{0.0475} = 10.897$$

Under independence, the square root of the sum is $\sigma_p(A + B) = \sqrt{(25.515 + 10.897)} = \sqrt{36.412} = 27.74$, which is smaller than 28.729.

48.3.3.3 Portfolio Diversification

The EL is not sensitive to the diversification effect, but the risk reduction effect appears in σ_p since:

$$\sigma_p(A + B) = 28.729 < \sigma(A) + \sigma(B) = 25.515 + 10.897 = 36.412$$

The gain in loss volatility is a metric of the diversification effect: $36.412 - 27.744 = 8.668$. Since risk, measured by loss volatility, do not add arithmetically, allocating the overall portfolio risk to each obligor is an issue. The risk allocations are dealt with in the capital allocation chapters (section 13).

48.4 COMPARISON OF THE DEPENDENT AND THE INDEPENDENT CASES

Correlation implies the following changes:

- the joint default probability is now higher than the products of the unconditional (standalone) default probabilities of A and B
- the conditional default probabilities now differ from the unconditional (standalone) default probabilities.

As a result, the distribution fat tail gets thicker and the upward shift of joint default probability implies that other probabilities for other credit states get lower.

Full calculations are easy to conduct, as in the independent default case. Table 48.10 shows that the portfolio EL remains the same while the loss volatility increases with correlation. In addition, the probabilities of larger losses are larger than in the independent case, as expected (Table 48.10).

With this simple example, we address the issue of loss percentiles when no value of loss matches the percentile selected. Economic capital is a loss value matching a percentile minus the expected loss.

Consider the case of a single obligor, with A only in the portfolio. There are only two states: either A defaults with probability 7% or A survives with probability 93%. Assume that we look for a 5% loss percentile defined by $P[L \leq L(5\%)] = 5\%$. This probability is lower than the standalone default probability of A, which is 7%. In such a case, and, in general, when discrete values of a loss distribution do not match a selected loss percentile, how should we define the loss percentile?

We know that $P(\text{loss} \leq 100) = 7\%$ and that there is no loss value matching exactly 5%. The issue is to define the proper value of the loss that will not be exceeded in more than 5% of the cases. Being conservative implies considering the next upper loss. In this case the unique possibility is to use the 100, or A total loss. This is equivalent to matching the 5% loss percentile to the 7% loss percentile.

Adding B, we might also wonder how to define the 1% loss percentile, the loss that cannot be exceeded in more than 1% of all cases. Now, we have a choice of two values since we know that the loss is either 150 with probability 0.906% and 100 with probability 6.094%. Since can lose 100 with around 6% chance and we look for a value than cannot be exceeded with probability 1%, 100 is not acceptable. We have to revert again to the next upper loss, or 150. This loss will not be exceeded with a probability of 0.906%, therefore it will not be exceeded either with a probability of 1%.

TABLE 48.10 Comparison of loss statistics: independence versus 10% correlation

	Independence	Default correlation = 10%
Expected loss, EL^P	9.50	9.50
Portfolio loss volatility, σ^P	27.74	28.73

49

Analytical Loss Distributions

This chapter describes some analytical loss distributions under default mode only (no migrations).

The starting point is the simple case of independent losses. The portfolio distribution of the number of defaults is the well-known binomial distribution. The portfolio is granular and uniform: same exposure and same default probability for all obligors. The increase of loss volatility, in terms of the percentage of the total portfolio exposure, tends rapidly to zero when increasing the number of obligors.

Another distribution used builds on the structural model of default. It applies to a granular portfolio, with uniform size of exposure, uniform default probability and uniform correlation. The loss distribution is now dependent on the uniform correlation and is called "limit distribution." We introduce in the first step the standardized model of asset value, where all variables follow standard normal distributions, which can be correlated through a common factor. An important finding of such distributions, common to all full-blown models, is that the fat tail of the loss distribution is highly sensitive to the correlation between defaults.

Section 49.1 details the binomial distribution. Section 49.2 defines the asset value of a single obligor, considered as standalone (independently of any portfolio context) using the simplified "standardized" structural model, starting from asset value distribution, conditional on a single factor, which might represent the state of the economy. Using this standalone standardized model, we show how the Basel 2 stressed default probability is derived, explaining the core block of the risk weight functions of Basel 2. Section 49.3 details, in a sequence of simple steps, the limit distribution model, initially proposed by Vasicek[1].

---

1 See Vasicek, 2002 [76].

Contents

49.1 INDEPENDENT DEFAULT EVENTS: THE BINOMIAL DISTRIBUTION

When defaults events are independent, and have the same probability, the distribution of the number of defaults in a portfolio is the binomial distribution. Unfortunately, the binomial distribution cannot capture the effect of size discrepancies and of correlations. Nevertheless, the binomial distribution provides a good introduction to credit risk loss distribution. We use it here as a reference case and to show how diversification due to adding new facilities alters the distribution.

49.1.1 Simulating Increased Diversification with Loss Independence

Consider a portfolio with N loans of same maturity, each one with same exposure X net of recovery (or same LGD). Considering a unique horizon equal to the common maturity allows considering the loss distribution in default mode only. The default probability is identical for all obligors. This default probability is equal to the expected loss, if loss given defaults are also identical and equal to 1. The weights of each loan are identical.

Each random default is a Bernoulli variable with value 1 in the event of default, with probability α, and value 0 in the event of no default, with a probability $1 - \alpha$. It is the indicator function: $\mathbf{1}$ (default) = 1 under default and 0 if no default. The expected individual loss for obligor "i" is:

$$E(L_i) = X\alpha + 0(1 - \alpha) = X\alpha$$

The individual borrower's loss variance is $X^2\alpha(1 - \alpha)$. The number of defaults is the sum of all random individual defaults. The distribution of number of defaults is the binomial distribution.

The number of defaults has an expected value $N\alpha$. The portfolio number of defaults has a variance equal to the sum of all individual default variances, since defaults are independent of $N\alpha(1 - \alpha)$ or N multiplied by individual default variance. The portfolio loss variance is $N \times X^2\alpha(1 - \alpha)$ and the total portfolio loss volatility is the square root, or $X\sqrt{N\alpha(1 - \alpha)}$.

With N exposures, of which unit value size is $X = 2$, and $\alpha = 10\%$, the unit variance in value is $10\%(1 - 10\%) \times 2^2 = 0.36$ and the total variance is $0.36N$. The loss distribution volatility in value is the square root, or $\sqrt{(0.36N)}$. Note that with a large number of obligors, the binomial distribution would tend to the normal distribution under independence. In a later section, we will see how the limit normal distribution for large uniform granular portfolios behaves when there is a positive uniform correlation.

49.1.2 The Effect of Diversification

It follows that each additional exposure adds the same constant amount to the portfolio loss variance $X^2\alpha(1 - \alpha) = 0.36$. The loss volatility increases with the square root of N, less than the loss variance that is proportional to N. The additional volatility is the difference between the loss volatility with $N + 1$ exposures and the loss volatility with N exposures.

The behavior of the same statistics measured as percentages of the total exposure, or NX, differs. The portfolio loss variance in percentage of total exposure is:

$$[N \times X^2\alpha(1 - \alpha)]/[NX] = X\alpha(1 - \alpha)$$

This is a constant value since the unit exposure X and α are both constant. The ratio of the portfolio loss variance to the total exposure is proportional to the uniform exposure X. This value is $2 \times 10\% (1 - 10\%) = 18\%$. The ratio of the portfolio loss volatility to the total exposure is:

$$\frac{\text{portfolio loss volatility}}{N\,X} = \frac{\sqrt{N\,X\alpha(1-\alpha)}}{N\,X} = \sqrt{\frac{\alpha(1-\alpha)}{N}}$$

Increasing the number of obligors reduces the loss volatility without affecting the mean loss. The portfolio loss volatility, in percentage of total exposure, decreases with $\sqrt{N}$ and converges to zero when N increases.

In the sample calculation below, N increases from 1 to 10,000, with the same other parameters as above. Table 49.1 shows the variance and the volatility, in value and in percentage of total exposure, when increasing the number of obligors N from 1 up to 10,000. The ratio of variance to exposure remains constant at 18%. The additional volatility in value is also constant but it decreases in percentage (Figure 49.1).

This confirms the well-known result that the loss volatility in percentage of portfolio size tends towards zero and that the portfolio loss converges to its expected value. In the section on the limit distribution (Section 49.3), we examine what happens when the correlation is positive.

TABLE 49.1 Variation of portfolio loss variance and volatility with diversification and size in $ value and in % of portfolio size

N	Variance in value	Volatility in value	Variance/exposure	Volatility/exposure
1	0.36	0.60	18%	30.00%
2	0.72	0.85	18%	21.21%
10	3.60	1.90	18%	9.49%
100	36.00	6.00	18%	3.00%
200	72.00	8.49	18%	2.12%
1000	360.00	18.97	18%	0.95%
5000	1800.00	42.43	18%	0.42%
10000	3600.00	60.00	18%	0.30%

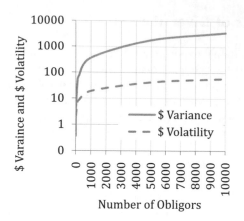

FIGURE 49.1 Variation of portfolio loss variance and volatility in value with diversification

49.2 THE "STANDARDIZED" STANDALONE STRUCTURAL MODEL

In this section, we consider a single obligor as a standalone entity. There is no portfolio effect and the obligor's risk is independent of any factor. The default probability is unconditional. It could represent the default probability through-the-cycle of that obligor, for example.

We start from the standard normal variable representing asset value. The default probability, α, is the probability that the asset value falls below a threshold $A(\alpha)$ depending on α, or the α quantile of the asset value distribution. Using a standard normal distribution of asset value, the default point of asset value is the inverse distribution matching the default probability (Figure 49.2).

$$P[A \leq A(\alpha)] = \alpha = \Phi[A(\alpha)]$$

$$A(\alpha) = \Phi^{-1}(\alpha)$$

This relation allows mapping the $A(\alpha)$ triggering default to various confidence levels representing the default probabilities. Extending the spectrum of credit states to rating classes, we can find probabilities that the obligor belongs to any rating class. This simplified version of the structural model of default is called subsequently the "standardized structural default" model because it relies on a standardized normal distribution asset value at horizon.

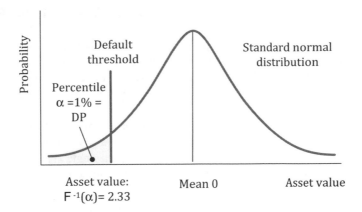

FIGURE 49.2   Standardized asset model

For example, if the default probability is 1%, then $A(\alpha = 1\%) = \Phi^{-1}(1\%) = -2.33$. The probabilities matching a rating class are usually mapped to each rating class, for example, average long-term historical frequencies of defaults from Moody's scale. For the Aaa rating class, we use the Basel 2 minimum default probability for non-sovereign obligors instead of the Moody's statistic. For defining a default threshold, we use the α loss percentiles matching each rating class. Table 49.2 shows the default thresholds of asset values for each rating class, derived from the structural standardized model of default and matching the inverse normal standard distribution. All threshold values for default are negative since the percentiles match negative variations of the standardized asset value.

TABLE 49.2   Default thresholds of asset value for each rating class

Rating class	α	$\Phi^{-1}(\alpha)$
Aaa, Basel 2 (1)	0.03%	−3.432
Aa	0.05%	−3.291
A	0.08%	−3.156
Baa	0.20%	−2.878
Ba	1.80%	−2.097
B	8.30%	−1.385
Default	20.00%	−0.842

[a]For Moody's the annualized default probability is 0%, but Basel 2 imposes a minimum threshold of 0.03%.

49.2.1 A Single Obligor Dependent on the State of the Economy

In general, the obligor credit standing depends on general economic conditions materialized by a single factor. We find out the default probability from the standardized model of default adding a correlation with the single factor. The main issue to be addressed is: what is the default probability of the obligor conditional on a given state of the economy? This default probability is a conditional percentile.

Assume that there is a uniform correlation ρ across asset values of each pair of obligors. The correlation results from the common dependence on the state of the economy, which is represented by a single common factor Z. When considering a single obligor, the asset value A depends on two independent variables, normal standard, the common factor and an independent random specific risk.

$$A = \rho Z + \sqrt{(1 - \rho^2)} X$$

A and Z follow a standard bivariate distribution with correlation ρ if, and only if, both Z and X are independent normal standard variables. Moreover, for one obligor, the unconditional long-term default probability d is given, and the unconditional default point of asset value, $A(d)$, follows. The default point $A(d)$ for the asset value such that $P([A \leq = A(d)] = d$ and the relation between d and $A(d)$ is $A(d) = \Phi^{-1}(d)$.

The specific risk X is:

$$X = \frac{A - \rho Z}{\sqrt{1 - \rho^2}}$$

Note that specific risk X is not different from the standardized value of A and follows a standard normal distribution $\Phi(X)$ with mean 0 and standard deviation 1. We retain this second view in subsequent developments. Furthermore, when the correlation and Z are given, A is a monotonous increasing function of X. For the particular percentile value $A(d)$ of A, there is a corresponding value $X(d)$, from the above equation. Because X is always standard normal, we translate all conditions on A into conditions on X.

The default probability is always defined as the asset value being below the default point of A. In what follows, we consider two cases. The standalone default probability and default points are d and $A(d)$, respectively. The default probability and asset value conditional on the state of the economy are called $\alpha(Z)$ and $A(Z)$, respectively. The default condition is always, either one of the unconditional condition or the conditional condition on Z:

$$d = P[A \leq A(d)]$$

$$\alpha(Z) = P\{[\alpha(Z)] \leq A[\alpha(Z)]\}$$

The second condition is a conditional percentile. The factor Z is the conditioning variable. When $Z = z$ fixed, A is conditional on Z. For making explicit the conditioning role of Z, we use a particular value z of Z in subsequent developments. The asset value distribution is normal but non-standard with mean ρZ and standard deviation $\sqrt{(1 - \rho^2)}$, or $N[\rho z, \sqrt{(1 - \rho^2)}]$, with mean $\mu = \rho z$ and standard deviation $\sigma = \sqrt{(1 - \rho^2)}$. The standardized asset value X follows $\Phi\{[A - \rho z]/\sqrt{(1 - \rho^2)}\}$.

The default probability d is defined by unconditional values:

$$d = P[X \leq X(d)]$$

The conditional default probability $\alpha(Z)$ is defined by:

$$\alpha(Z) = P[X(Z) \leq X(d)]$$

49.2.2 The Asset Value and Default Probability Conditional on the State of the Economy

When we make the asset value dependent on Z, both the asset value and the default probability become conditional on the state of the economy. The default point remains $A(d)$. But the conditional asset value on Z, $A(z)$, now follows a normal and non-standard distribution $N[\rho z, \sqrt{(1 - \rho^2)}]$ conditional on z. On the other hand, the standardized asset value X follows a normal standard condition $\Phi(0,1)$.

When $Z = z$ increases, the default point $A(d)$ is unchanged, but the normal distribution of asset value $A(z)$ shifts to the right, because its expectation increases, when the correlation is positive. The conditional default probability is defined by the condition:

$$\alpha(z) = P[A(z) \leq A(d)] = P[X(z) \leq X(d)]$$

The two main issues of interest are:

1 finding the conditional default probability $\alpha(z)$ conditional on the state of the economy z
2 conversely, finding the value of Z that matches a particular value of the conditional default probability.

49.2.3 The Default Probability Conditional on The State of the Economy

Using the monotonous increasing relation between A and X, given Z and the correlation:

$$\alpha(z) = P[A \leq A(Z)] = P[X(Z) \leq X(d)]$$

Using the definition of $X(d)$:

$$X(d) = \frac{\Phi^{-1}(d) - \rho Z}{\sqrt{1 - \rho^2}}$$

We find the conditional default probability on Z as the percentile of X, or $P[X(Z) \leq X(d)]$:

$$\alpha(z) = \Phi\left[\frac{\Phi^{-1}(d) - \rho Z}{\sqrt{1 - \rho^2}}\right]$$

As an example, we start from a range of values for the state of the economy.

We use the standardized value X, from the formula $X = (A - \rho Z)/\sqrt{(1 - \rho^2)}$. If A were unconditional and standard normal, the default point would be, for a given percentile $\alpha = 1\%$, $A(1\%) = -2.3263$. Next, Z changes, keeping the unconditional default point constant. The default point for A remains $A = -2.3263$. Using $Z = 2$, the conditional default point of X is:

$$(-2.3263 - 30\% \times 2)/0.9539 = -3.0676$$

The corresponding conditional default probability is 0.108%, much lower than the original 1%.

Table 49.3 shows what happens when Z varies between -2 and $+2$ by steps of one. The table shows the default points of both the unconditional asset value A, which is constant, and of the standardized asset value X, conditional on Z, which depends on Z. The conditional default probability derives from either variable, and is identical, provided that we use the correct normal distribution of asset value, non-standard or standardized. The default probability is the 1% asset value percentile.

The parameters of the normal distribution of the asset value are $E(A) = \rho z$ and $\sigma(A) = \sqrt{(1 - \rho^2)}$. $E(A)$ increases with Z and $\sigma(A)$ remains constant. The default point $A(d)$ remains constant. Since the distribution of the asset value A shifts to the right and the default point remains constant, the conditional default probability declines. Given the default point of asset value, the conditional default probability $\alpha(z)$ is the normal inverse of its default point $A(d)$ calculated with the distribution of A, $N^{-1}[\rho z, \sqrt{(1 - \rho^2)}]$.

When Z increases from 0 to 2, the mean of the distribution of the asset value shifts to the right, increasing from 0 to 0.6 (dashed line) (Figure 49.3). The calculation involves calculating the normal inverse of -2.3263 using the corresponding densities $N(0, 0.9539)$ and $N(0.6, 0.9539)$. Since the same default point -2.3263 applies for both curves, the default probability is lower when Z increases, making the density shift to the right. The conclusion is that an increase of Z corresponds to an improved credit standing and upgraded economic conditions.

TABLE 49.3   **Default point, specific risk and default probability conditional on the state of the economy**

ρ	0%	30%	30%	30%	30%	30%
z	0	-2.0	-1.0	0.0	1.0	2.0
α	1%	1%	1%	1%	1%	1%
$E(A) = \rho z$	0	-0.6	-0.3	0	0.3	0.6
$\sigma(A) = \sqrt{(1 - \rho^2)}$	1.0000	0.9539	0.9539	0.9539	0.9539	0.9539
Z	0	-2.0	-1.0	0.0	1.0	2.0
Default point of A	-2.3263	-2.3263	-2.3263	-2.3263	-2.3263	-2.3263
Conditional DP(z)	1.00%	3.517%	1.683%	0.737%	0.295%	0.108%
Default point of X	-2.3263	-1.8097	-2.1242	-2.4387	-2.7532	-3.0676
Conditional DP(z)	1.000%	3.517%	1.683%	0.737%	0.295%	0.108%

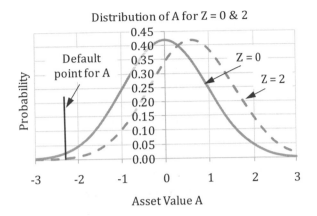

FIGURE 49.3   Asset value distributions: quantile 1%, Z equals 0 and 2

Using instead the normal standard distribution of X, the distribution of X does not change with Z. Instead, when z increases, the default point shifts to the left, keeping other inputs, correlation and long-term default probability constant. This left shift of the default point makes the conditional default probability decline. Again, when Z shifts from 0 to 2, a higher Z makes the default point shift to the left, showing again that the default probability is lower (Figure 49.4).

The figure relates the state of economy to the conditional probability. This conditional default probability $\alpha(Z)$ varies inversely with Z (Figure 49.5).

The example is extended by allowing both Z and the correlation to vary (Figure 49.6). The conditional probability varies inversely with Z and increases with the correlation. The upper curve corresponds to a 30% correlation, the middle curve to a 20% correlation, and the lower curve to a 10% correlation. The unconditional default probability is 1%. The default probabilities with Z positive are close to zero and are not shown.

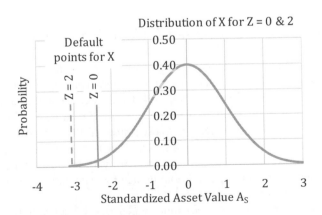

FIGURE 49.4   Left shift of conditional default point of Z

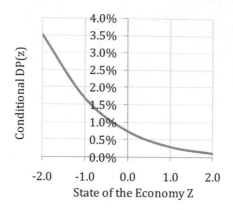

FIGURE 49.5 Conditional default probability on the state of the economy

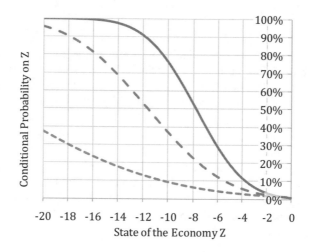

FIGURE 49.6 Conditional default probability when correlation varies

49.2.4 Application: The Stressed Default Probability under Basel 2

Basel 2 uses risk weight applicable to exposure using "through-the-cycle," or unconditional long-term default probabilities, derived from mapping internal ratings to such annualized default probabilities. This long-term PD is supposed to be fixed since it matches a long-term state of the economy. The risk weights apply to the exposure less recoveries or LGD.

The rationale for deriving risk weights is to use a stressed PD instead of the long-term PD. The formula for risk weight has a core module that relies on the stressed default probability assigned to the facility. For stressing the default probability, Basel 2 uses the single factor model as above and stresses downward the conditioning factor Z. The only difference is that Basel 2 specifies the Z percentile for stressing Z.

Using the subscript "B2" for stressed values under Basel 2 rules, the conditional default probability is $\alpha_{B2}(Z) < d$, d being the unconditional default probability. Let us call the Z percentile $Z(\beta)$, or the value of Z matching this percentile β. By definition of the percentile β: $\beta = P\{Z \le Z(\beta)\} = \Phi[Z(\beta)]$ and $Z(\beta) = \Phi^{-1}(\beta)$.

Basel 2 sets a confidence level of 99.9%, stressing the conditional default probability. The stressed Z value shifted downward matches the confidence level 0.1%. The percentile 0.1% for Z is such that $P[Z \le Z(0.1\%)] = 0.1\%$. The Basel 2 confidence level, 99.9%, matches the 0.1% Z percentile. From the standard normal distribution:

$$Z(0.1\%) = \Phi^{-1}(0.1\%) = -3.0676$$

From the stressed Z value, the stressed conditional default probability follows, as above:

$$\alpha(Z = z_{B2}) = \Phi(X_{B2}) = \Phi\{[A(d) - \rho z]/\sqrt{(1 - \rho^2)}\}$$

With $d = 1\%$ and zero correlation, $A(d) = -2.3263$. The conditional default point of the standardized asset value X is $X(z) = [A(d) - \rho z]/\sqrt{(1 - \rho^2)}$:

$$X(-3.0676) = [-2.3263 - 30\% \times -3.0676]/\sqrt{(1 - 30\%^2)} = -1.4740$$

The stressed default probability is:

$$\alpha_{B2}[Z(0.1\%)] = \Phi(-1.4740) = 7.025\%$$

The calculations comparing the unstressed and the Basel 2 stressed cases are shown in Table 49.4 and Figure 49.7, using a correlation of 30% and the standardized value of asset value A, or X. Note that Basel 2 specifies the correlation to be used.

Basel 2 expresses Z as the inverse function of the percentile or $\Phi^{-1}(\beta)$. Similarly, the default point of asset value is $A(d) = \Phi^{-1}(d)$. Replacing, the general equation providing the conditional quantile for Basel 2:

$$\alpha_{B2} = \Phi\left(X \le \frac{\Phi^{-1}(d) - \rho \Phi^{-1}(\beta)}{\sqrt{1 - \rho^2}}\right)$$

In our notations, the percentile β is 0.01%. The Basel 2 formula uses a percentile 99.9%. Changing β by $1 - \beta = 99.9\%$, results in values of Z matching β and $1 - \beta$ that are opposite

TABLE 49.4 Calculations comparing the unstressed and the Basel 2 stressd cases

Basel 2 Stressed DP	$Z = 0, \rho = 0$	Z_{B2}
ρ	0%	30%
Z	0	-3.0676
Unconditional DP	1%	1%
$E(A) = \rho z$	0	-0.92028
$\sigma(A) = \sqrt{(1 - \rho^2)}$	1.0000	0.9539
$A = \Phi^{-1}(d)$	-2.3263	-2.3263
Default point of X	-2.3263	-1.4740
Conditional stressed $DP(z_{B2})$	1.000%	7.025%

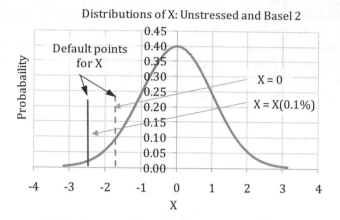

FIGURE 49.7 Standardized asset value distribution: default probability 1%, Z equals 0 and 2

because the normal distribution is symmetric: $Z(\beta) = -Z(1 - \beta)$, or $\Phi^{-1}(\beta) = -\Phi^{-1}(1 - \beta)$. Such change serves only for showing up $(1 - \beta)$ as in the Basel 2 formula. The changes results in a formula identical to that of the Basel 2 reference document.

$$\alpha(Z_{B2}) = \Phi\{[\Phi^{-1}(PD) + \rho\Phi^{-1}(0.999)]/\sqrt{(1 - \rho^2)}\}$$

In Basel 2, the risk weight formula multiplies this conditional quantile by the loss given default. Furthermore, Basel 2 adds a correlation and a maturity adjustment for deriving the full formula for the risk weights. But the core module of the formula is the above one.

49.3 MODELING DEFAULTS IN A UNIFORM PORTFOLIO: THE LIMIT DISTRIBUTION

The limit distribution refers to the loss distribution of a granular portfolio widely diversified, with a uniform correlation resulting from systematic risk due to a single common factor. Each obligor is characterized by a standard normal asset value and a default threshold.

49.3.1 The Uniform Granular Portfolio

The default probability is identical for all obligors and all pairs of asset values have the same uniform correlation. This default probability is equal to the expected loss, if loss given defaults are also identical and equal to 1. The weights of each loan are identical. This is a limit case, but a proxy for a widely diversified granular portfolio of which exposures and correlations are similar. Loans are assumed to have same maturity M. This simplifies the modeling of the loss distribution, since we stay in default mode, ignoring migrations if horizon extends beyond maturity.

Such restrictive assumptions can be relaxed by using Monte Carlo simulation. For example, single factor models allow generating correlated asset values without making any restrictive assumptions on the default point, or default probability, and size of exposure. The Cholesky decomposition can impose a variance-covariance structure on obligor's asset values. In the next chapter on modeling loss distribution for credit portfolio (Chapter 50), the equal exposure and equal default probability assumptions are relaxed.

The case of uniform correlation is of interest for "homogeneous portfolios" with same default probability and uniform asset correlation in the same credit class, such as Basel 2 pools of loans. The portfolio is made of N credits, with subscript i, with all asset values A_i following bivariate normal distributions correlated with a single factor Z, with a uniform correlation ρ:

$$A_i = \rho Z + \sqrt{1 - \rho^2}\, X_i$$

X_i is the specific risk of the obligor "i," equal to the standardized normal asset value variable. For A_i and Z to follow a bivariate distribution, Z and all X_i have to be independent standard normal variables.

Each individual loss is l_i. The individual exposures l_i are equal to a common value l, equal to the exposure multiplied by the percentage loss under default. Default is a Bernoulli variable 1_i with value 1 when an obligor defaults and 0 under no default, or an indicator function. Using the indicator function of default allows expressing the random individual loss as $1_i l$. The random portfolio loss L_P is the summation of losses of individual obligors, or $L_P = \sum_{i=1,N} 1_i l$.

The individual probability of default is equal to d. Each individual loss $1_i l$ has an expected value for a single loan equal to default probability times the loss:

$$E(1_i l) = dl + (1 - d)\, 0 = dl$$

The portfolio loss L_P has an expectation equal to the sum of the expectations of individual loans: $E(L_P) = \sum_{i=1,N} E(1_i l) = Ndl$. The portfolio loss, in percentage of total portfolio exposure, is l_P. It is the ratio of total portfolio loss divided by the total of individual exposures $\sum_{i=1,N} l = Nl$. The expected value of the portfolio loss percentage is:

$$E(l_P) = \sum_{i=1,N} E(1_i l)/Nl = Ndl/Nl = d$$

If the default probability depends on the state of the economy, all conditional default probabilities are equal to the same α, conditional on the state of the economy, and named $\alpha(Z)$.

$$E(l_P \mid Z) = \alpha(Z)$$

The portfolio loss is equal to conditional default probability on the state of the economy. It is random because asset values depend on Z, and any value of asset value lower than the default point matching the unconditional default probability triggers default. As shown above, conditional default probability varies inversely with the state of the economy.

49.3.2 Modeling Defaults under the Structural Model

The basic idea of the limit distribution model portfolio is that the expected value of the portfolio loss percentage converges to the conditional default probability when the number of obligors is large. Therefore, the percentage portfolio loss sums up to the modeling of the expected portfolio loss, in percentage of total loss, or to modeling distribution of the conditional default probability.

If all individual loans have the same loss under default and the same default probability, and if all losses were independent, the distribution of the portfolio loss would be the binomial distribution with parameter equal to the default probability. It would converge, following the central limit theorem, to a normal distribution as the portfolio size increased.

Because defaults are not independent, the conditions of the central limit theorem are not met and the limit distribution when the number of assets, N, grows is not normal. The main issue addressed by the limit distribution model is to find out the portfolio loss in percentage of portfolio exposure as a function of the unconditional default probability d and the uniform correlation, conditional on Z.

Since the correlation of asset values is uniform, the decomposition of specific risk between systematic and specific risk is identical for each firm. All obligors have the same default point and default probability. The relationships defining the percentile matching default probability and default points are identical to those above.

The unconditional default probability is d, equal to 1%, and matches a default point for the asset value, under independence and correlation zero: $A(d) = \Phi(1\%) = -2.3263$. The conditional default probability, $\alpha(Z)$, varies inversely with Z and is:

$$\alpha(z) = \Phi\left(\frac{A - \rho Z}{\sqrt{1 - \rho^2}}\right)$$

The conditional probability declines when $Z = z$ increases.

49.3.3 The Limit Distribution

The key point is that the portfolio loss, in percentage of portfolio exposure, given Z, converges, by the law of large numbers, to its expectation $\alpha(Z)$, conditional on Z, when N tends towards infinity.

Assuming that the default probability is $\alpha(z)$ given $Z = z$ is equivalent to assuming that the diversification of the portfolio is large enough for the default probability to become almost certain. This implies that the portfolio loss volatility is entirely due to its sensitivity to the factor and that the specific risk tends towards zero. In that case, there is a one-to-one correspondence between the portfolio loss and the z value.

The portfolio loss distribution, or l_p, is the same as $\alpha(Z)$ because the portfolio loss in percentage terms is equal to the default probability. This unique distribution depends on the probability distribution of $\alpha(z)$. Since the conditional default probability varies inversely with z:

$$P\{\alpha(z) \leq \alpha\} = P\{Z \geq z(\alpha)\} = P\{Z \leq -z(\alpha)\}$$

The value $z(\alpha)$ is the particular value of z that matches a value of the conditional default probability α. For writing this last inequality, the symmetry property of the standard normal distribution is used:

$$P\{Z \geq z\} = P\{Z \leq -z\}$$

Since the portfolio loss, in percentage of exposure, is equal to the conditional default probability $\alpha(z)$, the probability that l_p remains below or equal to a particular value x defines the percentile x such that $P\{l_p \le x\}$. The portfolio loss percentile x is:

$$P\{l_p \le x\} = P\{\alpha(z) \le x\} = P\{Z \ge z\} = P\{Z \le -z(x)\}$$

$$P\{Z \ge z\} = P\{Z \le -z(x)\} = \Phi^{-1}[-z(x)]$$

The default probability conditional on Z uses $\alpha(z) = \Phi[(A - \rho Z)/\sqrt{(1-\rho^2)}]$ with $A = \Phi^{-1}(d)$ and $Z = z$:

$$\alpha(z) = \Phi\left\{\frac{\Phi^{-1}(d) - \rho z}{\sqrt{1-\rho^2}}\right\}$$

Replacing $\alpha(z)$ by l, the value $z(x)$ of Z follows:

$$z = \frac{\Phi^{-1}(d)\sqrt{1-\rho^2} - \Phi^{-1}\left[\alpha(z)\right]}{\rho}$$

The value of $\alpha(z)$ is defined by $P\{\alpha(z) \le x\} = \Phi(x)$, and $\Phi^{-1}[\Phi(x)] = x$, which allows replacing $\Phi^{-1}[\alpha(z)]$ by $\Phi^{-1}(x)$.

$$z = \frac{\Phi^{-1}(d)\sqrt{1-\rho^2} - \Phi^{-1}(x)}{\rho}$$

Since $P(l_p \le x) = P[Z \le -Z(x)] = \Phi^{-1}[-Z(x)]$, the distribution of the portfolio loss distribution is the inverse standard normal distribution of $-Z$:

$$P(l_P \le x) = \Phi^{-1}\left[\frac{\Phi^{-1}(x) - \Phi^{-1}(d)\sqrt{1-\rho^2}}{\rho}\right]$$

The last equation provides the portfolio loss conditional on Z, given the correlation and the unconditional default probability d. Allowing x to vary between 0 and 1 generates the full distribution.

49.3.4 Application: Finding the Factor Value Matching a Given Portfolio Loss Percentile

Assume that the default probability of any one loan is 5%, and that the uniform correlation is 30%. The starting point is $\alpha(z) = P(l \le x) = 1\%$. A first step calculates z and the conditional default probability $\alpha(z)$, which equals the portfolio loss percentage x. The second step calculates the probability that such loss percentage is lower or equal to some threshold x. The input values are $d = 5\%$, $x = 1\%$ and $\rho = 30\%$. The next equation provides the value of z matching the conditional probability 1%.

$$z = \frac{\Phi^{-1}(d)\sqrt{1-\rho^2} - \Phi^{-1}(x)}{\rho}$$

Replacing, we find:

$$z = \frac{\Phi^{-1}(5\%)\sqrt{1-30\%^2} - \Phi^{-1}(1\%)}{30\%}$$

Using $\Phi^{-1}(5\%) = -1.6449$ and $\Phi^{-1}(1\%) = -2.3263$, we find $z = 6.6983$. We can check the formula below provides the correct conditional probability:

$$\alpha(z) = \Phi\left\{\frac{\Phi^{-1}(d) - \rho z}{\sqrt{1-\rho^2}}\right\}$$

The formula provides 1%, which matches $P(l \leq x) = 1\%$. The second step derives the probability that the percentage portfolio loss is lower or equal to 1%. The formula for this percentile is:

$$P(l_P \leq x) = \Phi^{-1}\left[\frac{\Phi^{-1}(x) - \Phi^{-1}(d)\sqrt{1-\rho^2}}{\rho}\right]$$

Replacing with the above inputs:

$$P(l_P \leq 1\%) = \Phi^{-1}\left[\frac{\Phi^{-1}(1\%) - \Phi^{-1}(5\%)\sqrt{1-30\%^2}}{30\%}\right]$$

The result is 2.78%. In other words, the probability that the portfolio loss does not exceed $x = 1\%$ is 2.78%.

For generalizing, both the percentage portfolio loss x and the correlation are allowed to vary. The fraction of portfolio loss varies between 0.20% and 20%, and the correlation has three values: 10%, 20% and 30%. Figure 49.8 shows the cumulative probability above. We can check that the probability of having a loss lower than 4% is 46.65% with correlation 30%, 36.23% with correlation 20% and 16.59% with correlation 10%. In other words, the probability of losing 4% of the portfolio increases with correlation.

This is in line with expectations. The loss percentiles are higher when correlation increases, on the left-hand side of the graph. The ranking of curves is reversed when we reach a higher threshold. This is a mechanical result. If small losses are more likely, then large losses have to be less likely for the sum of probability of all losses remaining equal to 1.

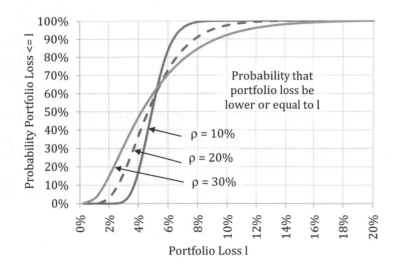

FIGURE 49.8 Portfolio loss distributions in percentage of exposure

50

Simulation of Credit Portfolio Loss Distributions

This chapter explains and illustrates the Monte Carlo simulation methodology along two main lines of credit portfolio modeling: simulations of correlated asset values are based on the structural model of default and simulations of dependent times to default of a portfolio of obligors. The main purposes of this chapter are twofold:

- illustrating the essentials of simulations along different modeling lines
- demonstrating the high sensitivity of the shape of the simulated distributions of defaults to dependency.

Since the main purpose is to focus on the effect of dependencies across defaults on the loss distribution, it is sufficient to use a granular uniform portfolio (same default probability, same exposure, and same correlation). The sample simulations rely on a single factor model for generating the dependency between the firms within the sample fictitious portfolio. Note that, using the same principles, we relax some of those assumptions in Chapter 57 on portfolio analysis and reporting.

Section 50.1 describes the main principles for conducting credit simulations. Sections 50.2 and 50.3 describe the simulation algorithm for the standardized asset value model of default and for the intensity model of default. The distribution of defaults when running multiple simulations is described in Section 50.2, when allowing correlation to vary. This chapter should be completed by the review of credit portfolio models that follows in the next chapter (Chapter 51).

Contents

50.1 PRINCIPLES OF SAMPLE SIMULATIONS

The major credit portfolio models use three types of simulations:

- asset value simulations dependent on a single factor, along the principles of the "structural default model" implemented by Moody's-KMV Portfolio Manager
- simulation of times to default dependent on a single factor, along the lines of the "reduced form" model of default detailed originally by Li [48].

This chapter explains the algorithm of simulations, leaving aside econometric simulations of default rates of portfolio segment as modeled in Credit Portfolio View, which are expanded in the next chapter.

The simulation algorithms used here are simplified. All firms depend on a single common factor. There is a common block for simulations in the methodology used for making asset values or times to default of the various firms within a portfolio dependent on a common factor.

For asset value simulation, the core block is a one-factor model applied to the asset values Y_i of each obligor, where the common factor Z represents the state of the economy, or general risk, and X_i is the specific risk. The subscript "i" refers to each obligor within the portfolio or to a homogenous segment within a portfolio. We use the simplified standardized asset value model, where asset values are standard normal and the default point is defined according to the default probability of each firm.

$$Y_i = \rho Z + \sqrt{1-\rho^2}\, X_i$$

The appropriate technique for correlating the standardized asset values of firms is the Cholesky decomposition. All asset values of all obligors within the portfolio should depend on the same common factor Z. Hence the normal standard variable Z is identical for all lines of the portfolio. The simulation of dependent asset values is an intermediate step for triggering default by comparing the simulated asset value with the default threshold. Default is modeled by a dummy variable, 1 being default when asset value is lower than the default point and 0 being no default. The count of defaults within the portfolio is the sum of the dummy variables representing default.

For portfolio simulations based on the reduced model of times to default exponentially distributed, the appropriate methodology is the copula approach. The dependency is obtained by generating dependent uniform standard variables. One variable represents the single common factor of all firms within the portfolio. The second dependent uniform variable is obtained by plugging in the dependency structure using:

$$V = \Phi\left[\rho\Phi^{-1}(U) + \sqrt{(1-\rho^2)}\,\Phi^{-1}(\alpha)\right]$$

The second uniform variable is specific to each firm. The "target" dependent variables, for any pair of firms within the portfolio, are times to default "TD," obtained by using the inverse of the exponential distribution with arguments U and V. Because we deal with a portfolio, the dependency of times to default is obtained by making the first uniform variable common to all lines of the portfolio. The variable U plays the role of the common factor. Differentiated and dependent times to default of all obligors are obtained by generating a specific second uniform variable V_i for each obligor. Times to default have to be compared to a given horizon, for example one year, for triggering default. If the simulated time to default is lower than a year, a default is triggered, materialized by a dummy variable taking the value 1. If not, there is no default, and the dummy variable is equal to zero. The count of defaults within the portfolio is the sum of the dummy variables representing default.

In the general case, firms might differ by exposure size, default probability and correlation with the rest of the portfolio. In our simulations, correlation is uniform, and we also use a common default probability and a common exposure. These two last assumptions are easily relaxed.

50.2 MONTE CARLO SIMULATIONS OF DEFAULT EVENTS BASED ON THE STRUCTURAL MODEL OF DEFAULT

The example uses the standardized normal distribution of distance to default model, given the default probability of obligors. The model operates in default mode only, and exposures are at book value. There is a uniform preset asset correlation and a uniform preset default probability.

50.2.1 Asset Distribution and Default Probability

We use the standardized normal distance to default model, considering that the default probability embeds all information relevant to default and on unobservable asset values. Considering a single firm "i" with the default probability α_i, there is a default point $A(\alpha_i)$ of the random asset value A_i such that the default probability is α_i. If Φ is the cumulated standardized normal distribution, then:

$$\Phi[A(\alpha_i)] = \alpha_i, \text{ or } A(\alpha_i) = \Phi^{-1}(\alpha_i)$$

Φ^{-1} is the normal inverse distribution. The normal inverse distribution provides the given threshold $A(\alpha_i)$ given the default probability α_i. For instance, with $\alpha_i = 1\%$, the default point is $A(\alpha_i) = \Phi^{-1}(1\%) = -2.33$, and so on. Generating a default event requires that the asset value A_i be lower than $A(\alpha_i) = \Phi^{-1}(\alpha_i)$.

A dummy variable represents the default event. It has a value of 1 if the asset value is below the threshold (default), and zero otherwise (non-default):

$$d_i = 1 \text{ if } A_i \leq A(\alpha_i) = \Phi^{-1}(\alpha_i)$$

$$d_i = 0 \text{ if } A_i > A(\alpha_i) = \Phi^{-1}(\alpha_i)$$

The dummy variables are intermediate variables serving for determining the portfolio number of defaults.

50.2.2 The Multiple Simulations

There are N obligors in the portfolio. The number of simulations of all asset values of all obligors is K. Each simulated asset value determines a 1 or 0 value for each d_i, one for each of the N obligors, with i varying from 1 to N. Each simulation generates as many asset values as there are obligors, or N asset values. For each obligor, the discrete default variable d_i takes the values 0 or 1. The sum of all d_i is the portfolio number of defaults for one simulation.

The simulations are repeated K times. For each simulation, we have N asset values, N values for the dummy variable, and a total count of defaults. With K simulations, we have K numbers of portfolio defaults. The K counts of portfolio defaults form a distribution. With a large number of simulations, we have a smoother distribution. From the distribution of the number of portfolio defaults, all statistics, standard deviations of defaults, mode of the distribution, and percentiles of the count of portfolio defaults are derived.

50.2.3 The Simulation Algorithm

For illustrating the process, we show the first simulations, following the copula sequence of calculations. The copula approach is equivalent to the Cholesky approach in this case. For conduction simulations, the pre-required inputs are:

- the correlation between asset values ρ, which is allowed to vary for showing the effect on the distribution of portfolio defaults in Moody's-KMV Portfolio Manager
- the default probabilities d_i of each obligor.

In the sample simulations of this chapter, the portfolio is uniform. The common default probability is $d = 5\%$, and the threshold point of asset value $\Phi^{-1}(d) = -1.645$. The uniform correlation is allowed to vary but the values are those of uniform correlation. There is no size discrepancy either. In the further example of Chapter 57, we relax the assumptions of uniform probability and of constant size, while keeping the uniform correlation. In this chapter, the simulation algorithm is detailed.

The sequence of calculations of each simulation for all firms within the portfolio is in rows. The first row corresponds to the common factor. The subsequent rows correspond to each firm, as many as there are obligors in the portfolio. The sample calculations are illustrated for three firms only, out of a portfolio with as many lines as there are firms within the portfolio. The full simulation uses a portfolio of 100 firms.

The first uniform standard variable $U = U_1$ is equal to $\Phi(Z)$, the common factor. For making all firms dependent on the same common factor, we impose that all U_1 variables of the first column are equal to the first one, which represents the common factor. Table 50.1 (below) shows a single simulation, with only the first three firms of the portfolio of 100 firms. In this single simulation[1], $U_1 = 0.5$ and the common factor is $Z = \Phi^{-1}(U_1) = 0$. Those values are common to all lines of the portfolio.

The second uniform variable is an intermediate variable corresponding to specific risk $X = \Phi^{-1}(U_2)$. The bivariate variable $V = \Phi_2(U_1, U_2, \rho)$ is a normal variable calculated with the formula:

$$Y = \Phi_2(U_1, U_2, \rho) = \rho \Phi^{-1}(U_1) + \sqrt{1 - \rho^2}\, \Phi^{-1}(U_2)$$

The function $\Phi_2(U_1, U_2, \rho)$ is abbreviated to Φ_2. It embeds the dependency between the two uniform variables, which is the same as the dependency between Z and the asset value Y. In the case of normal variables, it is equal to asset value Y.

Note that $V = \Phi(\Phi_2)$ is the third uniform variable correlated with $U = U_1$. The asset value dependent on Z is calculated twice in Table 50.1[2], as Φ_2 and as $Y = \Phi^{-1}(V)$. This makes the table structure identical to the second case where we use dependent times to default. In the present case, the last column is the asset value Y, also calculated in fifth column. The fifth column Φ_2 is simply the formula of the Cholesky transformation in the case of normal standard variables. The last column shows the asset values of firms dependent on the factor.

For modeling defaults, we need to append a second table (Table 50.2), which calculates whether there is a default or not. Each row of this second table corresponds to a row of the previous table. The dummy variable is derived from the firm asset value, in the last column. It equals 1 when this asset value is below the default point. In this case, we use the same default probability, 5%, for all firms. The default point in the standardized asset value model is -1.645. There is a default only when the simulated asset value is below the default point. In the example,

TABLE 50.1 Simulation of the asset values of the three first firms of the portfolio

	$U = U_1$	U_2	$X = \Phi^{-1}(U_2)$	$\Phi_2(U, U_2, \rho)$	$V = \Phi(\Phi_2)$	$Z = \Phi^{-1}(U_1)$	$Y = \Phi^{-1}(V)$
Factor	0.500	0.567	0.170	0.162	0.564	0.000	0.162
Firms							
1	0.500	0.039	−1.765	−1.684	0.046	0.000	−1.684
2	0.500	0.471	−0.072	−0.068	0.473	0.000	−0.068
3	0.500	0.511	0.027	0.026	0.510	0.000	0.026

TABLE 50.2 From asset value to default event

d	$\Phi_{-1}(d)$	Default
5.0%	−1.645	0
5.0%	−1.645	1
5.0%	−1.645	0
5.0%	−1.645	0

---

1 Since U_1 represents a cumulative probability of a normal standard variable, 0.5 matches the mean 0 of the standard normal variable.
2 It is obvious with normal standard variables that $Y = \Phi_2$ and $Y = \Phi^{-1}(V)$ since $V = \Phi(\Phi_2)$ and therefore $\Phi^{-1}(V) = \Phi_2$.

this happens for the first firm (firm 1, fourth row in the table) since the asset value is -1.684 < -1.645. The default column only has values 0 for no default and 1 for default. For the first three firms, there is only one value that equals 1. For the entire portfolio, it is sufficient to sum up the dummy default variable across firms for obtaining the number of defaults.

Note that this table corresponds only to one of the K simulations. For running K simulations, we need to calculate K times the same table, inputting for each one the same random value of U in the first row, duplicated for all firms within the portfolio, as explained above, and as many uniform random values for U_2 as there are lines in the portfolio. The next steps imply deriving the asset value Y, comparing with threshold point, assigning a default whenever asset value falls below default point, and summing up across rows to have the count of defaults.

50.2.4 Simulations of Default Distributions

The simulations serve for visualizing the distributions with increasing correlation. Generating a range of portfolio default distributions corresponding to various uniform asset correlations makes it possible to see how loss statistics vary with correlation. Asset correlation varies from 0% to 50% in steps of 10%, generating five loss distributions.

Running simulations in Excel™ would be tedious, since we need to duplicate as many tables as there are simulations, which could range from 100 to 1000 or more. We used a simulation software for running 1000 simulations with a portfolio of 100 lines.

When the uniform correlation increases, we observe that the mode of the distribution moves to the left. Simultaneously, the fat tail, grouping high counts of portfolio defaults with low frequencies, extends to the right. The curve is asymmetric and highly skewed. The standard deviation of portfolio defaults, the skewness and the kurtosis increase with the correlation. The zero correlation distribution is very simple to derive since it is a binomial distribution. The distribution with a 100% correlation has only two points: zero default and 100 defaults. The mean of all distributions is unchanged since the expectation does not depend on correlation and should always be around 5 defaults (5% of 100 lines).

Figure 50.1 shows distributions of portfolio defaults for correlation values 0, 10%, 20%, 30%, 40% and 50%. The highest mode matches the highest correlation and vice versa. The lowest mode corresponds to a zero correlation and is the binomial distribution since we use uniform exposure and uniform default probability. For highlighting the differences between default distributions, the x-axis shows that only the most frequent losses, showing only default lower than 10 although the fat tails will extend further to the right. In fact, default losses having higher values than 10 occur in the simulation: for a 50% correlation, some simulations generate 40 to 50 defaults, close or equal to half of the total exposure. When correlation increases, the probability of the mode increases and the tail extends to the right while getting "thicker."

Getting to the far end of the right-hand tail implies a much greater number of simulations to stabilize the tail for reducing simulation noise. The simulation noise is the variation of the values of the count of portfolio defaults across different runs of simulations. It decreases proportionally to the square root of the number of the simulations. The loss percentiles, measured by a count of defaults in this example, are numbers not exceeded in more than 5%, 1%, or fewer cases. They serve for measuring the Credit VaR and deriving capital as loss percentile minus expected loss (the latter being equal to 5 in our example).

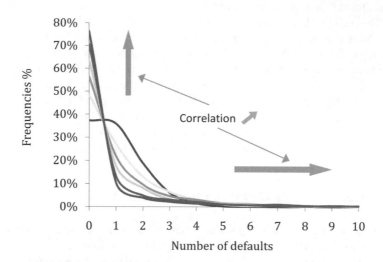

FIGURE 50.1 **Loss distributions and loss correlation (uniform portfolio, uniform default probability and uniform asset correlation)**

50.2.5 Dealing with Different Default Probabilities and Discrepancies of Exposures

Differentiating exposures is not an issue. Once we have generated dummy variables that represent default, we simply multiply them by the loss given default assigned to each line of the portfolio for converting the count of default into a sum of losses. Summing up the product of the dummy variable and the exposure attached to each firm would provide a portfolio loss rather than a count of defaults. Differentiating default probability is also easy. With the asset value model, it is sufficient to differentiate the normalized default point. For example, using a default point of -2.3263 matches a default probability of 1%, and another, -1.96, would match 2.5% default probability. Then, for each line of the portfolio, the simulated asset value is compared to the differentiated default point. The default point should be selected from the actual default probability of each line of the portfolio. For attaching a different correlation for each lines, the dependency function $\Phi_2(U_1, U_2, \rho)$ could use a different correlation across lines. Hence none of the simplifying assumptions are restrictive.

Such simulations are used in Chapter 57 (on portfolio analysis and reporting) for illustrating how the outputs are organized. In this chapter we keep uniform default probability, exposure and correlation because the focus is on the effect of dependency on the loss distribution.

50.3 SIMULATIONS OF TIMES TO DEFAULT

Under the reduced model of default, the distributions of defaults are exponential. For obtaining dependent default distributions across firms of the portfolio, we replicate the copula methodology. The intermediate variables are the uniform variables, and the target variables are times to default. The simulation of dependent times to default was introduced first by Li [48], and has been widely implemented in the industry for credit portfolio models.

50.3.1 The Simulation Algorithm

For illustrating the algorithm of simulations, we set the intensity of default as 5%, and the uniform correlation is 30% in the sample below. The intensity is constant[3]. The correlation input is user-defined according to standard practices of others for making the first-year default frequencies in line with alternate models, such as the Moody's-KMV Portfolio Manager model. Note that the reduced form of the model makes it very easy to implement, but questions were raised to the reliabilities of inputs once defaults of portfolios grew higher in the financial crisis.

The structure of the table used for simulating dependent times to default is the same as for asset values. The difference is that we derive the dependent time to default as the inverse function of the exponential distribution. Once times to defaults are simulated, we count the defaults occurring within a specified horizon, here one year.

For illustrating the process, we show again the first simulations, following the copula sequence of calculations. The purpose is to simulate times to default (TD) dependent on a common factor. For simulations, we use the above inputs: the uniform correlation ρ is 30% and the uniform default intensity λ of each obligor is 5%. The sequence of calculations for all firms within the portfolio, for each simulation, is in rows. The first row corresponds to the common factor. The subsequent rows correspond to each firm.

The sample table (Table 50.3), with three firms only, out of 100 firms, corresponds only to one simulation. The first uniform standard variable $U = U_1$ represents the common factor. All first uniform variables are equal to that of the factor. In this example $U = 0.5$, which matches a time to default equal to 13.863, identical across firms. The second uniform variable is an intermediate variable corresponding to specific risk. The bivariate variable $\Phi_2(U_1, U_2, \rho)$ embeds the dependency. The formula for $\Phi_2(U_1, U_2, \rho)$ is the same as in the case of asset values. The uniform standard variable V is dependent on $U = U_1$.

Times to default t are obtained from U and V values by inverting the exponential distribution $F(T) = 1 - \exp(\lambda T)$. The inverse function of the exponential distribution is $T = \ln[1 - F(T)]/\lambda$. Replacing $F(t)$ by the values of U and V, we find the matching values of T_1 and T_2 as $\ln(1 - U)/\lambda$ and $\ln(1 - V)/\lambda$. The times to default are in the last two columns. They all depend on U_1. The first time to default matches the factor and is the same across rows. The second time to default is that of the firm, in rows.

For modeling default events, we need to append a second table (Table 50.4) with the dummy variable representing default. Each row of this second table corresponds to the row of the previous table (Table 50.3). The values of dummy variables are derived from the firm's time to

TABLE 50.3   Simulation of times to default for the three first firms of the portfolio

	$U = U_1$	U_2	$X = \Phi^{-1}(U_2)$	$\Phi_2(U, U_2, \rho)$	$V = \Phi(\Phi_2)$	$T_1 = \Phi^{-1}(U_1)$	$T_2 = \Phi^{-1}(V)$
Factor	0.500	0.092	-1.326	-1.265	0.103	13.863	2.171
Firm							
1	0.500	0.382	-0.300	-0.286	0.388	13.863	9.805
2	0.500	0.011	-2.299	-2.194	0.014	13.863	0.285
3	0.500	0.997	2.718	2.593	0.995	13.863	106.951

---

3 Using piece-wise constant intensities is feasible in a multi-period setting, each intensity being calibrated with historical default probabilities.

TABLE 50.4　From time to default to default event

Horizon	Default
1	0
1	1
1	0

default, in the last column. Default occurs within the horizon when the time to default is lower than or equal to 1, which happens for the second firm in this sample simulation, because the time to default for this firm is 0.285, lower than 1.

Each single simulation run provides the number of defaults for the portfolio by summing defaults across firms. For obtaining a frequency distribution for the portfolio defaults, we need to run a large number of simulations. For running K simulations, we would need to calculate K times the same table, inputting for each one the same random value of U in the first column and as many uniform random values for U_2 as there are lines in the portfolio. For a single simulation, we find a number of defaults of 5.5% for each firm, or 11% for the pair of firms.

The simulations are conducted by generating as many tables as above, with 100 lines, 1000 times. For reducing the simulation sample error in the fat tail of the distribution of portfolio defaults, we need to increase the number of simulations until the portion of the tail matching the default percentile is stable enough. Figure 50.2 shows the number of defaults of the 100-line portfolio using the copula method, over a horizon of one year. The mean of the distribution is 4.84. The 5% percentile occurs at 2 defaults and the 95% percentiles at 13 defaults.

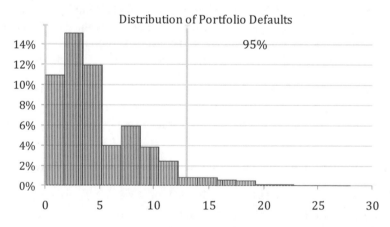

FIGURE 50.2　Distribution of portfolio defaults

50.3.2 Dealing with Different Default Probabilities and Discrepancies of Exposures

For using varying default probabilities across each firm, we would change the time intensities across firms, which would imply attaching to each line a different intensity of default, instead of using the same. For considering varying exposures for each firm, we would simply modify the last module, replacing each dummy variable by a product of the current dummy variable and the exposure attached to each firm. The sum of the products across lines of portfolio would provide the portfolio loss instead of the count of defaults. For changing the horizon, we simply extend the horizon for modeling defaults. Both changes are easy. For changing correlation across lines, it is necessary to input in the dependency function $\Phi_2(U_1, U_2, \rho)$, a different correlation, hence, none of the simplifying assumptions is restrictive.

51

Credit Portfolio Models

The purpose of this chapter is to provide an overview of the main "vendors" models, building on the principles of credit portfolio modeling already explained. We review here four models:

- Moody's-KMV Portfolio Manager
- Credit Metrics
- Credit Portfolio View ("CPV")
- CreditRisk+.

The two first models are self-contained, and can be relatively readily implemented by end-users. They are full valuation models and rely on Monte Carlo simulations for generating a distribution of portfolio values at a final horizon, from which loss statistics are derived. The other models provide an open framework. Credit Portfolio View is an econometric model of default rates using observable economic and country-industry factors. CreditRisk+ relies on actuarial techniques and provides an analytical distribution of default, within an open framework. A comparative view of models is in Gordy [32].

The four models provide a global view of the lines along which credit portfolio models can be constructed. The only omitted "best practice" model is the dependent times to default model, which is extensively used because it is easy to implement, and which is described in the previous chapter (Chapter 50).

The presentation of credit portfolio models follows a structure by building block as described in the first section, which provides a summarized overview of all four models. The overview lists the main building blocks of each model: The underlying conceptual framework is introduced first, how defaults and migration events are modeled, the dependencies building block applying to risk factors, the revaluation at horizon, and the simulation block. Subsequent sections describe the specifics of each model.

Contents

51.1 CREDIT PORTFOLIO MODEL OVERVIEW

The structure of the presentation deals with the main building blocks that tend to be common to all credit portfolio models (Table 51.1). The sources are in [80], [81] and [82].

1 The underlying conceptual framework, such as the structural model of default (Moody's-KMV) or the econometric approach (CPV).
2 The modeled credit events, ranging from default events only to full migrations, with special cases where the target variables are default and migration rates of sub-portfolios.
3 Modeling dependencies and risk factors.
4 Revaluation at the final horizon implemented by models, when applicable (full migration mode).
5 Generating portfolio values and portfolio loss distributions at horizon, such as Monte Carlo simulation or the actuarial techniques used in CreditRisk+.

51.2 MOODY'S-KMV CREDIT MONITOR AND MOODY'S-KMV PORTFOLIO MANAGER

As with other models, we follow the structure of Section 51.1 for presenting the model. Moody's-KMV Portfolio Manager is considered as the most comprehensive portfolio model and provides all necessary outputs for calculating a credit VaR[1].

51.2.1 Conceptual Framework

Moody's-KMV Portfolio Manager is an implementation of the structural default model. Default is triggered when asset value falls below a threshold matching the default probability assigned to each facility. When there is no default, the final credit state is modeled as the distance to default, or the distance between asset value simulated at horizon and the default point. The default point is the debt value projected as of horizon.

---

1 This presentation is derived from publications on Moody's-KMV Portfolio Manager and from Kealhofer in [45] and [46].

TABLE 51.1 Vendors' models basic techniques for generating loss distributions

	KMV Portfolio Manager	Credit Metrics	CPV	CreditRisk+
Credit events	Default and migration through EDF© range for individual obligors	Default and migration through ratings and default probabilities class for individual obligors	Default and migration rates for portfolio segments by country, industry and risk class	Default and migration rates for portfolio segments by country, industry, risk class and band size
Horizon credit state of each facility	Simulated EDF© value	Simulated rating class	Simulated default rate of portfolio segments	Default intensity
Correlation structure	From orthogonal multiple factors model of assets returns	From multiple factors model of equity returns	From economic factors and residuals from: • the ARIMA models predicting economic factor values • the multifactor model of the index of the Logit function	From end user defined relation of segment default intensities with external factors
Generation of portfolio value distribution	Monte Carlo simulations of correlated assets values	Simulation of credit states with joint migration matrices Simulation of credit states with Monte Carlo simulations	Monte Carlo simulation of predicted economic factor values and predicted index values. Segment default and migration rates are a Logit function of the predicted index values	Segment-specific defaults follow a mixed Poisson distribution. The mixing variable is a linear function of factors. The portfolio loss distribution aggregates segment distributions as if independent
Revaluation at horizon	Credit spreads Risk-neutral default probabilities Book value (default mode)	Credit spread of horizon rating class	Credit spread of horizon rating class	Book value (default mode only)

51.2.2 Credit Events and Credit State at Horizon

Moody's-KMV Portfolio Manager operates in full valuation mode, since it assigns a random distance to default to each facility. The distance to default is a metric mapped to default probabilities. Hence, the model simulates all credit states feasible at horizon. The model allows using book values, and it operates then under default mode only, since it simulates only default and non-default states at horizon.

51.2.3 Risk Factors and Dependence Structure

The underlying "first level" risk factors, from which the credit events derive, are the asset values of firms. The unobservable asset values are modeled under the default option model. The asset values depend on common "second level" risk factors for generating dependencies. The "second level" factors influence asset returns from statistical fits. Statistical fits provide also the characteristics of the error terms. This is the case for all firms included in Moody's-KMV Credit Monitor universe, and the data is delivered with the model.

The correlations between modeled asset values are derived from a multifactor model, using orthogonal factors such as regions, or industry indices, obtained using principal component analysis. Orthogonal factors facilitate the calculation of asset value correlations since they derive directly from the coefficients of the multifactor model.

Frequently, the universe of bank portfolios does not include such firms, and there is no modeling available of factor influences. This requires providing an estimate of the fraction of specific variance resulting from the error term (or, alternatively, of the variance from all common factors, which is general risk). In such a case, the specific risk becomes a control parameter of the model. The higher is the specific risk, the lower is the correlation effect and, conversely, increasing the systematic risk generates a higher correlation. The final loss distribution is very sensitive to the correlation effect, so that the control values used for systematic risk are important.

Moody's-KMV Portfolio Manager allows defining the ratio of systematic risk to total risk. The ratio of general risk to total risk is the R^2 of the multifactor regression model. Stressing this R^2 is equivalent to increasing the general risk and, therefore, the correlations. The "R-square" of the regression – measuring general risk – is the output of the multifactor model linking assets returns to factors. When inputting directly the default probability, this "R-square" is necessary since it defines the relative weights of specific versus general risk. It becomes an input rather than an output of the multifactor model in the KMV universe. When no fit is available, for private firms for example, it is necessary to specify the R^2 using for instance the average over all firms, which is the range of 20% to 30% for listed companies in the main stock exchanges. The "R-Square" can be used as a stress variable. For example, country risk creates a "contagion" effects on firms, increasing the correlation between defaults. A contagion scenario within a country would reflect in a higher than usual value of the "R-Square."

51.2.4 Revaluation of Facilities at Horizon

The KMV model operates in full valuation mode, using either credit spreads or risk-neutral valuation to revalue any facility at horizon. Valuation depends on modeled asset values. The modeled asset values are those of the KMV universe, if the user chooses so. With preset default probabilities, rather than KMV modeled EDFs©, the model uses the reduced form of the full model of asset value, considering that all relevant information on asset value is in the assigned default probability.

Revaluation at horizon uses either credit spreads corresponding to the final credit state or the KMV-specific risk-neutral valuation process that uses the "risk neutral EDF©." Risk-neutral probabilities are derived from credit spreads, since they embed risk aversion. When using credit spreads, the model maps the final distance to default of each firm, for each simulation, to a rating class. Then, each facility is revalued at horizon using such credit spread. Because the revaluation depends on the cross-tabulation of ratings class to credit spreads, the process is called "matrix revaluation," each cell of the matrix providing the credit spread by rating class and maturity. Matrix revaluation is also used by Credit Metrics.

51.2.5 Generation of Portfolio Value Distribution

Moody's-KMV Portfolio Manager uses Monte Carlo simulation for generating correlated asset values and final distances to default of each firm. The portfolio value sums up all facility values for each draw of a set of correlated assets values for all facilities. Since all facility values follow a distribution, the aggregation provides a portfolio value distribution as well. The portfolio value distribution results from migrations altering the value of facilities maturing after horizon and from default events between now and horizon.

In Moody's-KMV Portfolio Manager, the loss given default is a random variable whose mode is an end user input. It is possible to specify its parameters, but the beta distribution is common to all facilities. This results in an additional component to the loss volatility, one resulting from the value volatility, and the other resulting from the independent random LGD volatility.

The model operates both within the KMV universe of listed firms or with end-users preset default probabilities mapped to internal ratings. For listed firms, it is possible to use modeled asset values.

51.2.6 Portfolio Optimization

Moody's-KMV Portfolio Manager provides a portfolio optimization module. Once revenues and risk for a portfolio are available, it becomes possible to alter the risk–return profile of the portfolio by changing the structure of the portfolio. The rationale follows the classical portfolio optimization theory: minimize risk given return or maximize revenues given risk, or maximize the Sharpe ratio (expected return/volatility) of the portfolio by changing the exposure weights.

Portfolio optimization under a global funding constraint means:

- reducing risk, at a constant return
- increasing revenue, at the same risk.

If we assume the spread in percentage is constant, the issue is to define the portfolio weights leading to a more efficient risk–return profile. Formally, this the well-known problem of maximizing return given risk or minimizing risk given return, a constrained optimization problem. In practice, enhancing the risk–return profile through trade-off of exposures requires only simple calculations as a first approximation (Table 51.2). The following example is based on the credit

TABLE 51.2 Enhancing the risk–return profile of the portfolio*

	Base case	High risk exposure + 20%	Low risk exposure + 20%
Loss volatility	221	252	244
Portfolio EL	101	114	107
Loss percentile 1%	1055	1190	1196
Capital in excess of EL	954	1076	1089
Portfolio AIS	401	446	436
Portfolio RaRoC	31.48%	30.81%	30.17%
Portfolio SVA	62	62	56

* AIS is the "all-in-spread." SVA is the "shareholder value added." RaRoC is the "risk-adjusted return on capital." All definitions, calculations and examples are in Section 14, Chapters 55 and 56.

portfolio analysis (Chapter 57), with base case matching the example. Other cases change the size of high-risk and low-risk exposures by plus or minus 20%, and replicating the simulations.

In this example, the base case provides the highest Sharpe ratio of return to risk. Portfolio optimization follows these lines. Rebalancing exposure weights generate new risk–return combinations. Some dominate others. These make up an efficient frontier. Then, it becomes a simple matter to see how to move to various points in the efficient frontier by changing the exposure weights. This requires a full optimization module in the portfolio model because both capital allocation and return are allowed to vary.

Optimization under funding constraints differs from optimizing the portfolio expansion (Figure 51.1). A full optimization model should not recognize the limits imposed on business volume, by risk class, industry and country because, economically, limits might be sub-optimal. The optimization module might help refining limits, but is not a substitute to business policy and limits.

Moody's–KMV Portfolio Manager embeds an optimization module and provides various optimized outputs, such as:

- optimization at constant risk
- optimization at constant return
- the efficient frontier.

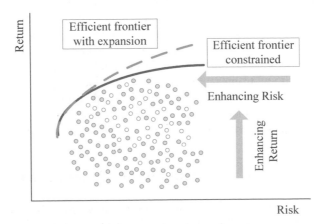

FIGURE 51.1 Optimization functions with portfolio models

51.3 CREDIT METRICS

Credit Metrics is described in the technical document of J. P. Morgan [37]. It follows the general principles outlined with Moody's-KMV model. It is a full revaluation model. The main difference is that Credit Metrics derives correlations from equity values rather than asset values. It does not adjust asset values and correlations for the obligors' leverage that influences both equity values and correlations. By contrast, Moody's-KMV usage of asset values and correlations "undoes" the leverage effect in order to use unlevered assets values and correlations. The dependencies are generated from equity returns correlations, themselves resulting from a multifactor model, as in Moody's-KMV model.

Credit Metrics is a full valuation model. The principle is similar to Moody's-KMV Portfolio Manager. However, Credit Metrics relies more on credit ratings than Moody's-KMV model. It uses Monte Carlo simulations for generating the distribution of portfolio value at horizon. The model uses matrix valuation at horizon for revaluing each facility.

51.4 CREDIT PORTFOLIO VIEW: ECONOMETRIC MODELS

This section presents the macro-economic modeling of default and migration rates. This is the Credit Portfolio View framework, which addresses explicitly the cyclical dynamics of these variables. Credit Portfolio View differs substantially from the two previous models in that it models default and migration rates of portfolio segments using an econometric approach. Accordingly, we expand the building block implemented for moving from economic variables to default and migration rates. The sources are Wilson [80], [81] and [82].

The econometric techniques model the default rates of "portfolio segments" or sub-populations of firms by risk class, from times series of default rates and economic factors. The Credit Portfolio View model ("CPV") provides a framework for capturing the cyclical dynamics of credit risk. The principle underlying CPV is to relate default and migration rates to external factors. It uses standard times series models combined with a Logit model for obtaining default rates by portfolio segment. Time series models serve for predicting economic variables, industry and economic indexes, related to default and migration rates. The predicted values are combined into an economic index that relates directly to default rates of a specific segment through a Logit model. The two steps, from economic factors to an economic index, and from the economic index to default rates, effectively relate economic variables to defaults and migrations. CPV extends the modeling of default rates to migrations between risk classes, complying with the constraint that default plus all migrations rates should some up to one.

The model focuses on portfolio segments, rather than individual obligors, and default or migration rates rather than probabilities. The credit standing of firms has a homogeneous behavior within a portfolio segment. However, CPV allows defining segments with more than one criterion, such as industry product-type, or counterparty type and risk.

51.4.1 Credit Portfolio View Conceptual Framework

Credit Portfolio View models default rates of sub-portfolios as Logit functions of an economic index Y. This economic index is a linear function of economic factors, analogous to a multifactor model. Credit Portfolio View relies on several modeling options.

- Default events depend on economic conditions materialized by economic indices Y_i defined for each portfolio segment "i." Each economic index depends on country-industry factors X_{ki}, where "k" designates each specific factor.
- The default events modeled are default rates, or ratios of default frequencies to the initial number of firms within each portfolio segment. CPV works with grouped data rather than individual data. These sub-populations are banking portfolio segments, grouped by risk class, for example, plus other criteria.
- For looking forward, it is necessary to use predicted values of economic indices. Future values of an index depend on future values of the factors influencing the index. For this purpose, CPV needs modeling the predicted values of factors using standard time series models.
- For converting the predicted values of factors into default rates of each segment, CPV uses a Logit function, the index summarizing the predicted factors that influence default rates.

The economic factors driving the credit risk of obligors are economic, geographic or industry variables X_k. The usage of common factors generates dependency across firms, which allows capturing the cyclical dynamics of credit risk of firms. The factors X_k represent the "general" risk of obligors, while the residual of the fit of default rates to the index Y_i represents the specific risk. CPV uses three main building blocks for modeling of default and migration rates of portfolio segments.

51.4.1.1 Logit Model of Default Rates

A first block models default rates DR_i by portfolio segment i, as a function of the economic index Y_i. The Logit model ensures that the default rate remains in the 0 to 1 range of values, no matter what the index value is. It converts predicted values of economic factors into default rates DR_i for each portfolio segment using the Logit equation:

$$DR_i = 1/[1 + \exp(-Y_i)]$$

Credit Portfolio View looks forward by using predicted values of the index. The predicted value of the economic index $Y_{i,t+1}$ is a linear combination of several industry-country factors $X_{k,t+1}$, the index "k" referring to economic factor. The date "t" is the current date. Values of variables are certain as of current date t and are random at the future date $t + 1$.

51.4.1.2 Using Predicted Values of the Index

The second block models the future values of the economic-industry factors $X_{k,t+1}$ as a function of their past values and error terms, using an ARIMA time series model. These factors are common to all portfolio segments, hence there is no index i. This feature allows the model to "look forward" using predicted values of economic factors.

The predicted index depends on the set of $X_{j,t+1}$ values for k economic factors that influence the credit risk of all portfolio segments:

$$Y_{i,t+1} = \beta_{i,t} + \beta_{i,1} X_{1,t+1} + \beta_{i,2} X_{2,t+1} + \ldots + \beta_{i,k} X_{k,t+1} + \varepsilon_{i,t+1}$$

Each economic factor predicted value $X_{j,t+1}$ at date $t + 1$ results from an ARIMA time series model, using lagged observations and past errors as predictors of the future values. The general functional form is a linear lagged function of these past observations and errors:

$$X_{j,t+1} = \alpha_1 X_{j,t} + \alpha_2 X_{j,t-1} + \ldots + \gamma_1 e_{j,t} + \gamma_2 e_{j,t-1} + e_{j,t+1}$$

The model fit provides the ratio of specific to systematic risk, or the ratio of the variance explained by common factors to the variance of the residual term of the fit. Accordingly, the ratio of specific risk, the risk unrelated to external factors, varies across risk class and increases relatively for the upper risk classes. The second block plugs in the Logit equation the predicted values of the index rather than its current value.

51.4.1.3 Modeling Migration Rates

The third block models the migration rates $MR_{i,t+1}$ of transitions matrices consistently with the variations of the default rates, allowing migration probabilities to shift upward or downward according to the values of the default rates. This block allows the model to use full valuation. The risk status at horizon determines the valuation of the facility using market spreads corresponding to this risk class (matrix evaluation).

In CPV, migration rates are conditional on the state of the economy through the modeled default rates. Credit Portfolio uses the default rates for deriving what migrations rates should be. Historical long-term migration statistics are considered as long-term averages, or "unconditional migration probabilities." Conditional migrations are dependent on the state of the economy, as much as default rates are. Migration rates between any pair of risk classes should remain consistent with default rates, imposing that all migration rates, including the default state, sum up to one. When default rates vary, the migration rates vary for complying with this constraint. CPV uses a "shift" factor that modifies the migration rates in accordance with modeled default rates.

The default rates of portfolio segments result from the model. When the default rates get higher than average, all migration probabilities to non-default states shift toward lower values. When the default rates get lower than average, all migration probabilities to non-default state increase. For quantification purposes, the shifts of migration rates are proportional to the deviation of the modeled default rate from its average long-term value. Moreover, the shifts differ for investment grade risk classes and speculative grade risk classes, recognizing that investment grade obligors are less sensitive to economic movements than speculative grade obligors.

51.4.2 Credit Events and Credit State at Horizon

According to the above, the target variables are the default rates and the migration rates by portfolio segment. Each segment is defined, at least, by risk class. Additional criteria can be used. For example, under Basel 2, the large corporates are segregated from the retail portfolio. The CPV framework can accommodate various segmenting criteria.

51.4.3 Risk Factors and Dependence Structure

The "first level" risk factors in CPV are the economic indices (Y_i) applicable to each segment, used as inputs in the Logit functions. Such economic indices are a linear function of several other country-industry risk factors. These second-level factors have two purposes for obtaining predicted values of the index and, since they are common to all portfolio segments, they generate dependencies between the default and migration rates of all segments. These are end-user defined as well as the economic indices. Note that a simplified single factor index could theoretically be plugged in the Logit function. But this simplification might not allow capturing the underlying factors that drive such an index, and generate too much specific risk.

51.4.4 Revaluation of Facilities at Horizon

Because CPV models joint migrations conditional on the state of the economy, they allow defining the future credit state at horizon. The full revaluation of facilities is feasible using the "matrix valuation" methodology.

51.4.5 Generation of Portfolio Value Distribution

By generating random predicted values of economic factors, it becomes possible to generate correlated random values of these default rates. The predicted values of common economic factors derive from ARIMA time series models and depend on their lagged historical values and error terms. ARIMA models allow deriving future values from past ones. In addition, they provide the uncertainty of the predicted variables and the error term. Both can serve for generating random predicted values. The methodology is the Monte Carlo simulation.

The technicalities of the econometric approach result from the multiple models involved in the process. The default rates of portfolio segment are a Logit function of an economic index, which is a linear combination of economic factors plus an error term. Looking forward, all economic factors have uncertain values.

Each predicted value of each factor depends on X_k, their lagged values and the residuals. The default rates are a Logit function of the predicted index $Y_{i,t+1}$, which depends on the $X_{i,t+1}$ through a linear multifactor model. The economic factors and residuals of the function $Y_{i,t+1}$ ($X_{1,t+1}$, $X_{2,t+1}$, $\ldots$, $X_{k,t+1}$, $\varepsilon_{i,t+1}$) are not independent in general and have a variance-covariance structure. It would be restrictive to impose zero cross-correlations across residuals. This makes it overly complex to implement the model.

The CPV open framework allows customization to any observable data set, but requires end user modeling as a prerequisite. In addition, it provides an explicit link with the economic cycle dynamics, using observable factors. These features are strengths of the econometric framework of CPV. In addition, the model allows explicit testing of a discrete number of economic scenarios by selecting a discrete sample of values of factors and/or economic indices.

The main merit of CPV is to have made explicit all that is ideally required to implement an econometric approach. The drawback is that it is quite complex to implement the full model. CPV provides flexibility to end-users who can implement a more or less comprehensive model and picking up the relevant factors of their choices. CPV is not a self-contained model such as Moody's–KMV Portfolio Manager, which provides the outputs using its own proprietary model rather than requiring modeling by end users.

51.5 CREDITRISK+ AND ANALYTICAL DISTRIBUTIONS

CreditRisk+ is a default model that generates loss distributions based on default event, recovery rates and exposure at book value. It is described in the Credit Suisse reference document "CreditRisk+: A Credit Risk Management Framework" published in 1997 [23]. It is not a full valuation model, since exposure value does not change according to risk.

51.5.1 Conceptual Framework

CreditRisk+ utilizes an analytical framework, which avoids the full-blown Monte Carlo simulations. CreditRisk+ relies on the Poisson distribution, widely used in insurance modeling. The Poisson distribution applies when defaults are independent, which is a major drawback. Accordingly, CreditRisk+ has two versions: the basic version relies on independent defaults; the second version allows introducing dependencies using factor models by using the mixed Poisson distribution, which allows preserving the analytical attractiveness of the model.

The Poisson distribution tabulates the frequency of observing k defaults when the default intensity, or the number of default per unit of time, has a fixed value n. This default intensity is the Poisson parameter (Figure 51.2). The density function of the Poisson distribution has been introduced in the chapter on probability distributions (Chapter 12). The basics of the Poisson distribution are:

- probability density function (PDF): $P(K = k) = \exp(-n)n^k/k!$
- n is the default intensity per unit of time, for instance one year, or the average number of defaults in a one year period – it is identical to the default intensity: λ
- k is the random number of defaults, from 0 to the maximum number of exposures in a portfolio segment and $k!$ is the factorial of k.

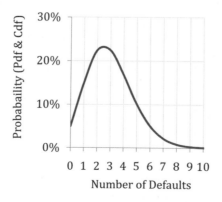

FIGURE 51.2   The Poisson probability function. Poisson parameter = 3

Using the value 3 for the Poisson parameter, the loss percentile corresponding to 99% is around 7 defaults. Converting the loss percentiles into loss is straightforward with equal unit sizes.

The Poisson distribution does not allow dealing with size discrepancies of exposure, but models only counts of defaults. For turning around such restrictions, the model necessitates dividing the portfolio into segments by risk class and size band of exposure, or of loss under default. Each segment is defined by cross-tabulating rating class and size band. This allows bypassing the limitations of the Poisson distribution that generates the distribution of the number of defaults, without considering size discrepancies. For instance, a 1000$ unit loss would result in 7000$ loss percentiles at 1% confidence level in the preceding example. Dividing the portfolio into segments by risk class and exposure bands generate some complexities.

CreditRisk+ uses the "mixed Poisson distribution." The mixed Poisson distribution uses a "mixing variable," Q. The mixed Poisson distribution conditions the Poisson parameter with a random mixing variable "Q." The Poisson parameter becomes nQ, instead of the original n. The mixing variable Q can be a simple scaling factor, but it is in general random. The added value of the mixing variable is to allow the default intensity to fluctuate randomly and to make it a function of risk factors. For making the analytics simple, it is necessary that $E(Q) = 1$. When $Q > 1$, the default intensity increases above the average, and conversely when $Q < 1$.

This allows modeling the entire aggregated loss distribution over the entire portfolio and opens the door to interdependencies between individual distributions as long as only the mixing variables embed them.

51.5.2 Credit Events and Credit State at Horizon

CreditRisk+, like CPV, applies to portfolio segments, each of them being defined by bands of exposure size and uniform default probability. Therefore, CreditRisk+, like CPV, models default rates, not individual default probabilities, although not for the same reason. For CreditRisk+, the segmenting is required because of the usage of analytical distributions that do not allow dealing with size discrepancies of exposures. For CPV, segmenting is used only to have sub-portfolios meaningfully related to factors and to end up with default rates and migration rates by rating class. In CreditRisk+, the segmenting allows generating an analytical loss distribution for sub-portfolios defined by cross-tabulating size bands and rating class.

51.5.3 Risk Factors

The mixing variable acts as the "first-level" risk factor, allowing default intensity to change with risk factors. For addressing dependencies, the second version of CreditRisk+ makes the mixing variable a factor model, a linear combination of external "second-level" factors, such as economic conditions. The mixing variable allows the default intensity to vary according to whatever risk factors are relevant or to run scenarios of default intensity by using discrete values of interest.

CreditRisk+ uses specific properties of the mixed Poisson distribution. When individual mixed Poisson distributions are independent, or if they depend on each other through the mixing variable only, the sum of the mixed Poisson distributions remains a mixed Poisson. Since CreditRisk+ makes only the mixing variable dependent on external factors, it complies with this condition.

51.5.4 Dependency Structure

The first version of CreditRisk+ does not allow to model dependencies, a major drawback. The second version of CreditRisk+ makes the mixing variable of individual distributions dependent upon a set of common factors. This common dependence across segments of the mixing variable to the same factors makes default intensities of segments dependent. CreditRisk+ adds a factor independent of all others for generating a specific random noise. The resulting ratio of specific to total risk becomes an input.

51.5.5 Generation of Portfolio Value Distribution

An attractive property of CreditRisk+ is that loss distributions are entirely analytically tractable with adequate assumptions. The mixing variable allows making the default intensity a function of common risk factors.

For correlating defaults of portfolio segments, CreditRisk+ makes the default intensities of portfolio segments a linear function of common factors, using "sensitivities" as coefficients. When using a mixed Poisson, it is not possible, in general, to stick to analytical loss distributions. Therefore, CreditRisk+ relies on a special case that allows a full analytical formulation of the distribution. When the mixing variable, Q, follows a standardized gamma distribution, the resulting mixed distribution follows the negative binomial distribution. The gamma distribution is briefly described in the appendix (Section 51.6).

The CreditRisk+ approach is an elegant methodology because it is entirely analytical. It relies on the mixed Poisson distribution, whose parameter is the density of defaults per unit of time, a parameter similar to an annual default probability. The time intensity parameter makes defaults dependent on time, which is useful for modeling the times to default. When aggregating distribution over all segments, it is possible to identify the time profile of worst and best cases. Moreover, it is also a simple task to consider various scenarios by changing the values of the mixing variables. Since the loss distribution is analytical, it is simple and fast to calculate. On the other hand, CreditRisk+ does not model the relative magnitude of general and specific risk, which is user-defined, is a default model only, and also imposes restrictions with respect to the definition of portfolio segments.

51.6 APPENDIX: THE GAMMA DISTRIBUTION

The gamma distribution is such that:

$$P(X) = \frac{a^r}{\Gamma(r)} e^{-aX} X^{r-1} \text{ and } \Gamma(r) = \int_0^\infty e^{-u} u^{r-1} du$$

Since the mean value of the gamma distribution is r/a, we should set $r = a$ to adopt the scaling convention of the mixing variable Q, so that $E(Q) = 1$. Using the common value h for r and a, the mixing variable function follows gamma(h, h), and its analytical density function is:

$$H(q) = \frac{1}{\Gamma(h)} \int_0^{hq} e^{-z} z^{h-1} dh$$

With these rules, the expectation and the volatility of the mixing variable are:

$$E(Q) = 1$$

$$\sigma(Q) = 1/\sqrt{h}$$

The expectation and the volatility of the number of defaults K following the mixed Poisson, with Q following the standardized gamma, are:

$$E(K) = n \text{ and } \sigma^2(K) = n + n^2/h$$

The smaller h, the larger is the standard deviation of K, which corresponds to a larger volatility of gamma(h, h), the distribution of Q. In addition, simple algorithms allow calculating the distribution.

SECTION 13

Capital Allocation

Linking global risk management with business policies is not simple. The transfer pricing system provides a first pillar for linking global risk management to business policies by allocating income to individual transactions. The two basic "pillars," the fund transfer pricing (FTP) scheme and the capital allocation scheme, provide the two major links between the aggregated view of the portfolio and its individual lines. Without such links, banks would not be able to send signals to business lines consistent with global views on risks and returns (top-down process). Conversely, without proper aggregation of the risk–return profiles of transactions, they cannot monitor how well business lines do, compared to projected targets (bottom-up process).

For portfolios, the risk allocation is an economic capital allocation to each transaction. Economic capital is credit risk capital or market risk capital. Both result from VaR measures for credit and market risks. Without such allocation of risks, it is not feasible to compare profitability across portfolio lines because they are not risk-adjusted. The risk metric for risk-adjustment is allocated capital.

The capital allocation issue, for a given existing portfolio, does not exist for regulatory capital because it is mechanically assigned to individual transactions through the risk-weight functions. Hence capital allocation issues arise only when dealing with economic capital. The capital allocation issue results from the sub-additive property of individual risks stemming from diversification effects. The standalone risk of a transaction portfolio is intrinsic to a facility ignoring the diversification effects within a portfolio. The risk contribution is the risk retained by a facility, or a sub-portfolio, after, or "post," diversification. Risk contributions make up the foundation of the capital allocation system. Risk contributions are additive if properly defined.

The three chapters of this section address the following issues:

- the definition of economic capital or credit VaR from percentiles of the value distribution plus the various methods for defining the zero-loss point, for accounting economic provisions and accrued revenues from today up to horizon (Chapter 52)
- the definition of risk contributions, which are capital allocations within a given existing portfolio, with specific properties (Chapter 53)
- the definition of marginal risk contributions, or incremental capital allocations, when new transactions are added to an existing portfolio, or when existing transactions expand in size (Chapter 54).

Risk allocations, together with the FTP system, allow implementing bank-wide consistent risk management. Once properly defined, they open the door to risk-adjusted measures of performances, which are expanded on in the next section (14).

52

Economic Capital and Credit Risk VaR

The measures of portfolio credit risk are statistics, expectation, volatility and loss percentiles, derived from the portfolio value distributions at some horizon. Assuming that it is possible to derive a portfolio distribution, some options remain open and there are intermediate steps to move from such distributions to economic capital calculations and related measures.

This chapter addresses these questions:

- what is the horizon of the calculations?
- what are the alternate measures of capital, given economic provisioning and portfolio revenues?

This section is based on a review of various options used by different credit portfolio models.

Section 52.1 discusses the choice of the horizon for constructing the portfolio value distribution. Section 52.2 reviews the choices for calculating capital and expected loss, and discusses time lag between future losses and current capital. Section 52.3 opens the discussion of risk-adjusted measure of performances, which are then presented in Chapter 55, because they depend on alternative metrics for defining allocated capital to a transaction or a sub-portfolio.

Contents

52.1 HORIZON FOR CREDIT CAPITAL

Portfolio models generate a value distribution at a future horizon selected by the end user. Note that all portfolio models use a "static" view of the portfolio, like ALM does, since they calculate loss statistics for the current portfolio at a point in time. However, all credit portfolio models require setting a horizon for measuring credit risk. This horizon applies to all facilities regardless of their maturities.

Portfolio management implies restructuring of the risk–return profile of the portfolio through limits, syndications, securitizations, loan trading and usage of credit derivatives. The "originate and hold" business model of banks changed with the emergence of securitizations and credit portfolio management. From a portfolio prospective, the relevant horizon is a period that allows:

- restructuring the portfolio to bring its risk in line with the bank goals
- raising capital, if the existing capital is less than required to ensure adequacy with the portfolio risk.

Both actions take time. Hence, an intermediate period between long maturities and the minimum time for adjusting portfolio risk and/or capital seems adequate. Such a horizon might perhaps extend to 1, 2 or 3 years. From a practical standpoint, the one-year horizon offers many benefits. It is in line with the budget process. It matches the time of disclosure of financial statements and regulatory reports.

All models use a fixed horizon, typically one year, and some offer the possibility of making calculations for longer periods. With a fixed horizon, it is necessary to deal with intermediate dates when facilities mature.

- If a facility matures before horizon, the risk exposure extends to the maturity, and no further, and the value of the facility at horizon is zero. The default probability should be adjusted to the actual maturity. The loss statistics calculations should include the loss under default of these facilities.
- If the facility matures after the horizon, its value at horizon is random. Such randomness should be included in full valuation models, due to migration risk. The valuation at horizon embeds any migration between current dates and horizon plus the roll-down effect due to amortization. The roll-down effect depends on the facilities excess spreads over market credit spreads.

There is a case for considering longer horizons than the management horizon for the credit portfolio and/or bank's capital. Long maturity facilities have more exposure to credit risk simply because default probabilities increase with the duration of the credit exposure and because migrations might have a larger magnitude. Facilities with longer life should generate more capital charge. Considering credit risk until horizon only does not capture the full credit risk. Full valuation at horizon extends to maturity, but does not consider migrations beyond horizon.

Extending the horizon generates technicalities. It implies breaking down the period from horizon to maturities longer than a year into several sub-periods, and applying to each sub-period forward migrations and default probabilities. Valuation models of bonds do consider such forward probabilities up to maturity. In practice, it is easier to assign a single forward default probability $d(1, T)$ from horizon (1) to maturity (T).

The regulatory view on maturity is that the capital weights should increase with the maturity of exposures, subject to a cap, which is intended to capture migration risk. Basel 2 regulatory capital includes an adjustment for effective maturity, along those lines.

Another practical view is that extending the horizon for measuring risk generates offsetting effects for the portfolio as well as for amortizing facilities. Exposure to credit risk is longer, an effect analogous to the diffusion effect of potential future exposure (PFE) of derivatives. But, as with PFEs, the amortization effect reduces the size of exposure and credit risk of a facility is zero at maturity. We have the usual offsetting effects of increasing uncertainty with time plus the amortization effect. Hence, there might be a maximum risk at some point in time for a facility and for the credit portfolio. This makes horizons that are shorter than maturities relevant.

For practical reasons, using several years allows exploring how credit risk evolves with horizon. Calculations over a single horizon are much simpler. Although practices vary across banks, the single horizon calculation seems common.

The single horizon, for example one year, does not resolve all issues. Facilities mature before one year and default time can occur at intermediate point in time between the current date and the horizon selected. Moreover, default probabilities should match the time profile of exposures. Amortizing exposures are packages of bullet facilities, so that addressing the issue for bullet facilities is sufficient (Figure 52.1). In theory, the default probabilities broken down by sub-period should be the marginal default probabilities applying to each successive period for a given rating class.

In practice, for a facility maturing before horizon, the default probability should be time adjusted because it does not make sense to assign a full annual default probability to a three-month exposure. A proportional time adjustment is sufficient for short periods. For instance with an horizon of $H = 1$ year and a maturity $T < H$, the time-adjusted default probability could be the product $d(0, 1)T$ (with $T < 1$).

Default dates serve for discounting to present future losses. For shorter than 1-year facilities, dating default at maturity makes more sense than waiting until the horizon date one year ahead. In practice, the rule of dating default at maturity or horizon, if maturity is longer than horizon, is simpler to handle.

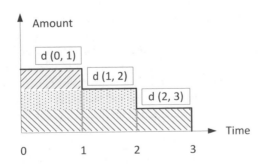

FIGURE 52.1   Stripping amortizing facilities into bullet facilities

52.2 FROM PORTFOLIO VALUE DISTRIBUTION TO CREDIT CAPITAL

The loss distribution results from the portfolio value distribution. The loss distribution is the mirror image of the portfolio value distribution. From the loss distribution, all loss statistics including credit risk VaR and economic capital derive. However, there are alternative options for calculating them. The loss calculations from the value distribution require a starting point for determining the downside variation that measures loss. All loss statistics result from the loss distribution and such cut-off point for calculating losses at horizon. The current value is the simplest zero point loss, and is sometimes used. But it is not the unique choice. We discuss alternative choices in the next section. The notations are:

- current date = 0
- horizon date = H
- portfolio loss percentile at the confidence level $\alpha = L_p(\alpha)$
- portfolio capital at the confidence level $\alpha = K_p(\alpha)$
- portfolio expected loss = EL_p
- portfolio contractual revenues = R_p
- revenues net of EL_p = expected spread (ES) = $R_p - EL_p$

The capital K_p depends on confidence level and on the reference value at horizon for determining losses of value. Simulations generate the distribution of future values at horizon, for a single facility as well as with the portfolio. From the distribution, we need to derive a loss distribution and loss percentiles $L_p(\alpha)$. The starting point is the portfolio value distribution. Open issues are:

1 what is the zero loss point from which losses should be calculated?
2 how should we define expected loss?
3 does capital calculation depend on expected loss or not at the aggregated portfolio level?
4 does capital depend on accrued income between now and horizon?
5 how should we derive the current value of capital given that the portfolio values are calculated at a future date?

Economic capital depends on the portfolio value used for zero loss. Capital $K_p(\alpha)$ at confidence level α is a loss percentile $L_p(\alpha)$ minus expected loss and minus the value corresponding to the zero-loss point. Net income generated over the period can serve as an additional cushion against losses (Figure 52.2).

There are various solutions for defining the zero loss point. For example, Credit Metrics uses the current value of the portfolio. Other options are to use as zero loss point the future expected value under no prior default, and deduct revenues generated between current date and horizon because they serve as an additional safety cushion. Expected loss can be defined in various ways as well because it also depends on the zero point for losses.

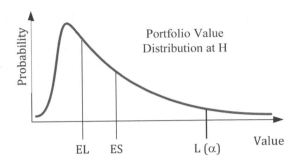

FIGURE 52.2   **Future loss distribution and statistics and capital**

52.2.1 Capital Under Default Mode

For a default-only model, ignoring migrations, and using book values only, the issue is simple. The value under no prior default is the book value. Hence, the zero-loss point is the aggregated book value as of horizon, conditional on no prior default, which is the current book value minus amortization until horizon. Capital should be net of expected loss EL, which includes both principal and accrued revenues. For a default model, the expected loss is the expectation of all book value losses at horizon. It is equal to book value multiplied by the default probability and multiplied by the loss given default. Considering the accrued portfolio net revenues, R_p, as an additional cushion for absorbing losses is another option. Only accrued portfolio revenues conditional on no prior default provide a cushion against losses. The most comprehensive value of capital is net of expected loss, and, eventually, net from accrued revenues conditional on no prior default.

$$K_p(\alpha) = L_p(\alpha) - (R_p \mid \text{no default}) - \text{EL}_p$$

52.2.2 Capital Under Full Migration Mode

For a full valuation model, the expected value at horizon is random and depends on excess spread of facilities over market spread and the related "roll-down" effect, migrations, the forward risk-free rates plus the forward credit spreads matching the final credit state.

For a single facility, the expected value results from all migrations, including migrations to the default state. For the default state, the expected value depends on value if there is no default plus the recoveries under default. Without prior default, the value at horizon is an expectation over all possible credit states other than default. The expected value is the weighted average of expected values under no prior default, multiplied by the survival probability, plus the value given default (recoveries) multiplied by the default probability. The equation is:

$$E(V_H) = E(V \mid \text{no default}) \, [1 - d(0, H)] + E(V \mid \text{default}) \, d(0, H)$$

It is simpler to assume that $(V \mid \text{default})$ is certain, as recoveries, which is restrictive. Otherwise, we should consider the expected value under default, which is the expectation of the recovery distribution. Such expected value embeds expected loss. The zero point for potential loss is the expected value conditional on no prior default, or $E(V \mid \text{no default}) [1 - d(0, H)]$. At this point, we can simply use the following notations:

$$E(V \mid \text{no default}) = E(V \mid \text{no default}) [1 - d(0, H)]$$

$$E(V \mid \text{default}) = E(V \mid \text{default}) \, d(0, H)$$

The expected loss EL is the difference between the value under no default and the value under default.

$$EL_p = E(V \mid \text{no default}) - E\,(V \mid \text{default})$$

The capital is in excess of EL, or equal to the loss percentile minus expected loss, ignoring excess spread.

$$K(\alpha) = L(\alpha) - [E(V \mid \text{no default}) - E(V \mid \text{default})]$$

If we choose to consider excess spread as an additional cushion against future losses, we deduct it from the above:

$$K(\alpha) = L(\alpha) - [E(V \mid \text{no default}) - E(V \mid \text{default})] - (\text{ES} \mid \text{no default})$$

For a portfolio, the expected value also includes expected loss and expected excess spread. Capital should be determined with the same principles than above for a default mode model. The most general capital formula is similar to above equation:

$$K_p(\alpha) = L_p(\alpha) - E(V_p \mid \text{no default}) - (\text{ES}_p \mid \text{no default}) - EL_p$$

The zero point for measuring potential losses, or capital, is $E(V_p \mid \text{no default}) + (\text{ES}_p \mid \text{no default}) - EL_p$. The capital is valued as of horizon.

Moody's-KMV Portfolio Manager follows these principles. Credit Metrics uses the current value, and does not calculate the expected value under no prior default. Both are feasible choices for calculating the capital.

52.2.3 Expected Loss

Under full valuation, the expected loss depends on the starting point, current value or expected value under no prior default. Using current value as the zero loss point, the expected loss is:

$$EL_p = \text{expected value of portfolio} - \text{current value}$$

Using expected value of portfolio at H under no default as the zero loss point, the expected loss is, as above:

$$\text{EL}_\text{p} = E(V \mid \text{no default}) - E(V \mid \text{default})$$

Moody's-KMV Portfolio Manager provides the calculations of both terms to get the expected loss.

52.2.4 Economic Capital and Loss Volatility

A common practice is to express economic capital as a multiple of loss volatility LV_p of the portfolio. This multiple derives from the prior determination of the loss distribution and the loss statistics serving as the zero point for capital. It is not a parametric multiple, such as the one embedded in the normal distribution. Rather it is derived from capital using the simulated loss distribution. But it is convenient to write capital as a scaled factor of loss volatility:

$$K_\text{p}(\alpha) = m(\alpha)\text{LV}_\text{p}$$

The multiple of loss volatility embeds the skewness and the kurtosis of the loss distribution. It does not mean at all that the loss volatility calculated from the loss distribution summarizes all moments of this distribution.

The most important application of this formulation is capital allocation based on the risk contributions of facilities to the portfolio loss volatility. Such risk contributions, properly defined, sum up exactly to the portfolio loss volatility. With the multiple $m(\alpha)$, it is easy to convert these "risk contributions" to the portfolio loss volatility into capital allocations.

52.2.5 From Future Values to Current Capital

The economic capital calculated as above is the Credit VaR. However, it is calculated as of horizon. Another adjustment is required to find the economic capital as of today.

Since loss values are at horizon, they should be brought back to current date to determine capital properly. The rationale for the choice of the discount rate is as follows. Since capital is available today to meet future loss, we can invest it risk free and get $(1 + y_f)$ times the current capital at the horizon of one year. If the risk-free rate is 5% and we have 100 today as capital, we will have 105 in one year. Future losses should match the future value of capital at the risk-free rate. This is equivalent to matching the current capital with future losses discounted at the risk-free rate.

This rule implies that capital be actually invested in risk-free assets. Otherwise, capital would generate additional risk, requiring additional capital, etc. Note that this rule is not neutral for calculating risk-adjusted return, using capital as a metric for risk. It implies adding up to the revenues of any facility the revenues from capital invested at the risk-free rate.

52.3 RAROC CALCULATIONS AT PORTFOLIO AND FACILITY LEVELS

This section anticipates Chapter 55 on risk-adjusted performance. Risk-adjusted measures of performance include the RaRoC ratio and shareholders' value added (Sva). Both measures use the capital as risk metrics. Summarizing the risk adjustment, RaRoC is a ratio of revenues to capital while Sva is the difference between revenues and the cost of capital.

Because capital can be defined in various ways, the RaRoC ratio depends on consistent definitions of the numerator and the denominator and the Sva depends as well on the definition of capital. We discuss here the RaRoC calculations. There are two choices for revenues. Either we use gross revenues or net expected loss. Expected revenues should apply only to those facilities that do not default since accrued revenues before defaulting count in recoveries. For capital, the various definitions are listed above.

If the revenues are net of expected loss, the capital should also be, otherwise, the expected loss would count twice. If the revenues are the contractual revenues, not netting the EL, capital should include both expected and unexpected loss. If the revenues net from expected loss serve to absorb losses, capital should be net of expected revenues. Table 52.1 shows examples of alternate calculations of RaRoC. We assume that the revenues from capital at the risk-free rate, or $y_t K_p(\alpha)$, are included in the total revenue figures.

With revenues netted from capital, the RaRoC ratio is not any more proportional to revenues because revenues are both on the numerator and the denominator. It is easy to increase revenues and observe that all RaRoC ratios increase with contractual revenues. The RaRoC based on capital in excess of expected revenues or in excess of EL_p are both lower than the RaRoC on total expected and unexpected loss. When netting expected loss from revenues, negative values are possible because the expected loss might be bigger than revenues. In addition, risk-free exposures generate a zero capital, or a negative one when considering revenues! RaRoC is irrelevant in such cases, and it is still possible to determine target revenues as mark-ups over operating costs (Chapter 55).

The actual RaRoC values within a mark-to-model framework are more complex than they look. Under full economic valuation, the loss percentile and the EL_p depend both on contractual revenues because of the mark-to-model calculation discounts the revenues. Such revenues appear only implicitly in the above ratios because $L_p(\alpha)$ and EL_p derive from mark-to-model values that embed revenues.

TABLE 52.1   RaRoC values under various definitions of capital

Revenues, R_p	80	80	80
EL_p	50	50	50
$L_p(\alpha)$	400	400	400
Capital	$L_p(\alpha)$ 400	$L_p(\alpha) - EL_p$ 350	$L_p(\alpha) - R_p - EL_p$ 270
RaRoC Numerator	Revenues 80	Revenues $- EL_p$ 30	Revenues $- EL_p$ 30
RaRoC formula	$R_p/[L_p(\alpha)]$	$(R_p - EL_p)/[L_p(\alpha) - EL_p]$	$(R_p - EL_p)/[L_p(\alpha) - R_p - EL_p)]$
RaRoC	20.00%	8.57%	11.11%

53

Capital Allocation and Risk Contributions

The loss distribution is a prerequisite for determining risk contributions, since all loss statistics, expected loss, portfolio loss volatility and portfolio capital, derive from the loss distribution.

There are several risk contributions. The first ones are the risk contributions of facilities within an existing portfolio. These risk contributions are defined as a decomposition of the portfolio loss volatility. Marginal risk contributions are the changes of risk "with and without" an additional unit of exposure, a facility or a sub-portfolio of facilities. Both risk contributions to capital are derived from risk contributions to portfolio loss volatility.

The risk contributions serve as the basis for the capital allocation system, which serves for determining how much capital is utilized by a single facility or a sub-portfolio. They also serve as a metric for risk-adjusting performances and making them comparable across the bank's portfolio. The purpose of this chapter is to define risk contributions and to demonstrate their basic properties that differentiate their respective usages.

Section 53.1 discusses normative capital allocations as opposed to effective capital utilizations resulting from existing exposures. Section 53.2 provides definitions of alternate measures of risk contributions. Section 53.3 defines standalone individual losses of facilities, or risk measures independently of the portfolio context. The next section (Section 53.4) discusses risk contributions within a portfolio context, when a fraction of the standalone risk is diversified away by the portfolio. Section 53.5 summarizes the basic properties of risk contributions, which are demonstrated in Section 53.6. Section 53.7 uses the example of the two-obligor portfolio for illustrating the properties of risk contributions. The last section (Section 53.8) is an appendix that shows how to derive risk contributions for any number of obligors in matrix format.

Contents

53.1 NORMATIVE CAPITAL ALLOCATIONS AND CAPITAL EFFECTIVE UTILIZATIONS

Two important risk metrics are expected loss and economic capital, measured by unexpected loss in excess of expected loss at a given confidence level, or credit VaR. Economic capital, when used in conjunction with expected loss, is the most comprehensive risk metric because it embeds all components of risk. For market risk, VaR embeds sensitivity and risk factors, volatility and dependencies. For credit risk, credit VaR embeds default probabilities and recoveries, size of exposure, and dependency across losses.

Expected loss allocations do not raise any issue since expected losses are additive whatever the loss correlations. On the other hand, risks are sub-additive and measures of capital allocation have to transform individual facility risk or sub-portfolio risk in additive capital allocations. The first section discusses the distinction between normative capital allocations and effective utilizations of capital, or capital charges due to existing exposures.

53.1.1 Normative Risk Allocations Versus Capital Utilizations

The risk allocation issue exists only for capital because unexpected losses are highly sensitive to loss correlations, or diversification effects. They do not add up arithmetically, and are "sub-additive:" the sum of individual risks is less than the risk of the sum. Capital allocation requires a methodology for defining the risk allocated to a transaction or a sub-portfolio, called the "retained risk" post-diversification effect, consistent with the total diversified risk. Consistency means here "additive." We are looking for an allocation key making the total risk equal to a sum of terms called risk contributions.

Capital allocations have two different meanings, which are unfortunately identical in the current risk terminology. They might refer either to "normative" allocations or to actual allocations of capital to the existing bank's portfolio. Normative allocations are like authorizations. They define how much capital should not be exceeded by a subset of transactions. They act as a limit, by industry for example. Like authorizations they depend on management policies. Normative allocations are authorizations, or caps, on capital utilizations of risk contributions. Should we need to refer to normative allocations, we would designate them as capital authorizations. Although normative capital allocations are business decisions, such capital allocations would be myopic if capital utilizations cannot be measured.

53.1.2 Capital Utilizations

When addressing capital allocations as the measure of capital used up by those transactions, technical issues arise because risks are "sub-additive." Considering an existing portfolio, or an existing portfolio plus some new transactions, the issue is to define the fraction of the global and diversified risk of the portfolio that should be allocated to any existing transaction or sub-portfolio, or to new transactions. Those are capital utilizations.

There is a key difference between regulatory capital and economic capital. Regulatory capital is calculated by transaction and then summed up to make up total regulatory capital. Hence, there is no issue for regulatory capital charged for credit risk which adds up the capital charges for transactions. Regulators defined capital charges for credit risk as embedding some average correlation effect, but not the actual diversification effect that is specific to a portfolio.

When using economic capital, either credit VaR or market VaR, dependencies, or diversification effects, make risks non-additive. The issue is to define some methodology for moving top-down or bottom-up from total capital to individual transactions or sub-portfolios. The capital allocation system provides the top-down and bottom-up links between the global, diversified, risk of the bank's portfolio and individual transactions or sub-portfolios.

Capital utilizations serve as a risk metric. As a measure of risk, they make up a basis for limit management. They also serve for defining risk-adjusted performance, since such measures require a measure of risk.

Such capital allocations are called risk contributions of facilities or sub-portfolios to the overall portfolio risk. The terminology applies to both credit risk and market risk when using economic measures of risk rather than additive regulatory capital charges. The economic risk contributions should also add up arithmetically to obtain the total risk, for reconciling allocated risks with the overall risk. For pricing purposes, they should also be such that pricing based on risk contributions should keep the portfolio risk-adjusted return in line with the overall risk-adjusted target.

There are many types of risk contributions. Risk contributions include those applying to the existing transactions, others are variations of the portfolio risk "before and after" inclusion of new transactions. The convention in this text is that "risk contributions" apply to the existing portfolio, whereas "marginal risk contributions" measure the incremental risk due to new transactions. The modeling of risk contributions necessitates defining risk contributions to the portfolio loss volatility and risk contributions to the portfolio capital. Some also consider the risk contributions to the "fat tail" of the loss distribution as being relevant for some issues, such as reducing the capital given the confidence level, or simply identifying those transactions that contribute more to extreme risk. For common usages, the former two types of risk contributions are sufficient: risk contributions and marginal risk contributions. Risk contributions are defined in such a way that they add up to the existing portfolio capital or loss volatility.

For allocating existing risks, risk contributions apply. They measure the current risk, or capital utilizations, within the existing portfolio. The gap between capital utilizations and normative capital authorizations measures the capability of expanding businesses subject to capital constraints. When considering new transactions, the issue is to determine the additional risk to the existing portfolio. Measuring additional risk requires marginal risk contributions for limit management and for risk-based pricing, which should compensate for the additional risk.

53.2 DEFINITIONS OF RISK CONTRIBUTIONS

In this section, we define three risk metrics relevant for a facility or a sub-portfolio. The standalone risk of a facility X is the risk of a transaction considered in isolation from any portfolio, when its risk is not diversified by the portfolio. The risk contribution of a facility within a portfolio P is the risk of the same transaction, considering diversification within a portfolio. It designates the fraction of risk retained, post diversification, or "retained risk," which is considerably less than standalone risk. Note that the risk contribution depends both on the transaction and on the portfolio. Within a small portfolio, there would be less diversification and retained risk should be higher. Within a large portfolio, everything else being held equal, the retained risk should be much lower.

The marginal risk contribution of a new facility added to a portfolio P is the incremental risk of the portfolio when adding such a facility. It is defined as the difference of the portfolio risk with the facility and the portfolio without the facility. Incremental risk can be positive or negative.

In terms of notations, we designate:

- the risk contribution of any facility "i" within the existing portfolio P as RC_i^P
- the marginal risk contribution of an additional facility X to the portfolio P as $MRCX^{P+X}$.

Even though risk contributions should add up to capital, we use as intermediate variables the portfolio and facility loss variances and volatilities. The benefit of starting from variance is that the variance of portfolio loss can always be decomposed into additive terms. With N facilities, there are N variance terms and $N(N-1)$ covariances terms embedding correlations. Volatilities do not sum up arithmetically as variances do. Still, it is more convenient to define risk contributions as contributions to portfolio loss volatility. The portfolio variance is the sum of variances and covariances. Contributions to loss volatility should also be additive. Since portfolio loss volatility is the portfolio loss variance divided by portfolio loss volatility, by definition, risk contributions to portfolio loss volatilities can be defined by dividing each term of the sum of variances and covariances by the same portfolio loss volatility. After scaling them with this common factor, they add up to the portfolio loss volatility.

Moving from definitions to risk measures:

- the standalone risk is the loss volatility of a single facility
- the marginal risk contribution is the algebraic change in portfolio loss volatility when adding a facility "X" to the portfolio
- the risk contribution of a facility I to a portfolio P is the covariance of the random loss of this single facility I with the random portfolio loss aggregated over the entire portfolio (including I), and divided by the loss volatility of this aggregated loss. Such risk contribution is also called "absolute" risk contribution to avoid confusion with the marginal risk contribution
- risk contributions to capital derive from portfolio volatility.

Among the definitions above, the first two are intuitive and the third sounds mathematical. The fourth item needs further explanation since the ratio of capital to volatility depends on the shape of the portfolio loss distribution and the loss percentiles used for defining capital. Next, we examine the properties of these definitions and show why they are relevant.

53.3 STANDALONE INDIVIDUAL LOSSES

Risk contributions always refer to a facility of obligor i and to a reference portfolio P. The portfolio P is made of N facilities. Each facility i relates to a single obligor. The notations apply to both default mode and full valuation mode models. However, all examples use calculations in default mode only for simplicity.

The losses are random variables. For the single facility i, $i = 1$ to N, the random loss is L_i. The exposures, X_i, $i = 1$ to N, are supposedly deterministic. The loss under default for each facility "i," or L_i, equals the product of exposure and loss given default, LGD_i. The random loss takes values 0 or $L_i = X_i \times LGD_i$.

For introducing randomness in the default loss for individual facilities, L_i, $i = 1$ to N, we model default as a Bernoulli variable D_i taking the value 1 in case of default and zero otherwise, or an indicator function of the default event. The random loss is $L_i = L_i \times D_i$. The default probability is the probability of D_i having value 1, equal to d_i in default mode. Consider a single exposure with loss under default having the value L_i. From the formula deriving the expectation, variance and volatility for such an exposure (see Chapter 49):

$$E(X) = L_i \times d_i$$

$$V(X) = L_i^2 \times d_i(1 - d_i)$$

$$\sigma(X) = L_i \sqrt{[d_i \times (1 - d_i)]}$$

Since all risk contributions refer to a common portfolio P, it is convenient to use a superscript P for designating such reference portfolio in the subsequent notations.

The random portfolio loss L^P sums up arithmetically all random individual losses L_i of each obligor. The aggregated random portfolio loss is $L^P = \Sigma_{i=1,N} L_i$ for the N obligors. Since we sum up random individual losses, the expectation of the sum is $E(L^P) = \Sigma_{i=1,N} E(L_i)$.

The loss volatility is the standard deviation of a loss. It is σ_i for a single facility and σ_P for the entire portfolio. For a single facility, it is the standalone loss volatility. For the portfolio, the portfolio loss volatility is the volatility of a sum of the random individual losses and depends on correlations between individual losses L_i.

The "unit exposure" loss volatility of a single facility is the loss volatility for an exposure equal to one unit. In default mode, the unit exposure loss volatility is the usual $\sigma_i = (1 - d_i) \sqrt{d_i}$. The exposure weighted loss volatility is:

$$l_i \sigma^1_i = l_i \sqrt{[d_i \times (1 - d_i)]}, \text{ where } l_i = X_i \times LDG_i$$

The correlation coefficients between individual losses L_i and L_j are $\rho_{ij} = \rho_{ji}$. The standalone loss volatilities are σ_i calculated with the above standard formulae. Hence, $\rho_{ij} = Cov(L_i, L_j)/\sigma_i \sigma_j$.

In default mode, the loss results from default only. In the full valuation model, the loss for one facility follows a distribution and we should replace each d_i unique default probability by a discrete variable of which values are not limited to 0 and 1, but takes as many values as there are credit risk classes, including the default state, or by a continuous variable such as the distance to default. In both the discrete case and the full valuation mode, we should assign a probability to each final credit state. Such probabilities are transition probabilities from the initial credit state to the final credit state, including the default state, in the full valuation matrix model. They define the distribution of asset values under the structural default model, given initial asset value.

53.4 RISK CONTRIBUTIONS AND MARGINAL RISK CONTRIBUTIONS TO PORTFOLIO LOSS VOLATILITY AND TO CAPITAL

This section summarizes in the first subsection the key properties of risk contributions to portfolio loss volatility and capital, making them pivotal in the capital allocation system. The demonstration of the properties follows.

53.4.1 Risk Contributions, Portfolio Loss Volatility and Capital

The standalone risk is the loss volatility of a single facility. The risk contribution RC_i^P to the loss volatility of the portfolio is the contribution of an obligor i to the overall loss volatility σ^P. A risk contribution is additive, unlike risk. Therefore, by definition, the sum of all risk contributions should be the portfolio loss volatility:

$$\Sigma_{i=1,N}RC_i^P = \sigma^P$$

Risk contributions to the portfolio loss volatility differ from the risk contributions to the portfolio capital. For converting risk contributions to portfolio loss volatility into risk contributions to capital, we use the ratio $m^P(\alpha)$, the multiple of portfolio loss volatility σ^P to capital $K^P(\alpha)$:

$$K^P(\alpha) = m^P(\alpha)\sigma^P$$

The multiple depends on the loss distribution of the portfolio and the confidence level. If we know how to define risk contributions, we know the absolute contributions to capital, by multiplying each risk contribution by $m^P(\alpha)$.

53.4.2 Marginal Risk Contributions

We expand marginal risk contribution in the next chapter. But we define them now for contrasting them with risk contributions detailed here.

The marginal risk contribution to loss volatility is the change in portfolio loss volatility when adding an additional unit of exposure, a new facility, a new obligor, or a new portfolio. For instance, the marginal risk contribution of a new obligor "X," (or a subset portfolio "X" of obligors), is the variation of the loss volatility with and without an obligor "X" (or a subset of obligors).

Marginal risk contributions are MRC_X^{P+X}. The portfolio now becomes the initial portfolio plus the new obligor's facility "y." The marginal risk contribution of a single obligor "X" in a portfolio of N obligors without y, and $N + 1$ with X, is:

$$\mathrm{MRC}_X^{P+X} = \sigma^{P+X} - \sigma^P$$

The marginal risk contributions to the portfolio loss volatility and the marginal contribution to capital differ. The marginal risk contribution is the variation of the portfolio σ^P when adding x facility or obligor. The marginal contribution to capital is the corresponding variation of capital. These distinct marginal contributions do not relate in a simple way. The capital is $K^{P+y}(\alpha)$, with confidence level α. The two marginal risk contributions are:

$$\mathrm{MRC}_X^{P+X}(\mathrm{LV}^P) = \sigma^{P+X} - \sigma^P$$

$$\mathrm{MRC}_X^{P+X}[K(\alpha)] = K(\alpha)^{P+X} - K(\alpha)^P$$

The multiple $m^P(\alpha)$ changes when the portfolio changes, and becomes $m^{P+X}(\alpha)$, and it is not possible to move from marginal risk contribution to capital with a simple multiplication, because the portfolio $P + X$ does not have the same loss distribution as P. Unless otherwise specified, we use marginal risk contribution as the marginal change of the loss volatility of the portfolio.

53.4.3 Usages of Risk Contributions and of Marginal Risk Contributions

Marginal risk contributions serve for determining the additional capital consumed by an additional facility or the capital saved by withdrawing a facility from the current portfolio and for pricing purpose. We show in the next chapter that:

- pricing in such a way that the revenues of an additional facility equals the target hurdle rate of return times the marginal risk contribution of the new facility ensures that the target return of the portfolio on capital remains constant or above the minimum hurdle rate
- marginal risk contributions to the portfolio loss volatility are lower than absolute risk contributions to the portfolio loss volatility; however, marginal risk contributions to the portfolio capital can be higher or lower than contributions to the portfolio capital.

Risk contributions and marginal risk contributions address different issues. The key distinction is ex post versus ex ante applications. Risk contributions serve for ex post allocations of capital based on effective usage of line while marginal risk contributions serve for making ex ante risk-taking and risk-based pricing decisions.

53.5 BASIC PROPERTIES OF RISK CONTRIBUTIONS

The formal definitions and properties of risk contributions are expanded in the next section. In this section, we summarize the basic properties as an overview of this next section. Risk contributions resolve the issue of breaking down the portfolio risk into additive contributions to global risk of each facility or sub-portfolio. We provide evidence that risk contributions defined as follows have the subsequent properties in the next section.

The risk contribution to the portfolio loss volatility of a facility i to a portfolio P is the covariance of the random loss of this single facility i with the aggregated random portfolio loss over the entire portfolio (including i), and divided by the loss volatility of this aggregated random loss.

Risk contributions to loss volatility, multiplied by the multiple of overall capital to overall portfolio loss volatility, sum up exactly to the portfolio capital. This is the key property making them the foundation for the capital allocation system resolving the issue of allocating risks.

For an existing facility, we show that the risk contribution is proportional to the standalone risk. The ratio of the risk contribution of a given facility to the facility loss volatility is lower than 1. It measures the diversification effect at the level of a facility. This ratio is the "retained risk," or the risk retained within the portfolio, as a percentage of the standalone risk of a facility. This retained risk, or RR_X, measures the un-diversifiable risk of the facility by the portfolio. The complement to one measures the gain from diversification. By definition of risk contribution, the retained risk is:

$$RR_X = \text{undiversified risk/standalone risk} = RC_X/\sigma_X$$

The facility RR_X depends upon the entire correlation structure with the portfolio. The higher is the RR_X ratio, the higher is the undiversifiable risk of the facility. It is important to track the retained risks for identifying facilities contributing more to portfolio risk. Conversely, for diversification purposes, low RR_X values identify transactions that increase the diversification of the existing portfolio.

53.6 THE CAPITAL ALLOCATION MODEL AND RISK CONTRIBUTIONS

This section provides the theoretical formulas of portfolio loss variance and volatility, their decomposition in risk contributions and shows how to derive the capital allocations. This is the basic capital allocation model. The next section illustrates these theoretical formulas and provides a fully detailed numerical example using the two-obligor portfolio example (Chapter 48).

53.6.1 Risk Contributions to Portfolio Loss Volatility

All variances and covariances include the size effect of exposures in this section. The portfolio loss volatility is the square root of the portfolio loss variance σ^2_P. The loss variance of a portfolio is the variance of a sum of individual losses:

$$\sigma^2_{\,P} = \mathrm{Cov}(\Sigma_i L_i, \Sigma_i L_j) = \Sigma_i \mathrm{Cov}(L_i, L_P)$$

The variance is also the sum of the covariances between each individual facility loss and the portfolio loss. It is also equal to the summation, for all combinations of i and j, of the $\rho_{ij}\,\sigma_i\,\sigma_j$ terms:

$$\sigma_p^{\,2} = \Sigma_i\, \Sigma_j\, \rho_{ij}\,\sigma_i\,\sigma_j$$

The correlation coefficient between the losses of i and j is:

$$\rho_{ij} = \mathrm{Cov}(L_i, L_j)/\sigma_i\,\sigma_j$$

The variance of the portfolio loss is the summation of all covariances across the entire set of pairs of facilities. In order to check this formula, it is useful to decompose it into its risk contribution components. The portfolio loss variance is:

$$\sigma_p^{\,2} = \Sigma_{i=1,n}\, \mathrm{Cov}(L_i, L_P)$$

The portfolio loss variance is the sum of all covariances of individual obligors' losses with the portfolio. This allows utilizing a shortcut for demonstrating directly that the absolute risk contributions to loss volatility are additive.

$$\sigma_p^{\,2} = \mathrm{Cov}(L_P, L_P) = \mathrm{Cov}(\Sigma_i L_i, L_P) = \Sigma_i \mathrm{Cov}(L_i, L_P)$$

The portfolio loss volatility is, by definition, the portfolio loss variance divided by the portfolio loss volatility:

$$\sigma_p = \Sigma_i \mathrm{Cov}(L_i, L_P)/\sigma_p$$

Each term of the summation is the covariance of each single obligor's loss and the portfolio loss divided by the portfolio loss volatility. The risk contribution to portfolio volatility, RC_i^P, is defined as:

$$RC_i^P = \mathrm{Cov}(L_i, L_P)/\sigma_P$$

Risk contributions defined as this ratio sum up to the portfolio loss volatility:

$$\Sigma_i RC_i^P = \Sigma_i[\mathrm{Cov}(L_i, L_P)]/\sigma_P = \sigma_P$$

Writing that $\mathrm{Cov}(L_i, L_P) = \rho_{iP}\,\sigma_i\,\sigma_P$ and dividing both terms by σ_P, we find that the absolute risk contribution $\mathrm{Cov}(L_i, L_P)/\sigma_P$ is:

$$RC_i^P = \mathrm{Cov}(L_i, L_P)/\sigma_P = \rho_{iP}\,\sigma_i$$

The absolute risk contribution of a facility is proportional to the correlation with the rest of the portfolio and with the facility standalone risk. These very simple rules relate risk contributions to portfolio volatility, by summing up each risk contribution:

$$\Sigma_i RC_i^P = \Sigma_i [Cov(L_i, L_P)]/\sigma_P = \Sigma_i \rho_{iP} \sigma_i = \sigma_P$$

This simple relation shows explicitly why risk contributions are higher than others. They combine the correlation effect with the portfolio and the magnitude of the standalone risk.

We have found that $RC_i^P = \rho_{iP} \sigma_i$. Therefore, the retained risk RR_i of an individual facility, the ratio of risk contribution to standalone risk, is identical to its correlation coefficient with the entire portfolio: $RR_i = \rho_{iP}$. Since all correlations coefficients are lower than or equal to 1, this demonstrates the general result: $RC_{iP} \leq \sigma_i$.

53.6.2 Specific Cases

A specific case is that of independence, where all covariances terms are zero. Then:

$$\sigma_P^2 = Cov(L_P, L_P) = Cov(\Sigma_i L_i, L_P) = \Sigma_i V(L_i)$$

The total portfolio variance is the sum of all individual variances and the portfolio loss volatility becomes the square root of this summation. The risk contribution becomes:

$$RC_i^P = V(L_i)/\sigma_P = \sigma_i^2/\sigma_P$$

or the ratio of the standalone loss variance of the facility to the loss volatility of the portfolio. The undiversifiable risk ratio becomes $RR_i = \sigma_i/\sigma_P$, the ratio of the standalone risk of the facility to the portfolio loss volatility.

Another reference case is the uniform portfolio, with uniform equal exposures, loss given default, and the same correlation across all pairs of facilities. Such portfolio has a loss volatility and loss percentiles that depends on its correlation. According to the above, all risk contributions in the limit distribution obtained with standard normal variables become equal since $RC_i^P = \rho_{iP}\sigma_i$ becomes simply the uniform correlation. Capital allocation, or risk contributions, under uniform correlation, is equivalent to allocation of overall economic capital at the pro-rata of standalone loss volatilities of facilities.

53.6.3 From Risk Contributions to Capital Allocation

The risk contributions sum up to the portfolio loss volatility, but do not add up to capital. In order to proceed to capital allocation, we use the multiple of loss volatility providing the capital at a given confidence level. The loss distribution provides both loss volatility and capital at a given confidence level, from which the multiple derives. If capital $K(\alpha)$ is the capital at the confidence level α, there is always a multiple $m(\alpha)$ such that $K(\alpha) = m(\alpha)LV_P$. We also know that $LV_P = \Sigma_i RC_i^P$. For obtaining the capital allocations, we multiply the risk contributions by the multiple $m(\alpha)$, the ratio of portfolio capital to loss volatility, both resulting from the loss distribution:

$$K(\alpha) = m(\alpha)LV_P = \Sigma_i m(\alpha)RC_i$$

The capital allocation system simply allocates the fraction $m(\alpha)RC_i^P$ of capital to the facility or the sub-portfolios i. For a sub-portfolio, such as those of business units, the capital allocation

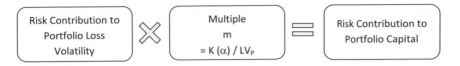

FIGURE 53.1   Risk contributions to portfolio loss volatility and capital allocation

simply sums up all $m(\alpha)RC_i^P$ over all facilities of the sub-portfolio, using the additive property of risk contributions (Figure 53.1).

53.7 SAMPLE CALCULATIONS OF RISK CONTRIBUTIONS

This section uses the example of the two-obligor portfolio and a default correlation of 10%. All calculations are in Chapter 48, where we detail the loss distribution of a portfolio of two obligors, with default correlation. We only need to replicate the results here. Tables 53.1 and 53.2 replicate the details of exposures and the loss distribution for this same portfolio.

The cumulated loss probabilities provide the loss percentiles. For instance, the loss at the 7% confidence level is 50, and the loss at the 0.906% confidence level is 100. The second percentile is roughly the loss at the 1% confidence level. For confidence levels lower than or equal to 0.906%, the loss is maximum, or 150. Between 7% and less than 0.906%, the loss is 100. Between 11.094% and less than 7.00%, the loss is 50.

The sequence of calculations is as follows:

- calculate standalone loss volatilities and expected loss for each obligor
- calculate the portfolio (A + B) loss volatility, given diversification effect: this is the starting point for risk allocation
- define portfolio capital according to loss percentiles at various confidence levels
- finally, derive the risk contributions to portfolio loss volatility and to portfolio capital.

TABLE 53.1   Standalone default probabilities and default correlations

	Default probability	Exposures, X_A and X_B
A	7.00%	100
B	5.00%	50
ρ_{AB}	10.00%	

TABLE 53.2   Loss distribution (default correlation = 10%)

	Probabilities	Cumulated probabilities
A & B default	0.906%	100.000%
A defaults	6.094%	99.094%
B defaults	4.094%	93.000%
None default	88.906%	88.906%

53.7.1 Standalone Expected Loss and Portfolio Expected Loss

The expected loss of obligor i is $E(L_i) = d_i \times L_i$ in value. The expected loss for the portfolio of obligors is the summation of individual obligors expected losses: $EL_p = \Sigma_i(d_i \times L_i)$. The expected losses are the exposures times the standalone default probabilities. The expected loss of the portfolio is independent of the correlation and is the sum of standalone expected losses. The expected losses of A and B are the default probability multiplied by the exposure or 100 multiplied by 7% = 7 and 50 multiplied by 5% = 2.5 respectively for A and B.

53.7.2 Standalone Loss Volatilities and Portfolio Loss Volatility

The standalone loss volatility of obligor i, with i = A, B, in value is:

$$\sigma_i = L_i\sqrt{d_i(1-d_i)}$$

The loss volatility of obligor i per unit of exposure value is:

$$\sigma_i^1 = L_i\sqrt{d_i(1-d_i)},$$

which is a percentage of exposure. The loss volatility of obligor i is equal to $\sigma_i^1 l_i$. The unit exposure volatilities are:

$$\sigma_{1A} = \sqrt{d(A)\left[1-d(A)\right]} = 25.515\% \text{ for A}$$

$$\sigma_{1B} = 21.794\% \text{ for B}$$

The loss volatilities of A and B are:

$$\sigma_A = 100\sqrt{7\%(1-7\%)} = 25.515$$

$$\sigma_B = 50\sqrt{5\%(1-5\%)} = 10.897$$

In Table 53.3, we provide in the last line the arithmetic summation of exposures and of standalone loss volatilities, which is higher than the portfolio loss volatility due to diversification effects.

TABLE 53.3   Unit exposure loss volatilities and loss volatilities

Facility	Exposure	Default probability	Unit exposure volatility	Exposure weighted loss volatility
A	100	7%	25.515%	25.515
B	50	5%	21.794%	10.897
Portfolio[a]	150			36.412

[a] Arithmetic sums and no diversification effect.

TABLE 53.4 Loss distribution statistics

EL	9.50
Loss volatility	28.729
Loss variance	825.36

53.7.3 The Portfolio Loss Volatility

The direct calculation of loss statistics is in Chapter 48 (Table 53.4). The loss volatility is the square root of the portfolio loss variance or 28.729. It is the starting point for allocation of risk. The portfolio loss volatility is lower than the sum of the standalone volatilities, the difference measuring the diversification effect, equal to $36.412 - 28.729 = 7.683$.

53.7.4 Risk Contributions to Volatility

Table 53.5 provides the standalone loss volatilities, the portfolio loss volatility, and the risk contributions to loss volatility and capital (the latter being the capital allocations). The issue is how to derive the risk contributions RC to the total portfolio A + B. The direct calculation proceeds as defined above by calculating the contributions to the portfolio variance divided by the portfolio loss volatility. The risk contributions are:

$$RC_i^P = \text{Cov}(L_i, L_P)/\sigma_P$$

$$= \text{Cov}(L_i, L_A + L_B)/\sigma_P$$

$$= [\text{Cov}(L_i, L_A) + \text{Cov}(L_i, L_B)]/\sigma_P$$

The covariances are functions of standalone volatilities and correlation coefficient using:

$$\text{Cov}(L_X, L_Y) = \rho_{XY}\sigma_X\sigma_Y$$

The two risk contributions can be expanded, making explicit all terms making up each risk contribution:

TABLE 53.5 Risk contributions to the portfolio loss volatility

	A	B	Portfolio
Loss volatility (weighted by exposure)[a]	25.515	10.897	36.412
RC to loss volatility	23.628	5.101	28.729

[a] The sum of standalone loss volatilities is 36.412, higher than the portfolio loss volatility of 28.729 derived from the loss distribution.

$$RC_A^P = [\rho_{AA}\sigma_A\sigma_A + \rho_{AB}\sigma_A\sigma_B]/\sigma_P$$

$$RC_B^P = [\rho_{BA}\sigma_B\sigma_A + \rho_{BB}\sigma_B\sigma_B]/\sigma_P$$

We know all terms of this equation:

- $\rho_{AA} = \rho_{BB} = 1$
- $\rho_{BA} = \rho_{AB} = 10\%$
- $\sigma_A = 25.51$
- $\sigma_B = 10.90$.

In this case, RC_A^P and RC_B^P are:

$$RC_A^P = (25.51^2 + 10\% \times 25.51 \times 10.90)/28.73 = 23.628$$

$$RC_B^P = (21.79^2 + 10\% \times 25.51 \times 10.90)/28.73 = 5.101$$

It is easy to verify that the risk contributions sum up to the loss volatility:

$$RC_A^P + RC_B^P = 28.729$$

53.7.5 Capital Allocation

The ratio of capital to loss volatility depends on the confidence level. With a confidence level of 0.906%, the loss percentile is 150 and capital is the loss percentile in excess of the expected loss or $K(0.906\%) = 150 - 9.5 = 140.5$. Since the portfolio loss volatility is 28.729, the ratio $m(0.906\%)$ of capital to loss volatility is $m(0.906\%) = 140.5/28.73 = 4.89$. The risk contributions to the portfolio capital are the multiples of the allocated loss volatilities times the multiple. There are, respectively, for A and B, $23.628 \times 4.891 = 115.55$ and $5.101 \times 4.891 = 24.95$, summing up to the capital 140.50. They are the capital allocations. We can now complete the previous table (Table 53.5) with capital allocations (Table 53.6).

The capital allocation uses the risk contributions. Nevertheless, we could also use other criteria such as the ratios of individual standalone risks to their sum for performing the same task. What are the drawbacks and benefits of these two alternate schemes?

The risk contributions of A and B are respectively 23.63 and 5.103, summing up to 28.73. The percentage allocations are 23.63/28.73 and 5.103/28.73, or, respectively, 74.43% and 16.07%. We could use another key for allocating capital, such as standalone risk. The standalone loss

TABLE 53.6 Absolute risk contributions to the portfolio loss volatility

Capital in excess of EL	140.5		
Multiple of Loss Volatility	4.891		
RC to LV of portfolio	23.63	5.10	28.73
RC to Capital of portfolio	115.55	24.95	140.50

volatilities of A and B are respectively 25.515 and 10.897, also summing up to 36.41 > 28.73. The corresponding percentage allocations would be 25.515/36.412 and 10.897/36.422, or 70.07% and 29.93% respectively. The capital allocation to B with risk contributions is heavier than with standalone risks, and the opposite occurs for A.

The major difference is that the risk contributions embed the correlation structure, while standalone risks do not. In the following, we use contributions to loss volatilities. In the final section we provide the general formula that applies with more than two obligors and uses a matrix format.

53.8 APPENDIX: CALCULATION OF ABSOLUTE RISK CONTRIBUTIONS FROM THE VARIANCE-COVARIANCE MATRIX

The absolute risk contributions derive from the simple matrix formula of the variance of the portfolio loss. This matrix extends to any number of obligors. For proceeding, we stick to the default model with two obligors, but the formulas are general and apply to full valuation models as well (Table 53.7). The variance of the portfolio loss distribution is:

$$\text{portfolio loss variance } \sigma_P^2 = \mathbf{X} \, \Sigma \, \mathbf{X}^T$$

- $\mathbf{X}$ is the row vector of exposures, or 100 and 50
- $\mathbf{X}^T$ is the column vector of exposures, the transpose of the above
- Σ is the unit variance-covariance of the portfolio of exposures, with each term equal to $\rho_{AB} \sigma_A \sigma_B$
- ρ_{AB} is the default correlation between A and B.

The "unit exposure" variance-covariance matrix, Σ, combines the correlation matrix and the unit exposure volatilities. The unit exposure loss volatility of X is $\sqrt{d_i(1-d_i)}$, for any obligor X. The generic formula of covariance: $\text{Cov}(A, B) = \rho_{AB} \sigma^1_A \sigma^1_B$ provides all terms of the unit exposure variance-covariance matrix (Table 53.8). For example:

TABLE 53.7 Exposures, default probabilities, loss volatilities and default correlation

Exposure	Weight	Default probability	Unit standalone volatility
100	66.67%	7%	25.515%
50	33.33%	5%	21.794%
150	100.00%		
Default correlation, ρ_{AB}	10%		

TABLE 53.8 "Unit exposure" variance-covariances matrix

6.5100%	0.5561%
0.5561%	4.7500%

$$\rho_{AB}\sigma^1_A\sigma^1_B = 10\% \times 25.515\% \times 21.794\% = 0.5561\%$$

The matrix format applies to the calculation of any portfolio loss volatility, as illustrated in the chapter on correlations. Here, we focus on a specific additional step allowing obtaining the vector of risk contributions. The sequential steps are the following.

- Multiplying the row-vector of exposures X by the "unit" variance-covariance matrix Σ results in a row vector of the unit covariances of individual obligors A and B with the portfolio loss, or 6.788 and 2.931. A sample calculation is as follows. The covariance of A with portfolio P = A + B, Cov(A, P), depends only on unit covariances and on A's exposure: Cov(A, P) = $100 \times 6.51\% \times 50 \times 0.5561\% = 6.788$. In order to find the risk contributions, we simply need to divide these by the portfolio loss volatility obtained in the next step.
- Multiplying this row vector by the transpose of X, we get the variance of the portfolio loss 825.358, and the square root is the portfolio loss volatility 28.729.
- Equivalently, we can directly calculate the covariance of each exposure with the portfolio by the multiplication of unit covariances by the exposure of the obligor, instead of using the entire vector X^T. For example $X_A \times Cov$A, P) = $100 \times 6.788 = 679$ is the covariance of A with the portfolio P. Similarly, $X_B \times Cov(B, P) = 50 \times 2.931 = 147$. Obviously, these two covariances add up to the same portfolio variance than before 825.358.
- Dividing these covariances, 679 and 147, by the portfolio loss volatility, we obtain the absolute risk contributions of A and B in value, as a row vector, 23.628 and 5.101. They are $RC_A^P = 679/28.729 = 23.628$ and $RC_B^P = 147/28.729 = 5.101$.
- Summing up these two risk contributions in value, or 23.628 + 5.101, gives the portfolio loss volatility 28.729.
- Using the risk contributions in percentage of the portfolio loss volatility, we obtain the capital allocation coefficients based on risk contributions, or 82.24% and 17.76%.
- Finally, the risk contributions to capital are directly derived from the absolute risk contributions to loss volatility using the multiple $m(1\%) = 3.15$, this multiple necessitating the knowledge of the entire loss distribution.

All risk calculations in matrix format are in Table 53.9. The final table (Table 53.10) summarizes the capital allocation process.

TABLE 53.9 Calculations of portfolio loss variance and volatility and of absolute risk contributions

Default correlation matrix

I	10.00%
10.00%	I

Variance-covariance matrix

Transposed $\mathbf{X}^T$ vector

Σ (unit exposure)

6.5100%	0.5561%
0.5561%	4.7500%

100
50

X vector

100	50

σ_{AP}	σ_{BP}	Variance
6.788	2.931	825.358

$X_A \sigma'_{AP}$	$X_B \sigma'_{BP}$	Variance
679	147	825.358

ARC to LV (value)

$X_A(\sigma'_{AP}/\sigma_P)$	$X_B(\sigma'_{BP}/\sigma_P)$	Volatility
23.628	5.101	28.729

ARC to LV (%)

σ_{AP}/σ_P	σ_{BP}/σ_P	
82.24%	17.76%	100.00%

TABLE 53.10 Risk contributions to loss volatility and to capital

Multiple, $m(1\%) = 3.15$	A	B	Portfolio
RC to LV (value)	23.628	5.101	28.729
RC to capital (value)	74.430	16.070	90.500

54

Marginal Risk Contributions

Marginal risk contributions are the incremental risks due to a new facility or a new sub-portfolio added to an existing portfolio. They are risk differences before and after inclusion of a new facility or a new sub-portfolio. Marginal risk contributions serve essentially for risk-based decisions and pricing while risk contributions are the basis for the capital allocation system for the existing portfolio.

The subsequent chapter on risk-adjusted performance (Chapter 55) shows that marginal risk contributions are the correct references for risk decisions and for risk-based pricing because they guarantee that the return remains in line with the target overall return on capital.

Section 54.1 defines marginal risk contributions to portfolio loss volatility and provides sample calculations, using the simple two-obligor portfolio. Section 54.2 defines the marginal contribution to capital, with sample calculations, and shows that they always add up to the final portfolio capital. Section 54.3 is a summary of the properties of marginal risk contributions. Section 54.4 shows that marginal risk contributions to the portfolio loss volatilities are always lower than the risk contributions and lower than standalone loss volatilities.

Contents

54.1 MARGINAL RISK CONTRIBUTIONS TO LOSS VOLATILITY

For illustrating what happens with marginal risk contributions, we again refer to the same two-obligor portfolio. This is not as restrictive as it looks like, because we could consider that A is the existing portfolio and that B is another portfolio, rather than single obligors. The main mechanisms are more explicit when we concentrate on this extremely simple case of two such sub-portfolios.

Determining the marginal contributions of either B or A to the portfolio loss volatility or to capital is extremely simple. The final portfolio (A + B) is always the starting point. The marginal risk contributions are differences between the risk of A + B and the risks of A or B. We consider in most cases that A is the initial portfolio and A + B is the final portfolio. The marginal risk contributions are noted as MRC(B) or MRC(A), depending on whether B or A are second to enter into the portfolio. The risk metric is the loss volatility. The starting point in Table 54.1 is the standalone loss volatilities of A and B plus the final portfolio loss volatility.

When the initial portfolio is A, the marginal contribution of B to the portfolio loss volatility is the latter minus the loss volatility of A (Table 54.2):

$$MRC(A) = 28.729 - 25.515 = 3.214$$

This simple table (Table 54.2) shows that the marginal risk contribution of B is lower than its risk contribution and its standalone risk:

$$MRC(B) < RC(B) < \text{standalone risk (B)}$$

$$3.214 < 5.101 < 10.897$$

We now shift the entrance order, using B as the initial portfolio, and B + A as the final portfolio, and we repeat the calculations (Table 54.3). The marginal risk contribution of A is:

$$MRC(A) = 28.729 - 5.101 = 17.832$$

We observe again the same properties as above:

$$MRC(A) < RC(A) < \text{standalone risk (A)}$$

$$17.832 < 23.628 < 25.515$$

TABLE 54.1   Loss volatility for A, B and the portfolio, A + B

	A	B	Portfolio	Sum
Loss volatility, LV_i	25.515	10.897	28.729	36.412

TABLE 54.2   Marginal risk contribution to the final portfolio loss volatility

	A	B	A + B
RC to LV of final portfolio	23.628	5.101	28.729
MRC to LV of initial portfolio		3.214	

TABLE 54.3   Shifting the order of entrance in the final portfolio

	A	B	A + B
RC to LV of final portfolio	23.628	5.101	28.729
MRC to LV of initial portfolio	17.832		

The marginal risk contributions of A or B to the same final portfolio A + B depend on who is "first in." But once all obligors are in the portfolio, risk contributions to loss volatility always sum up to the portfolio loss volatility.

Note a final property of marginal contributions. When summing up the marginal contributions to portfolio loss volatility of the second entrant, with B or A as second entrant, we find: 17.832 + 3.214 = 21.046. The sum of the marginal risk contributions to the same portfolio is lower than the loss volatility of the final portfolio. This is expected since both marginal contributions are lower than risk contributions, and the latter sum up to this final portfolio loss volatility.

54.2 MARGINAL RISK CONTRIBUTIONS TO CAPITAL

When considering capital, the loss distributions of the initial and the final portfolios differ. Therefore, we cannot derive the risk contributions to capital as multiples of the loss volatility, because the multiple changes when adding the second obligor. Nevertheless, we do know the final portfolio capital, and it serves as a starting point for calculating marginal contributions to capital.

We start again with a portfolio with A only, the biggest exposure, and add B for finding the incremental capital charge allocated to B. As already mentioned, there is no loss value matching the 1% probability, and we conservatively take the next upper value of loss. Starting with A only, this is A's total loss. The expected loss is 7, so that capital at 1% is the total exposure of A minus the expected loss, or $100.0 - 7.0 = 93.0$. Adding B, the portfolio capital becomes again 140.5. The marginal contribution to capital of B is $140.5 - 93.0 = +47.5$.

For calculating marginal contribution to capital, we start from the end, and take the difference between the final portfolio capital and the initial portfolio capital. The calculation now needs an additional input: the standalone capital of the first obligor in the portfolio, which is a loss percentile minus the expected loss.

We can repeat the process starting with B as the "first in" exposure. The capital at the 1% confidence level is the entire exposure of B minus its expected loss, or $50 - 2.5 = 47.5$. When adding A to B, we reach again the capital of the final total portfolio, 140.5, resulting in a positive incremental risk contribution of A of 93.0.

Note that negative marginal risk contributions to loss volatility and capital make sense for several reasons. Negative exposures, or exposures with negative correlations with the portfolio, can decrease the portfolio risk, measured by loss volatility or capital. This happens when hedging credit risk with credit derivatives[1].

Ignoring credit hedges, a new asset has, in general, two effects. The new asset increases the exposure of the portfolio, and, simultaneously, it diversifies away some of the risk of existing assets. In usual cases, the first effect more than offsets the second effect, and the net effect on portfolio risk, using as metric loss volatility or capital, is an increase.

Even though the sequence is not neutral for additions to a portfolio, marginal risk contributions to capital always sum up to the capital of the final portfolio, whichever is the first in, because we end up anyway with the same final portfolio A + B. Risk contributions also do, even though each one is above marginal contribution to portfolio volatility.

54.3 GENERAL PROPERTIES OF RISK CONTRIBUTIONS AND MARGINAL RISK CONTRIBUTIONS

We found empirically some rules applying when we compare risk contributions to marginal contributions and some properties of marginal risk contributions. In the next section, we show why those rules and properties are general. It is more convenient to provide an overview of these properties in this section before getting into the details.

First, consider portfolio loss volatility. The marginal risk contributions to the portfolio loss volatility are lower than the risk contributions, and the latter are also lower than standalone loss volatilities. Accordingly, marginal risk contributions to portfolio loss volatility add up to a value lower than portfolio loss volatility. This remains to be demonstrated in the general case.

Second, consider capital. Marginal risk contributions to portfolio capital can be higher or lower than risk contributions to capital, which are derived from the additive risk contributions to volatility. But, they always add up to the final portfolio capital, because this final portfolio capital is determined once we know A or B. Marginal risk contributions to capital are additive. Moreover, they cannot be derived directly from loss volatility because the multiple capital/loss volatility changes when moving from initial to final portfolio.

Third, this finding contrasts with the observation that the sum of marginal contributions to the portfolio loss volatility is always lower than the portfolio loss volatility, since each one of them is lower than the risk contribution of each component, according to the first property.

Fourth, with any asset that is not a credit hedge, marginal contributions to the portfolio capital can be positive or negative, while risk contributions to loss volatility of the final portfolio cannot be negative.

Finally, marginal risk contributions of the first entrant and of the second entrant depend on who is first and who is second, and on the confidence level.

Such properties are non-intuitive. They become apparent here because we use a two-obligor portfolio, and because individual exposures are large compared to total exposure. In real cases, the new exposures are usually small fractions of the portfolio exposure, and we do not have such drastic concentration effects.

The discrepancies between marginal risk contributions and between contribution to loss volatility and capital have implications. When considering risk-based pricing for new facilities, the correct measure of risk contribution is the marginal risk contribution. When considering risk-

---

1 Provided that the underlying of the credit derivatives is one of the obligors or an obligor's issue which is positively correlated with one of the obligor's credit risk.

based performance within an existing portfolio, or when considering capital allocation (utiliza-tion) within an existing portfolio, the correct measure is the non-marginal risk contribution.

In the subsequent paragraphs, we refer only to marginal risk contributions to loss volatility. The conclusions are relevant as well for capital, unlike in the above example, to the extent that new transactions are small compared to the reference portfolio, which makes it acceptable to use a constant ratio of capital to portfolio loss volatility. When considering risk-adjusted performances, we will refer to capital rather than loss volatility because capital is the metric used for risk adjustment.

Even though, with large portfolios, risk contributions to portfolio loss volatility and to capital are proxies of marginal risk contributions, potential discrepancies might be important in some cases and cannot be ignored. Vendor's models provide different outputs in terms of risk contributions. Moody's-KMV Portfolio Manager calculates risk contributions, while Credit Metrics calculates marginal risk contributions. Both sum up to capital in the end, but the terms of the sum might differ.

54.4 MARGINAL RISK CONTRIBUTIONS TO VOLATILITY VERSUS RISK CONTRIBUTIONS

Marginal risk contribution to volatility MRC_X is the difference of loss volatility of the portfolio with and without the facility X. Note that, when considering the marginal contribution of X, we always start from P, the initial reference portfolio before the new facility is added[2]. When we consider risk contributions, the reference portfolio becomes the final portfolio P + X. The superscript, P or P + X, designates the reference portfolio.

The starting point is the existing portfolio P. By definition, the marginal risk contribution of X, or MRC_X, is:

$$MRC_X = \sigma(P + X) - \sigma(P)$$

Also, since all risk contributions within portfolio P + X are additive and sum up to the loss volatility of "P + X":

$$\sigma(P + X) = RC_P^{P+X} + RC_X^{P+X}$$

For comparing the marginal contribution of X to the risk contribution of X, once X is in the portfolio, we replace the loss volatility of P + X, $\sigma(P + X)$, by the sum of the risk contributions of the two terms P and X to the final portfolio P + X:

$$MRC_X = RC_X^{P+X} + [RC_P^{P+X} - \sigma(P)]$$

Adding the new facility X to the initial portfolio P triggers two effects. The new facility increases the exposure and the risk of the initial portfolio. However, simultaneously, it diversifies away some of the risk of this initial portfolio. In other words, all existing facilities within the initial portfolio have lower risk contributions within the larger final portfolio. Hence, the risk con-tribution of the initial portfolio to the final larger portfolio has to be lower than its standalone

---

2   Unlike when dealing with non-marginal risk contributions.

volatility. This implies that the second term within brackets of the marginal risk contribution has to be negative. It is negative because it measures the incremental diversification effect due to the new facility. The retained risk (RC_P^{P+X}) allocated to the initial portfolio within the larger final portfolio is lower than its standalone risk $\sigma(P)$. Therefore, the marginal risk contribution of the new facility to the initial portfolio P has to be lower than its risk contribution within the final expanded portfolio P + X. Mathematically, $RC_P^{P+X} \leq \sigma_P$, which implies that $MRC_X^P < RC^{P+X}$.

Moreover, the standalone loss volatility of facility "X" is always larger than its risk contribution within the portfolio P + X because the latter risk contribution is the retained risk post-diversification effects.

Combining both results, we find the general property that the marginal risk contribution to loss volatility is lower than the risk contribution, which is also lower than the standalone loss volatility:

$$MRC_X^P < RC_X^{P+X} < \sigma_P$$

This explains the inequalities observed in our simple example.

54.5 MARGINAL RISK CONTRIBUTION AND SIZE OF AN EXISTING EXPOSURE

Instead of adding an additional exposure, we start with both A and B in the portfolio, but we increase B's exposure. It is much easier to look at risk contributions to portfolio loss volatility, because the loss volatility is easier to calculate than the marginal capital which depends on the loss distribution shape and confidence level. The risk contribution remains proportional to allocated capital to B. Using the same two-obligor portfolio, we increase gradually B's exposure size from zero to, for example, 200, higher than A's exposure. We obtain the graph shown in Figure 54.1, with the size of B along the horizontal axis and risk contributions along the vertical axis. As a check of the above, the risk contribution of B remains always above its marginal contribution to portfolio loss volatility.

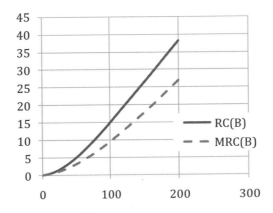

FIGURE 54.1 Risk contribution when exposure increases

Moreover, both contributions increase more than proportionally to exposure. This is the rationale of economic limits. If we assume that the revenue from B is proportional to B's exposure, then the return on capital allocated to B declines. At some point, it might become uneconomical to expand further B's exposure because the return would fall below a minimum required return. When we discuss risk-adjusted performance, we will measure the return on allocated capital as the all-in-revenues of B minus expected loss to allocated capital. Such a result relies on the assumption that revenue is a constant percentage of exposure, which is quite restrictive.

SECTION 14

Risk-adjusted Performance

Traditional measures of performances are book returns on equity and capital (ROE or ROC), or ratios of profit to equity and to the capital base. The book return on asset (ROA) is the ratio of the all-in income from lending to the size of the loan. For the trading book, the profitability is its P & L, measured as the variation of value over a period.

But such ratios are not risk-adjusted and cannot serve for comparing performances across facilities or sub-portfolios with different risks or for making explicit the relationship between risk management guidelines and the bank's profitability. The metric for risk-adjusting performances are the capital allocations, or risk contributions.

The standard measures of risk-adjusted performance are "RaRoC," or "risk-adjusted return on capital" and "SVA," or "shareholders value added"[1]. In simple terms, RaRoC measures a profit divided by risk, using capital as a metric of risk, while SVA measures whether facilities add value by charging to client more that the cost of risk of a position.

This section includes two chapters.

- Chapter 55 explains the rationale for defining risk-adjusted measures of performance. It makes a distinction between risk-adjusted performance of existing portfolio lines and risk-based pricing for new transactions, which relate, respectively, to risk contributions and marginal risk contributions.
- Chapter 56 focuses on implementations: economic income statements, monitoring risk-based performance and consistency of risk-based pricing with the overall return required for the bank's portfolio.

---

1   See Bennett, 1991.

55

RaRoC and Shareholders' Value Added

In the financial universe, there is no expected performance without a price to pay in terms of risk. Since only risk–return combinations are meaningful, comparing performances across transactions or business units is inconsistent, and pricing risk to customers without risk adjustment is not feasible.

The cost of capital "fallacy" refers to using a single value for the cost of capital, embedding the average risk of the bank's equity to activities of which risks differ. The cost of capital should be differentiated according to risks. In risk-adjusted performance, we keep the cost of capital constant, but we account for risk by allocating capital to transactions or sub-portfolios. If the risk increases, the capital allocation increases and the cost of the capital charge increases, even though the cost of capital to the bank remains the same.

Section 55.1 defines the cost of capital, which combines the required return of equity, the capital allocated to each transaction of the sub-portfolio and the risk-adjusted performance measures, the risk-adjusted return on capital (RaRoC) and shareholders' value added (SVA). Section 55.2 discusses risk-based pricing for new transactions and shows that pricing is consistent with marginal risk contributions. Section 55.3 details the calculation of the RaRoC ratio. Section 55.4 makes explicit the risk premium due to capital charge, or the value of capital-based risk. Section 55.5 introduces SVA measures of performance and shows the consistency with RaRoC measures. Section 55.6 focuses on discrepancies between the market price of credit risk and the capital-based price of the same risk. Such discrepancies lead to arbitrages by banks that are further illustrated in Chapter 59 on credit portfolio management.

Contents

55.1 RISK-ADJUSTED MEASURES OF PERFORMANCE

In risk-adjusted measures of performances, the risk metric used is the capital allocation. The two traditional measures of risk-adjusted performances are the RaRoC ratio, or "risk-adjusted return on capital," and the "SVA," or shareholders' value added.

55.1.1 Definitions

The RaRoC ratio is a profitability percentage comparable to minimum risk-adjusted benchmarks, or hurdle rates. The SVA is a value which combines both percentage profitability and size of transactions, for finding out whether a transaction or a sub-portfolio creates or destroys value for shareholders. In both cases, the risk adjustment is based on both expected loss and the economic capital allocated, which is a risk contribution. RaRoC is the ratio of income netted from expected loss and operating costs to economic or regulatory capital used as the risk-adjustment metric. SVA is the revenue net of debt cost minus the expected loss and the cost of regulatory or economic capital. The cost of capital is valued using a hurdle rate representative of the cost of raising capital times the amount of capital allocated. Before detailing the calculations, we highlight the merits of both measures.

A ratio ignores the size effect, so that we do not know, when using RaRoC only, whether a transaction generates much income or not without looking at its size. The SVA figure is a value depending on size, but a high value does not indicate whether it results from a low percentage RaRoC combined with a large size of transaction or the opposite, a high profitability by unit of capital allocated combined with a small size. Both measures are useful and should be used together.

Finally, there is a distinction between the trading book and the banking book. For market transactions, defining a relevant P & L requires some historical experience and conventions for isolating revenues from sales and revenues from trading. Hence, what follows is easier to implement with credit risk of the banking portfolio.

As a reminder, two systems are pre-requisites for this process: the funds transfer pricing system, which serves for allocating income; and the capital allocation system, which serves for allocating risks.

55.1.2 The Hurdle Rate and the Cost of Capital

The reference for hurdle rate is the cost of capital of the bank. The cost of capital of a bank differs from the cost of capital of a corporation. In a non-financial corporation, the cost of capital is defined as the weighted cost of equity and debt, the weights being the target weights of equity and debt. Such cost of capital, or weighted average cost of capital ("Wacc"), is the discount rate applicable to investment projects for calculating the net present value of the project.

In a bank, we do not consider debt because income is already defined in excess of cost of debt. The hurdle rate is the cost of equity, which is defined, as in non-financial corporations, as the required return on equity by shareholders.

The cost of debt remains mostly important, however. It depends on the credit rating of the bank, which influences the credit spread applicable to the bank. Also the cost of funding short-term is also critically affected by the inter-bank cost of liquidity, defined as a Libor. Such cost of liquidity includes a spread, which normally matches the average risk of the banks used as references for calculating a Libor. But the interbank rates can become much higher either because there are fears for the future of a particular bank, or because the financial system faces a liquidity crisis, such as the 2007–2008 crisis.

The hurdle rate, or cost of equity for the bank, is the equity risk premium above the risk-free rate that the market assigns to a particular bank. The cost of equity is theoretically defined by the well-known CAPM model, which adds to the risk-free rate a premium that depends on the systematic risk of the stock measured by the β of the stock.

When using risk-adjusted measure of performances, the cost of risk has only two components, the expected loss and the capital allocated to a transaction or a portfolio. The cost of allocated capital also has two components, the amount of capital charged and the percentage compensation, or hurdle rate, applicable to bank's capital. The cost of capital is the cost of equity for the equity portion of bank's capital. For Tier 2, or subordinated debt, there is also a cost, which is the excess spread of subordinated debt above the spread applicable to bank's debts that are senior to Tier 2. Both ROE and ROC, inclusive of Tier 2 capital, are relevant.

55.1.3 The "Ex Ante" and the "Ex Post" Views

"Ex ante" means before a risk decision is made and "ex post" after it is made. Before making a risk decision, the issue is to define the incremental risk and the adequate target pricing. "Ex post," we need to break down the portfolio risk, measured by capital, into additive items, which are called the risk contributions.

Similar views apply for risk-adjusting performances. "Ex ante," we need to define how much to charge for a new facility of a client. "Ex post," we need risk-adjusted performances of facilities for monitoring and comparison purposes.

For making such distinction explicit, we define risk-adjusted performance measurement, or RAPM, as the "ex post" measure." Risk-based pricing is used for new deals, under an "ex ante" prospective. In both cases, the risk adjustment relies on expected loss and on allocated capital. The latter is a risk contribution. For RAPM, the risk contributions of existing assets are relevant. For risk-based pricing, the correct capital allocation is the marginal risk contribution. Note that it should be checked that marginal risk contributions are relevant for pricing, which means that they allow maintaining the risk-adjusted return of the existing portfolio, before and after including the new transactions, above the minimum target return.

55.1.4 The Reference Capital for Risk Contributions

Risk contributions add up to the bank's capital. But there are several possible references for capital.

The first one is the actual capital of the bank. This capital is usually above the required regulatory capital in order to avoid adjustments of capital depending on the transactions and the portfolio turnover. The regulatory capital is rule based. Regulatory capital charges are risk-adjusted in Basel 2, but they use standard diversification parameters that might not match the particular portfolio of the bank. The economic capital is the credit VaR and fully reflects the specifics of the portfolio. All three references are relevant.

Let us assume that we measure risk contributions to economic capital, lower than actual capital. For using actual capital as reference, the risk contributions should be scaled up using the ratio of actual to economic capital, normally higher than one. If available capital is higher than economic capital, and if the required return on available capital is 20%, the return on economic capital is higher than 20%, and vice versa. For instance, with available capital of 100, the target profit is $20\% \times 100 = 20$. If economic capital is lower, for example 80, the effective return on economic capital is higher and equal to $20/80 = 25\%$.

$$\text{return of economic capital} = 20\% \times (\text{available capital/economic capital})$$

$$\text{return of economic capital} = 20\% \times 100/80 = 25\%$$

A side issue is whether such discrepancies make sense economically. For instance, is it normal to require 25% on economic capital because it is smaller than available capital? Or is it normal to require 20% on available capital and have $20 \times 100/80 = 25\%$ on economic capital? Assume that economic capital is lower than actual capital. The higher return on economic capital is an incentive to take on more risks since the economic capital-based pricing is lower than actual capital-based pricing. Actual capital overstates the true risk of the portfolio. If we consistently price on economic capital, the bank will effectively take on more risks and, in the end, economic capital should tend towards available capital. Once they converge, there is a common base. Whatever the reference, risk-adjusted measures are scaled up or down when changing reference.

55.2 RISK-BASED PRICING AND MARGINAL RISK CONTRIBUTIONS

The goal of risk-based pricing is to determine the minimum target return for a new transaction, in line with the transaction risk and with shareholders' requirements. The cost of bank's capital is the benchmark for a RaRoC ratio. It also serves for the calculation of SVA. When referring to regulatory capital, the allocated capital is rule based. When referring to economic capital, we need to specify which capital allocation is relevant for pricing.

55.2.1 Risk-based Pricing and Marginal Risk Contribution to Capital

The existing portfolio is the initial reference portfolio P. Economic capital is a multiple of this portfolio loss volatility, $\sigma(P)$, or $m \times \sigma(P)$, and m is supposed to be constant. The constant assumption means that new transactions do not alter significantly the portfolio loss distribution. Otherwise, capital and the multiple m, have to be redefined when adding new transactions to the existing portfolio.

The required pre-tax and net of operating expense return is $k\%$, equal to the bank's hurdle rate or cost of equity. The target operating income is $k\% \times m \times \sigma(P)$. From there, the target all-in revenue of a new transaction is easily determined.

For example, a portfolio has a loss volatility of 100. The multiple m (capital/loss volatility) is 2. The hurdle rate is 25% pre-tax and after operating expenses. Assuming that the initial portfolio has a return of 25%, it would generate earnings initially equal to $25\% \times 2 \times 100 = 50$. A new transaction increases the portfolio loss volatility to 110. The marginal risk contribution to loss volatility of this new transaction is 10, and the incremental capital of this transaction is $2 \times 10 = 20$. The target net income when the new transaction is included in the portfolio is $25\% \times 2 \times 110 = 55$. This is an increase of $55 - 50 = 5$. This increase is exactly $25\% \times (220 - 200) = 5$, or the hurdle rate times the incremental capital. Pricing on a different base than marginal risk contribution would not maintain the portfolio minimum return on capital.

55.2.2 Risk-based Pricing and Risk Contribution to Capital

We now generalize the example. The initial portfolio is P and it becomes P + X, X being the new transaction. By definition, the marginal risk contribution to P is:

$$\text{MRC}_X^P = \sigma(P + X) - \sigma(P)$$

What should be the return required for the additional facility "X?" The hurdle rate is a percentage k on the capital of the existing portfolio. We assume again that the capital K is $m \times \sigma(P)$.

The facility percentage return r on capital allocated should be at least equal to the percentage hurdle rate k on capital. The required revenue in value is $k \times m \times \sigma(P + X)$. The return on capital without the new facility is $r \times m \times \sigma(P)$. The revenue from the new facility "X" should be at least $k \times m \times [\sigma(P + X) - \sigma(P)]$. The required return, in percentage of capital, on the new facility r is such that the return on the portfolio P + X, summing the income on the existing portfolio plus the income on the new facility, is at least $k \times m \times \sigma(P + X)$:

$$k \times m \times \sigma(P) + r \times m \times [(\sigma(P + X) - \sigma(P)] \geq k \times m \times \sigma(P + X)$$

Dropping the multiple m, the condition implies that $r \geq k$. Since the risk contribution (RC) of the transaction within the new portfolio is higher than the marginal risk contribution, pricing on the non-marginal risk contribution would overestimate the required income. The marginal risk contribution is the correct risk contribution for preserving a portfolio return higher than or equal to the cost of capital.

55.2.3 The Pricing Paradox with Marginal Risk Contributions

The usage of marginal risk contributions, lower than risk contributions, for pricing purpose sounds puzzling at first sight. It implies that pricing based on marginal risk contributions is lower than pricing based on risk contributions.

An example helps to understand the apparent paradox. For example, the marginal risk contribution to capital is 15 and the required return on capital is 20%, resulting in target income of 20% × 15 = 3. When the facility enters in the portfolio, it has a risk contribution within the final portfolio, for instance 17, higher than its marginal risk contribution to the initial portfolio, 15. The revenue of 3 does not provide 20% on 17. How could the revenue of 3 maintain the overall portfolio return?

In fact, 3 is the additional revenue required to compensate the overall portfolio capital after inclusion of the new facility. Suppose that all risk contributions before including the new facility sum up to 100. After inclusion of the new facility, all risk contributions sum up to 115, since 15 is the incremental capital. If the new facility has a risk contribution of 17 once it is included in the initial portfolio, this implies that the sum of all risk contributions over all facilities existing before the inclusion of the new one dropped down from 100 to 98. This is the only way for the final portfolio capital to be 115, given that the incremental capital is 17, since 98 + 17 = 115.

This illustrates the two effects of adding a new facility to an existing portfolio. The first effect is the direct increase of capital, and the second effect is the increased diversification of the existing facilities. The value of this increased diversification, in terms of capital, is equal in this example to 17 − 15 = 2. The new facility increases the overall risk incrementally and simultaneously diversifies the existing risks. This solves the pricing paradox. Pricing according to risk contribution of the new facility in the final portfolio would ignore the diversification effect, which makes all other risk contributions of existing facilities decrease. On the other hand, pricing on marginal risk contributions captures both the incremental risk and the increased diversification.

Mispricing is defined as the discrepancy between the theoretical target price and the effective price. Discrepancies often exist. Sometimes under-pricing is due to competition. Sometimes, banks choose to under-price some transactions because they expect to sell other products and services to a client. In the latter common case, the client's portfolio only is relevant for measuring risk-adjusted performance.

55.2.4 Risk-adjusted Performance versus Risk-based Pricing

Once a facility is entered in the portfolio, its return on capital drops, compared to the ex ante return on capital based on marginal contributions. This phenomenon results from the risk contribution of the new facility within the final portfolio being higher than the marginal risk contribution. In the above example, the facility generates an income of 3, and a return on marginal contribution to capital of 3/15 = 20%. Once it is in the portfolio, the new risk-adjusted performance becomes 3/17 = 17.65%. On the other hand, all other risk-adjusted performances rise because their risk contributions to capital get lower. This is the same paradox as above.

Still, the ex post risk-based performances using risk contributions remain relevant for comparing the risk–return profiles of facilities, clients, products and business units within the final portfolio. For comparing risk-adjusted performances, we simply need to be able to calculate the RaRoC of credit facilities or sub-portfolios using risk contributions to the final portfolio.

55.3 RAROC CALCULATIONS

Once the economic effects of adding a new facility are made explicit, we can detail the RaRoC calculation. The RaRoC ratio nets expected loss (EL) from earnings and further risk-adjusts performance by dividing net earnings by allocated capital.

55.3.1 Revenues

For credit risk, revenues include the interest margin, plus any upfront and recurring fees. The upfront fee increases the margin during the early life of the transaction. This makes the all-in spread higher in the early stage and lower in the later periods. The subsequent revenues would not be representative of the profitability of the transaction. In order to avoid such distortion and to use representative revenues across periods, it is common to use "all-in revenue" or "all-in spread" (AIS). The all-in revenue is an annualized value of interest income and fees calculated over the life of the transaction. The all-in spread is the spread over the cost of debt. It is a more relevant measure of excess revenues over cost of debt that the simple difference between the interest rate charged to a borrower minus cost of debt, which was named "commercial margin" in the ALM chapters. The all-in spread should be used instead, since there are always non-recurring fees and recurring fees.

55.3.2 Expected Loss

The expected loss netted from revenues has different interpretations depending upon whether it applies to individual transactions or to portfolios of transactions. For an individual transaction, the expected loss looks theoretical since the loss will either occur or not. The loss is never equal to the expected loss, since the effective loss is either zero or the loss given default, under default mode. For portfolios, expected loss has a statistical meaning because there is always a loss distribution. This is the rationale for economic provisioning. Setting aside a fraction of income of all transactions will, after aggregation, result in an economic provision meeting the overall expected loss requirement (as estimated on an ex ante basis). The expected loss of a single transaction should be viewed as an allocation of the overall expected loss of the portfolio. But the allocation is much simpler than capital allocation because expected losses add up arithmetically whatever the dependencies across transactions.

55.3.3 Other Costs

Finally, all other costs that enter into the profit calculations should ideally be considered. The operating costs allocated to a transaction or portfolios include direct costs and overheads. It is not easy to determine direct costs, although banks operating in the retail segment have experience of the average direct cost by type of transactions. When direct costs remain inaccurate, some normative allocation is used instead of the actual costs. The normative allocation, whatever the key for allocating costs, should sum up to actual operating costs. The calculation will remain identical, as the expanded formula below shows.

55.3.4 Expanded RaRoC Formula

We need some notations to designate all items, as we did in Chapter 29 on transfer pricing. As noted earlier, it is more convenient to make calculations before tax, because pricing is before tax, and to express all items as percentages of assets because the required all-in spread is in percentage of the exposure. Capital letters refer to values and small letters refer to percentages of exposure, except for the required return on capital, k, which is a percentage of capital. Duplicating the notations used previously:

- exposure: X
- asset all-in revenue: r (%)
- risk-free rate: i_f (%)
- cost of debt: i (%), inclusive of the credit spread applicable to the bank
- allocated debt: D
- operating costs: oc (%)
- expected loss: el (%)
- allocated capital RC (K), in monetary units
- required return on capital: k, as a percentage of capital, not exposure.

Target revenues should absorb the cost of debt, the operating expenses and generate a minimum required return k on capital. The RaRoC formula is:

$$\text{RaRoC} = [r \times X - i \times D - \text{el} \times A - \text{oc} \times X]/K$$

RaRoC is defined as long as capital K is not zero, meaning as long as risk is not zero. For risk-free transactions, the ratio is undefined. But, in such a case, the issue is to find the all-in rate charged to a risk-free borrower that would absorb all costs other than the cost of risk. Note that SVA is not subject to infinite or undefined ratios because it is a simple difference.

55.4 THE RISK PREMIUM EMBEDDED IN RISK-BASED PRICING

When using risk-based pricing, we have to make sure that RaRoC $\geq k$. The RaRoC numerator is simply the earnings before tax, or EBT. EBT should at least equal to $k \times K$.

$$\text{EBT} = r \times X - i \times D - \text{operating costs (OC)} - \text{expected loss (EL)} \geq k \times \text{capital}$$

If we substitute capital to debt for the amount of allocated capital, there is an excess cost equal to the differential between the cost of capital and that of bank's debt. But capital should be invested risk-free, otherwise it would generate additional risk. Therefore, we can consider that the exposure is entirely financed with the bank's debt and that we have the additional risk-free revenue from capital allocated. This modifies the revenue component of the earnings before tax, which becomes the all-in rate applicable to the borrower plus the risk-free revenue for the invested capital:

$$\text{all-in revenues} = r \times X + i_f \times K$$

The cost of debt becomes the bank's percentage cost of debt, inclusive of the bank's credit spread, multiplied by the exposure, or $i \times X$.

The financial earnings before tax are equal to:

$$r \times X + i_f \times K - i \times X$$

Operating costs and EL are often expressed as percentage of exposure, which is consistent with all-in rate charged to the borrower. The condition for meeting target profit follows:

$$r \times X + i_f \times K - i \times X - (\text{OC} + \text{EL}) \times X \geq k \times K$$

Next, we make explicit the risk premium due to credit risk, which is $(k - i_f) \times K$, and we divide by exposure to make all terms percentages of exposure:

$$(r - i) - (\text{OC} + \text{EL}) \geq (k - i_f) \times K/X$$

The differential $(r - i)$ represents, in the ALM chapters, the commercial margin in percentage of exposure, or the difference between the (annualized) all-in rate charged to the borrower and the cost of the debt that exactly mirrors the asset (the transfer price):

$$(r - i) \geq (\text{OC} + \text{EL}) + (k - i_f) \times K/X$$

The target risk-based all-in rate charged to the borrower should be such that:

$$r \geq (\text{OC} + \text{EL}) + i + (k - i_f) \times K/X$$

Deducting the risk-free rate from both sides, we have a condition on spreads over the risk-free rate, a single common reference for the borrower and the bank:

$$(r - i_f) \geq (\text{OC} + \text{EL}) + (i - i_f) + (k - i_f) \times K/X$$

The target all-in spread above the risk-free rate is proportional to a premium equal to $(k - i_f) \times K/X$. This premium is proportional to the ratio of capital to exposure and to the excess of cost of capital over the risk-free rate. It is called a risk premium since allocated capital is the metric for the risk of the asset.

This calculation is slightly different from the pricing calculation used in the ALM chapters. The risk premium was calculated as the excess cost of substituting capital to debt, in proportion of the capital allocated to the transaction, due to risk. The simpler relation ignored the fact that allocated capital for credit risk should be invested risk-free. The debt was lower than exposure by the amount of capital. The above rationale is more consistent because it eliminates the credit risk resulting from having capital invested in risky assets. Accordingly, since we saved the full cost of the bank's debt i, the risk premium was a function of $r - i$, not $r - i_f$. A numerical example of a RaRoC calculation follows in the next chapter.

Consider operating costs. If we set them to zero, the calculation of all-in revenues becomes a contribution for absorbing these costs. The minimum target all-in revenues has to be higher by the amount of such costs. Therefore, the cost allocation should be added to the required all-in revenues in Euro value or in percentage of exposure to obtain the required all-in revenue or the all-in spread in percentage of exposure.

55.5 SVA MEASURES

The "shareholders' value added" (SVA) is a measure in monetary units. SVA adjusts the revenues with expected loss, then with operating costs, and finally with the cost of the risk-based capital, equal to the hurdle rate k multiplied by allocated capital. Note that hurdle rate now appears explicitly in the calculation.

$$SVA = EBT - EL - k \times K$$

By definition, when the RaRoC is above the hurdle rate, the SVA is positive, and conversely. However, using both of them improves the reporting by providing both percentage profitability and size of profits. In the SVA equation, debt equals exposure, which implies that capital is invested risk-free.

$$SVA = r \times X + i_f \times K - i \times X - (EL + OC) \times X - k \times K$$

The risk premium over risk-free rate appears again as the spread of cost of capital over risk-free rate multiplied by capital allocated:

$$SVA = (r - i) \times X - (EL + OC) \times X - (k - i_f) \times K$$

A positive SVA implies the same condition that RaRoC $> k$, or:

$$SVA/X = (r - i) - (EL + OC) - (k - i_f) \times (K/X) \geq 0$$

By definition, a RaRoC above or equal to the bank's cost of capital $k\%$ is equivalent to SVA positive or zero, or creation of value. However, it is not equivalent to set as target a minimum ratio or a SVA value, because the SVA targets implicitly embed a target volume. Since both business volume and profitability per unit of capital are desirable, using both measures makes sense.

A well-known drawback of RaRoC is that the ratio becomes infinite or undefined when risk tends towards zero, such as with Aaa counterparties. When capital drops to zero, the target earnings are the operating costs, plus the cost of debt, plus any markup. Nevertheless, very high RaRoC and infinite ratios appearing in reports create confusion. SVA does not have this flaw. If risk is zero, the SVA equals earnings minus operating costs and remains meaningful. Sometimes, the earnings are negative. A negative RaRoC remains meaningful but is not easy to use. In such a case, the SVA will be negative as well. A negative SVA means that the business destroys value for shareholders and tells how much.

The rationale for using clients as reference for measuring RaRoC and SVA is that individual facility spreads often do not generate a RaRoC in line with target bank risk-adjusted profitability. Market spreads of large corporates do not compensate the bank's risk, although that depends on country and geographic areas. In Europe, typical spreads to large corporates in the bond market are in the 10 to 20 basis point range, and, substantially higher for small businesses. With such spreads, negative RaRoC might appear. The picture changes when aggregating all revenues, fees and spreads, over all facilities and services sold to single customers. Fees increase substantially the profitability and represent an increasing fraction of revenues. The client's RaRoC or client's SVA provide a more relevant image than single facility spreads, RaRoC or SVA.

55.6 THE PRICE OF RISK AND ARBITRAGE

In general, the capital-based price of credit risk will not coincide with the market price of credit risk. The risk premium derived from risk-based pricing using capital as risk metric has no reason to coincide with the market price of credit risk. For example, the market spread on a 1000 loan is 0.2% while the required capital is $4\% \times 1000 = 40$. The capital-based return should be $20\% \times 40 = 8$, or 0.8% of the book value of the loan. It is quite different from the market spread over the risk-free rate that is 0.2%. The implied capital in the market spread is the capital that would provide the required 20% return with the actual market spread. The market spread in monetary units is $0.2\% \times 1000 = 2$. The capital proving a 20% return with such spread is $2/20\% = 10$, instead of 40. This is the implied bank's capital in market credit spreads. Note that, theoretically, such an issue does not exist with expected loss, since credit spreads equal the loss rate. But it does when referring to capital measuring unexpected loss.

The example illustrates the discrepancy between market price of risk and the capital-based price of risk. Neither regulatory capital nor economic capital will coincide with the market-based price of credit risk, or spreads. Referring to two prices for the same risk will mechanically generate arbitrage. In the above example, lending at 20 basis points is not profitable for the bank. It would make sense only if other clients' revenues compensate the gap between the facility spread and the required return on capital.

Arbitrage emerges in general as soon as two measures of the same risk differ. A well-known case of possibly under-priced risk is that of securitizations, such as CDOs or other securitizations. The returns provided to investors by each asset-backed note is rating based. But if banks believe that the risk is lower than the risk measured by ratings, they will generate excess returns from CDOs. The CDOs would generate revenues, net of losses, higher than the rating-based revenues required by investors because actual losses are lower than rating-based losses. More generally, securitizations are economical for the bank as soon as they allow increasing the bank's return on capital while still offering the market spread to investors matching the ratings assigned to the various tranches issued by the securitization vehicle. Chapter 59 on credit portfolio management provides examples of regulatory arbitrage, through securitizations and usage of credit derivatives, which allow banks to generate a higher return on capital by taking advantage of such discrepancies.

According to the CAPM, the required return on capital results from the market price of systematic risk of the stock. The cost of equity depends on the systematic risk of the bank's stock in the equity market. The "internal price of risk" charged to a borrower depends on its contribution to the bank's portfolio capital. It translates into a minimum all-in spread that does not match, except by chance, the market credit spread applicable to the borrower.

Bond credit spreads above the risk-free rate relate to default probabilities, recovery rates, risk aversion and bond market liquidity. There are several sources of discrepancy between the bond spreads compensating market investors for credit risk and the all-in spread compensating the bank.

First, economic capital measures the contribution of the bond to volatility of losses of the bank's portfolio and is specific to each bank. Second, the required return on capital depends only on the general risk of the bank's stock, whether capital depends on both the general risk and the specific risk of the bank's portfolio. Therefore, the bank uses a cost of capital that depends on its systematic risk only through the β of its stock, for defining compensation to both systematic and specific risk. Finally, the market values credit risk through the bond credit spread, which depends on factors that are not related to a particular bank. Such discrepancies between the market price of credit risk and the capital-based pricing of the same credit risk create inevitably arbitrage opportunities.

56

Economic Income Statements

The primary purpose of this chapter is to present practical calculations when implementing risk contributions and risk-adjusted profitability measures. It details calculations of risk contributions, and of risk-based profitability, with ex post risk-adjusted performance measurements (RAPM) versus ex ante risk-based pricing (RBP). The calculations illustrate the general properties of the risk contributions and of risk-adjusted profitability, as introduced previously.

Economic income statements serve for reporting risk-adjusted measures of performance. When addressing risk-based pricing, the target price, or all-in revenue, results from moving up from target income to price piling up all costs, including the necessary mark-ups for risks. Assuming that prices are in line with both risk and the target compensation of risks, ex post RaRoC and SVA measures differ from the ex ante measures because the risk contributions replace the marginal risk contribution to capital once a facility is in the portfolio. Moreover, these measures drift with time, as risk does, when time passes.

The examples used for illustrating how risk contributions differ also show how they translate into differing risk-adjusted measure values. They also illustrate, through examples, that RBP using marginal contributions does ensure that the "ex post" RAPM of the portfolio using risk contributions is effectively in line with the target return.

Section 56.1 details the calculations of RaRoC and SVA and presents economic income statements, or risk-adjusted performance reporting on an ex post basis. Section 56.2 shows how to derive the target price from target return and risk and contrasts ex ante versus ex post views of risk-adjusted measures. Section 56.3 contrasts RaRoC and SVA based on the two types of risk contributions. It also shows through examples that ex ante pricing on marginal contribution guarantees ex post RAPM overall performance target for the portfolio during a period of portfolio expansion. For that purpose, the two-obligor portfolio used in Chapter 48 is used as an example. Section 56.4 is a reminder of the drift of risk-adjusted measures when time passes, suggesting that recording initial values, at origination, make sense.

Contents

56.1 THE CALCULATION OF RAROC AND SVA FOR CREDIT RISK

This section provides sample calculations of RaRoC and SVA using the formulas detailed in the previous chapter (Chapter 55). There is a required return on capital of 20% before tax, for calculating the charge for capital in SVA calculations and for comparing RaRoC to this minimum threshold target return on capital.

56.1 Calculation of RaRoC and SVA

Table 56.1 details a sample calculation. Simplifying assumptions are used:

- the horizon is one year
- the loss is identical to exposure (zero recoveries)
- the AIS is 2% of exposure
- the expected loss is 1%
- the economic capital is 3%
- the economic capital is a risk contribution

TABLE 56.1   RaRoC and SVA calculations before operating costs

Year	I
Exposure	1000
Parameters in % of outstanding balances	
Expected loss	1.0%
Economic capital	3.0%
AIS	3.0%
Cost of capital (before taxes)	20.0%
Yearly RaRoC and SVA	
Expected loss	10
Capital	30
AIS	30
− expected loss	−10
= AIS − EL	20
Cost of capital (20% × 20)	4.0
RaRoC	66.7%
SVA	16

TABLE 56.2 Economic income statement post operating costs

+ revenues (margins and fees)	30
− expected loss	10
= revenues net of expected loss	20
− direct costs[a]	3
− overhead allocation	2
= profit pre-tax	15
Capital	30
− cost of capital[b]	6.0
RaRoC	50%
SVA	9.0

[a] Allocated by product line.
[b] Hurdle rate = 20% pre tax.

- the cost of capital is the required return on equity, or 20% pre-tax
- finally, this is a pre-operating cost calculation.

Since RaRoC is above 20%, the SVA is positive. However, the RaRoC is pre-operating costs. A full calculation, post operating costs, should refer to the hurdle rate of 20%. If allocating of costs is not done, RaRoC and SVA are only contribution margins before operating costs. In Table 56.2, operating costs are 5. They include direct costs and overhead. The operating income nets them from revenues before calculating RaRoC and SVA.

56.2 RISK-BASED PRICING

A direct application of RaRoC and SVA is to determine the appropriate customer price, given risk. The approach is identical to the one used to derive price from a target ROE applied to the regulatory capital. The only difference is that the economic capital replaces regulatory capital. Instance of moving down from revenues to RaRoC and SVA, we move bottom up, from target return to target pricing.

The example shown in Table 56.3 shows the difference of target prices resulting from risk-sensitive measures of capital, either Basel 2 regulatory capital or economic capital. The example uses an exposure net of recoveries of 100, with a 100% weight for the capital charge, a cost of debt of 5%, and operating costs equal to 2% of exposure. The target customer rate covers the cost of debt and operating expenses, and provides a return on capital of 20% before tax (hurdle rate). The risk-free rate is 4.5%.

The cost of capital is equivalent to adding a risk premium proportional to capital multiplied by the differential cost of equity and debt, when using a 100% debt funding of assets. This premium collapses to zero when there is no risk, and, otherwise, it increases proportionally with capital.

Table 56.4 is a top-down calculation, with the same inputs as above. The all-in rate is 8.62% or 10.55%, applicable to the exposure of 1000 and capital equal to, respectively, 40 or 100. The resulting RAPM is 20%.

TABLE 56.3   Bottom-up calculation of risk based pricing (RaRoC ≥ 20%)

In € or % of exposure	Low risk	High risk
Exposure (X) €	1000	1000
Economic capital (K) €	40	100
Risk-free rate %	4.5%	4.5%
Cost of bank's debt %	5.0%	5.0%
Expected loss %	1.0%	2.0%
Operating expenses %	2.0%	2.0%
Total cost %	3.0%	4.0%
Risk premium = $(k - i_f) K / X$		
Cost of capital k (% of capital)	20.0%	20.0%
Cost of capital k – risk free rate i_f	15.5%	15.5%
Capital / X %	4.0%	10.0%
Risk premium = $(k - i_f) K / X$	0.62%	1.55%
Target risk-based all-in price and all-in spread		
Target all-in rate	8.62%	10.55%
Target all-in spread over risk-free rate	3.62%	5.55%

TABLE 56.4   Top-down calculation of RAPM

In €		
Exposure	1000.0	1000.0
All-in revenue	86.2	105.5
Risk-free rate	4.5%	4.5%
Revenue from investing capital	1.80	4.50
Total revenues	88.0	110.0
Cost of bank's debt %	5.0%	5.0%
Cost of bank's debt, debt = 1000	50.0	50.0
Operating cost	20.0	20.0
All-in earnings before tax	18.0	40.0
RaRoC calculation		
EL	10.0	20.0
All-in earnings before tax – EL	8.0	20.0
Capital	40.0	100.0
RAPM or RaRoC	20.0%	20.0%

When it is not feasible to calculate operating costs or to allocate them properly to transactions, they are replaced by a normative allocation. If we calculate the RaRoC by setting those as zero, the required all-in spread will decline by 2% in both cases. The all-in earnings become contributions that should absorb operating costs. If this standard contribution is 2% of exposure, identical to the one used above, the all-in spread will increase by 2% and the required all-in revenue will increase by the Euro amount (20). The calculation is identical, using normative allocation of costs for finding post operating costs RaRoC and required spread or revenues.

56.3 RISK-BASED PERFORMANCE, PRICING AND CAPITAL ALLOCATION

As an example, we expand the calculations of RaRoC and SVA for the same two-obligor portfolio used previously to illustrate the properties of marginal risk contributions and risk contributions once a transaction is within the portfolio. For simplification purposes, we ignore the operating costs included in the detailed calculations above. Note that, in all cases, the all-in spreads are additive and sum up to the portfolio all-in spread. Marginal as well as non-marginal risk contributions also sum up to total portfolio-allocated capital.

The characteristics of a portfolio divided in two sub-portfolios A and B (as in Chapter 48) are replicated in Table 56.5. The portfolio is used to compare risk-based pricing with ex post risk-adjusted performance, when the initial portfolio is A and when B is added for forming the final portfolio.

The capital is defined for the 1% confidence level. For the initial portfolio, capital is 93 and for the final portfolio, capital is equal to 140.5 and portfolio loss volatility is 28.729 (Table 56.6). The marginal contribution of B to loss volatility is 3.214 and the marginal risk contribution of B to capital is 47.5.

We assume that A has a RaRoC equal to 20%, the minimum required risk-adjusted return, and we consider adding B to get the final portfolio A + B. For ensuring the minimum return of 20% of the final portfolio, the pricing of B should be based on its marginal contribution to capital.

56.3.1 Risk-based Pricing

The RaRoC formula, without operating costs is:

$$RaRoC = (AIS - EL)/MRC$$

TABLE 56.5   Portfolio of two obligors

	Default probability	Exposure
A	7.00%	100
B	5.00%	50
ρ_{AB}	10.00%	

TABLE 56.6   Initial and final portfolio characteristics

	Initial	Final	
	A	A+B	Variation
Exposure	100.0	150.0	50.0
EL	7.0	9.5	2.5
Loss volatility	25.515	28.729	3.214
Capital at 1%	93.0	140.5	47.5

where MRC is the marginal risk contribution to capital. For the initial portfolio A, the capital required for A is 93. Equating its RaRoC equation to 20%, we find the corresponding target AIS for A:

$$\text{AIS} = \text{EL} + k \times \text{MRC} \times (K) = \text{EL} + 20\%\text{MRC} \times (K)$$

$$\text{AIS(A)} = \text{EL(A)} + k\% \times \text{MRC(A)} = 7 + 20\% \times 93 = 25.60$$

The next step is to find the target AIS for B, given its marginal contribution to capital, 47.5. The RaRoC formula, without operating costs, allows us to determine the target AIS of B as second entrant in the portfolio, given the required cost of capital of 20% pre-tax. Starting with A as the initial portfolio, the required AIS for B from the minimum RaRoC on its marginal contribution to capital is:

$$\text{AIS(B)} = \text{EL(B)} + k\% \times \text{MRC(B)} = 2.5 + 20\% \times (47.5) = 12.00$$

We check that the total RaRoC ratio for the final portfolio is again equal to 20%. We simply add up the AIS, the EL and the marginal contribution to capital, and apply the RaRoC formula to the portfolio A + B:

$$\text{RaRoC(A + B)} = [\text{AIS(A)} + \text{AIS(B)} - \text{EL(A + B)}]/K \times (\text{A + B})$$

$$\text{RaRoC(A + B)} = [25.60 + 12.0 - 9.5]/140.5 = 20\%$$

These calculations are summarized in Table 56.7, where the RaRoC of A + B is calculated as above.

TABLE 56.7   Incremental risk contribution and risk-based pricing

	Initial	Marginal	Final
Risk-based pricing	A	B	A+B
Required return on capital	20.0%	20.0%	20.0%
EL	7.00	2.50	9.50
MRC (capital)	93.00	47.50	140.50
Target AIS	25.60	12.00	37.60

56.3.2 Risk-based Performance

Once we have the final portfolio, the RAPM of each facility differs from the initial RaRoC because the calculation is based on the risk contributions to capital of the final portfolio. For the added sub-portfolio B, the marginal risk contribution to capital is higher than its risk contribution, once in the portfolio. The reverse is true for the initial sub-portfolio A. But the portfolio risk-adjusted return remains 20% because marginal contributions to capital and all-in revenues net of expected loss are additive. The risk-based pricing on marginal contributions to capital does maintain the overall portfolio return on target (Table 56.8).

TABLE 56.8 Risk-adjusted performance (ex post)

Capital allocations	A	B	A+B
RC (loss volatility)	23.628	5.101	28.729
RC (loss volatility) %	82.24%	17.76%	
RC (capital)	115.553	24.947	140.500

RAPM	A	B	A+B
AIS	25.600	12.000	37.600
EL	7.000	2.500	9.500
AIS − EL	18.600	9.500	28.100
RAPM (AIS − EL) / RC(K)	16.10%	38.08%	20.00%

The final portfolio return remains 20% but the risk-adjusted return of each facility changes due to the variations of risk contributions before and after entrance of B.

56.4 ORIGINATION AND POST-ORIGINATION FOLLOW UP

This latter format would apply to RAPM calculations when using them as ex post risk-adjusted measures of performance because we effectively start from given all-in spreads charged to borrower. For ex post calculations, the capital allocations would change. The risk contributions should be those that apply when transactions are within the portfolio, whether marginal risk contributions apply before they are included.

For reporting purposes, the risk-adjusted measures are historical. Before the risk decision, the capital allocations are marginal, and risk contributions increase after the transactions are included in the portfolio. Since the all-in spread is the same, the RaRoC declines after origination.

Moreover, RaRoC and SVA differ at origination and after because both risks and valuation change when time drifts. The drift results both from revenue and from risk drifts through time if both are measured until maturity of a transaction. Risk under default mode would decrease when residual maturity declines because the cumulative default probability declines when time passes (under constant valuation of exposure[1]). Such drifts are limited when using a single horizon for all exposures, making calculations more tractable.

There is a case for keeping track of RaRoC and SVA values at origination, and to guarantee these values to the origination business unit because they are not in control of ex post drifts. The issue is similar to that of transfer prices in ALM, which should be assigned to each transaction on an historical basis (as of date of origination) for avoiding exposure to interest rate risk of the commercial margin.

After origination, the transaction could be transferred to the credit portfolio management unit. Capital is then transferred to the credit portfolio management unit, which manages the loan portfolio using securitizations or credit derivatives (Chapters 58 and 59).

---

1 Under full valuation, the drift of time causes the valuation to migrate upward or downward, simultaneously with a declining exposure period when getting closer to maturity. The net effect of valuation and risk drift might be positive or negative.

SECTION 15

Credit Portfolio Management

Credit portfolio management starts with adequate descriptions of the portfolio, of risk concentrations and of the various risk metrics that can serve as credit limits. This static view is the point of entry for more active portfolio management.

Enhancing the risk–return profile of the portfolio can minimize risk given return, increase return at constant risk, or improve both if the portfolio structure is inefficient. Optimization is always subject to funding and capital constraints.

Credit portfolio management optimizes the existing portfolio within constraints, and, then goes beyond by freeing-up capital for facilitating origination while keeping credit risk concentration within limits.

The techniques for expanding origination under capital and funding constraints are essentially to off-load the risk from the balance sheet of the bank. Securitizations have been critical for expanding the origination business. Credit derivatives have a wide set of usages, such as customizing the credit portfolio risk profile and complying with limits, either hedging portfolio risk by buying credit derivatives or taking exposures synthetically by selling credit derivatives.

Both techniques have become hot issues in the financial crisis since they were vectors of contagion to the entire system. However, there is a difference between the sound economics of securitizations and using credit derivatives for hedging and transactions that can be seen as pure arbitrage transactions, arbitrage between the price of credit risk in the balance sheet and the price in capital markets, or arbitrage of regulations and rating agencies. The current status of securitization and credit derivative is mitigated. Some argue that they are the necessary vehicles for financing the economy while others see more their recent adverse effects of excess securitizations. The future will strike a compromise between the two views. Whatever the regulations will be, those techniques deserve full recognition as credit portfolio management as well as origination facilitating tools, in as much as they remain in line with sound economics.

This section covers credit portfolio management in three chapters.

- Portfolio analysis under a static view of the portfolio structure along risk metrics and business dimensions is an intermediate step. Portfolio optimization follows well-known principles, as inspired from market portfolio optimization by rebalancing exposures for improving the Sharpe ratio (Chapter 57).
- Credit portfolio management relying on securitization is fully expanded in several steps, from the setting up of securitization SPEs to the structuring of asset-backed notes issued by SPEs, the economic consistency of securitization vehicles, their economical effects on the originating bank, and up to assessing the resilience of these structures (Chapter 58).
- Credit portfolio management relying on credit derivatives, which completes the main aspects of active credit portfolios (Chapter 59).

57

Portfolio Analysis

This chapter presents sample reporting and analysis of the outputs of a portfolio model. For generating such analyses, a sample portfolio with different risk classes and sizes of exposures was created. A simulation based on the structural model of default was used to generate the loss distributions and statistics. The simulation used the standardized asset model of default, as described in Chapter 50 on simulations. Asset values are standard normal variables, dependent with a uniform correlation, and with a default point defined by the default probability assigned to each line. A default occurs when the asset value falls below the default point, and the loss, which equals the loss given default defined for each exposure, is assigned to each simulated default. The full process allows generating the entire loss distribution of the sample portfolio. The process developed throughout this chapter replicates all steps of implementation of credit portfolio models, from the original risk data, to simulations of the loss distribution, and up to typical reports from credit portfolio models.

The chapter provides various sample reports. The details of the sample portfolio are described in Section 57.1. The loss distribution generated with Monte Carlo simulations is described in Section 57.2. Section 57.3 provides a portfolio overview. It groups all aggregated statistics, starting from the simulated loss distribution and up to the portfolio capital and RaRoC, using definitions provided in previous chapters, plus a standard measure of size concentration. The capital allocation is based on risk contributions to portfolio volatility.

The next three sections (Section 57.4–57.6) provide three types of typical portfolio reports, drilling down into portfolio facilities. Section 57.4 cross-tabulates alternative metrics for risk, such as, for example, exposure versus expected loss and so on. Section 57.5 relates to performance and mis-pricing, or gaps between target values of performance measures and actual values across facilities. The third series of reports (Section 57.6) provide the links between risk and performance measures with business dimensions, such as business units, specialized, for instance, by product line, and by type of borrowers, or asset classes. This series of reports illustrates a business-oriented breakdown of the portfolio.

The details of the portfolio are provided in appendices, the first one (Section 57.7) with portfolio data and the second one (Section 57.8) with all outputs of the calculations and the simulations by individual line within the portfolio, such as capital allocation and risk-adjusted profit ratios. The last appendix (Section 57.9) describes the basic specifications of information technology systems allowing one to cross-tabulate the various dimensions that serve for analysing any portfolio and to drill down from any aggregated data set to individual lines of the portfolio.

Contents

57.1 THE SAMPLE PORTFOLIO AND THE SIMULATIONS

The portfolio description is in Appendix 1 (Section 57.7). The major characteristics are:

- 50 obligors
- uniform loss correlation of assets of obligors
- two risk classes, each with a default probability
- two business units and two industries
- unequal exposures and various percentages of exposure defining loss given default.

For illustrating the process of portfolio analysis, we do not need to use large numbers of risk classes or industries. The principle would be identical with more numerous segments.

57.1.1 Portfolio Data

The portfolio data is summarized in Appendix 1 (Section 57.7). The portfolio has 50 lines. The facility data is available in Appendix 2 (Section 57.8). There is one facility per obligor, with different exposures, loss given default percentages, default probabilities and all-in spreads. The maturity is one year for all facilities, so that there is no VaR at the one-year horizon. Facilities are in two risk classes, of which default probabilities are 1% and 2.5% respectively. There are two business units (V and W) and two industries (A and B). Facilities have unequal exposures, from 50 to 500, and loss given default percentages ranging from 20% to 100%. Exposures are at book value. The total exposure is 11,000, before recoveries. The total portfolio of loss given default is 6000. The portfolio uniform asset correlation is 30%. The revenues are all-in spreads. The accounting return on asset is the ratio of the AIS over total exposure.

57.1.2 Portfolio Simulations

For generating the loss distribution, the standardized asset model of default was implemented. The simulation is in default mode only, with only two credit states, default or survival. The standardized asset model of default follows the structural approach. Each asset value of each obligor is a normal standard variable. The asset values are dependent with uniform correlation, using the Cholesky methodology. The default point of the standardized asset value is defined by the default probability assigned to each line. Each default is materialized by a dummy variable equal to 1 when the line defaults and zero otherwise. Multiplying the dummy variable by the loss given default provides the line loss. Summing up across lines provides the aggregated portfolio loss. For each simulation, we have a portfolio loss.

For generating a smooth loss distribution, we conducted 50,000 simulation runs. The various portfolio loss statistics are derived from this empirical distribution, and include all loss percentiles, the average loss, or expected loss, and the portfolio loss volatility.

For each line, the expected loss and the unexpected loss are calculated. The unexpected loss for a default/survival distribution is simply $\sqrt{[d(1-d)]}$ multiplied by the loss under default, where d is the default probability of the line. For a uniform portfolio, it was shown that the risk contribution to the portfolio loss volatility is proportional to the uniform correlation times the loss volatility of each line. Therefore, the capital allocation is proportional to the ratio LV(i)/LV(P), or the individual loss volatility divided by the sum of the individual loss volatilities across the entire portfolio. In other words, the capital allocation is proportional to the standalone loss volatilities of each individual line.

The portfolio capital is defined from the 1% loss percentile of the simulated distribution. The portfolio capital is calculated as the loss percentile minus the expected loss, which sums up all individual expected losses. The revenues generated by the portfolio are not used for calculating capital. The capital in excess of expected loss at the 1% confidence level is equal to 955. The portfolio loss volatility is 221.1, resulting in a ratio of capital to loss volatility of 4.32. This multiple is used for allocating the portfolio capital to each line of the portfolio.

An all-in spread is assigned to each line. The RaRoC ratio is calculated as (AIS – EL)/RC, or the excess of all-in spread over expected loss to the capital allocation. Operating costs are ignored, implying that the ratio is a risk-adjusted contribution. The SVA of each line is calculated as AIS – EL – $k \times$ RC, or the excess of all-in spread in monetary units over expected loss and the cost of capital allocated. The required return on capital k is 25% pre-tax. Most of the outputs of such calculations for each line of the portfolio are replicated in Appendix 2 (section 57.8), which details results for each line.

57.2 PORTFOLIO LOSS DISTRIBUTION

The entire loss distribution, plus a zoom on the fat tail, for both the probability density distribution and the cumulated distribution are shown in Figures 57.1 and 57.2. The losses are in value. The density function exposure in the fat tail area shows irregularities, reflecting the differentiated frequencies of default and of the sizes of defaulted exposures.

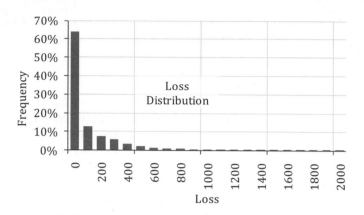

FIGURE 57.1 **Portfolio loss distribution and "fat tail"**

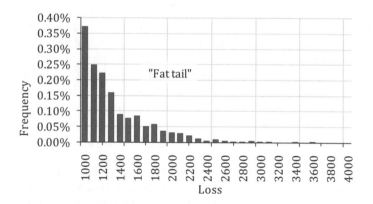

FIGURE 57.2 **Portfolio loss distribution: zoom on the "fat tail"**

Figures 57.3 shows the cumulative distribution, from which loss percentiles derive, and the fat tail frequency distribution. The loss percentile at the confidence level 1% is 1055, or 9.59% of the total exposure of 11,000, and 17.58% of the total loss given default of 6000. These are relatively high numbers, resulting from the choice of both a small portfolio and high default probabilities, which are in the speculative grade zone of the rating scale.

57.3 PORTFOLIO OVERVIEW

The portfolio overview provides some basic aggregated characteristics of the risk/reward profile. The table below (Table 57.1) summarizes some of these aggregated characteristics. The loss given default percentages have a direct significant effect on losses, but exposures serves to normalize the data since the spreads are exposure based.

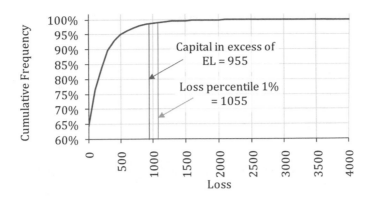

FIGURE 57.3 Cumulative loss distribution

57.3.1 Loss Statistics and Capital

The definitions used in the calculations below are self-explaining. The expected loss is 101, or 0.91% of exposure. It is lower than the default probabilities 1% and 2.5% because of recoveries. The loss percentile $L(1\%)$ is 1.41 times the portfolio loss volatility LV_p. As a reminder, $L(1\%)$ with a normal distribution would be 2.33. The actual multiple, 1.41, is lower because of diversification effects. This in an interesting observation showing that normal distribution multiples have comparable orders of magnitude to the actual correlated loss distribution because the fat tail effect and the diversification effect compensate to some extent.

There are two possible calculations of capital:

- as the loss percentile in excess of expected loss or K_{EL} (1%),
- as the loss percentile in excess of expected spread or K_{ES} (1%).

The 1% loss percentile is 9.59%, and capital in excess of EL is 8.67%, in percentage of total book value exposure. The capital in excess of EL minus expected spread is not used because it is not allowed by regulations.

A simple measure of the diversification effect is the ratio of the portfolio loss volatility, 221.1, to the sum of individual standalone loss volatilities, 750.17, or 29.47% in our example. The portfolio diversifies away close to 70.53% of the sum of standalone loss volatilities (Table 57.1).

57.3.2 Portfolio Risk Return Profile

The "all-in spread" (AIS) is the annualized revenue from each obligor, including interest margin and fees, both upfront flat fees and recurring fees, averaged over the maturity of the facility. The aggregated contractual spread, or total AIS under no default, is 401, while expected loss is 101. The expected spread is the contractual AIS minus the EL, or 401–101 = 300 (rounded value).

TABLE 57.1   Portfolio overview

Total exposure value, X	1100.00
Total LGD value: LGD	6000.00
Average LGD (%)	54.55%
Expected loss value, EL	100.58
EL/X	0.91%
Portfolio loss volatility: LV_P	221.1
Loss volatility % of X: LV_P/X	2.01%
Sum of transactions loss volatilities $\Sigma\, LV_i$	750.17
Diversification effect, or retained risk: $\Sigma\, LV_i/LV_P$	29.47%
Loss percentile 1%: $L(1\%)$	1055.00
$L(1\%)/X$	9.59%
$L(1\%)/LV_P$	1.41
$L(1\%)/\Sigma\, LV_i$	4.77
Capital in excess of EL: $K(1\%) = L(1\%) - EL$	954.43
$K(1\%)/X$	8.674%
$K(1\%)/LV_P$	4.32
$K(1\%)/\Sigma\, LV_i$	1.27
AIS	401.00
Expected spread $ES = AIS - EL$	300.43
AIS/exposure, or ROA	3.65%
ES/X, or expected ROA	2.73%
Cost of capital k, pre-tax and pre-operating costs	25%
Sharpe (RaRoC) ratio: $(AIS - EL)/[L(1\%) - EL]$	31.48%
$SVA = ES - k \times K$ (%)	61.82

The portfolio Sharpe ratio is its overall RaRoC. The calculation with capital in excess of expected loss is:

$$RaRoC = (AIS - EL)/K(1\%) = 31.48\%$$

The RaRoC is equal to the Sharpe ratio, because the spread AIS is net of the risk-free rate. The ROA is the spread in percentage of exposure. The SVA is the difference between the AIS, the EL, and the cost of the economic capital of the portfolio, pre-tax and pre-operating costs, set at 25%. Since RaRoC = 31.48% > 25%, the SVA is positive and equal to 62 (rounded). The book return on asset, ROA, is the ratio of contractual AIS to exposure, and equals 3.65%, gross of expected loss. The ratio is the overall spread above the risk-free rate, in percentage of exposure. The book return on equity, ROE, is not risk adjusted, and is the contractual AIS divided by capital:

$$(401-300)/954 = 31.6\%$$

It is quite close to the Sharpe ratio.

57.3.3 Portfolio Concentration and Correlation Risk

Both correlation risk and concentration risk are related measures of portfolio risk. Correlation risk relates to the loss dependency. High correlation results in a large number of losses occurring simultaneously. The effect is similar to a large loss. Concentration designates the effect of size discrepancies. A high size concentration implies that some lines have a much bigger size than other lines.

Concentration risk is the risk of large losses due to default of large transactions. Concentration characterizes size discrepancies. The individual loss given default weights, ratios of the individual loss given default to the total loss given default (6000), measure exposure sizes. It is common to report the lines having the largest weights in the portfolio. The alternate synthetic views of portfolio size concentration include the diversity score and the concentration curve.

The diversity score is an index synthesizing the discrepancies of exposures of individual facilities. There are as many concentration indices as there metrics for risk. Alternate metrics include exposure, losses given default, standalone risk measured by individual loss volatilities, or capital allocation. Concentration implies significant discrepancies of the weights of the individual facilities to the total portfolio size (whatever metric is used for measuring risk, size, loss given default, etc.). A concentration index, or diversity score, can be defined for each metric. The diversity score is a number that is always lower than the actual number of facilities. The ratio of diversity score to the number of exposures is the concentration index, always lower than one, except when the portfolio has uniform exposures. The concentration risk is higher when the diversity score is lower.

The diversity score is the number of equal size exposures equivalent to the weight profile of individual exposures. The diversity score (DS) is the following ratio:

$$DS = \frac{1}{\sum_{i=1,n} w_i^2}$$

The w_i are the weights of facilities, using one risk metric, the most common one being the size of exposure. For interpreting the diversity score, we consider the case where all weights are equal to $1/n$, n being the number of obligors. In this case, the ratio would be:

$$DS = \frac{1}{\sum_{i=1,n} \frac{1}{n^2}},$$

or $1/(n/n^2) = n$. This allows the interpretation of the diversity score as the number of uniform exposures "equivalent" to the number of actual unequal exposures.

The ratio of the diversity score to the actual number of exposures is always lower than 1 whenever there are size discrepancies, and the gap measures the size concentration. As an example, consider the simple two-obligor portfolio, with exposures 100 and 50 respectively. The exposure weights are 66.667% (100/150) and 33.333% (50/150). The diversity score is:

$$DS = \{1/[(1/66.667\%)^2 + (1/33.333\%)^2]\} = 1.80$$

It is the "equivalent" number of equal size exposures. The concentration index is the ratio of the diversity score to the actual number of exposures, 2 in this case. This is 1.8/2 = 0.9. The ratio is lower than 1 because the exposures are unequal.

TABLE 57.2   Concentration risk

Diversity score of exposure	35.02
Concentration index of exposure	70.04%
Diversity score of capital (in excess of EL)	33.22
Concentration index of capital	66.45%

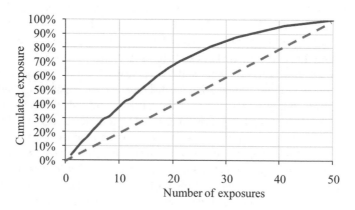

FIGURE 57.4   Gini concentration curves of exposures

Table 57.2 provides the diversity scores for exposure and capital allocation, equal to 35.02 and 33.22 respectively. Both numbers compare to the actual number of exposures, 50. The ratio of the diversity scores to the actual number of exposures measures the concentration in terms of weight discrepancies. Note that the capital diversity score combines both effects of size concentration and of diversification, since capital allocations capture the retained risk post-diversification effect.

A second measure of concentration risk is the "concentration" curve, or "Gini" curve. The curve shows the cumulated exposure, or any alternate risk metric, such as capital, as a function of the number of exposures. The curve cumulates the exposures starting with the largest exposures and ranked by descending values. A uniform exposure portfolio would have a straight-line concentration curve. The higher the curve is above the straight line, the higher is the concentration risk.

In the exposure concentration curve (Figure 57.4), the first five biggest obligors represent 21% of the total portfolio exposure; the first ten biggest obligors represent 40% of the total portfolio exposure, and so on. The curve hits 100% when all 50 exposures cumulate. The slope is steeper at the beginning of the curve because the largest exposures are the first along the x-axis.

57.3.4 From Portfolio Risk to Individual Facilities

The loss volatility of each facility is $\text{LGD}\sqrt{[d(1 - d)]}$, d being the default probability. The standalone loss volatility of a facility is intrinsic to that facility and does not depend upon any portfolio effect. For a uniform correlation portfolio, allocating capital to each facility follows the simple rule of the pro-rata of the standalone facilities. For each facility, the ratio of the individual standalone loss volatility, calculated as above, to the sum over the entire portfolio, is the percentage of total capital allocated to each facility.

Together with the all-in spread, the capital allocation allows one to calculate the RaRoC and SVA of each individual facility as well. Once the allocation is available, all facilities have a risk–return profile. The subsequent sections provide detailed reports on individual facility risk and return.

57.4 REPORTING ALTERNATE METRICS OF RISK

All subsequent reports provide information about individual facilities within the portfolio, and, occasionally, about sub-portfolios. Exposure measure is in value or in percentage of total portfolio. Exposure weights are convenient for measuring size discrepancies. It is convenient to cross-tabulate risk measures to demonstrate that they are far from being strongly correlated in general, and show that exposure is not, in general, a good measure of risk. The direct implication is that setting limits on exposure has a significantly different effect than setting limits on alternate risk metrics. In fact, exposure is not risk, and limits on expected loss or capital allocations are more efficient for capping the risk of facilities.

57.4.1 Exposures, Default Probability and Loss Given Default

The two basic underlying drivers of credit risk, besides exposure, are the default probability, or EDF©, and the loss given default, LGD. They are the two ingredients of the EL = DP × LGD, or loss rate. Exposure does not capture either default or recovery risk. In this sample portfolio, the default probabilities and the LGD do not correlate with exposure weights. Figure 57.5 illustrates the loose link between exposure and LGD.

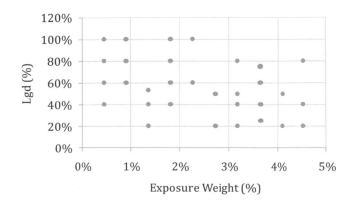

FIGURE 57.5   Facility exposure and loss given default (%)

57.4.2 Exposure and Expected Loss

The EL, in percentage of exposure, combines both default probability and severity of loss. The EL/exposure graph (Figure 57.6), both in percentage of total portfolio exposure, illustrates again the loose relation between the two metrics and the fact that "exposure is not risk." Because of such a loose relation, capping the exposure does not cap high EL, and, conversely, capping EL does not necessarily eliminate high exposures. It is not equivalent to set limits in terms of EL and in terms of exposure.

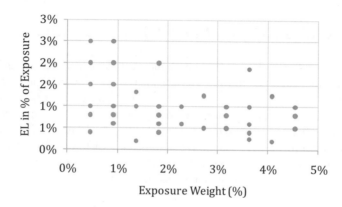

FIGURE 57.6   Expected loss (% of exposure) and exposure weight (%)

57.4.3 Exposure and Capital Allocation or Loss Volatility

Loss volatility is the basis for capital allocation in a uniform correlation portfolio. Plotting capital allocation against exposure (in monetary value) shows that limits on risk contributions (in monetary value) differ from limits on exposure. Because we use monetary values, risk contributions increase with exposure (Figure 57.7). But caps on capital allocations, measured

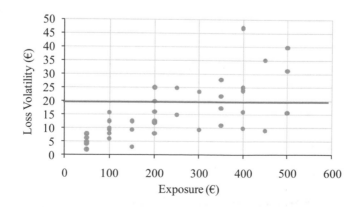

FIGURE 57.7   Capital allocations and exposures in monetary units

by loss volatility, would allow taking large exposures. For example a cap at €20 allows keeping some of the largest exposures.

57.5 RISK-ADJUSTED PERFORMANCE AND MIS-PRICING REPORTS

The performance measures relate revenues to exposure or economic risk measures. Revenues are all-in spreads, including interest margin and fees annualized over the life of the facility, either in value or percentage of exposure. The book ratios, ROA and ROE, and the risk-adjusted measures, are calculated for each individual line as they are for the overall portfolio.

As a first step, we contrast book measures of profitability versus risk-adjusted measures. Next we show mis-pricing reports that provide gaps between the target values of profitability measures and the actual values across facilities.

57.5.1 Book Measures of Profitability versus Risk-adjusted Measures

Book measures of profitability (ROA) and risk-adjusted measures (RaRoC) are similar for the whole portfolio. The ROA by facility is the contractual all-in spread divided by exposure. But, at individual facility level, they differ significantly. The loose relation is the primary reason for risk-adjusting performance measures. Negative RaRoC appear in real portfolios whenever the spread does not compensate the EL. There are no negative RaRoC ratios in this sample, but several are below the threshold of 25%, resulting in negative SVA. The overall portfolio RaRoC ratio is 38% (Figure 57.8).

57.5.2 Mis-pricing Reports

Mis-pricing reports visualize the gaps between the target values of RaRoC and SVA and help focusing on corrective actions (ex post view) or future decisions (ex ante view). For RaRoC, the

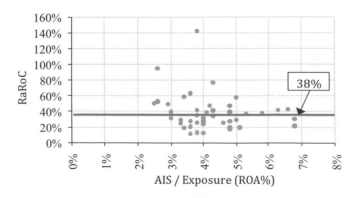

FIGURE 57.8   ROA (%) or spread (%) versus RaRoC

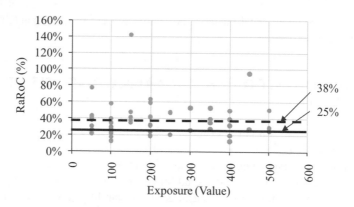

FIGURE 57.9   Mis-pricing report based on RaRoC

minimum value is the cost of capital, here 25% before tax. The minimum SVA is zero. When the RaRoC is higher than 25%, the SVA is positive, and vice versa. Positive SVAs measure creation of value and negative SVAs measure destruction of value. Mis-pricing reports serve for identifying which facilities contribute to the "richness" of the portfolio and which do not. There are two mis-pricing reports.

The first mis-pricing report provides the gaps between the target minimum return and the effective return for each facility. For RaRoC, the benchmark is the minimum return on capital, 25%. For SVA, it is the zero value showing that a facility breaks even on the cost of risk (Figures 57.9 and 57.10).

A second type of mis-pricing report is relative to the portfolio average. The averages of RaRoC and SVA across facilities are also shown in Figures 57.9 and 57.10. It shows whether a facility is more or less profitable, after risk adjustment, than the average portfolio risk-adjusted return. For the RaRoC, the average value (not weighted by exposure size) across all facilities is 38%. For SVA, it is possible to use the average SVA as a benchmark. The aggregated SVA over the portfolio is 61.82 and the arithmetic average is 1.24. However, SVA depends on size, so that the actual reference value for the portfolio should be the SVA per unit of exposure, or

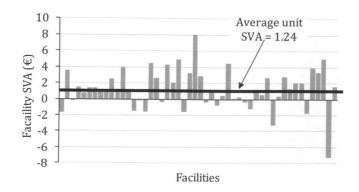

FIGURE 57.10   Mis-pricing report based on SVA

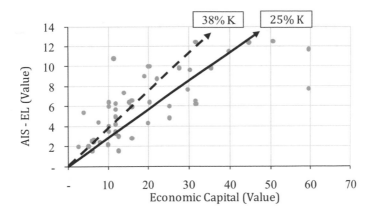

FIGURE 57.11   Mis-pricing report based on expected spread and capital

61.82/11,000 = 0.56% (not shown). Mis-pricing would become the gap between the SVA per unit of exposure for each facility and the portfolio average unit exposure SVA.

A third type of mis-pricing report shows the gap between the required expected spread, or between the average expected spread of the portfolio, and the facility expected spread. It is convenient to plot expected spread against capital allocation, because they are, respectively, the numerator and the denominator of the RaRoC ratio. AIS – EL, in value, plotted against capital shows the numerator and the denominator of the RaRoC ratio. All dots above the 25% line create value and all dots below the line destroy value. All dots above the 38% line represent facilities "richer" than the portfolio average and conversely. Mis-pricing are gaps between the dots and the two lines representing $25\% \times K$ and $38\% \times K$. Figure 57.11 shows what the pricing should be (in terms of risk-adjusted return) and what it is effectively. It also allows identifying the facilities that are over- and under-priced compared either to the hurdle rate or to the average spread.

57.6 REPORTING RISK AND RETURN VERSUS BUSINESS DIMENSIONS

All previous reports show risk metrics and measures of profitability across facilities, without relating them to business dimensions. Business dimensions are, for example, the asset class of the borrower and business units, who could be in charge of different products. Both risk and profitability measures should be cross-tabulated with these "business dimensions" for providing links with business management. For such reports, facilities should be grouped in sub-portfolios according to these two new dimensions.

As examples of such reports, tri-dimensional representations allow showing risk or return vertically, aggregated or averaged, for clients' industries "A" and "B" or business units "V" and "W," used as the horizontal dimensions. Note that because of grouping in sub-portfolios, it is convenient to be able to "drill down" in portfolio segments for identifying those facilities that contribute most to possible discrepancies across portfolio segments. There are two types of useful charts. The first type (Figure 57.12) cross-tabulates risk metrics with business units and industries, and the second type (Figure 57.13) uses risk-adjusted profitability measures. All charts are self-explanatory and use either aggregated measures or arithmetic averages.

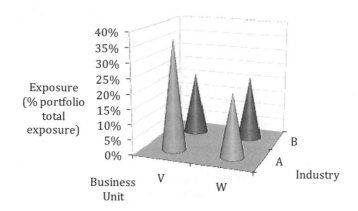

FIGURE 57.12 Exposure by industry and business unit segments

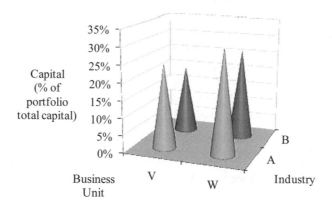

FIGURE 57.13 Capital by industry and business unit segments

Since capital combines default probability and loss given default, it should be similar to the same report using expected loss as the risk metric (Figure 57.14). The risk is higher with business unit W and across industries (Figures 57.15 and 57.16). It is convenient to provide the decomposition along the two risk drivers, default probability and loss given default. We expect that at least one of them, or both of them, are higher in business unit W and across industries. The reports show that the average default probability is higher for industry B and that the average LGD is higher in industry A, and that both tend to be higher than or approximately equal to averaged values for the business unit W.

Figures 57.17 and 57.18 should show how profitability measures compare across segments. Risk-adjusted measures are expected to be lower for the business unit W because the risk, measured by capital or expected loss, is higher for this business unit. This is verified in the figures.

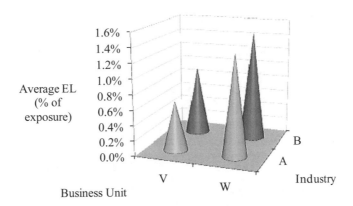

FIGURE 57.14   EL (%) by industry and business unit segment

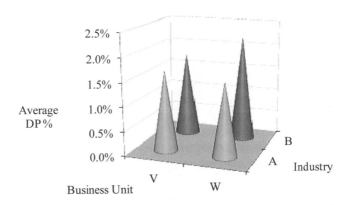

FIGURE 57.15   Default probability by industry and business unit segment

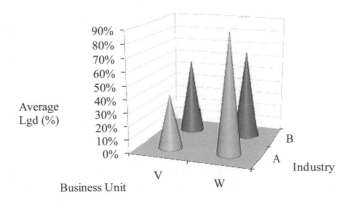

FIGURE 57.16   LGD by industry and business unit segment

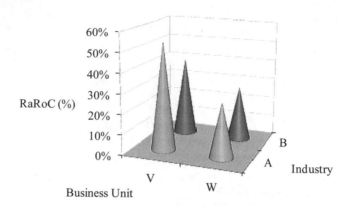

FIGURE 57.17   RaRoC by industry and business unit segment

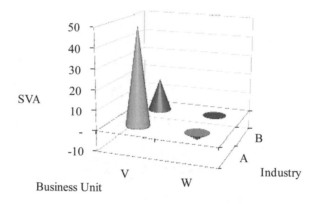

FIGURE 57.18   SVA by industry and business unit segment

For setting up such charts, appropriate systems allowing aggregation and cross-tabulation along multiple dimensions are required. In addition, they should allow to drill down within sub-portfolios whenever required. Appendix 3 (Section 57.9) provides some basic and well-known specifications of such reporting systems.

57.7 APPENDIX 1: SAMPLE PORTFOLIO INPUTS

Facility	Exposure, X	EDF© (%)	LGD (%)	X × LGD	Industry	Spread (%) X	Business unit	Weight (%) X
1	400	1.0%	20%	100	A	1.8%	V	3.64%
2	200	1.0%	40%	80	B	1.6%	V	1.82%
3	500	1.0%	80%	400	A	1.5%	W	4.55%
4	100	1.0%	80%	80	A	3.0%	W	0.91%
5	50	1.0%	80%	40	A	3.0%	V	0.45%
6	200	1.0%	80%	160	B	2.2%	W	1.82%
7	50	1.0%	40%	20	A	2.5%	V	0.45%
8	50	1.0%	100%	50	A	4.5%	W	0.45%
9	50	1.0%	100%	50	A	4.0%	W	0.45%
10	100	1.0%	60%	60	B	3.2%	V	0.91%
11	100	1.0%	80%	80	A	2.5%	W	0.91%
12	200	1.0%	20%	80	A	1.8%	V	1.82%
13	350	1.0%	80%	280	B	1.8%	V	3.18%
14	250	1.0%	100%	250	B	1.8%	V	2.27%
15	100	1.0%	100%	100	A	2.2%	W	0.91%
16	100	1.0%	100%	100	A	2.2%	W	0.91%
17	150	1.0%	20%	30	A	2.0%	V	1.36%
18	200	1.0%	60%	120	A	2.0%	V	1.82%
19	200	1.0%	100%	200	A	2.2%	W	1.82%
20	250	1.0%	60%	150	A	2.4%	V	2.27%
21	400	1.0%	60%	240	B	1.2%	W	3.64%
22	400	1.0%	40%	160	A	1.1%	V	3.64%
23	200	1.0%	100%	200	A	1.6%	W	1.82%
24	350	1.0%	50%	175	B	1.2%	V	3.18%
25	450	1.0%	20%	90	A	0.8%	V	4.09%
26	350	2.5%	40%	140	A	2.0%	V	3.18%
27	50	2.5%	100%	50	A	5.0%	W	0.45%
28	50	2.5%	60%	30	B	4.8%	V	0.45%
29	100	2.5%	100%	100	A	5.0%	W	0.91%
30	50	2.5%	80%	40	A	5.0%	W	0.45%
31	400	2.5%	40%	160	A	2.3%	V	3.64%
32	50	2.5%	60%	30	B	2.8%	V	0.45%
33	300	2.5%	50%	150	A	2.0%	W	2.73%
34	50	2.5%	100%	50	B	5.0%	W	0.45%
35	100	2.5%	80%	80	B	3.0%	W	0.91%
36	450	2.5%	50%	225	B	2.2%	W	4.09%
37	100	2.5%	60%	60	B	3.2%	W	0.91%
38	200	2.5%	20%	80	A	2.5%	V	1.82%
39	400	2.5%	80%	300	A	3.0%	W	3.64%
40	100	2.5%	60%	60	B	3.0%	W	0.91%
41	150	2.5%	40%	60	A	3.0%	V	1.36%
42	150	2.5%	40%	60	A	2.0%	V	1.36%
43	150	2.5%	40%	60	A	2.5%	V	1.36%
44	150	2.5%	60%	80	B	3.5%	V	1.36%
45	200	2.5%	80%	160	B	3.3%	W	1.82%
46	350	2.5%	20%	70	B	0.8%	W	3.18%
47	300	2.5%	20%	60	B	0.8%	V	2.73%
48	500	2.5%	20%	100	A	0.7%	V	4.55%
49	400	2.5%	60%	300	B	2.0%	W	3.64%
50	500	2.5%	40%	200	B	1.5%	V	4.55%
	Total 11,000			Total 6,000				Total 100%

57.8 APPENDIX 2: SAMPLE PORTFOLIO OUTPUTS

Facility	Exposure, X	Spread (%) X	Spread (€)	EL (€)	Spread (€) – EL	UL ($)	UL (%) UL (€) = K%	K (€)
1	400	3.6%	2.5	1.00	1.50	9.95	1.33%	12.66
2	200	3.4%	6.8	0.80	6.00	7.96	1.06%	10.13
3	500	3.3%	16.5	4.00	12.50	39.80	5.31%	50.64
4	100	4.8%	4.8	0.80	4.00	7.96	1.06%	10.13
5	50	4.8%	2.4	0.40	2.00	3.98	0.53%	5.06
6	200	4.0%	8.0	1.60	6.40	15.92	2.12%	20.25
7	50	4.3%	2.2	0.20	1.95	1.99	0.27%	2.53
8	50	6.3%	3.2	0.50	2.65	4.97	0.66%	6.33
9	50	5.8%	2.9	0.50	2.40	4.97	0.66%	6.33
10	100	5.0%	5.0	0.60	4.40	5.97	0.80%	7.60
11	100	4.3%	4.3	0.80	3.50	7.96	1.0611	10.13
12	200	3.6%	7.2	0.80	6.40	7.96	1.06%	10.13
13	350	3.6%	12.6	2.80	9.80	27.86	3.71%	35.45
14	250	3.6%	9.0	2.50	6.50	24.87	3.32%	31.65
15	100	4.0%	4.0	1.00	3.00	9.95	1.33%	12.66
16	100	4.0%	2.6	1.00	1.60	9.95	1.33%	12.66
17	150	3.8%	5.7	0.30	5.40	2.98	0.40%	3.80
18	200	3.8%	7.6	1.20	6.40	11.94	1.59%	15.19
19	200	4.0%	8.0	2.00	6.00	19.90	2.65%	25.32
20	250	4.2%	10.5	1.50	9.00	14.92	1.99%	18.99
21	400	3.0%	12.0	2.40	9.60	23.88	3.18%	30.38
22	400	2.9%	11.6	1.60	10.00	15.92	2.12%	20.25
23	200	3.4%	6.8	2.00	4.80	19.90	2.65%	25.32
24	350	3.0%	10.5	1.75	8.75	17.41	2.32%	22.15
25	450	2.6%	11.7	0.90	10.80	8.95	1.19%	11.39
26	350	3.8%	13.3	3.50	9.80	21.86	2.91%	27.81
27	50	6.8%	3.4	1.25	2.15	7.81	1.04%	9.93
28	50	6.6%	3.3	0.75	2.55	4.68	0.62%	5.96
29	100	6.8%	6.8	2.50	4.30	15.61	2.08%	19.86
30	50	6.8%	3.4	1.00	2.40	6.24	0.83%	7.95
31	400	4.1%	16.4	4.00	12.40	24.98	3.33%	31.78
32	50	4.6%	2.3	0.75	1.55	4.68	0.62%	5.96
33	300	3.8%	11.4	3.75	7.65	23.42	3.12%	29.80
34	50	6.8%	3.4	1.25	2.15	7.81	1.04%	9.93
35	100	4.8%	4.8	2.00	2.80	12.49	1.67%	15.89
36	450	4.0%	18.0	5.63	12.38	35.13	4.68%	44.69
37	100	5.0%	5.0	1.50	3.50	9.37	1.25%	11.92
38	200	4.3%	8.6	2.00	6.60	12.49	1.67%	15.89
39	400	4.8%	19.2	7.50	11.70	46.84	6.24%	59.59
40	100	4.8%	4.8	1.50	3.30	9.37	1.25%	11.92
41	150	4.8%	7.2	1.50	5.70	9.37	1.25%	11.92
42	150	3.8%	5.7	1.50	4.20	9.37	1.25%	11.92
43	150	4.3%	6.5	1.50	4.95	9.37	1.25%	11.92
44	150	5.3%	8.0	2.00	5.95	12.49	1.67%	15.89
45	200	5.1%	10.2	4.00	6.20	24.98	3.33%	31.78
46	350	2.6%	9.1	1.75	7.35	10.93	1.46%	13.90
47	300	2.6%	7.8	1.50	6.30	9.37	1.25%	11.92
48	500	2.5%	12.5	2.50	10.00	15.61	2.09%	19.86
49	400	3.8%	15.2	7.50	7.70	46.84	6.25%	59.59
50	500	3.3%	16.5	5.00	11.50	31.22	4.16%	39.73
	Total 11,000	Mean – A 4.300%	Total 401.00	Total 100.58		Total UL (€) 750.17	Total (%) 100%	Total 954.43

57.9 APPENDIX 3: PORTFOLIO ANALYSIS AND REPORTING ISSUES

Risk data is continuously getting richer and new models, running at the bank-wide scale, produce new measures of risk. Bringing these measures to life necessitates appropriate tools for decision makers. Decision makers extend from traders, sales and account officers dealing with clients, to risk managers, plus top management who cannot rely only on aggregated measures.

Risk data extends from observable inputs, such as market prices, to all various credit risk metrics, dis-aggregated at sub-portfolio and facility levels. Risk data warehouses are critical for organizing the data-gathering process and building up risk data, such as inputs required by the Basel 2 Accord. Moreover, VaR measures require all data for producing market risk and credit risk reports. Bringing the information to life is, in addition to being a bank-wide management challenge, an information technology challenge.

Information technology (IT) plays a key role in banks. Due to the scale of operations of systems of banks, creating the required risk data warehouse with the inputs and outputs of models, and providing links to front ends and reporting modules for decision makers are major challenges. It requires modern tools capable of on-line queries and analyses embedded in front ends and reporting. "Online analysis and processing" (OLAP) systems are presumably tools capable to forward relevant information to end-users whenever they need it. We review some of the reporting and management issues that they need to address.

57.9.1 Traceability of Aggregated Measures and Risk Management

Aggregated measures have a limited usage if it is not possible to trace back the inputs. VaR is not a substitute to all others inputs even though it provides a synthesis of multiple measures. The drawback is that it embeds synthetically underlying the sources of risks. Synthetic measures are convenient but not intuitive anymore and generate a "black-box" effect. "Why is risk high for a particular segment?" is not a simple question for modeled loss volatility or capital. How is the end-user going to disentangle such interdependencies?

Moreover, without access to underlying sources of risks, it is not feasible to control VaR, and VaR remains a passive, although useful, report. VaR type measures of risk require a two-way implementation: from underlying parameters to VaR, and from VaR to the different sources of risk that they represent.

57.9.2 Dealing with Multiple Dimensions

Second, there are many dimensions of interest, both from a risk perspective and a business perspective. Multiple risk measures generate several new metrics for risks, which supplement traditional and pro-forma reports required by supervisors. Expected loss and unexpected loss, capital and risk contributions, risk-adjusted measures, ex ante and ex post measures are required at all levels (facilities, sub-portfolios, bank-wide). Their availability is a condition for the feasibility of best practices. Simultaneously, the business line prospective, with dimensions such as transactions, product families, market segments or business units' sub-portfolios, should be cross-tabulated with such metrics for providing an integrated and consistent bank-wide risk oversight and management.

Combining that many risk and profitability dimensions with business dimensions is a conceptual and practical challenge. Multi-dimensional views of the banks portfolio are complex to handle. Modern IT systems can handle the task. However, IT still needs to format risk, profitability and business reporting so that they integrate smoothly within the bank's processes.

In OLAP terminology, these multiple dimensions are called "axes." Multi-dimensional reporting along many axes requires a more extensive of usage of new tools:

1 Slicing and dicing the portfolio across any one of these dimensions, or combinations of them, such as reporting the risk-adjusted profitability by client, market segment or business unit, or for both. Credit committees, credit officers and risk managers are major end-users on the business side.
2 Drilling-down function to find out which transactions are the sources of risk of subsets of transactions. The simplest example would be to find which transactions and obligors contribute most to the risk of a business unit, measured along any risk metric (exposure, expected loss, risk allocation).
3 "What-if" simulation capabilities to find out what would happen when adding or withdrawing a transaction or a business line, conducting sensitivity analyses for finding which risk drivers influence risk more, or when considering rebalancing the bank's sub-portfolios. Best-practice decision-making processes should ideally have those functions readily available.

57.10 PORTFOLIO ANALYSIS AND REPORTING TECHNICAL CHALLENGES

In order to avoid falling into the trap of managing reports rather than business, online customization is necessary to produce the relevant information on time. Front-ends tools with "what-if" and simulation functions, producing risk–return profiles both for the existing portfolio and new transactions, become as important in the credit universe as they are in the market universe. Figure 57.19 illustrates the multiple dimensions and the reporting specifications. We explain why these seemingly "logistical" and IT issues closely relate to bank-wide management and portfolio analysis issues for decision makers.

57.10.1 Basic Specifications of Reporting Systems

Data mining is considered to be a technical issue. But this is not the case for risk management. Developing new reports or new models relies entirely on the capability of extracting relevant data. More often than not, this remains an issue that is dealt with partially, causing time intensive efforts.

"Data mining" and "drill-down" functions trace back inputs leading to an aggregated risk metric, such as VaR or capital. More commonly, it allows finding out why a particular sub-portfolio or client portfolio has a high or low risk. Subsets of risk–return outliers, clients or products, suggest "drilling-down" for finding why there are outliers, what their characteristics are, and identifying them.

"Slicing" the data, for example according to ratings, allows one to see whether spreads are indeed higher with higher risks, and then to investigate whether the recovery rate mitigates the findings or help understanding the findings. The criteria for "slicing" the banks' portfolios

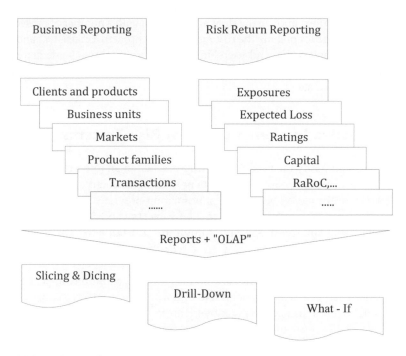

FIGURE 57.19   Information technology and portfolio reporting

for business purposes are multiple: excess utilization over risk limits, transaction data for risk assessment purposes and preparing credit risk decisions, cross-sectional data by country or rating, and others in addition to the usual business views such as customers, products and business units. Moreover, modeling adds new metrics to classical measures, expected and unexpected loss, capital, and so on. This magnifies the number of dimensions of risks to deal with for risk management purposes.

57.10.2 Stress Testing and What-if Analyses

Stress tests are essentially "what-if" analyses. They become critical if unexpected events occur. OLAP can potentially store scenarios and outputs of scenarios, or even run new scenarios in real time, putting powerful "what-if" functions available to end-users in the right formats for interpreting the outputs. Second-level indirect effects pose a real challenge (collateral calls are an example). Few banks seem capable of isolating such scenarios and fully stress-test their portfolios, and have to limit their scenarios to first-level effects for lack of integration across risk systems.

Bank-wide risk management requires two-way processes, top-down and bottom-up, for implementation. OLAP and data mining addresses these issues efficiently. OLAP allows drilling down, slicing, and what-if analyses, along with viewing data along several perspectives, combining several axes.

Embedding the risk information in the right architecture, with a number of preset interactive functions, is a prerequisite for making the risk management process a consistent and integrated, truly bank-wide reality and makes end-users' interactions easier through adequate front ends. According to experience, and given complexity of banks' risk systems, there is still a long way to go before we reach that stage.

57.10.3 Interactive Implementation of Risk Systems

Multiple dimensions magnify the need for filtering the data in an interactive way. First report findings inspire new investigations, making data mining an interactive exercise for end-users. The search for new information becomes conditional on previous findings, suggesting new investigations. Examples abound. Discovering a new excess exposure over limit necessitates understanding why such an excess appears. It might result from new transactions, or simply from the risk drift of existing transactions. Corrective actions depend on the sources of excess risks.

Risk management is also event driven. Should risk concentrations appear suddenly, or unexpected events emerge, it is mostly helpful to find where they emerge and why. The sudden financial crisis highlighted the need to urgently identify which transactions were most at risk. Many banks struggled because of outdated risk systems for isolating such toxic assets.

58

Securitization and Capital Management

Securitizations have been a core technique for expanding the financing offered by banks under the "originate and distribute" business model. Securitizations were, originally, a technique for financing based on simple mechanisms and economics. A securitization is economically sustainable if assets securitized, net of operating set-up costs of the SPEs (special purpose entities), provide an expected return in line with the expected compensations required by investors in asset-backed notes issues by SPEs. However, being in line does not mean matching. If the loss of the underlying asset portfolio deviates to a lower than expected loss by any amount, such adverse deviation would impair the credit standing for all asset-backed notes. Hence the expected return from the portfolio should be higher than the expected return to investors, creating a safety cushion that would preserve the securitization economics under stressed conditions. Such rationale is very similar to the capital adequacy principle.

Securitizations, which were supposed to provide a better diversification of risk across all investors in SPE vehicles, became a major contagion factor in the 2007 financial crisis. This does not imply that securitization techniques are flawed. Rather it shows that risks were not addressed properly, raising methodology and discipline issues, notably since ratings agencies and banks tends to use different techniques for assessing the resiliency of securitization structures. The wave of securitizations went into an abrupt stop when it appeared that the risk under stressed conditions was vastly underestimated by arrangers as well as rating agencies. However, they should develop again when imposing a more stringent discipline on risk-assessing methodology plus imposing risk sharing between the originating bank and the investors by making it an obligation to the bank to maintain an interest in the securitized portfolio.

This chapter details these mechanisms and the associated techniques. Section 58.1 addresses the variety of securitizations and shows how some simple principles can be used to finance virtually any asset subject to consistent economics of the securitization vehicle. It reminds us of the basic rationales and motivations that fostered the development of this technique, and, finally, the section details the basic ingredients necessary for arranging a securitization. Section 58.2 explains how securitizations can differentiate the risk of the pools of assets securitized from the risk of notes issued in the markets. Such differentiation is obtained by issuing notes with cascading seniority claims on the cash flows generated by assets of SPEs, or the "waterfall mechanism." Section 58.3 details the economics of a securitization through a simplified case study and illustrates the arbitrage mechanism between financing the same assets on balance sheet versus financing in the market. Finally, Section 58.4 addresses issues for assessing the risk and the resiliency of securitization structures. Stress testing rules are factor-push scenarios. But since only portfolio models provides the loss distribution of asset portfolio, and since each tranche can be shows as being a correlation product, portfolio models remain a mandatory technique for assessing the risk of the underlying pool of assets, in addition to factor-push stress tests.

Contents

58.1 ECONOMICS OF SECURITIZATIONS

A securitization is feasible whenever the asset securitized provides an expected return high enough for compensating the investors investing in the notes issued by a securitization vehicle, plus an add-on to this minimum asset return for absorbing unexpected downsides and plus the operating costs of setting up the SPE.

There are various schemes for securitizing assets. The first of the two basic structures are pass-through securities, whereby assets were assigned to each class of notes issued to investors, and each class of notes bears the risk of only those assets assigned to it. Pools of assets are ranked according to risk, and so are assigned notes to each pool. In the second version, the waterfall model, the asset cash flows are routed to notes issued according to their seniority level. Hence the risk of senior notes depend on the risk of the pool of assets and the subordination level measured by its lower attachment point, or the size of notes subordinated to the note considered. When using sequential amortization, it is worth noting that prepayment risk is much less an issue for investors, because prepayment cash flows go first to senior notes, which amortize faster. An added value, for mortgage-backed securities, of the waterfall model combined with sequential amortization is that investors bear less prepayment risk, while pass-through securitizations made them bear entirely the prepayment plus default risks. (See Figure 58.1.) The rest of the chapter discusses the waterfall model.

58.1.1 Expected Return on Assets and Compensations to Investors

A securitization implies selling assets to an SPE who issues a series of notes of various risk acquired by investors. The compensation comes from the cash flows generated by the pool of

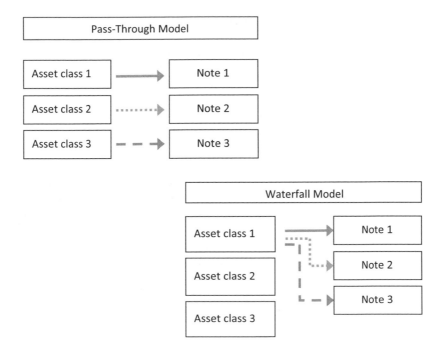

FIGURE 58.1 Two securitization models: pass-through and waterfall

assets sold to the SPE. The required compensation for investors depends on the risk of each note issued by the vehicle. Investors rely on external risk assessment of these notes by rating agencies. The return required by investors is ratings driven.

The weighted average required return by investors measures the cost of financing the assets through securitizations. The expected return from assets should remain in line with such weighted cost of financing. If the match was perfect, securitizations would fail whenever stressed conditions prevail. Economics of securitization vehicles should provide a safety cushion between expected asset returns and the threshold that meets the required return by investors.

For the expected return from assets to comply with the economic consistency of a securitization, the losses from the pool of assets have to be low enough. The economic feasibility of a securitization backed by pools of assets depends on the diversification of the portfolio backing the notes issued and on the dependencies between losses within such pools. Credit portfolio models should demonstrate that the unexpected deviations of return, given loss correlations, do not alter significantly the economics of the SPE.

A securitization is economically sound if the measures of risk are not flawed. For example, the portfolio risk depends on correlations between assets defaults and migrations, and such correlations are sensitive to economic conditions. For investors, the unique risk assessments available are credit ratings of the different notes, which should be in line with actual risks. Sound practices should stress-test the asset returns and their correlations to ensure that the structure is "resilient" to adverse conditions. In theory, rating agencies should provide correct and reliable credit ratings of notes issued for investors.

58.1.2 Variety of Securitizations

Any asset or pool of assets that complies with such economics can be securitized. Accordingly, there are many types of securitizations. Originally, pools of mortgages were the first ones to be securitized. Subsequently, a wide variety of assets were securitized. Securitizations vary widely according to the nature of assets securitized, from credit cards to loans or leasing receivables, CDO (collateralized debt obligation), CBO (collateralized bond obligation) and CLO (collateralized loan obligation). An office building generates rents, which might be high enough to compensate market investors, and can be securitized as well. Synthetic securitizations use credit derivatives for selling only the credit risk of a pool of assets, or a fraction of their risk, without actually selling the underlying assets of the credit derivatives. For providing a yield rather than only a spread, investors might provide cash invested in the risk-free assets. The compensation will add up the risk-free rate and the spread from credit derivatives for reconstructing a risky yield.

Securitizations are not limited to banks. Corporations securitize pools of commercial credits. The securitization of commercial real estate is arranged by banks but the sponsor is not the bank.

Such conditions were not necessarily met, as the financial crisis illustrates in 2007–2008. Moreover, incentives for securitization need to be sound. Originators might take advantage of securitizations by including a fraction of "toxic assets" within the portfolios securitized, which makes the SPE riskier than it appears. Practices might depart from such sound principles. Rating agencies face difficulties for monitoring all structures that have been rated. Their methodologies might not be adequate for assessing the risk of portfolio, if they do not rely on credit portfolio models.

Nevertheless, as long as the economic consistency of a securitization can be substantiated, notably by using correct measures of risk for both assets and liabilities of the SPE, the securitization mechanism is sound.

58.1.3 Rationales For Securitizations

The rationale of traditional securitizations by banks has to do with the "originate and sell" business model of banks. Holding loans within the balance sheet, notably large mortgage portfolios, consumes capital which could be freed if the bank can sell the assets into the capital markets. Selling the assets, without recourse, frees up capital and allows the development of new business. This is the basic rationale of saving freeing capital to originate new business by off-loading assets onto the capital market. Securitizations aiming at freeing up capital are sometimes called "balance sheet" securitizations.

Another rationale, which is common to all securitizations, is the arbitrage between the costs of financing on-balance sheet and through the market. The cost of financing the same assets in the market is the weighted cost of financing through the various notes issued by the SPE, plus any other non-financial cost for setting up the vehicle and for servicing the loans. This rationale is directly related to the price discrepancies of credit risk in the balance sheet and in the market. The price of credit risk on-balance sheet is capital-based. The cost of financing the same credit risk in the market is credit-rating based. They have no reason to coincide, as was pointed out in Chapter 55. Such securitizations are regulatory arbitrages, similar to an arbitrage between the capital-based cost of risk through and the cost of risk when using credit derivatives (see Chapter 59). Note that for securitizations to be feasible, the gap between the market cost of financing and on-balance sheet financing should remain positive even under stressed conditions.

The discrepancies might originate from differing perceptions of the same risk by banks and credit-rating agencies. A synthetic securitization is made of a portfolio of credit derivatives that provide compensation to sellers with the recurring premium. It does not necessitate any sale of assets, since credit derivatives allow separating assets from their credit risk. The investors buy notes, but instead of receiving the full yield of the portfolio, inclusive of the credit spread, they are compensated with the recurring premium. Investors might also buy bonds that provide the risk-free rate plus the recurring premium. The risk-free rate is provided by investing the cash from investors in risk-free assets. The principal is secured by the risk-free assets, and only the spread in excess of the risk-free rate is at risk. This class of securitization is "synthetic," because it is made of credit derivatives that create synthetic credit exposure on the underlying assets. It is even simpler than a traditional cash securitization.

In the case of synthetic securitizations, banks base their assessment of the risk of the pool of credit derivatives on portfolio models and consider that rating agencies over-estimate the risk of the pools. The arbitrage is based on different assessments of the same risk rather than assuming that there are two prices of the same risk, one being capital-based and the other rating-based. Such securitizations are also called "arbitrage securitizations." They are effectively pure arbitrage transactions if the banks do not sell the credit risk of their own exposures, but simply assemble derivatives with other underlying assets than those that they have on their balance sheet.

58.1.4 The Securitization Organization

Securitizations are conducted through a special purpose entity (SPE), a legal entity like a fund which is bankruptcy-remote from sponsors. The SPE buys the assets from a bank and issues "asset-backed bonds" in the market. The investors buy the bonds, thereby providing the necessary financing for the SPE to acquire the assets sold by the bank. Once the assets are sold without recourse to the SPE, they do not appear in the bank's balance sheet. Financing of investors substitutes to the bank's funding.

Figure 58.2 summarizes the basic organization of a securitization. The seller of the assets is often a bank, or it is a corporate firm looking for attractive funding of account receivables. The SPE assets generate cash flows, made of interest and principal payments, plus prepayments of mortgages that serve for paying the bonds holders. The SPE does not issue a single class of bond that would bear the entire risk of the portfolio of assets securitized. Instead, it issues several types of notes of different seniority levels. A specific feature of a securitization is that the default of one class of notes, such as the riskiest notes, does not trigger the default of other more senior notes and of the SPE. Bonds backed by assets are called "notes" or "structured notes." The variety of notes issued allows customizing the risk of these various issues to the profiles of potential investors. Defining how many classes of notes should be issued and the risk of each one is called "structuring."

Investors cannot buy the notes unless they have a risk assessment of what they buy. Rating agencies assign a rating for each class of structured note, which is sufficient information for investors to make a decision to invest or not and for making the notes tradable. The credit rating defines the risk of a class of notes, and the corresponding credit spread compensates investors

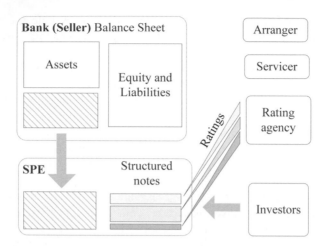

FIGURE 58.2   Structuring a securitization

for credit risk. Risk-adverse investors buy the lowest credit risk notes, while some investors are attracted the higher spread above the risk-free rate of riskier notes.

There are other players in securitizations, besides the bank, the investors and the rating agencies. The "arranger" structures the transaction. The "servicer" takes care of day-to-day relations with the borrowers whose loans have been securitized during the life of the transaction. Figure 58.2 provides a synthetic view of the securitization.

The SPE isolates the pool of assets from the seller. The non-recourse sale implies that the seller is not responsible of losses within the pools of assets sold to note holders. The investors bear the credit risk of the pool, broken down across classes of notes issued.

The structuring of the transaction relies on covenants that rule the governance of the transaction during its life. It also defines to the sizes and seniority level of claims to SPE cash flows. Seniority level remains a key element in securitizations which determines the risk of investors.

58.2 STRUCTURING AND THE WATERFALL MECHANISM

Differentiating the seniority levels of notes issued means that investors have different priority claims on the cash flows of the SPE, some being "senior" and others being "subordinated" claims. This differentiates the risks across notes issued by the SPE while simultaneously ensuring a protection for the more senior notes. The protection against credit risk of senior investors results from the fact that equity, the most subordinated note issued, and subordinated notes provide a loss protection for more senior notes.

The simplest way to provide a safety cushion for investors that are not willing to suffer from the first losses of the portfolio is to use an oversized pool of assets. The collateralized assets have a higher volume than claims acquired by senior investors. Since only a fraction of the pool suffices to compensate these investors, the over-collateralization of senior notes provides a safety cushion against adverse deviations of the flows generated by the pool. For instance, a pool of assets can generate 100, and only 60 are necessary to compensate senior investors if the subordinated notes compensation is 40% of the total pool cash flow. The risk of loss for these investors materializes only when the actual cash flow goes under 60. The structure pays the flows promised to investors as long as the flows generated by the assets do not decrease by more than 40%. However, in this description, we ignore the loss of value by investors due to changes of market parameters or to a downgrade of notes issued by rating agencies.

58.2.1 Structuring of Notes

The structuring of the transaction consists of defining the amounts of the various notes issued and their risk–return profile. Structuring defines the seniority level and the thickness of each note issued. All subordinated notes to a given senior note absorb losses first. They serves as a safety cushion protecting the senior notes. When cash flows do not suffice to pay the all obligations to all note holders, the deficiencies first hit the subordinated notes. At the lower end of subordination, the risk is highest, since the most subordinated notes concentrate all the risk of the pool of assets. At the upper range of senior notes, the risk is near zero because it is nearly impossible for losses to reach a level such they would hit this upper class notes (Figure 58.3).

The subordination level of a note is defined by two parameters: the thickness of the notes (the size in percentage of total assets funded), and the attachment point. The attachment point defines the size of the subordinated notes ranking below the note. The higher this "safety cushion," the lower the risk of the notes protected by the more subordinated notes.

Agencies rate notes according to their risks. Senior notes can be investment grade because the likelihood that the pool of assets losses exceed the safety cushion provided by the subordinated notes is near zero for the highest grades. When moving down the scale of seniority, the loss franchise provided by the subordinated notes shrinks. The last subordinated note, which is like equity, gets all first losses and has no rating. Either the seller of assets or a third party, acting as a "credit enhancer," holds the last tranche. Since the equity tranche bears all the risk of the assets, the spread compensating credit enhancers is high. Since this note is likely to disappear once the losses exceed the amount of the note, this tranche is sometimes called the "zero-equity tranche." Its return depends on how long the equity tranche survives, hence on the timing of defaults of the pool of assets.

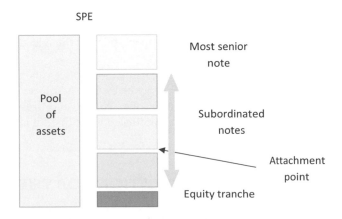

FIGURE 58.3   Structuring of notes

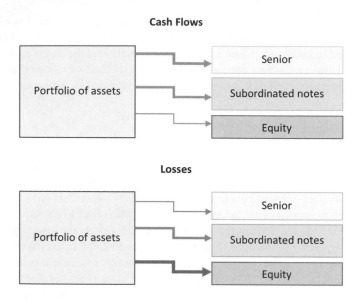

FIGURE 58.4   **Waterfall of cash flows and of losses**

58.2.2 The Waterfalls of Cash Flows and Losses

The structure routes the flows generated by the pool of assets to investors using priority rules based on the seniority level, first to senior notes and last to the "equity" tranche. This is the "waterfall of cash flows." The "waterfall of losses" follows symmetrical paths. They hit the equity tranche first, then the subordinated notes, and finally the senior notes. The first cash flows go to the senior notes. The first losses go to the subordinated notes. Figure 58.4 shows the waterfall of cash flows and losses, with the thickness of arrows measuring the priority level ruling the routing of cash flows or losses to destination.

Structuring through differentiated seniority levels allows issuing several types of securities differing in terms of their risk–return profiles and their maturities. Issuing several classes of structured notes of different seniority levels makes the securities attractive to various populations of investors, over the entire spectrum of risk. High-risk notes are of interest to investors looking for a higher than expected spread in compensation for the added risk. Investors in senior notes benefit from a good rating.

The amortization of notes can be parallel or sequential. Maturities vary across notes, under the sequential amortization scheme, because the payments flow first to senior notes, thereby amortizing them quicker. The concurrent amortization scheme amortizes notes in parallel, but any deficiency of cash flows still hits the subordinated notes first. In all cases, the equity tranche gets fully amortized first.

58.3 ECONOMICS OF SECURITIZATION FOR THE BANK

In this section, we consider "balance sheet" cash securitizations whose purpose is to free up capital for expanding business volume. Any securitization must be economically consistent, in that the expected return of assets should overcompensate the weighted cost of financing through the tranches issued by the SPE. But economic consistency of a securitization does not necessarily imply that the securitization is economical for the bank.

For making sense for the bank, the securitization should also improve the RaRoC of the bank. Full modeling of the effect of a securitization on the bank's portfolio would rely on credit portfolio models. However, this is not necessary for highlighting the main factors that drive the RaRoC post-securitization. Key factors that affect the economics include:

- the extent of capital savings
- the price at which assets (loans) are sold by the bank to the SPE
- the direct costs of setting up a securitization.

The capital saving from selling assets makes the economic capital of the bank smaller, which, everything else held constant, tends to increase the return on the remaining capital. The pricing depends on the return required by the investors in the SPE. The latter depends on both the credit quality of the portfolio sold to the SPE and the structure of the notes issued by the SPE and their risks. Such pricing meeting expectations of investors might result in a capital gain or a capital loss for the bank.

Moreover, a lower cost of financing through securitization than on-balance sheet financing makes a case for considering securitization. The direct cost of setting up a securitization, which includes legal costs or payment to the arranger, offsets some of the benefits. Through the structuring of notes, securitization dissociates the quality of the original flows generated by the pool of assets from the quality of the promises of flows to investors, since the original flows are routed to notes according to priority rules. As result, the cost of financing will generally be different from the cost of funding on-balance sheet for the seller. The cost of financing is always a weighted average cost of funds. It is the weighted average of cost of equity and debt in the bank balance sheet, and it is the weighted average of the costs of the various notes issued by securitization vehicles. We use the familiar weighted average cost of capital (Wacc) for comparing the Wacc on balance sheet with the Wacc of securitization.

58.3.1 Analysis of a Securitization Transaction (Case Study)

The analysis below uses an example of a balance sheet cash securitization. Its purpose is to determine the costs and the benefits of the transaction and to assess the impact on return on capital for the bank. The analysis progresses through four steps:

- the description of the original situation before securitization
- the calculation of the funding cost for the originating bank
- the funding cost through securitization
- the impact on the return on equity (ROE) or on capital (RaRoC).

We use the book ROE in the example because it allows by-passing the modeling of economic capital, and still highlights the key parameters.

The portfolio of loans of a bank has an annual expected return net of expected loss (EBT/ assets) of 10.10%. The risk-free rate is 9%. The debt on the balance sheet of the bank is rated A, corresponding to a 1% spread over the risk-free rate. The capital charge for such loans is 4%

equity (tier 1). The subordinated debt in the balance sheet is assumed to cost the same as other financial debts issued by the bank, which is a simplifying but not restrictive assumption. The required return on equity before tax is 20%. Although such a return should be a market return, we consider that it is expressed as minimum book ROE[1]. The bank considers securitizing an amount of loans equal to 1000, a fraction of the total loan portfolio, whose size is 10,000.

In the securitization, the pool of loans will be funded with tranches sold to investors by a SPE. There are two classes of tranches issued to investors. The subordinated tranche (junior) is the riskiest and represents 25% of the amount securitized. Given the risk of the junior tranche, the credit spread required over the 9% risk-free rate is 2.00% (200 bps). The senior tranche represents 75% of the pool of loans, is investment grade (senior shares), with a rating of AA, and a credit spread of 0.50% above the risk-free rate. The direct costs of the securitization include the legal cost, 0.20%, and the servicing cost, 0.10%, expressed as a percentage of the value of securitized loans.

For the purpose of simplification, we assume that the notes issued by the SPE have a single year maturity and are zero-coupons. This assumption simplifies calculations and is not restrictive. A sequence of issues is addressed below.

1 What is the cost of funding the loans in the balance sheet of the bank (Wacc of bank's balance sheet)?
2 Given the loan portfolio profitability, what is the resulting return on equity (before tax)?
3 Given the return to investors of the junior and senior tranches, and their weights, which is the overall cost of issued notes? We assume that both classes of notes have the same duration, equal 1 year.
4 Given the direct cost of securitization, what is the yearly all-in cost of securitization?
5 Given the cost of funding through securitization, what is the selling price of the securitized portfolio? Does the sale generate a capital gain or a capital loss?
6 The bank saves capital by securitization. However, the securitization changes the book return on equity. Consider that the above pool of 1000 is a fraction of total loan portfolio, which is originally 10 000, with the same characteristics as the 1000 above. Securitizing 1000 brings down the total assets to 9000. The original equity was $4\% \times 10,000 = 400$ and the securitization saves 40, bringing down the total new equity to 360. What is the return on remaining equity once 1000 of loans are securitized and the gain/loss from its original value pre-securitization?

58.3.2 The Costs of Funding On Balance Sheet and through Securitization

The cost of financing loans on balance sheet is the Wacc of the bank (Table 58.1). With the above assumptions, the calculation is straightforward, given the bank's rating and the corresponding cost of the bank's debt. The weights of equity and debt are 4% and 96% respectively. The required return on equity is given and the cost of debt results from the credit rating of the bank. The bank's Wacc is 10.4%.

---

1 Using the book ROE is a common practice. Furthermore, it can be shown that it is consistent with a minimum market return under some assumptions, notably a constant PER (stock price to earnings ratio).

TABLE 58.1 Wacc calculations, on-balance sheet

Funding structure		Cost BS
Riskless rate		9%
Rating		A
Spread		1.00%
Interest cost		10.00%
	Weights	Cost
Debt	96%	10.00%
Equity	4%	20.00%
		BS Wacc
WACC		10.400%

TABLE 58.2 Effective ROE of the bank

	Balances	Yield	Revenue and costs
Assets	10,000	10.10%	1010
Debt	9,600	10.00%	960
Earnings before tax (BT)	400		50
Effective ROE = EBT/capital			12.50%

58.3.3 The Effective Return on Capital for the Bank

The calculation of the book return on bank's capital is the ratio EBT (earnings before tax) to capital (Table 58.2). Given expected return on assets, the book ROE is 12.50%, lower than the required 20%.

58.3.4 The Cost of Financing through Securitization

The cost of financing through securitization is also a weighted average cost of the notes issued, using the credit spreads matching the ratings assigned to the two classes of notes (Table 58.3). The direct operating costs of setting up the securitization vehicle are not included at this stage.

The cost of financing loans through securitization is lower than on balance sheet. This cost depends on the structuring of notes (the weights assigned to each one of them), the credit spreads prevailing in the market and the risk-free rate. This is a key benefit of securitization in this example. It is not a general rule since the market spreads can narrow or widen depending on prevailing conditions.

TABLE 58.3 Wacc of securitization

Cost senior	Cost junior
9%	9%
AA	Ba
0.50%	2.00%
9.50%	11.00%

Weights	Cost
75.00%	9.50%
25.00%	11.00%

Wacc
9.875%

58.3.5 The Annualized All-in Cost of Financing through Securitization

The all-in cost includes the direct operating costs of setting up the SPE and the servicing fee. The service fee is also a cost usually born by the bank that has the relationship with the clients. Note that none of these two cost items are paid to investors, and they are not considered when addressing the pricing issue for selling the loans to the SPE. This additional operating cost is 0.3%. Adding this value to the Wacc of securitization, we obtain an all-in cost of financing of 10.375%, still lower than the balance sheet Wacc. This is not yet the full all-in cost of securitization, since we need to add up algebraically any capital gain or loss resulting from the sale of assets to the SPE at mark-to-market values.

58.3.6 The Pricing of Assets Sold to the SPE

We can use a simple calculation for 1 year. The pool of loans returns 10.10% for 1 year, so that 1000 provides 1101 in 1 year. The discounted value at 10.10% is equal to par value by definition:

$$1101/(1 + 10.10\%) = 1000$$

This price at which assets are sold to the SPE is such that the investors acquiring the notes issued by the SPE get their average required return. This price is:

$$1101/(1 + 9.875\%) = 1002.048$$

It is easy to check that, if investors pay 1002.048 for something that provides 1101.0 in 1 year, their return is effectively:

$$(1101 - 1002.048)/1002.048 = 98.95/1002.48 = 9.875\%$$

Because the Wacc for securitization is lower than the return on the portfolio of loans, the sale generates a capital gain equal to $1002.048 - 1000 = 2.048$, or 0.2048% of the amount securitized. Such a capital gain should be deducted from all other cost items for finding the all-in cost of securitization.

Before proceeding, it is shown that the 1-year maturity assumption is not restrictive. In the general case, the price of assets sold results from discounting all cash flows of the pool by the required Wacc of investors in the SPE. The discounted value of future flows generated by the assets at 10.10% is exactly 1000. With another discount rate, the present value differs from this face value. The value is V, a function of the portfolio yield is r, and of the new discount rate is y. The duration provides the variation of value of a debt, $V(y) - V(r)$ due to a change of yield[2] from r to y: $V(y) - V(r) = -\text{duration}(y - r)V(r)$. The formula allows finding the price of the debt sold to investors as a percentage of an initial value $V(r)$ equal to par, or 100%. The proxy of the new value $V(y)$ derives from the duration formula[3], according to $(V - 100\%)/100\% = -\text{duration}(y - r)$ and $V(\%$ of face value$) = 100\% + \text{duration}(r - y)$.

58.3.7 The All-in Cost of Funding through Securitization

The all-in cost of financing through securitization starts from the securitization Wacc, adds all direct costs (set-up cost and serving fee) and deducts any capital gain from the sale of assets to the SPE (Table 58.4). A capital loss should be added. The cost is again lower than the cost of financing in the balance sheet both because the securitization Wacc is below this cost and because the bank makes a capital gain when selling the assets to the SPE.

In general, not all effects will be positive because the cost of financing through securitization could be lower than the cost on balance sheet, but still be higher than the portfolio yield, thereby generating a capital loss when selling the assets to the SPE.

TABLE 58.4   The all-in cost of financing through securitization

Weighted cost of securitization notes	9.875%
Sale price of loans (% of value)	100.205%
Capital gain (+) / loss (−)	0.205%
Direct cost of securitization (not paid to investors)	0.200%
Servicing fee (not paid to investors)	0.100%
All-in cost of securitization	9.970%

---

2   We ignore the factor $1 + r$ in this proxy calculation.
3   Since the duration is one year in our example, and the yield is $r = 10.10\%$, the value at the discount rate $y = 9.875\%$ is: $100\% + 1 \times (10.10\% - 9.875\%) = 100.225\%$. This means that the sale of the assets to the SPE generates a capital gain of 0.225% of an amount of 1000, a proxy of the above exact value 0.2048%. In the general case of maturities longer than one year, the same formula could serve for finding a proxy mark-to-market value of the pool of loans by changing their duration. For example, under a more realistic case, the loan duration could be 10 years, and the proxy value as percentage of initial value would be: $100\% + 10 \times (10.10\% - 9.875\%) = 1002.25\%$ and the capital gain would be 10 times as much, or 2.25% instead of 0.225%.

TABLE 58.5   Book ROE post-securitization

Original assets	10,000
Amount securitized	1,000
Remaining assets	9,000
Original amount of equity	400
Equity saved	40
Ending value of equity	360
Ending value of debt	8,640
Portfolio loan yield (%)	10.100%
Additional yield (% of securitized assets 1000)[a]	0.205%
Additional yield (% of remaining assets 9000)	0.023%
Direct cost (% of securitized assets 1000)[a]	0.200%
Direct cost (% of remaining assets 9000)	0.022%
Total yield	10.101%
Portfolio yield value 9000 × total yield%	924.400
Cost of debt (% of debt)	10.000%
Cost of debt (value) 8640 × cost of debt	864.000
EBT	60.400
ROE post-securitization, equity 360	16.778%
Original yield pre-securitization	12.50%
Gain of ROE	4.278%

[a] In % of assets securitized

58.3.8 Securitization Economics and the Return on Equity

For calculating the resulting return on capital of the bank, we need to include all items in the calculation. Note that capital gain/loss is obtained as a percentage of the face value of the amount securitized. Percentages of asset value have to be converted into percentages of the remaining portfolio on balance sheet after securitization. This implies multiplying the percentage capital gain/loss by 1000/9000. For example, a capital gain of 0.205% of 1000 is converted into $0.205\% \times 1/9 = 0.023\%$, a percentage of the remaining portfolio. The full calculation of the return on capital post securitization is summarized in Table 58.5. Compared to the original return on capital, 12.50%, the securitization improved the final return by 4.278%.

The sale of assets generates a capital gain for the seller only when the cost of financing (Wacc) with securitization is lower than the asset yield, which is 10.20%. In such a case, the capital gain from sale will effectively increase the revenues, thereby increasing the average return of assets on the balance sheet. This is not a sufficient condition to improve the return on capital because we need to add up direct operating costs of setting up the SPE.

58.3.9 Enhancing the Bank's Return on Capital through Securitization

We consider two cases. If capital is a linear function of the amount securitized, it is relatively easy to determine whether the securitization enhances the ROE, by how much, and what are the limitations. Under full economic capital analysis, the capital is not any more a preset percentage of assets but results from a direct calculation with a portfolio model pre and post securitization. Whatever the method used, securitization makes more sense if it enhances the return on capital.

If capital is approximately proportional to amount securitized, and if securitization improves the ROE, it is tempting to increase the amount securitized. The bank would benefit even more from the positive relationship between the amount securitized and the ROE. This is sometimes called the "leverage effect of securitization." Leverage is positive as long as the all-in cost of financing through securitization remains fixed. The higher the amount securitized, the higher the final ROE after securitization. However, there are limits to such leverage effect. It is unlikely that the return on asset remains constant when the amount securitized changes. If the credit quality of securitized assets declines, the junior tranche should become higher and the cost of financing through securitization will increase. The lower quality of new assets securitized might set up a practical limit to the amount securitized[4].

All the above equations are oversimplified. The true economic capital savings would result from the portfolio risk before and after securitization. A prerequisite for evaluating the benefits of the transaction, and for assessing the resiliency of the structure, is to find out the distribution value of the securitized assets directly from a credit portfolio model. The composition of the assets, their risks, and their correlations would play a significant role, notably for making sure that the expected returns of loans remains above the returns expected by investors.

58.4 ASSESSING THE RISK OF ASSET-BACKED NOTES

The resiliency of a structure designates its ability to sustain variations of the risk factors without generating losses to the various classes of structured notes. Rating agencies focus on the risk of issued notes, while credit portfolio models make up the foundation for modeling the risk of the underlying credit portfolio. Both methodologies serve for assessing how resilient a securitization structure is and should be used in conjunction.

58.4.1 Rating Methodologies for Structured Notes

Critical parameters that determine the resiliency of structures depend on the type of structure. For consumers or mortgages loans, typical critical parameters include:

- the delinquency rate (delays in payment)
- the charge-off rate (losses due to default)
- the payment rate (both monthly payments of interest and principal)
- the recovery rate (both percentage amount and timing of recoveries)
- the average yield of the portfolio of loans.

The degree of over-collateralization of each note measures the risk, when such factors are stress-tested.

The stress tests serve for rating the notes, in addition to measuring the resiliency of the structure. The main purpose of such stress scenarios is finding out the stress level of each factor that each note can sustain without impairing its risk. For example, a common way of assessing the risk of an

---

4 This might not applies to securitizations of short-term assets, such as credit cards, since the rapid amortization of such loans makes it necessary to periodically replenish the pool of assets with new short-term loans, of which quality is not necessarily downgraded simply because they are new loans.

asset-backed note is to use multiples of expected charge-offs for finding out when the credit risk of notes is impaired. For a given note, the higher the multiple sustainable by the note without any loss, the higher the rating. For instance, the required minimum multiple for an "AAA" scenario is highest compared with a riskier subordinated note. An "AAA" scenario designates the minimum multiple required to preserve the AAA rating. Minimum required multiples of charge-off rates are, for example, 5 or 6 times the expected average charge-off rate for senior notes.

One easy way to assign ratings to notes is to map these minimum multiples with the note ratings. Evidently, the minimum multiple required to have a given rating also depends on the quality of the assets. Hence, the AAA scenario, or the "AAA multiple" of expected loss, is lower when the average risk of assets is low than when it is higher. This is a shortcut to the full modeling of the risk of the portfolio of assets. The full assessment of the structured note ratings requires plugging these scenarios to the "spreadsheet" model of the waterfall of cash flows. Various simulations show when losses hit each note.

Such methodologies make sense to the extent that the stress scenarios are in line with past experience. They are not inconsistent with modeling the portfolio loss distribution, since they stress risk factors that affect this distribution.

But such methodologies are no substitutes for credit portfolio models that generate the loss distribution of the underlying asset portfolio and allow modeling the risk of each note. Notably, stress testing the correlation of losses within the portfolio of assets is mostly important for at least two reasons. First, the portfolio loss distribution is highly sensitive to the uniform correlation; and, second, it has been shown that default correlations are sensitive to economic conditions. One of the lessons of the 2007–2008 crisis is that the risk of notes issued by securitization vehicles was massively under-estimated. Portfolio models did not help either since securitization arrangers use them, but a model is as good as the inputs are. Models should have allowed conducting more stringent stress tests, both on the quality of inputs and on loss correlations. In any case, they remain the unique tool for better addressing dependencies than simpler techniques such as those described above.

58.4.2 Credit Portfolio Models and Securitizations

For securitizing retail portfolios, consumer lending or mortgages, a single factor model is often used with a uniform correlation, using simulations similar to those explained in the portfolio simulation chapter (Chapter 50). The most common model used by banks is a simulation using either the structural model or the time-intensity model. Time-intensity models would use various intensity of defaults across successive periods, in a piecewise way. Default correlation plays a major role in securitizations, since it drives the thickness of the fat tail of the loss distribution.

For addressing structuring with portfolio models, the waterfall of losses serves for allocating losses to each tranche. A simple pass-through model[5] allocates each randomly generated loss to the various notes according to the seniority of notes. The pass-through model is an over-simplification because of the many covenants that apply for routing the losses and the

---

5 "Pass-through" in this section does not refer to the first generation of securitizations. It refers here to the assumption that asset cash-flows are "passed-through" the notes according to the waterfall model, but ignoring covenants that require, for example, that a fraction of excess cash-flows are retained within the SPE as an additional protection for investors until the SPE reaches maturity. In other words, we ignore covenants governing the SPE.

TABLE 58.6 Example of a structuring of notes

Structured notes	Size
Senior 3	20
Senior 2	20
Senior 1	20
Sub 2	20
Sub 1, or equity	20
Total	100

various triggers to be considered. The pass-through model allows easier generation of the loss distribution for each tranche and assigning an expected loss, which is an objective basis for assigning a rating.

The loss of any structured note depends upon the aggregated level of losses of portfolio of loans. Losses flow to structured notes according to their seniority level. Any note benefits from the protection of all subordinated notes, whose size determines the level of over-collateralization of the note. The total size of all subordinated notes under a specific structured note is a loss franchise of benefit to the next senior tranche.

The principle for allocating random losses to each tranche is simple under a pass-through model. A portfolio has a size of 100. There are five classes of structured notes, each having an equal size of 20 (Table 58.6). Tranches get more senior when moving up. The lowest tranche is "Sub 1," serving as "equity" for the others since it is hit by the first losses of the portfolio. The most senior tranche is Senior 3, on top.

The exercise is to allocate losses. The portfolio loss can range from 0 up to 100, although this 100 loss will never happen. The distribution of portfolio losses results from simulation or relies on the limit distribution (Chapter 49) for granular uniform retail portfolio. If the simulated loss is lower than 20, it hits only Sub 1. If it is above 20, the excess over 20 hits the upper tranche. Hence a 25 portfolio loss results in a total loss of 20 for Sub 1 and a loss of $25 - 20 = 5$ for Sub 2. Following the same rationale, the allocation of a portfolio loss of 45 would be 20 for Sub 1, 20 for Sub 2 and 5 for Senior 1, and 0 for both Senior 2 and 3.

The loss distribution of each note has a lower bound of zero. For example, the Senior 1 note has a loss of zero when the portfolio loss is 40 and a loss of 1 when the portfolio loss reaches 41. The loss distribution of each note is also capped by its size. In our example, Senior 1 cannot lose more than 20. In order to reach this loss level, the portfolio loss should hit the value 60.

The random loss of the portfolio is L, the random loss for the note N_{ab} benefiting from the seniority level defined by its attachment point, "a," is L_{ab}. The size of the note N_{ab} is $b - a$, and it is equal to the maximum loss of the note. For any value of simulated portfolio loss L, the loss allocation for each note follows the waterfall. Figure 58.5 shows both portfolio loss and the loss for the note N_{ab}. Analytically, the loss for the note is simply: $L_{ab} = \min[\max(L - a, 0), b - a]$. The first loss appears only when L passes the lower bound a. If the portfolio loss L gets bigger, the loss L_{ab} remains bounded by $b - a$. Any excess above this cap hits the next structured note. The expected loss[6] results from the portfolio loss distribution truncated at the levels a and b.

---

6 Formally, if $f(L_p)$ is the PDF of the portfolio loss: $E(L_{ab}) = \int_a^b L_p f(L_p)\, d(L_p)$.

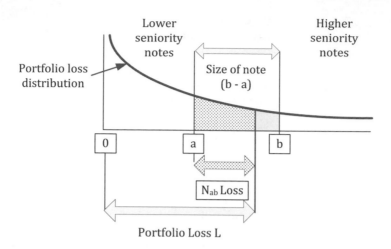

FIGURE 58.5 **Loss distributions of the portfolio and of a structured note**

In order to illustrate the above methodology, we use the above simple example of a portfolio funded by five classes of structured notes. The portfolio characteristics are:

- 100 obligors
- a uniform unit exposure
- a uniform default probability of 5%
- recoveries of zero
- a uniform asset correlation of 30%.

There are five classes of structured notes, all equal to 20% of the portfolio, or 20, following the above example.

In order to determine expected losses, multiple simulations serve for generating the underlying asset loss distribution. The number of simulations is 1000. Allocating the portfolio loss to all structured notes at each run also generates the loss distributions of the structured notes. The expected loss of each note is simply the arithmetic average of losses hitting each tranche across all 1000 trials. Table 58.7 summarizes the results.

With 30% correlation, there is no loss in the 1000 trials for Senior 1 and Senior 2. The 3 most senior notes are investment grade, since the expected loss is 0.06% for Senior 1. The average simulated loss of the portfolio is 4.98%, close to the 5% value. For the subordinated notes, the

TABLE 58.7 **Simulation of the expected loss of a portfolio and of the notes**

	Portfolio loss	Senior 3	Senior 2	Senior 1	Sub 2	Sub 1 (equity)
Maximum	58.00%	0.00%	0.00%	18.00%	17.00%	19.000%
Mean	4.98%	0.00%	0.00%	0.06%	0.21%	3.71%

expected loss is lower because each note loss is bounded upward and downward.

58.4.3 Tranches are Subject to Correlation Risk

The tranches issued by a securitization are similar to N-to-default derivatives. The rationale is the same as for first-to-default derivatives. With securitizations, the probability that a single tranche defaults is equal to the probability that a minimum fraction of all assets defaults. Its risk is that of an N-to-default basket, N being a fraction of the total number of assets within the portfolio. This makes securitization tranches correlation products, as are N-to-default products.

The rationale can be explained through simple cases. Consider a portfolio of two assets financed by two tranches, a junior one and a senior one. Moreover, assume the size of each tranche is identical to the size of each asset.

- For the senior tranche to default, both assets should default. This happens only when the joint probability of default is high. The risk of the senior tranche increases with the correlation.
- The junior tranche defaults if only one asset defaults, like a first-to-default basket of two assets. The risk of the junior tranche increases when the probability that any one of the two assets defaults increases. The probability of triggering this first-to-default product is one minus the joint survival probability. The risk of the junior tranche varies inversely with credit loss correlation, when the joint survival probability increases. The risk that any one asset default declines (one minus joint survival probability). The risk of the junior tranche declines when credit correlation increases.

In general for the senior tranche to default, many assets should default jointly – implying a high correlation. For a subordinated tranche to default, any one of several assets should default, and the probability of such an event is always 1 minus the joint probability that the other assets survive. The risk of a subordinated tranche increases when the joint survival probability of these assets declines, or, equivalently, when the correlation declines. The tranches embed different correlations and are correlation products. Unless we address correlation properly, the risk of tranches is not adequately assessed. One consequence is the effect of a correlation increase, like in stressed conditions. This will make the senior tranche riskier, and subject to credit downgrades. Downgrading of senior tranches is presumably related to an underestimation of the stressed loss correlation in the financial crisis.

59

Credit Portfolio Management

This chapter explains how credit portfolio management techniques, notably credit derivatives, help customizing the needs of both bankers and investors by trading separately the credit risk component of assets. It discusses several areas and illustrates them with a simplified case study.

- Active portfolio management: credit derivatives provide all the features necessary for actively reshaping the risk–return profile of a portfolio. Securitization techniques previously discussed are also within the scope of portfolio and capital management.
- Hedging credit risk: hedges result from matching asset credit risk with the mirror credit risk of a credit derivative. In addition, credit derivative hedges apply to single assets, baskets of assets, or the entire bank's portfolio.
- Creating synthetic exposures and taking credit exposures: the seller of a credit derivative can take synthetic exposures that would, otherwise, be out of their direct reach. Selling a credit default swap is a substitute to taking cash credit exposure. On the other side of the deal, the lender hedges its risks.

Section 59.1 expands the rationale for active credit portfolio management. Section 59.2 is a reminder of the techniques for trading credit risk. Section 59.3 discusses applications of credit derivatives. Section 59.4 illustrates, through an example, how credit derivatives can serve for enhancing the risk–return profile of a portfolio, through regulatory arbitrage. The last section (Section 59.5) generalizes the principle of taking advantage of discrepancies between the prices of the same risk. For banks, the price of credit risk is capital-based. For investors, the price is rating-based. Both capital-based and rating-based prices of a given credit risk will generally differ, leading to profitable arbitrage between the two prices.

Contents

59.1 THE RATIONALE FOR CREDIT PORTFOLIO MANAGEMENT

Credit portfolio management is closely related to the business model of banks. Under the "buy and hold" business model, the bank originates loans and keeps them in its balance sheet until maturity (or default). Under the "originate and distribute" business model, the bank originates loans but resells them, thereby freeing up some capital for originating new business, the main technique for doing so being securitization.

Traditional banking builds up on relationship management. Banks build a relationship with clients and sell customized solutions, notably to the large clients. The traditional relationship model has its drawbacks. Relationship banking creates a customer base, but it also tends to creates concentration and specialization. Credit portfolio management refers to all actions serving for re-shaping and "optimizing" the risk–return profile of the credit portfolio of the bank.

There are many incentives for developing active portfolio management. A primary motivation is expanding new business, while still complying with risk limits, by off-loading credit risk onto the markets. Off-loading credit risk can be done through securitizations or the use of credit derivatives that transfer risks to the seller. Another motivation is to increase diversification and reduce risk concentration. Originating new loans in different industries would be the classical way. Selling credit derivatives to gain credit exposures without entering into cash transactions is more flexible.

Portfolio management techniques aim at enhancing the profile of the portfolio and on the means to achieve such goals. The first major innovation in this area is the implementation of portfolio models. The second innovation is the flexibility provided by credit derivatives, such as credit default swaps (CDSs), whose market expanded considerably. Active portfolio management emerged when techniques and instruments developed allowing direct sales of loans, securitizations, or credit risk hedging.

Transfers of assets from origination to a loan portfolio management unit requires transfer prices between origination and portfolio management, for allocating income to each of these two poles. In terms of organization, the credit portfolio management unit buys internally all or some of the portfolio of loans of the bank. It is separated from the originating unit, which is dedicated to developing new business. The transfer within the bank between the two units should be done at mark-to-market values, since the portfolio management unit operates in capital markets. It implies the transfer of risk, measured as the cost of allocated capital. Once the two units are organized, credit portfolio management acts in a way similar to asset-liability management (ALM) for liquidity and interest rate risk, in that it operates over the whole portfolio, rather than on focusing on single transactions, as the origination unit does. Credit portfolio management can be seen as an equivalent of ALM for credit risk.

Portfolio management makes lending activities of banks closer to the trading philosophy since it implies changing the structure of portfolios for optimizing its risk–return profile. The portfolio management unit becomes a profit center and lives with its own goals, tools and techniques to achieve "optimization." Securitizations have been used for a long time for managing credit portfolios. Credit derivatives further facilitated this task and added new degrees of freedom.

At the time of writing, the future of active portfolio management and securitizations is subject to uncertainty because these techniques are associated to the contagion of risk to the entire financial system. However, the issues raised by the 2007 financial crisis do not dismiss such techniques. The economics of reshaping portfolios through securitizations and credit derivatives can and should be economically sound. To a large extent, the crisis is more the outcome of improper usage of these techniques, rather than flaws embedded in the techniques.

59.2 TRADING CREDIT RISK

There are various traditional techniques for trading credit risk. Syndication is the classical process of lending large amounts, with a bank serving as underwriter, and selling fractions of such loans to other banks for diversification purpose. The "final take" is the fraction of the loan retained by the underwriter.

Loan trading consists of direct sales of loans by banks to other institutions. Historically, loan trading remained limited. However, a loan trading market emerged in New York, with standard contracts facilitating direct sales of loans. The market emerged with distressed loans because they were sold at low prices offering a significant potential of capital gains. However, the emergence of the credit derivatives market in the last 10 years is of much larger dimensions and today offers liquidity and flexibility, making direct loan trading less attractive.

Securitization consists of selling pools of credits to a dedicated entity, an SPE, refinanced in the market. The asset cash flows serve for compensating investors who buy the asset-backed bonds issued by the SPE. Securitization is feasible as long as assets held in the SPE generate a return sufficient for compensating investors in the bonds issued by the SPE, given the risk of the portfolio of assets held by the SPE and the risk of bonds acquired by investors.

Credit derivatives (mainly CDSs) are far more flexible because they are traded, while setting up a securitization vehicle is a more complex operation. Credit derivatives provide protection against credit loss, the ability to exchange one credit risk for another (for example, exchange a poor rating credit with a better credit rating assets), or allow to take exposures to credit risk by selling them.

59.3 APPLICATIONS OF CREDIT DERIVATIVES

Credit derivatives serve for three main activities that relate directly to credit portfolio management:

- hedging credit risk
- trading credit risk
- customizing credit risk.

59.3.1 Hedging Credit Risk

Credit derivatives allow separating the trading of the credit risk of assets from trading the asset itself. The most common derivatives are credit default swaps, which pay to the buyer the loss given default under default of the underlying asset. They are insurances against default risk. Credit spread products provide protection against a widening of credit spreads and offset the loss of mark-to-market value due to wider spreads.

Syndication implies several risks:

- keeping a larger amount of the funds for a longer than expected time
- selling a fraction to other banks at a lower than predicted spread, if not agreed in advance.

This makes it useful to customize the size of the intermediate exposure, the term of the exposure and the spread. Credit derivatives allow customizing of all three items for the expected horizon of syndication, from inception and up to final take. Buying a protection would offset the exposure to credit risk beyond the expected horizon for distributing the loans to banks. A spread derivative would cap the spread.

The same issue arises for all uncertain exposures from committed lines of credit or from the potential exposures of the derivative portfolio of the bank. Credit derivatives serve for insuring potential excess exposures.

59.3.2 Trading Credit Risk

Investors look at credit derivatives as instruments for taking exposures to which they have no access, for searching yields, and for trading credit risk expectations. Investors also look at credit derivatives as providing return enhancements through the revenue of the seller. They also consider them for replicating exposures to which they have no direct access, as well as a way for increasing diversification by buying exposures that diversify away some of the risk of their concentrations, on certain industries for example.

Investors or traders also look at these instruments as providing an enhanced return when they perceive credit events as having a low probability. The "search for yield" makes credit derivatives attractive in spite of default risk.

Credit derivatives allow trading different expectations on the same risks. Default probabilities and recoveries are uncertain parameters. Internal ratings or default probability models are not necessarily reliable. Credit spreads embed expectations of default probabilities and recoveries. If different parties have different views on probabilities of default and/or on future recoveries, they can trade these views through CDSs. In practice, differing expectations translate into varying perceptions of loss rates across investors. The loss rate combines the default rate with the loss given default rate. For instance, a default probability of 1% combined with a recovery rate of 20% results in a loss rate of $(1 - 20\%) \times 1\% = 0.8\%$. Conceptually, the spread equals $\lambda \times LGD$, or the loss rate, under risk-neutral probabilities. A trader might estimate a loss rate of 1%, while the CDS price implies a loss rate of 0.6%. Such discrepancies are incentives for trading the different expectations about loss rates. The trader can see the CDS as under-pricing the risk and buys it in the hope of a gain in value if the embedded loss rate in the fee increases as expected.

59.3.3 Customizing Credit Risk

Tailoring and customizing exposures is a major function of credit derivatives. This helps reshaping individual and portfolio credit risk profile so that they meet eligibility criteria, for both lenders and investors.

Credit derivatives allow one to engineer the credit risk quality and spreads using baskets. First-to-default baskets have a credit standing lower than any one of the standalone assets in the basket. Therefore, it is possible to engineer any credit risk independently of what exists in the market by customizing the basket so that it has the desired credit standing. This is like creating a portfolio, but with fewer constraints since we build up the rating by assembling a small number of assets in the proportions consistent with the target credit standing. Note that such products are correlation products, as explained in Chapter 9.

Finally, customizing its own credit risk is feasible by buying credit insurance or selling it. When buying credit protection, the buyer hedges its exposure. When selling a credit derivative, the seller gains exposure without holding the underlying asset. Both CDSs and total return swaps serve for hedging or gaining exposure to the underlying credit risk.

Usually there is no need to invest cash to get a credit exposure. But replicating a credit-risky cash asset is easy with credit derivatives. An investor can invest in a risk-free asset and sell a CDS. The recurring fee from the CDS provides the compensations for credit risk, in addition to the risk-free rate. Note, however, that many credit derivative contracts impose posting collateral for mitigating counterparty risk.

59.3.4 Applications for Credit Portfolio Management

The customization of credit risk through credit derivatives has many applications, one of them being active credit portfolio management by banks. In general, the purposes of credit derivatives include replicating, transferring, or hedging credit risks.

If the bank holds a concentration in an industry, it is a protection seeker. It has number of choices, such as capping exposures or diversifying the loan portfolio in other industries. Credit derivatives offer additional options. Buying a direct protection for some of the assets held is a simple solution. The bank hedges a fraction of this concentration by buying credit protection. The bank can also diversify away some risk of its portfolio by taking synthetic exposures and selling CDSs. The protections sold would provide revenue that would offset some of the cost of protections bought, while still benefiting from gains of diversification.

Transferring credit risk can be of mutual interest. Two banks, one heavily concentrated in industry A and the other in industry B, might be willing to exchange or transfer their risks to each other in order to achieve a better balance in their portfolios.

Credit portfolio managers look both for protection against risky assets and for increased diversification by selling protection against exposures that diversify some of the risk of the portfolio, while, simultaneously, increasing the return with the recurring premium received. The example provided in Section 59.4 illustrates the economics of the process.

59.3.5 Evolution of Credit Risk Models

The evolution of credit risk models and tools illustrates how credit trading progressively emerged.

- March 1991: Credit Monitor launched.
  The firm KMV, today a unit of Moody's, introduces Credit Monitor, which models default probabilities for companies with publicly traded equity.
- 1992: credit derivatives emerge.
  The ISDA, a professional association dedicated to the development of derivatives, first uses the term "credit derivatives" to describe these new contracts which are traded over-the-counter.
- 1993: Portfolio Manager released.
  KMV introduces the first version of its Portfolio Manager model, the first credit portfolio model. Credit portfolio models allow determining economic capital (credit VaR) and the risk contributions to the overall risk of the portfolio of any single asset or sub-portfolio. This allows measuring whether it is economical, given risk contributions and spreads of assets to keep them or to sell them, and to do so on an active basis when risk and return changes through time.
- 1994: credit derivatives market begins to expand.
  At this early stage, some commentators doubt the new credit derivatives market will take off, but by the end of the year, the volume of credit derivatives sold is $4–5 billion. The majority of contracts, whose usage expanded considerably in the last decade, are credit default swaps. Pricing models provided a conceptual framework for assigning a value to such derivatives.
- September 1996: the first CLO, or collateralized loan obligation, a new type of securitization.
  The UK's National Westminster Bank issues the first collateralized loan obligation, securitizing $5 billion of its corporate loan book to shed regulatory capital. Formerly, securitizations had been used for decades for selling pools of retail banking loans into the capital market. Since then, various types of securitizations expanded very quickly until the 2007 financial crisis.

59.4 PORTFOLIO CREDIT RISK MANAGEMENT (CASE STUDY)

The usages of credit derivatives for portfolio management are multiple: increasing diversification by taking synthetic new exposures as well hedging existing excess exposures and risk concentrations. By doing so, they also alter the portfolio return. The economics of the transactions should enhance, in the end, the return on capital (ROC).

Enhancing the ROC results from the joint effect of credit derivatives on the capital base, which depends on exposures hedged or gained, and on return, through fees paid for hedging or fees received from selling credit protection. "Regulatory arbitrage" is a classical example. Regulatory arbitrage is the direct outcome of differing prices for the same credit risk. As pointed out in Chapter 55, the capital-based price of credit risk and the market price of the same credit risk will not match in general. By taking advantage of such discrepancies, it becomes feasible to enhance the ROC. The same type of arbitrage applies to securitizations, for which an example is provided in the next chapter. Both are examples of credit portfolio management of which main purpose is to increase the risk-adjusted return by using credit derivatives.

We expand the example using regulatory capital. The weight assigned to corporations is 100% and the weight with a banking counterparty drops to 20% under the Basel 1 regulations. The capital charge with a direct loan is 4% (50% × 8%) and becomes 1/5 of 4% = 0.80% for a bank. Next consider two banks. Bank A is the lending bank and bank B is the counterparty for buying and selling credit derivatives. Bank A's pre-tax revenue decreases by the fee paid when it buys credit protection from bank B, say 0.80%, while bank B's revenue increases by the same fee. Bank B has no funding cost but earns the recurring fee from the sale of the CDS. The capital charge for a sold credit derivative is identical to a direct exposure to a corporation, if the underlying asset is a corporate issue, and equal to the full 4%, identical to lending directly to a corporation. Bank A can also sell a CDS for minimizing its cost. It earns the recurring fee for the CDS sold but has an additional exposure to credit risk, which offsets partially the gain of credit exposure from the bought CDS for credit protection purpose. By entering into such trades, the bank might enhance its risk-adjusted return.

For making explicit the economics of such transactions, we use a typical case study.

A credit portfolio of 1000 has an average risk weight of 100% and uses up 4% capital or 40. The spread on loans over funding cost is 100 bps. The cost of regulatory or economic capital is the product of the required return on capital (k) by capital, or $k \times K$. The original return on capital is 25% before tax. Table 59.1 provides some lines for adding protection bought and protection sold, which are zero initially.

According to these data, the economic income statement shows the initial return on capital, equal to the target return. The original return is that of the original portfolio or 100 bps × 1000 = 10 (Table 59.2).

TABLE 59.1   Initial situation: capital

Capital calculation	Notional	Risk weight	Capital
Portfolio	1000	100%	40.0
Credit trading			
Protection bought	0	20%	0.0
Protection sold	0	100%	0.0
Capital from trading CDS			0.0
Capital after trading CDS			40.0

TABLE 59.2   Initial situation: earnings

Earnings calculation	Spread of loans (bps)	Cost/revenue CDS (bps)	P&L (€)
Portfolio	100		10.0
Credit trading			
Protection bought	0	60	0.0
Protection sold	0	80	0.0
Net P&L after trading CDS			10.0

TABLE 59.3 Initial situation: economic income statement and return on capital (ROC)

Economic income statement	Original portfolio
Net capital after trading CDS	40.0
Net P&L after trade	10.0
ROC	25.00%

The capital is calculated as 4% of the original portfolio risk-weighted 100% and return of capital is calculated with original values. Note that, for return to capital, we ignore expected loss, which means that we consider returns as net of expected loss (Table 59.3).

It is possible to hedge the portfolio with credit derivatives issued by a bank. The cost of the protection bought is 60 bps. The risk weight applicable to the bank is 20%, or a capital charge of 20% × 4% = 0.8% multiplied by the amount of protection acquired. It is also possible to sell protection through credit derivatives. The purpose of such a sale would be to reduce the cost of the hedge for example. In such case, the banks earns a spread estimated to 80 bps (the premium of the CDS), but this protection sold has a capital charge corresponding to a 100% risk weight or 100% × 4% = 4%.

The cost of a credit risk hedge (a credit default swap, CDS) includes two cost components. The direct cost is the premium of CDS times the exposure hedged. The second component is the cost of the Basel 1 or Basel 2 capital allocated to the exposure to the seller of the CDS, a bank with risk weight 20% instead of 100%. Under Basel 2, such a capital charge would depend on the rating of the bank. But only numerical values would change and we can proceed as if we are subject to Basel 1 capital charges. Selling a CDS provides the premium but costs additional capital, as if the bank were exposed to the underlying asset risk weighted 100%.

If the bank buys a credit protection of 1000 for the total portfolio, earnings decline by the cost (premium) of the CDS bought, but capital also declines. The bank can also buy a protection for 1000 (total portfolio) and sell a credit protection for 300 in order to offset some of the cost of the protection. Again, earnings, capital and return on capital change.

We now proceed for the calculations of earnings, capital and return on capital in the two cases:

- when buying full protection for the portfolio
- when buying and selling protection.

59.4.1 Buying Protection for the Portfolio from Another Bank

Tables 59.4–59.6 provide the calculations of capital, earnings and return on capital for the initial bank portfolio. The protection acquired matches the total portfolio and reduces both earnings and capital of the bank. Note that the calculation of capital now uses a capital charge with a risk weight of only 20%. By buying protection, the exposure remains 1000, but has a reduced risk weight. We substitute the new capital to the initial capital because we substitute entirely the exposure to the bank to the exposure to the corporation. The new earnings combine algebraically the initial revenue with the cost of the hedge. Finally the return on capital has improved, moving from 25% to 50%.

TABLE 59.4   Buying protection: capital

Capital calculation	Notional	Risk weight	Capital
Portfolio	1000	100%	40.0
Credit trading			
Protection bought	1000	20%	8.0
Protection sold	0	100%	0.0
Capital from trading CDS			−8.0
Capital after trading CDS			8.0

TABLE 59.5   Buying protection: earnings

Earnings calculation	Spread of loans (bps)	Cost/revenue CDS (bps)	P&L (€)
Portfolio	100		10.0
Credit trading			
Protection bought	1000	60	−6.0
Protection sold	0	80	0.0
Net P&L after trading CDS			4.0

TABLE 59.6   Buying protection: economic income statement

Economic income statement	Original portfolio	Portfolio after trade
Net capital after trading CDS	40.0	8.0
Net P&L after trade	10.0	4.0
ROC	25.00%	50.00%

Under a more realistic calculation, we would substitute actual risk weights under Basel 2, which now depend on the ratings assigned to the corporation and the bank. Depending on these ratings and the associated risk weights, and on the actual cost of protection, the return on capital might increase or decrease, but the sequence of calculations would be the same.

59.4.2   Buying Protection for the Portfolio and Selling Protection

The bank now sells protection to the bank, on a reference asset that is a corporation risk-weighted 100%. This reduces the cost of protection by buying the CDS from the bank. The capital is reduced to that of substituting the exposure to the corporation to an exposure to a bank, plus the additional capital from selling protection on a corporation, although for a lower amount. The capital again declines but to a lower amount than in the preceding case because of protection sold (Table 59.7).

TABLE 59.7   Buying and selling CDSs: capital

Capital calculation	Notional	Risk weight	Capital
Portfolio	1000	100%	40.0
Credit trading Protection bought Protection sold	 1000 300	 20% 100%	 8.0 12.0
Capital from trading CDS			4.0
Capital after trading CDS			20.0

TABLE 59.8   Buying and selling CDSs: earnings

Earnings calculation	Spread of loans (bps)	Cost/revenue CDS (bps)	P&L (€)
Portfolio	100		10.0
Credit trading Protection bought Protection sold	 1000 300	 60 80	 −6.0 2.4
Net P&L after trading CDS			6.4

The calculation of earnings now adds up the proceeds from selling protection for 300 at a premium of 80 bps (Table 59.8). Finally, both effects show up as an improved return on capital compared to the original situation. Note that we assume no change of diversification due to the new synthetic exposure, since we add up capital, as regulatory capital does. Economic capital could increase by less than the additional capital due to selling protection if the new exposure to the corporation, from selling a credit derivative, has a favorable diversification effect on the new portfolio (Table 59.9). The return on capital moves up from 25% to 32%.

Credit derivatives have an obvious potential for portfolio management because they are new tools helping to reshape the risk–return profile of portfolios without cash sales of assets or to extend exposure beyond limits by transferring excess risks to others. The market for credit risk allows them to rebalance their specific portfolios by exchanging risk concentrations, hedging credit risk and gaining synthetic exposure.

TABLE 59.9   Buying and selling CDSs: economic income statement

Economic income statement	Original portfolio	Portfolio after trade
Net capital after trading CDS	40.0	20.0
Net P&L after trade	10.0	6.4
ROC	25.00%	32.00%

59.5 OTHER ARBITRAGE BETWEEN ECONOMIC PRICES AND RATING-BASED PRICES

Credit derivatives provide a direct way for taking advantage of the discrepancies of prices for the same credit risk. Another example is that of synthetic securitizations.

Synthetic securitizations assemble a portfolio of credit derivatives, and sell the portfolio to investors by issuing bonds. For providing the full yield of credit-risky bonds, the arranger of securitization might invest in the risk-free asset to generate the risk-free return. The fees from selling protection through credit derivatives provide the additional risky return to investors. Normally, the compensation of investors should match exactly the return of the synthetic portfolios. In practice, the return required by investors depends on credit ratings assigned by rating agencies. On the other hand, the bank will model the return of the portfolio, inclusive of dependencies. The bank assessment of the risk and return of the synthetic portfolio will not, in general, match the risk assessment of rating agencies. Banks take advantage, in this case, of the discrepancy between rating-based returns and economically modeled returns of the synthetic portfolio. This is the familiar outcome of having two prices for the same risk, except that arbitrage is between rating-based prices and economic prices, instead of between capital-based prices and economic prices of credit risk.

SECTION 16

Conclusion and Financial Reforms

60

The Financial System and Reforms

At the time of writing, recommendations with respect to the prevention of financial crises were listed in formal reports, such as the Financial Stability Forum Report of the G20 [29], or in the White Paper from the White House [78]. Reports provide recommendations and further reassessment of existing and new regulations. Most of them are inspired by common sense and refer to the framework broadly described in the first chapter of this book, addressing the causes of the financial crisis. We provide a brief summary of the orientations of these two documents. They essentially look for more risk oversight, better practices, and wider and stronger regulations.

A more macro-prudential view of the financial system seems very likely to emerge for addressing the issue of assessing the risk of the final system rather than the risk of specific financial firms only. This point in time overview of ongoing reforms concludes this text[1]. Such macro-prudential regulations would finally provide some views of the level of system-wide risk, contrasting with the former focus on specific risks of financial firms.

Contents

---

1 There are other reports from the FSA in UK for "strengthening liquidity" [31] as well a draft from the BCBS [6].

60.1 THE FINANCIAL STABILITY FORUM RECOMMENDATIONS

The Financial Stability Forum (FSF) work adopted the framework of "procyclicality" of the financial system as the foundations for its recommendations. It identified three areas as priorities for policy action:

- "the capital regime
- bank provisioning practices
- the interaction between valuation and leverage."

It set up fourteen main recommendations, grouped in these three main areas. In addition to reinforcing the resiliency of financial entities through various enhancements, it also introduced "system-wide" measures and monitoring. Recommendations are to be implemented by the Basel Committee on Banking Supervision (BCBS) and coordinated with other standard setters (IFRS).

The FSF did not address explicitly issues raised elsewhere, such as extending the scope of regulations to hedge funds and rating agencies, or the contagion mechanism of credit derivatives and the related clearinghouses proposals.

60.1.1 Capital

Recommendations on capital are mainly inspired by few simple principles:

- the capital buffers should be increased
- reducing the procyclical effects of regulations
- a more extensive usage of stress-testing.

1 "The BCBS should strengthen the regulatory capital framework so that the quality and level of capital in the banking system increase during strong economic conditions and can be drawn down during periods of economic and financial stress."

The rationale is that capital should be counter-cyclical. The current Basel 2 capital is driven by inputs that are supposed to be "through-the-cycle." This does not eliminate procyclicality because extending credit and increasing profit is easier in strong expansion phases, while capital required tends to shrink in recession phases. For making the capital buffer counter-cyclical, banks should build up capital above the regulatory minimum for making their capital base stronger in stressed environments. A variety of ways for making capital counter-cyclical rather than cyclical is to enhance the capital quality (meaning core capital as opposed to Tier 2 capital) and capital planning by financial institutions. This item is related to the buildup of reserves in anticipation of losses.

2 "The BCBS should revise the market risk framework of Basel 2 to reduce the reliance on cyclical VaR-based capital estimates."

Moreover, market VaR is cyclical in nature. The FCF observes that losses occurred mainly on the trading book and were in excess of VaR-based capital. The FCF considers defining an incremental capital charge, notably through stress-testing. The report does not mention explicitly the underestimation of VaR due to lack of liquidity.

3 "The BCBS should supplement the risk-based capital requirement with a simple, non-risk-based measure to help contain the build-up of leverage in the banking system and put a floor under the Basel 2 framework."

The FSF addresses mismatch risk through this recommendation. It emphasizes the usage of simple and transparent measures of leverage. In some countries, mismatch risk used to be controlled by a mismatch ratio, a ratio of long-term assets to long-term sources of funds, which ceased to be enforced. A form of minimum liquid asset holding is considered, among other points relating to off-balance sheet commitments. Note that ALM should normally enforce such policies within banks, but that ALM risk does not currently imply any capital charge nor any rule. The FSF does not call for a capital charge but refers rather to simple measures of leverage.

4 "Supervisors should use the BCBS enhanced stress testing practices as a critical part of the Pillar 2 supervisory review process to validate the adequacy of banks' capital buffers above the minimum regulatory capital requirement."

Stress testing is a generally implemented practice in banking. However, by how much factors should be stressed remains a matter of judgment. In addition, stress testing is often based on historical data and remains limited to first-level direct effects in many instances. One might infer that the financial crisis will be a scenario for future stress tests, a scenario that no one expected over the modern period of finance.

5 "The BCBS should, on a continuing basis, monitor the impact of the Basel 2 framework and make appropriate adjustments to dampen excessive cyclicality of the minimum capital requirements."

The idea is that monitoring capital will help capturing cyclical movements and allow taking additional measures when capital appears volatile.

6 "The BCBS should, on a continuing basis, carry out regular assessments of the risk coverage of the capital framework in relation to financial developments and banks' evolving risk profiles and make timely enhancements."

The FSF mentions extensions of the capital framework in several areas: Capital for liquidity lines of credit, securitizations and VaR-based capital, and counterparty risk plus re-assessing the role of external ratings.

60.1.2 Provisioning

7 "The FASB and IASB should issue a statement that reiterates for relevant regulators, financial institutions and their auditors that existing standards require the use of judgment to determine an appropriate provisioning of loan losses."

The FSF observes that there are a variety of practices with respect to impairment, which are essentially based on past experience and have been insufficient. It recommends more forward-looking measures, considering economic trends and the business policy. The main idea is to recognize higher impairment losses earlier in the credit cycle, by incorporating judgments regarding factors that might cause losses differing from historical levels.

8 "The FASB and IASB should reconsider the incurred loss model by analyzing alternative approaches for recognizing and measuring loan losses that incorporate a broader range of available credit information. The FSF recommends that the FASB and IASB establish a resource group to provide input on technical issues and complete this project on an expedited basis."

The recommendation refers to moving from the current "incurred loss model" to alternate measurement of impairments that would rely on a wider scope of risk information for improving fair value, expected loss and dynamic provisioning. The feasibility is to be assessed by the standard setters. Such policy was implemented in Spain and helped to reduce the adverse effect of the crisis.

9 "The BCBS should undertake a review of Basel 2 to reduce or eliminate disincentives for establishing appropriate provisions for loan losses."

The regulatory treatment of loan losses is subject to rules for recognition of capital gains and losses that the FSF recommends to review with the objective of facilitating higher loss provisioning.

60.1.3 Valuation and Leverage

10 Authorities should use quantitative indicators and/or constraints on leverage and margins as macro-prudential tools for supervisory purposes. This recommendation is twofold:
   - "Authorities should use quantitative indicators of leverage as guides for policy, both at the institution-specific and at the macro-prudential (system-wide) level." Work by the BCBS to supplement the risk-based capital requirement with a simple, non-risk-based measure, such as simple leverage ratios, "is welcome."
   - "Authorities should review enforcing minimum initial margins and haircuts for OTC derivatives and securities financing transactions."

The FSF recommends the usage of a leverage ratio, both at the individual institution level and at the "macro-prudential," or system-wide, level. The "leverage ratio" should consider off-balance sheet commitments. Oversight of maturity/liquidity mismatch should be enhanced. It recognizes the difficulty of defining such "leverage ratio" system wide due to inter-bank lending and borrowing, and commits to conduct further study at the macro level. The "macro-prudential" view is the first material incursion along the route of assessing the financial system risk, rather than the classical route of risk-assessing financial firms on a standalone basis. The same "macro-prudential" view also appears in the White Paper of the White House, which proposes a special treatment of "highly interconnected financial firms" that can impair the stability of the whole system.

Increased margins and haircuts refers to increasing over-collateralization, and is viewed as a way to reducing the incentive for leverage and minimizing the adverse feedback effect of "loan-to-value" ratios under downside movements of value.

11 "The BCBS and the CGFS should launch a joint research program to measure funding and liquidity risk attached to maturity transformation, enabling the pricing of liquidity risk in the financial system."

The key component of this agenda is to define measures of funding and liquidity risk.

12 "Based on the conclusions of the above research program, the BIS and IMF could make available to authorities information on leverage and on maturity mismatches on a system-wide basis."

The goal is to have system-wide monitoring and measurement of mismatch risk.

13 "Accounting standard setters and prudential supervisors should examine the use of valuation reserves or adjustments for fair valued financial instruments when data or modeling needed to support their valuation is weak."

The recommendation refers to model valuation in inactive markets and possible valuation reserves for valuation uncertainty. It also suggest to "de-link" valuation from profit and loss when significant uncertainty exists, using the valuation reserve as a "filter" between uncertain valuations and direct impacts on profit and losses, considering profit and loss are less reliable in presence of such uncertainty.

14 "Accounting standard setters and prudential supervisors should examine possible changes to relevant standards to dampen adverse dynamics potentially associated with fair value accounting."

This recommendation refers to the adverse effect of fair values and markdowns of portfolios in adverse conditions that erode core capital, increase leverage and eventually result in insolvency. The FSF mentions the following as possible ways to reduce this potential impact.

- Enhancing the accounting model so that the use of fair value accounting is carefully examined for financial instruments of credit intermediaries.
- Transfers between financial asset categories.
- Simplifying hedge accounting requirements.

60.2 THE WHITE PAPER FROM THE WHITE HOUSE

The White House document basically supports the FSF document and adds other dimensions, in addition to proposing a reform of the US regulation system. The five key objectives of the proposed reforms are:

1 "promote robust supervision and regulation of financial firms"
2 "establish comprehensive supervision and regulation of financial markets"
3 "protect consumers and investors from financial abuse"
4 "improve tools for managing financial crises"
5 "raise international regulatory standards and improve international cooperation."

For those purposes, the report proposes new roles for the Federal Reserve and to create new agencies for enhancing risk supervision and coordination. The Federal Reserve and the Federal Deposit Insurance Company, the SEC and the Commodity Futures Trading Commission (CFTC) will retain their previous roles.

60.2.1 Supervision

The report proposes that any firm that poses a "significant risk" to the financial system should be regulated. Those firms are the "largest, most interconnected and most highly leveraged" firms, also called Tier 1 "FHC" (Financial Holding Companies). For such firms, cost of failure should be "internalized" rather than imposed on the society, through tighter regulations than for other financial firms and should be "system-wide." This includes capital requirements, liquidity standards, liquidity risk management and liquidity stress tests, with both firm-specific and market-wide scenarios.

It proposes that the Federal Reserve be in charge of supervision of these firms, stronger capital requirements and the registration of all hedge funds to the SEC (Security and Exchange Commission – the authority in charge of regulating the financial markets). The regulation within the US should be unified through a National Bank Supervisor.

Under this section, the report proposes that capital and liquidity requirements were "simply too low" and that regulation was insufficient. It emphasizes the adverse effect of the fragmentation of supervisory authorities in the US. A new Financial Services Oversight Council should be in charge of filling out gaps in regulations and to facilitate national coordination.

The federal regulator should better align compensations practices with long-term shareholder value, notably by providing the faculty of shareholders to influence the compensations of senior executives. Standard setters should promote more forward-looking loss provisioning and provide greater transparency on fair value and cash flows.

60.2.2 Establish Comprehensive Supervision and Regulation of Financial Markets

Enhanced regulation should extend to securitizations, credit rating agencies, and OTC derivatives. For securitizations, issuers and originators should retain an interest in securitized assets.

The report observes that such instruments were supposed to better distribute risks and promote efficiency. Rather, in fact, it concentrated the risk in opaque ways. Securitizations were an incentive to lack of market discipline on granting credit. Investors were overly reliant on credit rating agencies, which failed to accurately describe the risk of issues.

The report addresses the case of derivatives, emphasizing that those were a major contagion vector. It proposes to enforce record keeping and reporting requirements on all OTC derivatives and to trade standardized derivatives through clearinghouses. The Federal Reserve authority over market infrastructure (clearing and settlements) should be enhanced.

60.2.3 Protect Consumers and Investors from Financial Abuse

This section proposes the creation of a new "Consumer Financial Protection Agency" (CFPA). It emphasizes that consumer protection is a critical foundation of the financial system, while regulations should promote growth, efficiency and innovation in the long run. The CFPA should have an independent role as a supervisory and enforcement authority and promote effective regulations. It should ensure transparency, simplicity, fairness and access to all consumers. For investors, the SEC is in charge to promote transparency and accountability.

60.2.4 Improve Tools for Managing Financial Crises

The report recognizes that financial authorities have currently no other choice than bailouts or financial collapse when a major institution fails, and proposes to define a new regime to address the "too big to fail" issue. The report recommends that a "new resolution regime" be implemented to avoid the "disorderly resolution" of failing bank holding companies and Tier 1 Financial Holding Companies, but it does not specify how such a "new resolution regime" would be defined.

60.2.5 Raise International Regulatory Standards and Improve International Cooperation

The report aims at coordination of supervision internationally on strengthening the capital framework and enhanced crisis management tools. For coordination, a "Financial Services Oversight Council" would gather the principal federal regulators, a national bank supervisor would coordinate national efforts and an Office of National Insurance will extend the scope of coordination to insurance companies. Arbitrage across different regulation regimes towards the "loosest" standards imposes more consistency across statuses of financial firms and across boundaries. The paper supports the international efforts on core issues, regulatory capital standards, and oversight of financial markets, supervision of internationally active firms and crisis prevention and management.

The paper supports the guidelines of FSF paper, with a prominent role of the BCBS on reviewing Basel guidelines. This includes a variety of recommendations, beyond reinforcing the FSF mandate:

- new regulations on liquidity risk
- new regulations on the clearing of OTC derivatives

- extension of the scope of regulations
- better compensation practices
- improvement of accounting standards
- more forward-looking accounting standards for impairment
- tighter oversight of rating agencies
- macro-prudential focus.

60.3 AREAS UNDER SCRUTINY BY FINANCIAL AUTHORITIES: SUMMARY

The reports recognize deviations from sound practices and the deficiencies of regulations. Recommendations and proposals are still to be refined and undergo feasibility assessments. Some are specific enough to sound readily feasible. Others have to be better refined and some have yet to be fully defined.

- Capital reinforcement and solvency.
- Dynamic and more forward-looking provisioning.
- Supervision of liquidity, mismatch risk and leverage.
- Governance and alignment of compensations towards longer-term goals.
- Simpler and more flexible accounting standards.
- Clearinghouse for credit derivatives and traceability of OTC derivatives.
- Obligation of financial firms to maintain a financial commitment in pools of securitization vehicles.
- Extension of supervision to un-regulated players, notably funds, to a degree left open at this stage.
- Extension of supervision to rating agencies, and fuller disclosure of differentiated rating methodologies.
- Focus on system-wide monitoring and oversight, beyond monitoring of individual entities.
- Focus on "Tier-1 FHCs" or "too big to fail and interconnected" financial firms.
- Recognition for the need of a new regime for compelling such firms to internalize costs and for handling eventual failure.
- Consumer and investor protection.

There are pending issues with respect to implementation and how far supervisors will go. In some cases, technical solutions and feasibility are question marks.

Some general remarks stems from such "lessons from the crisis." Perhaps, two points deserve to be mentioned as concluding remarks.

First, the business model of financial entities is not questioned and current reports fail to address, except indirectly through the Tier 1 firms, the sustainability issue of giant banks forming a global monopoly. There is a case for casting doubt on how to escape the asymmetrical treatment of internalized gains and externalized losses. More practically, there are doubts as well with respect to the manageability of such large banks.[2]

---

2 Among others, the "UBS Shareholder Report" discloses some deficiencies when reviewing the internal management of the bank facing the crisis.

Second, there seems to be a consensus on some core corrective actions. This is not very surprising. With respect to practices, models and risk management tools, it is striking that all recommendations converge towards best practices and techniques and deficiencies of regulations of which many were known, but not fully recognized, before the systemic crisis.

The near future will let us know what will prevail in terms of enhancements of supervision and regulations, and, in the medium term, how the system as a whole will evolve.

References

1 Alexander, C. (2008) *Practical Financial Econometrics*, John Wiley & Sons.
2 Altman, E.I., Haldeman, R., Narayanan, P. (1977) ZETA Analysis: A New Model to Identify Bankruptcy Risk of Corporation, *Journal of Banking and Finance*, 29–55.
3 Altman, E.I., Caouette, J., Narayanan, P. (1998) *Managing Credit Risk: The Next Great Financial Challenge*, John Wiley & Sons.
4 Artzner, P., Delbaen, F., Eber, J.-M., Heath, D. (1997) Thinking Coherently, *Risk*, **10** (11).
5 Asarnow, E., Edwards, D. (1995) Measuring Loss on Defaulted Bank Loans: A 24-Year Study, *The Journal of Commercial Lending*, **10** (2), 11–23.
6 Basel Committee on Banking Supervision (2008) *Principles for Sound Liquidity Risk Management and Supervision* (Draft), Bank for International Settlements, Basel, Switzerland.
7 Basel Committee on Banking Supervision (June 2006) *International Convergence of Capital Measurement and Capital Standards – A Revised Framework, Comprehensive Version*, Bank for International Settlements, Basel, Switzerland.
8 Basel Committee on Banking Supervision (1996, updated 2005) *Amendment to the Capital Accord to Incorporate Market Risk*, Bank for International Settlements, Basel, Switzerland.
9 Basel Committee on Banking Supervision (1994) *Risk Management Guidelines for Derivatives*, Bank for International Settlements, Basel, Switzerland.
10 Basel Committee on Banking Supervision (1988) *International Convergence of Capital Measurement and Capital Standards*, Bank for International Settlements, Basel, Switzerland.
11 Bierwag, G. (1987) *Duration Analysis – Managing Interest Rate Risk*, Ballinger Publishing Company, Cambridge, Massachusetts.
12 Black, F., Derman, E., Toy, W. (1990) A One-Factor Model of Interest Rates and its Application to Treasury Bond Options, *Financial Analysts Journal*, **46** (1), 33–39.
13 Black, F., Scholes, M. (1973) The Pricing of Options and Corporate Liabilities, *Journal of Political Economy*, **81** 637–659.
14 Bodie, Z., Kane, A., Marcus, A. (2008) *Investments*, 7th edition, Irwin.
15 Brace, A., Gatarek, D., Musiela, M. (1997) The Market Model of Interest Rate Dynamics, *Mathematical Finance*, **7**, 127, 154.
16 Brooks, C. (2008) *Econometrics for Finance*, Cambridge University Press.
17 Carty, L.V., Lieberman, D. (1998) *Historical Default Rates of Corporate Bond Issuers, 1920–1996*, in S. Das (ed.) (2003) *Credit Derivatives: Trading and Management of Credit and Default Risk*, John Wiley & Sons, 317–348.
18 Cherubini, U., Luciano, E., Vecchiato, W. (2004) *Copula Methods in Finance*, John Wiley & Sons.

19 Commission of The European Communities (2008) Proposal for a Regulation of The European Parliament and of The Council on Credit Rating Agencies, Brussels.

20 Cooper, I., Mello, A. (1991) The Default Risk of Swaps, *Journal of Finance*, **46** (2), 597–620.

21 Cornett, M.M., Saunders, A. (2006) *Financial Institutions Management: A Risk Management Approach*, McGraw-Hill.

22 Cox, J.C., Rubinstein, M. (1985) *Options Markets*, Englewood Cliffs, N.J., Prentice Hall.

23 Credit Suisse (1997) *CreditRisk+: A Credit Risk Management Framework*, Credit Suisse Financial Products.

24 Danielsson, J. (2007) *The Value at Risk Reference: Key Issues in the Implementation of Market Risk*, Risk Publications, London.

25 Das, S. (ed.) (2005) *Credit Derivatives: CDOs and Structured Credit Products*, John Wiley & Sons.

26 Das, S. (2003) *Swaps and Financial Derivatives: Products, Pricing, Applications and Risk Management*, 3rd edition, John Wiley & Sons, New Jersey.

27 Daykin C.C., Pentokäinen, T., Pesonon, M. (1994) *Practical Risk Theory for Actuaries*, Chapman & Hall, London.

28 Duffie, D., Singleton, K.J. (2003) *Credit Risk: Pricing, Measurement and Management*, Princeton University Press, New Jersey.

29 Financial Stability Forum (2009) *Addressing Procyclicality in the Financial System*.

30 Frye, J. (1997) *Principals of Risk: Finding VaR through Factor-Based Interest Rate Scenarios*, in *VaR: Understanding and Applying Value at Risk*, 275–288, Risk Publications, London.

31 FSA (2009) *Strengthening Liquidity Standards*, London.

32 Gordy, M.B. (2000) A Comparative Anatomy of Credit Risk Models, *Journal of Banking and Finance*, **24**, 119–149.

33 Gordy, M.B. (2003) A Risk Factor Model Foundation for Rating-Based Bank Capital Rules, *Journal of Financial Intermediation*, **12**, 199–232.

34 Gordy, M.B., Howells, B. (2006) Procyclicality in Basel II: Can we treat the disease without killing the patient? *Journal of Financial Intermediation*, **15**, 395–417.

35 Grimmett, G.R., Stirzaker, D.R. (2002) *Probability and Random Processes*, Oxford University Press.

36 Hull, J. (2008) *Options, Futures and Other Derivatives*, 6th edition, Prentice Hall.

37 J.P. Morgan (1997) *CreditMetrics Technical Document*, New York, J.P. Morgan Bank.

38 J.P. Morgan (1995) *Risk Metrics Technical Manual*, New York, J.P. Morgan Bank.

39 J. de Larosière, Chairman, *The High-Level Group of Financial Supervision in the EU*, Brussels, February 2009.

40 Jarrow, E. (1998) *Volatility*, Risk Publications, London.

41 Johnson, N.L., Kotz, S., Balakrishnan, N. (1994) *Continuous Univariate Distributions*, Volume I, John Wiley & Sons.

42 Johnson, N.L., Kotz, S., Balakrishnan, N. (1995) *Continuous Univariate Distributions*, Volume II, John Wiley & Sons.

43 Johnson, N.L., Kotz, S., Balakrishnan, N. (1997) *Discrete Multivariate Distributions*, Volume II, John Wiley & Sons.

44 Jorion, P. (2000) Risk Management Lessons from Long-Term Capital Management, *European Financial Management*, **6**(3), 277–300.

45 Jorion, P. (2007) *Value-at-Risk*, 3rd edition, McGraw-Hill, New York.

46 Kealhofer, S. (2003) Quantifying Credit Risk I: Default Prediction, *Financial Analysts Journal*, **3**, 30–44.

47 Kealhofer, S. (2003) Quantifying Credit Risk II: Debt Valuation, *Financial Analysts Journal*, **59** (1), 78–92.

48 Kleinbaum, D.G. (1994) *Logistic Regression*, Springer.

49 Li, D. (2000) On Default Correlation, a Copula Approach, *Journal of Fixed Income*, **9** (4), 43–54.

50 Matten, C. (2000) *Managing Bank Capital*, 2nd edition, John Wiley & Sons.

51 McNeil, A.J. (1999) *Extreme Value Theory for Risk Managers, Internal Models and CAD II*, Risk Books, London.

52 Merton, R.C. (1973) Theory of Rational Option Pricing, *Bell Journal of Economics and Management Science*, **4** (1), 141–183.

53 Merton, R.C. (1977) On the Pricing of Contingent Claims and the Modigliani-Miller Theorem, *Journal of Financial Economics*, **5**, 241–249.

54 Modigliani, F., Miller, M.H. (1958) The Cost of Capital, Corporation Finance, and the Theory of Investment, *American Economic Review*, **48**, 261–297.

55 Moody's (2008) *European Corporate Defaults and Recovery Rates: 1985–2007*, London.

56 Neftci, S.N. (2000) *Introduction to the Mathematics of Financial Derivatives*, 2nd edition, Academic Press, New York.

57 Neftci, S.N. (2008) *Principles of Financial Engineering*, Academic Press, New York.

58 PriceWaterhouseCoopers Publications (2009) *IFRS Manual of Accounting 2009: Global Guide to IFRS*.

59 PriceWaterhouseCoopers Publications (2009) *Pocket Guide to International Financial Reporting Standards*.

60 Ramirez, J. (2007) *The Theoretical Framework*, in *Accounting for Derivatives*, John Wiley & Sons, London.

61 Rebonato, R. (2002) *Volatility and Correlation: In the Pricing of Equity, FX and Interest Rate Options*, John Wiley & Sons, New Jersey.

62 Risk Publications (1996) *Vasicek and Beyond*, London.

63 Risk Publications (2003) *Liquidity Black Holes: Understanding, Quantifying and Managing Financial Liquidity Risk*, London.

64 RiskMetrics Group (2002) *CreditGrades: Technical Documents*, New York.

65 Ross, S. (1993) *Probability Models*, Academic Press, San Diego.

66 Saunders, A., Cornett, M.M. (2008) *Financial Institutions Management*, McGraw-Hill.

67 Schmid, M.M., Walter, I. (2009) Do Financial Conglomerates Create or Destroy Economic Value?, *Journal of Financial Intermediation*, **18**, 193–216.

68 Schönbucher, P. (2003) *Credit Derivative Pricing Models: Models, Pricing and Implementation*, John Wiley & Sons.

69 Sharpe, W. (1964) Capital Asset Prices: A Theory of Market Equilibrium Under Condition of Risk, *Journal of Finance*, **19**, 425–442.

70 Smith, G.D. (1985) *Numerical Solution of Partial Differential Equations: Finite Difference Methods*, 3rd edition, Oxford University Press.

71 Standard & Poors (2003) *Corporate Ratings Criteria*, McGraw-Hill, New York.

72 Stern, J., Stewart, G.B., III (1991) *The Quest for Value: The EVA © Management Guide*, HarperCollins, New York.

73 Taleb, N.N. (1996) *Dynamic Hedging: Managing Vanilla and Exotic Options*, John Wiley & Sons, New Jersey.

74 Taleb, N.N. (2004) *Fooled by Randomness*, The Random House Publishing Group.

75 UBS (2008) *Shareholder Report on UBS's Write Downs*.

76 Vasicek, O. (1997) An Equilibrium Characterization of the Term Structure, *Journal of Financial Economics*, **5**, 177–188.

77 Vasicek, O. (2002) *Loan Portfolio Value*, Risk Publications.

78 Walpole, R.E., Myers, R.H. (1993) *Probability and Statistics for Engineers and Scientists*, MacMillan Publishing Company.

79 White House (2006) The White Paper from The White House, June, Washington.

80 Willmott, P. (2000) *Paul Wilmott on Quantitative Finance*, John Wiley & Sons, New Jersey.

81 Wilson, T. (1997) Portfolio Credit Risk I, *Risk*, **10** (9), 111–117.

82 Wilson, T. (1997) Portfolio Credit Risk II, *Risk*, **10** (10), 56–61.

83 Wilson, T. (1998) *Credit Portfolio View*, McKinsey & Co.

Index